Syntactic Theory and
First Language Acquisition:
Cross-Linguistic Perspectives

VOLUME 2
BINDING, DEPENDENCIES, AND
LEARNABILITY

Syntactic Theory and First Language Acquisition: Cross-Linguistic Perspectives

VOLUME 2
BINDING, DEPENDENCIES, AND LEARNABILITY

Editors:
Barbara Lust
Gabriella Hermon
Jaklin Kornfilt

Co-editors:
Suzanne Flynn
Shyam Kapur
Isabella Barbier
Katharina Boser
Claire Foley
Zelmira Nuñez del Prado
Edward J. Rubin
Lynn Santelmann
Jacqueline Toribio

LEA LAWRENCE ERLBAUM ASSOCIATES, PUBLISHERS
1994 Hillsdale, New Jersey   Hove, UK

Lawrence Erlbaum Associates, Inc., Publishers
365 Broadway
Hillsdale, New Jersey 07642

Cover design by Mairav Salomon-Dekel

Library of Congress Cataloging-in-Publication Data

Syntactic theory and first language acquisition: cross-linguistic perspectives.
    v.   cm.
    Papers from a symposium held at Cornell
University, April 24–26, 1992.
    Includes bibliographical references and indexes.
    Contents: v. 1. Heads, projections, and
learnability. — v. 2. Binding, dependencies,
and learnability / editors, Barbara Lust,
Gabriella Hermon, Jaklin Kornfilt; coeditors,
Suzanne Flynn . . . [et al.].
    1. Language acquisition—Congresses.
2. Grammar, comparative and general—Syntax—
Congresses. I. Lust, Barbara, 1941–   .
II. Suñer, Margarita. III. Whitman, John, 1954–   .
    ISBN 0-8058-1350-0. — ISBN 0-8058-1575-9 (set)
    P118.S937 1994   401'.93   93-42783
                                                       CIP

Books published by Lawrence Erlbaum Associates are printed on acid-free
paper, and their bindings are chosen for strength and durability.

Printed in the United States of America
10 9 8 7 6 5 4 3 2 1

To our dear friend and colleague
Dede Kaufman

Contents

List of Contributors

Isabella Barbier   Department of Modern Languages and Linguistics, Cornell University.

Katharina Boser   Human Development and Family Studies, Cornell University.

Yu-Chin Chien   Department of Psychology, California State University.

Gennaro Chierchia   Dipartimento Di Filosofia, Universita Degli Studi De Milano, Department of Modern Languages and Linguistics, Cornell University.

Robin Clark   Department of Linguistics, University of Pennsylvania.

Katherine Demuth   Department of Cognitive Science & Linguistics, Brown University.

Viviane Deprez   Department of Linguistics, University of Massachusetts and Rutgers University.

Jill De Villiers   Department of Psychology, Smith College.

Suzanne Flynn   Department of Foreign Languages & Literature, Massachusetts Institute of Technology.

Janet Fodor   Department of Linguistics, Graduate Center, City University of New York.

Claire Foley Department of Linguistics, Cornell University.

Henry Gleitman Department of Psychology, University of Pennsylvania.

Lila Gleitman Department of Psychology, University of Pennsylvania.

Jane Grimshaw Department of Linguistics and Center for Cognitive Science, Rutgers University.

Liliane Haegeman Department of Linguistics, Université de Genève.

Kenneth Hale Department of Linguistics & Philosophy, Massachusetts Institute of Technology.

Gabriella Hermon Department of Educational Studies, University of Delaware.

C.-T. James Huang Department of Linguistics, University of California at Irvine.

Nina Hyams Department of Linguistics, University of California at Los Angeles.

Celia Jakubowicz Laboratoire de Psychologie Expérimentale, CNRS/EPHE/Université René Descartes.

Aravind Joshi Department of Computer Information Science, University of Pennsylvania.

Shyam Kapur Department of Computer Science, James Cook University, Australia.

Diane Kaufman 7949 Montgomery Avenue, Elkins Park, PA 19117.

Jay Keyser Department of Linguistic & Philosophy, Massachusetts Institute of Technology.

Jaklin Kornfilt Department for Languages and Linguistics, Syracuse University.

Charlotte Koster Department of Linguistics, University of Groningen.

Jan Koster Department of Linguistics, University of Groningen.

Yafei Li Department of Linguistics, University of Wisconsin, Madison.

David Lightfoot Department of Linguistics, University of Maryland.

Diane Lillo-Martin Linguistics Department, University of Connecticut and Haskins Laboratories.

Barbara Lust Human Development and Family Studies and Department of Modern Languages and Linguistics, Cornell University.

Gita Martohardjono Linguistics Department, Queens College of the City University of New York.

Reiko Mazuka Department of Psychology, Duke University.

Cecile McKee Department of Linguistics, University of Arizona, Tucson.

Zelmira Nuñez del Prado Department of Modern Languages and Linguistics, Cornell University.

Yukio Otsu Institute for Cultural and Linguistic Studies, Keio University, Tokyo.

Amy Pierce MIT Press, Cambridge, MA.

Andrew Radford Department of Language and Linguistics, Essex University.

Eric Reuland Research Institute for Language and Speech (OTS), Utrecht University.

Luigi Rizzi Department of Linguistics, Université de Genève.

Thomas Roeper Department of Linguistics, University of Massachusetts.

Edward Rubin Department of Modern Languages and Linguistics, Cornell University.

Lynn Santelmann Department of Modern Languages and Linguistics, Cornell University.

Carlota Smith Center for Cognitive Science, University of Texas.

Margarita Suñer Department of Modern Languages and Linguistics, Cornell University.

Chih-Chen Jane Tang Institute for History & Philology, Academia Sinica, Nankang, Taipei, Taiwan.

Jacqueline Toribio Department of Spanish and Portuguese, University of California, Santa Barbara.

Virginia Valian Department of Psychology, Hunter College and Graduate Center, City University of New York.

Jürgen Weissenborn Max Planck Institut für Psycholinguistik, Netherlands.

John Whitman Department of Modern Languages and Linguistics, Cornell University.

Preface

The collected works in these two volumes were first presented at a symposium held at Cornell University, April 24–26, 1992, entitled Syntactic Theory and First Language Acquisition: Cross-Linguistic Perspectives. At this symposium, about 200 scholars, working on many different languages, gathered to hear about 45 papers, commentaries, and debates, and to participate in discussions of the most recent research results. The papers were grouped into panels, in order to bring together scholars who were working on similar issues across different languages, and in order to encourage active debate on vital issues in the field.

We hope that these volumes can bring to the reader a sense of the great energy, intense enthusiasm, and highly positive (albeit pointed) debate at the symposium. That energy and highly focused intellectual exchange convinced us that our field had reached a new dimension of scientific inquiry.

This new dimension is essentially interdisciplinary. The chapters in these volumes (like the symposium itself) conjoin research in linguistic theory (i.e., the theory of natural language representation), with research in first language acquisition. The acquisition research is conducted in a precise manner, guided by linguistic theory as well as by scientific method. The strongest, most general result of this research convergence is that there is now a new and closer relation between theoretical research and acquisition research. The strengthened interaction across these fields has produced new energy, new significance, and new validation for each. In addition, the research reported here integrates, in a new, more precise manner, the field of formal learnability theory emerging from computer science.

ACKNOWLEDGMENTS

To a large degree, the new energy in this field owes much to the relatively new field of cognitive science, which has provided a structural umbrella of support for interdisciplinary interactions. At Cornell, the Cognitive Studies program provided the essential initial support, both financial and intellectual, for the symposium, as well as for the volumes. In this way, the personal support of codirector Frank Keil was crucial. At the National Science Foundation, concern for interdisciplinary Cognitive Studies programs led to substantial assistance, which made both the symposium and the volumes possible. Paul Chapin and Joe Young collaborated in helping to provide this support. In addition, the wise and knowledgeable editorial support of Amy Pierce, at Lawrence Erlbaum Associates, provided both intellectual and structural support for this publication.

The coeditors of these volumes contributed true editorial scholarship as well as intellectual energy and support for the symposium.

The symposium organizing staff at Cornell consisted of several outstanding undergraduates: Elizabeth Abrams, Lisa Cindolo, Danielle Cleveland, Rosita Juvera, and Dan Metrick. Without their energy and responsible direction, the Cornell Symposium could not have proceeded as it did. Indirectly, but fundamentally, they helped to make these volumes possible.

Finally, Qing Xie provided the essential core of organization and communication among the 200 persons who attended the symposium and the many scholars whose work appears in these volumes. We are all deeply indebted to her exceptional and invaluable assistance. Yafei Li's support, both practical and intellectual, was present throughout. Sue Wurster's competent direction pervaded the whole project. Vicki Griffin's tireless assistance in manuscript preparation is deeply appreciated. Marion Potts' early and seminal idea for the symposium was critical. Claire Foley and Zelmira Nuñez del Prado assumed responsibility for the preparation of these volumes from beginning to end. James Gair's constant support is deeply appreciated.

We thank the following for their financial support: NSF (#DBS9210789), and several divisions at Cornell: Cornell Cognitive Studies Program, Department of Modern Languages and Linguistics, Cornell Linguistics Circle, College of Human Ecology, the Einaudi Center and Western Societies Program, Africana Studies and Research Center, East Asia Program, South Asian Program, Latin American Studies, Soviet and Eastern European Studies.

—*Barbara Lust (for the editorial board)*

Contents of Volume 1

Syntactic Theory and
First Language Acquisition:
Cross-Linguistic Perspectives

VOLUME 1
HEADS, PROJECTIONS, AND
LEARNABILITY

III LEARNABILITY

General Introduction
Syntactic Theory and
First Language Acquisition:
Cross-Linguistic Perspectives

The chapters in these two volumes reflect a new and exciting convergence between developments in linguistic theory and developments in the study of natural language acquisition.

This convergence has long been motivated by the linguistic theory of Universal Grammar (UG), a theory under which both (1) and (2) hold.

(1) UG is "a general theory of linguistic structure that aims to discover the framework of principles and elements common to attainable human languages; this theory is now often called 'universal grammar' " (Chomsky, 1986, pp. 3–4).

(2) "UG may be regarded as a characterization of the genetically determined language faculty. One may think of this faculty as a 'language acquisition device' " (Chomsky, 1986, pp. 3–4).

In spite of this fundamental motivation, however, scholarship directed to a convergence between linguistic theory and actual first language acquisition has, until recently, been limited to the work of only a few scholars and their students. After a brief period of intense interaction in the early 1960s (e.g., between Chomsky, Miller, Lenneberg, and Brown; see Fodor, Bever, & Garrett, 1974, for review), this scholarship was generally not central to work in linguistic theory or in any other field (e.g., developmental psychology).

There were several apparent reasons for this divergence. Linguists, lacking adequate methodology or theory for studying development, often tended to dismiss an endeavor that would require scholarship in the area of language acquisition. Concurrently, as linguistic theory developed (growing in both technical precision and complexity, changing more quickly as time went on), psychologists, often lacking adequate methodology or theory in the area of linguistics, tended to avoid more and more any study of first language acquisition that involved linguistic theory.

This situation could have resulted in a highly developed, highly technical, and precise formal linguistic theory, with little or no connection to the empirical facts of first language acquisition or to biological reality. This result would undermine the theory of UG as stated in (1) and (2). It did not occur, however.

The chapters in these volumes attest to this by demonstrating the closest interaction between the field of linguistic theory and the study of first language acquisition to date. The fact that the field has seen this resurgence of interaction (and now, arguably, a more articulated and precise interaction) between linguistic theory and actual study of first language acquisition may be one of the strongest arguments for the viability and promise of the UG paradigm articulated in (1) and (2).

There are two critical aspects of current research in the UG paradigm that, together, characterize the specific thrust of this collection of papers and the source of much of its current energy: (a) the deliberate cross-linguistic aspect, and (b) the confrontation of real development in first language acquisition.

THE CROSS-LINGUISTIC RESEARCH PARADIGM

The research that appears in this collection specifically pursues a cross-linguistic perspective in combination with its focus on convergence between linguistic theory and acquisition. This approach has long been insinuated by the UG paradigm but has only gradually come to the fore, and it provides a new strength to argumentation in this paradigm.

It is clear that a theory of UG must be mapped to a theory of specific languages. It must be able to account for cross-language variation as well as for language universals, a fact that closely links it to issues of first language acquisition. Chomsky (1986) has articulated this point:

> (3) It is important to bear in mind that the study of one language may provide crucial evidence concerning the structure of some other language, if we continue to accept the plausible assumption that the capacity to acquire language, the subject matter of UG, is common across the species. . . . A study of English is a study of the realization of the initial state S_o under particular conditions. Therefore it embodies assumptions, which should be made explicit concerning S_o. But S_o is a constant; therefore Japanese must be an instantiation of the same

initial state under different conditions. Investigation of Japanese might show that the assumptions concerning S_o derived from the study of English were incorrect; these assumptions might provide the wrong answers for Japanese, and after correcting them on this basis we might be led to modify the postulated grammar of English. Because evidence from Japanese can evidently bear on the correctness of a theory of S_o, it can have indirect—but very powerful—bearing on the choice of the grammar that attempts to characterize the I-language attained by a speaker of English. (pp. 37–38)

The chapters in these volumes take this cross-linguistic perspective one step further. In accordance with (3), a theory of UG requires cross-linguistic analyses. This is true whether one is pursuing the theory from the point of view of adult language, where UG characterizes a critical component of the internalized language (I-language) attained by a speaker, or from the point of view of language acquisition, where UG is viewed as a model of the initial state (S_o). Therefore, if the converging study of linguistic theory and first language acquisition can strengthen research in the UG paradigm, the combined cross-linguistic approach in both fields should provide the strongest paradigm possible. All of the chapters in these volumes apply this cross-linguistic approach.

Development

The research in these volumes reflects a remarkable shift in assumptions in the field, such that there is now a shared assumption that development in language acquisition is real. The premise now is that neither (4) nor (5) alone can be assumed to provide a sufficient research paradigm, even if they are true. There is an implicit acknowledgment of (6).

(4) "Acquisition of language is something that happens to you: . . . You are just designed to do it at a certain time" (Chomsky, 1988, p. 174).

(5) "What I am describing is an idealization in which only the moment of acquisition of the correct grammar is considered" (Chomsky, 1965, p. 202).

(6) "The 'simplifying assumption' of 'instantaneous learning' of language is 'obviously false' " (Chomsky, 1975, pp. 119, 121).

This shift in assumptions has had major theoretical consequences, as is seen in the following.

The issue now becomes: Does the real development in language, which we see during language acquisition, reflect a real development in grammatical knowledge? If so, how should this grammatical development be represented? If not, what does explain the language change?

Although early work in linguistic theory had set out to explain the relative speed and efficiency of successful universal language acquisition (e.g., Chomsky, 1965), current research, reflected in these volumes, directly confronts (6).

OVERVIEW OF THE VOLUMES

Reading through this collection may leave the impression that major issues remain open both in linguistic theory and in the study of first language acquisition. This is veridical. None of the particular issues raised in these two volumes is totally solved in any of the individual chapters, or elsewhere in the field. Rather, each of the chapters represents a particular position of scholarly debate in the field today. Each chapter must be interpreted in conjunction with the others that appear with it. Only the collection as a whole represents the true state of the field today.

Many of the chapters diverge dramatically, just as many of them converge dramatically. We do not view this as an unhappy outcome. Rather, the collection as a whole reflects the development of a paradigm for scientific investigation regarding both linguistic theory and the language faculty, a paradigm that is truly interdisciplinary. With this paradigm, the field has reached new strength in its capacity for scientific debate of issues, a strength that was not possible on the basis of purely theoretical or purely empirical argumentation. The debates themselves, focused and developed, informed by both theoretical arguments and arguments from first language acquisition, are significant; they provide the necessary foundation for the scientific understanding of the issues they involve. They bring the field to a point where work on first language acquisition can truly inform linguistic theory, and vice versa.

RECURRENT DEBATES

Several major debates, arising from the UG paradigm, recur in both of the volumes and provide the focus for most of the research reported in them. In the following, we summarize emerging consensus in these debates and remaining divergence.

Continuity or Discontinuity of UG

The acceptance of (6) has immediate theoretical consequences for the interpretation of UG in (1) and (2); in particular, it has consequences for fundamental questions that concern the interpretation of UG as a model of the initial state. Given change over time (i.e., noninstantaneity), does UG itself stay constant, as in (the Strong Continuity Hypothesis (SCH), or does UG change over time, as in various possible Discontinuity Hypotheses (DH)? If the SCH (of UG) is supported, what then accounts for real change in language? If the DH is supported, then what explains change from a nonadult grammar to an adult grammar? If the DH is supported, in what sense is (2) true?

Chomsky (1988) suggested what has been termed a maturational solution to questions like these, as in (7).

(7) "It seems hard to explain these transitions without appeal to maturational processes that bring principles of universal grammar into operation on some regular schedule in a manner to be described and accounted for in a genetic way" (p. 70).

This attempt at a maturational solution immediately divorces the real facts of development of language from linguistic theory, however, as no independent theory of UG change exists in linguistic theory. In addition, once we accept (7), then (2) is no longer directly interpretable as it stands. No independent explanation at the level of biology or neuroanatomy currently exists, either, for a maturationally staged UG. Although it is possible to describe different forms of child language in general linguistic terms, or in terms that borrow from a general theory of UG, in what sense is this explanatory? (We might compare such descriptions to generative descriptions of particular adult languages based loosely on analyses of English without any regard to the principles and parameters of UG. It is noteworthy that in the field of comparative syntax such studies have been almost completely superseded.) Every chapter in these volumes is concerned with these issues and reaches for some solution.

Several years ago, the field was characterized by dramatically different approaches to the UG paradigm in the study of first language acquisition. Some earlier proposals argued for qualitative change in the child's access to UG over the course of first language acquisition. Under these proposals, a complete UG actually characterized only the end state in language development. These approaches contrasted with a Strong Continuity Hypothesis in which a full UG was argued to provide a model for both the initial state and continuous constraint on the course of first language acquisition (see, e.g., Lust, 1986, 1987; Whitman, Lee, & Lust, 1991).

In contrast to the literature a few years ago (e.g., early Clahsen, 1982; Lebeaux, 1988; Radford, 1990), many of the chapters in these volumes now argue against a radical version of a Discontinuity Hypothesis (e.g., against complete absence of functional categories or of particular binding theory principles; see Radford's chapter 7 in volume 1, for example), and they thus challenge the proposal in (7). This is true for volumes 1 and 2.

Several chapters debate more specific issues. For example, does apparent change in child language reflect change in grammatical competence at the level of UG or of specific language grammars, or does it reflect structural representations of particular utterances (e.g., Grimshaw, volume 1, chapter 4) but not grammatical competence in general? Many chapters investigate the optional or obligatory nature of the child's knowledge in one or both of these areas. For example, the questions whether or not the child has knowledge of CP in the X-bar system of phrase structure at initial periods of acquisition, and whether he or she accesses this knowledge obligatorily (a distinct volume 1 issue), recur throughout many of the proposals in volume 2 as well (cf. Rizzi's proposal regarding *pro*-drop in chapter 10 of volume 2, for example).

Principles or Parameters

The foregoing issues involve a fundamental subissue: To what degree does cross-linguistic variation, and therefore UG, involve parameter setting? In parallel, to what degree does language acquisition involve parameter setting? Which are the true parameters? In addition, if acquisition does involve parameter setting, in what sense does this explain language acquisition? How should parameter setting be related to (6)?

In strong statements, which may be taken as reflecting the classical theory of parameters, Chomsky suggested (8).

(8) The initial state of the language faculty consists of a collection of subsystems, or modules as they are called, each of which is based on certain very general principles. Each of these principles admits of a certain very limited possibility of variation. We may think of the system as a complex network, associated with a switch box that contains a finite number of switches. The network is invariant, but each switch can be set in one of two positions, on or off. Unless the switches are set, nothing happens. But when the switches are set in one of the permissible ways, the system functions, yielding the entire infinite array of interpretation for linguistic expressions. A slight change in switch settings can yield complex and varied phenomenal consequences as its effects filter through the network. . . . To acquire a language, the child's mind must determine how the switches are set. (Chomsky, 1987, p. 68)

Acquisition of language is in part a process of setting the switches one way or another on the basis of the presented data, a process of fixing the values of the parameters. (Chomsky, 1988, p. 63)

On this view, parameter setting is necessary to language acquisition, presumably instantaneous, and probably binary valued.

In confronting cross-linguistic variation, each of these two volumes assesses parameter setting theory, asking: What is the nature of the parameter that may underlie observed variation, and how can it account for language acquisition? In volume 1, phrase structure is an issue, as in the investigation of the head direction parameter in X' theory and its proper formulation, and that of various forms of a head raising (in particular, *verb raising*) parameter that may operate on phrase structure to derive surface word-order variation across languages (e.g., German and English). In volume 2, these questions implicate the Binding Theory module (especially the component that handles lexical anaphors and pronouns) and the related module that deals with *pro*-drop phenomena. Binding Theory parametrization and the *pro*-drop parameter are debated.

One striking result across both volumes is an apparent diminished role for parameters both in the explanation for cross-linguistic variation and for language acquisition. In chapter 1 of volume 1, Huang argues for a simple form of a phrase structure parameter of head direction, even in the problematic case of Chinese, but against separate parameters for direction of case and theta role assignment (see, e.g., Travis, 1984). Deprez (chapter 12) presents a nonparametric account of V-2. In volume 2, Koster (chapter 1), Tang (chapter 2), Li (chapter 3), and Hermon (chapter 4) each argue for a treatment of Binding Theory that is independent of any parametrization of locality.

Similarly, in the acquisition literature, Lust (volume 1, chapter 5) argues for the role of a head direction parameter and pursues its formulation in terms of a functional head (i.e., C^0). This is a restricted, abstract version of the head direction parameter. In volume 2, Hermon's (chapter 4), Jakubowicz's (chapter 5), and Mazuka and Lust's (chapter 6) accounts of acquisition in the area of Binding Theory are nonparametric. In the area of *pro*-drop in volume 2, several of the chapters, including Valian (chapter 11) and Rizzi (chapter 10), challenge the view that a classic *pro*-drop parameter explains the observed acquisition data, that is, main clause null subjects in child language when they occur. Rizzi's can be considered a nonparametric approach to early null subjects, because it does not analyze missing subjects in main clauses in early English as exhibiting the [+] setting of a *pro*-drop parameter.

In fact, although the classic parameter setting paradigm of switch setting, as described in (8), would appear to explain apparently instantaneous acquisition, it would not in itself account directly for real delay in language development. Switch setting alone, would appear incompatible with delay. To deal with this problem, the acquisition literature has frequently resorted to variations on the original parameter setting paradigm in (8). These variations involve either an inborn, unmarked, privileged parameter setting that must then be undone over time and that leads children acquiring certain languages to hold false grammatical hypotheses about their language, initially (e.g., Hyams, 1986); or a "hill climbing" interpretation of parameter setting in place of switch setting (Lebeaux, 1988, 1990).

Lust (volume 1, chapter 5) argues with regard to phrase structure that the classic switch setting view of early parameter setting is compatible with real developmental change in language knowledge, and she argues against the hill climbing interpretation. Valian (volume 2, chapter 11) argues against the unmarked inborn setting hypothesis of parameters on the basis of pro-drop–related acquisition data that reveal critical differences between children acquiring Italian and children acquiring English from early ages. (See also Valian, 1990.)

Tension Between Inductive and Deductive Learning

A distinction between I-language and E-language is essential to the UG paradigm, as summarized in (9), and it obviously underlies the approach in these volumes to cross-linguistic variation and acquisition.

   (9) a. *E-language:* E-language is " 'externalized language' . . . in the sense that the construct is understood independently of the properties of the mind/brain" (Chomsky, 1986, p. 20).

   b. *I-language:* "Let us refer to this 'notion of structure' as an 'internalized language' (I-language). The I-language, then, is some element of the mind of the person who knows the language, acquired by the learner, and used by the speaker-hearer. . . . The grammar would then be a theory of the I-language, which is the object under investigation" (Chomsky, 1986, p. 22).

The theory of UG requires this distinction and is explicitly a theory of I-language:

   (10) "UG now is construed as the theory of human I-languages, a system of conditions deriving from the human biological endowment that identifies the I-languages that are humanly accessible under normal conditions" (Chomsky, 1986, p. 23).

Although most chapters in these volumes do not address this distinction directly, it is essential to the solution of the full set of issues debated here (see, e.g., Kapur, Lust, Harbert, & Martohardjono, 1993, in preparation, on the Binding Theory). Just as the I-language/E-language distinction must be recognized in the study of UG through adult language, so it must be in the study of UG through child language. Observed utterances are always manifestations of E-language but are at best only indirect manifestations of

I-language. The complete data set from any particular language or any particular child's corpus reflects I-language only indirectly, to the degree that it reflects UG. Even then, UG is only a part of I-language.

This distinction between E-language and I-language has consequences both for methodology and for interpretation, as is reflected in these volumes. Methodologically, almost all of the chapters here reflect a distinct shift from earlier research that studied structures individually. For instance, utterances with or without V-2 position in German were investigated in order to assess children's knowledge of German word order (Clahsen, 1982). In contrast, knowledge of the grammar of German V-2 in first language acquisition is studied in these volumes through widespread aspects of grammar, such as knowledge of CP phrase structure, knowledge of each step of the V-to-I-to-C movement that underlies V-2, and knowledge of other operations on CP and SPEC of CP such as WH-movement and topicalization. See Boser, Lust, Santelmann, and Whitman (1991, 1992) for an example of this type of argumentation regarding grammatical knowledge of V-2 in German, and Deprez and Pierce (1993) for related analyses. All of the chapters in these volumes in this area of V-2 knowledge involve such extensive data analyses in order to justify their argumentation.[1]

In addition, it is clear that certain debates about grammatical knowledge have resulted in a debate about what constitutes E-language and what constitutes I-language in observed child behavior. The debate between Valian and Hyams provides a precise example of this issue. (See also the earlier literature on this debate, including Bloom, 1990, and Mazuka, Lust, Wakayama, & Snyder, 1986.) Recognition of the E-language/I-language dichotomy is necessary to the final resolution of that debate. There it becomes clear that unless processing and performance constraints can be clearly identified, it is not possible to identify whether a particular E-language phenomenon, absence of a subject in a short child utterance (e.g., *Ø push car*), is due to a grammatical hypothesis about possible null subjects (e.g., some version of a *pro*-drop parameter, an I-language factor), or due to the attested processing/performance factors that restrict a child's utterances across all structures in all languages at early periods of development (presumably an E-language factor).

On the level of interpretation, understanding of acquisition and identification of the role of UG in acquisition requires an analysis of the degree to

---

[1]This paradigm was nicely illustrated in Hyams' (1986) pursuit of evidence regarding the child's grammar of pro-drop. This methodology characterizes the study of children's natural speech and is the primary method used in many of the studies of children's earliest language, given the fact that the younger children are, the less amenable they are to experimental methods. The incorporation of experimental methods, however, is clearly motivated by a concern for the measurement of I-language (cf. Lust, Chien, & Flynn, 1987). New and refined methods extending experimentation to infants are now being developed (e.g., Gerken, Landau, & Remez, 1990; Jusczyk, Mazuka, Mandel, Kiritani, & Hayasaki, 1993).

which inductive (E-language based) and deductive (I-language based) processes are at work. As a related question, we must ask to what degree a separate learnability module (that informs inductive learning) is necessary as a supplement to the language faculty informed by UG (see, e.g., Manzini & Wexler, 1987), or not (Kapur et al., 1993, in preparation). Even a highly deductive UG-based acquisition theory must deal with induction. For example, parameters require data/experience to be triggered. In general, specific language data (E-language) and specific language grammars must be mapped to UG principles, as well as to parameters.

Whereas all of the chapters in these volumes are indirectly related to these issues, several confront them directly. In volume 1, Gleitman (chapter 14), who has repeatedly articulated the need for study of the deductive/inductive links in a comprehensive theory of language acquisition, summarizes a wide set of coherent research, which essentially argues that knowledge of syntax (presumably linked closely to deductive knowledge) guides and constrains inductive knowledge (of the lexicon). Although Gleitman focuses on acquisition of the verbal lexicon, Chierchia (volume 1, chapter 15) develops the possibility of treating acquisition of the nominal lexicon in this framework. The results of this research must be brought to bear on all of the studies in each of the two volumes, wherein a major debate concerns whether an early stage of child language reflects a solely lexicon-based grammar (and thus is discontinuous with adult grammar). The research of Hale and Keyser (e.g., volume 1, chapter 3) may provide the basis for the extensive cross-linguistic research that is necessary to a full account of possible mapping between syntax and lexicon, both in theory and in acquisition. Several of the chapters in volume 2 investigate the role of specific triggering data in determining language or grammatical knowledge. Kapur's chapter 22 most specifically concerns the inductive/deductive tension.

Relation Between UG and Specific Language Grammars

Once one adopts the cross-linguistic approach and confronts the real fact of development of language, one is immediately and necessarily led to what may be the most fundamental issue of all, the hypothesis in (11):

(11) "At the steady state attained in language acquisition, the UG principles remain distinct from language-particular properties" (Chomsky, 1989, p. 72).

Flynn and Martohardjono (volume 1, chapter 16) confront this hypothesis directly, using research in adult second language acquisition as a paradigm by which to investigate it. This issue implicitly underlies much of the debate about the nature of language development. Notice that if UG and specific language principles are distinct, then a version of the Strong Continuity Hypothesis is possible as consistent with real change in language acquisition (i.e., (6)). Here, a mapping between UG and specific languages must be accounted for, even though UG principles and parameters stay constant and continuous over this mapping (see, e.g., Cohen Sherman & Lust, 1993; Lust, volume 1, chapter 5). If UG and specific language principles do not remain distinct, then it is not clear how the course of language development can be so described. In fact, if UG and specific language principles do not remain distinct, but instead UG becomes the I-language (of a specific L) and is thus modified, then this would appear to require a form of discontinuity in acquisition.

THEORY OF FIRST LANGUAGE ACQUISITION

The most recent research, as exemplified in these volumes, with its debates on the preceding four issues, leads to the development of a theory of first language acquisition. In fact, it may lead to a significant paradigm shift in the way we now pursue this theory.

Typically, in work within the UG paradigm, a theory of first language acquisition (where the emphasis is on (6), not (5)) has generally attributed acquisition to growth of the lexicon, parameters, and possible maturation (see, e.g., Chomsky & Lasnik, 1992). Although the current research in the field pursues all of these ideas, the results lead us further toward a true theory of language acquisition, one that calls for a refinement and a complication of the way in which each of these factors is held to play a role. In these four general areas, we see (a) a diminished role of parameters, and (b) a skepticism regarding UG change (maturation) in explaining real change in children's language over time. In our view, these results do not weaken the UG paradigm in ((1) and (2)); in fact, they strengthen it.

Any arguments for a Strong Continuity Hypothesis allow us to interpret the principles and parameters of UG as an explanation for the relatively fast, efficient success of the child as language learner (the original intent of the Language Acquisition Device or LAD), not as an explanation for the real time delay in actual child language.

However, we are led to seek an answer to the fundamental and distinct question: What does explain the real change in children's language knowledge over time, if and when such change does exist? More specifically, what role does UG play in this developmental course? If the SCH is adopted, this would appear to lead to a classical interpretation of UG as a filter and constraint on the acquisition process (Chomsky, 1980, 1988). However, this ironically means that UG explains the eventual success of the learner, not the developmental delays per se. Many of the chapters in these two volumes point to a more refined paradigm for approaching this developmental question, one that involves a detailed theory of UG. If neither cross-linguistic variation nor language acquisition can be totally reduced to parameter setting, this too requires a more refined theory of UG.

Many of the chapters in both volumes provide an account of acquisition that views the child as engaged in working out the nitty-gritty details of how the lexicon, PF effects (e.g., whether or not an element can be lexically null in a language), and other language-specific principles (e.g., the INFL or agreement system or the WH system of the language) interact indirectly with UG principles. These include principles of X′ theory and of SPEC-head agreement (as in Haegeman, volume 1, chapter 2, for example). This approach can be generalized if we view the acquisition course as reflecting an interaction between UG modules, an interaction that is not itself prescribed by UG but must be worked out in a language-specific manner (as in Lust, volume 1, chapter 5; see also Deprez, volume 1, chapter 12; Flynn & Martohardjono, volume 1, chapter 16; Hermon, volume 2, chapter 4). The child must work out this modular interaction on the basis of positive, language-specific data to which he or she is exposed.

THEORY OF UG

The results of this more refined approach to a theory of first language acquisition have consequences for a theory of UG in general. To the degree that an SCH is supported, the theoretical definition of principles and parameters in linguistic theory has validation as a model of the initial state in a strong sense. That is, both (1) and (2) hold directly and in close accord with each other. The specific trends that are emerging in the acquisition literature (such as the restriction of the number of parameters, combined with a support for parameter setting as instantaneous and efficacious when it does occur), are in accord with a strengthening of this theory of UG. Clearly, the proliferation of proposed parameters to describe all cross-linguistic variation had become one of the major threats to the explanatory strength of the theory in recent years. We may view this streamlining of the parametric component of UG as in accord with the independent changes toward a minimalist approach to the linguistic theory of UG (Chomsky, 1992). In fact, several of the chapters in both volumes articulate this connection specifically. See, for example, J. Koster (volume 2, chapter 1) and Tang, (volume 2, chapter 2).

All of the chapters that deal directly with language acquisition have consequences for linguistic theory per se. (See C. Koster, volume 2, chapter 8, for example). In the same way, all of the chapters that deal directly with theoretical issues have consequences for the interpretation of first language acquisition.

THEORY OF LEARNABILITY

The results in each of these four debates also accord with certain major changes in formal learnability theory.

Learnability theory forms the third corner of a triad that includes linguistic theory and the theory of natural language acquisition. It provides interesting constraints on both and is in turn informed by their special needs. The origins of learning theory can be traced back to the pioneering work of Gold (1967), who showed that, in general, even simple families of languages cannot be learned through induction from positive evidence alone. The impact of his conclusion was extensive, and linguistic theory was altered substantially so as to overcome this problem. In the current formulation of UG theory, there are only a finite number of parameters, each with only a finite number of values, that the child needs to fix in order to identify the core of his or her language. Such parameter spaces are always learnable even from positive evidence.

Recently, the problem of overgeneralization that arises only in the absence of negative evidence has received some interesting formal treatment. Berwick (1985) and, later, others, including Manzini and Wexler (1987), proposed the Subset Principle as an essential mechanism by which the child could overcome this learnability problem. The child obeys the Subset Principle when he or she guesses the smallest language consistent with a body of evidence. Some, however, have argued that such a special principle is neither necessary nor efficacious (e.g., Kapur et al., 1993, in preparation).

Because, in principle, parameter setting reduces the learning problem that Gold identified to a solvable one (especially if one assumes stochastic input as in Kapur, volume 2, chapter 22), then the major remaining learning problem involves feasibility: How can learning proceed in a feasible manner amid considerably varied circumstances such as those involving noise, and in a plausible amount of time? Even if there were only 20 parameters, the search space would still be large enough to pose a problem, especially if the input were noisy. Because the actual input can be quite misleading—sometimes parameters conspire in particularly malicious ways (e.g., Fodor, chapter 19, volume 2)—an exhaustive search may not be feasible. Thus, the solution remains mysterious, but in different ways than previously supposed. At this point, the first steps in this new direction are being taken. The previous goal was to explain learnability in the abstract, where, for example, the child as learner was idealized to be all-powerful. In contrast, the chapters on learnability, although diverse in their approach and assumptions, all attempt to account for learnability under more realistic conditions, addressing the problem of learning in a feasible manner.[2]

---

[2]Any proposal showing feasible learning would necessarily have to account for the course of language development as well, but, for the moment, that remains beyond the purview of the research reported here.

Many of the previous approaches to learnability theory failed precisely at the point of feasibility. Traditionally, the approach to learning has always been inductive (i.e., data driven). In fact, an even stronger implicit assumption has been that learning is error driven. According to this prevailing view, the child tries to revise the values of parameters only if there is explicit contradiction in the input. In such a setting, the notion of a trigger as a specific data item that reveals some value of a particular parameter has been taken to be very important (see, e.g., Gibson & Wexler, 1992). Frank and Kapur (1992), however, argued that the amount of time required for the child to succeed in a real parameter space, even if such triggers exist, is far beyond what can be reasonably assumed. Many other approaches assume that the child has the ability to build, maintain, and evaluate a large number of parsers simultaneously. It is also far from clear that this is a plausible assumption to make, because no serious mechanisms to explain this hypothesis have been discussed. Certain other previous models fail even when a small amount of noise is permitted in the input.

More recent approaches to learnability theory attempted to overcome these shortcomings. In volume 2, Clark (chapter 21), Fodor (chapter 19), Kapur (chapter 22), and Lightfoot (chapter 20) share a common concern for these formal aspects of the parameter setting problem. They emphasize the ambiguity in the input the child receives and suggest ways in which learning can nevertheless proceed. Lightfoot is concerned with the complexity of the data needed to trigger particular parameter settings. He challenges Roeper and Weissenborn's (1990) claim that children primarily use data from embedded clauses to set parameters. He argues instead that the theory of learnability must include a degree-0 complexity restriction; namely, only structurally simple data (i.e., data drawn from unembedded domains) are used by the child to set parameters.[3] Clark emphasizes that there must be definite bounds not only on the complexity of data for triggering but also on the interaction between different parameters in order to achieve computationally feasible parameter settings. He concludes with a sketch of an interesting learning proposal based on genetic algorithms. Fodor concentrates on alternative analyses of some linguistic phenomena to minimize the conflation of the core and the periphery.

Kapur's proposal has a more deductive flavor. In his approach, the data that constitute evidence are not simply a sentence or even a set of utterances as such, but rather the whole corpus of input (or a substantial fraction of it), interpreted in whichever way is revealing to the child. There is then no trigger in the conventional sense, and thus the issue of the complexity of the trigger is not directly relevant. The issue of ambiguity in the input is also considerably diminished, because a statistical average is likely to be

---

[3]See Lightfoot (1989) and related peer commentary for extensive debate on this proposal.

robust under most circumstances. In this approach, a strong form of UG can be brought into closer coherence with formal learnability theory and can be viewed as guiding and constraining induction.

In summary, the changes reviewed here in learnability theory parallel changes in the theory of natural language acquisition and in linguistic theory. Across all domains we see a new concern for a more realistic view of language learning (one that involves real time and real evidence); a more constrained view of the number and types of parameters in UG; and a closer, more precise link between these.

ORGANIZATION OF THE VOLUMES

The first volume addresses issues surrounding the theory and knowledge of phrase structure; the second addresses issues surrounding the theory and knowledge of anaphora and related issues (e.g., WH and quantifier dependencies). These are arguably the two most central, and most unifying, areas of research in a theory of UG and, correspondingly, in a theory of the language faculty. The two volumes are profoundly related. Each of the four recurrent issues raised in the foregoing discussion appears in both volumes. For example, research on phrase structure principles during acquisition (volume 1) is central to an understanding of the child's knowledge of Binding Theory, of the distribution and interpretation of empty categories, and of quantifier or WH scope (volume 2).

Each of the volumes is organized around central domains of debate. Each begins with a set of chapters that pursue the theoretical formulation of these domains. Each concludes with a set of chapters that are concerned in particular with formal properties of learnability. The central core of each volume involves the sets of chapters that deliberately attempt to integrate linguistic theory and the study of acquisition around focal areas of debate concerning precise issues, such as the knowledge of V-2 in German and related languages (volume 1), or the knowledge of principles in the Binding Theory (volume 2).

Each of the volumes includes a brief introduction. In it, the editors (a) sketch the necessary background for the volume; (b) introduce the specific issues under debate; (c) summarize the individual chapters, placing them in the context of the debates; and (d) provide an overview of major points of convergence and divergence that emerge from each of the central debates.

Barbara Lust, Isabella Barbier,
Claire Foley, Gabriela Hermon, Shyam Kapur,
Jaklin Kornfilt, Zelmira Nuñez del Prado,
Margarita Suñer, John Whitman

REFERENCES

Berwick, R. (1985). *The acquisition of syntactic knowledge.* Cambridge, MA: MIT Press.

Bloom, P. (1990). Subjectless sentences in child language. *Linguistic Inquiry, 21,* 419–509.

Borer, H., & Wexler, K. (1987). The maturation of syntax. In T. Roeper & E. Williams (Eds.), *Parameter setting* (pp. 123–172). Dordrecht: D. Reidel.

Boser, K., Lust, B., Santelmann, L., & Whitman, J. (1991). *The theoretical significance of auxiliaries in early child German.* Paper presented at the 16th Annual Boston University Conference on Language Development, Boston, MA.

Boser, K., Lust, B., Santelmann, L., & Whitman, J. (1992). The syntax of CP and V-2 in early child German: The Strong Continuity Hypothesis. *Proceedings of the North Eastern Linguistics Society, 22.*

Chomsky, N. (1965). *Aspects of the theory of syntax.* Cambridge, MA: MIT Press.

Chomsky, N. (1975). *Reflections on language.* New York: Pantheon Books.

Chomsky, N. (1980). *Rules and representations.* New York: Columbia University Press.

Chomsky, N. (1986). *Knowledge of language: Its nature, origin, and use.* New York: Praeger.

Chomsky, N. (1987). *Language in a psychological setting.* Tokyo: Sophia Linguistica, Sophia University.

Chomsky, N. (1988). *Language and problems of knowledge.* Cambridge, MA: MIT Press.

Chomsky, N. (1989). Some notes on economy of derivations. In I. Laka & A. Mahajan (Eds.), *WPL, X, Functional heads and clause structures* (pp. 43–74). Cambridge, MA: MIT.

Chomsky, N. (1992). A minimalist program for linguistic theory. *MIT Occasional Papers in Linguistics, 1.* Cambridge, MA: MIT, Department of Linguistics and Philosophy.

Chomsky, N., Lasnik, H. (1992). Principles and parameters theory. In J. Jacobs, A. vanStechow, W. Sternfeld, & T. Venneman (Eds.), *Syntax: An international handbook of contemporary research.* Berlin: Walter de Gruyter.

Clahsen, (1982). *Spracherwerb in der Kindheit* [Language Acquisition in childhood]. Tübingen: Gunter Narr.

Cohen Sherman, J., & Lust, B. (1993). Children are in control. *Cognition, 46,* 1–51.

Deprez, V., & Pierce, A. (1993). Negation and functional projections in early grammar. *Linguistic Inquiry, 24,* 25–67.

Fodor, J., Bever, T., & Garrett, M. (1974). *The psychology of language.* New York: McGraw Hill.

Frank, R., & Kapur, S. (1992). *On the use of triggers in parameter setting.* Paper presented at the 17th Annual Boston University Conference on Language Development, Boston, MA.

Gerken, L., Landau, B., & Remez, R. (1990). Function morphemes in young children's speech perception and production. *Developmental Psychology, 26,* 204–216.

Gibson, E., & Wexler, K. (1992). *Parameter setting, triggers and V2.* Paper presented at GLOW, Lisbon.

Gold, E. M. (1967). Language identification in the limit. *Information and Control, 10,* 447–474.

Hyams, N. (1986). *Language acquisition and the theory of parameters.* Dordrecht: D. Reidel.

Jusczyk, P., Mazuka, R., Mandel, D., Kiritani, S., & Hayasaki, A. (1993, March). *A cross-linguistic study of American and Japanese infants' perception of acoustic correlates to clausal units.* Paper presented at SRCD 60th anniversary meeting, New Orleans, LA.

Kapur, S., Lust, B., Harbert, W., & Martohardjono, G. (1993). Universal Grammar and learnability theory: The case of binding domains and the subset principle. In E. Reuland & W. Abraham (Eds.), *Knowledge and language: Vol. 3. Issues in representation and acquisition* (pp. 185–216). Dordrecht: Kluwer.

Kapur, S., Lust, B., Harbert, W., & Martohardjono, G. (in preparation). *On relating UG and learnability theory: Intensional and extensional principles in the representation and acquisition of Binding Domains.*

Lebeaux, D. (1988). *Language acquisition and the form of the grammar.* Unpublished doctoral dissertation, University of Massachusetts, Amherst.

Lebeaux, D. (1990). The grammatical nature of the acquisition sequence: Adjoin-α and the formation of relative clauses. In L. Frazier & J. de Villiers (Eds.), *Language processing and language acquisition.* Dordrecht: Kluwer.

Lightfoot, D. (1989). The child's trigger experience: Degree 0 learnability and open peer commentary. *Behavioral and Brain Sciences, 12,* 321–375.

Lust, B. (Ed.). (1986). *Studies in the acquisition of anaphora: Vol. 1. Defining the constraints.* Dordrecht: D. Reidel.

Lust, B. (Ed.). (1987). *Studies in the acquisition of anaphora: Vol. 2. Applying the constraints.* Dordrecht: D. Reidel.

Lust, B., Chien, Y.-C., & Flynn, S. (1987). What children know: Comparison of experimental methods for the study of first language acquisition. In B. Lust (Ed.), *Studies in the acquisition of anaphora: Volume 2. Applying the constraints* (pp. 271–356). Dordrecht: D. Reidel.

Manzini, R., & Wexler, K. (1987). Parameters, binding theory and learnability. *Linguistic Inquiry, 18,* 413–444.

Mazuka, R., Lust, B., Wakayama, T., & Snyder, W. (1986). Distinguishing effects of parameters in early syntax acquisition: A cross-linguistic study of Japanese and English. In *Papers and Reports on Child Language Development* (pp. 73–82). Stanford, CA: Stanford University.

Radford, A. (1990). *Syntactic theory and the acquisition of English syntax.* Oxford: Basil Blackwell.

Roeper, T., & Weissenborn, J. (1990). How to make parameters work: Comments on Valian. In L. Frazier & J. de Villiers (Eds.), *Language processing and language acquisition* (pp. 147–162). Dordrecht: Kluwer.

Travis, L. (1984). *Parameters and effects of word order variation.* Unpublished doctoral dissertation, MIT, Cambridge, MA.

Valian, V. (1990). Logical and psychological constraints on the acquisition of syntax. In L. Frazier & J. de Villiers (Eds.), *Language processing and language acquisition* (pp. 119–146). Dordrecht: Kluwer.

Whitman, J., Lee, K.-O., & Lust, B. (1991). Continuity of the principles of Universal Grammar in first language acquisition: The issue of functional categories. In NELS *Proceedings of the North Eastern Linguistics Society, 21,* 383–397.

Introduction to Volume 2

Constraining Binding, Dependencies, and Learnability: Principles or Parameters?

One of the most active areas in the study of Universal Grammar during the last decade has centered around a universal theory of various forms of syntactic dependencies, specifically, both A and A' (argument and nonargument) dependencies. Intensive research has concerned both lexical proforms and empty categories. Cross-linguistic investigation into this area of UG has led to a wide set of discoveries about natural language variation and has raised fundamental issues about its proper representation in formal theory. As the chapters in this volume document, these theoretical issues are closely paralleled by issues in first language acquisition.

In this volume, general issues concern the degree to which parameters can account for cross-linguistic variation and acquisition. Recent shifts toward a more restrictive theory of UG (i.e., minimalist theory) call into question both the number and the nature of parameters, relying (whenever possible) on a few universal principles rather than a profusion of parameters. This more restrictive theory requires parameters to be general (i.e., not limited to specific domains) and to refer to observable properties of language. Possibly, it requires that parametrization be linked to functional categories (e.g., Borer, 1983; Chomsky, 1992; Ouhalla, 1991).

Specific issues concern the locality constraints that govern dependency relationships. Apparent cross-linguistic variation in locality had led, in some earlier work, to a parameter-based approach to locality in UG. Some scholars proposed different definitions of locality for different types of dependency. Now, a more restrictive, universal definition of locality is sought. This change has arisen in part due to concerns about learnability. The classic theory of

1

parameter setting promised an explanation for early, efficient language acquisition because experience (presumably a small amount of it), under this theory, would quickly allow switch setting and a wide array of deductive consequences (Chomsky, 1988b) in grammar construction. As the learnability section in this volume makes explicit, however, this leading idea of parameter setting raised a number of questions that must be solved if the program it inspires is to succeed. If parameters constrain cross-linguistic variation and acquisition, how are they triggered? How does experience work to set parameter values? How many parameters must be set? How do they interact?

The parameter-setting approach to UG promised major explanatory power for first language acquisition, as well as for cross-linguistic variation. But if there are no constraints on parameters, and no limits to what can be parametrized, then this theory of UG is not restrictive and thus not explanatory. The critical issue now is: *How can cross-linguistic variation and, correspondingly, first language acquisition be explained in terms of principles and a finite set of parameters?*

Chomsky's (1992) minimalist program addressed many of these issues. In terms of the recent shift to a minimalist theory of UG, our explanation may "assume that S_0 (the 'Initial State') is constituted of invariant principles with options restricted to functional elements and general properties of the lexicon" (Chomsky, 1992, p. 6).

Each of the contributions to this volume pursues these issues, challenged by cross-linguistic variation; many of the scholars support their arguments with evidence from first language acquisition.

Locality

Perhaps the most central notion that has guided research on universal principles and has led to a rich array of proposed parameters of various kinds is that of *locality.* This volume reports research on locality in three areas that have received intensive study both theoretically and in first language acquisition. Researchers have applied parameter theory in a UG framework to each of these areas in order to account for cross-linguistic variation and to develop a model of the initial state (S_0). The bulk of the volume concerns the first two areas. The three areas are:

1. *Binding Theory (BT):* The principles constituting BT constrain proforms (i.e., anaphors and pronominals) and characterize the A(rgument)-system. Locality is essential to the BT, because the Binding Principles (A and B) apply within certain syntactic domains (so-called governing categories or binding domains) whose exact extension is determined by means of universal principles. Because these local domains do (or at least seem to) differ cross-linguistically, parameters have been proposed to account for such variation.

2. *Empty categories (ECs):* The principles that govern the distribution of ECs involve various types of null elements. The possibility for null subjects, generally referred to as *pro*-drop (e.g., in Spanish or Italian), is one of the most heavily studied areas of cross-linguistic variation in this domain and was proposed as a paradigm area of parametrization. The first such proposals in a generative framework include Taraldsen (1978) and Chomsky (1982).

For at least some instances of ECs, the issue of locality needs to be referred to. For example, the Empty Category Principle (ECP), however formulated, is a locality principle that tells us something about the distance (among other factors) between a phonologically empty (nonpronominal) element and its licenser (i.e., its proper governor). Similarly, in those instances where a pronominal EC (i.e., *pro*) needs to be licensed and/or identified by an overt element, it is important to determine not just the nature of the licenser/identifier, but also the structural relationship and syntactic distance between that element and *pro*. For example, in a language where a subject *pro* must be identified by rich agreement, *pro* and the AGR element in question must be in the same IP; this local domain cannot be extended. Thus, even where *pro* is bound by an element outside its IP (and has its content identified thus), its formal identifier (i.e., the rich AGR) must still be in the same IP. The situation is the same even where an outside binder of a subject *pro* is itself coindexed with a rich AGR element (and where the outside binder would be identified by that AGR element if that binder is itself a *pro*). The identifying and licensing ability of the higher AGR cannot be transmitted via a binder to the lower *pro*; that *pro* needs its own direct identifier in the local domain. (For some discussion of locality in the identification and licensing of *pro* in Turkish, a *pro*-drop language with obvious similarities in this respect to better-studied languages like Spanish and Italian, the reader is referred to Kornfilt 1984, 1988, 1991.)

3. *Quantifier and WH-related dependencies:* These involve a different type of proform (i.e., a variable bound by the WH- form or quantifier) and characterize the A'-binding (i.e., nonargument) system. The notion of locality has played a seminal role in generative treatments of such (apparently) unbounded dependencies. For WH-movement, whether this notion was expressed in terms of Subjacency (cf. Chomsky, 1973; Rizzi, 1986; and related work), antecedent-government (cf. Chomsky, 1986a, and others), or some other analysis, it has become clear that the relationship between an A' binder and its bindee is either directly local or mediated via local links (i.e., links in binding chains).

In this introduction, we briefly introduce each of these three domains, connected by the notion of locality, and we identify issues of current debate. We summarize each of the chapters in this volume, placing each in the context of these debates. We conclude by noting where we see essential convergence and divergence in results, and we sketch directions for future research. We begin to draw fundamental connections among the three areas, as a basis for future research. We assume that the results with greatest scientific impact involve converging evidence across theoretical, cross-linguistic and acquisition studies. In fact, research into first language acquisition provides a check on the validity of the ultimate formal theory of UG.

THE BINDING THEORY (BT)

BT: Major Issues of Debate

That module of UG termed the Binding Theory has been traditionally formulated as in (1), incorporating three distinct principles (cf. Chomsky, 1981):

(1) Classical BT (Schematic)
   A. An anaphor is locally bound.
   B. A pronominal is locally free.
   C. An R-expression is free everywhere.

In this theory, the nominal elements in the lexicon are categorized as anaphor, pronoun, or name (i.e., referring expression). The principles in (1) predict anaphors and pronouns to have complementary distribution.

Over the last decade, mainly through the pursuit of cross-linguistic evidence regarding this module of UG, the Binding Theory has been continually challenged, at the same time that it has revealed a wide set of regularities in the pronominal and anaphoric systems of languages across the world (cf. Harbert, in press, for review).

One persistent issue concerns *the productive evidence for long-distance anaphora with lexical forms that resemble anaphors, as in the case of reflexives in, for instance, Japanese, Korean, Chinese, Sinhala, and Marathi.* The existence of such long-distance anaphora calls into question the definition of locality, the nature of Principle A, and the relation between anaphors and pronouns. The behavior of these lexical forms also calls into question the proper representation of an interaction between linguistic principles and extralinguistic or pragmatic factors, as in, for instance, logophoric properties of pronouns. (See Koster & Reuland, 1991, for a recent collection of papers that deal with these issues.) This issue has motivated the postulation of special learning principles that interact with UG principles to guarantee learnability. (See, for example, Berwick, 1982; a debate between Manzini & Wexler, 1987; and Kapur, Lust, Harbert, & Martohardjono, 1993, on this issue; and papers collected in Reuland & Abraham, 1993.)

Several distinct approaches to this problem have been proposed. These proposed solutions fall into the following classes:

1. *Parametrization of the local domain* (e.g., Manzini & Wexler, 1987; Yang, 1984; although see Manzini, 1992, for an opposing view). Here UG is said to allow locality to vary in every way observed.

2. *Movement at LF of the anaphor* (initiated by Lebeaux, 1983; and further developed in Chomsky, 1986b; Cole, Hermon, & Sung, 1990, 1992; Huang & Tang, 1991). Here LF movement is assumed to be locally constrained in a similar manner across languages, despite surface variation. Under this approach, long-distance phenomena are explained not by Binding Principles (BP), but by (cyclic) properties of LF movement.

3. *Reanalysis of the long-distance anaphors* as not true anaphors (e.g., the logophor analysis, as in Sells, 1987).

4. *Lexical analyses*, as in the analysis of the verbal lexicon in terms of morphological licensing of reflexivity (cf. Reinhart, in press; Reinhart & Reuland, 1991), or the morphemic status (compound or monomorphemic) of anaphors and its possible relation to movement at LF (e.g., Pica, 1985, 1987).

A related problem for the BT concerns *overlap of pronouns and anaphors in the same domains*. For example, even in English, Zribi-Herz (1989), Pollard and Sag (1992), and Baker (1993a) identified apparent long-distance reflexives that offend Principle A. Others identified offenses of Principle B in local domains in English (e.g., Fiengo & May, in preparation). Bouchard's (1984) functional approach reflected one attempt to solve this problem. Here the structural domain in which a form appears determines its properties.

So-called pronominal anaphors in a wide range of languages extend this problem of distributional overlap and the Binding Principles (e.g., Mohanan, 1982; Wali & Subbarao, 1991; Wali, Subbarao, Gair, & Lust, in preparation; see also Keenan, 1988). This distributional overlap presents a major problem for learnability in the area of the BT (cf. Lust, Mazuka, Martohardjono, & Yoon, 1989).

Another fundamental issue that has arisen in the BT concerns a *possible lack of homogeneity among and within the Binding Principles (BPs)*. For example, it has been suggested that there may be a fundamental difference between Principle A and the other BT Principles, B and C. The latter are concerned with obligatory disjoint reference, whereas the former is concerned with direct binding that need not involve reference at all, as in *no man revealed himself*. It has, in fact, been argued that these facts reflect a fundamental theoretical distinction between binding and reference and thus fractionate the BT (e.g., Fiengo & May, in preparation; Reinhart, 1983a, 1983b). This has motivated Reinhart, for example, to argue for the elimination of Principle C and may possibly ultimately lead to the elimination of Principle B, or to a fractionation of Principle B (its bound variable application versus its disjoint reference properties). Principle B on this view would become nonhomogeneous (see Reuland, this volume, chapter 9). (In contrast, see Lasnik, 1976, 1989.)

Finally, Chomsky's (1992) minimalist theory provoked a fundamental reassessment of the position of BT in UG. Here BT, along with principles governing other dependencies, was argued to apply at LF exclusively.

Clearly, the representation of the BT in UG, and the explanation for its ostensible cross-linguistic variation, must now be reassessed. We may look to first language acquisition research for evidence in the resolution of these issues.

Research on first language acquisition has also provided debate. For example, with regard to the Binding Theory, although some have argued for a parametrized locality (e.g., Chien & Wexler, 1990), other researchers have argued for a strict grammatical interpretation of locality in the young child (e.g., Padilla-Rivera, 1990).

Related Chapters in This Volume

How Can Binding Work in a Minimalist Framework?   In this volume, J. Koster (chapter 1) presents a new theory of binding in terms of Chomsky's minimalist program. Koster argues that so-called anaphors and pronouns should not be distinguished in terms of traditional NP classification—that is, in terms of morphology. Koster's approach is related to previous functional or definitional approaches, where locality determines the status of a lexical element (e.g., Bouchard, 1984; Lust et al., 1989), and to approaches that analyze long-distance anaphors as logophors (cf. Clements, 1975; Hagége, 1974; Koster & Reuland, 1991; Sells, 1987). It is also related to other current work on the role of the verbal lexicon in the Binding Theory, as well as to proposals involving pronominal morphology.

In Koster's analysis, the Binding Theory universally determines what constitutes a local domain. No parametrization of locality is adopted. Elements can then be bound and identified in local domains through general local identification mechanisms; elements that are not bound are identified by other means (e.g., context). Pronouns and logophors are not locally bound, whereas the same morphological forms are anaphors if they are locally bound. Koster adopts Chomsky's minimalist theory feature-checking approach in suggesting that morphologically marked anaphors are marked with a strong anaphoric feature that must be checked in a SPEC-head agreement relationship with a strong head of an agreement phrase (AGR-S or AGR-O). Cross-linguistic variation can be explained, in that various languages either (a) reflect no anaphoric agreement, in the absence of morphologically marked anaphors; (b) check features in AGR-S; or (c) check features in AGR-O. Koster accounts for facts in English, French, German, Dutch, Frisian, and Spanish under this analysis.

In Koster's revised analysis of the BT, no special parameter setting is necessary for describing cross-linguistic variation in the area of the Binding Theory (except for the general parametric option of checking features in AGR-S or AGR-O, which is not particular to the BT). Presumably, what a child has to learn in each language is which system of anaphoric relations a certain morphological form belongs to.

Koster's proposal, like other current work, observes a difference between Principle A and the other Binding Principles. In fact, he advocates a radical revision of the Binding Theory, where Principle A is made more specific and Principle B is eliminated. This particular move is debated in later chapters in this volume.

The Case of Chinese. The Chinese long-distance reflexive *ziji* (as opposed to other reflexive forms in Chinese) has provided a challenge to locality in Principle A. To account for Chinese, Tang (this volume, chapter 2) also works within the minimalist program, presenting a new nonmovement analysis of long-distance binding in Chinese (thus replacing the earlier movement proposal in Tang, 1989).

Tang proposes that Chinese has AGR, which provides a local domain for binding, but that it is not overt. Two functional heads (AGR) are anaphorically linked if they have identical anaphoric ϕ-features. Extension of the binding domain to allow long-distance *ziji* occurs through successive agreement of anaphoric ϕ-features in functional heads. The Chinese *ziji* can be long-distance bound under this analysis if the SUBJECT is linked to (has anaphoric *phi*-features identical to those of) the closest potential SUBJECT.[1] AGR is the only acceptable SUBJECT for an X reflexive. A morphologically simple reflexive (such as Chinese *ziji*) can be either an X or an XP, whereas a morphologically complex reflexive (e.g., *ta ziji*) is always an XP.

Tang, affirming the independent status of INFL/AGR, argues that "a binding domain may be extended in different ways, depending on whether a language has overt AGR or not." Finally, she argues that "functional heads that license anaphoric linking may be parametrized." Whether or not a head allows this anaphoric linking depends on a morphological property of the functional head.

Tang's chapter relies not on LF movement, but on the notion of relativized SUBJECT (a principle of agreement between heads), on cross-linguistic variation in morphology (a property of overtness of AGR) and on the structure

---

[1]Here Tang follows Progovac (1991, 1992), who proposed that the notion of SUBJECT in a local domain for reflexive binding be relativized. According to Progovac, if the reflexive is a head, the SUBJECT must be a head; if the reflexive is an XP, the SUBJECT must be an XP. However, the editors note that the issue of how to define morphological simplicity remains open (cf. Kornfilt, 1993, on Turkish; also Li, this volume, chapter 3).

and morphological complexity of bare and compound reflexives, to account for long-distance binding in Chinese. No locality parameters are necessary in this approach, because long-distance orientation falls out of the X' status of the reflexive in various languages. Only X' reflexives can extend their binding domain, because only these forms choose functional heads as their SUBJECTs. Languages that create binding chains of functional heads then exhibit long-distance (LD) reflexives. Crucially, all features associated with LD reflexives follow from the interaction of the X' status of the reflexive with UG principles, and parametrization needed elsewhere in the grammar.

An Abstract Compositional Approach to Morphology: Uniting Japanese and Chinese. Li (chapter 3) presents an alternative compositional account of reflexives for both Japanese and Chinese, analyzing four reflexive forms in a Japanese dialect.

Li observes that in certain Japanese dialects, the Japanese reflexive *zisin* does not allow long-distance binding, whereas *zibun* does (see also Mazuka & Lust, this volume, chapter 6). If *zibun* and *zisin* are both monomorphemic reflexives, he argues, then under the relativized SUBJECT analysis, both should allow the extended domain for binding, and both should allow long-distance antecedents. However, they do not. Li points out that the only way to maintain the relativized SUBJECT analysis is to assume that *zisin* is not underlyingly monomorphemic. The consequence of this is that, like J. Koster, he argues that "it is no longer possible to make use of the correlation between the binding properties of a reflexive and its overt morphological form."

In sum, Li views the distribution of anaphors as resulting from the underlying NP structure and the particular feature composition for each form. Li argues that on these terms a simple and uniform analysis of Japanese and Chinese is possible; Chinese *ziji* corresponds to both *zibun* and *zisin*. Comparison of the possible binders for forms like *zibunzisin* 'selfself' and *karezisin* 'himself' and for *zibun* and *zisin* leads Li to propose that "the set of possible antecedents of a reflexive is simply the intersection of the sets of antecedents of its components." On this view, he argues that "we can still treat *ziji* as a logophor."

Li thus proposes an account based on a more abstract view of morphology and the lexicon, converging with general UG principles of antecedent selection and binding, and other even more general principles such as SPEC-head agreement, as well as general pragmatic factors related to logophoricity. Again, no locality parameters are needed, because the distribution of various forms follows from the interaction of the lexical specification of the item with general UG principles.

Is There Movement? (Chinese Again). Hermon's (chapter 4) proposal, like Tang's, does not parametrize locality and consults the morphology of reflexive type. Contrary to Tang (this volume, chapter 2) and to Li, Hermon bases her account on the LF head-movement approach proposed in Pica (1985, 1987), Sung (1990), and Cole et al. (1990, 1992). Hermon argues that LD orientation, subject orientation, and an observed blocking effect for reflexives all follow from the interaction of the X' status of the reflexive and the type of AGR in a particular language with UG principles governing head movement and feature percolation. Both Hermon and Tang obviate various independent parameters settings, such as governing category (GC) and subject orientation, relying instead on UG principles needed elsewhere in the grammar. Hermon derives several predictions for language acquisition that may distinguish these closely related proposals.

Cross-Linguistic Study of First Language Acquisition. Each of the chapters discussed thus far predicts that morphology and UG principles interact to explain acquisition in the area of BT in specific ways. Two chapters in this volume specifically test versions of this type of hypothesis.

Jakubowicz (chapter 5) provides a nonparametric account for reflexives in Danish and French. In her account, what determines the locality for reflexives is their X' status combined with the lexical properties of the predicates governing the reflexive. Some predicates allow incorporation (allowing a local reading), whereas others do not, forcing an LD interpretation (by forcing movement to INFL).

In particular, Jakubowicz discusses the distribution of the Danish elements *sig* and *sig selv*, and the French elements *se* and *lui-même*. Under her analysis, *se* and *sig* are featureless core reflexives and must be locally bound; the only exception is long-distance binding of *sig*. *Sig* undergoes covert movement and is lexically incorporated into its governor; long-distance binding is a last resort option when incorporation is ruled out by lexical properties of the governor. In contrast, *se* undergoes overt movement and has affixlike properties; its movement does not depend on lexical properties of a governor. *Lui-même* is analyzed as the adjunction of the reflexive morpheme *meme* to the element *lui*, which has *phi*-features.

Jakubowicz argues that her analysis predicts that the acquisition of *se* and *sig(selv)* should be almost instantaneous, whereas long-distance *sig* and *lui-même* may be acquired later. She presents French and Danish acquisition data in support of these hypotheses.

When Is an Anaphor Not an Anaphor? (Japanese). Mazuka and Lust (chapter 6) distinguish between knowledge of the syntactic Binding Principles and knowledge of the lexicon that may instantiate these principles in a language. They argue that although the Binding Principles themselves may be biologically programmed, children cannot assume prior knowledge of the language-specific lexical classification as anaphor or pronoun in the BT sense, just as different languages do not have uniform morphological classes for these types. On the basis of combined cross-linguistic analysis of Japanese and first language acquisition data from Japanese, they argue for a definitional interpretation of the Binding Theory (cf. Lust et al., 1989). (Theoretically, this proposal is related, although not identical, to a functional theory, e.g., Bouchard, 1984.) According to this interpretation, the BT (including a universal principle of locality) is definitional because it determines the lexical differentiation of classes of different syntactic proform types. The BT provides syntactic features for a lexical item, if it can. Guided by the BT, and restrictive locality determined by UG, children must learn on the basis of direct and indirect evidence. They must consider the distribution of various lexical items in their language and determine which items are anaphors and which are pronouns, assigning both positive and negative syntactic features to the lexicon being acquired. In the case of Japanese, because the full set of positive and negative features cannot be assigned, *zibun* is determined not to be an anaphor or a pronoun in the syntactic BT sense of these terms. One implication is that not all languages will instantiate the BT classes lexically; for instance, Japanese does not. Mazuka and Lust suggest that the domain of empty categories (not lexical categories) is most directly related to the BT in Japanese. (In this context, see our remarks on the binding properties of empty categories in the concluding section of this introduction.) This proposal thus predicts quite profound differences across languages, although these differences are syntactically explained.[2] Again, no parametrization of locality is involved.

Principle B or P: Binding Theory or Pragmatics? Two chapters in this volume are central to the current debate over the status of Binding Principles B and C. They address the debate concerning a hypothesized revision of the Binding Theory, where Principle B is to be viewed as constraining binding in the bound variable interpretation of pronouns, and an independent pragmatic principle constrains coreference in other interpretations (Chien & Wexler, 1990; Grodzinsky & Reinhart, 1993; Reinhart, 1983a, 1983b).

In these chapters, Kaufman and C. Koster argue that there is no evidence that children lack either Principle B or that part of Principle B that assigns the bound variable interpretation of pronouns. They debate the interpretation of the important finding of Chien and Wexler (1990) that children often do not initially assign disjoint reference to pronouns in the local domain, thus appearing to offend Principle B.

Kaufman argues that children can perform as well with referential pronoun interpretation as with bound or quantified pronoun interpretation.

---

[2]As a sign of this profound cross-linguistic difference, note that the set of verbs that (in Mazuka and Lust's analysis) most clearly precludes local binding of *zibun* in object position in Japanese, includes verbs that may lexically license local binding in other languages (cf. Reinhart & Reuland, 1991).

C. Koster also argues, based on experimental results from Dutch VP ellipsis, that a reformulated Binding Theory (that excludes issues of coreference) is not an improvement over traditional Binding Theory. In essence, both Kaufman and C. Koster argue that standard Binding Theory for Principle B is in place from early on. If children make mistakes, these are due to a number of factors not directly related to structural binding (cf. C. Koster, 1993). C. Koster's results on Dutch VP ellipsis accord with those from Foley, Nuñez del Prado, Barbier, and Lust (1992a, 1992b, 1992c, in press); see also Thornton and Wexler (1991), for English. The combined Kaufman and C. Koster results also accord with Grimshaw and Rosen (1990); Crain and McKee (1986); and Lust, Eisele, and Mazuka (1992), who argue on the basis of empirical evidence that standard Binding Theory for Principle C is in place from earliest periods of acquisition.[3]

For a more detailed discussion of this set of chapters, and in particular those of Kaufman and C. Koster, see Reuland's commentary in chapter 9 of this volume.

Integrating the Pragmatic Dimension. Smith develops, in chapter 15, a cross-linguistic analysis of reference (both coreference and disjoint reference or obviation) connected with pronoun systems, supplementing this with report of research on Chinese language acquisition. She, too, develops a pragmatic theory of reference that does not replace the Binding Theory (e.g., Principle B) but interacts with it. In addition, Smith raises the critical learnability issue, which remains open in the field today: How does the child learn what is not possible, that is, that "certain pairings of forms and interpretation cannot be made" (cf. Mazuka & Lust, chapter 6, and Kapur, chapter 22, in this volume; see also Baker, 1993b). This is the crucial question regarding the acquisition of knowledge reflecting Principles B and C of the BT.

BT: Summary. In general, the first set of chapters in this volume, based on both theoretical and acquisition research, converge in eliminating parameter setting in the area of the BT; that is, they all argue that no BT-specific parametrization of locality (e.g., of governing category) is necessary to capture (i.e., either describe or explain) the facts of cross-linguistic variation or the facts of first language acquisition. (In this regard, they converge with Manzini, 1992, who argued for a "single locality principle and a single locality domain" [p. 161] in UG.) Instead, the observed cross-linguistic variation is argued to result from configurational and

---

[3]Notice that if these results hold, then in accord with the minimalist program of UG, they implicate the critical role of a level of LF representation (at which bound variable knowledge must be computed) throughout first language acquisition (cf. Foley et al. 1992a, 1992b, 1992c, in press).

morphological factors, along with UG principles needed elsewhere: for instance, whether AGR (a property of phrase structure) is overt or not across languages, whether functional determination of anaphors and pronouns is possible through reference to configuration, what the underlying phrase structure of NP is, and what the morphological properties of the anaphors or pronouns are. No major revisions in the Binding Principles themselves are motivated, although the Binding Principles are seen as interacting with several other grammatical and pragmatic aspects of language knowledge, such as logophoricity. Evidence is presented against a fractionation of Principles A, B, and C, distinguishing, for instance, between referential and nonreferential cases, or grammatical and pragmatic principles, while acknowledging that these distinctions are independently necessary in the grammar as a whole. (See J. Koster, this volume, chapter 1, however.) Evidence supports a strong and continuous role of the BT and a restrictive locality in first language acquisition. Most of the chapters in this volume that deal with acquisition, in fact, provide support for a universal and restrictive locality (e.g., Chien, chapter 17; Jakubowicz, chapter 5; Kaufman, chapter 7; Mazuka & Lust, chapter 6; Roeper & de Villiers, chapter 16). No evidence is provided for discontinuity in UG in this area during any period of acquisition. Several authors argue explicitly against such discontinuity (e.g., Kaufman, C. Koster).

Specific debates remain open regarding the precise level of representation at which the BT applies, and the precise mechanism by which it is represented. (For instance, although many of the proposals here do not involve movement in the area of BT, Hermon argues for a movement analysis.) A fundamental issue remains: What exactly constitutes the universal theory of locality for cross-linguistic variation and for the child? (See Manzini, 1992, for one approach to this problem.)

EMPTY CATEGORIES (ECs)

The domain of empty categories provides a particularly important area for the study of UG, because evidence so critically underdetermines the grammar of ECs for the learner, and because the distribution of ECs is so precisely constrained (cf. Chomsky, 1982, 1988a).

The range of empty categories within a language and across languages has provoked intense study within the UG paradigm, leading to numerous discoveries regarding the principles of language structure (e.g., locality) that underlie and constrain the distribution, interpretation, and differentiation of the empty categories (Chomsky, 1982, 1988).

Research has accrued regarding each of the types of ECs, including *NP-traces* (as in passive structures), *PRO* (as in control structures), *variables* (as in WH-binding or other forms of operator-variable binding), and the empty category termed *pro*, which is highly productive in some languages (e.g., the Romance languages, Chinese, Japanese and the South Asian languages). These category types have been the focus of much study in linguistic theory and in related studies of first language acquisition. The theory of UG is concerned with the relation between the subsystem of principles that apply to the empty categories, including locality principles, and the other subsystems such as the Binding Theory module.

Much research has focused on null subjects, generally subsuming their distribution and interpretation under the parameter commonly termed *pro*-drop and originally focusing on this property of the Romance languages in contrast to English. (In fact, empty categories elsewhere, as in object omission, have received less study, although see, for example, Authicr, 1989, Cole, 1987; Huang, 1984, 1989; Rizzi, 1986. More widespread argument omission, in languages such as Sinhala, Turkish, Japanese, or Bengali, has, likewise, drawn less attention.) This domain (subject suppression) has become a paradigm area for study of the parameter-setting component of UG.

In this volume, some of the research focuses on persistent issues regarding a parameter-setting model of subject *pro*-drop. We first address these issues. In addition, several chapters in this volume anticipate a link between the study of the empty categories and the study of lexical proforms involving the Binding Theory (Mazuka & Lust, chapter 6; Pierce, chapter 14; Smith, chapter 15). We consider this issue in the final section of this introduction. Two chapters introduce the area of operator-variable constructions or quantifier-variable constructions (Chien, chapter 17; Roeper & de Villiers, chapter 16).

The formulation of a *pro*-drop parameter to explain subject omission in some languages has undergone numerous revisions over the years since its original formulation in Chomsky (1981) and Perlmutter (1971). Motivation for this reformulation came from extended cross-linguistic study in which the following facts became apparent:

1. The original deductive consequences proposed for the *pro*-drop parameter were disconfirmed. For example, the predicted correlation between *that*-trace effects and [+/−*pro*-drop] languages was disconfirmed, as was the predicted correlation with inversion (e.g., Gilligan, 1987; Safir, 1985, 1986; Suñer, 1989).

2. Separate explanatory principles appeared to be required in order to explain the licensing of this null subject EC, and its identification or interpretation (Hermon & Yoon, 1989; Huang, 1984; Rizzi, 1986). This result severely weakened the strength of the proposed parameter.

3. Evidence was raised showing widespread productive occurrence of main clause null subjects in adult language, independent of parametric

grammatical differences across languages, as in Haegeman's (1990a, 1990b) diary studies.

4. Precise licensing by local AGR was called into question as the main criterion for *pro*-drop, by cross-linguistic studies (e.g., Gilligan, 1987; Hermon & Yoon, 1989; Jaeggli & Safir, 1989).

Major Issues of Debate

In general, the basic issues in the study of empty categories are the following:

1. How are the empty categories licensed?

2. To what degree are the principles of licensing universal or language-specific?

3. How do the principles that determine and constrain the licensing of ECs relate to principles that are concerned with their identification or interpretation (cf. Adams, 1987; Hermon & Yoon, 1989; Jaeggli & Safir, 1989; Rizzi, 1986 and references therein)?

4. In cases where a language allows either a null argument (e.g., *pro*) or a lexical pronoun in subject position, where are these in actual free variation? Where is only one option allowed? How do these (null and phonetically realized lexical items) interact (e.g., Kornfilt, 1984, 1987; Montalbetti, 1984)?

More narrowly, with regard to the proposed *pro*-drop parameter (subject position) the debated issues then became the following:

5. Is there a *pro*-drop parameter? Alternatively, are null subjects to be explained by control theory (e.g., Huang, 1984) or by other aspects of grammar (e.g., topic-drop), rather than by a uniformly defined *pro*-drop parameter?

6. If there is a parameter, what is its proper formulation? (See Lillo-Martin, this volume, chapter 13, for a summary of several alternative formulations.)

7. What is the relation of subject *pro*-drop to other ECs? Further studies have begun to investigate the degree to which ECs in subject and object position might not be equivalent, possibly at the level of UG (subject-object asymmetry). Does a discourse null operator license object but not subject omission (e.g., Huang, 1984, 1989)?

These theoretical issues regarding a *pro*-drop parameter (PDP) all have correlates in the domain of first language acquisition. They concern the formulation of hypotheses regarding what the child knows in the initial stages of first language acquisition, how the child uses this knowledge to deal with cross-linguistic variation (i.e., the various specific language data to which he or she is exposed), and whether this knowledge reflects *pro*-drop parameter setting. In fact, issues regarding first language acquisition can be articulated quite precisely:

8. Is there an unmarked setting of a PDP? If so, parameter resetting would be involved in first language acquisition. Hyams' (1986) early seminal proposal argued that in acquisition, there appeared to be evidence in the speech of young English learners for an unmarked [+*pro*-drop] setting of this parameter, thus raising the important issue of markedness in a theory of parameter setting, and its relevance to language acquisition (cf. Gair, 1988). Subsequent research questioned various aspects of this original proposal (e.g., P. Bloom, 1990; Hyams, 1992; Mazuka, Lust, Wakayama, & Snyder, 1986; Valian, 1991). Critically, the empirical evidence showed that proposed deductive consequences of a [+*pro*-drop] setting were not confirmed in acquisition data; and it was suggested that patterns of subject omission were not universal (see Hyams, 1992, for a review of several problems that emerged with the original proposal). For example, one prediction for the early [+*pro*-drop] grammar was the initial universal absence of modals, and the development of such modals in correlation with the development of a [−*pro*-drop] grammar that licensed lexical elements in INFL. Several lines of evidence have disconfirmed this prediction. (See, for example, Valian, 1991, on this issue.) Similarly, a prediction for a close correlation between the acquisition of expletive subjects and nonnull subjects has also been challenged (cf. Valian, 1991) on empirical grounds.

9. If there is parameter setting or resetting, what is the trigger for the setting or resetting (Lightfoot, 1991; Roeper & Weissenborn, 1990)? How simple or complex must the triggering data be?

The severity of the problem raised in the last point can be seen when one considers cases like German or Dutch, which under certain views are "limited *pro*-drop" languages (e.g., Jaeggli & Hyams, 1988; Jaeggli & Safir, 1989; Koster, 1986) and allow either overt or little *pro* expletives. Clearly, in these languages, the presence of an overt expletive could not be simply considered diagnostic of a general non-*pro*-drop language. It is possible that if the child already knew the licensing facts for null expletives, he or she could deduce the relevant knowledge. But clearly this would not explain the child's discovery of the relevant licensing principles. It is exactly the emergence of this knowledge that must be explained.

Related Chapters in This Volume

This volume includes chapters that reflect the results of years of converging scholarship on both cross-linguistic variation and first language acquisition with regard to a theory of *pro*-drop and related issues. It reflects a number of new accounts of *pro*-drop (i.e., missing subjects in adult and child language) that do not involve parameter resetting.

Root Null Subjects

Rizzi's account in chapter 10 of Early Null Subjects (ENS) in child language relies on the differences between null subjects in adult languages like Italian and ENS in languages like English, to develop a new theory of main clause null subjects. Essentially, Rizzi's is a nonparametric approach to Early Null Subjects (ENS), because it does not analyze main clause missing subjects in early English acquisition as exhibiting the [+] setting of a *pro*-drop parameter. Rather, it proposes that such ENSs reflect a different phenomenon; they are "root null subjects," which are found in certain special registers of English and other languages (such as the diary register studied by Haegeman, 1990a, 1990b). ENSs in main clauses represent a different type of null element; they may not be identical to *pro* or to a variable bound by a discourse-bound null operator. If we followed Rizzi's approach, we would not have to claim that children in English ever reset a parameter for null subjects. One could assume that children determine from very early on whether their language licenses genuine null subjects or not. In fact, Rizzi's initial analysis of some early child speech suggests that children make very little, if any, error regarding *pro*-drop in the CP-embedding domain. Under Rizzi's account, children also have access universally to the linguistic principles licensing root null subjects, as do adults.

This new proposal of Rizzi's builds on previous proposals that separate licensing from identification or interpretation of *pro* and relate licensing of *pro* to the CP-embedding domain (cf. Adams, 1987; Rizzi, 1986).

The Pro-Drop Debate

Valian (chapter 11) also argues against parameter resetting in first language acquisition, citing experimental data that indicate that although all children appear to drop some subjects at early MLU levels, American children's earliest productions of English utterances with verbs show a significantly higher use of overt subjects than do either Italian or Greek children's. Valian argues that this evidence provides a critical argument for early knowledge of correct parameter setting. Lillo-Martin (this volume, chapter 13) reports on a study of Chinese acquisition (Wang, Lillo-Martin, Best, & Levitt, 1992) that supported this argument.

Both Valian and Rizzi assume that languages can differ in determining the value for null subjects as either [+] or [−]. Crucially, however, there is no need, on their view, to assume that there is a preset value for a parameter or that children ever reset a parameter. These chapters then support a form of a Strong Continuity Hypothesis, because the grammar for null subjects does not mature or change in the course of acquisition.

As the Hyams, Valian, Rizzi, and Lillo-Martin chapters in this volume suggest, the issues regarding *pro*-drop in linguistic theory and first language acquisition are not yet resolved. (See, for example, P. Bloom, 1993), for extension of the debates.) In fact, the debates regarding these issues concerning *pro*-drop are only now reaching the precise level of analysis that will be necessary to resolve them fully. In this introduction, we attempt not to resolve these debates, but to clarify the fundamental issues that underlie them and to point the way to the further research that they appear to require. The issues are both interesting and significant because they raise fundamental questions about the study of first language acquisition in relation to linguistic theory.

We begin by focusing on the Hyams and Valian proposals, because these point up several of the most basic issues of debate.

Issue 1: Continuity or Discontinuity. The most fundamental issue that distinguishes the Hyams and Valian proposals concerns the basic nature of language acquisition: *Do children hold a qualitatively different grammar, with regard to UG principles and parameters, from adults?* (Compare the chapters in volume 1 for related debates.) Hyams' answer to this question is yes (Strong Discontinuity Hypothesis); that is, children initially hold an incorrect grammar for their language in the case where they are acquiring a non-*pro*-drop language (e.g., English). (They hold a correct grammar for a *pro*-drop language.) Valian's answer is no: Children's grammar with regard to the *pro*-drop parameter (as well as other basic principles of phrase structure) is properly set (Strong Continuity Hypothesis), whether the language is [+*pro*-drop] or [–*pro*-drop]. Although children in all languages may be observed to reduce subjects, for Valian, this does not result from a mistaken grammatical hypothesis on the part of the child, regarding either a [+] or [–] *pro*-drop parameter setting.

Issue 2: Grammar (Competence) or Processing (Performance). Much of the literature has adopted a dichotomy, labeling the Hyams proposal a grammatical account and the Valian proposal, a performance account. Although there is some motivation for this contrast, we would like to avoid these dichotomous labels here, because they risk begging the real issues that appear to underlie these two proposals and thus obfuscate the important agreement between them.

Clearly, as can be seen from Issue 1, both scholars agree that grammatical competence critically determines child language. Both adopt a parameter-setting model. The issue is not whether grammar is functioning, but which aspect of the grammar explains which aspect of child language data, to explain a child's language performance. For Valian, for example, it is the correct grammar that explains Italian–English child language differences in performance.

Clearly, too, both proposals are in agreement in that they are concerned with separating performance factors from competence (grammar) factors in the study of child language. No one would deny, we assume, that the putative telegraphic speech of child language (following the even more length-restricted one-word speech) must reflect some general performance or processing constraints, which are to some degree independent of whatever limitations may or may not hold of the child's grammatical knowledge. Hyams, for example, refers to Clark's (this volume, chapter 21) discussion of the child as "computationally bounded." In fact, extensive experimental evidence (e.g., Egido, 1979; Gerken, 1991; Shipley, Smith, & Gleitman, 1969) as well as earlier in-depth studies of this early child speech (L. Bloom's reduction hypothesis, for example) provide evidence that children's grammatical knowledge goes beyond their surface speech. Thus both proposals must agree that grammatical knowledge (competence) and performance cannot be equated. This distinction presumably accords with an I-language/E-language distinction, such as we recognize in adult language (cf. the general introduction to these volumes).[4] In fact, subject omission is in itself an E-language phenomenon.

The real issue that appears to separate the Hyams and the Valian proposals, then, is a more precise one: Does a certain E-language phenomenon, the observed subject omissions in early English child language (e.g., Ø *want milk*) reflect a grammatical hypothesis on the part of the child, in fact, a hypothesis about a particular grammatical parameter setting (Hyams)? If not, that is, if the child's grammatical knowledge is not incorrect, then what does explain this phenomenon? Can the explanation for this particular datum (i.e., observed language behavior), lie outside the grammar, for instance, in some type of performance limitations? Thus (like other child language phenomena) can ENSs lead one to underestimate the child's grammatical competence (Valian)? Or are ENSs constrained by some universally available root null subject principles of grammar (Rizzi)? A priori, some combination of these proposals would also be possible.

Issue 3: Methodology. This debate appears to raise an issue about methodology, that is, whether frequency of occurrence of a phenomenon in child language can provide the critical evidence needed to pursue the

---

[4]Actually, a rather profound issue is implied here. The length constraint observed universally in early child language, during what has been called the holophrastic/one word and telegraphic speech stages, is still not truly understood. The universality of this length constraint suggests that it is in some way biologically determined and so general that there is no direct linguistic explanation. On the other hand, careful analyses of this early child speech led L. Bloom (1970, 1973) originally to an indirect linguistic explanation for both holophrastic and telegraphic periods: Children were learning the specific linguistic rules of their grammar and, because of this, could not produce full adult language.

foregoing issues. Here, too, we think there is more agreement than disagreement across the Valian and Hyams proposals. (See also Rizzi on this issue.)

Clearly, grammar (I-language or competence) itself makes no direct predictions about relative frequencies of occurrence of any E-language phenomena, either across languages or in language acquisition. At the same time, argumentation with regard to I-language must consult empirical evidence; and this evidence can consist only of actual language data, and actual language behaviors. For example, if children omit not only subjects but in fact all other arguments or constituents with equal frequency, it would not be possible to argue that the evidence supported a *pro*-drop hypothesis. Children do, in fact, also omit objects, as in, for example, *Kathryn ∂ make again* (L. Bloom, 1970). In English, it is only the relatively lower frequency of this phenomenon, when compared to subject omission, that has allowed scholars to argue for a [+*pro*-drop] parameter setting (cf. also P. Bloom, 1990).

Issue 4: Subject-Object Asymmetry. In fact, one particular issue that emerges now in this literature, across all proposals, involves the proper explanation for an observed asymmetry in both child and adult language in frequency of subject and object omission (in all languages, with or without *pro*-drop, in which it has been observed). Further research must investigate the degree to which this asymmetry is explained by a *pro*-drop parameter. At this time, explanations range widely and include a proposed special relation between topic and subject (cf. Reinhart, 1981), a relation between operator-variable binding and object (Jaeggli & Hyams, 1988), grammatical configuration (Mazuka et al., 1986), processing (L. Bloom, 1970; P. Bloom, 1990, 1993; Hyams & Wexler, 1993).

Issue 5: The Proper Formulation of the Pro-drop Parameter: The Special Significance of the CP Domain. All proposals must be concerned with the proper formal representation of the *pro*-drop parameter, because, by all accounts, this representation is associated with a precise hypothesis regarding the mind.

Rizzi (this volume, chapter 10) supports the proposal by Roeper and Weissenborn (1990) that the critical domain for *pro*-drop parametric variation across languages may be not the main clause subject domain, but the embedded domain of CP. This proposal raises two parallel issues that must guide further research:

1. Empirically, is there evidence of children's knowledge regarding correct or incorrect *pro*-drop in this (CP) embedding domain? (This issue overlaps with issues addressed explicitly in volume 1, *viz.* the child's

knowledge of phrase structure and functionally headed phrase structure, as in CP.) For initial studies in this regard, see Valian (1991); Nuñez del Prado, Foley, and Lust (1993); Nuñez del Prado, Foley, Proman, and Lust (in press). 2. Theoretically, if such evidence exists, how are subject *pro*-drop and the CP domain related? Is a reformulated parameter necessary, or can the phenomenon now be restated in terms of the features of COMP (i.e., C°) across languages? How should licensing be expressed in this CP domain?

Issue 6: Cross-Linguistic Variation in Lexical Pronominal Systems. Pierce's chapter 14 points the way to a new, more precise analysis of possible cross-linguistic variation in lexical pronoun systems, and its relation to zero pronouns. For example, Pierce uses French first language acquisition evidence to distinguish two competing theories regarding French pronouns, arguing that they are clitics and thus not in A-position. Pierce's proposal raises the important issue that *pro*-drop phenomena may be related to facts about the lexical pronoun system of a language in ways not yet fully addressed. (See also Hyams, this volume, chapter 12 on pronoun trade-off; and Smith's analysis in chapter 15 of this volume of zero and lexical pronoun forms in Chinese. For related proposals, including arguments from first language acquisition that ostensible lexical pronouns are not themselves in A-position, see Lust, Bhatia, Gair, & Sharma, 1990, for Hindi; Lust, Chien, Chiang, & Eisele, 1991, for Chinese.) This issue may lead to a new approach to parameter setting and learnability in the *pro*-drop domain.

With respect to the relationship between the lexical pronoun system and the null subject phenomenon, Pierce suggests that French, contrary to some views, is a null subject language in both its child and its spoken adult forms.[5]

Issue 7: The Formulation of Processing/Parsing Models. All proposals for a *pro*-drop parameter, like all other parameter-based proposals, must ultimately be responsible for a model of processing/parsing. In general, the parameter-setting model of UG provides an apparently vicious circularity that can be resolved only by an analysis of processing. Data must be processed in order that parameter values can be established and set; yet without parameter setting, how can grammatical analyses of these data occur? See, for example, Lightfoot (1991, chapter 10 in this volume), Mazuka (1990, in press), Mazuka and Lust (1990), and Valian (1990a, 1990b, 1991) (and ensuing debate by Kim, 1993, and Valian, 1993) for explicit attempts to deal with this problem.

In general, on the original view of UG (e.g., Chomsky, 1981), parameters originate unset; only after experience with a specific language can parameter setting occur. On the other hand, if parameters are preset in UG, this does

---

[5]Pierce claims that French has two types of null subject: the *pro*-drop variant, with clitic, and the null subject variant (root null subjects, cf. Rizzi's proposal), without clitic.

not obviate the role of experience because, for the marked language at least, experience must be invoked. On both accounts, the issue is how and when experience works to determine parameter values, not whether it works.

In this volume, Valian attempts to develop a processing/parsing model that would work for *pro*-drop, whereas Hyams debates this model. Clearly, further research in this area is necessary in order to develop the parameter-setting model of UG. All of the chapters in the last learnability section of this volume take on these issues.

WH-QUESTION AND QUANTIFIER (Q) DEPENDENCIES

In the area of WH-dependencies, the notion of locality is particularly provocative. Although natural languages clearly allow long-distance WH-dependencies (at surface structure or LF or both), research has shown that these dependencies are constrained by locality in interesting ways. Major issues in the theory of UG in this area are:

1. What is the nature of the local links in these long-distance binding chains? To what degree do these local links involve properties of the verbal lexicon, and/or configuration?

2. Are A(rgument)-binding and non-A(rgument) (A′) binding dependencies, and the locality these involve, related? The debate regarding movement or nonmovement in the area of the Binding Theory (cf. Hermon, this volume, chapter 4) anticipates these questions; see also Bailyn (1992) for a study of Russian acquisition that addresses these issues.

3. A related issue concerns the nature of the proform in these long-distance dependency domains. For instance, is the variable involved in a WH-construction an empty category or a lexical element (e.g., a resumptive pronoun), and does the empty category necessarily bear the features of a variable?

4. Do the principles that constrain long-distance A′ dependencies, as in WH-binding, hold at LF, at surface structure, or at every level?

In the area of quantifier dependencies, another area of A′-binding, cross-linguistic research indicates strict locality of quantifier binding domains (e.g., May, 1985). Again, theoretical issues similar to those adduced here arise as to the nature of the local domain and how the local domain can be extended, for instance, through quantifier raising (QR) at the level of Logical Form. In particular:

5. How are Q- and WH-dependencies related?

These theoretical issues are paralleled by issues regarding first language acquisition:

6. Are children universally constrained by locality with respect to A'–binding dependencies as well as A-binding dependencies? (See the earlier section on the BT.)

7. If so, what is the nature of this locality? Is it based on configuration, and/or on lexical properties? If it is based on configuration, what are the properties of configuration to which the child is sensitive?

Two chapters in this volume directly address the last two issues, chapter 16 by Roeper and de Villiers on WH-dependencies, and chapter 17 by Chien on quantifier scope relations. In doing so, they provide evidence pertinent to the first five issues in linguistic theory.

Drawing on evidence from English, German, and French first language acquisition, Roeper and de Villiers provide evidence for a strong knowledge of locality in WH-extraction domains, at early ages. They show that not only are children initially capable of long-distance extraction, but empirical evidence of local scope marking and partial movements as well as blocked extractions from adjuncts (e.g., relative clauses and temporal adverbial clauses) in child language demonstrate that this extraction is sensitive to locality and is constrained by it. They argue that where mistaken extractions appear to occur in the children's language, these do not reflect a breakdown of UG-determined constraints, but rather a deficit in word-specific syntactic subcategorization learning, which is independent of lexical thematic knowledge, and which may correspond to grammatical options in other languages.

Chien's chapter introduces the area of quantifier scope, that is, the issue of locality applied directly to the level of Logical Form. Chien's experimental data from Chinese children and adults provide several lines of evidence that Chinese children as well as adults are sensitive not only to surface linear order but also to underlying configuration, in their establishment of quantifier scope. Chien's data provide the foundation for further evaluation of the mapping from surface structure to Logical Form, and the maintenance of locality in this mapping. For example, Chien calls into question an isomorphism principle in the initial state (i.e., the assumption that LF and surface structure cohere in structural scope relations, argued for Chinese by Huang, 1982). Chien's data point to a crucial difference between the 3- and 4-year-olds in her study, and the 5-year-old (and older) children and adults, provoking further research in this area. They also implicate lexical learning (involving, in this case, specific quantifiers).

For further discussion of both of these chapters and the theoretical issues they bear on, see the commentary by Whitman (this volume, chapter 18).

LEARNABILITY

Formal learnability theory provides another perspective on the issues raised here. It constrains the nature of both the knowledge to be acquired and the mechanisms of learning.

In pioneering work of Gold (1967), it was shown that in the *identification in the limit* paradigm of learning, positive evidence alone is very restrictive. That is, many apparently simple theories of language knowledge were shown, on the basis of Gold's work, to be nonlearnable, given positive evidence alone, in this model. Subsequent developments in linguistic theory have diminished the significance of this formal result because, in the principles and parameters framework, there is only a finite number of possible natural languages (or at least of core grammars for languages), and such families are always in principle learnable. Finite cardinality of natural languages would in itself assure learnability in Gold's paradigm. Nevertheless, the absence of negative evidence in the child's input continued to intrigue linguists, and this issue in particular became a central issue in the study of natural language acquisition. For example, because a learner exposed only to positive evidence can fail by overgeneralizing, principles such as the Subset Principle (SP), which derive from a separate learning module (outside of UG), were proposed to help the learner avoid this trap (Berwick, 1985). In particular, the Subset Principle was proposed to account for both cross-linguistic variation and acquisition in the area of the Binding Theory (Jakubowicz, 1984; Manzini & Wexler, 1987). (This apparent overgeneralization problem assumes a *conservativeness* constraint on the part of the learner, i.e., a constraint against changing a hypothesis unless there is explicit counterevidence. See Kapur, this volume, chapter 22.)

In recent work, it has been argued on both formal and empirical grounds that no special learning principle is required, and in fact no separate learning module is necessary, in order to explain either cross-linguistic variation or acquisition in the area of the Binding Theory (see Kapur, Lust, Harbert, & Martohardjono, 1993, in preparation; Wexler, 1992; as well as Joshi, this volume, chapter 23, for debate). Formally, such a principle is by no means necessary because the child need not be conservative, and learning is always possible where only a finite number of parameters need to be set. Kapur et al. (1993, in preparation) argued that a restrictive hypothesis on the part of the child regarding strict locality is predicted by a strong form of a theory of UG. The SP does not predict this universally, because it is an inductive principle that proposes that the learner chooses the smallest language compatible with the input data. If input data is "large," the hypothesized language is predicted to be large. If the SP did predict strict locality (in spite of input language), it would be redundant to UG in this way. In addition, a number of problems with the SP have been identified, with respect to linguistic predictions and learnability predictions (Hermon, this volume, chapter 4; Jakubowicz, this volume, chapter 5; Joshi, this volume, chapter 23; Kapur, this volume, chapter 22; Kapur et al., 1992, in preparation). These developments have led to a new focus on what appears to be the major remaining learnability problem in this paradigm. How can the child set parameters in a feasible manner? Even if there are only 20 parameters, the search space is large enough to pose a problem, especially if the input is noisy. Because the actual input can be quite misleading—sometimes parameters conspire in particularly malicious ways—and exhaustive search is not feasible, the solution remains mysterious, but in different ways than previously supposed.

In this volume, Fodor (chapter 19), Lightfoot (chapter 20), Clark (chapter 21), and Kapur (chapter 22) share a common concern for the formal aspects of the parameter-setting problem by looking at it in this new perspective. They emphasize the possibilities for confusion in the input the child receives and suggest ways in which learning can nevertheless proceed. Fodor, in particular, lays out these problems with linguistic precision in terms of a core–periphery distinction and argues for a number of core–periphery "ambiguities in the input data." Clark argues, in addition, for a number of parameter-parameter ambiguities.

In "Degree-0 Learnability," Lightfoot argues for one example of a simplicity constraint on triggers. He reviews arguments that the theory of learnability must include a restriction that only structurally simple data—data of "degree-0 complexity" drawn from unembedded domains (plus a little bit more)—are used by the child to set parameters. Evidence is drawn from a number of linguistic phenomena to show that, with adequate reanalysis, triggers that satisfy this restriction can be found. This is used as an argument to challenge the Roeper and Weissenborn (1990) claim that children primarily use data from embedded clauses, which is in direct opposition to degree-0 learnability.[6]

Clark and Kapur, as well as Fodor, discuss the computational costs of the learning task in a parameter-setting paradigm and suggest interesting, although very different, proposals for learning. Clark and Kapur both propose general solutions with a probabilistic character. However, Clark abandons the linguistic deductive paradigm, whereas Kapur does not. Clark argues that the deductive model is impractical because it is computationally too costly. His solution is to rely on a nondeductive, selection-based approach to parameter setting, using genetic algorithms that introduce a general fitness metric. The fitness metric determines how well a certain parametric option fits the environment, and a differential reproduction model ensures the selection of

---

[6]For discussion and debate of this proposal, see commentary in Lightfoot (1989).

the option with the best fit. Clark argues that in order to achieve computationally feasible parameter setting, there must be definite bounds both on the complexity of triggering data and on the interaction between different parameters.

Fodor begins to draw a different conclusion. Faced with problems of indeterminacy of input (caused by the fact that learners cannot a priori decide whether input is relevant to core or periphery of the grammar), Fodor investigates an approach in which triggers are highly specified, to the extent that every generalization is unambiguously triggered. She hypothesizes that UG establishes a finite set of triggers, each associated innately (via parameter setting) with the generalization it introduces into the language.

Although robustness in the data for learnability must result from positive evidence in the proposals of Fodor, Clark, and Lightfoot, it arises from statistical averaging over both positive data and data that should exist but does not (indirect negative evidence) in Kapur's model. In that model, linguistic principles provide constraints on learning, that is, averaging, thus obviating constraints on the complexity of the trigger for every parameter. Kapur argues that groups of parameters are set entirely on the basis of the verification of linguistically motivated hypotheses. The learning algorithm is simple, uniform, and robust.

Open Issues of Debate

The learnability chapters in this volume raise several issues for future research. First, Kapur's proposal to link linguistic theory and learning theory raises the important issue of the role of indirect negative evidence in the language acquisition process. This issue is complementary to the Clark-Lightfoot one, where the concern is for simplifying the quality of the positive evidence necessary for acquisition. Although this issue has been raised in linguistic theory (e.g., Chomsky, 1986), it remains an open question in the field of first language acquisition (cf. Lust, Mazuka, Martohardjono, & Yoon, 1989; Mazuka & Lust, this volume, chapter 6); and in the field of formal learnability theory (cf. Kapur, 1992; Kapur & Bilardi, 1992). Second, although some of the chapters concentrate on the specific nature of single sentences as evidence either for or against parameter setting (e.g., Fodor, Lightfoot), others begin to suggest that not single sentences but whole data sets actually provide the critical data base for the child (e.g., Clark, Kapur). The error-driven (or failure-driven) model for language acquisition, which has been assumed in much previous work (cf. the debate regarding *pro*-drop acquisition) is now called into question (e.g., Kapur, Clark). Finally, Fodor's proposal, like the others, raises the question whether parameters are even necessary, once the triggers are made so explicit that they could be connected directly to generalizations. After all, if (like Fodor) one adopts the Reinhart and Reuland approach to reflexives, parameters for BT are not necessary.

CONCLUSIONS

The full set of chapters in this volume reflect fundamental developments in the theory of UG as a research paradigm. Together they reflect the emergence of a strengthened, more constrained, and more realistic theory of UG.

The theory is more constrained in that it reflects a diminished number of parameters, and stronger constraints on the nature of the parameters. Both theoretical and acquisition research generally converge in eliminating domain-specific parameters, while investigating theory-general ones. In many cases, UG principles alone are argued to account for both cross-linguistic variation and acquisition. A nonparametrized definition of locality emerges. Parameters are held accountable to learnability theory.

With this strengthening of the theory comes a change in the nature of the link between acquisition data and linguistic theory. The link is more direct.

In earlier work, the link between linguistic theory and first language acquisition data had been frequently treated as more indirect. For example, in the area of the Binding Theory studied in this volume, the postulation in some earlier work of a learning module with principles specific to this module (e.g., the Subset Principle [SP]) provided mediation between the UG module and language acquisition data. It was the learning module and this Subset Principle, for example, that had been proposed to define the actual data and stages of first language acquisition, not the UG module. The SP itself was not directly connected with any particular linguistic theory, or with the linguistic module per se. A weaker version of UG interacted with this learning module. This learning module and the Subset Principle could have, in fact, appeared to account for an unlimited number of parameters and parameter values in UG. As Manzini (1992) observed, for example, regarding an earlier application of the SP to the Binding Theory, "the type of locality parameter presented by Manzini and Wexler (1987) as well as by previous authors, including Yang (1984), can be roughly characterized as *ad hoc*, in that differences in locality behavior are directly coded in different definitions of locality domain" (p. 156).

In the chapters in this volume, however (like those in volume 1), we see in effect a research paradigm where the UG module itself is viewed as directly accounting for observed acquisition data. Its greater restrictiveness obviates the learning module. Its principles and its limited, finite set of parameters are viewed as predicting and accounting for language acquisition and learnability directly.

At the same time, at another level of representation, the precise links between the principles and parameters of UG and actual language data (either cross-linguistic variation or acquisition data) are in a sense more indirect, and ostensibly less simple, as the theory has become at once more restrictive and more refined.

Reuland makes this point in his commentary. For example, the restrictive Binding Principles themselves, and a universal restrictive knowledge of locality, do not apply independently of knowledge of reference and pragmatic influences on reference. For example, relations between an antecedent and a bound element may reflect properties of a chain that involve detailed properties of both the binder and the bindee, as well as possible barriers between them. Cross-linguistic variation in inflectional and/or agreement systems may provide a true source of parametric variation; ostensible differences in binding domains may reflect indirect, deductive consequences of variation in other domains.

Morphological/lexical variation across languages may interact with syntactic parametrization. For example, morphological variation in pronouns and anaphors across languages may consult various semantic features (e.g., +/− "affective", Jakubowicz, this volume, chapter 5; or +/− "intrinsically reflexive predicate", Reinhart & Reuland, 1991); as well as the syntactic features relevant to the Binding Theory (+/− anaphor, +/− pronoun, Mazuka & Lust, this volume, chapter 6). Even lexical learning must be viewed now in a less simplistic manner.

Morphological/lexical variation in pronouns in a language link the BT to *pro*-drop phenomena (e.g., Kornfilt, 1984, 1987; Montalbetti, 1984; and, in this volume, Mazuka & Lust, chapter 6; Pierce, chapter 14; Smith, chapter 15). It may no longer be possible to continue to study these domains independently.

In what follows, we attempt to specify these latter proposed interactions as foundations for future research.

Interactions Between BT and ECs

One kind of interaction between ECs and the BT is tied to the fact that *pro*-drop languages have two types of pronominals available to them (i.e., *pro* as well as phonologically realized pronouns) in certain syntactic contexts. This can give rise to situations where the effects of Principle B of the BT are obscured. (For a discussion of other factors that render apparent Principle B effects rather complex, see Reuland's chapter 9 in this volume.) More specifically, it appears that in such languages, when both *pro* and a lexical pronoun are available, *pro* is the pronominal that obeys Principle B in having to be free within the relevant local domain. A corresponding lexical pronoun is, in general, disjoint in reference in the same domain, although its potential antecedent is outside that domain. We have in mind structures schematized as follows:

(2) $[_\alpha A_i \ldots [_\beta [B] \ldots]]$

Suppose that the syntactic domain β contains the element B and a governor for B. Suppose further that, in a non-*pro*-drop language, the position B is occupied by a lexical pronominal. If we find that such a pronominal is not disjoint in reference from A, that is, it can share the index of A, we would conclude that β is the relevant local binding domain for B. Now, in a *pro*-drop language, if we encounter the same configuration, and, further, if β contains a licenser/identifier for B, a lexical pronoun occupying B will most likely (although not always) be disjoint from A, which is outside β.

It is clear in such situations that the disjoint reference of the lexical pronoun is due not to the BT per se, but rather to some other (perhaps functional) principle (cf. Kornfilt, 1984, 1987, for Turkish; Montalbetti, 1984, for Spanish)—possibly some special version of the Avoid Pronoun Principle (cf. Chomsky, 1981). It is interesting to note that if such a lexical pronoun is treated in the same way as a pronoun in a non-*pro*-drop language, such disjoint reference would be taken to signal an extended binding domain—a domain large enough to include the pronoun itself and the antecedent from which it is disjoint. In our schema, the relevant local domain would thus not be β, but α. Thus, it would appear on the surface that for the purposes of Principle B, the relevant local domain would be larger in *pro*-drop languages than in non-*pro*-drop languages.

Furthermore, replacing the lexical pronoun that is disjoint in such an extended domain with an anaphor would lead to ungrammaticality, due to a violation of Principle A. But if β is not the local domain for the element in B, but rather α, this would be a problem, because in α, the anaphor in B should be properly bound by the antecedent in A. Hence, for the purposes of Principle A, we would have to conclude that the local domain is not α, but β—thus positing different local domains for pronominals versus anaphors. In other words, it would appear that in *pro*-drop languages, the local domain for Principle A would be systematically smaller than the local domain for Principle B, if the lexical pronouns are taken to be the representatives of the class of pronominals. This seems to be an initially interesting characterization of the workings of the BT in *pro*-drop languages (cf. Enç, 1985, 1986, for an analysis along such lines for binding facts in Turkish, and Kornfilt, 1987, 1988 for an opposing view). However, note that when position B in our schema is occupied by *pro*, it can indeed share the index of A. This would show that β is the relevant local domain for pronominals as well as anaphors in this case—surely a more desirable outcome a priori, and one that makes the claim that BT treats *pro*-drop languages like non-*pro*-drop languages. This treatment is possible if BT looks at *pro* rather than at lexical pronouns as the representative of the class of pronominals.

Our point here involves more than just the issue of the distribution of lexical pronouns versus *pro*. Facts of language can lend themselves to different analyses, and it is important to decide which aspects of a given phenomenon (here, the apparent lack of complementary distribution between pronominals and anaphors) are best analyzed via which module of the syntactic model. (Here, the choice is between UG principles of BT and the principles referring to ECs.)

The Problem of Noncomplementary Distribution

It should be noted that instances where the complementary distribution between anaphors and pronominals predicted by Principles A and B of the BT breaks down were noticed early on in various studies of binding phenomena (cf. Chomsky, 1982, 1986; Huang, 1983, among many others). As a matter of fact, it is due in part to just such data in non-*pro*-drop languages like English that the BT was revised from the form given in (1), taken essentially from Chomsky (1981), to the following statement in Chomsky (1986) (where I stands for a specific indexing):

> (3) I is BT-*compatible* with (α, β) if:
>   (A) α is an anaphor and is bound in β under I
>   (B) α is a pronominal and is free in β under I
>   (C) α is an r-expression and is free in β under I
>   (Chomsky, 1986, p. 171)

This version of the BT makes the prediction that, for those instances where anaphors and pronominals are not in complementary distribution, the local domain for Principle A will be larger than the local domain for Principle B. Crucially, this is precisely the reverse situation from what we found earlier to hold in *pro*-drop languages for the distribution of lexical pronouns in contexts where *pro* would be licensed. Furthermore, this version of the BT still predicts that in most instances, anaphors and pronominals will be in complementary distribution. It follows, therefore, that for *pro*-drop languages, the type of pronoun whose distribution reflects the workings of the BT is *pro* rather than overt pronouns in those instances where the *pro* is independently made licit by the theory of ECs. Why should this be so? The Avoid Pronoun Principle goes some way toward answering this question but doesn't solve the problem completely, because that principle is itself a stipulation—unless it is made to follow from some more general principle (e.g., laziness), if the latter principle can be motivated independently.

The decision to attribute the different binding behavior of phonologically overt versus nonovert pronominals in part to the BT and in part to the theory of ECs has repercussions not only for syntactic theory but also for predictions about first language acquisition. Although it would transcend the scope of this introduction to develop a detailed system of such predictions, suffice it to say that the discussion so far would predict that (apparent) effects of Principle B would take longer to be acquired by the child than effects of Principle A. The latter are all genuine BT facts, whereas the former actually consist of complex interactions of two distinct syntactic modules, the first including Principle B and the second including principles referring to ECs.[7]

Sentence Grammar and Discourse Grammar

Actually, the distribution of pronominals might be determined by interactions that are even more complex than what has been outlined so far. If our treatment of pronominals in *pro*-drop languages has been on the right track, the interacting principles, although in distinct syntactic modules, are all part of sentence grammar. However, there are good reasons to believe that principles of discourse and pragmatics form yet another component that contributes to the complex phenomenon in question.

In our discussion so far, we have seen that in *pro*-drop languages, in those syntactic contexts that allow for both *pro* and lexical pronouns, *pro* rather than lexical pronouns tends to reflect the workings of Principle B. (It should be noted, however, that this is a very strong preference, but not an all-or-nothing grammatical principle. This is not surprising, if this preference is indeed due to a functional principle like Avoid Pronoun.) However, there are situations where the lexical pronoun is preferred—indeed, seems to be the only choice. Although the exact factors behind this choice seem to differ somewhat cross-linguistically, it seems to be generally linked to a topic change in discourse (for some discussion on pertinent facts in Turkish, see Enç, 1986). Thus, where a new topic needs to be introduced in the discourse or in a given pragmatic situation, the subject must be phonologically overt, even if a *pro* in the same syntactic position would be licit. (In another approach, Larson & Lujan, 1991, proposed that Spanish lexical pronouns are focused.)

Such a discourse principle, because it is not part of sentence grammar, must be acquired separately by the child, and it stands to reason that such acquisition is a complex task, given that purely sentence-oriented principles of grammar dictate just the opposite choice of pronominal element, between *pro* and overt pronoun. We assume, as seems reasonable, that the child's production will first reflect effects of principles governing sentence grammar, before reflecting discourse principles and their interaction with sentence grammar. (See, e.g., Chien & Lust, 1985; Eisele, 1988; Eisele & Lust, 1993; and Lust, 1986, for early studies confirming this assumption.) If so, this might

---

[7]As an indication of the need for further cross-linguistic study here see also Lust, Bhatia, Gair, & Sharma (1990), for a study of Hindi, in which OPC constraints observed for Spanish appear to be reversed for Hindi (i.e., lexical pronouns are required in certain cases where zero pronouns are required in Spanish).

be a contributing factor to the frequent observation (cf. Hyams, this volume, chapter 12; Valian, 1991; and others) that young children use fewer lexical subject pronouns (than older children) irrespective of their target language, and that the use of lexical subject pronouns becomes more frequent in the course of linguistic development even in *pro*-drop languages.[8] In this context, it would also be interesting to investigate the distribution of lexical pronouns in non-*pro*-drop languages where there is a choice of more than one pronominal paradigm, as in *er, sie* versus *der, die* in German (the latter in their nondemonstrative use). If the binding properties (with respect to sentential BT) differ, it would be interesting to see whether something like Avoid Pronoun is at work here, as well. If so, such a functional principle would obviously have to be reformulated and generalized to cover such instances. Such investigation should also be carried out with respect to the behavior of these pronominals in discourse; it is likely that the distribution, if it exhibits interesting diversity, would also have repercussions on our theory of acquisition.

Summary

In general, these results converge with a new emphasis on the E-language–I-language distinction in linguistic theory (see the General Introduction to these volumes). Principles and parameters cannot be viewed as having a direct, simplistic one-to-one connection to surface language data. Both our theory of grammar and our theory of learnability must take this into account.

The final result is a more realistic theory of UG. This greater realism strengthens the scientific foundations of the theory. The realism is complemented by greater complexity in linguistic analyses of child language data, and more intense attempt to separate performance from competence in analysis of E-language facts.

Explanation for Developmental Change. This stronger, more direct application of UG to language acquisition data, however, provokes intense concern with the following question. We see most of the contributors to this volume (like those in volume 1, who deal with phrase structure) wrestling with it in some sense. *If child language is not identical to the adult language, what accounts for the difference, and for the developmental change between child and adult?*

Is the difference only an apparent one or is it real? If it is real, at what level should the difference be represented? Does it involve grammar or

---

[8]Note, however, that this precise empirical claim requires further testing and analysis. Clifford (1984) reported, for example, that young children acquiring English use lexical pronouns, mainly in subject position, in earliest speech. Pronouns occurred, on average, in 26% of utterances in her speech samples from her 8 subjects, with MLUs from 1.97 to 2.91.

performance effects or both (e.g., the Hyams-Valian debate)? Is it at the level of UG principles and parameters (Strong Discontinuity) or not (Strong Continuity)? Most (although not all) of the chapters in this volume support a strong continuity of UG approach. However, if strong continuity of UG is supported, and the change is not at the level of UG, and yet there is change in grammar, how and where is the change to be represented? Several alternative approaches are explored in various chapters in this volume (as in volume I):

1. One approach is to revise our theory of adult grammar (e.g., Rizzi), so that it accounts for both the child and the adult Root Null Subjects. (This is similar to the approach Grimshaw takes in volume 1 on phrase structure issues.)

2. Another approach involves a "wobbly grammar". Competence of the child is proposed to be variable (e.g., two values of parameters are entertained at once, as in Lillo-Martin's analysis; or CP phrase structure representation exists for some structures and not for others, e.g., Rizzi, this volume, chapter 10).

3. A third approach involves mapping from continuous UG to specific language grammars, with mediation by the lexicon and/or language-specific grammatical features such as INFL/AGR (e.g., in this volume, Hermon, chapter 4; Jakubowicz, chapter 5; Mazuka & Lust, chapter 6). The deductive consequences of UG principles and parameters are realized in language-specific terms (cf. Flynn & Martohardjono, volume I, chapter 16).

Clearly, no single chapter in this volume provides a complete solution to any of the fundamental issues and debates discussed earlier. Many issues still remain open. Each chapter, however, and the collection as a whole, lays the foundation for new, more finely focused research in both linguistic theory and acquisition. This new research can be guided by a strengthened and more realistic theory of UG, one that is enriched by an invigorating interchange between linguistic theory, cross-linguistic variation, and first language acquisition.

—Barbara Lust, Jaklin Kornfilt,
Gabriella Hermon, Claire Foley,
Zelmira Nuñez del Prado, and Shyam Kapur

REFERENCES

Adams, M. (1987). From old French to pro-drop. *Natural Language and Linguistic Theory, 5,* 1–32.

Authier, J.-M. P. (1989). Arbitrary null objects and unselective binding. In O. Jaeggli & K. Safir (Eds.), *The null subject parameter* (pp. 45–67). Dordrecht: Kluwer.

Bailyn, J. (1992). LF movement of anaphors and the acquisition of embedded clauses in Russian. *Language Acquisition, 2*, 307–336.

Baker, C. L. (1993a). *Learnability issues in the study of anaphora.* Unpublished manuscript, University of Texas, Austin.

Baker, C. L. (1993b). *Some observations on British English reflexives.* Unpublished manuscript, University of Texas, Austin.

Berwick, R. (1982). *Locality principles and the acquisition of syntactic knowledge.* Unpublished doctoral dissertation, MIT, Cambridge, MA.

Berwick, R. (1985). *The acquisition of syntactic knowledge.* Cambridge, MA: MIT Press.

Bloom, L. (1970). *Language development: Form and function in emerging grammars.* Cambridge, MA: MIT Press.

Bloom, L. (1973). *One word at a time: The use of single-word utterances before syntax.* The Hague: Mouton.

Bloom, P. (1990). Subjectless sentences in child language. *Linguistic Inquiry, 21*, 491–504.

Bloom, P. (1993). Grammatical continuity in language development: The case of subjectless sentences. *Linguistic Inquiry, 24*, 721–734.

Borer, H. (1983). *Parametric syntax: Case studies in Semitic and Romance languages.* Dordrecht: Foris.

Bouchard, D. (1984). *On the content of empty categories.* Dordrecht: Foris.

Chien, Y.-C., & Lust, B. (1985). The concepts of topic and subject in first language acquisition of Mandarin Chinese. *Child Development, 56*, 1359–1375.

Chien, Y.-C., & Wexler, K. (1990). Children's knowledge of locality conditions in binding as evidence for the modularity of syntax and pragmatics. *Language Acquisition, 1*, 225–295.

Chomsky, N. (1973). Conditions on transformations. In S. Anderson & P. Kiparsky (Eds.), *A Festschrift for Morris Halle* (pp. 232–286). New York: Holt, Rinehart & Winston.

Chomsky, N. (1981). *Lectures on government and binding.* Dordrecht: Foris.

Chomsky, N. (1982). *Concepts and consequences of a theory of government and binding.* Cambridge, MA: MIT Press.

Chomsky, N. (1986a). *Barriers.* Cambridge, MA: MIT Press.

Chomsky, N. (1986b). *Knowledge of language: Its nature, origin, and use.* New York: Praeger.

Chomsky, N. (1988a). *Language and problems of knowledge.* Cambridge, MA: MIT Press.

Chomsky, N. (1988b). *Language in a psychological setting.* Tokyo: Sophia University, Sophia Linguistica.

Chomsky, N. (1992). *A minimalist program for linguistic theory. MIT Occasional Papers in Linguistics, 1.* Cambridge, MA: MIT, Department of Linguistics and Philosophy.

Clements, G. N. (1975). The logophoric pronoun in Ewe: Its role in discourse. *Journal of West African Languages, 2*, 141–177.

Clifford, T. (1984). *Acquisition of pronouns in the first language acquisition of English: A study of natural speech.* Unpublished master's thesis. Cornell University, Ithaca, NY.

Cole, P. (1987). Null objects in universal grammar. *Linguistic Inquiry, 18*, 597–612.

Cole, P., Hermon, G., & Sung, L. M. (1990). Principles and parameters of long distance reflexives. *Linguistic Inquiry, 21*, 1–22.

Cole, P., Hermon, G., & Sung, L. M. (1992). Feature percolation. *Journal of East Asian Linguistics, 1*, 1–28.

Crain, S., & McKee, C. (1986). Acquisition of structural restrictions on anaphora. *Proceedings of the North Eastern Linguistics Society, 16*, 91–110.

Egido, C. (1979). *The functional role of the closed class vocabulary in children's language processing.* Unpublished doctoral dissertation, MIT, Cambridge, MA.

Eisele, J. (1988). *Meaning and form in children's judgments about language.* Unpublished master's thesis, Cornell University, Ithaca, NY.

Eisele, J., & Lust, B. (1993). *Children's judgments about pronouns.* Manuscript submitted for publication.

Enç, M. (1985). *Agreement and governing categories.* Unpublished manuscript, University of Southern California, Los Angeles.

Enç, M. (1986). Topic switching and pronominal subjects in Turkish. In D. I. Slobin & K. Zimmer (Eds.), *Studies in Turkish linguistics* (pp. 195–208). Amsterdam: John Benjamins.

Fiengo, R., & May, R. (in preparation). *Indices and identity.*

Foley, C., Nuñez del Prado, Z., Barbier, I., & Lust, B. (1992a, January). On the strong continuity hypothesis: A study of pronoun coindexing. Paper presented at the annual meeting of the Linguistic Society of America, Philadelphia, PA.

Foley, C., Nuñez del Prado, Z., Barbier, I., & Lust, B. (1992b, June). *Quantifier raising in VP ellipsis.* Paper presented at the University of Massachusetts 'wh' workshop, Amherst, MA.

Foley, C., Nuñez del Prado, Z., Barbier, I., & Lust, B. (1992c, October). *LF representation of pronouns in VP ellipsis: An argument for UG in the Initial State.* Paper presented at the 17th Annual Boston University Conference on Language Development, Boston, MA.

Foley, C., Nuñez del Prado, Z., Barbier, I., & Lust, B. (in press). LF operator-variable binding in the Initial State: An argument from VP ellipsis. *Cornell University Working Papers* (special issue on language acquisition). Ithaca, NY: Cornell University.

Gair, J. (1988). Kinds of markedness. In S. Flynn & E. O'Neil (Eds.), *Linguistic theory in second language acquisition* (pp. 225–251). Dordrecht: Kluwer.

Gerken, L. A. (1991). The metrical basis for children's subjectless sentences. *Journal of Memory and Language, 30*, 1–21.

Gilligan, G. (1987). *A cross-linguistic approach to the pro-drop parameter.* Doctoral dissertation, University of Southern California, Los Angeles.

Gold, E. M. (1967). Language identification in the limit. *Information and Control, 10*, 447–474.

Grimshaw, J., & Rosen, S. (1990). Knowledge and obedience: The developmental status of the binding theory. *Linguistic Inquiry, 21*, 187–222.

Grodzinsky, Y., & Reinhart, T. (1993). The innateness of binding and coreference. *Linguistic Inquiry, 24*, 69–102.

Haegeman, L. (1990a). Non-overt subjects in diary contexts. In J. Mascaro & M. Nespor (Eds.), *Grammar in progress* (pp. 167–174). Dordrecht: Foris.

Haegeman, L. (1990b). Understood subjects in English diaries. *Multilingua, 9*, 157–199.

Hagége, C. (1974). Les pronoms logophoriques [Logophoric pronouns]. *Bulletin de la Société de Linguistique de Paris, 69*, 287–310.

Harbert, W. (in press). Binding theory. In G. Webelhuth (Ed.), *Government and binding theory.* Oxford: Basil Blackwell.

Hermon, G., & Yoon, J. (1989). The licensing and identification of *pro* and the typology of AGR. *Proceedings of the Chicago Linguistic Society, 25*, 174–192.

Huang, C.-T. J. (1982). *Logical relations in Chinese and the theory of grammar.* Unpublished doctoral dissertation, MIT, Cambridge, MA.

Huang, C.-T. J. (1983). A note on binding theory. *Linguistic Inquiry, 14*, 554–561.

Huang, C.-T. J. (1984). On the distribution and reference of empty pronouns. *Linguistic Inquiry, 15*, 531–574.

Huang, C.-T. J. (1989). Pro-drop in Chinese: A generalized control theory. In O. Jaeggli & K. Safir (Eds.), *The null subject parameter* (pp. 185–214). Dordrecht: Kluwer.

Huang, C.-T. J., & Tang, J. (1991). The local nature of the long distance reflexive in Chinese. In J. Koster & E. Reuland (Eds.), *Long distance anaphora* (pp. 263–282). Cambridge: Cambridge University Press.

Hyams, N. (1986). *Language acquisition and the theory of parameters.* Dordrecht: Reidel.

Hyams, N. (1992). A reanalysis of null subjects in child language. In J. Weissenborn, H. Goodluck, & T. Roeper (Eds.), *Theoretical issues in language acquisition* (pp. 249–268). Hillsdale, NJ: Lawrence Erlbaum Associates.

Hyams, N., & Wexler, K. (1993). On the grammatical basis of null subjects in child language. *Linguistic Inquiry, 24*(3), 421–459.

Jaeggli, O., & Hyams, N. (1988). Morphological uniformity and the setting of the null subject parameter. *Proceedings of the North Eastern Linguistics Society, 18*, 238–253.

Jaeggli, O., & Safir, K. (1989). The null subject parameter and parametric theory. In O. Jaeggli & K. Safir (Eds.), *The null subject parameter* (pp. 1–44). Dordrecht: Kluwer.

Jakubowicz, C. (1984). On markedness and binding principles. *Proceedings of the North Eastern Linguistics Society, 14*, 154–228.

Kapur, S. (1993). Monotonic language learning. In *Proceedings of the workshop on algorithmic learning theory* (pp. 147–158). Tokyo: JSAI.

Kapur, S., & Bilardi, G. (1992). Language learning from stochastic input. In *Proceedings of the Fifth Conference on Computational learning theory* (pp. 303–310). San Mateo: Morgan-Kaufman.

Kapur, S., Lust, B., Harbert, W., & Martohardjono, G. (1993). Universal Grammar and learnability theory: The case of binding domains and the subset principle. In E. Reuland & W. Abraham (Eds.), *Knowledge and language: Vol. 3. Issues in representation and acquisition* (pp. 185–216). Dordrecht: Kluwer.

Kapur, S., Lust, B., Harbert, W., & Martohardjono, G. (in preparation). *On relating Universal Grammar and learnability theory.* Unpublished manuscript, Cornell University, Ithaca, NY.

Keenan, E. L. (1988). On semantics and the Binding Theory. In J. Hawkins (Ed.), *Explaining language universals* (pp. 105–144). Oxford: Basil Blackwell.

Kim, J. (1993). Null subjects: Comments on Valian. *Cognition, 46*, 183–193.

Kornfilt, J. (1984). *Case marking, agreement, and empty categories in Turkish.* Unpublished doctoral dissertation, Harvard University, Cambridge, MA.

Kornfilt, J. (1987). Beyond binding conditions: The case of Turkish. In H. Boeschoten & L. Verhoeven (Eds.), *Studies on modern Turkish* (pp. 105–120). Tilburg: Tilburg University Press.

Kornfilt, J. (1988). A typology of morphological agreement and its syntactic consequences. *Proceedings of the Chicago Linguistics Society, 24, Papers from the Parasession on Agreement in Grammatical Theory,* 117–134.

Kornfilt, J. (1991). Some current issues in Turkish syntax. In H. Boeschoten & L. Verhoeven (Eds.), *Turkish linguistics today* (pp. 60–92). Leiden: Brill.

Kornfilt, J. (1993). *A note on morphological simplicity.* Unpublished manuscript, Syracuse University, Syracuse, NY.

Koster, C. (1993). *Errors in anaphora acquisition.* Research Institute for Language and Speech Utrecht, The Netherlands.

Koster, J. (1986). *The relation between pro-drop, scrambling and verb movements.* Groningen Papers in Theoretical and Applied Linguistics. TTT nr.1. Groningen, The Netherlands.

Koster, J., & Reuland, E. (Eds.). (1991). *Long Distance Anaphora.* Cambridge: Cambridge University Press.

Larson, R., & Lujan, M. (1991). *Focused pronouns.* Paper presented at the Rochester Workshop on Japanese Linguistics, Rochester, NY.

Lasnik, H. (1976). Remarks on coreference. *Linguistic Analysis, 2,* 1–22.

Lasnik, H. (1989). *Essays on Anaphora.* Dordrecht: Kluwer.

Lebeaux, D. (1983). A distributional difference between reciprocals and reflexives. *Linguistic Inquiry, 14,* 723–730.

Lightfoot, D. (1989). The child's trigger experience: Degree-0 learnability. *Behavioral and Brain Sciences, 12,* 321–375.

Lightfoot, D. (1991). *How to set parameters.* Cambridge, MA: MIT Press.

Lust, B. (Ed.). (1986). *Studies in the acquisition of anaphora: Vol. 1. Defining the constraints.* Dordrecht: Reidel.

Lust, B., Bhatia, T., Gair, J., & Sharma, V. (1990). *On the acquisition of Hindi pronominal anaphora: A test of the null hypothesis in Hindi jab clauses.* Paper presented at University of Delhi Conference on Anaphora, Delhi, India.

Lust, B., Chien, Y.-C., Chiang, C.-P., & Eisele, J. (1991). *Chinese and English children's interpretation of pronouns: A test of the linear precedence hypothesis.* Paper presented at the NAACCL III (Annual Conference on Chinese Linguistics). Cornell University, Ithaca, NY.

Lust, B., Eisele, J., & Mazuka, R. (1992). The binding theory module: Evidence from first language acquisition for Principle C. *Language, 68,* 333–358.

Lust, B., Mazuka, R., Martohardjono, G., & Yoon, J. (1989). *On parameter-setting in first language acquisition: The case of the binding theory.* Paper presented at GLOW, Utrecht.

Manzini, R. (1992). *Locality.* Cambridge, MA: MIT Press.

Manzini, R., & Wexler, K. (1987). Parameters, Binding Theory, and learnability. *Linguistic Inquiry, 18,* 413–444.

May, R. (1985). *Logical form: Its structure and derivation.* Cambridge, MA: MIT Press.

Mazuka, R. (1990). *Japanese and English children's processing of complex sentences: An experimental comparison.* Unpublished doctoral dissertation, Cornell University, Ithaca, NY.

Mazuka, R. (in press). *Grammatical parameter-setting and language processing: A developmental study of Japanese and English children's processing.* Hillsdale, NJ: Lawrence Erlbaum Associates.

Mazuka, R., & Lust, B. (1990). On parameter-setting and parsing: Predictions for acquisition. In L. Frazier & J. de Villiers (Eds.), *Language processing and acquisition* (pp. 163–206). Dordrecht: Kluwer.

Mazuka, R., Lust, B., Wakayama, T., & Snyder, W. (1986). Distinguishing effects of parameters in early syntax acquisition: A cross-linguistic study of Japanese and English. *Papers and Reports on Child Language Development, 25,* 73–82.

Mohanan, K. P. (1982). Pronouns in Malayalam. *Studies in the Linguistic Sciences, 11,* 67–75.

Montalbetti, M. (1984). *After binding.* Unpublished doctoral dissertation, MIT, Cambridge, MA.

Nuñez del Prado, Z., Foley, C., & Lust, B. (1993). The significance of CP to the pro-drop parameter: An experimental study of English-Spanish comparison. In E. Clark (Ed.), *The Proceedings of the Twenty-Fifth Annual Child Language Research Forum* (pp. 146–157). Stanford University, Stanford, CA.

Nuñez del Prado, Z., Foley, C., Proman, R., & Lust, B. (in press). Subordinate CP and pro-drop: Evidence for degree-n learnability from an experimental study of Spanish and English acquisition. *Proceedings of North Eastern Linguistics Society, 24.* Amherst, MA: University of Massachusetts.

Ouhalla, J. (1991). *Functional categories and parametric variation.* London: Routledge.

Padilla-Rivera, J. A. (1990). *On the definition of binding domains.* Dordrecht: Kluwer.

Perlmutter, D. (1971). *Deep and surface constraints in syntax.* New York: Holt, Rinehart & Winston.

Pica, P. (1985). Subject, tense and truth. In J. Gueron, H. Obenauer, & J.-Y. Pollock (Eds.), *Grammatical representation* (pp. 259–291). Dordrecht: Foris.

Pica, P. (1987). On the nature of the reflexivization cycle. *Proceedings of the North Eastern Linguistics Society, 17,* 483–499.

Pollard, C., & Sag, I. (1992). Anaphors in English and the scope of Binding Theory. *Linguistic Inquiry, 23,* 261–304.

Progovac, L. (1991). *Subjunctive: Transparency of functional categories.* Unpublished manuscript, Wayne State University, Detroit, MI.

Progovac, L. (1992). Relativized SUBJECT: Long-distance reflexives without movement. *Linguistic Inquiry, 23,* 671–680.

Reinhart, T. (1981). Pragmatics and linguistics: An analysis of sentence topics. *Philosophica, 27,* 59–94.

Reinhart, T. (1983a). *Anaphora and semantic interpretation.* London: Croom Helm.

Reinhart, T. (1983b). Coreference and bound anaphora: A restatement of the anaphora questions. *Linguistics and Philosophy, 6*, 47–88.

Reinhart, T. (1986). Center and periphery in the grammar of anaphora. In B. Lust (Ed.), *Studies in the acquisition of anaphora: Vol. I. Defining the Constraints* (pp. 123–150). Dordrecht: Reidel.

Reinhart, T., & Reuland, E. (1991). Anaphors and logophors: An argument structure perspective. In J. Koster & E. Reuland (Eds.), *Long distance anaphora* (pp. 283–322). Cambridge: Cambridge University Press.

Reinhart, T., & Reuland, E. (1993). Reflexivity. *Linguistic Inquiry, 24*, 657–720.

Reuland, E., & Abraham, W. (Eds.). (1993). *Knowledge and language: Vol. 1. From Orwell's problem to Plato's problem.* Dordrecht: Kluwer.

Rizzi, L. (1986). Null objects in Italian and the theory of *pro. Linguistic Inquiry, 17*, 501–557.

Roeper, T., & Weissenborn, J. (1990). How to make parameters work. In L. Frazier & J. de Villiers (Eds.), *Language processing and language acquisition* (pp. 147–162). Dordrecht: Kluwer.

Safir, K. (1985). *Syntactic chains.* Cambridge: Cambridge University Press.

Safir, K. (1986). Subject clitics and the NOM-drop parameter. In H. Borer (Ed.), *The syntax of pronominal clitics, syntax and semantics* (Vol. 19, pp. 333–356). New York: Academic Press.

Sells, P. (1987). Aspects of logophoricity. *Linguistic Inquiry, 18*, 445–481.

Shipley, E., Smith, C., & Gleitman, L. (1969). A study in the acquisition of language: Free responses to commands. *Language, 45*, 322–342.

Suñer, M. (1989). *Subject clitics in the Northern Italian vernaculars.* Unpublished manuscript, Cornell University, Ithaca, NY.

Sung, L. M. (1990). *Universals of reflexives.* Unpublished doctoral dissertation, University of Illinois, Urbana.

Tang, J. (1989). Chinese reflexives. *Natural Language and Linguistic Theory, 7*, 93–121.

Taraldsen, T. (1978). *On the NIC, vacuous application and the that-t filter.* Bloomington: Indiana University Linguistics Club.

Thornton, R., & Wexler, K. (1991). *VP ellipsis and the binding principles in young children's grammars.* Paper presented at the 16th Annual Boston University Conference on Language Development, Boston, MA.

Valian, V. (1990a). Logical and psychological constraints on the acquisition of syntax. In L. Frazier & J. de Villiers (Eds.), *Language processing and language acquisition* (pp. 119–145). Dordrecht: Kluwer.

Valian, V. (1990b). Null subjects: A problem for parameter-setting models of language acquisition. *Cognition, 35*, 105–122.

Valian, V. (1991). Syntactic subjects in the early speech of American and Italian children. *Cognition, 40*, 21–81.

Valian, V. (1993). Parser failure and grammar change. *Cognition, 46*, 195–202.

Wali, K., & Subbarao, K. V. (1991). On pronominal classification: Evidence from Marathi and Telugu. *Linguistics, 29*, 1093–1110.

Wali, K., Subbarao, K. V., Gair, J., & Lust, B. (Eds.). (in preparation). *Anaphors and pronouns in some South Asian languages: A principled typology.* The Hague, Netherlands: Mouton.

Wang, Q., Lillo-Martin, D., Best, C., & Levitt, A. (1992). Null subjects versus null object: Some evidence from the acquisition of Chinese and English. *Language Acquisition, 2*, 221–254.

Wexler, K. (1993). The subset principle is an intensional principle. In E. Reuland & W. Abraham (Eds.), *Knowledge and language: Vol. 1. From Orwell's problem to Plato's problem* (pp. 217–239). Dordrecht: Kluwer.

Yang, B. W. (1984). The extended Binding Theory of anaphors. *Language Research, 19*, 169–192.

Zribi-Herz, A. (1989). Anaphor binding and narrative point of view: English reflexive pronouns in sentence and discourse. *Language, 65*, 695–727.

PART ONE

SYNTACTIC FOUNDATIONS: ANAPHORA AND BINDING

CHAPTER ONE

Toward a New Theory of Anaphoric Binding

Jan Koster
University of Groningen

CONCEPTUAL PROBLEMS OF THE BINDING THEORY

The theory of anaphoric binding, as first stated in Chomsky (1981), requires revision on both conceptual and empirical grounds. To see this, consider the theory that has guided anaphora research during the past decade:[1]

(1) A. An anaphor is bound in its governing category.
B. A pronoun is free in its governing category.
C. An R-expression is free.

If we compare these principles to others, we observe some striking differences. Generally, grammatical principles are concerned with local dependencies. From this perspective, Principle A is a bona fide principle of grammar, but Principles B and C are not. Principle B is concerned with pronouns, which are different from anaphors, traces, and licensed elements in that they can be nonlocally bound or not bound at all. Principle C has even less to do with the local dependencies commonly found in the grammars of natural languages. Prima facie, then, only Principle A merits incorporation into a theory of anaphoric binding as a subtheory of the more general theory of local dependencies.

---

[1]Of course, there have been many other attempts to revise this theory (see Koster & Reuland, 1991, for references). It seems to me that none of these attempts has succeeded in formulating a satisfactory alternative to the Binding Theory. In particular, theories stated in terms of argument structure have failed because anaphoric binding is not limited to coargument structure.

Even Principle A, however, is too anaphora-specific. An important aspect of it, local identification, is not limited to anaphora but is typical of grammatical dependencies in general (Koster, 1987). In a conceptually satisfactory theory of anaphoric binding, this function would be relegated to the more general theory underlying all types of local identification.

Another conceptual problem arises in Chomsky's recent minimalist program. Chomsky (1992) proposed to get rid of the notion of *government* in favor of the following more specific relations:

(2) a. head-complement
    b. SPEC-head

Theories incorporating (2) are more restrictive than those based on the standard notion of government and are therefore my focus in this chapter. (1) must then be revised: The notion *governing category* in Principles A and B is crucially based on the government relation, which no longer plays a role in theories incorporating (2). Ideally, a revision based on (2) also leads to empirical gains.

In this chapter, I sketch a new Binding Theory based on Chomsky's recent minimalist principles, and I suggest that this theory is empirically superior to the traditional Binding Theory.

EMPIRICAL PROBLEMS OF THE BINDING THEORY

The standard Binding Theory encounters several empirical problems that I do not discuss here (see Reinhart & Reuland, 1991, for recent discussion). I concentrate on a specific problem, namely the overlap between (so-called) anaphors and pronouns in the local domain. The Binding Theory (1) predicts complementary distribution between anaphors and pronominals in their minimal governing category. As has been documented in many languages, this prediction is not borne out. Contrary to what Principle B predicts, most languages, including English, have bound pronouns in local domains. A well-known example is (3), which has been with us since the earliest theories on anaphora (in this chapter, italics indicate intended coreference):

(3) *John* saw a snake near *him*.

Contrary to Principle B, a pronoun is not free in its minimal governing category in this example. In Dutch, we may even choose between an anaphor and a pronoun in this context:[2]

---

[2]Some speakers accept the bound pronoun *hem* here only in the reduced form *'um*. I do not share this judgment.

(4) *Jan* zag een slang naast   *zich/hem*.
    John saw a   snake next to self/him

Full overlap in the local domain is incompatible with the Binding Theory and the associated standard theory of NP classification. Curiously, there are also languages, like German and most of Slavic, that conform almost entirely to Principle B. Thus, a pronoun is totally excluded in snake sentences in standard High German:

(5) *Johann* sah eine Schlange neben *sich/*ihm*.
    John   saw a   snake   next to self/him

These examples from English, Dutch, and German suggest a revision of the Binding Theory (or the associated NP classification). Yet more striking examples can be found in Frisian, which does not have specialized, morphologically marked anaphors (G. de Haan, personal communication):

(6) a. *Jelle* wasket *him*.
       Jelle washes him
       'Jelle washes.'
    b. *Jelle* seach in njirre njonken *him*.
       Jelle saw   a viper near   him

Apparently, Middle English was like Frisian in this respect (Faltz, 1977):

(7) *He* cladde *hym*.
    he dressed him
    'He dressed.'

Modern English has an often overlooked residue of this type of binding. For many speakers of English, a bound pronoun is possible in examples like the following (Faltz, 1977):

(8) *John* bought *him* a new car.

The facts from Germanic alone suggest that we cannot simply say that pronouns must be free in a local domain.

In Romance, the situation is not very different:

(9) a. *Jean se* lave.
       John self washes
       'John washes.'

b. *Jean* parle de *lui.*
John talks of him
'John talks about himself.'

Apart from the reflexive clitic context (9a), French usually has bound
pronouns instead of reflexives, as in (9b), in the local domain.[3]
   Spanish also has the clitic reflexive in (10a), but it shows the same overlap
in PPs that we find in Dutch (10b–c) (I ignore here the role of extra
morphemes such as -*self* and *mismo*):

(10) a. *Juan se*   lava.
        John self washes
        'John washes.'
      b. *Juan* habla de   *sí mismo/él (mismo).*
        John talks about himself
      c. *Juan* vió una serpiente junto a *sí mismo/él (mismo).*
        John saw a   snake   near   him(self)

   It appears that in both Germanic and Romance, locally bound pronouns
are more the rule than the exception. If these observations are correctly
interpreted, Principle B must be reconsidered. An often overlooked problem
in this context is that the Binding Theory is never tested alone. It is tested
only in crucial conjunction with an independent theory of NP classification
that states that NPs like *himself* are [+anaphor, −pronominal] and that NPs
like *him* are [−anaphor, +pronominal]. Logically, either the Binding Theory
or the classification theory (or both) can be wrong.
   It is my claim that Principle A of the classical Binding Theory has survived
remarkably well. This is what we expect if Principle A is just an instance of
the very general local identification mechanism discussed in Koster (1987).
Most problems appear to originate from the independent theory of NP
classification. I demonstrate here how we can eliminate this theory, along
with the equally discredited Principle B.
   The trouble with the theory of NP classification is that it distinguishes
between anaphors and pronominals (in the sense of the Binding Theory)
on morphological grounds. I consider this approach hopeless and therefore
propose a radical configurational definition of anaphors:

(11) Anaphors are NPs that are locally bound.

According to this radical configurational definition, both *himself* in (12a)
and *him* in (12b) can be anaphors:

---

[3]Exceptions can be found in examples with quantified antecedents, like *On parle de soi.*

(12) a. *John* washes *himself.*
    b. *John* saw a snake near *him.*

The morphological distinctions, I claim, are independent of the Binding Theory and do not reflect the anaphor–pronominal opposition.

In general, there appear to be two kinds of morphological distinction: (a) specialized forms (like Dutch *zich*) versus nonspecialized forms (like English *him*), and (b) short forms (*zich*, *him*) versus long forms (*zichzelf*, *himself*). Although the latter distinction is briefly discussed, I concentrate on the former, in terms of the feature checking approach of Chomsky (1992). This approach has the virtue that it permits a radical reduction of options for parametrization. Basically, parametrization is reduced to a single type, namely the selection of strong versus weak morphological features that determine checking in SPEC-head configurations.

That the morphology-based theory of NP classification must be wrong is also clear from the well-known problem (Ross, 1970) that forms like *himself* can be bound outside their local domain:

(13) *John* said [that the book was written by Ann and *himself*].

It is generally assumed that nonlocally bound *himself* (as in (13)) is not an anaphor but a logophor (see Reinhart & Reuland, 1991). But if *himself* can be either an anaphor or a logophor, we have to find a criterion that distinguishes the two. Obviously, the criterion cannot be morphological. The theory I propose not only makes the correct predictions about bound pronoun distribution in local domains; it also provides a means to distinguish anaphors and logophors.

THE ROLE OF CASE

Recently, Eric Reuland and I have been exploring the idea that structural Case positions play a crucial role in anaphoric systems, an idea that also showed up in a different form in earlier work by Everaert (1986). Evidence can be found in Dutch. It appears that there is an interesting difference between oblique positions and (accusative) object positions.[4] In the oblique positions, the reflexive form *zich(zelf)* can optionally be replaced by the pronominal form *hem(zelf)* (see Koster, 1985):

(14) a. *Jan* sprak urenlang over *hemzelf* (*zichzelf*).
    John talked for hours about himself

---

[4]There appears to be no difference in Dutch between direct and indirect object, in the relevant respects. Therefore, in what follows, *oblique* means "in the context of a preposition." I return later on to the problem of double objects.

b. *Jan* zag een slang naast *hem* (*zich*).
John saw a snake near him
c. *Jan* sprak namens *hemzelf* (*zichzelf*).
John talked on behalf of himself

It is of interest that this alternation does not occur with nonoblique objects:

(15) *Jan* haat **hemzelf/zichzelf.*
John hates himself

Later, I argue that it is the same oblique–nonoblique distinction in English that is responsible for the difference between anaphors and logophors.

In Romance, the distinction between objective and oblique positions is even more obvious. Thus, in many varieties of Romance such as standard French and Spanish, the obligatory reflexive form is by and large limited to the object clitics. In prepositional phrases, we find pronominal forms to be optional (in Spanish, like Dutch) or even obligatory (in French) (see (9) and (10)). These facts suggest that the distribution of anaphors and pronouns within the local domain is somehow determined by Case or Case positions.

A SKETCH OF THE THEORY

As mentioned earlier, a satisfactory theory of anaphora states only what is specific to anaphora. More general aspects of local identification should be relegated to the more general theory of local identification, which handles not only anaphora but all local dependency relations (Koster, 1987). Thus, a dependent element δ (a trace or an anaphor, for instance) has to be bound within a minimal category β, where β is a major phrase node in the sense of the X' system:

(16) $[_\beta \ldots \delta \ldots]$

This general aspect of the theory of anaphora need not be repeated in the Binding Theory. What has to be stated is that (16) is not sufficient for anaphoric binding in that the relevant domain contains an opacity factor ω:

(17) $[_\beta \ldots \omega \ldots \delta \ldots]$

According to traditional opacity theories, ω is a subject accessible to δ or tense (cf. Chomsky, 1981).[5] It is questionable whether the notion *accessible subject* plays an important role in anaphoric systems. Even in English, tense

---

[5]Chomsky (1986) contains some rather complex elaborations of the Binding Theory that I ignore here.

leads to much stronger opacity effects, and presumably [± tense] is sufficient in a first approximation to opacity. In sentences with bare infinitives or small clauses, opacity effects are rather weak:

(18) a. *They* let [me help *each other*].
b. *John* considers [you better than *himself*].

In neither case does anaphoric binding across the embedded subject seem totally impossible. NPs introduce their own problem, to which I briefly return. In general, then, the domain statement for anaphora can presumably be limited to a specification of ω as [± tense] in (17). The relatively weak role of subjects in opacity is something I leave for further research.[6] For present purposes it suffices to say that local identification within a domain defined by tense is a rather common phenomenon in grammar and is by no means limited to the identification of anaphors (see Kaan, 1992, for discussion).

Note that according to my theory, the local domain has a dual role: It is the domain of both identification and definition. English, for instance, has both the traditional pronouns (like *him*) and logophors (like *himself*). Both have to be identified. Bound within a local domain, both are defined as anaphors and identified through the general local identification mechanism of grammar. If they are not bound within the local domain, identification follows other rules: Pronouns are contextually identified, whereas logophors show a much stricter pattern of identification (see Reinhart & Reuland, 1991, and the literature cited there). In general, both pronouns and logophors are elements that are not locally bound. The same morphological forms are anaphors if they are locally bound.

Crucially, now, we confront the unexplained distribution of morphologically specialized forms (like *zich* in Dutch) and the rather common occurrence of morphologically unspecialized anaphors (such as English *him*, in sentences like (3)). I propose that this distribution is not a matter of binding (identification) but a matter of licensing. Essentially, so it seems, the distribution of morphologically specialized anaphors is determined by a licensing agreement mechanism. Assuming that most agreement phenomena are typically determined by the functional nodes AGR-S and AGR-O, one may expect that these nodes also play a role in anaphor distribution.

By further assuming that licensing agreement is determined either by AGR-O or by AGR-S, I can begin to explain one of the most remarkable differences among anaphoric systems. As I noted before, many languages seem to have a "low" anaphoric orientation in that morphologically specialized

---

[6]Presumably, the relation between logophors and their antecedents is also affected by intervening subjects. See Koster (1978, 182–185).

anaphors are limited to the (nonoblique) verbal domain. French is a case in point. Other languages, like German, seem to have a "high" orientation in that obligatory specialized forms also occur in oblique contexts outside the immediate domain of the verb, for instance in adjuncts. Thus, compare again the following examples from English, (19a), and German, (19b), in which the brackets indicate the domains of AGR-S and AGR-O:[7]

(19) a. *John* [saw a snake **AGR-O**] near *him.*
b. *Johann* [**AGR-S** sah eine Schlange neben *sich*].
John saw a snake next to REFL

These examples suggest that English, like French, has the low orientation (obligatory licensing only in the domain of AGR-O) and that German has the high orientation (obligatory licensing in the larger domain of AGR-S). This difference exemplifies what is, to my knowledge, the most typical division we find in anaphoric systems. If this division is real, a theory of anaphoric binding is adequate only to the extent that it is able to account for it.

I now adopt an essential aspect of Chomsky's recent minimalist framework (Chomsky, 1992): the feature checking approach with respect to syntactic activity. Movements, for instance, are allowed in overt syntax only if strong morphological features of the moved categories must be neutralized by feature checking in certain configurations, particularly in SPEC-head configurations. The version of this theory that I adopt implies that feature checking matches strong features of a SPEC to features of the corresponding head, much along the lines of Rizzi's WH Criterion (Rizzi, 1990). So far, such theories have been applied only to movement phenomena. I would like to generalize such theories to all chains, including anaphoric chains.

Concretely, this further extension of the theory depends on the assumption that morphologically marked anaphors are strong and must be checked in a SPEC-head configuration against a corresponding strong head. This means that either the anaphor itself or its identifying antecedent has to be in the relevant SPEC position.[8] SPEC-head agreement of strong features always entails, therefore, that the element in SPEC must belong to a chain containing the strong feature that corresponds to the strong feature on the head.

It is assumed here not only that morphological anaphors are strong, but also that languages can have a corresponding strong anaphoric index on

---

[7]In the examples, I have indicated only the domains as determined by AGR-O and AGR-S. What I actually assume is that the object in (19a) is in [SPEC, AGR-OP] and that the finite verb in (19b) is adjoined to AGR-S (see Zwart, 1993, for a detailed justification of these assumptions).

[8]The main characteristic of chains is feature sharing (see Koster, 1987, chs. 1–2). This makes it possible to check features either directly (in the SPEC of the relevant head) or indirectly (through linking to this SPEC).

either AGR-S or AGR-O. In other words, licensing morphological anaphors means agreement with either AGR-S or AGR-O. These alternatives involve a parametric choice. There seem to be three possibilities. In the simplest case, languages have no anaphoric agreement at all. Such languages can have no morphologically marked anaphors, because there is no matching head. As suggested before, Frisian is such a language. Languages that do have a matching head appear to have a choice between AGR-S and AGR-O. Also, as suggested before, German and Slavic seem to select AGR-S, whereas English and French select AGR-O.

Reality is somewhat more complex in the sense that certain languages, like Dutch and Spanish, seem to have both possibilities. Such languages select either the German-Slavic option (AGR-S) or the English-French option (AGR-O). I return to some concrete evidence that Dutch can choose between two distinct grammars in this respect.

SOME EXAMPLES AND PROBLEMS

The theory outlined so far can best be elucidated by illustration. Consider the Frisian examples discussed before (repeated here for convenience):

(6) a. *Jelle* wasket *him.*
Jelle washes him
'Jelle washes.'
b. *Jelle* seach in njirre njonken *him.*
Jelle saw a viper near him

Because Frisian, by hypothesis, has no anaphoric indexing whatsoever, it cannot have morphologically marked anaphors, so that the anaphors in (6) (= *him*) have the same lexical form as nonanaphoric pronouns. This is confirmed by the fact that *him* in these examples can also have an antecedent outside the sentence, as can pronouns in general.

Frisian can also have the long form *himsels* in contexts like (6a):

(20) *Jelle* wasket *himsels.*
Jelle washes himself

Unlike what we observe for English -*self,* the intensifier -*sels* does not obligatorily mark the NP as either anaphoric or logophoric. It remains possible in (20) to refer with *himsels* to someone other than *Jelle.* I later return to the problem of long and short anaphoric forms.

Compare now the English examples (21a) and (21b):

(21) a. **John* washes *him.*

b. *John* washes *himself.*

Both examples are intended to involve local binding, so both cases involve anaphors. Example (21a) is ruled out, not by something like Binding Principle B, but by a morphological mismatch. Assuming that all English objects are in [SPEC, AGR-OP] for reasons of Case, we have an anaphor in (21a) in the relevant SPEC that does not agree with the strong anaphoric index on the head AGR-O.[9] The strong anaphoric index can be neutralized only by a corresponding strong anaphor. This is what saves (21b): the morpheme -*self* in English marks an NP as a specialized anaphor or logophor. We saw that English differs in this respect from Frisian. This is confirmed by the fact that, unlike what we saw in Frisian, *himself* cannot refer in (21b) to a person other than *John.*

In (21b), therefore, we have agreement between the strong anaphoric index on AGR-O and the anaphor that is marked as strong in this context. Consider snake sentences again:

(22) *John* saw a snake near *him.*

Him is locally bound, so it is an anaphor. It forms a chain with its antecedent *John*, which is in the SPEC of the AGR-SP. Because AGR-S has no strong anaphoric index in English, agreement is not necessary. This means that the anaphor is not obligatorily marked as strong by the morpheme -*self.* Note that the morpheme can still be added in examples like (22) under conditions of contrastive stress:

(23) *John* saw a snake near *himSELF.*

This example is unproblematic from the present theoretical perspective because -*self* marks a pronominal form as either strongly anaphoric or logophoric in English. Only strongly marked anaphors (checked in the SPEC of AGR-OP) must be matched by strong AGR-O. For logophors no such need exists, so that *himSELF* in (23) can be interpreted morphologically as a logophor and configurationally as a weak anaphor.

As for double object constructions, I adopt the small clause analysis familiar since Kayne (1981b). In fact, I assume that small clauses are like tenseless ECM constructions in that they involve two AGR-OPs, one for the Case of the embedded object, and one for the ECM of the embedded subject. Compare the following two examples:

---

[9]Note that I am assuming that the anaphoric index on the head is obligatorily present only if the SPEC contains an anaphor. This assumption is necessary to allow for nonanaphoric NPs in [SPEC,AGR-OP]. Note that I am also assuming that objective Case is checked in [SPEC, AGR-OP] in overt syntax (see also footnote 18).

(24) a. John let [Mary read the book].
    b. John gave [Mary the book].

In both examples, *the book* can be assumed to receive its Case from the lower AGR-O, whereas *Mary* receives its Case from the matrix AGR-O. Both objects are therefore nonoblique in English.[10] As I later claim, small clauses (and ECM constructions) also have their own AGR-SP.

This analysis of double object constructions implies that anaphors in both object positions must be marked as such by *-self.* This seems to be a correct result:

(25) a. *John* gave *himself* (*him*) a book.
    b. *John* gave Mary *himself* (*him*).

An intriguing problem, then, arises with respect to the exceptional case discussed earlier:

(8)   *John* bought *him* a new car.

I propose that such cases involve residual oblique case. Unlike structural objective Case, oblique case is not checked in [SPEC, AGR-OP], so that (8) is not ruled out by a mismatch. Obviously, nevertheless, it is more normal in current English to interpret (8) with a double structural Case as well, so that (26) is the preferred alternative for most speakers:

(26) *John* bought *himself* a car.

In those languages in which anaphoric agreement is determined by AGR-O, the morphologically specialized anaphoric forms are, as predicted by our theory, not found in oblique contexts. In modern English, obliqueness seems to be more and more limited to adjunct positions. Presumably, the indirect object was originally also oblique in English. In various historical and geographical variants of German, this situation is standard. Consequently, these forms of German have morphologically specialized anaphors only in the accusative direct object position. I return later to the relevant facts.

---

[10]Some evidence for this type of analysis can be found in Dutch, in which both objects undergo the intonation-neutral kind of scrambling that is often analysed as movement to [SPEC, AGR-OP] (see Vanden Wyngaerd, 1988). If this analysis is correct, there must be two AGR-Os. It should also be noted that I do not consider the possibility of passive formation a valid diagnostic for structural Case.

Incidentally, it should be noted that prepositional objects in English are not oblique but objective, and they are therefore checked in the SPEC of AGR-O.[11] Thus, *himself* in (27) is a relevant example:

(27) *George* approves of *himself.*

Following Kayne (1981a), many linguists have assumed that verb and preposition are in harmony here by assigning the same structural Case. This is also the Case absorbed under passive, a fact that is later shown to have interesting consequences:

(28) *George* was approved of *t.*

To summarize, it seems that all object types in modern English tend to have structural objective Case, which has to be checked in the SPEC of some AGR-O. Oblique cases are found only in adjuncts. Assuming that English has its strong anaphoric index in AGR-O, this also means that only reflexives in object positions are obligatory strong anaphors in English. Reflexives in adjuncts can also be logophors, that is, elements that can be bound outside the minimal local domain. I return later to English anaphora and some of its problems.

French has a rather straightforward anaphoric system from the present point of view. It has the low anaphoric orientation of English (agreement with AGR-O), and morphological marking of reflexives is by and large limited to clitics:[12]

(29) *Jean se* lave.
John refl washes
'John washes himself.'

In this example, it is assumed that the objective Case expressed by the clitic is checked in the SPEC of AGR-O. This is also the position where the strong anaphoric feature is neutralized.

As in all languages with anaphoric agreement determined by AGR-O, French morphologically marked anaphors are found only in the nonoblique

---

[11]Throughout this article I am using the term *prepositional object* for NPs contained in complement PPs.

[12]In principle, morphological marking seems necessary only to render strong those anaphors that are third person. The function of morphological marking could be disambiguation. Ambiguity never exists for first and second person anaphors in cases like *je me lave.* I therefore assume that it is universally the case that first and second person anaphors are either weak or strong, without obligatory marking of the distinction.

object positions. In oblique contexts, French has nonspecialized forms, like *lui(-même)*:[13]

(30) *Jean* parle de   *lui(-même).*
     John talks about him(self)

For double object constructions, I assume small clause structure with both embedded AGR-O and matrix AGR-O, as in English. This entails that an indirect object anaphor must also have an obligatory morphological anaphoric marking, because it has to be matched with the strong anaphoric index on AGR-O:

(31) *Jean se*   donne un livre.
     John refl give   a   book
     'John gives himself a book.'

In other words, a plausible case can be made for the hypothesis that both the indirect object and direct object clitic in French express structural Case, in spite of the fact that they can be morphologically distinct (*le* vs. *lui*). In general, surface form is not a reliable indicator of the underlying abstract Case. This is also clear from German, in which the complements of certain prepositions have oblique (nonstructural) accusative surface case. This is the same surface case found in most objects, which are usually in the nonoblique (structural) Case position [SPEC, AGR-OP].

Whereas French is a good example of a language with anaphoric agreement on AGR-O, German is an example of a language with anaphoric agreement on AGR-S. This entails that German has obligatory morphological marking of anaphors not only in object positions but also in the higher adjunct positions. The following simplified sentence structure may illustrate the differences:

(32)

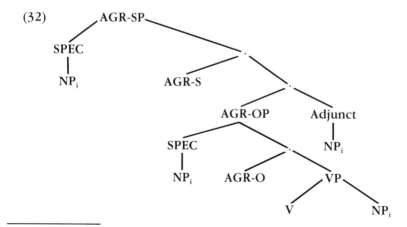

---

[13]Recall the well-known exception cited in footnote 3: *On parle de soi.* This can be seen as a residual form from an older system.

In languages like French and English, strong anaphoric features can be checked only in the SPEC of AGR-OP. In practice, this is possible because of the independently necessary movement of objects to [SPEC, AGR-OP] (for reasons of Case). In other words, Case and strong anaphoric index are checked in the same position. This entails that objects, and only objects, can be strong anaphors in these languages. In German and Slavic, in contrast, checking is done in the SPEC of AGR-SP. This implies that all anaphors in the sentence, including anaphors in adjunct position, must be checked: All NPs in (32) are in the c-command domain of the coindexed NP in the SPEC of AGR-S. As noted, actual movement to the relevant SPEC positions is possible but not necessary. Usually, checking of anaphoric features with respect to AGR-S occurs by anaphoric linking of the anaphor to the subject in the SPEC of AGR-SP.

This account also explains the different shape of anaphors in prepositional object position in the languages under discussion:

(33) a. *Jean* parle de   *lui/*soi.* (French)
     John talks about him/REFL
  b. *Johann* redet über **ihm/sich.* (German)
     John   talks about him/REFL

In (33a), the French anaphor is in a prepositional object position, an oblique position. Therefore, as a nonstructural object, it is not checked in [SPEC, AGR-OP] and cannot have the strong anaphoric shape expressed by the specialized form *soi.* It is bound by the subject *Jean,* but this connection to [SPEC, AGR-SP] cannot support a strong anaphoric form, because AGR-S does not bear the strong anaphoric index in French. In German, however, AGR-S does bear the strong anaphoric index, so that the connection in question leads to an obligatory strong anaphor, as shown in (33b). Naturally, the same contrast is found in adjuncts:

(34) a. *Jean* a   vu   un serpent à côté de *lui/*soi.*
     John has seen a snake   near   him/REFL
  b. *Johann* sah eine Schlange neben **ihm/sich.*
     John   saw a   snake   next to him/REFL

Although much research must be done in this area, there are strong indications that older variants of German behaved like French. Presumably, the specialized form *sich* was originally limited to structural object positions. According to Behaghel (1923, 295 ff.) it was only in the 17th century that the specialized form *sich* started to replace the pronominal forms (*im, ir, in*) in the dative. Luther's German still contains nonspecialized forms in the dative (Dal, 1962, p. 73):

(35) a. *Gott* schuf den Menschen *ihm* zum Bilde.
     God created man   in his image
   b. Andern hat er geholfen, und *er* kan *ihm* selber nicht helfen.
     others had he helped   and he can him self   not   help
     'He has helped others and cannot help himself.'

We can explain these facts by assuming that this historical variant of German has the low checking with respect to AGR-O. Of course, we must also assume that all nonaccusative objects are still nonstructural (oblique), like the objects of prepositions.[14] Nonspecialized anaphoric forms are commonly found in PPs, as is shown in examples from the 18th century author Wieland (Dal, 1962, p. 73):

(36) a. *Er* hat nicht mehr Mitleiden in *ihm* als   ein Hund.
     he had not   more sympathy in him than a   dog
     'There was no more sympathy in him than in a dog.'
   b. Wer hätte gedacht, dass *der alte Mann* so viel Blut in *ihm* gehabt hätte?
     who had thought that the old man so much blood in him had had
     'Who had expected that the old man would have had such vigor?'

In several current geographical variants of German this situation persists (see Keller, 1961; Lockwood, 1969). Very often, in the German dialects in question, the specialized anaphoric form is found only in structural accusatives. Oblique accusatives (in PPs) often have the expected nonspecialized form in southern German dialects (cf. Keller):

(37) *Er* hots für *in* selber gekhauft.
   he has-it for him self bought
   'He has bought it for himself.'

Such examples suggest that the relevant distinction is not in terms of surface case (accusative-dative) but in terms of abstract Case (structural-oblique). Much more research on historical and geographical variants of German must be done in order to test this hypothesis.

I have discussed two kinds of anaphoric systems distinguished by different settings of a parameter that might meet the narrow criteria formulated for parameters in Chomsky (1992). As mentioned before, some languages, like Dutch, can select either one of the permitted parameter settings. Standard

---

[14]In general, I am assuming that indirect objects are either structural (as in modern French, German, or English) or oblique (as in earlier stages of German or English). Perhaps, oblique indirect objects are complements to hidden prepositions in the sense of Kayne (1984, ch. 9).

Dutch is like German in that it has specialized anaphoric forms in all NP positions in the domain of AGR-S. Thus, specialized forms are found not only in structural object positions, as in (38a), but also in prepositional object positions, as in (38b), or adjunct positions, as in (38c):

(38) a. *Jan* wast *zichzelf.*
　　　 John washes himself.
　 b. *Jan* sprak over *zichzelf.*
　　　 John talked about himself
　 c. *Jan* zag een slang naast *zich.*
　　　 John saw a snake next to him

These facts are accounted for by assuming that Dutch is like German in that it selects AGR-S as the head at which to check the strong anaphoric feature of the specialized forms. However, as we mentioned earlier, Dutch can also select the nonspecialized forms, except in the structural object position, as in (39a):

(39) a. **Jan* wast *hemzelf.*
　 b. *Jan* sprak over *hemzelf.*
　 c. *Jan* zag een slang naast *hem.*

These data are accounted for by setting the parameter the other way, namely, by assuming checking in the SPEC of AGR-O. It seems to me that the two possible grammars for Dutch are clearly distinguishable in the sense that (39b) and (39c) are slightly substandard in comparison with the more normal (38b) and (38c). It should also be noted that (38c) and (39c) do not have exactly the same meaning. There seems to be a difference in terms of viewpoint: In (38c) the event is seen from John's point of view, whereas in (39c) the event is considered from the point of view of the speaker.

In any case, it seems reasonable to assume that Dutch may select either of the systems allowed by the possible parameter settings. The same might be the case in Spanish, as was briefly mentioned in connection with the examples in (10).

Before discussing some further problems in various languages, I digress briefly on the intriguing problems of short and long anaphoric forms.

HEAVY AND LIGHT ANAPHORS

In many languages, specialized anaphoric forms have either a long form or a short form. Dutch, for instance, has an obligatory long form *zichzelf* in (40a) and, in nonemphatic contexts, an obligatory short form *zich* in snake sentences like (40b):[15]

---

[15]Recall that I am limiting myself to the third person singular throughout.

(40) a. *Peter* bewondert *zichzelf.*
      Peter admires   himself
   b. *Peter* zag een slang naast zich.
      Peter saw a   snake next to him

Long and short forms do not have the same distribution, and up until recently I believed that the two forms were therefore governed by slightly different binding principles (see Koster, 1987, ch. 6). Because the theory presented here implies that there are no specific binding principles, another view on the distributional differences between long and short forms seems in order.

A complication in this area is the fact that long forms do not have the same status in all languages. Consider long and short forms in Dutch. In the majority of cases, Dutch must select the long form *zichzelf* (see (40a)). Exceptions are, among others, the syntactic objects of inherently reflexive verbs, as in (41a), and the complements of certain locational and directional prepositions, as in (41b) (see Koster, 1985, for discussion):[16]

(41) a. *Peter* vergist *zich* (**zelf*).
      Peter errs   refl (self)
      'Peter errs.'
   b. *Peter* keek   achter *zich* (**zelf*).
      Peter looked behind refl   (self)
      'Peter looked behind him.'

An extremely interesting case has been discussed by Vat (1980). According to Vat, prepositional objects obligatorily select the long form in simple sentences:

(42) *Peter* schoot op *zichzelf* (**zich*).
      Peter shot   at refl self   refl
      'Peter shot at himself.'

However, in the complements of ECM perception verbs and causatives, the short form must be selected for the same prepositional objects, provided that the antecedent is in the matrix clause:

(43) *Peter* liet [Jan op *zich* schieten].
      Peter let John at refl shoot
      'Peter let John shoot at him.'

---

[16]Adding -*zelf* in (41b) is possible under conditions of contrastive stress.

Although the distributional differences seem complicated, they can be accounted for under the traditional assumption that they follow from pragmatic factors. This idea was introduced into the modern discussion of anaphora by Zribi-Herz (1989). Although French shows a pattern somewhat different from Dutch, the main idea can be illustrated with the following examples:

(44) a. *Jean* parle de   *lui(-même)*.
        John talks about him(self)
    b. *Marie* est jaloux de *lui *(-même)*.
        Mary is jealous of her(self)

Usually, one is jealous not of oneself but of someone else. In the default case, jealousy is not self-oriented. So if one is the object of one's own jealousy, we have a marked situation that has to be expressed by adding the *self*-morpheme -*même*. (44a) suggests that the verb *parler* is more neutral in this respect. *Self*-morphemes are added in languages like French only if self-orientation is not expected. The same principle accounts for most, perhaps all, cases in Dutch. Naturally, inherently reflexive verbs in Dutch do not need addition of -*zelf*, because only self-orientation is possible:[17]

(45) a. *Peter* vergist *zich* (*zelf*)
        Peter errs   refl   self
        'Peter errs.'
    b. *Peter vergist Jan
        Peter errs   John

In contrast, the default orientation of a verb like *haten* 'to hate' concerns others. Consequently, the self-morpheme is required if self-orientation is to be expressed:

(46) *Peter* haat *zich* *(*zelf*)*.

Default orientation of the action or states expressed by verbs and other predicates is not a syntactic matter. Nevertheless, the generalization involved here is robust. Reinhart and Reuland (1991) demonstrated it with nominalizations that lack an overt object:

(47) Haten is niet gezond.
     hating is not healthy

---

[17]Inherent reflexive verbs in Dutch select a syntactic object without a theta role. I am not concerned here with the semantic aspects of inherent reflexivity, nor do I exclude clitic status of short reflexive objects (see Everaert, 1986).

In spite of the missing syntactic object, the intended target of the hatred here is someone other than the understood subject of *haten*. Other-orientation is the default meaning, so that self-orientation must be expressed by adding -*zelf.*

The other cases can also be explained along these lines. H. Nakajima (personal communication) has pointed out that the obligatory short form in snake sentences follows from the same principle. Compare the following sentences:

(48) a. John saw a snake nearby.
      b. John stood nearby.

If you see a snake nearby, the implication is that you see a snake nearby yourself. If, on the other hand, you stand nearby, the implication is that you stand nearby someone else. These nonsyntactic implications of the sentences in (48) are as hard as any linguistic facts. Again, we see that addition of a *self*-morpheme is a response to the default expectation. Because self-orientation is already implied in (48a), an added anaphor must be short:

(49) *John* saw a snake near *him.*

If, however, other-orientation is expected, the long form must be selected:

(50) *John* stood near *himself.*

As expected, Dutch follows the same pattern:

(51) a. *Jan* zag een slang naast   *zich.*
       John saw a   snake next to REFL
     b. *Jan*   stond naast   *zichzelf.*
       John stood next to REFL-self

These examples, incidentally, show that long and short forms are not lexically selected by certain prepositions, as was assumed in Koster (1985). The selection follows pragmatic pathways that are dependent on a context wider than that established by the preposition.

The same can be demonstrated with examples (42) and (43), repeated here for convenience:

(42) *Peter* schoot op *zichzelf*   (*zich).
     Peter shot   at   refl   self refl
     'Peter shot at himself.'

(43) *Peter* liet [Jan　op *zich* schieten].
　　　 Peter let　John at　refl　shoot
　　　 'Peter let John shoot at him.'

Here, too, we find two different forms (long vs. short) in the complement of the same preposition. Again, the distinction is based on a wider context. In all prepositional object positions, reflexive forms must be long in Dutch:

(52)　a. *Peter* spreekt over　*zich* *(*zelf*).
　　　　　 Peter talks　　about refl　(self)
　　　　　 'Peter talks about himself.'
　　　 b. *Peter* dacht　　aan *zich* *(*zelf*).
　　　　　 Peter thought of　refl　(self)
　　　　　 'Peter thought of himself.'
　　　 c. *Peter* houdt van *zich* *(*zelf*).
　　　　　 Peter loves of　refl　(self)
　　　　　 'Peter loves himself.'

In this respect, Dutch differs from French and German, which can also select short forms:

(53)　a. *Pierre* parle de　　*lui*. (French)
　　　　　 Peter　talks about him(self)
　　　 b. Peter redet über　sich. (German)
　　　　　 Peter talks　about REFL

It was already demonstrated by Everaert (1986, 204) that German *sich* does not have the same properties as Dutch *zich*. The German reflexive can be topicalized, as in (54a), or coordinated with another NP, as in (54b):

(54)　a. Sich,　　wusch er.
　　　　　 himself washed he
　　　 b. Er wusch　sich　　und seine Kinder.
　　　　　 he washed himself and his　　children

This is never possible in Dutch:

(55)　a. *Zich, waste　hij.
　　　　　 REFL　washed he
　　　 b. *Hij waste　　zich en　zijn kinderen.
　　　　　 He　washed REFL and his　children

These facts indicate that, contrary to what we find in Dutch, the German form can also be heavy in some sense when it is monomorphemic. E.

Reuland (personal communication) has suggested that German *sich* occupies the head position of the NP, whereas Dutch *zich* occupies a SPEC position. Let us adopt this suggestion and assume that French *lui* is like German *sich* in this respect (it can be topicalized and coordinated). We then end up with a three-way distinction. First of all, we have the truly light elements like the Romance clitics and Dutch *zich*. These elements cannot be topicalized or coordinated. They are used in contexts in which they cannot be replaced, syntactically or semantically, by a full NP (i.e., they occur in clitic positions and contexts of inherent reflexivity). Insofar as these forms are not clitics, they can also be used in contexts in which subject-orientation is, pragmatically speaking, the default expectation. This is what we find in snake sentences.

The heavy forms can either be monomorphemic (French *lui*, German *sich*) or consist of two morphemes (Dutch *zichzelf*). They are used in nonclitic contexts in which other- (nonsubject-) orientation is the default expectation. But even in languages with monomorphemic heavy forms, an extra morpheme (like French -*même* or German -*selbst*) can be added for purposes of contrastive stress or disambiguation.

Recall that English is not very transparent from this point of view. As I concluded earlier, the English morpheme -*self* marks an NP as either strongly anaphoric or logophoric. Because English has strong anaphor checking with respect to AGR-O, -*self* is always an obligatory part of reflexives in object positions. Outside AGR-OP, -*self* can only mark an NP as logophoric. To the extent that such logophors are locally bound (as weak anaphors), -*self* has a role very much like what we find in other languages: It is used for contrastive stress or to indicate deviation from an expected nonsubject-orientation. The phenomena in question are limited to adjuncts:

> (56) a. *John* saw a snake near *himSELF.*
>   b. *John* spoke on behalf of *himself.*

In both (56a) and (56b), the reflexive forms are in adjuncts, outside of AGR-OP, and are therefore weak anaphors in these contexts of local binding. For purposes of weak anaphoricity, the short form *him* would suffice in both cases. In fact, selection of the short form is normal in snake sentences like (56a) because of the expected subject-orientation. The extra morpheme, then, is added only to achieve contrastive stress. In (56b), we find the opposite situation. Here, the short form *him* would also be possible in principle. However, *speaking on behalf of X* clearly is associated with the default expectation that X is someone other than the subject. Therefore, the heavy form *himself* must be selected.

It is now time to return to the intriguing examples (42)–(43), repeated here for convenience:

(42) *Peter* schoot op *zichzelf* (*zich).
   Peter shot   at refl self   refl
   'Peter shot at himself.'

(43) *Peter* liet [Jan op *zich* schieten].
   Peter let John at refl shoot
   'Peter let John shoot at him.'

I concluded earlier that with prepositional objects the expected target of actions, for example, is someone other than the subject. Therefore, the heavy form must be selected, as in (42). However, with respect to NPs other than the local subject no such bias exists, so that these other NPs can bind the short form without problems (like *Peter* in (43)). In fact, with the ECM verbs in question, the matrix subject is often the expected orientation point, like the subject in snake sentences:

(57) a. Jan liet Peter komen.
         John let Peter come
     b. Jan liet Peter werken.
         John let Peter work

In (57a), the implied goal of *Peter*'s coming is *Jan*. Likewise, *Jan* is the understood beneficiary of *Peter*'s work.

In summary, the pragmatic concept of default orientation bias provides a very simple explanation for many of the intriguing facts concerning the distribution of light and heavy forms. My main conclusion is that extra morphemes like *-self* do not have the same function in all languages. In Dutch, the extra morpheme makes a light reflexive heavy for those cases in which subject-orientation is not the default. In German and French, the short forms themselves can be heavy, so that the extra morpheme is added mainly for purposes of emphasis (contrastive stress, disambiguation, strong deviations from standard expectations). In English, the extra morpheme indicates either a strong anaphor (to be checked in AGR-OP) or a logophor. In the latter case, the use of *-self* in local, anaphoric contexts is again governed by the familiar pragmatic notions.

SOME PREDICTIONS

Although the theory developed so far is not without problems, it is also promising in that it predicts several new facts. I limit myself here to some data from German and English.

With respect to anaphoric phenomena, small clauses behave like full clauses in many languages. In German, for instance, the following sentences are ambiguous (see Grewendorf, 1984, 1985):

(58) a. Peter konfrontierte [Maria mit sich (selbst)].
Peter confronted   Mary with herself
b. Hans überliess [die Schwester sich (selbst)].
Hans left   the sister [to] herself

Both the matrix subjects (*Peter, Hans*) and the embedded subjects of the small clauses (*Maria, die Schwester*) are suitable antecedents for the reflexives. Because I assume that the anaphoric checking domain in German is AGR-SP, I must also assume that the small clauses contain their own AGR-S, against which the strong anaphoric features must be checked through the small clause subjects in the SPEC of these AGR-Ss. From languages like Latin, for instance, it seems quite clear that there is agreement between small clause predicates and their subjects:

(59) a. Ferunt   eum   divitissimum esse.
they say him (Acc) very rich (Acc) to be
'They say he is very rich.'
b. Fertur   divitissimus esse.
[He, (Nom)] is said very rich (Nom) to be
'He is said to be very rich.'

If the small clause subject is in the accusative, as in (59a), the predicate shows the accusative ending as well. Passivization leads to a small clause predicate in the nominative form, as in (59b). On the basis of such facts, I consider it reasonable to assume an AGR-S in small clauses, so that the German facts in (58) do not come as a surprise.

Our theory predicts that if an object is not the subject of a small clause, it can bind an anaphor but not of the morphologically specialized kind. This prediction is borne out (Grewendorf, 1984, 1985):

(60) a. Hans erwartet *Maria* bei *ihr/*sich*.
Hans expects Mary at   her['s]
b. *Hans* hilft *dem Freund* bei *ihm/*sich*.
Hans helps the friend at his['s]

Assuming that the objects in these sentences (*Maria, dem Freund*) are not the subjects of small clauses, they are not connected to an extra embedded AGR-S. Therefore, the strong specialized form *sich* cannot be bound by these objects, because there is no AGR-S to match the strong anaphoric features. The unspecialized forms *ihr* and *ihm* are weak (as anaphors) and can be bound by antecedents unconnected to any AGR-S (as in (60)). In short, under the assumption that small clauses contain their own AGR-S, the contrast between (58) and (60) forms strong evidence for the theory presented here. The traditional Binding Theory cannot explain the difference and incorrectly predicts that (60) exemplifies a Principle B violation (under the connected assumption that the bound elements are pronominals).

I now turn to some hitherto unexplained facts of English. Reinhart and Reuland (1993) have pointed out an interesting difference between the following two sentences:

(61) a. *John* boasted that the queen had invited Mary and *himself.*
b. **John* boasted that the queen had invited *himself.*

The second example (61b) is in agreement with the standard Binding Theory: a reflexive cannot have an antecedent outside its local domain as defined by tense or a specified subject. The first example (61a) is problematic from this point of view, because it seems similar in all relevant aspects. Although the reflexive is bound by an antecedent external to its domain, as in (61b), the example seems grammatical. In other terms, *himself* must be a logophor rather than an anaphor in (61a).

How can we account for the difference? Under my approach, *himself* can be either an anaphor or a logophor, depending on context. In the checking domain of AGR-O, *himself* can be only a strong anaphor. Elsewhere, it is a logophor (or a weak anaphor if locally bound). In (61b), *himself,* as the object, is checked in the SPEC of AGR-OP.[18] Because it can be only a strong anaphor in this position, it must be locally bound. Because it is not, the sentence is ungrammatical.

Sentence (61a) can be saved by assuming that *himself* is somehow exempt from checking with respect to AGR-O. The fact that it is in a coordinated structure yields just this result, because there is independent evidence that coordination can block Case checking. Consider the existence of default cases. In Dutch, the nominative is usually assigned as a default case in contexts without tense:

(62) Ik een huis kopen? Nooit!
I a house buy? Never!

English typically has a nonnominative form in such cases:

---

[18]There seems to be disagreement whether to check the objective Case features in the SPEC of AGR-OP in overt syntax or at LF. Throughout, I am assuming checking in overt syntax and therefore actual presence of the object in [SPEC, AGR-OP] (see Zwart, 1993, for discussion).

(63) Me buy a house? Impossible!

Interestingly, this default case can presumably show up in coordinated structures, even if these coordinated structures as a whole are in structural Case positions. Compare the following alternatives:

(64) a. John and I were having a hard time.
      b. John and **me** were having a hard time.

The coordinated subject is in a position in which, normally, nominative Case is checked. In (64a), the nominative seems to be distributed over both conjuncts, as shown by the nominative pronominal form *I*. In the alternative (64b), possible for most speakers, the nominative is not distributed, as shown by the objective form *me*. We can explain this by allowing optionality of Case checking, not for the coordinated NP as a whole, but for the individual conjuncts. Mutatis mutandis, we can assume the same for the object position:

(65) They saw John and **me**.

As in (64), there could be two possible analyses here. Either Case checking is distributed, so that each conjunct is checked with respect to AGR-O, or Case checking is not distributed. In the latter case, **me** in (65) is assigned the default case that we also assumed for (64b).

With these assumptions, we can explain the logophoric character of *himself* in (61a). This form is only a strong anaphor if checked against AGR-O. But because this checking is only optionally distributed in coordinated structures, *himself* can also be a logophor.

Another fact that our theory explains has to do with the following example, discussed by Chomsky (1992):

(66) *John* wondered [which picture of *himself*]$_i$ *Bill* saw t_i

In this sentence, *himself* can be bound either by *John* or by *Bill*. Chomsky related the difference to two distinct LF representations resulting from two different reconstruction possibilities. The point can be illustrated further by replacing *saw* with *took*:

(67) *John* wondered [which picture of *himself*]$_i$ *Bill* took t_i

Again, there are two options in principle: Either *John* or *Bill* is the antecedent. Chomsky observed, however, that there is only one interpretation if *to take a picture* has the idiomatic sense of "to photograph." In that case, only *Bill* can be the antecedent. Chomsky explained this fact on the basis of the two different outcomes of reconstruction at LF with respect to (67):

(68) a. John wondered [which x, x a picture of himself] Bill took x
b. John wondered [which x] Bill took [x picture of himself]

In the first reconstruction (68a), *himself* is c-commanded only by *John*, the only possible antecedent. In (68b), *himself* is in the immediate domain of *Bill*, which is in this case the only possible antecedent. Chomsky further claimed that (68a) corresponds to the nonidiomatic reading of *take a picture*, whereas (68b) corresponds to the idiomatic reading (*take a picture* = "photograph"). Example (68b) is said to be a natural reconstruction for the idiomatic reading, because the idiomatic constituents are adjacent. These facts are considered a strong argument for LF.

Under the theory sketched in this chapter, the different interpretations find a natural explanation without recourse to the concept of LF. In comparing examples like (66) and (67) with their Dutch counterparts, we see at once that the ambiguity in the English examples has nothing to do with two modes of reconstruction but, rather, with the simple fact that English *himself* can be either an anaphor or a logophor. The Dutch reflexive *zichzelf* can be only an anaphor, with the interesting consequence that the equivalent of (67) is unambiguous in all readings:

(69) Jan vroeg zich af [welke foto van *zichzelf*]$_i$ *Bill* maakte t_i.
John wondered   which picture of himself Bill took

If there were two modes of reconstruction relevant for anaphoric binding, Dutch would have the two antecedent possibilities as well. This is not the case for the obvious reason that the Binding Theory works on pre-WH-movement c-command configurations. The relevant configurations belong to what van Riemsdijk and Williams (1981) called NP structure, a set of configurations that is in my opinion better described in a nonderivational framework (see Koster, 1987, ch. 2 for discussion). In any case, if the Binding Theory applies before WH-movement, *Bill* is correctly predicted to be the only possible antecedent in (69).

What about the ambiguity in the English examples? I claim that if English *himself* is an anaphor, only *Bill* can be the antecedent in (67), as in Dutch. In English, however, *himself* can be interpreted as a logophor, so that the external antecedent *John* is also possible. In accordance with our assumption that English has anaphoric checking with respect to AGR-O, *himself* is a strong anaphor only if it is checked in the SPEC of the AGR-OP. This is not the case in (66), so that *himself* is a logophor, and therefore an antecedent can occur outside the local domain.

Now consider (67). Under the idiomatic reading, a phenomenon sometimes referred to as reanalysis occurs, which I interpret along the lines of
Kayne (1981a) in terms of Case: the objective Case is assigned to the object
of the complex expression *take a picture of.* This view is confirmed by the
possibility of Case absorption under passive:

(70) *Bill* was taken a picture of *t.*

In other words, the object of the complex expression *take a picture of* has
to be checked in the SPEC of the AGR-OP immediately dominating the VP.
This explains the lack of ambiguity in (71) under the idiomatic reading:

(71) John wondered [which picture of *himself*]$_i$ *Bill* took t_i

As in Dutch, *Bill* is the only possible antecedent. This fact straightforwardly
follows from the Case checking position of *himself,* namely, the SPEC of
the AGR-OP immediately dominating the idiomatic VP. In this position, only
a strong anaphor and not a logophor is possible. Without reanalysis, in the
nonidiomatic reading, the Case of *himself* is checked in the PP.

In sum, it seems that the facts in question can be explained in a revealing
way under the theory sketched in this chapter. The same cannot be said of LF
explanations, because the Dutch facts strongly suggest that anaphoric binding
is based on pre-WH-movement configurations and not on the post-WH-move-
ment level of LF. Because the theory sketched here gives a uniform account
for the Dutch and the English facts, it is preferable to the LF-based explanation.

CONCLUSION

The theory sketched in this chapter was motivated by the many empirical
problems encountered by Principle B of the traditional Binding Theory
(Chomsky, 1981) and by the incompatibility of this theory with a restrictive
approach like Chomsky's (1992) minimalist framework. A secondary
motivation has been the conviction that much of the Binding Theory,
particularly the mechanism of local identification, is not anaphora-specific
but, rather, an instance of the more general theory of local identification
(Koster, 1987). What is specific to anaphoric binding is the mechanism
responsible for the distribution of specialized and nonspecialized (pronominal) anaphoric forms within the local domain. Because the traditional
Principle B is inadequate in this respect, it was replaced by a feature checking
mechanism that neutralizes strong anaphoric features, much along the lines
of the feature checking mechanisms proposed by Chomsky (1992) for
movement rules. In fact, this chapter represents one of the first attempts at

a broader application of feature checking. One outcome is the proposal that feature checking in SPEC-head configurations occurs either directly, in the relevant SPEC position, or indirectly, through linking of an anaphor to an antecedent in the relevant SPEC position.

As for the empirical facts, the languages studied generally show a high orientation, indicating checking in AGR-SP, or a low orientation, indicating checking in AGR-OP. Any adequate theory of anaphora must handle this difference in orientation. In the theory proposed here, the difference is accounted for by a fundamental parametrization such that either AGR-S or AGR-O is strong. German, Slavic, and versions of Dutch and Spanish are hypothesized to have the high orientation (strong AGR-S), whereas French, English, and other versions of Dutch and Spanish to have the low orientation (strong AGR-O). As it stands, the parametrization might appear arbitrary. Further research will reveal whether the parametrization is primitive, or whether it can be correlated with other properties of these languages. Nevertheless, the parametrization in question seems to be restrictive, in accordance with the minimalist framework. The strong AGR-S/AGR-O parametrization also seems to reach a high level of descriptive adequacy. Needless to say, there are still many problems, most of which have not been discussed here for reasons of space.[19] It is also likely that more serious revisions will be required when other languages are studied from the present point of view. It is, nevertheless, my hope that the new theory of anaphoric binding sketched in this chapter is a step in the right direction.

ACKNOWLEDGMENTS

I would like to thank Eric Reuland for the many stimulating discussions that led to this research. I would also like to thank Werner Abraham and Anko Wiegel for several of the German examples. Last but not least, I would like to thank Charlotte Koster and Marcel den Dikken for comments on an earlier version.

---

[19] To mention just two problems, consider sentences like *John let [Mary wash him]*, and the obligatory binding in NPs like *John's picture of himself*. The sentence is problematic in the reading in which *him* is bound by *John*. We are still within the local identification domain (determined by tense), so *him* would be an anaphor. Clearly, however, it does not have the required strong shape (*himself*). This problem can be solved by assuming that the AGR-OP of the lower clause can be skipped, because *him* is an anaphor only with respect to the matrix clause. Obligatory anaphoric binding in NPs is a very different problem. It is not obvious that it exists in English (see Pollard & Sag, 1992, for discussion), but it certainly exists in German and Dutch. The simplest solution is to assume that these languages have an AGR-S in NPs, or at least another structural Case checker. In the latter case, the parameter setting would involve not AGR-S but, more generally, the highest structural Case checker of a domain.

REFERENCES

Behaghel, O. (1923). *Deutsche Syntax. Eine geschichtliche Darstellung. Band I. Die Wortarten und Kasusformen.* Heidelberg: Carl Winter.

Chomsky, N. (1981). *Lectures on government and binding.* Dordrecht: Foris.

Chomsky, N. (1986). *Knowledge of language.* New York: Praeger.

Chomsky, N. (1992). A minimalist program for linguistic theory. *MIT Occasional Papers in Linguistics, 1.* Cambridge, MA: MIT, Department of Linguistics and Philosophy.

Dal, I. (1962). *Kurze deutsche Syntax.* Tübingen: Max Niemeyer.

Everaert, M. (1986). *The syntax of reflexivization.* Dordrecht: Foris.

Faltz, L. (1977). *Reflexivization: A study in universal syntax.* Unpublished doctoral dissertation, University of California, Berkeley.

Grewendorf, G. (1984). Reflexivisierungsregeln im Deutschen. *Deutsche Sprache, 12,* 14–30.

Grewendorf, G. (1985). Anaphern bei Objekt-Koreferenz im Deutschen. Ein Problem für die Rektions-Bindungs-Theorie. In W. Abraham (Ed.), *Erklärende Syntax des Deutschen* (pp. 137–171). Tübingen: Gunter Narr.

Kaan, E. (1992). *A minimalist approach to extraposition.* Unpublished master's thesis, University of Groningen, Groningen, The Netherlands.

Kayne, R. (1981a). On certain differences between French and English. *Linguistic Inquiry, 12,* 349–371.

Kayne, R. (1981b). Unambiguous paths. In R. May & J. Koster (Eds.), *Levels of syntactic representation* (pp. 143–183). Dordrecht: Foris.

Kayne, R. (1984). *Connectedness and binary branching.* Dordrecht: Foris.

Keller, R. (1961). *German dialects.* Manchester: MUP.

Koster, J. (1978). *Locality principles in syntax.* Dordrecht: Foris.

Koster, J. (1985). Reflexives in Dutch. In J. Guéron, H.-G. Obenauer, & J.-Y. Pollock (Eds.), *Grammatical representation* (pp. 141–167). Dordrecht: Foris.

Koster, J. (1987). *Domains and dynasties: The radical autonomy of syntax.* Dordrecht: Foris.

Koster, J., & Reuland, E. (Eds.). (1991). *Long-distance anaphora.* Cambridge: Cambridge University Press.

Lockwood, W. (1969). *Indo-European philology: Historical and comparative.* London: Hutchinson.

Pollard, C., & Sag, I. (1992). Anaphors in English and the scope of Binding Theory. *Linguistic Inquiry, 23,* 261–303.

Reinhart, T., & Reuland, E. (1991). Anaphors and logophors: An argument structure perspective. In J. Koster & E. Reuland (Eds.), *Long-distance anaphora* (pp. 283–321). Cambridge: Cambridge University Press.

Reinhart, T., & Reuland, E. (1993). Reflexivity. *Linguistic Inquiry.*

Rizzi, L. (1990). *Relativized minimality.* Cambridge, MA: MIT Press.

Ross, J. R. (1970). On declarative sentences. In R. Jacobs & P. Rosenbaum (Eds.), *Readings in English transformational grammar* (pp. 222–272). Waltham, MA: Ginn.

van Riemsdijk, H., & Williams, E. (1981). NP-structure. *The Linguistic Review, 1,* 171–217.

Vanden Wyngaerd, G. (1988). Object-shift as an A-movement rule. *MIT Working Papers in Linguistics, 11,* 256–271.

Vat, J. (1980). *Zich and zichzelf.* In S. Daalder & M. Gerritsen (Eds.), *Linguistics in the Netherlands 1980* (pp. 127–139). Amsterdam: North-Holland.

Zribi-Hertz, A. (1989). Anaphor binding and narrative point of view: English reflexive pronouns in sentence and discourse. *Language, 65,* 695–727.

Zwart, J.-W. (1993). *Dutch syntax: A minimalist approach.* Doctoral Dissertation, University of Groningen, Groningen, The Netherlands.

CHAPTER TWO

A Note on Relativized SUBJECT for Reflexives in Chinese

Chih-Chen Jane Tang
Academia Sinica, Taiwan

Within the Principles and Parameters approach, various kinds of theories have been posited to account for the contrast in long-distance binding between bare reflexives and compound reflexives in Chinese. Among these, one major distinction involves the derivation of long-distance binding possibilities and impossibilities from movement of bare and compound reflexives in LF. By examining long-distance binding of Chinese bare reflexives within a noun phrase, across a noun phrase, and across a noun phrase and a clause, I show in this chapter that the relevant facts may be explained under a revised version of the nonmovement theory of long-distance and local binding, in terms of the notion *relativized SUBJECT* proposed in Progovac (1991) as well as Progovac and Franks (1992). I first present the nonmovement account of binding of Chinese bare and compound reflexives in these two works (cf. Battistella, 1989; Cole, Hermon, & Sung, 1990; C.-T. J. Huang & Tang, 1991; Tang, 1985, 1989). I then revise the proposals of Progovac, and Progovac and Franks, so as to properly explain long-distance binding of Chinese bare reflexives. I conclude with a sketch of two remaining issues relevant to Progovac's and Progovac and Frank's theories.

Chinese has two reflexive forms: the bare reflexive with the invariant form *ziji* 'self' and the compound reflexive that appears as a pronoun+*ziji* sequence, as in *taziji* 'himself/herself', *woziji* 'myself'. As pointed out in Y.-H. Huang (1984) and Tang (1985, 1989), these two types of anaphoric elements exhibit distinct distributional and referential properties. As far as their reference is concerned, the bare reflexive, though not the compound reflexive, can have a long-distance antecedent outside its governing category, as in (1a) and (1b):

(1) a. Zhangsan$_i$ renwei [Lisi$_j$ da-le ziji$_{i/j}$].
   '(Lit.) Zhangsan$_i$ thought that Lisi$_j$ beat himself$_{i/j}$.'
b. Zhangsan$_i$ renwei [Lisi$_j$ da-le ta-ziji$_{\cdot i/j}$].
   'Zhangsan$_i$ thought that Lisi$_j$ beat himself$_{\cdot i/j}$.'

Long-distance binding with *ziji*, however, is restricted by a condition that requires the remote antecedent to agree in person and number features with all closer potential antecedents. In particular, a remote noun phrase can antecede *ziji* only if it agrees with the local noun phrase in the governing category of *ziji*. Thus, although *ziji* may have *Zhangsan* as its antecedent in (1a), where it agrees with *Lisi* in person and number, long-distance binding is blocked in examples like (2), where the remote noun phrase differs from the local noun phrase in person and/or in number. In these cases, *ziji* must be bound by the local noun phrase:

(2) a. Zhangsan$_i$ renwei [wo$_j$ da-le ziji$_{\cdot i/j}$].
   'Zhangsan thought that I beat myself.'
b. ni$_i$ renwei [Lisi$_j$ da-le ziji$_{\cdot i/j}$].
   'You thought that Lisi beat himself.'
c. wo$_i$ renwei [women$_j$ dui ziji$_{\cdot i/j}$ mei xinxin].
   'I thought that we had no confidence in ourselves.'

In (3), long-distance binding of *ziji* is also blocked, in spite of the fact that the remote noun phrase agrees with the most local noun phrase:

(3) Zhangsan$_i$ renwei [wo$_j$ zhidao [Lisi$_k$ chang piping ziji$_{\cdot i/\cdot j/k}$]].
   'Zhangsan thought that I knew that Lisi always criticized himself.'

The blocking of long-distance binding is due to the existence of the intervening noun phrase *wo* 'I', which agrees with neither *Zhangsan* nor *Lisi*. If *wo* is replaced by *Wangwu* as in (4), long-distance binding is again allowed:

(4) Zhangsan$_i$ renwei [Wangwu$_j$ zhidao [Lisi$_k$ chang piping ziji$_{i/j/k}$]].
   '(Lit.) Zhangsan$_i$ thought that Wangwu$_j$ knew that Lisi$_k$ always criticized himself$_{i/j/k}$.'

In general, potential local binders of bare and compound reflexives in Chinese are subject to (a) the subject-orientation condition, (b) the animacy condition, and (c) the c-command condition, except in cases where the antecedent represents an experiencer and where the noun phrase or the sentential subject containing the antecedent represents an inanimate entity. And the set of potential binders and blockers of long-distance *ziji* is exactly the same as the set of its potential local binders.[1]

PROGOVAC'S (1991) AND PROGOVAC AND FRANKS' (1992) ANALYSES

Various kinds of analyses have been proposed in terms of government-binding theory to account for the relevant Chinese binding facts. Among others, proposals made in Tang (1985, 1989), C.-T. J. Huang and Tang (1991), Battistella (1989), and Cole et al. (1990) have been much discussed. These analyses can be divided into three types, depending on the presence or absence of a movement analysis of bare and compound reflexives in LF. That is, Tang adopted a nonmovement analysis of both the bare reflexive and the compound reflexive in LF. In contrast, C.-T. J. Huang and Tang employed an LF movement analysis of both kinds of reflexives. Battistella and Cole et al., on the other hand, assumed that the bare reflexive, but not the compound reflexive, undergoes movement in LF. As for the type of movement involved, C.-T. J. Huang and Tang analyzed the LF movement of the bare and compound reflexives as an instance of movement by adjunction, whereas Battistella as well as Cole et al. treated the LF movement of the bare reflexive as head movement.

More recently, in arguing for a nonmovement analysis of the local and long-distance reflexives, Progovac (1991) and Progovac and Franks (1992) proposed the revision of Binding Principle A given in (5), based on the notion *relativized SUBJECT* in (6):

(5) A reflexive *R* must be bound in the domain *D* containing *R* and a SUBJECT.
   a. α is a SUBJECT for an X^0 reflexive iff X is a zero-level category (e.g., AGR).
   b. α is a SUBJECT for an XP reflexive iff X is an XP projection (e.g., [NP, IP] and [NP, NP]).

(6) The only relevant SUBJECT for X^0 is the X^0 SUBJECT, AGR.

Progovac and Franks' version of Binding Theory differs crucially from Chomsky's in two respects. First, Chomsky's (1981) Binding Theory requires a reflexive to be bound in its governing category as defined in (7):

---

[1]For a detailed discussion of potential local binders, long-distance binders, and blockers for reflexives in Chinese, see C.-T. J. Huang (1982), Tang (1985, 1989), and C.-T. J. Huang and Tang (1991), among others.

(7) α is a governing category for β iff α is the minimal category containing β, a governor of β, and a SUBJECT accessible to β.

According to Chomsky, an accessible SUBJECT is [NP, IP], [NP, NP], or AGR. But in (5) the notion accessible SUBJECT is replaced by SUBJECT. Second, a reflexive is further distinguished as an X^0 reflexive or an XP reflexive. As a result, the notion relativized SUBJECT is posited to define the SUBJECT for different types of reflexives.

Before turning to Progovac's account of Chinese reflexives, more needs to be said with respect to (5). In Progovac's theory, a morphologically simple reflexive can be an X^0 or XP reflexive, whereas a morphologically complex reflexive is an XP reflexive only. Although binding domain D in (5) is determined in accordance with the zero-level property of a simple reflexive, a coreferential reading between the simple reflexive and a potential XP binder is still allowed, because a simple reflexive is potentially an XP.

Consider now how Progovac accounted for local and long-distance binding of Chinese bare and compound reflexives on the basis of the foregoing assumptions. Progovac assigned the X' structures (8a) and (8b) to the bare and compound reflexives, respectively:

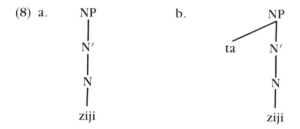

In (8b), where *ziji* is not exhaustively dominated by the node NP, the compound reflexive *taziji* is classified as an XP reflexive. On the other hand, the bare reflexive *ziji* in (8a) is an X or XP reflexive, because it is exhaustively dominated by NP. Being an XP reflexive, it follows from (5b) that *taziji* in object position needs to be bound by its clausemate subject and *taziji* in subject position needs to be bound by the closest potential antecedent outside of its containing clause, thereby ruling out a possible long-distance antecedent.

As already pointed out, the binding domain of the bare reflexive *ziji* is determined under (5a). Progovac posited two different ways of locating this domain. One way is to assume with C.-T. J. Huang (1982) that Chinese does not have AGR and thus *ziji* does not have the domain required in (5a); hence, the possibility of long-distance binding. The other is to assume with Borer (1989) that Chinese has an anaphoric AGR that is bound in a successive-cyclic manner, thereby extending the binding domain of *ziji* from its containing clause to the root clause. Attractive as it is, Progovac's theory of *ziji* is faced with certain empirical difficulties in dealing with blocking effects. In the case of Chinese as an AGR-less language, Progovac suggested that in examples like (9) *ziji* is bound by *Lisi* in accordance with (5b), and *ziji* is bound by *Zhangsan* in accordance with (5a) and a default principle of antecedent assignment to the matrix subject, thereby explaining the observation (9) in Y.-H. Huang (1984) and Tang (1985, 1989) (cf. (4), in which the *j* reading is permitted):

(9) Zhangsan$_i$ renwei [Wangwu$_j$ zhidao [Lisi$_k$ chang piping ziji$_{i/*j/k}$]].
  '(Lit.) Zhangsan$_i$ thought that Wangwu$_j$ knew that Lisi$_k$ always criticized himself$_{i/*j/k}$.'

This analysis, however, cannot explain: (a) why most native speakers consider grammatical the cases like (4), where *ziji* is bound by the intermediate subject; (b) why cases like (3) exhibit the blocking effect, where the intermediate subject does not agree with the local antecedent; and (c) why, as described in Tang (1985, 1989), although cases like (10) are acceptable for some native speakers, those like (11) are not:

(10) wo$_i$ renwei [Wangwu$_j$ zhidao [Lisi$_k$ chang piping ziji$_{i/j/k}$]].
  '(Lit.) I$_i$ thought that Wangwu$_j$ knew that Lisi$_k$ always criticized himself$_{i/j/k}$.'

(11) Zhangsan$_i$ renwei [wo$_j$ zhidao [Lisi$_k$ chang piping ziji$_{i/*j/k}$]].
  '(Lit.) Zhangsan$_i$ thought that I$_j$ knew that Lisi$_k$ always criticized himself$_{i/*j/k}$.'

In the case of Chinese as an anaphoric AGR language, Progovac (1991) and Progovac and Franks (1992) followed Borer (1989) and assumed that such AGR is bound to an A-element only if A'-binding fails. With this assumption, in cases like (1a) the lower AGR can be bound to the higher AGR because the matrix subject agrees with the embedded subject. As a result, *ziji* may be long-distance bound. On the other hand, in cases like (3), with the intervening subject as a blocker, the lowest AGR cannot be bound to the intermediate AGR because the subjects do not agree. Although the matrix subject does agree with the lowest subject, its AGR fails to bind the lowest AGR because they are too far away from each other. Hence, the impossibility of a long-distance antecedent.

Like the AGR-less account, the anaphoric AGR account also runs into problems. First, if the ungrammatical binding of *ziji* by the matrix subject in (3) is a consequence of the distance between *ziji* and the binder, why does such binding become well formed in (4)? To resolve this problem,

Progovac could claim that in (3) the ill-formed coreference reading between the matrix subject and *ziji* is attributed to a violation of anaphoric binding of the lowest AGR to the intermediate AGR. However, note that Borer's Chinese anaphoric AGR is posited to capture Huang's (1989) minimal distance condition on the antecedent of *pro* in Chinese. *Ziji* can nevertheless be bound by a long-distance antecedent.

Second, examine cases like (12)–(14), in which *ziji* is locally bound within a noun phrase:

(12) Zhangsan$_i$-de [youguan [ziji$_i$-de guojia]]-de baodao
'Zhangsan's reports of his own country'

(13) a. Zhangsan$_i$-de yi-pian [youguan [ziji$_i$-de guojia]]-de baodao
'Zhangsan's one report of his own country'

b. yi-pian Zhangsan$_i$-de [youguan [ziji$_i$-de guojia]]-de baodao
'one of Zhangsan's reports of his own country'

(14) a. Zhangsan$_i$-de zhe-san-pian [youguan [ziji$_i$-de guojia]]-de baodao
'(Lit.) Zhangsan's these three reports of his own country'

b. zhe-san-pian Zhangsan$_i$-de [youguan [ziji$_i$-de guojia]]-de baodao
'(Lit.) these three reports of his own country by Zhangsan'

Examples like (12)–(14) indicate that *ziji* and its local antecedent may be contained in the same noun phrase. Moreover, such binding possibilities are not restricted by the presence and absence of the (demonstrative-) quantifier-classifier sequence, nor are they constrained by the ordering of the antecedent and the (demonstrative-) quantifier-classifier sequence.

Based on the grammaticality contrasts in (15)–(19), Tang (1990, 1991) posited that in (12)–(14) the Chinese modifier marker *de* attached to the antecedent is not the counterpart of the English genitive marker *'s*; instead, it is a functional category with its own phrasal projection (Modifier Phrase, henceforth MODP) that is generated under an adjunct position:[2]

(15) John's wife, *new's books, *the letter [that John wrote]'s, *he heavily's beat me/Zhangsan-de taitai, xin-de shu, Zhangsan xie-de xin, ta henhen-de da-le wo

(16) he *('s) wife/ta (de) taitai

(17) a. *John's that book/Zhangsan-de na-yi-ben shu
b. *that John's book/na-yi-ben Zhangsan-de shu

(18) a. John's three books/Zhangsan-de san-ben shu
b. *three John's books/san-ben Zhangsan-de shu

(19) *John's yesterday's newspaper/Zhangsan-de zuotian-de baozhi

---

[2]See Tang (1991) for the discussion of different uses of *de*, under one of which *de* may be viewed as the Chinese counterpart of *'s* (cf. Li, 1985, 1990).

If this analysis is plausible, the modifier marker *de* is not the nominal AGR in Abney's (1987) DP hypothesis; hence, without any revision it cannot be anaphorically bound to the clausal AGR to account for the blocking effects in the (b) sentences in (20)–(23):

(20) a. Zhangsan$_i$-de na-san-pian Lisi$_j$-de [youguan ziji$_{i/j}$]-de wenzhang
     '(Lit.) Zhangsan's$_i$ those three articles about himself$_{i/j}$ by Lisi$_j$'
   b. Zhangsan$_i$-de na-san-pian wo$_j$-de [youguan ziji·$_{i/j}$]-de wenzhang
     '(Lit.) Zhangsan's those three articles about myself by me'

(21) a. Zhangsan$_i$-de yi-ben [Lisi$_j$ mai]-de [youguan ziji$_{i/j}$]-de shu
     '(Lit.) Zhangsan's$_i$ book about himself$_{i/j}$ that Lisi$_j$ bought'
   b. Zhangsan$_i$-de yi-ben [ni$_j$ mai]-de [youguan ziji$_{i/\cdot j}$]-de shu
     '(Lit.) Zhangsan's book about yourself that you bought'

(22) a. Zhangsan$_i$ you Lisi$_j$-de na-san-pian [youguan ziji$_{i/j}$]-de wenzhang.
     '(Lit.) Zhangsan$_i$ has Lisi's$_j$ those three articles about himself$_{i/j}$.'
   b. wo$_i$ you ni$_j$-de na-san-pian [youguan ziji·$_{i/j}$]-de wenzhang.
     '(Lit.) I have your those three articles about yourself.'

(23) a. Zhangsan$_i$ juede [Lisi$_j$-de [youguan ziji$_{i/j}$]-de baodao xie-de hao].
     '(Lit.) Zhangsan$_i$ thought Lisi's$_j$ report of himself$_{i/j}$ was well written.'
   b. women$_i$ juede [ni$_j$-de [youguan ziji·$_{i/j}$]-de baodao xie-de hao].
     '(Lit.) We thought that your report of yourself was well written.'

Cases like the (a) sentences of (20)–(23) also illustrate that long-distance binding of *ziji* may take place within a noun phrase (as in (20a) and (21a)), across a noun phrase (as in (22a)), and across a noun phrase and a clause (as in (23a)).[3]

A REVISION

Although Progovac's theory of *ziji* is still problematic, the notion of relativized SUBJECT is worth pursuing further. In the following, I would like to account for the relevant facts about *ziji* with a revised version of Progovac's hypothesis. Suppose Chinese does have AGR, but, unlike the case in languages like Italian, AGR in Chinese is not overt.[4] Also, suppose AGR may contain two kinds of ⌀-features: One type is syntactic ⌀-features specified via SPEC-head agreement, and another type is anaphoric ⌀-features marked via SPEC-head binding. In some languages syntactic ⌀-features are identical to anaphoric ones, whereas in other languages they are not. In the case of anaphoric ⌀-features relevant to Principle A of the Binding Theory, languages like Chinese that impose an

---

[3]For problems that cases like (12)–(14) and (20)–(23) may raise for C.-T. J. Huang and Tang (1991), Battistella (1989), and Cole et al. (1990), see Tang (1992).

[4]See Tang (1992) for the discussion of Chinese as an AGR-less language.

animacy condition on the potential binder of the reflexive do not have identical syntactic and anaphoric ø-features.[5]

In addition to these two assumptions, I posit that all functional heads, not just AGR, may contain both syntactic and anaphoric ø-features and thus may be said to be anaphorically linked to one another if they share certain identical anaphoric ø-features.

With these four claims, I can now explain long-distance binding of *ziji.* That is, as in Progovac and Franks' account, binding domain *D* of *ziji* in (5a) may be extended only if the X^0 in the minimal domain *D* is linked to a closest potential Y^0 in terms of identical anaphoric ø-features. Therefore, with possibilities and impossibilities of anaphoric linking among AGRs and MODs, cases like (1a), (2)–(4), (12)–(14), and (20)–(23) are all accounted for.[6] Moreover, extension of a binding domain by anaphoric linking captures the local and island-free nature of the Chinese long-distance *ziji* (see C.-T. J. Huang & Tang, 1991).

Yu (1991) pointed out that *ziji* can be bound by a base-generated topic:

(24) wo$_i$ (a), dao ge zai ziji$_i$-de bozi shang, wo ye bu pa.
'As for me, even with a knife at my own neck, I would not be frightened.'

Assuming that a base-generated topic is located in the SPEC of CP, examples like (24) suggest that in Chinese, C is also a relevant SUBJECT for *ziji,* thereby explaining the blocking effect in (25):

(25) ta$_i$ renwei wo$_j$ (a), dao ge zai ziji$_{*i/j}$-de bozi shang, wo ye bu pa.
'(Lit.) He thinks that as for me, even with a knife at my own neck, I would not be frightened.'

Cases like (24)–(25) also illustrate another important point; that is, *ziji* can be A'-bound, a phenomenon that also occurs in cases like (20)–(23), in which the antecedents are marked with the modifier marker *de.*[7]

---

[5] This is a variation that may be related to morphological properties of reflexives.

[6] Under this approach, functional heads with a nonoccupied specifier are not marked for ø-features and thus are not blockers for anaphoric linking.

[7] According to Aoun & Li (1993, p. 80), in raising costructions like (i) and (ii) *women* 'we' occupies an A'-position and in (i) its trace within the VP *hai-le* 'hurt' is invisible to the ECP due to the operation of reanalysis.

(i) women$_i$ keneng hai-le ziji$_i$.
'(Lit.) We are likely that hurt ourselves.'
(ii) women$_i$ bei ziji$_i$ hai-le.
'We were hurt by ourselves.'

If their analysis is correct, then in cases like (i) *and (ii) ziji* is also A'-bound.

Note that another way of looking at the issue in question is from the viewpoint of parametrization of the A/A'-nature of the specifier and adjunction positions crosslinguistically, as proposed in Yoon (1991). Under this approach, *ziji* may still be regarded as being A-bound.

It should be noted that even in English, not all phrases with the genitive marker *'s* are analyzed as arguments. In Grimshaw's (1990) theory, for example, they may be argument-adjuncts and modifiers that do not appear in a syntactic argument position. This, however, does not prevent them from acting as the binder of a reflexive:

(26) a. Albania's destruction of itself
    b. John's gift to himself

With the observation that specifiers of C, AGR and MOD are all potential antecedents of *ziji*, it seems that the so-called subject-orientation condition is too restricted in Chinese, though it is true that objects of verbs and prepositions cannot serve as antecedents of *ziji*.[8] The issue here does not seem to involve the specifier-complement distinction, however, given that objects of verbs and prepositions may be treated as specifiers, as proposed in Larson (1988) and Harbert (1990). Thus, what is relevant here seems to be the functional-lexical contrast. That is, only specifiers of functional categories (like C, AGR, Tense, Aspect, and MOD) can be the potential antecedents of *ziji*. I leave this to future research.

If this analysis has been on the right track, it has the following three implications. First, it suggests that INFL/AGR may still have its independent status in the Binding Theory, regardless of whether the *i*-within-*i* condition is valid (cf. Chomsky, 1986).

Second, it shows that binding domain D in (5a) may be extended in two different ways. For languages like Russian, with overt agreement elements, AGR seems to be visible to (5a) only when it is overtly present. For languages like Chinese, which never have any overt agreement elements, AGR seems to be always visible to (5a). And only to languages like Chinese is the posited anaphoric linking applicable. Consequently, although Russian and Chinese both have AGR, only Russian exhibits the finite–nonfinite asymmetry with

---

[8] The animacy condition seems to be too strong a condition, too. For example, as pointed out by P.-C. Wei (personal communication, January 21, 1992), names of planets can also serve as an antecedent:

(i) diqiu shun-zhe ziji-de guidao yunzhuan.
    'The earth follows its own path in its revolution around the sun.'

A closer examination of cases like (i) and (ii) shows that the relevant point is not just whether the NP is animate or inanimate, but whether the semantics of the NP may satisfy the selectional restriction of the predicate under its reflexive use:

(ii) a. [ta$_i$-de meimei]$_j$ hai-le ziji$_{*i/j}$.
      'Her sister hurt herself.'
   b. [ta$_i$-de jiaoao]$_j$ hai-le ziji$_{i/*j}$.
      '(Lit.) Her pride hurt herself.'

the long-distance reflexive (see Rappaport, 1986; Tang, 1985). The applicability of binding domain extension by anaphoric linking may reduce to morphological properties of AGR.

Third, functional heads that license anaphoric linking may be parametrized. For example, under Chomsky's (1992) minimalist program, both AGR-S and AGR-O are universal. If his claim is correct, then AGR-O cannot be a potential relativized SUBJECT for the Chinese bare reflexive. Again, the cross-linguistic distinction in the choice of potential relativized SUBJECTs in (5a) may be attributed to morphological properties of functional heads.

CONCLUSION

In this chapter, I have shown that the referential behavior of Chinese bare and compound reflexives may be accounted for under a revision of Progovac's (1991) and Progovac and Franks' (1992) Binding Theory in terms of the notion relativized SUBJECT, which is closely linked to the morphological complexity of the Chinese bare and compound reflexives in accordance with X'-theoretic structure rather than movement in LF.

In conclusion, two issues are worth mentioning. First, note that in Chinese *ta de ziji* 'he's self', in which the modifier marker *de* is inserted into the compound reflexive *taziji*, is ill formed. The observation that no instance of *de* is allowed between *ta* and *ziji* suggests another possible X' structure of *taziji* as in (27), where *ta* and *ziji* form a compound noun:

(27)

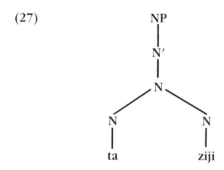

If there is any evidence that (27) is more plausible than (8b), then the difference in binding domain between *ziji* and *taziji* can no longer be distinguished in terms of the X-XP asymmetry alone.[9] As a result, it seems

---

[9]On the other hand, *ziji* has also been analyzed as *pro(-)ziji* (in Tang, 1985, 1989, and other references cited in Tang, 1992). See Tang (1992) for discussion of problems associated with the notion relativized SUBJECT under such an approach.

important to consider the contrast between them with respect to ϕ-features, as well. Here I do not discuss how (27) and (8a) may be approached under the nonmovement account of Chinese reflexives discussed earlier, but a possible hypothesis is that compound reflexives with ϕ-features are more referential than bare reflexives without ϕ-features, so that in LF the former need to be treated as XP rather than X with respect to (5).

Second, I have demonstrated that with the revision of the notion relativized SUBJECT, which is assumed in Progovac (1991) and Progovac and Franks (1992) to apply in LF, a proper interpretation of bare and compound reflexives in Chinese may be achieved without resorting to LF movement. However, if Chomsky's (1992) claim is correct and LF movement of reflexives is universal, it is still essential to solve problems raised by cases like (12)–(14) and (20)–(23) with respect to previously proposed movement theories (see Tang, 1992). I leave this to future research.

ACKNOWLEDGMENTS

This chapter is a shorter version of a paper presented at the 1992 Cornell Cognitive Studies Symposium. For helpful discussion of some of the issues addressed here, I am grateful to Wayne Harbert, C.-T. James Huang, John Whitman, Ting-Chi Tang, and Pei-Chuan Wei.

REFERENCES

Abney, B. (1987). *The English noun phrase in its sentential aspect*. Unpublished doctoral dissertation, MIT, Cambridge, MA.

Aoun, J., & Li, Y.-H. A. (1993). *Syntax of scope*. Cambridge, MA: MIT Press.

Battistella, E. (1989). Chinese reflexivization: A movement to INFL approach. *Linguistics, 27,* 987–1012.

Borer, H. (1989). Anaphoric AGR. In O. Jaeggli & K. Safir (Eds.), *The null subject parameter* (pp. 69–109). Dordrecht: Kluwer.

Chomsky, N. (1981). *Lectures on government and binding*. Dordrecht: Kluwer.

Chomsky, N. (1986). *Knowledge of Language*. New York: Praeger.

Chomsky, N. (1992). A minimalist program for linguistic theory. *MIT Occasional Papers in Linguistics, 1.* Cambridge, MA: MIT, Department of Linguistics and Philosophy.

Cole, P., Hermon, G., & Sung, L.-M. (1990). Principles and parameters of long distance reflexives. *Linguistic Inquiry, 21,* 1–22.

Grimshaw, J. (1990). *Argument structure*. Cambridge, MA: MIT Press.

Harbert, W. (1990). *Subjects of prepositions*. Unpublished manuscript, Cornell University, Ithaca, NY.

Huang, C.-T. J. (1982). *Logical relations in Chinese and the theory of grammar*. Unpublished doctoral dissertation, MIT, Cambridge, MA.

Huang, C.-T. J. (1989). Pro-drop in Chinese: A generalized control theory. In O. Jaeggli & K. Safir (Eds.), *The null subject parameter* (pp. 85–214). Dordrecht: Kluwer.

Huang, C.-T. J., & Tang, C.-C. J. (1991). On the local nature of the long-distance reflexive in Chinese. In J. Koster & E. Reuland (Eds.), *Long-distance anaphora* (pp. 263–282). Cambridge: Cambridge University Press.

Huang, Y.-H. (1984). Reflexives in Chinese. *Studies in English Literature and Linguistics, 10,* 163–188.

Larson, R. (1988). On the double object construction. *Linguistic Inquiry, 19,* 335–391.

Li, Y.-H. A. (1985). *Abstract case in Chinese.* Unpublished doctoral dissertation, University of Southern California, Los Angeles.

Li, Y.-H. A. (1990). *Order and constituency in Mandarin Chinese.* Dordrecht: Kluwer.

Progovac, L. (1991). *Relativized subject, long-distance reflexives, and accessibility.* Unpublished manuscript, Indiana University, Bloomington.

Progovac, L., & Franks, S. (1992). Relativized subjects for reflexives. *Proceedings of the North Eastern Linguistics Society, 22,* 349–363.

Rappaport, G. C. (1986). On anaphor binding in Russian. *Natural Language and Linguistic Theory, 4,* 97–120.

Tang, C.-C. J. (1985). *A study of reflexives in Chinese.* Unpublished master's thesis, National Taiwan Normal University.

Tang, C.-C. J. (1989). Chinese reflexives. *Natural Language and Linguistic Theory, 7,* 93–121.

Tang, C.-C. J. (1990). *Chinese phrase structure and the extended X̄-theory.* Unpublished doctoral dissertation, Cornell University, Ithaca, NY.

Tang, C.-C. J. (1991). *Hanyu-de* de *yu yingyu-de* 's [Chinese *de* and English 's]. Paper presented at the Third World Conference on Chinese Linguistics and Language Teaching, Taipei.

Tang, C.-C. J. (1992). *On movement/nonmovement analyses of reflexives in Chinese.* Paper presented at the Cognitive Studies Symposium, Cornell University, Ithaca, NY.

Yoon, J.-M. (1991). *The syntax of A-chains: A typological study of ECM and scrambling.* Unpublished doctoral dissertation, Cornell University, Ithaca, NY.

Yu, W. X. F. (1991). A-bound or not A-bound. *Linguistic Analysis, 18,* 210–234.

CHAPTER THREE

The Japanese Dialectal Monomorphemic Reflexive *Zisin* and Its Theoretical Implications: A Contrast With Chinese *Ziji*

Yafei Li
Cornell University

Based on Progovac's (1991) notion of relativized SUBJECT and two types of φ-features, Tang (this volume, chapter 2) proposed a nonmovement analysis of long-distance reflexivization in Chinese. The monomorphemic *ziji* 'self' is exhaustively dominated by NP, so it can be treated as either NP or N°. As N°, its SUBJECT must be another head (i.e., the closest AGR). If this AGR bears the same anaphoric φ-features as a higher AGR, the binding domain of *ziji* is extended, permitting long-distance binding. It is not my intention here to offer a thorough evaluation of Tang's interesting work or to propose an alternative full-scale analysis of *ziji*. Lust and Mazuka (this volume, chapter 6) showed that *zibun*, the Japanese counterpart of *ziji*, cannot be analyzed simply as an anaphor within Binding Theory. Many of the nonanaphoric behaviors of *zibun* are also found in *ziji* and are not well understood. The goal of this chapter is more modest: By examining the four reflexive forms found in the Kansei dialect of Japanese and among some older Japanese speakers, I show that an analysis of reflexivization based on relativized SUBJECT still needs independent motivation. The rest of the chapter focuses on a compositional account of the coreferential properties of complex reflexives in Japanese and Chinese.

ZISIN AND A COMPOSITIONAL ANALYSIS
OF JAPANESE REFLEXIVES

The crucial Japanese examples are given in (1), in which the well-known *zibun* is compared with the dialectal *zisin*:[1]

(1) a. Musasi$_i$-ga   Takuan$_j$-ni   Koziro$_k$-ga   zibun$_{i/*j/k}$/zisin·$_{i/*j/k}$-o
    Musasi-nom Takuan-dat Koziro-nom self self   -acc
    aisite-iru to hanasita.
    loved   C told
    'Musasi told Takuan the Koziro loved self.'
  b. Musasi$_i$-ga   Takuan$_j$-ni   zibun$_{i/*j}$/zisin$_{i/*j}$-ni kansuru hanasi-o sita.
    Musasi-nom Takuan-dat self   self -dat about   story-acc told
    'Musasi told Takuan a story about self.'

In environments like those in (1), *zibun*, like *ziji*, shows possible long-distance binding and obligatory subject binding. This is expected, given the relativized SUBJECT analysis. What is not expected is the behavior of the locally bound *zisin*. Because *zisin* is also exhaustively dominated by NP, it should be treated as N°, as is *zibun*. One would predict, incorrectly, that *zisin* would have an extended binding domain and could therefore take a long-distance antecedent. The only way out is to assume that underlyingly *zisin* is not a monomorphemic reflexive but, rather, is combined with some empty element (e.g., *pro*). This assumption is consistent with the fact that all overtly complex reflexives are local. However, if one wants to defend a relativized SUBJECT analysis of long-distance reflexivization, it is then no longer possible to make use of the correlation between the binding properties of a reflexive and its overt morphological form. Clearly, the motivation for relativized SUBJECT is now weakened, unless there is independent evidence for treating *zibun* as monomorphemic but *zisin* as multimorphemic.

   Zisin also raises a question of a different kind. *Zisin* is the constant component of the complex reflexives such as *karezisin* 'himself' and *zibunzisin* 'selfself'. But, as we will see shortly, it differs from them in coreferential properties. Why? In the rest of this chapter, I explore a possible answer to this question, illustrating the compositional approach to reflexives rather than defending a specific analysis. The basic idea may be implemented with somewhat different syntactic structures and equally plausible assumptions.

---

[1]All the Japanese examples are from Y. Li and Takahashi (1993). The crucial data are also verified with two other Japanese speakers. I thank Chioko Takahashi for insisting that there is something interesting going on in her dialect.

First, consider the behaviors of *karezisin* and *zibunzisin* in the environments in (1). Note that both reflexives are local, as in (2a) and *zibunzisin* must be subject bound, as in (2b).[2]

(2) a. Musasi$_i$-ga   Takuan$_j$-ni Koziro$_k$-ga   zibunzisin$_{i/*j/k}$/karezisin$_{i/*j/k}$
    Musasi-nom Takuan-dat Koziro-nom self-self   him-self
    -o aisite-iru to hanasita.
    -acc loved   C told
    'Musasi told Takuan that Koziro loved selfself/himself.'
  b. Musasi$_i$-ga   Takuan$_j$-ni zibunzisin$_{i/*j}$/karezisin$_{i/j}$-ni kansuru
    Musasi-nom Takuan-dat self-self   him-self -dat about
    hanasi-o sita.
    story-acc told
    'Musasi told Takuan a story about selfself/himself.'

Notice that when the matrix verb changes from *tell* to *hear*, the behaviors of *zibun* and *zisin* change ((1) vs. (3)), but those of *karezisin* and *zibunzisin* do not ((2) vs. (4)):

(3) a. Musasi$_i$-ga   Takuan$_j$-kara Koziro$_k$-ga   zibun$_{i/j/k}$/zisin$_{i/*j/k}$-o
    Musasi-nom Takuan-from Koziro-nom self   self -acc
    aisite-iru to kiita.
    loved   C heard
    'Musasi heard from Takuan that Koziro loved self.'
  b. Musasi$_i$-ga   Takuan$_j$-kara zibun$_{i/*j}$/zisin$_{i/j}$-ni kansuru
    Musasi-nom Takuan-from self   self -dat about
    hanasi-o kiita.
    story-acc heard
    'Musasi heard form Takuan a story about self.'

(4) a. Musasi$_i$-ga   Takuan$_j$-kara Koziro$_k$-ga   zibunzisin$_{i/*j/k}$/
    Musasi-nom Takuan-from Koziro-nom self-self
    karezisin$_{i/*j/k}$-o aisite-iru to kiita.
    him-self T-acc loved   C heard
    'Musasi heard from Takuan that Koziro loved selfself/himself.'
  b. Musasi$_i$-ga   Takuan$_j$-kara zibunzisin$_{i/*j}$/karezisin$_{i/j}$-ni kansuru
    Musasi-nom Takuan-from self-self   him-self -dat about

---

[2]Lust and Mazuka (this volume, chapter 6) adduced an example in which *zibunzisin* is not in an argument position and is long-distance bound. This example may bear a relationship to their discovery that children consistently resist using *zibun* in argument positions. I leave the theoretical implications of such cases to future investigation.

hanasi-o kiita.
story-acc heard
'Musasi heard from Takuan a story about selfself/himself.'

In particular, although *zibun* is still capable of long-distance binding and *zisin* is still local, both can be bound by an object when the matrix verb is *hear* (cf. (3)).

This sensitivity to the choice of verbs falls into the category of logophoricity discussed in Clements (1975), Kuno (1986), Sells (1987), and Koopman and Sportiche (1989). Roughly speaking, an anaphor is a logophor if it chooses as its antecedent an argument representing the source of information. Now *zibun* and *zisin* can be bound by the object of *hear* introduced by *from* because the latter is the source from which information (i.e., the story in (3b) or Koziro's loving someone in (3a)) is issued. In (1), the source of information is the subject of the verb *tell*; hence *zibun* and *zisin* are subject bound.[3] Note that *zibun* cannot be bound by the local object even when the latter is the source of information, as in (3b), in contrast to *zisin* in the same environment. The theoretical implications of this contrast are explored in Y. Li and Takahashi (1993). For now, I assume it and summarize the behaviors of the four reflexives in (5), with + standing for a possible binding relation, – for an impossible binding relation, and *source* for possible binding only if the argument is the source of information:

(5)		local subj	local obj	remote subj	remote obj
	i zibun	+	–	+	source
	ii. zisin	+	source	–	–
	iii. zibunzisin	+	–	–	–
	iv. karezisin	+	+	–	–

How much of this full paradigm of coreference possibilities in (5) is predictable?

Ideally, the properties of a complex reflexive should be derivable from those of its components. I refer to this as the compositional approach to reflexives and show that it is precisely what accounts for (5). Specifically, I propose (6):

(6) The set of possible antecedents of a reflexive is the intersection of the sets of antecedents of its components.

---

[3] *The source of information* is clearly an inadequate notion here, because in (3) the reflexives may also be bound by the subject, which is not the source of information but the recipient. It is possible that at the level of linguistic representation where logophoricity is determined, the subject of a sentence and the source of information share crucial properties. For the purpose of this chapter, however, it is neither possible nor necessary to explore the nature of logophoricity. For a formal definition of this notion, see Sells (1987).

To implement (6), the same syntactic structure is assigned to all the reflexive forms[4] except *zibun*, which I do not analyze further for the reasons discussed earlier:

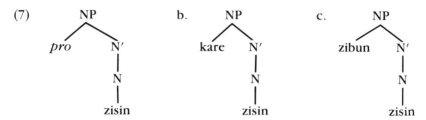

(7) NP · b. NP · c. NP

Furthermore, I make the following assumptions: (a) *zisin* is an anaphor that expects a local antecedent, (b) *pro* in (7a) is an empty logophoric pronoun that picks as its antecedent either the source of information or the subject (cf. footnote 3), and (c) there is a SPEC-head agreement relation between the specifier of NP and the reflexive N°.

First, consider *zisin* in (7a). In any sentence, the set of possible antecedents for the logophoric *pro* includes all the subjects and the source arguments, whereas the set of possible antecedents for *zisin* includes the arguments in the local clause. Clearly, the intersection of the two sets include the local subject and the local object if it happens to be the source of information, as confirmed by row (ii) in (5). This intersection is guaranteed through the SPEC-head agreement between the logophoric *pro* and the nominal head *zisin*—if either one of them is coreferential with an antecedent that the other cannot be coreferential with, the two cannot be in agreement. Next, consider *karezisin* in (7b). Occupying [SPEC, NP], the pronoun *kare* 'him' can refer to any argument outside the NP (cf. *John$_i$ told Bill$_j$ about [$_{NP}$ his$_{i/j}$ car]*). *Zisin* again confines its possible antecedents to the local clause, with the intersection being all the local arguments. This is exactly what row (iv) in (5) shows. Also note that this is a typical property of the *himself*-type reflexives, cross- linguistically. Because *himself* has been taken to represent syntactic anaphors (i.e., in the Binding Theory), Y. Li (1993) questions why a monomorphemic reflexive has logophoric properties when used alone but loses them in a complex reflexive. To my knowledge, the current analysis is the first attempt to answer this question systematically. Finally, in (7c), we know that *zibun* can refer to any subject or source argument except the local object (cf. row (i) of (5)). Because *zisin* can refer only to a local argument, the only possible antecedent shared by *zibun* and *zisin* is the local subject, as indicated in row (iii) in (5).

---

[4] The same NP structure is also used in Katada (1991). Again, I stress that (6) may be implemented in other ways. For instance, the idea can be expressed easily with a DP structure.

I add a few words about *zibun*. Its logophoric behavior strongly suggests, in my theory, that it is either a logophor in itself or part of a reflexive form that also contains an empty logophoric *pro*. The second possibility (minus logophoricity) is discussed for Chinese in Lust, Chien, and Eisele (1991). It is also worth noting that the analysis I proposed here treats *zisin* as a bimorphemic reflexive, which, according to the relativized SUBJECT analysis, must be local. But there is no reason that *zibun* must be monomorphemic, even underlyingly. I do not reject the notion of relativized SUBJECT, but I would like to see substantial independent evidence in its behalf, given that the overt morphological form of a reflexive is not reliable.

Because Tang's work is on Chinese, the validity of my remarks relies on the assumption that the conclusions regarding Japanese obtain in Chinese. Obviously, this assumption itself needs justification, given that the two languages have different inventories of reflexives with somewhat different behaviors. I now consider two obvious differences and show that a uniform analysis is defendable.

First, in contrast to Japanese, which has the two reflexive morphemes *zibun* and *zisin*, Chinese has only one reflexive morpheme *ziji* that both occurs by itself like *zibun* and forms a complex reflexive with a pronoun like *zisin*. Given my discussion of Japanese reflexives, the simplest analysis of *ziji* in Chinese is that it corresponds to both Japanese forms. It should be pointed out that my analysis presupposes that a child is born with the knowledge that only the local reflexive can combine with an overt pronoun to form a complex reflexive. It predicts that a Japanese child does not form a long-distance *karezibun* and a Chinese child does not use *taziji* 'himself' to refer to some remote antecedent. Presumably, a relativized SUBJECT analysis would not require such innate knowledge on the part of the child because the coreferential property of a given reflexive would correlate with its overt morphological form. But, as we have seen, no such simple correlation is possible for *zisin*. In fact, even for the standard Japanese dialect where *zisin* cannot be used alone, so that the correlation could be maintained, one must assume that the child knows how to treat *zibun* and *zisin* differently in order to exclude *karezibun*. Also notice that Japanese is not the only language in which different reflexive morphemes occur in distinct positions. Norwegian, for instance, also distinguishes among *seg* 'self', *ham-selv* 'him-self', and *seg-selv* 'self-self' (Hellan, 1986). Clearly, the *seg-selv* distinction patterns with the *zibun-zisin* distinction in Japanese.

If the Chinese *ziji* corresponds to both *zibun* and *zisin*, we have a second difference between the two languages. Recall that both *zibun* and *zisin* show logophoric properties in a possible coreference with the source object. One would expect that *ziji* used alone would show the same behavior. The fact is, however, that neither local nor long-distance object binding is possible with *ziji*.

(8) a. Youyou$_i$ [cong Taotao$_j$ nar] tingshuo Fanfan$_k$ bu xihuan ziji$_{i/*j/k}$.
       Youyou   from Taotao there   hear   Fanfan not like   self
       'Youyou heard from Taotao that Fanfan doesn't like self.'

   b. Youyou$_i$ [cong Taotao$_j$ nar] tingshuo-le yijian youguan ziji$_{i/*j}$
      Youyou   from Taotao there hear-asp   one about   self
      de chuanwen.
      's rumor
      'Youyou heard from Taotao a rumor about self.'

Apparently, (8) is sufficient to refute the claim that *ziji* is a logophor like *zibun*
and *zisin*, which in turn would indicate that, after all, Japanese reflexives and
their Chinese counterparts are actually not comparable. However, I show later
that (8a–b) are not the counterexamples they appear to be.

First compare the Japanese example (3b), repeated as (9a), with (9b):

(9) a. Musasi$_i$-ga   Takuan$_j$-kara zisin$_{i/j}$-ni kansuru hanasi-o kiita.
       Musasi-nom Takuan-from self -dat about   story-acc heard
       (cf. (2b))
       'Musasi heard from Takuan a story about self.'

   b. Musasi$_i$-ga   Takuan$_j$-no hon-kara   zisin$_{i/*j}$-ni kansuru
      Musasi-nom Takuan-gen book-from self -dat about
      hanasi-o siita.
      story-acc learned
      'Musasi learned from Takuan's book a story about self.'

Although the bare reflexive *zisin* can be bound by Takuan in (9a), it cannot
in (9b). The only difference between the two sentences is that in the latter,
Takuan is further embedded. I conclude, independently of any specific
theory, that a constituent embedded in the complement of *kara* 'from' cannot
be the binder of the bare reflexive. Now consider again the Chinese examples
in (8). Notice that inside each phrase headed by *cong* 'from', there are two
constituents, the nominal complement and a locative word *nar* 'there'. The
sentences immediately become unacceptable (under any reading) if the
locative word is dropped. More generally, most Chinese nouns cannot head
the complement of a locative or temporal preposition without a co-occurring
locative or temporal word (Lü, 1984):[5]

(10) a. cong Taotao nar/nali   vs.   *cong Taotao
        from Taotao there   from Taotao
        'from taotao'

---

[5]The only exceptions are for those nouns that directly denote places or time, such as *Beijing*
and *zuotian* 'yesterday'. But these nouns are not animate and hence cannot serve as the
antecedents of reflexives in Chinese.

b. zai zhuozi shang   vs.   *zai zhuozi
   at desk top   at desk
   'on the desk'
c. zai huiyi zhong   vs.   *zai huiyi
   at meeting middle   at meeting
   'at/during the meeting'

Given this peculiarity of Chinese syntax, it is natural to assume that in a PP like (10a), the complement of the preposition *cong* 'from' is not *Taotao* but the phrase headed by the locative word *nar* 'there', with *Taotao* modifying it (C. Li & Thompson, 1983). In other words, (10a) literally means "from Taotao's place." Returning to (8), we see that although *Taotao* is semantically the source of information, the structural correspondence is with the Japanese (9b) rather than (9a). So whatever prevents coindexation between *Takuan* and *zibun* in (9b) is responsible for the lack of object binding in the Chinese examples in (8). To conclude, we can still treat *ziji* as a logophor even though it demonstrates only subject binding.

REFERENCES

Clements, G. (1975). The logophoric pronoun in Ewe: Its role in discourse. *Journal of West African Languages, 10,* 141–177.
Hellan, L. (1986). On anaphora and predication in Norwegian. In L. Hellan & K. Christensen (Eds.), *Topics in Scandinavian syntax* (pp. 103–123). Dordrecht: Reidel.
Katada, F. (1991). The LF representation of anaphors. *Linguistic Inquiry, 22,* 287–313.
Koopman, H., & Sportiche, D. (1989). Pronouns, logical variables, and logophoricity. *Linguistic Inquiry, 20,* 555–588.
Kuno, S. (1986). Anaphora in Japanese. In S.-Y. Kuroda (Ed.), *Working Papers from the First SDF Workshop in Japanese Syntax* (pp. 11–70). La Jolla: University of California at San Diego.
Li, C., & Thompson, S. (1983). *Mandarin Chinese: A functional reference grammar.* Berkeley: University of California Press.
Li, Y. (1993). What makes long-distance reflexives possible? *Journal of East Asian Linguistics.*
Li, Y., & Takahashi, C. (1993). *Movement and logophoricity.* Unpublished manuscript, Cornell University, Ithaca, NY.
Lü, S. (1984). *Xiandai hanyu babai ci.* Beijing: Commercial Press.
Lust, B., Chien, Y.-C., & Eisele, J. (1991). *Chinese and English children's interpretation of pronouns: A test of the Linear Precedence Hypothesis.* Paper presented at NACCL III, Cornell University, Ithaca, NY.
Progovac, L. (1991). *Relativized subject, long-distance reflexives, and accessibility.* Unpublished manuscript, Indiana University, Bloomington.
Sells, P. (1987). Aspects of logophoricity. *Linguistic Inquiry, 18,* 445–479.

CHAPTER FOUR

Long-Distance Reflexives in UG: Theoretical Approaches and Predictions for Acquisition

Gabriella Hermon
University of Delaware and
National University of Singapore

Over the last few years there have been a number of analyses proposed to account for the locality restrictions on reflexives across languages. For example, as was discussed in Cole, Hermon, and Sung (1990), among others, reflexives in English must have local antecedents, whereas those in Chinese can take long-distance antecedents roughly in the domain of the root clause:[1]

(1) John think [Tom knows [Bill$_i$ likes himself$_i$]].

(2) Zhangsan$_i$ renwei [Lisi$_j$ zhidao [Wangwu$_k$ xihuan ziji$_{i,j,k}$]].
Zhangsan thinks Lisi knows Wangwu like   self
'Zhangsan thinks that Lisi knows that Wangwu likes himself.'

Most analyses of long-distance (LD) reflexives fall in one of the following classes. In one type of analysis the definition of binding domain for reflexives is parametrized. English is claimed to have a more restrictive setting for the parameter of governing category (GC) than Chinese, with perhaps other languages (like Icelandic) having intermediate settings. The parameter setting approach was described in detail by Manzini and Wexler (1987). A second class of analyses, based largely on Pica (1985, 1987), describes LD reflexives as a case of covert cyclic movement at LF. Although there may be disagreement in the literature about the details of LF head movement

---

[1] I do not attempt to review in this chapter the huge body of literature on long-distance binding. For a description of the situation in Chinese see Tang (1989), Huang and Tang (1991), Battistella (1989), and the various papers coauthored by Cole listed in the References.

exhibited by reflexives, these analyses all agree that the relationship between the antecedent and reflexive is local in some sense.

More recently, researchers have proposed a nonmovement variant of the head-movement analysis that extends the antecedent-reflexive binding chain beyond a local domain but without requiring that the reflexive actually move close to the antecedent. (See, for example, Progovac, 1992; Tang, 1992.)[2]

In this chapter, I argue that: (a) all nonparametric approaches to reflexives have common properties and capture basic correspondences in the data better than the parametric approach does, (b) head movement provides a better account of the properties of reflexives than competing nonmovement analyses, (c) parametric and nonparametric approaches make different predictions about the acquisition of reflexives cross-linguistically. More specifically, I argue that even though it seems at first glance that the developmental sequence supports a parameter-setting approach, a nonparametric head-movement approach is also capable of accounting for the L1 acquisition data.

I first describe how the various approaches account for what I consider to be the core facts regarding the distribution of reflexives, cross-linguistically. A number of problems for the head-movement approach are raised and possible solutions are offered. I then address the acquisition issues connected to LD reflexives.

HEAD MOVEMENT (HM), RELATIVIZED SUBJECT (RS), AND PARAMETER SETTING (PS)[3]

The analysis of head movement (HM) for reflexives is based on work by Pica (1985, 1987) and Battistella (1989) and is fully described in Cole, Hermon, and Sung (1990, 1992) and Cole and Sung (in press).[4] The basic insight is that LD reflexives are morphologically simple X^0 heads in all languages. These heads are subject to LF head movement to the I of their own clause and can optionally move (via C) to the I of the next clause up. All X^0 reflexives have to move in order to be interpreted and must end up adjoined to some I.[5] Morphologically

---

[2] Tang's chapter in this volume is a shorter version of the paper presented at the Symposium (cited here as Tang, 1992). All references here are to the full version, because the revised short version reached me after the completion of this manuscript.

[3] The following (nonstandard) abbreviations are used in this paper: BE = blocking effect, GC = governing category, HM = head movement, LD = long distance, PS = parameter setting, RC = relative clause, RS = relativized SUBJECT.

[4] See Huang and Tang (1991) for an approach that treats LD reflexives in Chinese as involving XP adjunction at LF rather than head movement.

[5] The hypothesis that LD reflexives have to move to a functional category in order to be interpreted was proposed in Hestvik (1990). Hestvik provided a detailed HM analysis for LD reflexives and pronouns in Norwegian.

complex XP reflexives (such as *himself*), on the other hand, can not adjoin to an X^0 head and hence are local.

A nonmovement variant of the head-movement account is the relativized SUBJECT (RS) approach, proposed in Progovac (1991, 1992) and adopted by Tang (1992) for Chinese. The RS approach claims that no movement is necessary at LF. Binding Theory is relativized in the sense that for the definition of governing category (GC), X^0 counts as a SUBJECT for X^0 reflexives, whereas only an XP counts as a SUBJECT for XP reflexives. Hence X^0 reflexives extend their GC to the first X^0 (namely AGR) and end up coindexed only with SPEC of AGR, whereas XP reflexives extend their GC up to the first XP SUBJECT (the SPEC of AGR).

It is also stipulated that AGR can end up in a chain with other AGR nodes in two distinct ways. If the language in question has an anaphoric AGR (Chinese), all AGR nodes in the sentence create a chain. Hence the GC for the X^0 reflexive is extended to the root clause. Other languages (in which AGR is overt and hence by definition not anaphoric) may extend their GC if AGR is absent (as in infinitival clauses).[6] Alternatively, according to Tang, in languages with overt AGR, a dependent tense (like subjunctive) also extends the GC of the X^0 reflexive by creating a chain of bound functional heads all the way up to the first independent (finite) tense. This explains why subjunctives in Icelandic and Italian allow LD X^0 reflexives. No such extension of GC is predicted to be possible from a finite clause with independent tense in languages that mark tense overtly. No chain extension is ever possible for XP reflexives, because the GC is defined not by a head but by an XP (SPEC of AGR). The clause is then invariably the GC for XP reflexives in object position, and finiteness and anaphoric AGR do not interact with the issue of domain for XP reflexives.

Finally, the parameter setting (PS) approach views the issue of GC for reflexives as an independent parameter with a number of possible settings. In this model the issue of deriving particular settings from other features of a language does not arise. Nor is there an attempt to correlate the issue of GC with the morphological form of the reflexives or with other properties of LD reflexives. The theoretical problems inherent in the PS approach were described in Hermon (1992) and Cole and Sung (in press). In what follows I describe the core issues connected to LD reflexives and evaluate how each of the three approaches described here handles the data. I show that, although both HM and RS can account for the cross-linguistic data without parameters, HM is preferred to a nonmovement approach because it accounts for a wider range of data.

---

[6] The assumption that infinitivals lack AGR may be problematic, because in many languages infinitivals allow overt AGR. The RS approach will then predict that LD reflexives should not occur inside inflected infinitival clauses.

The Categorial Status of LD Reflexives

HM. It is well known that in languages that allow both a local and an LD reflexive, the LD reflexive is morphologically simpler than the local reflexive. HM accounts for this fact by allowing only X^0 elements to adjoin to heads, as predicted by the typology of movement. XP reflexives could adjoin to VP but cannot move out of their clauses, because only a limited escape hatch is provided for XP-movement in the theory. This accounts for the difference between the possible antecedents for *ziji* (example (2)) and *taziji*:[7]

(3) Zhangsan$_i$ renwei [Lisi$_j$ zhidao [Wangwu$_k$ xihuan taziji$_{k/*i,*j}$]].
    Zhangsan thinks Lisi knows Wangwu likes   self
    'Zhangsan thinks that Lisi knows that Wangwu likes himself.'

The same situation seems to hold in all languages that have an X^0 and an XP reflexive: The X^0 form may be LD, whereas the XP form is always local.[8]

RS. In this approach the choice of SUBJECT (determining the GC) is relativized: For X^0 the SUBJECT is another X^0, whereas for XPs only XP elements act as SUBJECTs. Hence only AGR counts as the SUBJECT for X^0 reflexives. Because AGR can often be chained to a higher AGR, the GC for X^0 is larger than the one for XP, which simply selects the first subject.

Discussion. Let us evaluate which theory gives the right account for the X^0/XP distinction. Clearly, the parametric approach simply lists domains and hence makes no predictions about correlations with the categorial status of the reflexive, thus missing out on an important fact. HM relies on assumptions about different types of movements for X^0 and XP elements. HM also has to assume that the X^0 head of a larger XP (the *ziji* part of

---

[7] I need to explain why the *ziji* part of the complex reflexive *taziji* cannot move via LF head movement. I assume that this is due to the fact that the head cannot strand its SPEC *ta* by moving away. This leaves the question open whether other XP reflexives in which we find a different configuration may allow movement of the X^0 head, stranding the other constituent. For example, Malayalam has an X^0 form *tanne* that is LD, and a complex form *tanne tanne* that is also LD. As described in Jayaseelan (1991), the complex form is created by adjoining an inherent emphatic to the X^0 *tanne*. In our terms, the adjoined emphatic may create a new GC for *tanne* but does not prevent the head from moving.

[8] There are languages in which an XP form seems to be LD. Malay has the form *DIRI* 'self+*pronoun* that allows LD antecedents. However, as shown in Cole and Hermon (in preparation) these forms may be analyzed as a conflation of a pronominal with a local reflexive. Note, that there may also be independent reasons for limiting X^0 anaphors to a local domain. For example, if an X^0 is cliticized to the verb in the syntax (as is the case of Spanish *se*) further LF movement may be impossible. Cliticization is also suggested for local *sig* with certain verbs in Danish (Jakubowicz, this volume, chapter 5).

taziji) cannot be moved out, stranding the determiner *ta*. A similar stipulation is necessary in the RS approach. As noted in Tang (1992), the difference in X' structure between *ziji* and local *taziji* is as indicated below:

(4) a. $[_{NP}[_{N'}[_N \text{ ziji}]]]$
b. $[_{NP} \text{ ta } [_{N'}[_N \text{ ziji}]]]$

It is unclear what would prevent the head *ziji* in (4b) from choosing the X^0 setting for SUBJECT. Actually, as proposed in Progovac (1992), languages must be allowed to choose either the XP or the X^0 in (4a) as the relevant category for binding. Thus, for LD *sig* in Icelandic the X^0 node is the relevant category, whereas for local *sig* the XP node is the relevant category in determining the GC for the reflexive. This accounts for the fact that local *sig* allows object antecedents (as illustrated in (6)). It must be stipulated that if X^0 is not exhaustively dominated by XP, X^0 cannot be relevant to the choice of SUBJECT. Thus, despite the claims in the literature, not everything follows straightforwardly in this approach from a relativization of the notion of SUBJECT.

In summary, whereas HM relies on well-known differences among various types of movement to account for the different GCs of X^0 and XP reflexives, RS needs to introduce complications into Binding Theory by relativizing the notion of SUBJECT, thus making binding chains analogous to movement chains (which, according to Rizzi, 1990, obey relativized minimality). However, as discussed in Chomsky and Lasnik (in press), relativized minimality may be conceptually undesirable because it seems to miss an important generalization by presenting a list of arbitrary cases. Hence, it is questionable whether adopting the notion of relativized binding domain is a desirable move.

Subject Orientation (SO)

Another well-known fact about LD reflexives is that X^0 reflexives are generally bound only by subjects.[9] This is true in some languages for both local and LD X^0 reflexives (as in Chinese):

(5) Zhangsan$_i$ song gei Lisi$_j$ yipian guanyu ziji$_{i/*j}$ de wenzhang.
Zhangsan give to Lisi one   about   self DE article
'Zhangsan gave Lisi an article about himself (Zhangsan).'

---

[9] This generalization is challenged by data in which objects that are prominent in some way (they are, for instance, the source of the speech act) also serve an antecedents for reflexives. Many researchers analyze X^0 reflexives that allow orientation toward the speech act source as logophoric pronouns. See the description of logophoricity in Reinhart and Reuland (1991).

In other languages (like Icelandic), an X^0 may be object-oriented when used locally (from Hyams & Sigurjónsdóttir, 1990):

(6) Ég sendi Haraldi$_i$ föt   á sig$_i$
    'I sent Harald clothes for himself.'

In general, most researchers agree that local XP reflexives are not subject-oriented.[10] Well-noted problems in Chinese involve experiencer NPs that can serve as antecedents for *ziji* (Sung, 1990; Tang, 1989). Other problems have to do with the fact that in Chinese and Korean (but not in other languages) some subject antecedents are inside a larger NP (such as a possessive NP or a sentential subject) and thus technically do not even c-command the reflexive (Tang, 1989):

(7) [Zhangsan$_i$ de jiaoao]$_j$ hai-le   ziji$_{i/\ast j}$.
    Zhangsan 's pride   hurt-ASP self
    'Zhangsan's pride hurt himself.'

HM. HM predicts that after the X^0 reflexive adjoins to I (AGR-S), only an argument that c-commands this position in the tree can serve as an antecedent. Most commonly, the c-commanding NP is the SPEC of AGR-S (the subject). However, as argued in Cole and Wang (1992), if a language has other functional heads that c-command the I head to which the LD reflexive is adjoined, arguments of these should also be able to antecede the LD reflexive. Cole and Wang claimed that Chinese actually provides such examples in the form of NPs in the *bei* and *ba* construction that may serve as an antecedent of *ziji*:

(8) Lisi$_i$ ba wo$_j$ ling hui le   ziji$_{i/j}$ de jia.
    Lisi BA I   lead back ASP self DE home
    'Lisi took me back to his/my home.'

In their analysis, these phrases are part of a functional projection (Aspect P) that crucially is located above the I/AGR projection in which *ziji* appears after HM. Hence, these phrases c-command the LD reflexive. In general, then, HM claims that any argument NP that c-commands the reflexive (which is adjoined to I) can serve as an antecedent.

Another issue is how HM accounts for other antecedents that (at least at S-structure) do not seem to be in a position that c-commands I. As far as experiencers are concerned, it was argued in Hermon (1985) that in many

---

[10]Crucially, in Chinese, local *taziji* may refer to objects as well as subjects. See Cole and Sung (in press).

languages these are LF subjects. It is conceivable than that at LF, experiencers are higher in the tree than the adjunction site for reflexives. Sung (1990) adopted a version of this analysis for Chinese. As far as subjects of possessives and sentential subjects are concerned, Cole et al. (1992) argued that certain non-c-commanding antecedents in Chinese percolate the feature of ante-cedency up to the mother node (just in case the head of the node lacks that feature due to the fact that only animates can antecede reflexives in Chinese). The HM account uses assumptions about feature percolation to account for these cases, which were previously accounted for in Tang (1985) by stipulating a new relation of sub-command in Chinese.

RS. Tang extended the definition of SUBJECT for X^0 (which in the original account only included AGR) to include all functional heads. This allowed her to claim that NPs in SPECs of functional heads other than AGR can be antecedents for the reflexive, as long as these functional heads are bound to one another by sharing certain features. This extension is necessary because, as Tang argued, Chinese needs to include as antecedents NPs that are not in SPEC of AGR-S, such as specifiers of sentential subjects, possessive NPs, and possibly topics in SPEC of CP.

Discussion. I now evaluate which of the theories gives the best account of the limitations on antecedents for reflexives. Both HM and the RS approach correctly allow any c-commanding antecedent to be a potential binder for reflexives. HM, however, predicts that only NPs that c-command AGR-S (the adjunction site for X^0 reflexives) are binders. This may include complements of *ba* and *bei* phrases and experiencers that at LF are moved to a position higher than AGR-S, but it crucially excludes objects inside the VP. In the RS approach, the reflexive does not move. If, following Tang, the domain is extended via a chain to all functional heads, any SPEC of any functional head in the chain that c-commands the reflexive should be a binder. It is entirely unclear how, under the Split-INFL Hypothesis, objects (SPEC of AGR-O) are excluded from being a potential binder of an X^0 reflexive in a PP that follows the object. However, as discussed for Russian in Progovac (1992), objects are not possible antecedents:

(9) Milicioner$_i$ rasprašival arestovannogo$_j$ o sebe$_{i/*j}$.
     policeman questioned suspect   about self

Of course, one could explicitly exclude objects from the list of binders, but then subject-orientation (SO) would not follow from the theory of RS without stipulation.

Finally, PS does not predict any correlations among distinct parameters, such as GC and SO. Hence, PS wrongly predicts that local reflexives could be subject-oriented and that LD reflexives could have object antecedents.[11] Both HM and RS predict that all c-commanding arguments can be antecedents for LD reflexives, but RS has trouble excluding SPECs of AGR-O (objects) from this list.

Blocking Effects (BE)

Another well-known fact is that LD reflexives exhibit the BE in some languages but not in others. Blocking refers to the requirement that all the potential antecedents of an LD reflexives agree in person. For example, a first person intervening antecedent blocks a higher third person subject from being an antecedent for *ziji* in Chinese, even though the closest antecedent is also third person. Cole et al. (1992) claimed that although Chinese exhibits the BE, Icelandic and Italian do not:

(10) Zhangsan$_i$ renwei wo$_j$ zhidao Wangwu$_k$ xihuan ziji-$_{i/*j/k}$.
     Zhangsan think   I   know   Wangwu like   self

(11) Gianni$_i$ suppone che tu$_j$ sia inamorato della propria$_{i/j}$ moglie.
     Gianni supposes that you are in love   with self's   wife.

Theories of reflexives should ideally derive the BE from general principles of UG and should also account for the difference among languages without the need for parameters.

HM.   HM, in conjunction with the Feature Percolation Principle (FPP), will account for the BE. As claimed in Cole et al. (1992) the FPP (which is independently needed in UG) states that in cases of feature conflict between features of a head and features of other daughters, only features of heads are percolated up to the mother node. However, if the head lacks certain features, features may percolate up from nonheads (such as adjoined positions). This predicts that in languages with overt verb agreement, the adjoined reflexive will never pass up its features to the mother node, because AGR (the head to which X^0 adjoins) has ϕ-features of its own. Assuming a process of SPEC-head agreement checking at LF, we predict that in these languages, reflexives are never blockers, because their feature composition is never relevant at the time of feature checking. In Chinese, however, AGR has no ϕ-features. As a result, features of the adjoined reflexives end up on the mother node and play a role in feature checking, blocking the derivation if there is no agreement between the reflexive and the features of the binder.

---

[11]Manzini and Wexler (1987) suggested that one could link various parameters and require that if the setting on parameter X is marked (such as the setting *root clause* for Chinese) then the setting on parameter Y must be unmarked (+SO, in their terms). However, linking parameters this way is a violation of Wexler and Manzini's independence principle, an undesirable result, as discussed in Fodor (1990). See also the discussion in Hermon (1992).

Thus HM makes two strong predictions. The first prediction is that the set of antecedents is larger than the set of blockers. Because only SPEC of AGR-S is involved in agreement, only SPECs of AGR-S are potential blockers.[12] This prediction is borne out. As shown in Cole and Wang (1992), even though *ba* and *bei* phrases in Chinese can act as antecedents, they are never blockers (because these phrases are not in SPEC of AGR-S and hence do not participate in agreement):

(12) Wo$_i$ hui ba ni$_j$ ling hui le   ziji$_{i/j}$ de jia.
     I   will BA you lead back ASP self DE home
     'I would take you back to my/your home.'

The second prediction concerns the connection between verb agreement and the BE. Only languages in which there is no overt verb agreement (i.e., AGR-S has no ϕ-features) are predicted to have the BE. Languages with overt agreement will never exhibit the BE. This prediction is also correct. Italian and Icelandic have no BE, whereas Chinese has the BE. Languages like Malayalam and Kannada also illustrate the direct connection between AGR and BE. These languages are very similar and do not differ as far as domain restrictions on LD reflexives are concerned (i.e., they allow LD reflexives in tensed clauses as well as infinitival clauses). They crucially differ in that Malayalam has no overt AGR, having lost its verb agreement. Malayalam exhibits the BE, as described in Jayaseelan (1991):

(13) *Raaman$_i$ paRayunnu [nii/ñaan tan$_i$-te bhaarya-ye nulli   ennə].
     Raman   says   you/I   self-gen wife-acc pinched COMP
     'Raman says that you/I piched self's wife.'

Kannada, on the other hand has overt agreement and does not have the BE, as shown in Amritavalli (1991):

(14) [Ali tannanna$_i$ hoDeyuttaane anta] naanu yendukoNDe anta
     Ali self-acc   will hit   COMP   I   thought   COMP
     raama$_i$ heeLida.
     Rama said
     'Rama said that I thought that Ali would hit self.'

This minimal pair reconfirms the prediction that the BE in LD reflexives is linked to verb agreement. The FPP in conjunction with HM makes this prediction without having to stipulate a blocking parameter.

---

[12]However, subjects of a sentential subject and possessive NPs that percolate up their antecedency features (as discussed in Cole et al., 1992) may also percolate up ϕ-features that will then play a role in feature checking at LF. These NPs are therefore predicted to be blockers, even though they are not in a direct SPEC-head relation with the AGR of the clause.

RS. The RS approach predicts the BE will be present only if the GC was extended via an anaphoric AGR chain, that is, only in a language that has no tense distinctions (like Chinese) and no overt AGR. Because anaphoric AGR chains are created by coindexing all the AGR nodes in the chain, all AGR nodes have to agree in features. If, however, the language chooses to extend the GC via tense-dependency (as in Italian, Russian, or Icelandic) no identity of AGR is forced and hence no BE is expected. Crucially, Tang claimed that the BE is not connected to SPEC-head agreement per se and is not limited to SPECs of AGR-S in general. In this version of RS, once a chain is created via anaphoric AGR, all functional heads participate in that chain. Presumably then, all arguments of functional heads as well as SPECs of functional heads are potential antecedents and potential blockers.

Discussion. HM and RS differ in their account of blocking. Both theories roughly predict the same typological facts: Blocking will play a role only in languages without overt agreement. However, although RS claims that the set of potential binders and blockers is identical, HM predicts that binders that do not participate in SPEC-head agreement checking at LF will not be blockers. This was illustrated for Chinese in (12). HM can account for this fact, whereas the RS approach cannot.[13]

A potential problem for the HM approach involves the examples cited in Tang (1992). In (15) (Tang's (31b)), an NP is behaving as a blocker; yet it is unclear whether this NP is in SPEC of AGR:

(15) Wo$_i$ zhao-bu-dao   ni$_j$-de   na-san-pian [youguan ziji-$_{i/j}$]-de
      I   find-not-arrive you-MOD   that-three-CL about self-MOD
      wenzhang.
      article
      'I cannot find those three articles of yours about yourself.'

Blockers in these examples are expressions with *de*, which, Tang argued, appear in adjoined positions (and hence could not be involved in feature checking of SPEC-head agreement at LF). Clearly, HM will have to claim that these NPs are in fact in SPEC of AGR, assuming that NPs (or rather DPs) also have an AGR position, as evidenced in languages with overt agreement inside DP. Thus in (15), I assume a structure in which *ni-de* 'your-poss' is in SPEC of an AGR phrase internal to the DP. Hence it acts as a blocker for *ziji*. Tang's argument was based on her proposal that expressions with *de* appear in adjunct positions and not in SPEC positions.

---

[13]Progovac's original account limits antecedents to SPEC of AGR-S. Although this correctly accounts for the BE, it does not account for the set of possible antecedents, which needs to be extended to include all c-commanding NPs. Because all versions of RS equate the set of antecedents with the set of blockers, the correct prediction cannot be made.

It is unclear, however, how an NP in an A'-position can ever be a potential antecedent (even in an approach that chains together all functional heads). Thus, for many speakers, NPs in a nongap topic (A') position cannot be antecedents for *ziji*:

(16) Lisi$_i$ (a),   ta baba$_j$ bu xihuan ziji$_{i/j}$.
Lisi (top), his father not like self

I assume that these speakers do not allow antecedents in nonargument positions. Yet the same speakers accept the NPs with *de* in (15) (which Tang claimed are in adjoined positions) as antecedents and blockers. It is doubtful, then, whether *de* phrases really are adjuncts.

Finally, the PS approach has to consider the BE as a separate parameter that cannot be linked to other parametric options found in the language. PS cannot predict the correlation between the type of AGR and BE, nor can it predict which potential antecedents will be blockers.

Finite and Nonfinite Domains for LD Reflexives

Languages seem to vary as to whether they restrict LD reflexives to certain domains. Icelandic and Italian restrict LD binding to nonindicative clauses (subjunctives and infinitivals), whereas Chinese has no such restriction. Crucially, however, Kannada and Malayalam both allow X^0 reflexives in tensed as well as infinitival clause, even though clause type (unlike in Chinese) is overtly distinguished in these languages. (See (13)–(14), and the descriptions in Jayaseelan, 1991, for Malayalam and in Amritavalli, 1991, for Kannada.)

HM.   Because X^0 reflexives move at LF, HM predicts that such movement should not occur over an intervening barrier. Many researchers assume that HM at LF will never occur out of a tensed domain. Under this assumption, Chinese must be a language that does not distinguish tense (it has only ASPECT). This predicts that in languages that have a tensed/nontensed distinction in complement clauses, only HM out of nontensed clauses is permissible (subjunctives counting as tenseless).[14] This prediction is falsified by Kannada and Malayalam.

We are therefore forced by the data to deny that there is a universal restriction against LF head movement from a tensed domain. The HM approach can represent the cross-linguistic variation by assuming that some

---

[14]See, for example, Sigurjónsdóttir and Hyams (1991). They assumed that the restriction against LF movement from a tensed domain follows from the semantic principle restricting the piping of tense, as proposed in Reinhart and Reuland (1991). This was also proposed in Hermon (1992).

C heads are barriers, whereas others are not. For example, a subjunctive or an infinitival C will typically not be a barrier. As far as tensed C is concerned, languages can differ and perhaps randomly decide that a certain type of C is not a barrier for HM. This is the approach developed in Sung (1990), based on Pica (1987). In any case, HM will have to allow specification of which C elements count as opaque, and hence the question of domain does not directly follow from HM in any principled way.

RS. Both Progovac and Tang claimed that one of the strong points of the RS approach is the prediction that languages with weak AGR extend the binding domain via AGR-chaining, whereas languages with overt agreement will extend the domain only up to the first independent tense. Thus, they claimed that their approach makes much stronger predictions than the HM approach. Tang assumed two different ways of extending the binding domain for reflexives: In languages with strong AGR, extensions are permitted only when AGR is absent (infinitivals) or when certain bound functional heads are present (as in subjunctives).

Discussion. There are a number of empirical arguments against the strong view (inherent in the RS approach) on restricting domains for LD reflexives. First of all, RS does not allow for languages like Kannada, in which AGR is overt (and, hence, the only way to extend the binding domain should be by tense-chaining). Yet Kannada has LD reflexives in both tensed and infinitival domains. In the HM approach, both Kannada and Malayalam have indicative C heads that are not opaque (allowing HM), whereas in Icelandic and Italian, indicative Cs are opaque. HM then views the issue of domain as reflecting random variation among properties of C heads.[15]

Furthermore, there is some indication that the domain issue is best described as connected to the opacity of a C head rather than to notions like infinitival or subjunctive. As discussed in Progovac (1991), when the modal *by* in Russian cliticizes to the C *cto-*, *ctoby* makes both infinitival and subjunctive clauses opaque. Hence the domain for the LD reflexive *sebja* does not extend out of these clauses.

---

[15]Reinhart and Reuland (1991) argued that the LD reflexive in subjunctive domains is actually a logophoric pronoun (not subject to binding). Hellan (1991) and Thráinsson (1991) convincingly argued for the connection between logophoricity and subjunctive mood. Siggurðsson (1986) actually described a more permissive dialect of Icelandic, in which speakers allow *sig* in a finite clause embedded under certain semifactive verbs that impose a speaker perspective that permits the logophor *sig* even in indicatives. If we exclude subjunctives from the discussion of structural LD reflexives, arbitrariness of domains is reduced to the question whether a given language limits LD reflexives to infinitivals (like Icelandic) or allows LD reflexives in tensed clauses (Kannada).

I next turn to PS. PS claims that each reflexive randomly chooses a binding domain, as described in Wexler and Manzini (1987). Because parameters by nature best describe random variation, PS makes correct predictions regarding the domain issue. HM also treats the restrictions on clause type as subject to random variation, but the variation is due to the varying lexical properties of C heads that determine whether C is opaque in a given language. The locus of arbitrariness is then in the lexicon rather than in the principles determining the binding domain.

Islands and X^0 Reflexives

The general claim in the literature regarding European languages is that LD reflexives are allowed in adverbial clauses and relative clause (RCs), but typically only if the IP to which the adverbial clause is adjoined is preceded by a verb of saying with a perspective-taking subject that acts as an antecedent for the LD reflexive. The situation is the same in Chinese. Speakers accept *ziji* inside adverbial clauses, but only if the antecedent is one clause removed:[16]

(17) [Ruguo Lisi$_i$ haile ziji$_{i/*j}$], Zhangsan$_j$ jiu qu jian lao.
      'If Lisi hurts self, Zhangsan will go to jail.'

(18) Zhangsan$_i$ shuo [[ruguo Lisi$_j$ haile ziji$_{i/j}$], ta bu jiu qu].
      'Zhangsan said that if Lisi hurts self, then he will not go.'

If the reflexive is inside an RC, however, no such constraint applies. The antecedent of *ziji* can be either the head of the RC or a c-commanding NP in the next clause.

(19) Zhangsan$_i$ bu xihuan nei-ge piping ziji$_{i/j}$-de ren$_j$.
      Zhangsan not like that-one-CL criticize-MOD man
      'Zhangsan$_i$ does not like the man$_j$ who criticized self$_{i/j}$.'

I assume that the ban against reflexives in adverbial clauses in (17) is due to the fact that the subject of the clause to which the adverbial clause is adjoined does not c-command the reflexive, as shown in (20a). Hence, a higher subject is needed. Heads of RCs, however, c-command *ziji*, and hence no requirement for a higher subject is imposed, as in (20b):[17]

---

[16]Judgements on these and other similar sentences were collected from 10 native speakers of Mandarin.

[17]Researchers differ in how they interpret the facts about adverbial and relative clauses in European languages. Hellan (1991) and Thráinsson (1991) claimed that *sig* in Icelandic is a logophor that needs a perspective-holder as an antecedent. Hence, the requirement for a subject of a higher verb of saying. Crucially, they claimed that this applies in both RCs and adverbial

(20) a.

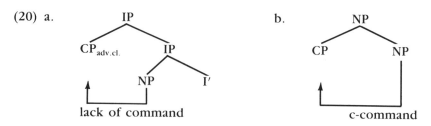

lack of command   c-command

HM. The fact that LD reflexives are allowed inside adjuncts and relative clauses poses a serious problem for the HM account. As discussed in Huang and Tang (1991) and Cole and Sung (in press), HM should obey the ECP and not allow extraction out of non-L-marked domains. In general, Chinese can be shown to obey the ECP as far as adjuncts are concerned, because no antecedent-government is possible into an adjunct or RC. A possible solution was presented by Cole and Sung (1991). They proposed that the adjunction of reflexives to the functional category C (which governs the adjunct CP adverbial clause) turns the C governor into a lexical governor. As a result, the C head L-marks the adjunct CP containing the offending trace of *ziji*.[18] In a similar fashion, RCs that are complements of a higher functional category of Classifier (as in Tang, 1990) are also de-barrierized by head movement of the reflexive to the Classifier head. It remains to be seen whether this is a viable solution.

Another option is to follow the suggestions made in Hellan (1991) and view the reflexive inside adverbial and relative clauses as a logophor. This would explain why speakers in many languages allow reflexives in RCs and adverbial clauses only if there is a higher perspective-taking entity (the subject of a verb of saying). Under this approach, reflexives in these environments are not subject to normal binding conditions (like c-command), and the ungrammaticality of reflexives inside these clauses is due to lack of context for logophors rather than lack of c-command. Indeed, Giorgi (1984) mentioned that in Italian, LD reflexives are sometimes acceptable in adverbial clauses without a higher perspective-taking subject, depending on the degree of involvement of the subject in the event described by the adverbial clause. A similar situation may exist in Chinese. Chinese, however, does not have overt clause-type marking, making it harder to distinguish between LD anaphors and logophors.[19]

---

clauses. Note, however, that independent RCs with LD reflexives are found in Latin (Benedicto, 1991) and Chinese. Hence, I claim that it is lack of c-command that bans the LD reflexive inside the adverbial clauses in these examples.

[18]The fact that adjunction of *ziji* to C turns C into a lexical head governor does not affect XP-movement. Because XPs cannot adjoin to C, the adjunct and the RCs are still barriers for XP-movement. The fact that head movement can de-barrierize the projection out of which the head is moved was first suggested for V-to-I movement in Chomsky (1986).

[19]The idea that Chinese may have logophoric *ziji* in adverbial clauses was suggested to me by E. Reuland (personal communication, April 1992).

RS. This account predicts that all chains into adjunct clauses and RCs are well formed, because these are binding (rather than movement) chains that are not sensitive to barriers. However, because the adjoined clause is not c-commanded by the clause it is adjoined to, a higher clause is needed to allow LD binding inside adjuncts. No such restriction is needed for LD reflexives inside RCs. It seems, however, that, as discussed in footnote 16, there is some disagreement in the literature about RCs. Hellan (1991) and Thráinsson (1991) claimed RCs need a higher clause to provide a perspective-taking antecedent for *sig* inside the RC. This fact remains unexplained in any account that views reflexives inside adverbial and RC clauses as LD anaphors rather than logophors.

Discussion. PS makes no particular predictions about adverbial and RC clauses. If the language has clauses that extend the binding domain (such as subjunctives), an LD reflexive should be acceptable. This is the view adopted by the RS approach as well. HM seems initially to make the wrong predictions. Two solutions were discussed: Either HM itself de-barrierizes the CP out of which the head moves, or (as suggested by some researchers) adverbial clauses and RCs allow LD interpretations of reflexives because these reflexives are logophoric. In any case, HM with some complications can account for the data. The occurrence of LD reflexives in islands does not, therefore, distinguish among the three analyses under consideration, because all three, given certain assumptions, make correct predictions.

Summary

Clearly, both HM and RS are far superior to the PS model, in that they try to derive all characteristics of reflexives from the interaction of general principles. The PS model does not attempt to correlate any of the core characteristics of reflexives, nor can it relate the existence of LD reflexives to any other features of the language (such as the categorial status of the reflexive).

I have argued that although HM and RS are very similar in predicting roughly the same range of data, HM is to be preferred as an account for reflexives across languages for a number of reasons. First of all, HM provides better empirical coverage for the data as far as SO, the BE, and the restrictions on domains are concerned. HM predicts that the set of blockers is a subset of the set of antecedents. As shown in Cole and Wang (1992), because blocking is a result of SPEC-head agreement checking at LF, only NPs in SPEC of AGR-S act as blockers. The competing nonmovement approach incorrectly predicts that the set of blockers is identical to the set of antecedents. Moreover, HM makes the right prediction in correlating blocking only with the type of AGR, viewing the issue of tense restrictions on LD reflexives as a separate issue. I argued that RS makes wrong predictions in that it limits LD reflexives to infinitival and subjunctive clauses in languages that have overt tense distinctions. Given the chain typology of RS, because Kannada has overt agreement, it should exhibit tense restrictions. However, neither Kannada nor Malayalam have any tense restrictions on LD reflexives.

Finally, on a conceptual level, as mentioned earlier, relativizing binding theory (and creating new typologies of binding chains) may not be a desirable move. In the HM approach, however, conditions quite independent of relativized minimality require that only heads move to head positions and only XPs move to specifier positions. I next consider how each of these approaches explains the development of LD reflexives in child language.

X^0 REFLEXIVES IN L1 ACQUISITION

Additional support for a particular theory can be sought in the developmental data. I do not review the acquisition studies of reflexives in this chapter.[20] It would be useful, however, to summarize some of the studies that examine the acquisition of X^0 reflexives. In general, the experimental studies try to determine at what age children exhibit a knowledge of LD reflexives. The studies seem to converge on one particular observation: LD reflexives come in at a variable age, around age 9 for Danish (Jakubowicz, this volume, chapter 5), around age 8 for Chinese (Chien & Wexler, 1987), around age 6;6 or later for Korean (Lee & Wexler, 1987), and around age 4;6–5;6 for Icelandic (Sigurjónsdóttir & Hyams, 1991). How can the various theories discussed here account for these facts? At first glance it seems that the bias toward early locality provides conclusive evidence that PS is on the right track, because this theory predicts that the local use (a subset of the LD use) should occur first.

PS indeed predicts that, given the Subset Principle, the child should go through a stage in which the setting for GC is local (the unmarked setting). Given positive evidence, the child will move to the larger setting. However, if early locality indeed indicates a first unmarked local setting, it is unclear why children, while exposed to years of positive input indicating the need for a wider setting, should maintain the subset setting until age 9 in some languages. Hence, PS (relying on the Subset Principle) cannot really account for the acquisition sequence without added complications.

I argue that nonparametric approaches can also account for this complicated developmental picture. For example, because HM views LD reflexives as reflecting the interaction of various principles with the X' status of the LD reflexive, we do not expect a fixed age at which LD reflexives

---

[20]For a review of the relevant acquisition literature see Hyams and Sigurjónsdóttir (1990) and Hermon (1992).

should appear in all languages. As pointed out in Sigurjónsdóttir and Hyams, the age at which children exhibit adultlike performance for LD reflexives in Icelandic depends on the interaction of various modules (syntax, pragmatics, and the lexicon). Hence, the age at which LD reflexives are instantiated may depend on the stage at which these modules operate on-line. Thus in Icelandic, with *raka* verbs (which for adults impose an LD preference), children get the LD reading in subjunctives at the age at which they begin to distinguish subjunctives from indicatives (around age 5;0). Sigurjónsdóttir and Hyams (1991) argued that this supports a model that treats *sig* in subjunctives as a logophor rather than an LD anaphor. With infinitivals, LD *sig* is delayed until around age 5;6. Sigurjónsdóttir and Hyams believed that this is due to the fact that the antecedent requirement for *sig* can optionally be satisfied locally, an option that is derivationally and computationally simpler than having to find an antecedent outside the local domain. In short, the choice of LD or local antecedent depends on knowing the verb type, the tense/mood options of the clauses containing the reflexive, and the feature composition of the reflexive.[21] Early locality is also a result of the child's preference for shorter derivations, all other things being equal. A similar view on this issue is taken in Jakubowicz (this volume, chapter 5), where it is argued that LD *sig* in Danish is delayed because this is an example of movement as a last resort.[22]

Next, consider another area in which PS makes very different predictions from both HM and RS. HM and RS attempt to derive all properties of reflexives from the interactions of principles of UG. This predicts that all core properties of reflexives should enter the grammar at roughly the same point. Crucially, the three theories reviewed here make slightly different predictions.

HM predicts that if children have LF HM, they could not possibly have an LD reflexive that is not subject-oriented, because SO follows from the c-command possibilities after movement of the reflexive to the I head. The BE, however, which in HM depends on the interaction of SPEC-head agreement at LF with feature percolation and the type of AGR, may or may not be acquired at the same time. The same is true of the domain issue. Children may extend the domain for LD reflexives if they have not yet learned the lexical properties of C heads that determine whether certain domains are opaque for HM. For example, Hyams and Sigurjónsdóttir (1990) claimed that at an early stage, before children learn what tense is in Icelandic, *sig* is possible not only in subjunctives and infinitivals but also in finite clauses. In the HM approach, this

---

[21]In many languages (like Icelandic and Malayalam), reflexives are both anaphoric and pronominal, forcing the LD reflexive to be obligatorily LD for adults. Early locality then may appear because the child allows Principle B violations for pronouns in these languages.

[22]A similar approach to the question of early locality was proposed in Hermon (1992). I argued that in the HM approach, early locality occurs before the principles and lexical specifications that result in LD reflexives become available to the child.

can be due to the fact that early on, children do not realize that certain domains are restricted for HM, because they do not distinguish between finite and infinitival C heads.

RS makes roughly the same predictions. For example, LD reflexives depend in Chinese on the realization that the language has anaphoric AGR and does not distinguish tense. SO should go hand in hand with LD reflexives because it is a result of extending the binding domain to all functional heads via chaining. Crucially, as distinct from HM, RS also predicts that the BE should automatically follow in languages like Chinese because the BE is a consequence of domain extension via an anaphoric AGR chain. Hence the BE should always be present if an LD interpretation is allowed in languages that have anaphoric AGR.

PS, on the other hand, does not predict any correlations among unrelated parameters. Hence SO and blocking may enter the language at different points, as positive evidence for setting these parameters becomes available. The two nonparametric approaches then predict certain correlations of properties connected to LD reflexives in child language, whereas PS makes no such prediction. The crucial question then is not the age at which LD reflexives become fully productive but whether subject orientation and blocking appear at the same time as the LD orientation.

In summary, it is crucial to obtain data from acquisition to determine when in development the various effects connected to LD reflexives become relevant. This may help us decide which theory of LD reflexives best represents the child's competence. Given sufficiently precise theories of grammar that make clear predictions for acquisition, language development can shed a light on crucial theoretical issues.[23]

CONCLUSIONS

HM and RS are similar in that they do not rely on parameters but attempt to derive the core properties of LD reflexives from the interaction of UG principles. I argued that the HM approach provides a superior account for SO, the BE, and the question of domain restrictions across languages. As far as the acquisition of LD reflexives is concerned, both HM and RS can account for the developmental sequence in particular languages by considering the lexical properties of various reflexive forms and their interaction with the UG principles governing the distribution of reflexives.

---

[23] The predictions made by HM and PS were investigated in L2 acquisition by Christie (1992). Christie concluded that neither model is supported by the L2 data. Crucially, she did not find that L2 learners exhibited the correlations predicted by HM for SO and BE. However, learners were also not engaged in parameter resetting. Christie viewed this as indicating the lack of access to UG in L2 acquisition.

The fact that young children prefer local rather than LD reflexives was seen as a possible consequence of a processing constraint that predisposes children to opt for the shortest derivation (or the minimal chain) when interpreting or producing reflexives, in line with the Economy of Derivation and Representation principle of Chomsky (1989).[24]

ACKNOWLEDGMENTS

This chapter is one of a number of works reporting on research on long-distance reflexives and related topics carried out by P. Cole, L.-M. Sung, C. Wang, and the author. This version incorporates many of the comments and criticisms provided by the participants and audience at the Cornell Symposium on Syntactic Theory and First Language Acquisition, April 1992. I would like to thank Peter Cole, K. P. Mohanan, and Anjum Saleemi for many valuable comments on ideas incorporated in this paper. The research reported here was supported in part by the National Science Foundation, grant number BNS-9121167.

REFERENCES

Amritavalli, R. (1991). *Lexical anaphora in Kannada*. Unpublished manuscript, Central Institute of English and Foreign Languages, Hyderabad, India.
Battistella, E. (1989). Chinese reflexivization: a movement to Infl approach. *Linguistics, 27*, 987–1012.
Benedicto, E. (1991). Latin long-distance anaphora. In J. Koster & E. Reuland (Eds.), *Long distance anaphora* (pp. 171–184). Cambridge: Cambridge University Press.
Chien, Y.-C., & Wexler, K. (1987). *A comparison between Chinese-speaking and English speaking children's acquisition of reflexives and pronouns*. Paper presented at the 12th Annual Boston University Conference on Language Development, Boston, MA.
Chomsky, N. (1986). *Barriers*. Cambridge, MA: MIT Press.
Chomsky, N. (1989). Some notes on the economy of derivations. *MIT Working Papers, 10*.
Chomsky, N., & Lasnik, H. (in press). Principles and parameters theory. In J. Jacobs, A. von Stechow, W. Sternefeld, & T. Vennemann (Eds.), *Syntax: An international handbook of contemporary research*. Berlin: Walter de Gruyter.
Christie, K. (1992). *Universal Grammar in the second language: An experimental study of the cross-linguistic properties of reflexives in English, Chinese and Spanish*. Unpublished doctoral dissertation, University of Delaware, Newark.
Cole, P., & Hermon, G. (in preparation). *Reflexives and pronouns in Malay*. Unpublished manuscript, National University of Singapore and the University of Delaware, Newark.
Cole, P., Hermon, G., & Sung, L.-M. (1990). Principles and parameters of long-distance reflexives. *Linguistic Inquiry, 21*, 1–22.

---

[24]The relevance of the principle of economy in derivations in child language has been recently proposed by Saleemi (1993).

Cole, P., Hermon, G., & Sung, L.-M. (1992). Feature percolation. *Journal of East Asian Linguistics*, *1*, 1–28.

Cole, P., & Sung, L.-M. (1991). *Long distance reflexives and islandhood in Chinese*. Unpublished manuscript, University of Delaware, Newark.

Cole, P., & Sung, L.-M. (in press). Head movement and long distance reflexives. *Linguistic Inquiry*.

Cole, P., & Wang, C. (1992, December). *Binding and phrase structure in Chinese*. Paper presented at the Linguistic Society of Hong Kong Annual Research Forum, Chinese University of Hong Kong.

Fodor, J. (1990). Parameters and parameter-setting in a phrase-structure grammar. In L. Frazier & J. de Villiers (Eds.), *Language processing and language acquisition* (pp. 225–255). Dordrecht: Kluwer.

Giorgi, A. (1984). Toward a theory of long distance anaphora: A GB approach. *The Linguistic Review*, *3*, 307–359.

Hellan, L. (1991). Containment and connectedness anaphors. In J. Koster & E. Reuland (Eds.), *Long distance anaphora* (pp. 27–48). Cambridge: Cambridge University Press.

Hermon, G. (1985). *Syntactic modularity*. Dordrecht: Foris.

Hermon, G. (1992). Binding theory and parameter setting. *The Linguistic Review*, *9*, 145–181.

Hestvik, A. (1990). *LF-movement of pronouns and the computation of binding domains*. Unpublished doctoral dissertation, Brandeis University, Waltham, MA.

Huang, C.-T. J., & Tang, C.-C. J. (1991). On the local nature of the long-distance reflexive in Chinese. In J. Koster & E. Reuland (Eds.), *Long distance anaphora* (pp. 263–282). Cambridge: Cambridge University Press.

Hyams, N., & Sigurjónsdóttir, S. (1990). The development of "long-distance anaphora": A cross-linguistic comparison. *Language Acquisition*, *1*, 57–93.

Jayaseelan, K. A. (1991). *Anaphors as pronouns*. Unpublished manuscript, Central Institute of English and Foreign Languages, Hyderabad, India.

Lee, H., & Wexler, K. (1987). *The acquisition of reflexive and pronoun in Korean*. Paper presented at the 12th Annual Boston University Conference on Language Development, Boston, MA.

Manzini, R. M., & Wexler, K. (1987). Parameters, binding theory and learnability. *Linguistic Inquiry*, *18*, 413–444.

Pica, P. (1985). Subject, tense and truth: Towards a modular approach to binding. In J. Gueron, H. G. Obenauer, & J.-Y. Pollock (Eds.), *Grammatical Representation* (pp. 259–291). Dordrecht: Foris.

Pica, P. (1987). On the nature of the reflexivization cycle. In *Proceedings of the North Eastern Linguistics Society*, *17*, 483–499.

Progovac, L. (1991). *Subjunctive: Transparency of functional categories*. Unpublished manuscript, Wayne State University, Detroit, MI.

Progovac, L. (1992). Relativized SUBJECT: Long-distance reflexives without movement. *Linguistic Inquiry*, *23*, 671–680.

Reinhart, T., & Reuland, E. (1991). *Reflexivity*. Unpublished manuscript, University of Tel Aviv and University of Groningen.

Rizzi, L. (1990). *Relativized Minimality*. Cambridge, MA: MIT Press.

Saleemi, A. (1993). *Small children's short derivations*. Unpublished manuscript, National University of Singapore.

Sigurjónsdóttir, S., & Hyams, N. (1991). *Reflexivization and logophoricity: Evidence from the acquisition of Icelandic*. Unpublished manuscript, University of California at Los Angeles.

Sigurðsson, H. (1986). Moods and (long distance) reflexives in Icelandic. *Working Papers in Scandinavian Syntax*, *25*.

Sung, L. M. (1990). *Universals of reflexives*. Unpublished doctoral dissertation, University of Illinois, Urbana.

Tang, C.-C. J. (1985). *A study of reflexives in Chinese.* Unpublished masters thesis, National Taiwan Normal University.

Tang, C.-C. J. (1989). Chinese reflexives. *Natural Language and Linguistic Theory, 7,* 93–122.

Tang, C.-C. J. (1990). *Chinese phrase structure and the extended X-theory.* Unpublished doctoral dissertation, Cornell University, Ithaca, NY.

Tang, C.-C. J. (1992, April). *On movement/nonmovement analyses of reflexives in Chinese.* Paper presented at the Cognitive Studies Symposium, Cornell University, Ithaca, NY.

Thráinsson, H. (1991). Long-distance reflexives and the typology of NPs. In J. Koster & E. Reuland (Eds.), *Long distance anaphora* (pp. 49–75). Cambridge: Cambridge University Press.

Wexler, K., & Manzini, R. M. (1987). Parameters and learnability in binding theory. In T. Roeper & E. Williams (Eds.), *Parameter Setting* (pp. 41–76). Dordrecht: Reidel.

PART TWO

LEXICAL ANAPHORS
AND PRONOUNS

CHAPTER FIVE

Reflexives in French and Danish: Morphology, Syntax, and Acquisition

Celia Jakubowicz
Université René Descartes, Paris

It is well known that certain properties of reflexives, such as binding domain and choice of antecedent, vary both between and within languages (Burzio, 1989, 1991; Everaert, 1991; Katada, 1991; Koster, 1987; Reinhart & Reuland, 1991; Yang, 1983, among others). In this chapter I argue that these differences result from the interaction between the feature composition of the reflexive morphemes, their status with regard to X′ theory, and general principles of Universal Grammar as formulated in Chomsky (1981, 1986, 1989, 1992). Such an account predicts that the acquisition of the core properties of reflexives should be almost instantaneous: Under the hypothesis that the child is constrained by Universal Grammar, acquisition will happen as soon as the child fixes the morphological properties of these expressions, on the basis of linguistic data. These claims are substantiated by contrasting syntactic and acquisition facts from French and Danish, a Romance and a Mainland Scandinavian language, respectively. The analysis of these facts supports the definition of *governing category* as formulated by Chomsky (1986): "A governing category of α is a maximal projection containing both a subject and a lexical category governing α (hence, containing α). A governing category is a 'complete functional complex' (CFC) in the sense that all grammatical functions compatible with its head are realized in it" (p. 169). The behavior of the reflexives is shown to comply with Principle A of the Binding Theory, as proposed by Chomsky (1981): An anaphor is bound in its governing category. Arguments are presented in favor of the hypothesis that the core case of binding is local binding and that long-distance binding results from a last-resort operation, triggered by morphological necessity.

115

FEATURE COMPOSITION OF *SE, SIG (SELV)*,
AND *LUI-MÊME*

Throughout this chapter, I am mainly concerned with the reflexive morphemes *se* and *lui-même* in French, and *sig* and *sig selv* in Danish. *Se* and *sig*
will be glossed as *REFL, sig selv* as *REFL-self,* and *lui-même* as *him- self.*

With regard to feature composition, the morphologically simple reflexives
se and *sig* are alike: Both are unspecified for gender, number, and case.
Both require a third person antecedent. However, *se* and *sig* can be bound
by an indefinite NP or to arbitrary PRO; these are not third person from a
semantic point of view. This is shown in (1) for Danish.

(1) a. Enhver$_i$/man$_i$ skal forsvare sig$_i$ fra politiet.
       everyone$_i$/one$_i$ must defend REFL$_i$ from police-the
    b. PRO$_i$ præsentere sig$_i$ for studenterne er kedeligt.
       PRO$_i$ introduce REFL$_i$ to students-the is boring

If, as proposed by Burzio (1989, 1991) true reflexives are elements that lack
φ-features and, crucially, can have an impersonal antecedent, both *se* and
sig qualify as true reflexives. The same holds for *sig* followed by the
morpheme *selv*. In modern Mainland Scandinavian languages, *selv* is
uninflected, occurring with all forms of person, gender, and number. I
tentatively posit that within the complex reflexive *selv* is nominal. In contrast
to the forms considered so far, *lui-même* has gender and number features:
elle-même 'she-self' and *eux-mêmes* 'them-selves'. It also has person features,
grammatically and semantically, and thus cannot be bound by a generic NP.
Même can function as an adverb or as an adjective. In the latter case alone
it is inflected for number and can appear in constructions in which the
nominal head is empty (Zribi-Hertz, 1990a). I assume that within *lui-même,*
même has adjectival status.

To summarize, *se* and *sig (selv)* are genderless and numberless. We have
seen that both can be bound by an impersonal NP. Following Burzio (1989),
it can be said that these expressions are personless as well, and when bound
to a definite NP they instantiate "pseudoagreement."[1] In contrast, *lui-même,*
constructed by adjoining the element *même* to the third person nonclitic
pronoun *lui,* has gender, number, and person features and thus cannot be

---

[1]According to Burzio (1991), α pseudoagrees with β if:

(i) β has no gender, no number, and no person, and,
(ii) α is third person.

Burzio argued that "person markings have a higher relative weight than either gender or number
markings since a featureless β pseudo-agrees with an α of any number and any gender, but
not with one which is 1st or 2nd person" (p. 14).

bound by an impersonal NP. As the translations of the French examples indicate, *himself* is similar to *lui-même* in this respect.

X' STATUS OF *SE*, *SIG (SELV)*, AND *LUI-MÊME*

Pronominal clitics differ from regular NPs with respect to a variety of syntactic processes (Kayne, 1975; Stefanini, 1962). Although the latter can be stressed, used to answer a question, coordinated, clefted, and topicalized, none of these processes is available for clitics. When these tests are applied to the reflexives considered here, it turns out that *sig selv* and *lui-même* behave as regular NPs (or DPs, along the lines of Abney, 1987), whereas *sig* behaves as a clitic, like *se*. This is shown in (2) through (6) for Danish.[2]

(2) *Stress:*
   a. Ida forsvarer SIG SELV / børnene.
      'Ida defends REFL-self/ the children'
   b. * Ida forsvarer SIG.
      Ida defends REFL

(3) *Answers to questions:*
   a. Hvem vasker Ida?   - Sig selv/Børnene.
      'Who does Ida wash?'   - REFL-self/The children.
   b. Hvem beskytter Julie?   - * Sig.
      'Who does Julie protect?'   - REFL.

(4) *Coordination:*
   a. Julie præsenterede studenten og sig selv.
      Julie introduced the student and REFL-self
   b. * Julie præsenterede studenten og sig.

(5) *Clefting:*
   a. Det var sig selv/studenten Peter udleverede.
      it was REFL-self/the student Peter delivered
   b. * Det var sig Peter udleverede.
      it was REFL Peter delivered

(6) *Topicalization:*
   a. Sig selv/turisten, udleverede Ida ikke til politiet.
      REFL self/the tourist, delivered Ida not to the police
   b. * Sig udleverede Ida ikke til politiet.
      REFL delivered Ida not to the police

These facts strongly suggest that the complex forms qualify as full phrases, whereas the simple ones do not. Muysken (1983) proposed that the levels

---

[2]The equivalent French examples are omitted due to space constraints.

118   JAKUBOWICZ

of categorial projection are determined in terms of two features: [+/−projection], [+/−maximal]. Under this view of X′ theory, *lui-même* and *sig selv* can be analyzed as [+projected, +maximal], and *se* and *sig* as [−projected, −maximal]. I assume that in terms of the standard X′ theory, the complex expressions correspond to full phrases (to which I refer as XP or DP), and that *se* and *sig* are heads (X°), exhaustively dominated by a functional phrase that I call a clitic-phrase: [$_{CIP}$ se/sig].[3]

There is, however, an important difference between Romance clitics like *se* or *le* 'him' in French and their counterparts *sig* and *ham* in Danish (and, more generally, in Mainland Scandinavian languages). Under the assumption that clitics are base-generated in argument position (Kayne, 1975, 1991), movement in French of an object clitic to its verb host is obligatory, and in modern French the clitic cannot be separated from its host. This is shown by the fact that the clitic moves with the verb, whether it is reflexive or not.

In contrast, in Danish main clauses, where the main verb raises to C, the weak forms (reflexive or pronominal) remain separated from the verb by the subject (as in (7a–b)), or its trace (as in (7c)).[4] Assuming that adverbs as well as the negative element are left-adjoined to the VP (Holmberg & Platzack, 1989), the fact that the clitic precedes the negation indicates that the clitic has left its base-generated position within VP and appears in second constituent position, that is, in IP.

(7) a. [$_{CP}$Igar udleverede [$_{IP}$Ida sig/ham [$_{VP}$ikke [$_{VP}$ . . . til politiet]]]].
Yesterday delivered Ida REFL/him not to the police
'Yesterday Ida did not deliver herself/him to the police.'
b. [$_{CP}$Hvor vasker [$_{IP}$børnene sig/ham [$_{VP}$ . . . .]]].
Where wash the children REFL/him
'Where do the children wash themselves/him?'
c. [$_{CP}$Børnene$_i$ klæder [$_{IP}$ t_i sig [$_{VP}$ . . . .]]].
'The children dress themselves.'

Following work by Halpern (1992), I assume that Danish clitics are syntactically independent prosodically bound words, whereas in modern

---

[3]It is crucial to my analysis that the clitic is head of a functional projection. Whether this category should be called clitic phrase (ClP), as proposed here, or DP, as in Jakubowicz (1992b), is without importance for the purpose of this chapter.

[4]Danish is a Verb-Second language. As in Norwegian and Swedish, the finite verb has overt tense features but lacks person features. In the literature dealing with Verb-Second, it is generally accepted that Verb-Second represents movement of the finite verb into COMP. However, authors differ with regard to the trigger of Verb-Second, the nature of the COMP position, and, more generally, the structure of the clause (Haider & Prinzhorn, 1985). For concreteness, I adopt here the proposal of Holmberg and Platzack (1989) concerning the structure of the sentence in Mainland Scandinavian languages.

French, *se* as well as *le* are clitics that select for morphological attachment. Thus *sig* and *ham* form only a prosodic constituent with their host and not a morphological one.

Let us now turn to the X' structure of *lui-même* and *sig selv*. Although both forms qualify as XPs, their internal structure differs. Rouveret (1991) suggested that pronouns are Number Phrases (NumP) in which the pronoun, inherently specified for person, occupies the NP position at D-Structure. Under the assumption that *même* is adjoined to the NumP, *lui-même* has the following representation.

(8) $[_{\text{NumP}} [_{\text{SPEC}} \text{lui}]_i [_{\text{Num'}} [_{\text{Num}} \text{sing}]_i [_{\text{NP}} [_{\text{NP}} \text{e}]_i]] [_{\text{AP}} \text{même}]_i]$

As presupposed earlier, *sig*, which is numberless and personless, heads a functional clitic projection. I assume that the complex reflexive results from the adjunction of the morpheme *selv* to the clitic phrase, as in (9).[5]

(9) $[_{\text{ClP}} [_{\text{ClP}} \text{sig}] [_{\text{NP}} \text{selv}]]$

DISTRIBUTION OF THE EXPRESSIONS

In what follows, I adopt Burzio's idea (but not his analysis) that a featureless, personless reflexive obtains its features through agreement. According to Koopman (1987), agreement is realized in a SPEC-head configuration. In a finite or infinitival sentence, the only element that is a head and carries overt or nonovert ϕ-features is INFL (which is coindexed with its SPEC, the subject). In order to satisfy the agreement requirement, therefore, the reflexive must adjoin to INFL. As a consequence, a personless reflexive is always subject-oriented. I also assume that clitics are base-generated in argument position: [. . . $[_{\text{VP}} [_{\text{V'}} \text{V} [_{\text{ClP}} \text{clitic}]]]$ (Kayne, 1975). However, in contrast to XPs, reflexive clitics, being functional heads, do not qualify as arguments.[6] To be case-marked and thus visible for theta-assignment, reflexive clitics need to move. If the clitic is subcategorized for lexical attachment, it undergoes overt movement; otherwise, movement takes place at LF. Thus s*e* incorporates overtly into the verb by head-to-head movement (cf. Baker, 1988). In contrast, movement of *sig* is covert. At PF, however, both *se* and *sig* are phonologically dependent elements. Let us now turn to the distribution of the expressions.

---

[5]If *sig* is not a projecting head, *selv* cannot be its structural argument, as suggested in Jakubowicz (1992b). A crucial aspect of both my former and my present analysis is that when *sig* is followed by *selv*, the complex expression qualifies as a full phrase.

[6]The intuitive idea is that a functional category, devoid of descriptive content, is not, by itself, able to function referentially. (See Jakubowicz, 1992b.)

French *Se*

It is well known that the French clitic reflexive must be locally bound. Thus (10a) is well formed, whereas (10b) and (10c) are ruled out, because *se* cannot pseudoagree with a first person antecedent (index i) or agree with a long-distance one (index j). I assume that at S-structure the clitic incorporates into the verb and, following Pollock's (1989) and Chomsky's (1989) proposals about verb movement, the clitic and the verb overtly adjoin to the Inflection in (10a) and (10b), and covertly, in (10c). The hypothesis that once a clitic is adjoined to some $X°$, it cannot be detached from it (Kayne, 1991) explains why *se* cannot move at LF to the matrix AGR phrase and be coindexed with the indefinite NP.

(10) a. Jean$_i$ se$_i$ présentera au directeur.
  Jean$_i$ REFL$_i$ will present to the director
  'Jean will introduce himself to the director.'
 b. * Tout le monde$_j$ pensait
  que je$_i$ se$_{i/j}$ présenterais au directeur.
  everybody$_j$ thought
  that I$_i$ REFL$_{i/j}$ would present to the director
  *'Everybody thought that I would introduce himself to the director.'
 c. * Tout le monde$_j$ m$_i$'a demandé
  de PRO$_i$ se$_{i/j}$ présenter au directeur.
  everybody$_j$ asked me$_i$ PRO$_i$ to REFL$_{i/j}$ introduce to the director
  *'Everybody asked me to introduce himself to the director.'

Danish *Sig*

Two properties of *sig* are well known: First, *sig* can be long-distance bound if it is contained in a nonfinite clause; and second, its binder must be a subject. These two conditions are satisfied in (11a); (11b) is excluded because the nonfiniteness constraint is violated. (11c) is excluded because, like *se*, *sig* cannot pseudoagree with a first person subject, and the object, with which it could pseudoagree, is not an available binder.

(11) a. Julie$_j$ bad mig$_i$ om [PRO$_i$ at præsentere sig$_j$].[7]
  Julie$_j$ asked me$_i$ about PRO$_i$ to introduce REFL$_j$
  'Julie asked me to introduce her.'

---

[7] In Mainland Scandinavian languages, some object-control verbs require a preposition: *bede om* 'ask for/about', *overtale til* 'persuade to', *tvinge til* 'force to'. Reinholtz (1989) observed that the preposition *om* should not be confounded with the complementizer *om*. Reinholtz showed that preposition stranding is allowed for the former and excluded for the latter. Henceforth I assume that *om* is reanalyzed with the verb and does not constitute a barrier for head government.

  b. *Julie$_j$ siger [at Jeg kritiserer sig$_j$].
    Julie$_j$ says that I criticize REFL$_j$
  c. *Jeg$_i$ lovede Julie$_j$ [PRO$_i$ at forsvare sig$_{i/j}$].
    I$_i$ promised Julie$_j$ PRO$_i$ to defend REFL$_{i/j}$

However, *sig* in argument position is not specialized for long-distance binding, contrary to what has been proposed in the literature (Hellan, 1988; Hestvik, 1989, 1990; Vikner, 1985). For instance, if PRO has third person features in a construction such as (12), both local and long-distance binding interpretations of *sig* are available.

(12) Julie$_j$ bad Ida$_i$ om [PRO$_i$ at præsentere sig$_{i/j}$].
   Julie$_j$ asked Ida$_i$ about PRO$_i$ introduce REFL$_{i/j}$
   'Julie$_j$ asked Ida$_i$ to introduce herself$_i$/her$_j$.'

Yet certain conditions must be satisfied for local binding of *sig*. One of these conditions involves the nature of the verb that governs the expression. In Jakubowicz (1992b) (see also Jakubowicz & Olsen, 1988), I argued that affectedness verbs (henceforth [+a]), in the sense of Anderson (1979), allow *sig* to be locally bound, whereas nonaffectedness verbs' ([−a]) prevent local binding.[8] Examples of the two types of transitive verbs are given in (13) and (14).

(13) [+a] verbs:

vaske	*børste*	*rede*	*sminke*	*barbere*	*frottere*
'wash'	'brush'	'comb'	'make up'	'shave'	'rub'
daekke	*beskytte*	*forsvare*	*redde*	*befri*	*løsrive*
'cover'	'protect'	'defend'	'save'	'liberate'	'untie'

---

[8]According to Anderson (1979), an affected object undergoes a physical or abstract change of state or location through the event denoted by the verb. See Tenny (1987) for a characterization of affectedness in aspectual terms, and Olsen (1992) for the application of a slightly modified version of Tenny's approach to Danish. Olsen observed, first, that verbs denoting nondelimited events exclude local binding of *sig*, and, second, that not all verbs that denote delimited events allow *sig* to be locally bound (e.g. *invite, find, recognize, meet*). Olsen concluded that local binding of *sig* is possible if the verb denoting a delimited event favors a coreferential interpretation between its two arguments. Note that under Anderson's characterization of affected objects, the verbs just mentioned belong to the category [−a] and are thus expected to exclude local binding of *sig*. Although the semantic notion of affectedness still awaits a more precise formulation than the one given by Anderson and adopted here, it is well known that affected and nonaffected objects behave differently with regard to various syntactic processes.

(14) [–a] verbs:

høre	betragte	beundre	respektere	elske	hade
'hear'	'look at'	'admire'	'respect'	'love'	'hate'
kende	invitere	naevne	forstå	huske	love
'know'	'invite'	'mention'	'understand'	'recall'	'promise'

Furthermore, when *sig* occurs within a prepositional phrase, its binding properties are dependent on the nature of the preposition that governs the expression. Whereas lexical prepositions, such as *bag* 'behind', *omkring* 'around', *under* 'under', and *over* 'over' allow *sig* to be bound to the subject of its own clause, functional prepositions, such as *om* 'about', *til* 'at' or 'to', *på* 'at', and *af* 'of' disallow local binding.

(15) a. Ida$_i$ lagde bøgerne bag sig$_i$.
   Ida$_i$ put the books behind REFL$_i$
   'Ida$_i$ put the books behind herself.'
   b. Ida$_i$ lyste omkring sig$_i$.
   Ida$_i$ shined (the light) around REFL$_i$

(16) a. * Ida$_i$ talte om sig$_i$.
   Ida$_i$ talked about REFL$_i$
   'Ida talked about herself.'
   b. * Ida$_i$ lyste på sig$_i$.
   Ida$_i$ shined (the light) at REFL$_i$

I do not consider here the constructions in which *sig* is governed by a lexical preposition. As for those in which it is governed by a functional preposition, I assume, as argued in detail in Jakubowicz (1992b), that these constructions should be analyzed as [–a] predicates. In the remainder of this chapter, the feature [–a] indicates transitive verbs like those in (14) and predicates in which *sig* is governed by a functional preposition.

Let us now consider the constructions in which *sig* is governed by a [+a] verb and is interpreted as locally bound. The following fact indicates that these constructions differ from intrinsically reflexive predicates. Verbs such as *vaske* 'wash' or *forsvare* 'defend' can take the complex reflexive or any other DP as argument, as in (17a), whereas intrinsically reflexive predicates with verbs such as *skamme* 'be ashamed' or *skynde* 'hurry', as in (17b), cannot.

(17) a. Ida vasker/forsvarer sig/sig selv/børnene.
   Ida washes/defends REFL/REFL-self/the children
   b. Ida skammer/skynder sig/*sig selv/*børnene.
   Ida is ashamed of/hurries REFL/*REFL-self/*the children

To explain why [+a] verbs admit but [–a] verbs exclude local binding of *sig*, I assume that at LF, [+a] verbs can incorporate the element projected in their internal argument position, producing a complex semantic predicate. This property—call it *P*—can be conceived as a distinctive lexical feature of [+a] verbs. Thus, [+a] verbs have the property *P*, whereas [–a] verbs lack this property.[9] How can property *P* account for the fact that [+a] verbs allow local binding of *sig*? Our argument is as follows: As stated earlier, *sig*, being the head of a functional projection, cannot be viewed as an argument and needs to move in order to be visible. Under the hypothesis that in contrast to *se*, *sig* does not overtly incorporate into the verb, its only option is to move at LF. If the verb has property *P*, *sig* can incorporate into the verb by head-to-head movement. By incorporation into the verb, *sig* acquires case and the chain [sig_i . . . . . t_i] can be theta-marked. Under Chomsky's (1989) assumption that in the absence of overt verb movement (either to I or to C), the verb must raise to I at LF, the verb plus the incorporated *sig* will therefore be in I at LF. Because I is coindexed with the subject through SPEC-head agreement, in this position *sig* can receive the necessary φ-features from the SPEC of IP. To illustrate, consider the LF representation of an embedded finite clause in which *sig* is governed by a [+a] verb.

(18) at [$_{IP}$ Ida$_i$ [$_{I'}$ forsvarer sig$_i$ [$_{VP}$ [$_{V'}$ $t_{[V-sig]i}$ [$_{CIP}$ t_i]]]]]
    that Ida defends REFL

Evidence in support of this hypothesis comes from the fact that, when governed by a [+a] verb, the simple and the complex reflexive give rise to different interpretations. Olsen (1992) observed that only one reading is available in a sentence in which *sig* occurs, like (19). In contrast, two readings arise in the presence of *sig selv*, as in (20).

(19) Line klædder sig på.
    Line dresses REFL part
    'Line dresses herself.'

(20) Line klædder sig selv på.
    (i) 'Line dresses HERSELF.'
    (ii) 'Line dresses herself by herself (without aid).'

---

[9] The idea that [+a] predicates allow their internal object to be incorporated into the verb is due to Zubizarreta (1987). This author was the first to observe that *zich* in Dutch can be locally bound if it occurs with a verb that affects its internal argument. However, my analysis differs from Zubizarreta's in that I assume that the element *sig* is syntactically projected. For Zubizarreta, a verb such as *wash* or *shave* is semantically dyadic but syntactically intransitive. In her account, locally bound *zich*, unlike long-distance bound *zich*, is not linked to a syntactic argument position.

Olsen also reported that in sentences such as these, the morpheme *selv* can be separated from *sig* and intensified by the adverb *helt* 'entirely', 'completely'.

(21) Line klædder sig på helt selv.
'Line dresses herself entirely by herself.'

These facts can be explained by the hypothesis put forth here, namely, that *sig* incorporates into its governor at LF if this governor has property *P*. The formation of a complex predicate through LF incorporation of *sig* into the [+a] verb allows *selv* to function as an IP (or VP) adjunct, giving rise to either an emphatic reading, as in (20i), or an adverbial reading ((20ii) and (21)). Under the hypothesis that [−a] verbs lack property *P*, incorporation of *sig* into the verb is excluded. Thus, sentence (22a) has no interpretation, and in (22b), because *sig* does not incorporate into the verb, *selv* cannot adjoin to IP (or VP) but must be adjoined to the clitic itself, and no emphatic or adverbial readings are available.

(22) a. *Ida$_i$ kritiserer sig$_i$.
Ida$_i$ criticizes REFL$_i$
   b. Ida$_i$ kritiserer sig selv$_i$.
Ida$_i$ criticizes REFL-self$_i$
'Ida criticizes herself.'

Further evidence in support of my hypothesis comes from VP-deletion constructions. As shown in (23), locally bound *sig* gets only a bound variable reading. If, as claimed, *sig* incorporates into the [+a] verb at LF, it cannot be evaluated independently of the complex predicate, and no coreferential reading is possible.

(23) Ida$_i$ præsenterede sig$_i$ for studenterne,
og det samme gjorde Julie$_j$ {O$_{j/*i}$}.[10]
Ida$_i$ introduced REFL$_i$ to the students and the same did Julie$_j$
'Ida introduced herself to the students and Julie did too.'

In contrast, in constructions in which *sig* must be long-distance bound, it gets a coreferential reading, like that of the pronominal *hende* 'her'.

(24) a. Ida$_i$ bad mig om at invitere/præsentere sig$_i$,
og det samme gjorde Julie$_j$ {O$_{j/i}$}.
Ida$_i$ asked me to invite/introduce REFL$_i$ and the same did Julie$_j$.
'Ida asked me to invite/introduce her and Julie did too.'

---

[10]The symbol /O$_j$/ indicates the bound variable reading: *Julie$_j$ introduced herself$_j$ to the students.* The asterisk preceding the index *i* indicates that the coreferential interpretation, *Julie$_j$ introduced Ida$_i$ to the students,* is not available in (23).

    b. Ida$_i$ bad mig om at invitere hende$_i$,
og det samme gjorde Julie$_j$ {O$_j$/$_i$}.
Ida$_i$ asked me to invite her$_i$ and the same did Julie$_j$
'Ida asked me to invite her and Julie did too.'

Given (24a), one might conclude that long-distance *sig* has pronominal properties.[11] However, the following indicates that such a conclusion would be incorrect. Although long-distance *sig* and the pronoun overlap in distribution, *sig* does not behave like the pronoun. In particular *sig*, in contrast to the pronoun, cannot have split antecedents. This fact, observed by Everaert (1991) for *zich* in Dutch, is also true of Danish.

(25) a. *Ida$_i$ hørte Julie$_j$ bede mig om at invitere sig$_{i+j}$.
           Ida$_i$ heard Julie$_j$ ask me to invite REFL$_{i+j}$
    b. Ida$_i$ hørte Julie$_j$ bede mig om at invitere dem$_{i+j}$.
          'Ida heard Julie ask me to invite them.'

However, if it is true, as I propose, that *sig* is uniformly a featureless reflexive head, it is puzzling that when it is long-distance bound, a coreferential reading is possible in VP-deletion contexts. One way to resolve this problem would be to give up or modify this idea and assume, as proposed by Bok-Bennema (1984) for Dutch and by Hestvik (1989) for Norwegian, that long-distance *sig* is in fact an overt pronominal anaphor, that is, a [+a, +p] expression. Such a solution captures the undeniable fact that long-distance *sig* does not give rise to a reflexive interpretation if, as in traditional terminology, reflexivity indicates identity or nondistinctness between the subject and the object (Maupas, 1607, quoted by Stefanini, 1962).

---

[11]Note that *sig selv*, although a true reflexive in Burzio's sense and strictly locally bound, nevertheless gets both a bound variable and a coreferential reading in VP-deletion constructions.

(i) Ida$_i$ kritiserede sig selv$_i$,
    og det samme gjorde Julie$_j$ {O$_{j/i}$}.
    'Ida criticized herself and Julie did too.'

This suggests that the fact that long-distance *sig* gets a coreferential reading does not indicate that it has pronominal properties. Note that in Danish, the possessive reflexive, analyzed as a DP by Dielsing (1988), functions like *sig selv*. In contrast, an X° reflexive that undergoes covert (*sig*), or overt (*se*) incorporation into its governor gets a bound variable reading only.

(ii) a. Ida$_i$ har last sin$_i$ bog og det samme gjorde Julie$_j$ {O$_{j/i}$}.
        'Ida read her (own) book and Julie did too.'
    b. Marie$_i$ se$_i$ présente aux étudiants et Jean$_j$ aussi {O$_{j/*i}$}.
        Marie REFL introduces to the students and Jean too

It is tempting to suggest that a reflexive may get a coreferential reading in VP-deletion contexts if it does not incorporate (overtly or covertly) into its governor.

However, because it suggests that the properties of *sig* are fundamentally different, depending on whether it is long-distance, locally bound, or followed by *selv,* this solution seems problematic from an acquisition point of view. Under the assumption that no negative evidence is available, how could a child conclude that one morpheme—*sig*—is listed two or three times in the lexicon? To avoid this problem, I continue to assume that *sig* has a single entry in the lexicon, and that its binding and interpretative properties derive from the interaction between its status as a featureless cliticlike element and general principles of Universal Grammar.

As argued here, locally bound *sig* is licensed by LF incorporation into a [+a] verb. If such licensing is excluded, namely, if complex predicate formation is banned, only one possibility is left to *sig:* The expression must move out from its base-generated position and land in a higher INFL where it can acquire features by SPEC-head agreement. Pica (1987) and Cole, Hermon, and Sung (1990) suggested that long-distance binding of $X°$ reflexives results from successive cyclic movement of the expression from the lower INFL to the matrix INFL via COMP. This derivation generates both a local and a long-distance reading of the $X°$ reflexive. However, in Danish as well as in the other Scandinavian languages, in the absence of complex predicate formation, local binding of the $X°$ reflexive is excluded and long-distance binding is obligatory. One must then conclude that in these languages the $X°$ reflexive moves directly from its base position to COMP, skipping the lower INFL. Under the assumption that in V-2 languages COMP and INFL are coindexed, once the embedded verb raises to the lower INFL at LF, the minimal domain of the $X°$ reflexive includes CP.[12] Chomsky (1992) proposed that two targets of movement are equidistant if they are in the same minimal domain. According to this notion of shortest movement, direct movement of *sig* from its base position to C gives rise to a permissible derivation. By way of illustration, consider the example in (26a) and its LF representation in (26b).

(26) a. at Ida$_i$ bad mig om at invitere sig$_i$
that Ida asked me to invite REFL

b. [$_{CP}$ at [$_{IP}$ Ida$_i$ [$_{I'}$sig$_i$ bad$_v$ [$_{VP}$ t_v mig [$_{PP}$ om$_v$
[$_{CP}$ [$_{C'}t'_i$ [$_{IP}$ PRO [$_{I'}$ at invitere$_v$ [$_{VP}$ t_v [$_{CIP}$ t_i]] . . .]

Once *sig* is in a position where it can receive the necessary φ-features, the chain [*sig*$_i$, t'_i, t_i] is visible for theta-marking. Movement of *sig* to a higher INFL must be seen as a last-resort device (Chomsky, 1992), driven by morphological

---

[12]Following ideas by Platzack (1986), I am assuming, first, that in Mainland Scandinavian languages, COMP contains the feature [+/− Tense], distinguishing finite and infinitival embedded clauses; and second, that the specific tenses are generated under INFL. One can think of COMP and INFL as a discontinuous constituent whose heads must have matching features.

necessity. This operation applies when it must, namely, when the governor of *sig* is a [–a] verb as in (26), or when its governor is a [+a] verb but the expression cannot agree or pseudoagree with the local subject, as in the following example:

(27) Julie$_j$ bad mig$_i$ om PRO$_i$ at forsvare sig$_{j/*i}$.
Julie asked me to defend REFL

Under the assumption adopted here that once a clitic is overtly or covertly incorporated into some X°, it cannot be detached from it, it follows that no complex predicate formation occurs in (27). As in (26), the embedded verb is in the lower INFL at LF, and *sig* moves to the matrix INFL via C. Finally, if the local subject has either no person or third person features, and the governor of *sig* has property *P*, as in (28), the derivation converges without application of the last-resort operation, that is, without long-distance movement.

(28) Julie bad Ida$_i$ om at forsvare sig$_i$.
Julie asked Ida to defend REFL

Because in this case LF incorporation of *sig* into its governor is possible, it must occur according to the *least effort* guidelines proposed by Chomsky (1989, 1992). This means that in cases such as (28), long-distance binding of *sig* represents a marked option. This prediction is borne out: As shown in the following, in modern Danish, long-distance binding of *sig* is rare and, crucially, it is less acceptable with [+a] verbs than with [–a] verbs. In general, subjects prefer to use a pronoun instead of *sig*.

First, Olsen's (1992) survey of two corpora (Maeggard & Ruus, 1981a, 1981b), obtained from 2,000 literary texts published by 172 Danish authors between 1970 and 1974, shows that among 3,519 occurrences of *sig*, only 4 come from sentences in which the expression is long-distance bound.

Second, two studies conducted by Olsen (1992) with 50 Danish native adult speakers, show the following results. In a sentence completion study, subjects were asked to choose between *sig* and a pronoun (*ham* 'him' or *hende* 'her'), to refer back to the matrix subject of an object-control sentence. On average, they used *sig* 23.7% of the time when the embedded verb was [+a], and 35.5% of the time when the embedded verb was [–a]. In the remaining cases they used the pronoun. In a grammaticality judgment study, sentences in which a pronoun in object position in an embedded clause was linked to the matrix subject were considered grammatical 100% of the time. In contrast, the same sentences with *sig* instead of the pronoun were judged grammatical 18.9% of the time when the embedded verb was [+a] and 47.7% of the time when the embedded verb was [–a].

Danish *Sig Selv*

We have seen that when *sig* is followed by *selv*, this element functions as either an IP (or VP) adjunct, or as a ClP adjunct, depending on the lexical properties of the predicate. If the verb is [–a], *selv* cannot be separated from *sig* and no emphatic or adverbial reading is available. In this case *selv* is adjoined to the ClP and, as indicated by stress patterns, *sig* gets cliticized onto *selv*. These facts suggest that when the verb is [–a], even if it is, morphologically, two separate elements, *sig selv* must be analyzed syntactically as a single nominal.[13] Under this hypothesis, the fact that *sig selv* must be locally bound follows straightforwardly. *Sig selv* qualifies as an XP and, as such, it can be adjoined to IP at LF. In this position, the agreement requirement of the featureless reflexive can be satisfied. Under the hypothesis that LF movement of *sig selv* is constrained by Relativized Minimality (Rizzi, 1990), a maximal projection intervening between the expression and its trace determines a domain impermeable to government. Thus, the specifier of IP constitutes a barrier for *sig selv*. Consequently, the expression cannot move further to become long-distance bound. By way of illustration, consider (29a) and its LF representation in (29b).

(29) a. at Ida$_i$ hader sig selv$_i$
          that Ida$_i$ hates REFL-self$_i$
          'that Ida hates herself'
      b. [$_{CP}$ that [$_{IP}$ Ida$_i$ [$_{IP}$ sig selv$_i$ [$_{I'}$ hader$_v$ [$_{VP}$ [$_{V'}$ t_v [$_{ClP}$ t_i]]]]]]]

Local binding is also obligatory when *selv* is IP- or VP-adjoined, namely, when the governor of *sig* has property *P*. In these constructions, through LF incorporation into the verb, *sig* is already locally bound. Note that when *selv* occurs without *sig* and is IP- or VP-adjoined, *selv* can modify only an expression occurring in its local domain. As the following examples illustrate, *selv* can modify only *PRO*. Note that the sentences are ungrammatical if *selv* is interpreted as modifying the subject of the matrix clause in (30a), or the object of the matrix clause in (30b).

(30) a. Eva$_i$ beder Anne$_j$ om PRO$_j$ selv$_{j/*i}$ at svare på brevet.
          'Eva asks Anne to answer the letter by herself.'

---

[13]Within possessive reflexive phrases, analyzed as DPs by Dielsing (1988), a "weak" adjective may occur between the reflexive and the nominal head.

(i) sin store bil
     REFL big car
     'his own big car'

The fact that nothing may intervene between *sig* and *selv* supports the proposal that *sig selv* must be analyzed as a compact nominal.

b. Eva$_i$ lover Anne$_j$ PRO$_i$ selv$_{i/*j}$ at svare på brevet.
'Eva promises Anne to answer the letter by herself.'

French *Lui-même*

In contemporary French, the distribution of the nonclitic featureless reflexive *soi* is limited, in that it can be used only with an indefinite impersonal antecedent (Ronat, 1982). If the antecedent is definite or specific, the third nonclitic pronoun *lui* occurs instead of *soi*. Zribi-Hertz (1980) observed that the adjunction of *même* to the pronoun *lui* is optional or obligatory according to the semantics of the predicate. Consider the following sentences:

(31) a. Jean$_i$ est content de lui$_i$-(même).
        Jean$_i$ is pleased with him$_i$-(self)
      b. Jean$_i$ est jaloux de lui$_i$*(-même).
        Jean$_i$ is jealous of him$_i$-*(self)

The contrast between (31a) and (31b) does not depend on syntactic shape alone (these sentences are identical in this respect), but, rather, on the interpretation of the expressions *être jaloux de* 'to be jealous of' and *être content de* 'to be happy with'. Whereas the former requires that its two arguments be disjoint in reference (henceforth [+DR]), the latter does not (henceforth [−DR]). Examples of the two types of expressions are given in (32) (from Zribi-Hertz, 1980).

(32) a. [+DR] expressions:

s'acharner contre	*être d'accord avec*	*bavarder avec*
'to be dead set against'	'to agree with'	'chatter with'
conspirer contre	*être en paix avec*	*être hargneux envers*
'conspire against'	'be in peace with'	'be cross towards'

      b. [−DR] expressions:

croire en	*douter de*	*se méfier de*	*avoir peur de*
'believe in'	'doubt'	'be suspicious of'	'to be frightened of'
avoir pitié de	*rêver de*	*penser d'abord à*	*parler de*
'have pity on'	'dream about'	'think of first'	'talk about'

According to Zribi-Hertz (1992), in the context of [+DR] expressions, adjunction of *même* may be "semantically analysed as a signal that the pronoun receives a marked index ('i') in its thematic domain (or Complete Functional Complex)." With [−DR] expressions, the adjunction of *même* "is unnecessary within its thematic domain, although it may be justified by a larger context implying, e.g., a contrastive reading of the object pronoun" (p. 13). The fact that the obligatory or optional character of the adjunction of *même* depends on lexical (semantic) properties, resembles what we have seen regarding the adjunction of *selv* to *sig* in Danish. In root sentences, adjunction of *selv* is obligatory if the governor of *sig* is [–a]. It thus appears that the adjunction of *même/selv* triggers an obligatory bound reading otherwise inaccessible (as in French) or allows an uninterpretable sentence to get an interpretation (as in Danish).

That the expression *lui-même* is subject to locality restrictions and does not behave as a pronoun is confirmed by the following: *Lui-même* cannot be used deictically; it cannot take split antecedents; and in noncontrastive environments, it must be A-bound, like *sig selv*.[14] However, the syntactic properties of *lui-même* and *sig selv* are not completely alike. First, *lui-même*, unlike *sig selv*, can be bound by an object. Second, as discussed in length by Zribi-Hertz (1989, 1990a), *lui-même*, like *himself*, can have a logophoric antecedent and can thus be discourse-linked. *Lui-même* can be free in its own clause and, in a contrastive environment a sentence antecedent does not have to c-command the reflexive. In contrast, neither *sig* nor *sig selv* can be used logophorically. Danish allows only *ham/hende selv* 'him/her-self' to be used logophorically, as discussed in Vikner (1985).

The fact that *sig selv* must be bound by a subject can be explained under the assumption put forth here that *sig selv*, being featureless, can receive the necessary features only through agreement in a SPEC-head configuration, as in IP. Because *lui* has φ-features, the complex expression does not need to move. It can be linked to any c-commanding antecedent in its Complete Functional Complex; hence its antecedent can be an object (I return to this presently).

I now investigate why *sig selv* cannot be used logophorically, whereas *lui-même* in French, *himself* in English, and *ham selv* in Danish can. According to Reinhart and Reuland (1991) only SELF anaphors in an argument (grid) position of a fully assigned predicate abide by the standard grammatical requirements on variable binding, whereas logophoric uses of SELF anaphors fall outside the scope of the grammar. This view, which does not take into account the properties of the element (*sig/lui*) to which the SELF morpheme is adjoined, seems to me problematic. First, note that in Danish, when *sig selv* is not itself a coargument of the verb but is contained within a subjectless NP, the personless reflexive is still in complementary distribution with the pronoun, contrary to what is observed in English. This shows that *sig selv* does not need to be an argument of the verb to fall within the scope of the grammar (Principle A of the Binding Theory). Second, the fact that *sig selv* cannot be used logophorically does not seem to be an idiosyncrasy of Danish. To my knowledge, similarly complex personless reflexives in the other Scandinavian languages (Hellan, 1988) as well as in Romance languages (e.g., *si mismo* in

---

[14]With respect to the properties of *lui-même*, see Zribi-Hertz (1990a) and Jakubowicz (1990).

Spanish and *se stesso* in Italian), cannot have a logophoric antecedent. It thus appears that *selv/même/self* can be used logophorically only when it is adjoined to a pronoun. Moreover, Reinhart and Reuland's important observation, that logophoricity is possible only where the SELF anaphor is not in a position on the theta grid of a verb, seems to be correct only in this case. Similarly, their proposal—that a SELF anaphor in a grid position of a predicate reflexivizes the predicate's grid—seems to be limited to languages in which a personless reflexive is completely unavailable (like English) or has a restricted distribution (like *soi* in French). Thus, Reinhart and Reuland's hypothesis, that *self* adjoins to the verb when the complex expression is in a theta position, may explain why *lui-même* in French and *himself* in English can be bound by either the subject or the object of their local domain.[15] Note, however, that in Danish, *ham selv* can never be linked to a subject and, as reported by Olsen (1992), although binding by an object is possible, it is rather rare. This seems to be related to the fact that *sig selv* is available both as an object of a verb and as an object of a preposition; but, as we have seen, its binder must be a subject.

(33) Ida$_i$ fortæller Julie$_j$ om hende selv$_{j/*i}$.
Ida tells Julie about her-self

Finally, the fact that *sig selv* cannot have a logophoric antecedent can be best explained under the hypothesis put forth here that *sig selv* should be analyzed as a maximal projection that adjoins to IP at LF. From this position, in which it can get the necessary ϕ-features, it cannot move further without violating the ECP. As a result, *sig selv* must always be locally bound.

WHAT DOES THE CHILD LEARN FROM EVIDENCE?

Under the foregoing analysis, the distribution of *se, sig (selv)*, and *lui-même* follows from the interaction between their morphological properties—feature composition and X′ status—and general principles of Universal Grammar: the principles of X′ theory, SPEC-head agreement, theta and government principles determining X°- and XP-movement, as well as the Binding Principles. Under this account, there is only one featureless core reflexive in French, *se*, and there is only one in Danish, *sig*. Both obey Principle A of the Binding Theory and must be locally bound, as proposed by Chomsky (1981). This is always the case for *se*, but not for *sig*. However, the fact that *sig* may marginally be long-distance bound does not contradict

---

[15]A similar result can be reached under Zribi-Hertz' (1992) proposal that *lui-même* may abide by theta-focalization or restrictive focalization. In her terms, the former, being dependent on argument structure, is subject to a locality condition; restrictive focalization may be discourse-linked and therefore does not obey locality.

Principle A. Recall that *sig* is a syntactically independent prosodically bound word that undergoes covert movement and is thus sensitive to the lexical properties of its governor. As argued, long-distance binding occurs as a last resort when covert incorporation of *sig* into its governor is excluded. In contrast, *se* selects for morphological attachment. Because *se* has affix-like properties, overt movement is necessary. This is why incorporation of *se* is not dependent on the lexical properties of its governor. However, if lexical properties such as [+/−a] are critical for LF (interpretative) phenomena, one should expect these properties to show no variation across languages and, thus, to have an effect in French as well. That this seems to be right is confirmed by the fact that adjunction of *lui-même* gives rise to different interpretations depending on whether the host of *se* is a [+a] or a [−a] verb. If the verb is [+a], adjunction of *lui-même* makes the sentence ambiguous. As shown, sentence (34) carries two readings: one in which the subject is said to have performed the activity without aid (cf. (i)), and another in which the subject is emphasized (cf. (ii)).

(34) Jean se lave/defend/présente lui-même.
    (i) 'Jean washes/defends/introduces himself by himself.'
    (ii) 'Jean washes/defends/introduces HIMSELF.'

In contrast, if the verb is [−a], only a single reading is available. Crucially, the adverbial interpretation accessible in the former case is excluded here.

(35) Jean se respecte/hait/aime lui-même.
    'Jean respects/hates/loves HIMSELF.'

These facts, similar to those previously reported with respect to the adjunction of *selv* to *sig* in Danish, confirm that the distinction between [+a] and [−a] predicates is well founded and give support to the hypothesis that *se* and *sig* undergo overt and covert movement, respectively.

Finally, recall that in French, the adjunction of *même* to the pronoun *lui* is obligatory only when *lui* is an internal argument of a [+DR] predicate (e.g., *être jaloux de* 'be jealous of'). In this case, the string *lui-même* is locally A-bound. The locality restrictions follow if one adopts Reinhart and Reuland's (1991) hypothesis that *même* (their SELF element) is adjoined to the predicate, or if, as suggested by Zribi-Hertz (1992), *même* qualifies as a focus marker, subject to theta-focalization when it is adjoined to *lui* in a [+DR] context.

If my analysis is correct, there is no need for parameters associated with binding domains.[16] Furthermore, the child need not be equipped with a

---

[16]See Hermon (this volume, chapter 4) for a similar view.

specific learning principle such as the Subset Principle (Wexler & Manzini, 1987). Under my proposal, the child is constrained by the principles of Universal Grammar and must rely on positive evidence to determine the morphological properties of the expressions considered here. Once these properties are identified, the distribution of *se* and *sig (selv)* will follow as a matter of course. (The acquisition of *lui-même* will be addressed later.) Note that on the basis of data like those presented here, the child can easily determine whether the reflexive is featureless or not, whether it is a clitic head or an XP, and if it is a clitic, whether it overtly or covertly incorporates into the verb. Because evidence identifying these properties is robust, one expects the acquisition of the binding properties of *se* and *sig (selv)* to be almost instantaneous. That is, the child should exhibit mastery of *se* and *sig (selv)* in comprehension and production studies, from the time he or she is willing (or able) to comply with the requirements of experimental tasks.

In contrast, long-distance *sig* is predicted to be acquired late. At the point at which the child has identified the morphological properties of *sig* and thus knows from Universal Grammar that *sig* moves at LF, he or she still needs evidence that *sig* can be long-distance bound. As shown, long-distance *sig* is rare in the linguistic input, and a pronoun can be used in the same configurations in which *sig* can be long-distance bound. Yet one fact distinguishes these two elements: *Sig* but not *ham* (or *hende*) must occur if the matrix subject is an impersonal NP, such as arbitrary PRO or the expression *man* or *enhver*. This is illustrated in (36):

(36) a. PRO$_i$ at lade [folk tale om sig$_i$/ham$_{*i}$] er kedeligt.
       PRO$_i$ to let people talk about REFL$_i$/him$_{*i}$ is boring
       'To let people talk about one/him$_i$ is boring.'
   b. Man$_i$ bad mig om at invitere sig$_i$/ham$_{*i}$.
       everybody$_i$ asked me to invite REFL$_i$/him$_{*i}$.

Nevertheless, if it is limited to examples like those given here, positive evidence that long-distance *sig* is obligatory in certain cases is rather poor. It is then likely that the child will need time to conclude that long-distance *sig*, even if marginal, is possible in Danish, in spite of the fact that the syntactic apparatus allows nonlocal binding of *sig*.

Let us finally consider how the child can acquire the binding properties of *lui-même*. Determining the morphological properties of the string seems rather unproblematic: Robust evidence is available to identify that the string has φ-features and behaves as a full phrase. However, knowledge of this type is not sufficient to conclude that *lui-même* may exhibit reflexivelike behavior. On the one hand, from a morphological point of view, *lui* and *lui-même* are alike: As analyzed earlier, the pronoun qualifies as a full phrase even when no adjunction of *même* takes place. On the other hand, as already mentioned, the distribution of the nonclitic oblique reflexive *soi* is limited in French, and a pronoun can be interpreted both ways: It can be free, or it can be linked to the subject of its thematic domain, unless the predicate is [+DR]. This is an idiosyncratic property of French that needs to be learned through experience. That learning this rule may not be easy is suggested by the following: The French child is confronted with data that show him that *même* can be used as an adverb ('even') or as an adjective ('same'). Given that *lui* can be free or bound, and *même* has different functions, the child may not be able to conclude right away that when *même* is adjoined to a pronoun in argument position, the pronoun must be A-bound. This leads me to predict that *lui-même* will be acquired later than *se*.

ACQUISITION STUDIES

In this section I report the main results of several interpretation and production studies conducted with native monolingual French- and Danish-speaking children. The design of the experiments, the linguistic materials, and the tasks were the same in both languages. The linguistic materials included a variety of sentence types (sentences with pronouns, passives, other raising constructions, etc.) in addition to constructions with reflexives. For the most part, the results obtained for sentence types other than reflexives will be ignored here. Comprehension was tested by an act-out task and by a sentence-picture matching task. Production was studied by an elicited-production task.[17] In each study, a set of pretest sentences preceded the test sentences. The pretest included both finite and nonfinite clauses, and the sentences were similar to test sentences in structure, but the former contained an R-expression instead of a reflexive. Children who did not succeed on the pretest materials were not included in the samples. For control purposes, a group of adults was incorporated in each study.

French Studies: *Se* and *Lui-même*

In French, six independent studies were conducted. Due to space limitation, I can only outline the results of these studies. For more information, the reader is referred to Jakubowicz (1989, 1990, 1992a).

---

[17]For the sentence-picture matching task, each array presented to the children contained three pictures. Of these, two represented a reflexive action (or event), and the third picture, a nonreflexive action (or event). Children were required to choose the picture that best matched the test sentence; only one picture of the three was the correct choice. The elicited-production task was as follows: The child was presented with an image representing a reflexive action (or event) and was asked to answer a question (for instance: *What is X [name of the character] doing?*).

The results of the first two studies showed that sentences with *se,* including the verbs *laver* 'wash', *brosser* 'brush', *peigner* 'comb', and *moucher* 'wipe his/her nose' were correctly interpreted by all the children, even the youngest, regardless of whether the antecedent of the reflexive was a quantified NP. Thus, 46 children between the ages of 3;0 and 3;5 gave correct responses 93.3% of the time. In the same age group, the mean percentage of correct responses was lower (54.1%) in two other studies in which we presented sentences with *se* including the verbs *viser* 'aim', *éclairer* 'shine the light', *montrer du doigt* 'point', *arroser* 'spray', *verser* 'pour', *servir* 'serve', *acheter* 'buy', and *préparer* 'prepare'. However, correct responses increased at ages 3;6–3;11 (78.1%), and no significant difference emerged between this age group and the older age groups (90% at 4;0–4;5; 95.3% at 5;6–5;11). All things considered,[18] these results suggest that the featureless reflexive is mastered when children are about 3 years old. In contrast, performance on the *lui-même* test sentences was very poor. Although correct responses in the comprehension studies increased with age, the scores obtained by the oldest children tested remained remarkably low (58.7% at 5;6–5;11) when compared to those of adults (100% correct responses). Furthermore, the children's performance on *lui-même* sentences was in general equally poor for [+DR] predicates (e.g., *parler avec* 'talk with', *crier après* 'yell at'), and [–DR] predicates (e.g., *parler de* 'talk about', *rêver de* 'dream about'). The most common error resulted from linking the expression to the matrix subject.

A similar contrast between *se* and *lui-même* was found in the elicited-production studies. The production scores for sentences including *se* was high and uniform across ages: Children aged 3;0–3;5 produced correct sentences with *se* 83.6% of the time and did not differ from the adults, who produced sentences with *se* 100% of the time. As for *lui-même,* unlike the adults, who used this expression productively (in 86.1% of the cases), the children rarely used the complex reflexive (*lui-même* was produced in 5.3% of the cases, data collapsed over age groups).

Taken together, these data indicate that the featureless reflexive is understood and used correctly when children are about 3 years old. In contrast, for *lui-même,* binding errors are very frequent even at age 5 in the comprehension tasks, and the expression is almost unobtainable in the production tasks, as would be the case if *lui-même* were not part of the child's vocabulary. These results confirm the predictions put forth earlier. Let us now turn to the acquisition studies for Danish.

---

[18]It is possible that the lower scores obtained by the youngest children in Studies 3 and 4 (mean age 3;2) are due to the fact that the graphics associated with the test sentences were more complex than in the previous studies. However, because this factor has not been independently tested, this explanation remains tentative.

Danish Studies: *Sig* **and** *Sig Selv*

I report here a short summary of the main results obtained in the acquisition studies conducted with native Danish-speaking children. A detailed presentation of these studies can be found in Olsen (1992); see also Jakubowicz and Olsen (1988). Consider first the comprehension studies.

Comprehension Studies. Three independent studies were conducted. In the first one, an act-out task was used.[19] A sentence-picture matching task, similar in all respects to the one used in the French studies, was used in the second and third studies. The test sentences and number of subjects participating in each study are given in (37)–(39).

(37) *Study 1* (80 children, 10 adults):
     Minnie beder Ida om at pege på/
     sigte på/ lyse på/ sprøjte på sig selv/sig.
     'Minnie asks Ida to point at /
     aim at/ shine (the light) at/ spray at herself/her.'

(38) *Study 2* (100 children, 10 adults):
     Bamse beder Minnie om at pege på/
     sigte på/ lyse på/ sprøjte på sig selv/sig.
     'Teddy bear asks Minnie to point at/
     aim at/ shine/ the light/ at/ spray at herself/him.'

(39) *Study 3* (100 children, 10 adults):
     Bamse beder Anders And om at tænke på/
     drømme på/ tegne / male sig selv/sig.
     'Teddy bear asks Donald Duck to think about/
     dream about/ draw/ paint himself/him.'

As can be seen, each study involved two conditions: test sentences with *sig* and test sentences with *sig selv*. Crucially, all the verbs occurring in the embedded clause were [−a] verbs. Consequently, if the test sentence contains *sig*, the expression must be long-distance bound. Note finally that each experimental condition was repeated eight times in the first study, and four times in the other two studies.

Let us now turn to the results. Consider first Table 5.1, in which the percentages of correct responses for *sig selv* are presented by age.[20] As can be seen, sentences with *sig selv* were correctly interpreted by all the children

---

[19]Note that for this task, the child was the actor in the event described in the embedded clause of the test sentences.

[20]The percentages presented on column 3 of Table 5.1 were reported from figures and thus may not correspond to the exact numbers found by Olsen. The same is true of the percentages in Table 5.3.

TABLE 5.1
Comprehension Studies. *Sig selv:*
Percentages of Correct Responses by Age

	Studies		
Age	1	2	3
3;0–3;5	98.4	77	
3;6–3;11	98.4		
4;0–4;5	96.9	90	84
4;6–4;11			
5;0–5;11		92	94
7;0–7;5	100	93	98
7;6–7;11			
9;0–9;5	100	97	94
9;6–9;11			
Adults	100	100	100

across the three studies. No significant differences among the percentages of correct scores were obtained in any of these studies. Consider now the percentages of correct responses by age for *sig*. These results are presented in Table 5.2. Note that the percentage of correct responses for *sig* obtained by the children younger than 9 years of age was remarkably low in the first two studies. Although a slight evolution occurred with age, the difference in percentages of correct responses between groups below 9 years was not significant. In contrast, a significant difference in correct scores emerged between the four younger age groups and the oldest children in Study 1, $F(1, 75) = 53.1$, $p < .0005$, and between the 7-year-olds and the 9-year-olds in the second study, $F(1, 38) = 15.1$, $p < .001$.

Consider now the third study. The scores obtained by the 4- and 5-year-olds were significantly higher than in Study 2 (4 years: $F(1, 38) = 6.2$, $p < .02$; 5 years: $F(1, 38) = 4.9$, $p < .05$). Yet children below age 9 interpreted *sig* correctly only about 50% of the time. Also, in this study, a significant difference in percentage of correct responses existed between the three first age groups and the oldest children, $F(1, 76) = 4.8$, $p < .05$. Nevertheless, across the three studies, the performance of the 9-year-olds was not faultless when compared to that of adults. At all ages, errors arose in binding the expression to the local antecedent about 95% of the time, on average.

Finally, between-condition comparisons revealed that in each study the children's performance was significantly better on *sig selv* than on *sig*, data

138

JAKUBOWICZ

TABLE 5.2
Comprehension Studies. *Sig*:
Percentages of Correct Responses by Age

Age	Studies		
	1	*2*	*3*
3;0–3;5	7		
3;6–3;11	13.3		
4;0–4;5	21.1	25	48
4;6–4;11			
5;0–5;11		27	53
7;0–7;5	35.1	40	59
7;6–7;11			
9;0–9;5	70	78	74
9;6–9;11			
Adults	100	100	100

collapsed over age groups (Study 1: $F(1, 75) = 542.3$, $p < .0005$; Study 2: $F(1, 95) = 197.5$, $p < .0005$; Study 3: $F(1, 76) = 51.6$, $p < .0005$).

Production Studies. I now report the results of two production studies from Olsen (1992). The purpose of the first one was to elicit sentences with *sig selv* and long-distance *sig*. The purpose of the second study was to elicit sentences with either *sig selv* or locally bound *sig*. In the first study, in order to elicit *sig selv*, testers presented the children with two different types of questions, (40) and (41), and each was repeated twice. Because of space limitation, the results for question type (41) are not presented here.

(40) Hvad laver X?
'What is X doing?'

(41) Hvem er det X peger på?
'Who is X pointing at?'

In order to elicit sentences with long-distance *sig*, testers asked the child to answer the following question, which was repeated four times.

(42) Hvad er det X beder Y om at gøre?
'What is X asking Y to do?'

The actions depicted in the pictures corresponded to the [–a] verbs used in the Comprehension Studies 1 and 2. Self-oriented actions were coupled with the question types (40) and (41); non-self-oriented actions, with the question type (42). Consider now Table 5.3, in which the percentages of sentences produced with *sig selv* or long-distance *sig* are presented by age. Table 5.3 shows that the mean percentage of sentences with *sig selv* was high and uniform across ages. In contrast, the percentages of sentences with *sig* were remarkably low. As can be seen, 9-year-olds behaved in this respect as the adults did, producing sentences with *sig* about 30% of the time. This result is thus similar to the one obtained in the sentence completion task presented earlier; recall that adults used long-distance *sig* no more than 35% of the time when the verb of the embedded clause was [–a]. Instead of long-distance *sig*, adults either produced a pronoun (40% of the time), or used the name of the matrix subject (28% of the time). Similar types of responses were given by the children: On average, a pronoun was produced about 60% of the time, and the name of the matrix subject, about 15% of the time. Other types of responses consisted of a verb that was sometimes followed by a prepositional object.

Let us now turn to the second study in which children of three age groups participated: eight 3-year-olds (mean age: 3;6), six 4-year-olds (mean age: 4;7) and six 5-year-olds (mean age: 5;3). Each subject was presented with 12 pictures in which reflexive or nonreflexive actions were represented. The verbs corresponding to the six reflexive scenes were all [+a] verbs admitting locally bound *sig* or *sig selv*. Children were asked to answer question type (40) (*What is X doing?*). The test question was repeated six times, once for each picture representing a self-oriented action.

An important result of this study was that all 20 children used locally bound *sig* productively. Percentages of sentences with *sig* are shown by verb:

(43) *tørre*: 98%   *barbare*: 85%   *stikke*: 74%
      'dry'   'shave'   'prick'
      gemme: 63%   *rede*: 60%   *vaske*: 50%
      'hide'   'comb'   'wash'

Although percentages of sentences with *sig* varied according to the verb, no child in this study used *sig selv*. When children did not use *sig*, particularly with the verbs *rede* and *vaske*, they produced sentences with the possessive reflexive or described the scene without a reflexive (see Olsen, 1992).

Notice now that children used locally bound *sig* productively. Yet none of the children produced *sig* when they were presented with pictures of self-oriented actions depicting [–a] predicates and they were asked to respond to the question types (40) and (41). This suggests that children know that [–a] verbs do not allow locally bound *sig*; they also may know

TABLE 5.3
Elicited-Production Studies.
Percentages of Sentencies with Sig Selv and Sig by Age

	Sentences	
Age	Sig Selv	Sig
3;0–3;11	83	5
4;0–4;11	90	0
5;0–5;11	88	2
7;0–7;11	84	10
9;0–9;11	100	30
Adults	100	38

that *sig* is a clitic-like element and thus cannot be used to answer a question such as (41).

To summarize: The data presented here show that *sig selv* and locally bound *sig* are understood and used correctly when children are about 3 years old. In contrast, long-distance *sig* is incorrectly interpreted as locally bound in the comprehension task. This error is made frequently by children below age 9, and to a lesser extent by the oldest children. However, such an error does not occur in the production task, when children are presented with a reflexive action involving a [−a] verb. If children thought that *sig* could always be locally bound, one would expect them to produce it across the board. But this does not happen. The fact that long-distance *sig* is almost never produced by children younger than age 9, and very rarely produced by the oldest children, cannot be invoked to explain why children do not use *sig* locally bound when local binding is disallowed. As we have seen, children use *sig* correctly with [+a] verbs that allow the expression to be locally bound. One must then conclude that children as young as 3 years old know the core properties of *sig*: They know that the expression is licensed by incorporation into a [+a] verb and disallowed by a [−a] verb. If so, the high number of binding errors made by the children below 9 years in the comprehension task is not attributable to lack of grammatical knowledge. As indicated earlier, subjects participating in these studies were tested on other sentence types, in particular, on sentences including a pronoun. As reported by Olsen (1992), although the 3- to 5-year-olds did less well than the 7-year-old children, the score for correct responses on pronouns obtained by the younger children nevertheless reached about 80% and differed significantly from their score on long-distance *sig*. Thus, binding errors on long-distance *sig* sentences cannot be due to their alleged incompetence with pronouns, as suggested by Hyams and Sigur-jónsdóttir (1990). Instead, these errors show that children did not confuse the featureless reflexive with a pronoun. When presented with a long-distance *sig* sentence and asked by the experimenter to provide a response, they bound the expression locally rather than treating it as a pronoun, perhaps in order to fulfill the task requirement. To assume that *sig* can be long-distance bound, the child will need evidence. However, as argued earlier, long-distance *sig* results from a last resort operation; as confirmed by the adults' performance on the elicited-production study, long-distance binding is rare in Danish. A reasonable conclusion would then be that young children have little opportunity to confirm that *sig* can be long-distance bound at all.

Final Comment

The French and Danish data reported here indicate that *se* and *sig (selv)* are acquired almost instantaneously. 3-year-olds understand and use these expressions correctly. If adequate procedures to test 2-year-olds were available, I would expect children of this age to be as successful as the 3-year-old children.

Such a result, expected under the analysis put forth here, supports the hypothesis that Universal Grammar principles operate on the inductions that children make. Namely, these constraints guide the child into determining the morphological properties of the reflexives available in the language to which he or she is exposed. Once these properties are established, binding properties are automatically derived by the syntactic principles to which the different expressions are subject. If the child were not constrained by such principles, it would be difficult to understand how the 3-year-old child could know, for instance, that *sig* cannot be used to answer a question. Moreover, it would be difficult to explain how that child could know that *sig* can be locally bound despite evidence indicating that, in an important number of cases ([–a] predicates), it is *sig selv* and not *sig* that occurs locally bound. The fact that long-distance *sig* is almost unobtainable from young children has been explained not in terms of lack of grammatical knowledge, but in terms of the absence or weakness of confirming input. However, such an explanation may not fully explain why *lui-même* seems not to be part of the French child's vocabulary. In argument position, *lui-même* may be relatively uncommon in the linguistic input (we have seen that the expression is obligatory in the context of [+DR] predicates only). But as an NP adjunct, *lui-même* is commonly used (see (44)).[21]

(44) Jean lui-même apportera les boissons.
'Jean himself will bring the drinks.'

Yet the expression does not seem to be part of the child's vocabulary, as suggested by the results of the production studies we carried out. Although

---

[21]See Zribi-Hertz (1990b) for an analysis of *lui-même* in adjunct position.

I expected French children to acquire *lui-même* later than *se*, the fact that their performance on this expression remains so poor even at the age of 5;8 is somewhat puzzling. Further research is necessary to understand when and how the complex French reflexive is acquired.

ACKNOWLEDGMENTS

I am especially indebted to A. Zribi-Hertz for valuable remarks and suggestions throughout the writing of this chapter. I would also like to acknowledge J. Emonds, J. Guéron, and L. Nash for helpful comments on Jakubowicz (1992b); G. Hermon for an insightful discussion of an earlier version of this paper; C. Rigaut for the analysis of the production data obtained in the French studies; and W. Isham for helping me to express my ideas in English. Parts of the French material included here were presented at the NELS 21 Conference, held at Montreal, October 1990; parts of the Danish data were presented at the 1988 Boston University Conference on Language Development and at the 1989 Paris Conference on Structure de la Phrase et Théorie du Liage, in collaboration with L. Olsen. The analysis and conclusions expressed in this chapter are solely my responsibility.

REFERENCES

Abney, S. E. (1987). *The English noun phrase in its sentential aspect.* Unpublished doctoral dissertation, MIT, Cambridge, MA.

Anderson, M. (1979). *Noun phrase structure.* Unpublished doctoral dissertation, MIT, Cambridge, MA.

Baker, M. (1988). *Incorporation: A theory of grammatical function changing.* Chicago, IL: University of Chicago Press.

Burzio, L. (1989). On the morphology of reflexives and impersonals. In *Proceedings of LSRL XIX.* Amsterdam: John Benjamins.

Burzio, L. (1991). The morphological basis of anaphora. *Journal of Linguistics, 27.*

Bok-Bennema, R. (1984). On marked pronominal anaphors and Eskimo-pro. In J. Gueron, H. Obenauer, & J. Y. Pollock (Eds.), *Grammatical representation.* Dordrecht: Foris.

Chomsky, N. (1981). *Lectures on government and binding.* Dordrecht: Foris.

Chomsky, N. (1986). *Knowledge of language: Its nature, origin and use.* New York: Praeger.

Chomsky, N. (1989). Some notes on economy of derivation and representation. *MIT Working Papers,* 10.

Chomsky, N. (1992). A minimalist program for linguistic theory. *MIT Occasional Papers in Linguistics, 1.*

Cole, P., Hermon, G., & Sung, L. (1990). Principles and parameters of long-distance reflexives. *Linguistic Inquiry, 21,* 1–22.

Delsing, L. O. (1988). The Scandinavian noun phrase. *Working Papers in Scandinavian Syntax, 42.*

Everaert, M. (1991). Contextual determination of the anaphor/pronominal distinction. In J. Koster & E. Reuland (Eds.), *Long distance anaphora*. Cambridge, MA: Cambridge University Press.

Haider, H., & Prinzhorn, M. (Eds.). (1985). *Verb second phenomena in the germanic languages.* Dordrecht: Foris.

Halpern, A. L. (1992). *Topics in the placement and morphology of clitics.* Unpublished doctoral dissertation, Stanford University, CA.

Hellan, L. (1988). *Anaphora in Norwegian and the theory of grammar.* Dordrecht: Foris.

Hestvik, A. (1989). Against the notion 'Governing Category.' Unpublished manuscript, Brandeis University, MA.

Hestvik, A. (1990). *LF movement of pronominals.* Paper presented at NELS 20, GLSA, University of Massachusetts, Amherst.

Holmberg, A., & Platzack, C. (1989). On the role of inflection in Scandinavian syntax. *Working Papers in Scandinavian Syntax, 43.*

Hyams, N., & Sigurjjonsddottir, S. (1990). The development of 'long distance anaphora': A cross-linguistic comparison. *Language Acquisition, 1,* 57–93.

Jakubowicz, C. (1989). Maturation or invariance of Universal Grammar principles in language acquisition. *Probus, 1,* 283–340.

Jakubowicz, C. (1990). *Binding principles and acquisition facts revisited.* Paper presented at NELS 21, University of Quebec, Montreal.

Jakubowicz, C. (1992a). Linguistic theory and language acquisition facts: Reformulation, maturation or invariance of binding principles. In E. Reuland & W. Abraham (Eds.), *Knowledge and language: Issues in representation and acquisition.* Dordrecht: Kluwer.

Jakubowicz, C. (1992b). *Sig* en Danois: Syntaxe et acquisition. In H. G. Obenauer & A. Zribi-Hertz (Eds.), *Théorie du liage et structure de la phrase.* Presses Universitaires de Vincennes.

Jakubowicz, C., & Olsen, L. (1988). *Reflexive anaphors and pronouns in Danish: Syntax and acquisition.* Paper presented at the 13th Annual Boston University Conference on Language Development, Boston, MA.

Katada, F. (1991). The LF representation of anaphors. *Linguistic Inquiry, 22,* 287–313.

Kayne, R. (1975). *French syntax: The transformational cycle.* Cambridge, MA: MIT Press.

Kayne, R. (1991). Romance clitics, verb movement and PRO. *Linguistic Inquiry, 22,* 647–686.

Koopman, H. (1987). *On the absence of case chains in Bambara.* Unpublished manuscript, UCLA.

Koster, J. (1978). *Domains and Dynasties.* Dordrecht: Foris.

Maegaard, B., & Ruus, H. (1981a). *Hyppige Ord i Danske Romaner.* København: Gyldendal.

Maegaard, B., & Ruus, H. (1981b). *Hyppige Ord i Danske Børnebøger.* København: Gyldendal.

Muysken, P. (1983). Parametrizing the notion head. *The Journal of Linguistic Research, 2,* 57–76.

Olsen, L. (1992). *Théorie linguistique et acquisition du langage. Etude contrastive des relations anaphoriques, syntaxe danoise et syntaxe comparée.* Universitée de Paris 8: Thèse.

Pica, P. (1987). On the nature of the reflexivization cycle. *Proceedings of NELS 17, GLSA, University of Massachusetts, Amherst.*

Platzack, Ch. (1986). The structure of infinitival clauses in Danish and Swedish. In O. Dahl & A. Holmberg (Eds.), *Scandinavian syntax* (pp. 123–137). University of Stockholm: Institute of Linguistics.

Pollock, J. Y. (1989). Verb movement, Universal Grammar, and the structure of IP. *Linguistic Inquiry, 20,* 365–424.

Reinhart, T., & Reuland, E. (1991). Anaphors and logophors: An argument structure perspective. In J. Koster & E. Reuland (Eds.), *Long-distance anaphora*. Cambridge, MA: Cambridge University Press.

Reinholtz, C. (1989). V-2 in mainland Scandinavian: Finite verb movement to AGR. *Working Papers in Scandinavian Syntax, 44.*

Rizzi, L. (1990). *Relativized minimality.* Cambridge, MA: MIT Press.

Ronat, M. (1982). Une solution pour un apparent contre-exemple à la théorie du liage. *Linguisticae Investigationes, VI*(1), 189–196.

Rouveret, A. (1991). Functional categories and agreement. *The Linguistic Review, 8,* 353–387.

Stefanini, J. (1962). *La voix pronominale en ancien et en moyen français.* Aix en Provence: Publication des Annales de la Faculté des Lettres.

Tenny, C. (1987). *Grammaticalizing aspect and affectedness.* Unpublished doctoral dissertation, Cambridge, MA: MIT.

Vikner, S. (1985). Parameters of binder and of binding category in Danish. *Working Papers in Scandinavian Syntax, 23.*

Wexler, K., & Manzini, M. R. (1987). Parameters and learnability in binding theory. In T. Roeper & E. Williams (Eds.), *Parameter setting.* Dordrecht: Reidel.

Yang, D. W. (1983). The extended binding theory of anaphora. *Language Research, 19,* 169–192.

Zribi-Hertz, A. (1980). Coréférence et pronoms réflechis: Notes sur le contraste *lui/lui-même* en français. *Linguisticae Investigationes, IV, 1,* 131–179.

Zribi-Hertz, A. (1989). Anaphor binding and narrative point of view: English reflexive pronouns in sentence and discourse. *Language, 65,* 4.

Zribi-Hertz, A. (1990a). *Lui-même* argument et le concept de pronom A. *Langages, 97,* 100–127.

Zribi-Hertz, A. (1990b). *NP* lui-même, *Recherches Linguistiques.* Klincksieck: Université de Metz.

Zribi-Hertz, A. (1992). Emphatic possessives in English and their anaphoric properties. Unpublished manuscript, Université de Paris 8.

Zubizarreta, M. L. (1987). *Levels of Representation in the lexicon and in the syntax.* Dordrecht: Foris.

CHAPTER SIX

When Is an Anaphor
Not an Anaphor?

Reiko Mazuka
Duke University

Barbara Lust
Cornell University

Cross-linguistic application of the Binding Theory (henceforth BT), that component of Universal Grammar that is concerned with anaphora, appears to require the assumption stated in (1).

(1) In each language, lexical items must be defined as *anaphors, pronouns,* or *R-expressions* independently and contrastively.

Otherwise it is not clear how BT Principles A, B, and C, as summarized in (2), can be instantiated (e.g., Chomsky, 1986).

(2) A: An anaphor is locally bound.
B: A pronoun is locally free.
C: An R-expression is free (everywhere).

In this chapter, we first show that linguistic evidence suggests that the Japanese lexical item *zibun* presents a problem for (1). We then present results from three studies of first language acquisition of Japanese that converge with these linguistic results.

We relate these results to a recent proposal for a particular interpretation of the BT, a definitional interpretation (Lust, Mazuka, Martohardjono, & Yoon, 1989). On this interpretation, it is not necessary to make the assumption in (1). We assume that the Binding Theory and Universal Grammar are linked to a theory of language acquisition, as well as to cross-linguistic variation with regard to the BT. On the definitional interpretation, minus features [–pronoun] or [–anaphor] as well as positive features [+anaphor] and [+pronoun] are necessary to lexical categorization by the BT in a language, and in acquisition. Lexical categorization (as in (1)) is not assumed to be predetermined. A uniform restrictive definition of locality is given by UG, and this provides the structure-dependent foundation by which the child achieves lexical categorization in keeping with the [+] and [–] BT features. (This theory shares fundamental properties of the functional determination theory of Bouchard, 1984.)

One implication of this proposal is that cross-linguistic variation with regard to the BT may include cases where the BT is not lexicalized.

THE LINGUISTIC FACTS

Japanese *zibun* has frequently been considered an anaphor comparable to the English reflexive *himself.* Semantically, *zibun* shares with the English reflexive a reference to *self.* However, analyses of *zibun* have motivated linguists to argue alternatively that *zibun* is a bound pronoun (e.g., Fukui, 1984; Ueda, 1984), a logophor (Clements, 1975), a variable (Akmajian & Kitagawa, 1976), both an anaphor and a logophor (Kuno, 1972; cf. Kuno, 1986), both an anaphor and a pronoun (Sportiche, 1986), a name in sentence grammar but a discourse anaphor (Oshima, 1986), or a noun (Tokieda, 1950). More recently, it has been argued that *zibun* is an operator anaphor (Katada, 1991) or a distributor like the *each* of each other (Abe, 1991).

The essential problem is that *zibun* appears to fail all the linguistic tests that would be criterial for the assignment of the feature [+anaphor], as summarized in (3).

(3) *Anaphor:* A nominal element with the feature [+anaphor]

    Criteria: 1. grammatical antecedent
                 2. lack of intrinsic reference
                 3. locally bound

                    a. *bound* = requires c-commanding antecedent
                    b. *local* = in its governing category[1]

We survey the facts with regard to each of these criteria.

---

[1]The exact definition of *locality* will not be central to our argument in this chapter (cf. Harbert, in press; Kapur et al., 1993; Lust et al., 1989). For our purposes here, it suffices that locality concerns a single clause or simplex S. Thus, we may assume either a definition like Bouchard's (1984) where the local domain is the minimal maximal projection containing the anaphor or pronoun, or a definition involving the notion of governing category.

Requirement for Grammatical Antecedent and Lack of Intrinsic Reference

Example (4) shows that *zibun* may occur without a grammatical antecedent and refer to the speaker.

(4) a. Muri   o   site, karada o   kowasita zibun o
overwork ACC did body   ACC broke   self   ACC
nasakenai to   omou.
pitiful   COMP think
I think of myself as pitiful because I overworked myself and fell ill.
'I didn't have the luxury, in thinking about myself hurriedly wolfing down animal feed as I was—to consider myself stripped of my dignity or pathetic, to feel that what I was eating wasn't fit for a human being.'

b. Zibun-no uchi-ga   sugu soko-ni   arimasu.
self-GEN house-NOM right there-LOC there is
'My house is right there.'

(5) shows that when an antecedent of *zibun* is available, it may occur not sentence-internally, but in discourse.

(5) *Discourse antecedent:*
a. A: Dareka-ga John$_i$-no kawari-ni   soko-ni itta no desu ka?
someone-NOM GEN substitute to there to went   Q
'Did someone go there in place of John$_i$?'
B: Iie, zibun$_i$-ga itta no   desu.
No, self-NOM went NOMINALIZER be
'No, SELF$_i$ went there.'

(Fukui, 1984)

b. A: Syoogakukin moraenakatta   n   desutte?
fellowship   was-unable-to-receive NOMINALIZER be isn't-it
Zannen desita nee.
regret   was I-tell-you
'I heard that you$_i$ couldn't get the fellowship. It was too bad.'
B: Ee, demo zibun$_i$-no chikara-ga tainakatta   sei desu kara.
yes, but   self-GEN ability-NOM insufficient due be because
'No, but it's because I$_i$ wasn't good enough for it.'

(6) shows that *zibun* can occur without a grammatical antecedent even when there is an alternative c-commanding antecedent available in the sentence. Syntactic antecedence requirements are lifted for *zibun*, not only in the long-distance domain but also in the local domain.

(6) a. Masao$_i$-wa   dooyoo sita. Tsuma$_j$-ga zibun$_i$-o uragitte
            TOP upset   was wife-NOM self-ACC betraying
        ita   koto-o   sitte   simatta   kara.
        was matter-ACC knowing ended-up because
        'Masao$_i$ was upset. Because he$_i$ came to realize that his$_i$ wife was
        betraying him$_i$.'
    b. Butai-ni agatta   Yoko$_i$-wa   kyuu-ni   kintyoo sita.
        stage-to appeared Yoko-TOP suddenly nervous
        'Yoko became nervous suddenly when she came out on stage.'
        Titioya$_j$-ga   saizenretsu-de   zibun$_i$-o miteita noda.
        Father-NOM in the front row self-ACC watching
        'Father was watching her$_i$ from the front row.'

Thus *zibun* can occur without a grammatical antecedent and can assign
intrinsic reference.

No Requirement for C-Commanding Antecedent

The contrast between (7a) and (7b) suggests that *zibun* does require a
c-commanding antecedent (Fukui, 1984).

(7) *C-commanding relationship:*
    a. Zibun$_i$-ga   ima gesyuku site iru ie ni
            NOM now boarding-be   house at
        Hirosi$_i$-wa   moo   gonen mo   sunde iru.
        TOP already 5-yrs to-the-extent living-be
        'In the house where he$_i$ boards now, Hirosi$_i$ has been living for
        as long as five years.'
    b. *Hirosi$_i$-ga   ima gesyuku site iru ie ni
            NOM   now boarding-be   house at
        zibun$_i$-wa   moo   gonen mo   sunde iru.
        TOP already 5-yrs to-the-extent living-be
        'In the house where Hirosi$_i$ boards now, he$_i$ has been living for
        as long as five years.'

(Fukui, 1984)

However, there are productive counterarguments to this claim. None of the
examples (4), (5), and (6) have c-commanding antecedents (they do not have
a sentence-internal antecedent). Oshima (1986) gave the examples in (8).

(8) *No c-commanding relationship:*
    a. Zibun$_i$-ga Mary-ni karakawareta koto-ga John$_i$-o
            NOM   by teased   matter-NOM ACC
        zetuboo-e oiyatta.
        despair to drove
        'That he$_i$ was made fun of by Mary drove John$_i$ to despair.'

(Oshima, 1986)

    b. Taroo$_i$-wa   inu-o   oikaketa sosite zibun$_i$ wa Ziroo$_j$-ni
       TOP dog-ACC chased   and   self$_i$-TOP   by
     oikakerareta.
     be-chased
     'Taroo$_i$ chased the dog and he$_i$ was chased by Ziroo.'
                             (Oshima, 1986, after Inoue, 1976)

It has also been proposed that *zibun* requires a subject antecedent when it does have a grammatical antecedent, as in (9). This would be in general accord with a c-command requirement. However, as the examples in (10) show, there are also counterexamples to this claim. *Zibun* may take nonsubject antecedents. (See also Kitagawa, 1986, for examples of *zibun* with split antecedents that include nonsubjects.)

  (9) *Subject antecedent:*
     a. John$_i$-ga Bill$_j$-ni zibun$_{i,*j}$-no koto-o   hanasita.
       NOM   to self-GEN matter-ACC talked
       'John$_i$ talked to Bill$_j$ about himself$_{i,j}$.'
     b. John$_i$-ga Mary$_j$-o zibun$_{i,*j}$-no ie   de korosita.
       NOM   ACC self-GEN house at killed
       'John killed Mary in his house.'
     c. Mary$_i$-ga John$_j$-ni zibun$_{i,*j}$-no ie   de korosareta.
       NOM   by self-GEN house at be-killed
       'Mary was killed by John in her house.'
                             (Kuno, 1972)

  (10) *Nonsubject antecedent:*
     a. Sono keiken-wa Mary$_i$-ni zibun$_i$-ga baka de aru
       that experience-TOP to   NOM fool be
      koto-o osieta.
      that-ACC taught
      'That experience taught Mary that she was a fool.'
                             (Kuno, 1972)
     b. Zibun$_i$-no zidoosya-ga kosyoo-sita John$_i$-o watasi$_j$-no
       GEN car-NOM   broke-down   ACC I-GEN
      zidoosya ni noseta.
      car   on load
      'I$_j$ gave a ride in my car to John$_i$, whose (self's$_i$) car broke down.'
           (Oshima, 1986, after Akmajian & Kitagawa, 1976)

No Locality Requirement

It is well known that *zibun* occurs in long-distance domains. For example, a *zibun* subject marked by *ga* can occur in various types of subordinate clauses with main clause antecedents, as in (11a–c). *Zibun* thus does not obey the locality criterion for an anaphor according to BT Principle A, in the way that the English reflexive does.[2]

(11) *Long-distance:*
   a. Zibun$_i$-ga   minikui node Mitiko$_i$-wa   kanasinde iru.
      NOM ugly   because   TOP sad   be
      'Because she$_i$ is ugly, Mitiko$_i$ is sad.'
                                                              (Akatsuka, 1972)
   b. Zibun$_i$-ga   nusunda to Sarah$_j$-ni iwareta to John$_i$-ga omotta.
      NOM stole that   by be-said that   NOM thought
      'John thought that Sarah said that he stole.'
                                                              (Akatsuka, 1972)
   c. John$_i$-wa zibun$_i$-ga   toosensuru koto-o   kitaisite   iru.
      TOP   NOM be-elected that-ACC expecting be
      'John$_i$ is expecting that he$_i$ will be elected.'[3]
                                                              (Kuno, 1972)

Examples (11d–f) show other forms of long-distance coindexing with *zibun*.

   d. John$_i$-wa Bill-ga zibun$_i$-o   mita toki   hon-o   yonde ita.
      TOP   NOM   ACC   saw when book-ACC reading was
      'John was reading a book when Bill saw self.'
                                                              (Kuroda, 1965)
   e. Satoo$_i$-wa Tanaka$_j$-ga Hara$_k$-ga zibun$_{i,j,k}$-no ie-   de korosareta
      TOP   NOM   NOM   GEN house at be-killed
      koto-o   Nakaura-ni hanasite simatte   no
      matter-ACC   to told   ending-up NOMINALIZER
      o   sitta
      ACC knew
      'Satoo$_i$ found out that Tanaka$_j$ had already told Nakaura that Hara$_k$ was killed in his$_{i,j,k}$ house.'
                                                              (Akatsuka, 1972)
   f. John$_i$-ga Bill$_j$-ga zibun$_{i,j}$-o hihan   sita to   omotteiru (koto).
      NOM   NOM self-ACC criticize did COMP be-thinking
      'John$_i$ thinks that Bill$_j$ criticized him$_{i,j}$.'
                                                              (Fukui, 1984)

It is true that *zibun* can sometimes occur in an object position and be coindexed with a subject in simplex sentences like (12a) and (12b), the paradigmatic anaphor domain or core anaphor domain for an English

---

[2]In these domains, as in several of the other domains we discussed earlier, the distribution of a Japanese lexical pronoun such as *kare* or *boku* overlaps with that of *zibun*.

[3](11c) is ambiguous; it allows more than one possible bracketing.

reflexive (e.g., *his/herself*). Here the reflexive may have a potential binder, which is the immediately c-commanding subject of the simplex S. However, as Akatsuka (1972) pointed out, this is a rather marked construction in Japanese, and in many cases, it is outright ungrammatical or highly unacceptable. Often, opinions about these sentences differ among Japanese speakers. For example, Oshima (1979) presented sentences such as (12a–c) as grammatical. However, for some, (12c) is much less acceptable than (12a) and (12b) (cf. Harbert, in press).

(12) a. John$_i$-wa zibun$_i$-o   bengo sita.
John-TOP zibun-ACC defended
'John$_i$ defended himself$_i$.'

(Oshima, 1979)

b. John$_i$-wa zibun$_i$-o   semeta.
John-TOP zibun-ACC blamed
'John$_i$ blamed himself$_i$.'

(Oshima, 1979)

c. John$_i$-wa zibun$_i$-o   mita.
John-TOP zibun-ACC saw
'John saw himself.'
(acceptable for Oshima, ? for some)

(Oshima, 1979)

d. *Tanaka$_i$-wa konboo-de zibun$_i$-o   nagutta.
Tanaka-TOP stick-with zibun-ACC hit
'Tanaka hit himself with a stick.'

(Akatsuka, 1972)

e. *John$_i$-wa zibun$_i$-o   aratta.
John-TOP zibun-ACC washed
'John washed himself.'

(Oshima, 1979)

Akatsuka proposed that some verbs obey an Unlike-NP constraint. With verbs like *arau* 'wash' and *naguru* 'hit', Akatsuka proposed that *zibun* is not acceptable in the object position. This cannot be attributed simply to the semantics of the verb because, as the acceptability of the English translation of (12d) and (12e) indicates, there is nothing in the meaning of those actions (i.e., washing and hitting) that prevents the referent of self from being the patient of the action. (See also Kitagawa, 1986.) Takezawa (1989, 1991) described this constraint in terms of (13).

(13) *Zibun* cannot be governed by V [+change].

Clearly, these facts indicate that the paradigmatic position for a core anaphor in English (i.e., one involving local binding) is not the paradigmatic position for the Japanese *zibun*.

Emphatic *Zibun*

Zibun has a productive emphatic use. In these cases, *zibun* is in a nonargument position and may be considered to be outside the range of the Binding Theory. For example, in (13), the occurrences of *zibun-de* would translate naturally as "by (him)self." Presumably *zibun-de* here is in an adjunct position. The nominal arguments modified by these constructions may be either lexical or null.

(14) *Emphatic zibun:*
    a. 84-sai-no   kooreesya-ga   *zibun-de* kuruma-o
       84 year-old-GEN aged person-NOM self-by   car-ACC
       unten-site   koosoku-dooro-o 150-kiro de tobasite,
       drive doing freeway-ACC   150-km/h at driving-fast
       suketti   ni iku no   ga   nikka
       sketching to go NOMINALIZER NOM daily-schedule
       datta to   itte   mo   dare mo sinzinai-   daroo.
       was COMP saying even nobody not-believe probably
       'If I told you that an 84-year-old man would go out to sketch
       every day, and drive himself there in his own car at 90 miles an
       hour, you probably wouldn't believe me.'
                               (Asahi Shinbun, October 15, 1986)
    b. Hironomiya-ga   zibun-de kimete watakushi-domo-ni
       Prince Hiro-NOM self-by   decide we-DAT
       syookai-site kureru koto ni naru   to   omoimasu to
       introduce   give   matter to become COMP think   COMP
       katarareta.
       stated-(honorific)
       '(Princess Michiko) said, "I think it will turn out that Prince Hiro
       will decide by himself and introduce (his future wife) to us." '
    (Asahi Shinbun, October 26, 1986, interview with Princess Michiko)

The lexical homonymy between an emphatic and a reflexive is a property of many languages, including English, as in *John cleaned up his office (by) himself* (e.g., Sinhalese *me*, Tamil *taan*, Hindi *apna*, Chinese *ziji*, Malayalam *taan*).

Conclusions Regarding Linguistic Evidence

Zibun thus does not require a grammatical antecedent, can have intrinsic reference, and is not locally bound, failing all of the criteria in (3) for the assignment of a Binding Theory [+anaphoric] feature. The possibility of intrinsic reference and absence of syntactic binding characterizes *zibun* in both local and long-distance domains. In fact, occurrence of *zibun* is highly restricted in the local core anaphor domains.

The distribution of *zibun* in long-distance domains of free anaphora as in (11), and the deicticlike properties illustrated in (5), might suggest that the proper lexical assignment for *zibun* is, or includes, [+pronoun]. However, because *zibun* may occur locally in some cases, as in (12), it is clear that it is not a Binding Theory pronoun, as is the English pronoun. *Zibun* does not obey Principle B consistently (cf. Kitagawa, 1986).

We return to these issues later in this chapter.

FIRST LANGUAGE ACQUISITION OF JAPANESE

We may ask, then, what is *zibun* in Japanese grammar? How does it relate to UG? Correspondingly, what is the Japanese child's initial (or early) hypothesis regarding the lexical item *zibun*? If we assume that the child is trying to assign the features [+anaphor] or [+pronoun] in order to categorize the lexicon (as in Lust et al., 1989), then on the basis of induction alone, the Japanese child may entertain any or all hypotheses. For example, the Japanese child could hypothesize that the lexical item *zibun* is [+anaphor] or [+pronoun], or [+anaphor] and [+pronoun]. Presumably, then, *zibun* could occur anywhere.

If the child consults the BT in a definitional manner, as hypothesized in Lust et al. (1989), then the linguistic evidence in Japanese should undermine, in fact negate, the possible categorization of *zibun* as either BT anaphor or BT pronoun. The data would not allow possible assignment of any negative features, either [−anaphor] or [−pronoun]. The Japanese child could thus conclude that these BT features are not relevant.

On the other hand, given a theory of UG as a model of the initial state, and the assumption in (1), we might expect the child's early hypotheses to be constrained by this theory in different ways. For example, the child could assume a restrictive hypothesis by which he or she assumed all relevant lexical items were anaphors unless proven otherwise on the basis of positive evidence.

Investigation of the acquisition of Japanese *zibun* then may shed light on the interpretation of the Binding Theory as a module of UG. In order to approach these issues, we first inquired whether the Japanese child's initial (or early) hypothesis treated the lexical item *zibun* as BT anaphor or BT pronoun. More specifically, we first tested the two hypotheses stated in (15) regarding the syntactic distribution of *zibun*.

(15) a. If the Japanese lexical item *zibun* is determined by UG to be a BT anaphor, then it should be acceptable by the child in a paradigmatic core anaphor position. Alternatively, if it is not con-

sidered an anaphor, then it should be resisted in those positions in Japanese acquisition.

b. If the Japanese lexical item *zibun* is determined by UG to be a BT pronoun, then it should be acceptable in a paradigmatic pronoun position. Alternatively, if it is not considered a BT pronoun, it should be resisted in those positions in Japanese. For our purposes here, we will assume these pronoun positions to be nonlocal or long-distant (cf. Bouchard, 1984; Lust et al., 1989, for discussion).

Design of Acquisition Studies

In this chapter, we report selected results from three experiments with Japanese children. We tested the Japanese children's production of complex sentences that contained *zibun* or an empty nominal category *pro* in various syntactic environments.

Materials

Study 1: Core Anaphor Domain. In this study, we tested *zibun* in the three constructions summarized in Appendix A. This design contrasts *zibun* in core anaphor position (which structurally allows *zibun* in an object A-position to be locally bound), that is, Type 1 in Appendix A, to two A′ occurrences of *zibun*, that is, Type 2, *zibun-no* (possessive, in PP adjunct), and Type 3, *zibun-de* (emphatic adjunct). Type 1 is a marked construction in adult judgments, as discussed earlier.[4] There are four sentences of this type, and four different verbs (*arau* 'wash', *huku* 'dry', *miru* 'see', *mitsukeru* 'find'). Two of the verbs used in this construction in our study (*arau* 'wash' and *huku* 'dry') are those that have been claimed to obey the Unlike-NP constraint. If the children's initial hypothesis is that *zibun* is an anaphor, then they should accept it in this paradigmatic core anaphor domain. If children are not initially sensitive to the Unlike-NP constraint (which is language-specific and lexically determined and therefore must require learning), then they should accept all sentences equally. If children accept *zibun* in this core anaphor position in principle yet are sensitive to the lexicon, they may resist the sentences with *arau* 'wash' and *huku* 'dry', although they accept those with *miru* 'see' and *mitsukeru* 'find'.

In the second construction, *zibun* is a possessive, modifying the object NP (i.e., (3) and (4) in Appendix A). This possessive would be a lexical pronoun in English (although in languages that have possessive reflexive forms, such as Hindi, the possessive would be a reflexive pronoun; cf.

---

[1] As discussed earlier, only a very restricted set of verbs, such as *hinansuru* 'criticize', *kaerimiru* 'reflect', can create natural simplex sentences with *zibun* in object position, and those verbs are not in a typical child's vocabulary (Akatsuka, 1972; Oshima, 1986).

Harbert, in press). In the third construction, (5) and (6) in Appendix A, *zibun* is placed in emphatic adjunct position.

All of the sentences involve left-branching complex sentences with adverbial subordinate clauses marked by *toki* 'when'. In each of the three structures, *zibun* is positioned in either the subordinate (first) clause or the main (second) clause. Sentences that contain *zibun* in the main clause are called *Forward* sentences, and those with *zibun* in the subordinate clause are called *Backward*.[5] There are 2 sentences of each type, making a total of 12 sentences. As the basic clause structure of the Japanese sentences is SOV, sentence Types 2 and 3 have an extra animate NP in the stimuli sentence.

Study 2: Pronoun Domain.[6] In Study 2, we tested *zibun* in several types of complex sentences. We concentrate on two types here. As shown in Appendix B, examples (1) and (2) include an adjunct structure, the adverbial subordinate *toki* clause, which corresponds to an English *when*-clause. These structures resemble those in Study 1, except that *zibun* is now in a long-distance case-marked subject A-position. Sentences (3)–(4) show a postpositional phrase construction. In the first type in Appendix B, which includes an adjunct ((1) and (2)), *zibun* occupies a long-distance paradigmatic pronoun position in comparable English sentences. The second type, involving a locative PP adjunct, has been the focus of much linguistic inquiry in English (cf. review in Lust, 1986; Reinhart, 1986); as well as in acquisition (Padilla-Rivera, 1990). Like Type 2 in Study 1, this second type involves *zibun* in an A'-position (*zibun-no*) when *zibun* occurs backward in the PP adjunct ((4) in Appendix B). When *zibun* appears in a Forward construction (e.g., (3)), it is nominative *zibun-ga*. These sentences correspond roughly to sentences like *Near John, he/self saw a snake* in English. This PP adjunct is a left-branching locative adjunct on the matrix S.

This design allowed a test of the Japanese children's acceptance of *zibun* in several paradigm pronoun positions. One sentence type ((3) in Appendix B) has been considered a Principle C violation in comparable English sentences (cf. Lust, Eisele, & Mazuka, 1992).[7]

Study 3: Null Pronoun (Subject) Study. In this study (see Appendix B), the adjunct sentence type (involving *toki*) that appeared in Study 2, as well as other structures, was tested with a null argument (i.e., *pro* or zero

---

[5] The directionality factor was designed to test independent hypotheses (Lust, in press; Lust, Eisele, & Mazuka, 1992; Lust & Mazuka, 1989). Here, it may be viewed as an experimental control.

[6] Initial portions of the data for Studies 2 and 3 were presented in Lust, Mazuka, Wakayama, and Oshima (1986). T. Wakayama and W. Snyder were actively involved in the data collection.

[7] The potential Principle C violation in Type 3, when a forward pronoun is involved, is discussed elsewhere (Lust et al., 1992) and briefly in this chapter.

pronoun). This allowed comparison of the lexical *zibun* constructions in Study 2 with constructions involving null anaphora in the same paradigm pronoun domains. Study 3 also provided a baseline measure of the children's basic competence for these complex sentence structures. The null pronoun is unmarked in these Japanese structures. In this way it was possible to calibrate children's acceptance or rejection of *zibun* in its various positions.

In all cases in Studies 2 and 3, the adjunct provides a long-distance domain for anaphora, that is, an option for free coreferential indexing between a name and a possible pronoun.

All sentences in the three studies were controlled in length within each study (they were equivalent in syllable length and as equivalent as possible in word length). All were controlled in other aspects of grammatical structure; for instance, they involved SOV sentence structure in both main and subordinate clauses, tensed main clauses (all past), and subordinate clauses (all in present or citation form). All were also controlled pragmatically, so as not to predetermine a semantic relation between *zibun* and the name antecedent in the sentence, but to allow it if the child's grammar allowed him or her to hypothesize an anaphora relation between them.

Summary of Experimental Hypotheses

If the child's initial hypothesis was that *zibun* is an anaphor and not a pronoun, then the child should accept *zibun* in a core anaphor position as [+anaphor] (e.g., Study 1, Type 1) to a degree significantly higher than in long-distance pronoun positions (e.g., Study 2). The reverse should be true if the child's hypothesis was that *zibun* is a pronoun. In addition, the design allowed a test of the role of the A/A' (argument/nonargument) factor in the children's hypotheses.

The emphatic condition in Study 1 allowed a test of whether the child accepted a correspondence between *zibun* and *emphatic* and allowed us to contrast results here with those on the paradigm BT anaphor and BT pronoun positions in Studies 1 and 2.

Finally, the children's acceptance of *zibun* can be tested for significance against the baseline of children's acceptance of comparable sentences with null (pronoun) anaphora in a paradigm pronoun position (subject position with adverbial subordinate clause embedding).

Method

An elicited imitation method was used.[8] There were two sentences for each condition in each study, providing a possible score range of 0–2.

---

[8] It is known from previous research that this method is applicable at young ages. Children must reconstruct the stimulus sentence through both their syntactic and their semantic knowledge in order to imitate correctly, and in imitating a sentence without context, children

Subjects

Forty-five children between ages 3 and 4 in four age groups were tested in Study 1, and 76 children between ages 3 and 5 were tested in six age groups in Studies 2 and 3. All were monolingual Japanese children from the Tokyo area with no apparent developmental problems.

The same children participated in Studies 2 and 3 in two separate sessions. The order of the two experiments was counterbalanced for each child.

Results

Zibun Is Not an Anaphor

We first present results from Study 1 that show that throughout the period studied, the Japanese children did not treat the lexical item *zibun* as an anaphor.

First, the overall correct imitation of the sentences in this study was extremely low at all four age groups. Overall correct imitation was at virtually 0% on all three types in Appendix A.[9] It was not the case, however, that children did not attempt the sentences. The children generally produced all or part of the sentence structure. Figure 6.1 shows the overall percentage of correct imitation across lexical items for each sentence type. Imitation of *zibun-o* (see arrows in figure) was much lower than imitation of other items in the sentences. Although children correctly imitated each lexical item approximately 60% of the time for this sentence type, the *zibun* NP was correctly imitated only 26% of the time.

The types of errors made by the children with regard to *zibun-o* are summarized in Table 6.1. As shown in the first column of Table 6.1, the children's responses were characterized with regard to the *zibun* constituent as *correct, dropped* or *changed.* In addition, another form or position of *zibun* was often *added,* as summarized in the second column of Table 6.1. The last four columns provide an analysis of the types of *zibun* additions that occurred.

As can be seen from this table, the most frequent error involved dropping the *zibun* object, leaving a null object. However, children inserted *zibun* in another form in the sentence 32% of the time, when they dropped *zibun-o* (26 out of 77 cases). An example of the most frequent type of error is given in (16a). Here, although the children dropped *zibun-o,* they inserted

---

appear to attempt to compute an anaphora relation between a possible antecedent and an anaphoric element in the sentence, if one is possible. If such an anaphoric relation is blocked grammatically, and children know it is blocked grammatically, imitation success is depressed. Imitation data have been found to provide converging evidence with comprehension data in many studies of the acquisition of anaphora (e.g., Cohen Sherman & Lust, 1993; Lust & Clifford, 1986; Lust et al., 1992; Lust, Solan, Flynn, Cross, & Schuetz, 1986).

[9]Error criteria are available from the authors on request. In general, any major change in syntax or semantics is considered an error in these standardized criteria.

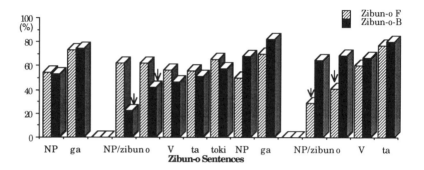

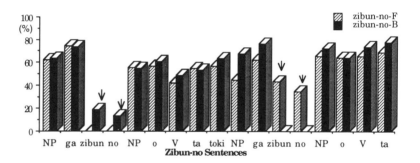

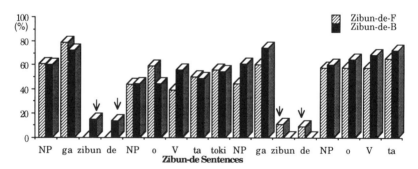

FIG. 6.1. Percentage of correct imitation for individual lexical items in *zibun-o, zibun-no,* and *zibun-de* sentences in Study 1 (location of *zibun* is indicated by arrow).

TABLE 6.1
Types of Errors With Regard to *Zibun* in Study 1

Zibun-o (Type 1) Sentences

Error Type			Additional Zibun Insertion					
					Breakdown of Inserted Zibun			
Zibun-o		Total	Total	*a	Z-ga	Z-de	Z-no	Z-o
Correct	46	(27%)	2		0	2	0	0
Dropped	77	(46%)	26	[3]	4	21	3	1
Changed	45	(27%)	10		2	6	5	0
Total	168	(100%)	38	[3]	6	29	8	1

Zibun-no (Type 2) Sentences

Error Type			Additional Zibun Insertion					
					Breakdown of Inserted Zibun			
Zibun-no		Total	Total	*a	Z-ga	Z-de	Z-no	Z-o
Correct	44	(29%)	6		0	1	5	0
Dropped	110	(71%)	20	[3]	0	17	3	3
Changed	0	(0%)	0		0	0	0	0
Total	154	(100%)	26	[3]	0	18	8	3

Zibun-de (Type 3) Sentences

Error Type			Additional Zibun Insertion					
					Breakdown of Inserted Zibun			
Zibun-de		Total	Total	*a	Z-ga	Z-de	Z-no	Z-o
Correct	18	(12%)	5		0	5	0	0
Dropped	136	(88%)	14	[2]	1	10	4	1
Changed	0	(0%)	0		0	0	0	0
Total	154	(100%)	19	[2]	1	15	4	1

Note. Children's responses that involved at least one verb were included in these analyses. Total number of sentences was 180 for each sentence type, based on 45 children.
[a]Number of times two instances of *zibun* were inserted in the same sentence.

zibun-de 'by self', an emphatic adjunct. In a few cases, a child added a *zibun-de* adjunct in both the subordinate and the main clauses, as in (16b).

(16) (*S* = *Stimuli, R* = *Response by a child*)

    a. S: Hirotyan-ga kami-o   aratta   toki, oniityan-ga   *zibun-o*
          name-NOM hair-ACC washed when brother-NOM self-ACC
          huita.
          dried

      R: Hirotyan-ga kami-o   aratta   toki, oniityan-ga
          name NOM hair-ACC washed when brother-NOM
          zibun-de Ø huita.
          self-by   dried
          'When Hirotyan washed (his) hair, big brother dried (himself) by himself.'

    b. S: Oneetyan-ga *zibun-o* mita toki, Zyuntyan-ga
          sister-NOM   self-ACC saw when name-NOM
          syasin-o   utusita.
          picture-ACC took
          'When the big sister saw self, Jun-chan took a picture.'

      R: Oneetyan-ga *zibun-de* Ø aruita toki, Zyuntyan-ga
          sister-NOM self-ACC   walked when name-NOM
          zibun-de syasin-o   totta.
          self-by   picture-ACC took

When children changed *zibun-o*, they often changed it into another NP. For example, in (17), a 3-year-old changed *zibun-o aratta* 'washed self' into *kao-o aratta* 'washed face'. (18) is an example where a child changed *zibun-o* into *zibun-no te* 'self's hand'. This type of change accounted for 17 of 45 cases of the Changed category (38%) in Table 6.1 (also see Table 6.2). In many cases, the children also added *zibun* in positions other than the object position (e.g., as a *zibun-de* adjunct).

(17) S: Oneetyan-ga *zibun-o* mita toki, Zyuntyan-ga syasin-o utusita.
        sister-NOM   self-ACC saw when name-NOM   photo-ACC took

    R: Oneetyan-ga *kao-o* mita toki, Ettyan-ga syasin-o utusita.
                 face   name-N
    'When big sister saw self, Juntyan took a picture.'

(18) S: Yukityan-ga *zibun-o* aratta   toki, Obaatyan-ga
        Name-NOM self-ACC washed when, Grandmother-NOM
        oyu-o   kunda.
        hot water-ACC got

    R: Yukityan-ga *zibun-no te-o* aratta toki, Obaatyan-ga oyu-o
                    self-GEN hand-ACC
        kumi-masi-ta.

TABLE 6.2
Numbers of Correct *Zibun* Imitations and Substitutions
in Relation to the "Unlike-NP Constraint"

Verb Type	Number Correct Imitations	Number Changes into Another NP	Number Changes Observing Unlike-NP Constraint
Violation *arau* 'wash', *fuku* 'dry'	15 (16%)	29	14
Nonviolation *miru* 'see', *mitsukeru* 'find'	31 (34%)	16	3

In the *zibun-no* and *zibun-de* sentences, Table 6.1 shows overwhelmingly that the children dropped *zibun-de* or *zibun-no* (88% and 71% of cases, respectively). In addition, in comparison to performance on *zibun-o* sentences, much fewer attempts were made to include additional *zibun* in their stimuli (38 for *zibun-o* sentences, 26 for *zibun-no* sentences and 19 for *zibun-de* sentences). In the *zibun-de* sentences, *zibun-de* was imitated correctly only 18 times out of 154 responses (and an additional 15 were inserted elsewhere in the sentence). This is in striking contrast to *zibun-o* sentences, where *zibun-de* was frequently produced even though the stimuli did not contain *zibun-de*.

Verb Type. Table 6.2 shows that the verb type had a significant effect. Children were significantly more likely to be incorrect regarding the *zibun* constituent when the verb violated the Unlike-NP constraint. This effect held across both verbs in both types. When the verb violated the constraint, the children were more likely to change or drop the *zibun-o*. In about half of those changes, *zibun-o* was changed into another NP such that the Unlike-NP constraint was observed, as in example (18). There were no significant developmental changes in this effect.

At the same time, even when there was no lexical violation of the Unlike-NP constraint (e.g., *miru, mitukeru*), Table 6.2 shows only 34% correct *zibun-o*, a significant contrast to the overall lexical imitation rate of 60%. (Productive addition of *zibun-de* did not significantly differ across verb types.) Thus, at the same time that the occurrence of *zibun* in an object position is lexically linked to some degree from the earliest stages, the resistance to *zibun* in this position is general and holds across verb types at all ages.

The results were especially surprising for the *zibun-de* (Study 1, Type 3) sentences. It might be thought that because children spontaneously inserted *zibun-de* in Types 1 and 2 (*zibun-o* and *zibun-no*), that the *zibun-de* construction was in some way necessary to propositional content whenever *zibun* occurred in the stimulus. The results were more subtle, however. On

Type 3 *zibun-de* sentences, children primarily deleted the *zibun-de* construction, leading to a minimal (12%) correct *zibun* constituent in this structure. This suggests that, in some way, the Japanese children believed this *zibun-de* (emphatic) construction in itself could be taken for granted. These results indicate that the children were dropping *zibun-de* and *zibun-no* selectively. They suggest that the children knew *zibun-de* and *zibun-no* occurred in nonargument positions; thus they did not show much of an attempt to preserve the meaning of *zibun* in these sentences, especially *zibun-de*. In contrast, in *zibun-o* sentences, the children showed an attempt to preserve the meaning of *zibun* by adding *zibun-de* or changing *zibun* into another NP. These results suggest that the Japanese children believe that in these cases simply replacing *zibun-o* with a null argument is not sufficient; *zibun* is in an A-position and thus should have semantic content in these sentences. At the same time, they show that *zibun* in an object A-position is largely unacceptable.

In sum, the children resisted *zibun* in the [+anaphoric] paradigm *zibun-o* position. The primary error was to resist *zibun-o* in an object A-position, either by deleting it or by changing it to a noun (e.g., *kao*). At the same time, children maintained the semantic content of *zibun*, which they showed by spontaneously inserting the emphatic adjunct *zibun-de* 'by self'. A sensitivity to reflexive relations within the verbal lexicon was also evident from the earliest stages, as seen in the results of the verb type test. In Study 1, *zibun* was resisted in a paradigm core [+anaphor] position, where a local c-commanding potential antecedent exists. The children seemed to attempt to represent the reflexive meaning of *zibun* (self), but this was incompatible with the paradigm [+anaphor] object position. It was compatible with an emphatic adjunct, *zibun-de* 'by self'. There were no significant developmental changes.

Study 1 further showed that the Japanese children also resisted *zibun* in an A'-position as possessive *zibun-no*, thus in a [+pronoun] position. In the next section, we evaluate the issue of *zibun* as pronoun.

Zibun Is Not a Pronoun

Figure 6.2 shows the mean number of correct imitations for *zibun-ga* sentences (Study 2) and null subject sentences (Study 3) with the *toki* 'when' construction, where there is a paradigm position for the pronoun (i.e., long-distance subject position in complex sentences with an adverbial clause adjunct). As can be seen here, *zibun-ga* sentences were continuously and significantly more difficult than null subject sentences ($F(1, 70) = 38.7$, $p < .0000$).

A very high proportion of the imitation errors for the *toki* sentences in Study 2 involved the possibility of anaphora. That is, they involved some

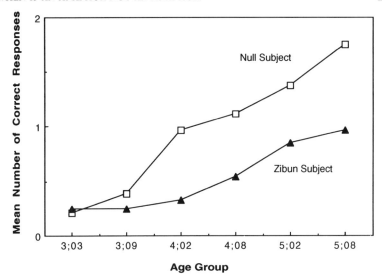

FIG. 6.2. Mean number of correct imitations for *zibun* and empty pronoun sentences in Studies 2 and 3.

change in either the name or the *zibun* subject and/or the relation between the two. Here again, a large number of errors involved insertion of *zibun-de*. Most frequent was the type exemplified in (19).

(19) a. S: Papa-ga   sakana-o yaku toki   *zibun-ga*
        Father-NOM fish-ACC grill   when self-NOM
        mado-o   aketa.
        window-ACC opened
        R: Papa-ga sakana-o yaku toki Ø *zibun-de* mado-o aketa.
                                          by self
        'When Father grills fish, self opened the window.'
    b. S: Zibun-ga ha-o   migaku toki Kazutyan-ga to-o
        self-NOM teeth-ACC brush   when   NOM door-ACC
        ketta.
        kicked
        R: Ø Zibun-de ha-o migaku toki Kazutyan-ga ha   ketta.ꞌ
          by self   teeth kicked

In both cases, *zibun-ga* was changed to *zibun-de* (most often in the same clause). *Zibun* here is removed from argument position; a null form replaces it, and *zibun-de* occurs as a modifier in a nonargument adjunct position.[10]

---

[10]*Zibun-de* in these examples could be taken as a modifier to a null argument (e.g., in an appositive reading), or as an adjunct or modifier to the predicate.

These results show that lexical *zibun* is also resisted in the long-distance subject position, a paradigm pronoun position. A null zero pronoun is clearly unmarked here. Here again, *zibun* was productively converted to a *zibun-de* adjunct. Simple omission of *zibun-ga* did occur more frequently than that of *zibun-o* in Study 1. However, it accounted for a smaller proportion of anaphora errors than did *zibun-de* insertion in Study 2. Once again, the children appeared to believe that the semantic aspect of *zibun* (self) should be preserved, but they found it incompatible with an argument [+pronoun] position; they productively converted *zibun* to its emphatic form. Free pronominal anaphora, apparently accessible with the zero pronoun, was resisted in the case of *zibun*.

Zibun in Nonargument Position Is More Accessible

The children dropped *zibun-no* frequently from the sentence type in (3)–(4) in Study 1, as seen in Appendix A. This might suggest a general resistance to *zibun*, even when not in an argument position. However, the nature of the errors was less severe with *zibun-no*. In Study 1, the children retained the basic propositional (i.e., SOV) structure of *zibun-no* sentences better than in *zibun-o* sentences. This was in spite of the fact that *zibun-no* sentences contained an extra NP compared to *zibun-o* sentences, causing extra processing load.

These results of Study 1 cohere with the results of Study 2, where *zibun-no* was maintained at a much higher rate than *zibun-ga*. In Study 2, *zibun-ga* ((1) and (2) in Appendix B) was converted to *zibun-de* more than ten times as often as was *zibun-no*.[11]

In general, these data cohere with the hypothesis that *zibun* in an A′-position is more natural/unmarked than *zibun* in an A-position for the Japanese child. Part of the difficulty with both *zibun-o* and *zibun-ga* in these constructions seems to lie in the attempt to resist *zibun* in the A-position.

Summary of Results

In summary, the results in this chapter (combined linguistic and acquisition data) have provided converging evidence that:

1. *Zibun* is not an anaphor (in the Binding Theory sense).

2. *Zibun* is not a pronoun (i.e., not a syntactic pronoun in the Binding Theory sense).

3. In general, *zibun* resists being in an A-position.

4. In both *zibun-o* (object) and *zibun-ga* (subject) sentences, one of the most common effects was the incorporation of *zibun* that had been modeled in argument position, into *zibun-de* 'by self', a PP adjunct that is [+emphatic].

---

[11]Note that a null argument is not acceptable in the locative PP.

This *zibun-de* insertion did not reflect a general need simply to represent *zibun-de*, because when this PP actually occurred in the stimulus sentences, the children usually omitted it. The children selectively dropped *zibun-de* from the adjunct position without attempting to replace it elsewhere. This selective behavior confirms that the children know the A/A' distinction. It shows that they do not have a need or preference for expressing *zibun-de*, unless motivated to do so. We suggest they are motivated to do so in the other examples by the conflict between maintaining the semantics of *zibun* and the A-position (either local [+anaphor] or long-distance [+pronoun]).

The facts suggest that the productive incorporation of *zibun-de* when it did occur (i.e., with stimulus sentences involving *zibun* in either subject or object position), was motivated by an attempt to maintain the semantics of *zibun* with a resistance to *zibun* in an argument position, and thus to the BT in general.

5. In the subject *zibun-ga* position, with long-distance anaphora, the null pronoun is unmarked.

6. Surprisingly, knowledge of the significance of verbal lexical factors in expressing reflexivity is present very early in the acquisition of Japanese.

7. The resistance to *zibun* in an argument position in the first language acquisition of Japanese coheres with linguistic facts. The occurrence of *zibun-o* in a paradigm anaphor local domain was seen to be marked in adult Japanese, and lexically sensitive in the same way as in the child. Although, to our knowledge, it has not yet been addressed in the linguistic literature, we believe that case-marked (*ga*-marked) *zibun* in [+pronoun] contexts as in (11) is also marked in adult Japanese.

8. In general, these results remove *zibun* from the A(argument)-theory domain of UG that is accounted for by the BT.

DISCUSSION

These results are compatible with the theory proposed in Lust and Martohardjono (1987), and Lust et al. (1989; cf. also Kapur, Lust, Harbert, & Martohardjono, 1993), which stated that we cannot assume predetermined lexical differentiation of the lexicon in a specific language as anaphor or pronoun. This leads to a learning paradox and is not consistent with observed cross-linguistic acquisition data. We proposed that the Binding Principles apply definitionally, in order to define categorically what constitutes a lexical anaphor or pronoun in a language in terms of the BT. The BT is efficacious in first language acquisition precisely because it guides the child's lexical learning of anaphor and pronoun in his or her language. A language may or may not lexically realize this distinction in BT features.

We argued there, on the basis of cross-linguistic data from both linguistic facts and acquisition studies, that the distribution of *zibun* in the adult Japanese language would not allow the assignment of both [+] and [–] values of features [+/–anaphoric], and [+/–pronoun], both of which are necessary to categorically lexicalize classes of syntactic anaphors and pronouns in the Binding Theory sense. Critically, the distribution for *zibun* would not allow assignment of minus features for the definition of either *anaphor* or *pronoun*. It was predicted that Japanese, like some other languages, might not categorically lexicalize the Binding Theory. The Japanese acquisition results reported in this chapter confirm this prediction. The Japanese child, presumably on the basis of the distributional evidence, is unable to accomplish a lexical characterization of *zibun* as either BT anaphor or BT pronoun.

The Nature of *Zibun*

This brings us to the question of defining the nominal category of *zibun*.
    The acquisition theory in Lust et al. (1989) proposed that nominal categories were first dichotomized categorically by the child as nominal (name or noun) or pronominal (in a general sense). The BP then applied to general pronominals to achieve their further differentiation as syntactic BT anaphors or syntactic BT pronouns. The first nominal/pronominal distinction was hypothesized to reflect the assignment of a [+/–R] feature (where [+R] has obligatory intrinsic reference and [–R] does not).
    We must first ask whether *zibun* has been characterized by features that represent this first dichotomy (i.e., nominal vs. general pronominal, [+/–R]). If so, is it a nominal or a general pronominal? *Zibun* does appear to have general pronominal properties to some degree, for instance, it may be coindexed with a local antecedent, favoring subject over object antecedents, and it may occur with long-distance antecedents in the same way as a pronoun. It is neither a proper noun nor a generic noun. On the other hand, *zibun* and other apparent lexical pronominals in Japanese (e.g., *kare* 'he', *kanojo* 'she', *boku* 'I—male', *watasi* 'I—female') appear to have nominal properties to a certain degree, as the following examples suggest.

(20) *Adjective*
    a. Minikui *zibun-ga*   iya ni natta.
        ugly   zibun-NOM   come to hate
        (lit. Ugly self is unbearable.)
        '(I) come to hate myself being ugly.'
    b. Kawaii *kanojo-ga* genkan de matteru yo.
        pretty   she-NOM entrance-at waiting
        (lit. Pretty she is waiting at the entrance.)
        '(Your) pretty girlfriend is waiting for you at the entrance.'

c. Hansamu-na *boku-wa* kurasu-no ninkimono sa.
handsome   I-TOP   class-GEN popular person
(lit. Speaking of handsome I, [I am] the popular man in the class.)
'I, who is handsome, am a popular guy in class.'

Zibun ga zibun de

a. *Zibun-ga*   zibun-de maita   tane desukara sikata   arimasen.
zibun-NOM zibun-by planted seed because no-way there is
(lit. There is nothing I can do since it is a seed I planted myself.)
'I cannot complain since it is my own fault.'

b. Hirosi-wa   *zibun-ga* zibun-de tsukutta otosiana ni otite
Hirosi-TOP self-NOM zibun-by made   hole-LOC   fell
kega-o   sita-n-desu.
injury-ACC did
'Hirosi got injured by falling into the hole he himself dug.'

Addressee

a. *Mother scolding child:*
Zibun-ga warui-n desyoo?
self-NOM bad
'It's your own fault.'

b. *An adult finds a boy crying in a park. She is a stranger:*
Boku-wa doo site naiteru no?
I-TOP   why   crying
(lit. Why am I crying?)
'Why are you crying?'

c. *A stranger sees a hat on the ground and asks the girl nearby:*
Kore watasi no oboosi?
this   I-GEN   hat
(lit. Is this my hat?)
'Is this your hat?'

Head of relative clauses

a. Tanaka-wa   ziko-o   okosita *zibun-ga*   warui to   itta.
Tanaka-TOP accident-ACC made   zibun-NOM bad COMP said
(lit. Tanaka said that *zibun*, who had the accident, was bad.)
'Tanaka said that it was his own fault since he was the one who had an accident.'

b. Kega-o   site byooin-ni hakobareta   *kanozyo-wa*
injury-ACC did hospital-LOC brought-PASS she-TOP
nagai aida   isikihumee datta.
for a long time unconscious
'She, who was brought to the hospital because of the injury, was unconscious for a long time.'

These facts may suggest that the [+/–R] nominal/pronominal distinction is also not lexicalized for *zibun*. These results would imply that *zibun* is a general nominal expression, [+/–R] unspecified. Perhaps, just as the BT has not lexicalized an anaphor/pronoun distinction in Japanese, neither has it lexicalized the nominal/pronominal distinction. (This idea was suggested to us by J. Bowers, personal communication, 1993.) If the absence of anaphor and pronoun lexicalization in Japanese results from the absence of lexicalization by Binding Principles A and B, and this absence of a nominal/pronominal distinction results from the absence of lexicalization by Principle C, then our results lead us to a general conclusion. The Binding Theory in UG is not lexicalized in the Japanese nominal system. If the Binding Theory is a coherent definitional system, then this full range of results would be predicted.[12]

Finally, if *zibun* is in fact an indeterminate nominal category (i.e., one that does not dichotomously represent the features [+/–R]), in addition to not representing the syntactic features assigned by the Binding Theory Principles A and B (i.e., [+/–anaphor], [+/–pronoun]), it still must be asked: What lexical features are associated with *zibun*? Here, too, our results have provided evidence. The productive association of *zibun* with *zibun-de* demonstrated that *zibun*, a reflexive signifying "self," is productively associated with a feature we may represent as [+emphatic]. The emphatic feature is conveyed by the general semantics of the lexicon and is independent of BT. The fact that this feature is represented by the *zibun-de* structure, a PP adjunct, documents that this feature is not related to the A-system (argument system), which is the domain of the Binding Theory.

---

[12]Although we have focused on *zibun* in this chapter, the theory in Lust et al. (1989) implies that the BT lexicon must be analyzed as a system. If there is no BT anaphor, then there is no BT pronoun. That the idea proposed in Lust et al. (1989) may be extended to Principle C was suggested to us by J. Bowers, personal communication, 1993.

These results would in fact be consistent with the fact that evidence for Principle C in Japanese is to some degree still inconclusive. For example, with two NPs/Ns, as in (i), some have proposed that Binding Principle C may not apply in Japanese (cf. Lasnik, 1989, for Thai; although see Lust et al., 1992).

(i) Tadasi-wa   Yoko-ga   Tadasi-to   issyo-ni ututte-iru
     name-TOPIC name-NOM name-with together photographed
     syasyin-o   taisetsu-ni mochiaruite ita.
     photograph-ACC care-with carry around - past
     'Tadasi was carrying around a picture of Yoko being photographed with Tadasi.'

Note that if a nominal/pronominal distinction is not made, and Principle C does not apply in the case of two names, then it may not be possible to determine whether or not Principle C should apply to a structure like that in (i). (See Lasnik, 1989, regarding the distinction between two forms of Principle C.) (iia) and (iib) would be indistinguishable.

(ii) a. [N [N/Pron. . . .]]
    b. [N/Pron. . . . .[N. . . .]]

Lexical Reflexivity

In contrast, although our chapter has only evaluated the verbal lexicon as an experimental control, our results have revealed surprising early sensitivity to a lexical constraint. For example, the knowledge that the verb *arau* 'wash' should not take what has been called a *like NP* or reflexive object appeared to be present even in the youngest children we tested.[13]

The surprising early sensitivity to verbal lexicon confirms that the children's behavior and knowledge of *zibun* were closely consistent with adult judgments. This result also suggests that reflexivity in Japanese may inherently be tied to lexicon, rather than to particular syntactic position. This is indicated both in the subtle sensitivity to verb types and in the *zibun-de* conversions. This is clearly an area for further research (cf. Reinhart & Reuland, 1993).

Zibun Homonymy

It might be proposed that it is possible to resolve the issues we raised here by postulating that there are in fact two *zibuns*, one corresponding to a paradigm BT anaphor and one corresponding to another form, such as a BT pronoun (e.g., Sportiche, 1986). We do not think this is a possible solution. We have argued (on the basis of both linguistic and acquisition data) that *zibun* is not accurately characterized in either of these ways. Because the requirements for neither a BT anaphor nor a BT pronoun are satisfied, a proposal for homonymy is irrelevant. Examples like (6) show that *zibun* in the local domain is interpretable with local, long-distance, or discourse antecedent. In the local domain, thus, *zibun* does not show the distinct properties of a BT anaphor, such as obligatory nonreferential coindexing with a local c-commanding antecedent. There is no way, therefore, that the child could acquire two distinct *zibuns*. (See also Wali & Subbarao, 1991, for arguments that this distinction is untenable.)

BT and Japanese

As argued in Lust et al. (1989), these results do not imply that the BT does not apply at all to a language like Japanese. On the contrary, our results have confirmed that null pronouns are unmarked in Japanese. We assume that, in accord with current theory, the BT does apply to these null elements (cf. Harbert, in press, for review of the issues regarding application of BT to ECs). For example, some evidence has suggested that Principle C may apply to these null elements in Japanese grammar and acquisition (cf. Lust,

---

[13]*Zibun-zisin* is more acceptable here. Therefore, the Unlike-NP constraint appears misnamed (cf. Kitagawa, 1986).

in press). These null elements do not require prior lexical learning. For example, even the [+/− intrinsic R] feature or the [+emphatic] feature would have no relevance to empty categories (cf. Lust, Mazuka, Wakayama, & Oshima, 1986; Nishigauchi & Roeper, 1987, for an opposite view). Thus, if the BT is biologically programmed, it can apply to null nominals without lexical learning.

In fact, it is not impossible that a form of grammaticization is underway in the Japanese language with regard to *zibun* (cf. Harbert, in press, for other examples of this). It is noteworthy that some evidence of Principle C may exist for *zibun* in acquisition data, as well as in adult grammar (cf. Lust et al., 1992).

Is There Another "Real" Lexical Anaphor *zibun-zisin* (Katada, 1991)?

It has been suggested, on the basis of data like (21), that *zibun-zisin* may be a local anaphor in Japanese (cf. Harbert, in press). If so, although our specific proposal for *zibun* may still be correct, it would contradict our general proposal for Japanese that the BT has not lexicalized (cf. Harbert, in press; Katada, 1991).

(21) Takahasi$_i$-wa [Masako$_j$-ga zibun$_{i/*j}$-o rikaisiteiru] to   itta.
          zibun-zisin?$_{*i/j}$-o
     TOP   NOM self ACC   understand COMP said
     'Takahasi said Masako understood self.'

It does not appear to us, however, that the claims made for *zibun-zisin* are correct. First, *zibun-zisin* does allow long-distance antecedents. As in (22), *zibun-zisin* can occur in the subject position of a main clause or a subordinate clause. This means that if *zibun-zisin* has an antecedent in the sentence, it can be a long-distance one.[14]

(22) a. John-ga   Bill-ni zibun-zisin-ga   katta to   itta.
        name-NOM name-DAT   NOM won COMP said
        'John said Bill that self won.'
                                                              (Katada, 1991)
     b. Yamada-wa zibun-zisin-ga   hatsumee sita kikai no okage de
        Yamada-TOP   NOM invented   machine due to
        okumantyoozya ni natta.
        millionaire to become
        'Yamada became a millionaire because of the machine he himself
        invented.'

---

[1]These examples correspond to Chinese examples given by Yu (1991) and Pan (1991) for *ta ziji* 'himself'.

In (23), *zibun-zisin* is scrambled out of an embedded clause, and it is coreferential with either the matrix subject *John* or the embedded subject *dareka*. When *zibun-zisin* is coindexed with *dareka* 'someone', *zibun-zisin* takes a non-c-commanding antecedent.

(23) John$_i$-ga Bill$_j$-ni [zibun-zisin$_{i/*j/k}$-o [dareka$_k$ ga *t* semeta]]to   itta.
     NOM   DAT   ACC someone-NOM blamed COMP said
     'John told Bill that self, someone blamed *t*.'

(Katada, 1991)

Also, *zibun* and *zibun-zisin* can occur interchangeably, as in (24). The fact that the distributions of *zibun* and *zibun-zisin* are not complementary invalidates the classification of *zibun* and *zibun-zisin* as local versus long-distance anaphor.

(24) a. John-ga zibun-o   semeta.
        John-ga zibun-zisin-o semeta.
        John-NOM   criticized
        'John criticized himself.'
     b. John-ga zibun-o   bengo sita.
        John-ga zibun-zisin-o bengo sita.
        John-NOM   defended
        'John defended himself.'

Therefore, any distinction between *zibun* and *zibun-zisin* that may exist does not appear to be due to differences in lexicalization that relate to BT. This result is consistent with our general proposal in this chapter, that the BT has not lexicalized in Japanese.

Conclusion

Japanese acquisition data have both cohered with and elucidated the linguistic theory of UG. In particular, they bear on the underlying nature of the Binding Theory, and the source and nature of cross-linguistic variation with regard to the BT. In adult grammar, as in first language acquisition of Japanese, *zibun* is not a BT anaphor and not a BT pronoun. It is not a long-distance anaphor.[15] These results suggest that the BT does not lexicalize in Japanese, that is, there are no contrasting lexical classes in the nominal system of anaphor versus pronoun in the BT sense of these terms. The assumption in (1) is not well

---

[15]Given this result, attempts at parametrization of governing category (GC) for *zibun* as long-distance anaphor are misguided. Inclusion relations where putative long-distance reflexives like *zibun* are considered a superset that includes anaphors of the English type must be invalid.

founded. Although our results pertain to Japanese they may have more general relevance to many, if not all, left-branching languages such as Korean, Sinhalese, and Tamil (cf. Gair, 1990, in press).

Our results have suggested that the domain of lexical anaphora may not always provide direct evidence for the BT in acquisition or theory. As we suggest in Lust et al. (1989), the domain of the EC may more directly reflect the BT, because it does not require mediation by the specific language lexicon.[16]

ACKNOWLEDGMENTS

An early version of this chapter was first presented at LSA, New York, 1986, based on an initial part of the data that we present here. We thank Shin Oshima, Akio Kamio, James Gair, Alice Davison, Kashi Wali, John Whitman, Tatsuko Wakayama, Wendy Snyder, and Yafei Li for comments. Kazuyo Otani provided many of the critical examples in this chapter and significant comments.

REFERENCES

Abe, J. (1991). Zibun as distributor and its interaction with pronominal kare. *Proceedings of the North Eastern Linguistics Society, 22*, 1–15.

Akatsuka, N. (1972). *A study of Japanese reflexivisation.* Unpublished doctoral dissertation, University of Illinois, Urbana.

Akmajian, A., & Kitagawa, C. (1976). Deep-structure binding of pronouns and anaphoric bleeding. *Language, 52*, 61–77.

Bouchard, D. (1984). *On the content of empty categories.* Dordrecht: Foris.

Chomsky, N. (1986). *Barriers.* Cambridge, MA: MIT Press.

Clements, G. N. (1975). The logophoric pronoun in Ewe: Its role in discourse. *Journal of West African Languages, 10*, 141–177.

Cohen Sherman, J., & Lust, B. (1993). Children are in control. *Cognition, 46*, 1–51.

Fukui, N. (1984). *Studies in Japanese anaphora.* Unpublished manuscript, MIT, Cambridge, MA.

Gair, J. (1990). *Pronouns, reflexives, and anti-anaphora in Sinhala.* Paper presented at South Asian Languages Association XII, Berkeley, CA.

Gair, J. (in preparation). Aspects of lexical anaphors and pronouns in Sinhala. In K. Wali, K. V. Subbarao, J. Gair, & B. Lust (Eds.), *Lexical anaphors and pronouns in some South Asian languages: A principled typology.*

Harbert, W. (in press). Binding theory. In G. Webelhuth (Ed.), *Government and binding theory.* Oxford: Basil Blackwell.

---

[16]Our results also show the importance of production data in acquisition studies. If a comprehension task alone had been used, the child's underlying representation for *zibun* might never have been discovered. Comprehension tests, however, should now be designed to complement the production studies reported here.

Kapur, S., Lust, B., Harbert, W., Martohardjono, G. (1993). Universal grammar and learnability theory: The case of binding domains and the subset principle. *Knowledge and language: Issues in representation and acquisition* (pp. 185–216). Dordrecht: Kluwer.

Katada, F. (1991). The LF representation of anaphors. *Linguistic Inquiry, 22*, 287–313.

Kitagawa, Y. (1986). *Subject in Japanese and English.* Unpublished doctoral dissertation, University of Massachusetts, Amherst.

Koster, J., & Reuland, E. (Eds.). (1991). *Long distance anaphora.* Cambridge: Cambridge University Press.

Kuno, S. (1972). Pronominalization, reflexivization and direct discourse. *Linguistic Inquiry, 3*, 161–195.

Kuno, S. (1986). Anaphora in Japanese. In S.-Y. Kuroda (Ed.), *Working papers from the first SDF workshop in Japanese syntax* (pp. 12–70). San Diego: University of California.

Kuroda, S.-Y. (1965). Causative forms in Japanese. *Foundations of Language, 1*, 31–50.

Lasnik, H. (1989). On the necessity of binding conditions. In H. Lasnik (Ed.), *Essays on anaphora* (pp. 149–167). Dordrecht: Kluwer.

Lust, B. (1986). Introduction. In B. Lust (Ed.), *Studies in the acquisition of anaphora: Vol. 1. Defining the constraints* (pp. 3–103). Dordrecht: Reidel.

Lust, B. (in press). *Universal Grammar and initial state.* Cambridge, MA: Bradford Books.

Lust, B., & Clifford, T. (1986). The 3-D study: Effects of depth, distance and directionality on children's acquisition of anaphora. In B. Lust (Ed.), *Studies in the acquisition of anaphora: Vol. 1. Defining the constraints* (pp. 203–243). Dordrecht: Reidel.

Lust, B., Eisele, J., & Mazuka, R. (1992). The binding theory module: Evidence from first language acquisition for Principle C. *Language, 68*, 333–358.

Lust, B., & Martohardjono, G. (1987). *On relations between binding theory and first language acquisition.* Paper presented at the 12th Annual Boston University Conference on Language Development, Boston, MA.

Lust, B., & Mazuka, R. (1989). Cross-linguistic studies of directionality in first language acquisition: The Japanese data—a response to O'Grady, Suzuki-Wei & Cho 1986. *Journal of Child Language, 16*, 665–684.

Lust, B., Mazuka, R., Martohardjono, G., & Yoon, J.-M. (1989). *On parameter setting in first language acquisition: The case of the Binding Theory.* Paper presented at GLOW, Utrecht.

Lust, B., Mazuka, R., Wakayama, T., & Oshima, S. (1986). *When is an anaphor not an anaphor?* Paper presented at the annual meeting of the Linguistic Society of America, New York.

Lust, B., Solan, L., Flynn, S., Cross, C., & Schuetz, E. (1986). A comparison of null and pronoun anaphora in first language acquisition. In B. Lust (Ed.), *Studies in the acquisition of anaphora: Vol. 1. Defining the constraints* (pp. 245–277). Dordrecht: Reidel.

Nishigauchi, T., & Roeper, T. (1987). Deductive parameters and growth of empty categories. In T. Roeper & E. Williams (Eds.), *Parameter setting* (pp. 91–121). Dordrecht: Reidel.

Oshima, S. (1979). Conditions on rules: Anaphora in Japanese. In G. Bedell, E. Kobayashi, & M. Muraki (Eds.), *Explorations in linguistics* (pp. 423–448). Tokyo: Kenku-sha.

Oshima, S. (1986). The Binding Theory: A case study. *Research Reports of Kochi University* (Vol. 35, pp. 1–46). Kochi University, Japan.

Padilla-Rivera, J. (1990). *On the definition of binding domains in Spanish.* Dordrecht: Kluwer.

Pan, H. (1991). *Pro and long distance reflexive ziji in Chinese.* Paper presented at NACCL3, Cornell University, Ithaca, NY.

Reinhart, T. (1986). Center and periphery in the grammar of anaphora. In B. Lust (Ed.), *Studies in the acquisition of anaphora: Vol. 1. Defining the constraints* (pp. 123–150). Dordrecht: Reidel.

Reinhart, T., & Reuland, E. (1993). Reflexivity. *Linguistic Inquiry, 24*, 657–720.

Sportiche, D. (1986). Zibun. *Linguistic Inquiry, 17*, 369–374.

Takezawa, K. (1989). *NP movement, anaphoric binding and aspectual interpretation.* Paper presented at OSU workshop on Japanese syntax and UG, Columbus, OH.

Takezawa, K. (1991). Judoo-bun, noukaku-bun, bunri-hukanoo-shoyuu-koobun to "teiru" no kaishaku [Passive voice sentences, active voice sentences, and nonseparable possessive sentences and the interpretation of *teiru*]. In Y. Nitta (Ed.), *Voice and transitivity in Japanese* (pp. 59–81). Tokyo: Kuroshio.

Tokieda, M. (1950). *Nihon bunpoo* [Japanese grammar]: *Part I. Koogo hen* [Colloquial Japanese]. Tokyo: Iwanami.

Ueda, M. (1984). *On a Japanese reflexive zibun: A non-parametrization approach.* Unpublished manuscript, University of Massachusetts, Amherst.

Wali, K., & Subbarao, K. V. (1991). On pronominal classification: Evidence from Marathi and Telugu. *Linguistics, 29,* 1093–1110.

Yu, W. X. F. (1991). *Logophoricity with Chinese reflexives.* Paper presented at NACCL3, Cornell University, Ithaca, NY.

APPENDIX A

Example Sentences
Japanese Study 1 (Core Anaphor Domain)

Type 1: Zibun-o

(1) *Zibun-o* Forward
Hirotyan-ga kami-o aratta toki, oniityan-ga *zibun*-o huita.
name   hair   washed   brother   self   dried
'When Hirotyan washed (his) hair, big brother dried self.'

(2) Zibun-o Backward
Oneetyan-ga *zibun*-o mita toki, Zyuntyan-ga syashin-o   utsusita.
sister   self   saw   name   photograph took
'When big sister saw self, Zyuntyan took a photograph.'

Type 2: Zibun-no

(3) Zibun-no Forward
Norityan-ga e-o   kaita toki, ozisan-ga *zibun-no* hon-o yonda.
name   picture   draw   uncle   self   book read
'When Norityan drew a picture, Uncle read self's book.'

(4) Zibun-no Backward
Mama-ga *zibun-no* pan-o yaita toki, Kentyan-ga miruku-o nonda.
mother   self   bread toasted,   name   milk   drank
'When mother toasted self's bread, Kentyan drank milk.'

Type 3: Zibun-de

(5) Zibun-de Forward
Obasan-ga gomi-o yaita toki, Tokityan-ga *zibun-de* hi-o tuketa.
aunt   trash   burnt   name   self   fire   started
'When Aunt burnt the trash, Tokityan started fire by self.'

(6) Zibun-de Backward
Marityan-ga *zibun-de* omotya-o simatta toki, mama-ga to-o simeta.
name   self   toy   tidied up   mother   door closed
'When Marityan tidied up the toys by self, Mother closed the door.'

APPENDIX B

Example Sentences
Japanese Study 2 (Pronoun Domain)
and 3 (Null Nominals)

Study 2	*Study 3*

Type 1:
Toki construction
Forward

(1) Papa-ga   sakano-o yaku toki,
father-NOM fish-ACC broil when
zibun-ga mado-o   aketa.
self-NOM window-ACC opened
'When Papa broil(s) fish,
self opened (the) window.'

(1) Otoosan-ga tokee-o   naosu
father-NOM clock-ACC fix
toki Ø hako-o   aketa.
when   box-ACC open-past
'When father fixes the clock,
Ø opened the box.'

Backward

(2) Zibun-ga e-o   miru toki,
self-NOM picture-ACC see   when
Akityan-ga momo-o   tabeta.
name-NOM peach-ACC ate
'When self saw (the) picture,
Akityan ate (a/the) peach.'

(2) Ø Hano-o   ueru toki,
flower-ACC plant when
obasan-ga mizu-o   hakonda
aunt-NOM water-ACC bring-past
'When Ø plants the flower,
the aunt brought the water.'

Type 2:
Postpositional phrase construction
Forward

(3) Oniityan-no mae de,   *zibun-ga* pen-o   otosita.
brother-GEN in front of self-NOM pen-ACC dropped
'In front of brother, self dropped (a/the) pen.'

Backward

(4) *Zibun-no* yoko de, Norityan-ga ningyoo-o mituketa.
self-GEN side at   name-NOM doll-ACC   found
'At the side of self, Norityan found (a/the) doll.'

CHAPTER SEVEN

Grammatical or Pragmatic: Will the Real Principle B Please Stand?

Diana Kaufman
Temple University

Among the principles that have been investigated as possible representations of children's grammatical knowledge, none have produced more mixed and controversial results than Principle B of the GB (government-binding) Binding Theory (Chomsky, 1981). What makes these results particularly puzzling is the fact that acquisition studies of Principles A and C of Binding Theory, both of which assume the same underlying grammatical knowledge as B, have resulted in more consistently good results.

This discrepancy in findings has motivated some acquisition researchers (Wexler & Chien, 1985) to propose a revision of GB Binding Theory in which a distinction is made between binding and coreference. Under this formulation, illicit binding is disallowed by a principle of the grammar, Principle B, and illicit coreference by a principle of pragmatics, Principle P. Such a revision fits nicely with versions of Binding Theory proposed by Reinhart (1983), Grodzinsky and Reinhart (in press), and Montalbetti and Wexler (1985).

In this chapter, I argue against the need for and adequacy of a modification of GB Binding Theory along the lines just suggested. In arguing against these particular revisions, I make the following points: First, the acquisition data from studies of Principle B appear to support the conclusion that children have knowledge of a grammatical principle, like Principle B, which constrains binding and coreference alike. Second, the most thorough attempt to revise the GB Binding Theory incorporating a pragmatic principle (Grodzinsky & Reinhart, in press; Reinhart, 1983, 1986) is arguably inadequate in its handling of aspects of the linguistic data and in its predictions about acquisition. Third, the pragmatic principles that have been proposed to rule out illicit coreference are in fact problematic in terms of either their learnability or their computational complexity.

Before addressing these points, I briefly describe the two alternative formulations of the Binding Theory that are most relevant to the debate. These are the Binding Theory proposals of Chomsky (1981)[1] and Reinhart (as presented in Grodzinsky & Reinhart, in press).[2]

TWO BINDING THEORY PROPOSALS

Chomsky's Formulation

Within the GB Binding Theory (Chomsky, 1981), noun phrases (NPs) are divided into anaphors, pronominals, and R-expressions (names).[3] Binding Theory determines whether the relations between NPs are allowed or disallowed within a particular sentence domain, called the governing category.[4] The Binding Theory principles state the permissible or required relations as in (1):

(1) Principle A: An anaphor is bound in its governing category.
Principle B: A pronominal is free in its governing category.
Principle C: An R-expression is free.

Some relevant English examples of the allowed and disallowed relations are given in (2)–(4):

---

[1]Since Binding Theory was first formulated by Chomsky (1981), there have been several proposals to modify it in order to improve its empirical coverage of the linguistic data (see, e.g., Chomsky, 1986). What is at issue here is not whether Binding Theory should. or will be revised, but whether revision along the lines discussed in the text is motivated by the acquisition data.

[2]The arguments for this version of Binding Theory are essentially those in Reinhart (1983). However, in response to empirical problems noted by several linguists (e.g., Lasnik, 1989), Reinhart replaced the speaker/hearer strategies governing intended coreference decisions (in the 1983 version) with a coreference rule, Rule I (in Grodzinsky & Reinhart, in press).

[3]The notion of c-command in this formulation of Binding Theory is that in Reinhart (1976).

[4]Chomsky (1981) gave the following definition of governing category in this formulation of Binding Theory:

(i) β is the governing category for α if and only if β is the minimal category containing α, a governor of α, and a SUBJECT accessible to α.

Within this formulation, the "SUBJECT . . . is the most prominent nominal element" (p. 209), and "an anaphor or pronominal searches for the closest SUBJECT to which it can be linked, where linking involves coreference for an anaphor and disjoint reference for a pronoun" (p. 211).

(2) a. Dan_1 washed $himself_1$.
   b. *Dan_1 cried when his mother washed $himself_1$.

(3) a. *$Sharon_1$ dried her_1.
   b. $Sharon_1$ told Jenny that she should dry her_1.

(4) a. *He_1 is scratching Dan_1.
   b. His_1 mom called Dan_1.

In this formulation of Binding Theory, Chomsky (1981) stated that *bound* is to be understood as antecedent-bound (A-bound), and not operator-bound (A'-bound). A-bound is bound by an element in an A (argument) position. Thus, Binding Theory constrains the syntactic binding of one NP by another NP, whether the antecedent is a definite NP (as in (5a)) or a quantified NP (as in (5b)), but it has nothing to say about the additional restrictions on quantifiers that allow binding in (6a) but not (6b). These additional restrictions, related to facts about quantifier scope and variable binding, are expressed by some other component of the grammar, possibly before the Binding Theory applies.

(5) a. The man_1 took his_1 turn.
   b. Every man_1 took his_1 turn.

(6) a. His_1 friends made a party for $John_1$.
   b. *His_1 friends made a party for every boy_1.

Finally, although GB Binding Theory is a theory of syntactic relations among NPs, its categories of indexed NPs have to have semantic import. Thus, NPs with identical indices (whether bound or free) are obligatorily coreferent, and NPs with distinct indices are obligatorily disjoint in reference.[5]

Reinhart's Formulation

In her proposal, Reinhart argued that stating the Binding Theory principles in terms of definite NP coreference (as discussed earlier) has resulted in enormous problems and complications in expressing anaphoric relations among NPs (see Grodzinsky & Reinhart, in press; Reinhart, 1983, 1986, for details). Consequently, Reinhart believed that the Binding Theory should state only the syntactic conditions under which anaphors and pronouns may be interpreted as variables bound to quantificational antecedents. Informally, these conditions are met whenever an anaphor or pronoun can be coindexed with a c-commanding antecedent, regardless of the nature of the antecedent, referential (as in (7a)) or quantificational (as in (7b)).

---

[5]See Lasnik (1989) for a discussion of the OB (*On Binding*) and GB indexing systems. Here, Lasnik discussed the need for set indices and for "pseudosemantic" rules to interpret identical, distinct, and intersecting indices in order to capture all of the possible NP relationships.

(7) a. Felix₁ thinks that he₁ is a genius.
   b. Everyone₁ thinks that he₁ is a genius.

Crucially, for this proposal to work with pronouns, c-commanding definite NP antecedents, such as *Felix* in (7a), must be analyzed as logically equivalent to c-commanding quantified NP antecedents, such as *everyone* in (7b), not an uncontroversial assumption.[6] Reinhart argued for this equivalence, showing that in a VP-deletion context, as in (8a), the pronoun *he* linked to *Felix* can have both the bound variable interpretation (8b) and the referential interpretation (8c), even with a referential antecedent.

(8) a. Felix thinks he is a genius and Max does too.
   b. Felix thinks Felix is a genius and Max thinks Max is a genius.
   c. Felix thinks Felix is a genius and Max thinks Felix is a genius.

Although both interpretations are available, only the bound variable one is relevant to Reinhart's Binding Theory.

It follows from this analysis, in which Binding Theory governs only bound variable anaphora, that there are only two principles or conditions. Condition A, given in (9a), states the restrictions on binding anaphors; and Condition B, given in (9b), the restrictions on binding pronouns. There is no Condition C.

(9) a. An anaphor is bound in its governing category.
   b. A pronoun is free in its governing category.

As in the GB formulation, all NPs are generated with free indices and anaphors and pronouns are bound by being coindexed with c-commanding antecedents. Some of these indexed interpretations are ruled out by the Binding Conditions A and B. The remaining ones are all interpreted as instances of variable binding.

Given that coindexation can express only bound variable anaphora in her formulation, Reinhart (in Grodzinsky & Reinhart, in press) argued that coreference interpretation is not captured by the mechanism of syntactic coindexation at all. Rather, it is governed by pragmatic knowledge that constrains the possible choices of referents for pronouns and R-expressions within a sentence. Thus, in place of Condition C and the coreference part of Condition B, she proposed an intrasentential coreference rule, Rule I.

---

[6] See Chomsky (1976) for a brief discussion supporting an analysis in which sentences with definite and quantificational NPs, as in (i) and (ii), have different logical representations.

(i) The man is here.
(ii) Every man is here.

(10) *Rule I:* NP A cannot corefer with NP B if replacing A with C, C A-bound by B, yields an indistinguishable interpretation.

Informally, what this rule does is rule out coreference interpretation in those structures that allow bound variable anaphora, unless the coreference interpretation is motivated by some aspect of the pragmatics or discourse context.

In summary, Chomsky's (1981) and Reinhart's (in Grodzinsky & Reinhart, in press) versions of the Binding Theory differ in two important respects. First, in Chomsky's formulation, BT constrains the possibilities for antecedent-anaphor relationships (for antecedents in argument position) regardless of antecedent type (referential or quantificational). However, the additional restrictions on quantifier/bound variable relations are handled by some other component of the grammar. In Reinhart's formulation, BT constrains the possibilities for antecedent-anaphor relations regardless of antecedent type. However, referential antecedents are considered to be ambiguous between a quantificational and referential interpretation, and BT is operative only in the former case. Second, in Chomsky's formulation, constraints on both binding and coreference possibilities are expressed within the grammar. In Reinhart's formulation, constraints on binding are grammatical, but all restrictions on coreference follow from pragmatic considerations.

The first acquisition studies focused on Chomsky's (1981) formulation of the Binding Theory, testing children's knowledge of Binding Theory with referential antecedents only.

THE EARLY STUDIES OF PRINCIPLES A AND B

In the early studies (Jakubowicz, 1984; Otsu, 1981; Padilla Rivera, 1985; Solan & Ortiz, 1982; Wexler & Chien, 1985), researchers tested the same children on Principles A and B.[7] The assumption here seems to have been that, because reflexives and pronominals are generally in complementary distribution in the object position with regard to their choice of antecedents, children who demonstrate knowledge of A should demonstrate knowledge of B and vice versa. What many researchers reported in these studies, however, was that children often performed better with reflexives (Principle A) than with object pronominals (Principle B), choosing the closest antecedent for both proforms. Nevertheless, a careful examination of these early studies, listed under Table 7.1,[8] shows that the results were more mixed than has been claimed.

---

[7] Studies of children's knowledge of Principle C were being carried out at the same time (see Lust, Eisele, & Mazuka, 1992, for a review), but they did not initially bear on the debate in question. The results of these studies are summarized later in the text.

[8] When not reported by the author(s), percentages in this table (and in all subsequent tables) are derived from the figures in the papers. Therefore, percentages may not be exact. The percentages correct by age for the Wexler and Chien (1985) study are as follows:

In Otsu's study, the results for pronouns and reflexives are comparable. Solan and Ortiz reported significantly better results for pronouns than reflexives. In Jakubowicz's study, the percentages for pronouns start out lower and are much more variable than the percentages for reflexives. However, by ages 4 to 5, children are getting 75% to 100% correct with pronouns. In the Wexler and Chien experiments, although performance with reflexives is better at the older ages, there are many younger ages, particularly in Experiment 3, at which performance with pronouns is equal to or better than that with reflexives. (See footnote 8 for the percentages by age in the Wexler & Chien study and the Padilla Rivera study.) Finally, in the Padilla Rivera study, the children do better at all ages with reflexives than with pronouns, not reaching 75% correct with the latter until age 9.

Taken together, these studies demonstrate that children's performance with pronouns is sometimes poorer and often more variable than their performance with reflexives. Nevertheless, the children's overall perform-ance in the studies is too good to support the conclusion that they have no knowledge of a grammatical principle like GB Principle B.

	Age	Pronominals	Reflexives
Experiment 1:	2;6	50%	45%
	3;2	50%	55%
	3;8	52%	65%
	4;4	55%	60%
	5;0	58%	85%
	5;6	50%	65%
	6;2	60%	80%
	6;6	65%	80%
Experiment 2	2;6	60%	48%
	3;2	65%	40%
	3;8	68%	48%
	4;4	60%	52%
	5;0	65%	55%
	5;6	65%	58%
	6;2	60%	82%
	6;6	65%	80%
Experiment 3	2;6	90%	13%
	3;2	80%	27%
	3;8	76%	42%
	4;4	63%	57%
	5;0	70%	67%
	5;6	65%	72%
	6;2	79%	76%
	6;6	64%	89%

The percentages correct for the Padilla Rivera (1985) study are:

3;0–3;11	5%	33%
5;0–5;11	25%	60%
7;0–7;11	57%	90%
9;0–9;11	75%	92%

TABLE 7.1

Studies of Principles A and B Before 1985

Authors	Language (Number of Subjects)	Task	Ages	Sentence Type	Pronouns Percentage Correct	Reflexives Percentage Correct
Otsu (1981)	English (60)	Act-out	3–7	SS	93	95
				CS	66	66
Solan & Ortiz (1982)	Spanish (clitics) & English (28)	Act-out	4–6	CS	57	41[a]
Jakubowicz, 1984	English					
Experiment 1	(28)	Act-out	3–5	CS	0–75	80–100
Experiment 2	(31)	Act-out	3–5	CS	50–100	80–100
Wexler & Chien (1985)	English (120)					
Experiment 1		Picture identification	2;6–6;6	SS[b]	50–65	45–85
Experiment 2		Picture identification	2;6–6;6	SS[c]	60–68	40–80
Experiment 3		Act-out	2;6–6;6	CS	63–90	13–89
Padilla Rivera (1985)	Spanish (clitics) (80)	Act-out	3;0–9;11	SS	5–75	33–92

Note. SS = simple sentence; CS = complex sentence.
[a]Difference is reported as significant. [b]Complex NP antecedent: possessive NP. [c]Complex NP antecedent: prepositional NP.

Wexler and Chien's (1985) Proposal

The researchers who did this early work seemed to agree that their results do not imply that children do not know Principle B, despite the disparity in performance on sentences with pronominals and reflexives. To account for the data, researchers like Jakubowicz (1984) suggested that children might not have figured out the difference between an anaphor and a pronoun and, consequently, did not know which principle to apply to which proform. Other researchers, specifically Wexler and Chien (1985), proposed that children know both Principles A and B, but, in the case of the latter, a reformulated version of B. In this reformulation, Principle B rules out only the binding of pronouns to quantified antecedents, as in (11a), and not the coreference between pronouns and referential antecedents, as in (11b). (Both examples are marked ungrammatical by GB Principle B.)

(11) a. *Every boy$_1$ washed him$_1$.
      b. *The boy$_1$ washed him$_1$.

In the Wexler and Chien proposal, the ostensibly poor performance of the children on pronominal sentences in the early studies would be accounted for by the fact that all of the test sentences had referential antecedents, for which GB Principle B was not sufficient to rule out coreference. What the children in these studies needed to know in order to rule out the illicit coreference in these sentences was a pragmatic principle they had not yet learned. It was in making this proposal that Wexler and Chien first made reference to Reinhart's (1983) theory of binding and a theory of binding developed by Montalbetti and Wexler (1985). A brief discussion of the latter indicates the role it plays in Wexler and Chien's proposal.

Montalbetti and Wexler's Binding Theory

Wexler and Chien (1985) stated that the essential notion in Montalbetti and Wexler's Binding Theory is not coreference, but linking, in the sense of Higginbotham (1983).[9] As in Reinhart (1983) and Grodzinsky and Reinhart (in press), pronouns link only to become bound variables, and linking applies only to NPs in a c-command relationship. But, unlike in Reinhart, a distinction

---

[9] Higginbotham's (1983, 1985) proposal differs from Montalbetti and Wexler's (1985) in that it handles not only binding but also coreference. As a matter of fact, Higginbotham argued that *obviativity*, which is similar to Lasnik's (1976) notion of disjoint reference, must be grammatical. Thus, Higginbotham did not replace coreference with linking, but coindexation with linking, arguing that linking captures more of the coreferential relationships than indexing could. (See Lasnik, 1989, for a discussion of linking versus indexation.)

is made between referential antecedents, to which pronouns may not link (even in a c-command configuration), and quantificational antecedents, to which pronouns (under a bound variable interpretation) must link in order to receive some interpretation in the domain of mental representations (see Montalbetti & Wexler, 1985, for discussion).[10]

Based on Montalbetti and Wexler's formulation, in which Binding Theory handles only linked elements (anaphors, variables, and pronouns bound to quantified antecedents), Wexler and Chien predicted that children, who know Binding Theory, should do well with sentences like (12a) but not with sentences like (12b). (The examples are from their paper.)

(12) a. Every bear$_1$ says Adam should give him$_1$ a pencil.
  b. The bear$_1$ says Adam should give him$_1$ a pencil

Both Wexler and Chien (1985) and Montalbetti and Wexler (1985) suggested that poor performance on sentences like (12b) resulted from the children's lack of knowledge of pragmatic principles to rule out local binding of the pronoun. However, none of these researchers offered any proposal as to how these pragmatic principles are learned or how they work. They did indicate that their position was not unlike Reinhart's (1983), suggesting that they assumed something like her pragmatic rule.[11]

In summary, the early studies of GB Binding Theory demonstrated considerable variability in children's performance regarding Principle B. Despite this variability, researchers were generally reluctant to assume that children had no knowledge of Principle B. Instead they looked for alternative explanations, one of which was that children had knowledge of a reformulated B that would predict good performance on sentences with quantified antecedents even in the face of poor performance on sentences with referential antecedents. This prediction was tested in the studies to follow.

---

[10]In Kaufman (1988), I discussed the fact that Montalbetti and Wexler's (1985) theory appears to run counter to the theory proposed by Montalbetti (1984) in his dissertation. Montalbetti and Wexler claimed that linking is restricted to cases of c-command. They also argued that the coreferential reading is just a special case of the free reading, linking being disallowed in both cases. However, in his dissertation, Montalbetti (1984) stated: (a) "linking itself is independent of the notion of c-command" (p. 33), and (b) "the coreferential reading [which is linked] is not a special case of the free one" (p. 60), which must never be linked, not even by accident.

Montalbetti argued that this three-way distinction—linking to a formal variable for binding interpretation, linking to some NP that must not be a formal variable for coreferential interpretation, and absolutely no linking for free interpretation—was needed to account for many facts in Spanish that could not be captured otherwise. Thus, it is difficult to know how this theoretical proposal of Montalbetti and Wexler could be motivated.

[11]Actually, when this proposal was first made, Wexler and Chien (1985) and Montalbetti and Wexler (1985) were referring to Reinhart's (1983) pragmatic strategies. These strategies were replaced by Rule I, in Grodzinsky and Reinhart (in press).

TESTING PRINCIPLE B WITH QUANTIFIED
AND REFERENTIAL ANTECEDENTS

The first test of children's knowledge of Principle B in sentences with referential and quantified antecedents was by Kaufman (1987, 1988). In this study, Kaufman used a modification of the truth-value judgment task (TVJT) (Crain & McKee, 1985) to test 60 children, ages 2;7 to 6;5. In the TVJT, the child and a puppet (Kermit) watched the experimenter act out a scene with toy animals and dolls. Following the act-out, Kermit said what had happened. The child then gave Kermit a cookie if he correctly described the event and a rag if he didn't. The act-outs in the task were either reflexive (one animal acting on himself in the presence of another animal) or transitive (one animal acting on another). The 16 test sentences (8 simple and 8 complex) uttered by Kermit all contained pronominals. Thus, half of the trials were *accept* trials in which a pronominal sentence described a transitive act-out, and half were *reject* trials in which a pronominal sentence described a reflexive act-out. Four filler sentences with R-expressions only (no pronouns) were interspersed among the test sentences so that the child would not hear sentences with pronouns only, and also as a check on whether the child was paying attention.

Each child was seen once for a test of sentences with referential antecedents and once for a test with quantified antecedents. (Order was counterbalanced.) Examples of the test sentences are given in (13)–(16).

(13) (The hippo chases the elephant.)
     The hippo hurt him.
(14) (The hippos chase the elephant.)
     Every hippo hurt him.
(15) (Here's the chicken watching the baby.)
     The baby fed her while the chicken was watching.
(16) (Here's the chicken watching the babies.)
     Every baby fed her while the chicken was watching.

Note that every test sentence was preceded by an antecedent sentence (in parentheses), because children's performance in the early studies and in pilot testing revealed that they needed a linguistic antecedent in order to track reference. Antecedent sentences were chosen to make either the reflexive or transitive act-out seem pragmatically possible.

There were a number of additional procedures and controls incorporated into the TVJT to ensure that the children be able to show what they knew (see Kaufman, 1988, for details). However, one in particular deserves mention. In designing the act-out scenarios with the referential and quantified antecedents, as in (13) and (14), the experimenter became concerned that there could be a serious confound in the way in which the two stimulus types were presented. The referential antecedent's depiction (with *the hippo*, for example) required only one agent acting or speaking once. However, the quantified antecedent's depiction (with *every hippo*, for example) needed multiple agents each acting or speaking in succession in order to convey a distributed reading. Thus, the quantified antecedent trial might be easier for the children to reference than the referential, not because the former was constrained by Binding Theory and the latter was not, but because it gave the children two more instances of the action (or the speech) in the scenario to use as a basis for judgment. In order to make the two act-outs more comparable in saliency, the experimenter had the single actor in the referential trial act out the scenario two or three times before Kermit described the act-out and the child judged Kermit's description.

The results of this study indicated that young children could perform very well on sentences with object pronouns regardless of antecedent type. As a matter of fact, as can be seen in Table 7.2, the children's performance for referential and quantified antecedents was essentially the same. Therefore, the Wexler and Chien (1985) prediction for quantified versus referential antecedents was not upheld.

TABLE 7.2
Mean Percentage Correct on the Truth-Value Judgment Task
With Pronouns Linked to Referential Versus
Quantified Antecedents (Kaufman, 1988)

	Quantified Antecedents (82)			
	Youngest (78%) (2;7–3;11)		Oldest (85%) (5;0–6;5)	
Sentence Type	Simple	Complex	Simple	Complex
Response Type				
Accept	88**	82**	96**	87**
Reject	82**	58	87**	70**

	Referential Antecedents (82)			
	Youngest (79%) (2;7–3;11)		Oldest (84%) (5;0–6;5)	
Sentence Type	Simple	Complex	Simple	Complex
Response Type				
Accept	93**	88**	93**	88**
Reject	77**	56	90**	64*

*Significant from chance at $p < .05$. **Significant from chance at $p < .01$.

Subsequent to the study by Kaufman, other researchers (Avrutin & Wexler, 1991; Chien & Wexler, 1990; Maxfield & McDaniel, 1991; McDaniel, Cairns, & Hsu, 1990; Thornton & Wexler, 1991) tested the prediction that children would do better with pronouns bound to quantified antecedents than with pronouns coreferential with referential antecedents, with English-, Chinese-, and Russian-speaking children. These results are summarized in Table 7.3.

In each case (with the exception of the Kaufman, 1988, study), the researchers reported that the children showed knowledge of B with quantified antecedents but not with referential antecedents. Again, as with the earlier studies, it seems the results were much more mixed than has been claimed. In the second study in Table 7.3 (McDaniel et al., 1990), the number of children treating the antecedent conditions differently is not very large. Thus, 10 children obeyed Principle B with referential antecedents, whereas 13 obeyed B with quantified antecedents. And 8 disobeyed B with referential antecedents, whereas 3 disobeyed B with quantified antecedents.

In the third study (Chien & Wexler, 1990), it appears that none of the children did well with anything before 4 years of age (raising the question whether these children have knowledge of any version of A or B). From 4 to 6 years of age the children did better on pronouns with quantified rather than referential antecedents, but from 6 to 7 years of age performance on the two was more comparable. In the fourth study (Avrutin & Wexler, 1991), performance on both the referential sentence condition, example (17a), and the quantified sentence condition, example (17b), seem to be poor, yielding scores of 44%/48% and 59%/50% on the two conditions, respectively. However, the researchers stated that *every* (*kazdyj*) in Russian has some referential properties, attributing the children's poor performance with that quantifier to this fact.

> (17) a. Father bear scrubbed him/his head.
> b. Every bear scrubbed him/his head.

These researchers also tested children with the quantifier *who*, in stimulus sentences like (18).

> (18) I know who scrubbed him/his head. Every bear.

The children did very well with these sentences, responding correctly 83%/ 80% of the time. In regard to the antecedent question, however, it is difficult to conclude anything on the basis of the *who* sentences alone. This is because the prominence of the quantified antecedent (uttered at the end of the sentence) might have made it easier for the children to track the referent of the pronoun. To compare the quantified antecedent condition with the

TABLE 7.3

Studies of Principle B With Referential and Quantified Antecedents

Authors	Language (Number of Subjects)	Task	Ages	Sentence Type	Referential Antecedent Percentage Correct	Quantified Antecedent Percentage Correct
Kaufman (1988)	English (60)	TVJT	2;7–3;11	SS	77	82
				CS	56	58
			5;0–6;5	SS	90	87
				CS	64	70
McDaniel, Cairns & Hsu (1990)	English (19)	Judgment task	2;9–6;7	SS	10 children[a] obey B	13 children obey B
					1 unsure	3 unsure
					8 children disobey B	3 children disobey B
Chien & Wexler (1990)	English (177)	YES/NO judgment	up to 4	SS	31	47
			4–5		39	60
			5–6		49	84
			6–7		77	87
Avrutin & Wexler (1991)	Russian (16)	TVJT	4–7	SS	44/48	59/50
				CS[b]		83/80
Maxfield & McDaniel (1991)	English (35)	Judgment task	3;1–6;10	SS[b]	17 children obey B	16 children obey B
					7 mixed	6 mixed
					11 children disobey B	9 children disobey B[c]
Thornton & Wexler (1991)	English (19)	TVJT	4;0–5;1	SS	42	92
				CS	78	90

Note. SS = Simple sentence; CS = Complex sentence; TVJT = Truth-value judgment task.
[a]No percentages were reported. [b]In the referential condition there was also a complex sentence. [c]The numbers do not equal 35, but they are as given on the handout.

referential antecedent condition, one would have had to construct a comparable example, something like (19). But this was not done.[12]

(19) I know that the bear scrubbed him. The bear.

In the fifth study (Maxfield & McDaniel, 1991), the results for referential and quantificational antecedents seem virtually the same. Thus, 17 of the children performed in accordance with Principle B for referential antecedents, and 16 did so for quantified antecedents. Eleven of the children disobeyed B with referential antecedents, and 9, with quantified ones. Finally, in the sixth study (Thornton & Wexler, 1991), the children, ages 4 to 5, appeared to do very well when tested on their knowledge of Principle B with quantified antecedents in VP-deletion contexts. Before testing the VP-deletion contexts, the researchers gave the children simple binding control sentences, like (20a) and (20b).

(20) a. Father bear washed him.
    b. Every bear washed him.

The children correctly rejected these sentences (following a reflexive act-out) 42% and 92% of the time, respectively. Thus, they did twice as well with the quantified antecedent sentence as they did with the referential antecedent one. However, the description of the act-outs suggests that these conditions were not comparable. In the referential condition, only father bear did the washing, whereas in the quantified condition, every bear did the washing in turn, conceivably making the second act-out more salient and easier to judge.

In the VP-deletion context, the children were given sentences like those in (21) and (22), following scenarios in which several toy figures acted out their parts one after the other.

(21) Gonzo washed him and Snuffy did too.

(22) Batman cleaned him and every turtle did too.

---

[12]Another indication that referential tracking might be an issue is given by the fact that the Russian-speaking children did somewhat better with sentences in which the pronoun was in preverbal position (66%), as in example (i), rather than in postverbal position (48%), as in example (ii).

(i) Father bear him scrubbed.
(ii) Father bear scrubbed him.

Avrutin and Wexler (1991) stated that the difference between these two conditions was almost significant, possibly indicating an effect. (Whether the effect was grammatical or a response bias, they did not know.) If such an effect can be found to be significant, it may be that the children were able to do better with (i) versus (ii) because the pronoun is closer to its antecedent, making referential tracking easier.

The results for these two sentences (78% correct rejection and 90% correct rejection) were also quite good. Again, it is difficult to know if these children did as well as they did because they know a Principle B that constrained binding only, or because the act-outs were salient enough to enable them to track the potential referents.[13]

These studies (like the earlier ones) have produced mixed results. In half of the studies the children's performance on the two antecedent types was comparable. In the other half, where the quantified antecedents yielded better scores than the referential ones, it is conceivable that a difference in the saliency of the act-outs for the two antecedent types was at issue.[14] Again, it does not seem that a strong case has been made either for children's performance on pronouns bound to quantified antecedents being better overall than their performance on pronouns coreferential with referential antecedents, or for a reformulated Principle B.

Not everyone agrees with this conclusion. In interpreting their results, Wexler and his colleagues argued that the children's good performance with quantificational antecedents demonstrated knowledge of a revised Principle B, one that deals only with variable pronoun binding. Further, they concluded that the children's poorer performance with referential antecedents revealed a lack of knowledge of a pragmatic principle. In these proposals, the pragmatic principle was given a name, Principle P. But, again, there was no discussion of what the pragmatic principle would be like, how it would operate, or how it would be learned. Thus, we are left to consider the only real candidate for a pragmatic principle (and for a Binding Theory incorporating one) that might explain children's apparently poor performance on tests of Principle B. This is Rule I of Reinhart's Binding Theory (Grodzinsky & Reinhart, in press).

EVALUATING THE REINHART AND THE GRODZINSKY AND REINHART PROPOSALS

Empirical Considerations

Several linguists, among them Lasnik (1986, 1989) and Higginbotham (1985), have argued that Reinhart's (1983) Binding Theory is unable to account for

---

[13] Thornton and Wexler (1991) also tested the children's knowledge of free indexing with pronouns and of reflexives and possessive pronouns in VP-deletion contexts. The children performed quite well with most of these sentences.

[14] A similar point can be made with the picture stimuli used in the Chien and Wexler (1990) experiment. For example, in the picture testing *Is Mama bear touching her?* Goldilocks is watching one bear touch her/herself. In the picture testing *Is every bear touching her?* Goldilocks is watching three bears. Here, too, it is possible that the quantificational stimulus is more salient than the referential stimulus, making judgments about the former easier.

the fact that there are ungrammatical instances of coreference with pronouns for which there is no bound variable alternative, as illustrated in (23).

(23) a. *We$_1$ like me$_1$. (We can't include me.)
        *We like myself.
     b. *John$_1$ and Mary saw him$_1$. (John can't be him.)
        *John and Mary saw himself.

Because illicit coreference is ruled out by the pragmatics, only where there is a bound variable alternative, both Lasnik and Higginbotham claimed that we need a grammatical principle like Principle B to prohibit the illicit coreferential binding in (23).[15]

In addition, Lasnik (1989) argued against any formulation of Binding Theory that excludes a grammatical Principle C. He contended that examples, such as those in (24), in which an R-expression need not be free (as it must in English), argue against a pragmatic approach to disjoint reference, "unless one is willing to posit that speakers of Thai, for example, are less interested in effective communication than speakers of English" (p. 153). What he called for was some modification of a grammatical principle (Principle C) that deals with this parametric variation (see Lasnik, 1989, for details).

(24) a. cɔɔn khít wâa cɔɔn chàlàat.
        'John thinks that John is smart.'   (Thai)
     b. John tin John sĕ thăáng.
        'John believes John will win.' (Vietnamese)
        (In Thai and Vietnamese an R-expression need not always be free.)
     c. cɔɔn chɔɔp cɔɔn.
        'John likes John.' (Thai)
     d. *John thuóng John.
        'John likes John.' (Vietnamese)
        (Within a clause the languages diverge.)

Finally, given the constraints against coindexation, or coindexed interpretation, of coreferential NPs in Reinhart's (1983) and Grodzinsky and Reinhart (in press) formulation, it seems there is no way to represent

---

[15] This argument was originally made in regard to Reinhart's (1983) Binding Theory proposal, in which the pragmatic strategies made reference to linguistic expressions. In Grodzinsky and Reinhart (in press), the possibility of coreference depends not on the availability of an alternative bound expression but on the availability of semantic binding. It is not clear to me how the latter formulation avoids the problems noted. (See Grodzinsky & Reinhart, in press, for discussion.)

obligatory noncoreference (see Montalbetti, 1984, and footnote 10, for discussion), and obligatory coreference and disjoint reference facts (see Finer, 1984; Kaufman, 1988) that appear to characterize the behavior of referential NPs in many languages.

Predictions for Acquisition

In regard to acquisition, Grodzinsky and Reinhart (in press) avoided the learnability problem that arises in relation to pragmatic Principle P (proposed by Wexler and his colleagues) by claiming that both Reinhart's Binding Conditions A and B and the noncoreference rule, Rule I, are innate. As a matter of fact, they even speculated that Rule I may be grammatical, stating that "in the long run [Rule I] may turn out to be just an instance of a more general rule of UG" (p. 27). However, they were then faced with the problem of explaining why some children do not appear to obey an innate principle or rule of UG. To do this, they claimed that the children do not have the computational capacity that is needed to execute the processes involved in judging Rule I–governed structures.

This proposal involving computational capacity appears to make the wrong predictions about acquisition. In regard to Principle B, if the supposedly poor performance of the children on pronouns with referential antecedents (in the studies in Tables 7.1 and 7.3) is to be accounted for by a lack of computational capacity, then children acquiring languages other than English (on which most of the earliest studies were done) should have the same difficulties. This does not seem to be uniformly the case. Looking at the percentages correct for the children in the studies in Table 7.4, one can see that many children do quite well on sentences with referential antecedents, testing knowledge of Principle B. Thus, it seems certainly more reasonable to assume that the cross-linguistic diversity in the children's performance is attributable to systematic variations in syntactic or morphological aspects of the languages being learned (Burzio, 1988; Jakubowicz, in press; Lust, Mazuka, Martohardjono, & Yoon, 1989), or to differences in the tasks used in the various studies (Hamburger & Crain, 1984), rather than to differences in computational capacity.

What about Principle C? Because the Binding Theory of Grodzinsky and Reinhart (in press) has no Principle C, Reinhart and Grodzinsky would have to predict that children, who cannot compute Rule I, will do very poorly with sentences testing Principle C. In Grodzinsky and Reinhart, this prediction is made explicitly. However, the studies in Table 7.5 show that this prediction is not substantiated. Most of the children in these experiments (who are the same ages as the children reported to do poorly with B) do very well in these tasks, correctly rejecting interpretations that are ruled out

TABLE 7.5
Studies of Principle C; A and B Reported Where Also Studied

Authors	Language (Number of Subjects)	Task	Ages	Sentence Type	Principle C Percentage Correct	Principle A Percentage Correct	Principle B Percentage Correct
Lust, Loveland, & Kornet (1980)	English (82)	Act-out	3;10 4;4 4;9 5;2 5;9 6;3 6;9 7;3	CS	80[a] 60[b] 80 70 92 60 90 35 95 50 90 80 80 70 75 96		
Solan (1983)	English (36)	Act-out	5;2–8;5	CS	84		
Lust, Mazuka, Wakayama, & Oshima (1986)	Japanese (76)	Imitation task	3;1–5;11	CS	89% correct imitation where C doesn't block; 72% correct where C does block[c]		
Crain (1986)	English (62)	TVJT	Mean age 4;2	CS	88		
Crain & McKee (1987)	Italian	TVJT	3–5	SS CS SS/CS	88 63		
Eisele (1988)	English (54)	TVJT	4;0–7;11	CS	68	93	83
Eisele & Lust (1990)	English (18)	TVJT	3;0	CS	75		
Grimshaw & Rosen (1990)	English (12)	TVJT	4–5	SS/CS SS	62.5		
McDaniel, Cairns & Hsu (1990)	English (20)	Judgment tasks	3;9–5;4		16 obey C 2 partial 2 no C	16 obey A 4 no A	58 9 obey B 4 partial 7 no B

Note. SS = Simple sentence; CS = Complex sentence. [a]Without pragmatic lead. [b]With pragmatic lead biased toward Principle C violation. [c]Difference is significant.

194

TABLE 7.4

Studies of Principles A and B After 1985, All With Referential Antecedents

Authors	Language (Number of Subjects)	Task	Ages	Sentence Type	Pronouns Percentage Correct	Reflexives Percentage Correct
Deutsch, Koster & Koster (1986)	Dutch (96)	Picture selection (among 4 pictures)	6 8 10	SS	54 71 81	53[a] 87 90
Crain & McKee (1987)	Italian (NR)[c]	TVJT	3–5	SS/CS	83	93
Chien & Wexler (1987)	Chinese (NR)	Picture identification act-out	2;6–6;6	SS/CS	75–90	85–100
Lee & Wexler (1987)	Korean (90)	Act-out	3;7–6;7	SS/CS	35–20	60–100
Solan (1987)	English (37)	Act-out	4–7	CS	38–48	76–92
Jakubowicz & Olsen (1988)	Danish (80)	Act-out	3 4 7–9	CS	70 70 100	100 98 100
Jakubowicz (1989) Experiment 1	French (88)	Picture match	3;0–3;5 3;6–7;0	CS	60 80–90	90 100
Experiment 2		Picture match	3;6–7;0	CS	le = 60–100 lui = 80–100	
McKee (1992)	Italian (30) English (60)	TVJT TVJT	3;7–5;5 2;6–5;3	SS/CS CS/CS	90 61	95 91
Hyams & Sigurjónsdóttir (1988, 1990)	Icelandic (105)	Act-out	2;6–6;0	CS	83–93 (by 4;0)	88–100 (by 3;8)
Chien & Wexler (1990) Experiment 2	(142)	English Act-out	2;6–6;6	CS	52–85	36–95
Experiment 3	(174)	Act-out	2;6–6;6	CS	(say) 37–68 (want) 48–66	44–99 42–99
Sigurjónsdóttir & Hyams (1991)	Icelandic (55)	Act-out TVJT	3;0–6;0	CS	65–100 10–40	58–90 63–100

Note. SS = Simple sentence; CS = Complex sentence; NR = Not reported. [a]Chance = 25%.

195

by Principle C[16] (also see Lust, Eisele, & Mazuka, 1992, for a review of studies supporting children's knowledge of Principle C).

In sum, Reinhart's proposed version of Binding Theory, in which bound variable anaphora is determined by one module of the grammar and coreference is determined by pragmatics (or perhaps another module of the grammar), seems problematic in many respects. First, it does not explain a number of the adult linguistic facts. Second, it does not seem to make the right predictions regarding the acquisition of either Principle B or Principle C. Third, it runs into difficulty explaining the variable (and often good) performance of children whose computation is claimed to be too immature for them to make judgments about coreference relations. Thus, it appears to complicate the grammar without being theoretically or empirically justified.

But if the Binding Theory revision separating bound variable and coreferential anaphora is theoretically and empirically unmotivated, how do we account for the mixed results with Principle B? It seems we must look to the factors involved in tasks designed to test children's knowledge of Principle B. Some of the factors to be considered (involving attention, memory, presuppositions, beliefs, discourse processing, etc.) may also affect children's performance in tests of Principles A and C. But they seem to be particularly problematic in tests of Principle B. (See Kaufman, 1988, for discussion of these differences for Principles A, B, and C.)

Considering the Experimental Task

In many of the studies of Principle B discussed here, children have had to be able to pay attention to actions (or pictorial depictions of actions), to discern the potential actors and recipients of the actions, to track reference across utterances, and to discriminate between matched and mismatched stimuli. In addition, they have had to accommodate what they see to their own biases, presuppositions, and desires regarding how they want the world to be (see Eisele, 1988; Eisele & Lust, 1990; Kaufman, 1988, for discussion

---

[16]Some of the studies gave the following percentages for correct acceptance as well:

Crain and Mckee (1987)
    Principle C—simple sentences—97% acceptance
                    complex sentences—92% acceptance
   Principle A—simple and complex—97% acceptance
   Principle B—simple and complex—97% acceptance
Eisele (1988)
   Principle C—complex sentences—94% acceptance
Eisele and Lust (1990)
   Principle C—complex sentences—74% acceptance
Grimshaw and Rosen (1990)
   Principle C—simple and complex—83% acceptance
   Principle B—simple—83% acceptance

of these issues, particularly in relation to the TVJT). It is not hard to see how such complexity could lead to multiple sources of performance error.

Many researchers have suggested factors that might further complicate the task of establishing and designating the sentential referent for an object pronoun. Some of these complicating factors include: the absence of a linguistic antecedent (Grimshaw & Rosen, 1990; Kaufman, 1988), the effects of contrastive stress (Grimshaw & Rosen, 1990; Maxfield & McDaniel, 1991), the relative rarity and uninformativeness of pronouns in the object position (Limber, 1976), and the effects of sentence complexity (Kaufman, 1988).[17]

Although it is beyond the scope of this chapter to consider any of these factors in detail, a brief discussion of two studies indicates the way in which referential tracking can complicate the task of demonstrating knowledge of Principle B. In the first, Deutsch, Koster, and Koster (1986) asked children, ages 6, 8, and 10, to choose the correct picture for sentences with pronouns and reflexives (see Table 7.4 for results). This study differed from most of the other studies of Principles A and B in giving the children the opportunity to choose among potential actors as well as potential recipients of the action. Thus, it was possible to see whether, in designating reference, the children were having difficulty with the choice of the proform (and by implication with the Binding Principles) or with the choice of the antecedent (a reference tracking problem). With the Principle B examples, the children mistakenly chose the picture in which the antecedent (actor) was different but the type of action (self or other) was the same as that described by the stimulus sentence, 30% (age 6), 20% (age 8), and 10% (age 10) of the time. This contrasts with their incorrectly choosing the picture in which the action (self or other) was different from that described by the stimulus sentence, 11% (age 6), 8% (age 8), and 10% (age 10) of the time.

The second study was by Kaufman (1989). Sixty children, ages 2;7 to 6;5, were asked to evaluate the grammaticality of sentences with first person pronominals and reflexives. In this study, in which the pragmatic effects of designating reference are neutralized, the children were very successful in designating which sentences with both pronominals and reflexives were ungrammatical. The younger children categorized 77% of the ungrammatical reflexive sentences and 73% of the ungrammatical pronominal sentences as baby talk. And the older children designated 85% of the ungrammatical reflexive sentences and 88% of the ungrammatical pronominal sentences as baby talk. Thus, where the problem of referential tracking was no longer an issue, children not only performed very well on sentences testing Principle B, they did as well as on those testing Principle A.

---

[17]It is clear that most of the children tested in these studies of Binding Theory could understand and use sentences of the complexity given in the tasks. Thus, the claim is not that sentence complexity per se is the problem. It is, rather, that in tasks requiring the tracking and designation of reference, increased sentence complexity can cause an increase in overall task difficulty.

In sum, it seems clear from the children's performance on tests of Principle B that they have knowledge of a grammatical principle, like B. It also seems apparent that the children have difficulty consistently demonstrating this knowledge. For those of us who have been hopeful about being able to devise tasks that transparently demonstrate children's grammatical knowledge, an appeal to a multiplicity of pragmatic factors to explain children's variable performance with Principle B may not seem very satisfying. However, given the complexity of performance in this case, it seems unlikely that a single pragmatic principle (whatever form it takes) will ever explain children's performance either in accord with or in violation of the grammar.

ACKNOWLEDGMENTS

I would like to thank Henry Goehl, Barbara Lust, Gary Milsark, and an anonymous reviewer for their many helpful suggestions.

REFERENCES

Avrutin, S., & Wexler, K. (1991). *Development of binding and LF movement in Russian.* Paper presented at the 16th Annual Boston University Conference on Language Development, Boston, MA.

Avrutin, S., & Wexler, K. (1991). *Development of principle B in Russian: Coindexation at LF and coreference.* Unpublished manuscript, MIT, Cambridge, MA.

Burzio, L. (1988). *On the non-existence of disjoint reference principles.* Paper presented at the annual meeting of the Linguistic Society of America, New Orleans, LA.

Chien, Y.-C., & Wexler, K. (1987). *A comparison between Chinese-speaking and English-speaking children's acquisition of reflexives and pronouns.* Paper presented at the 12th Annual Boston University Conference on Language Development, Boston, MA.

Chien, Y.-C., & Wexler, K. (1990). Children's knowledge of locality conditions in binding as evidence for the modularity of syntax and pragmatics. *Language Acquisition, 1,* 225–295.

Chomsky, N. (1976). Conditions on rules of grammar. *Linguistic Analysis, 2,* 303–351.

Chomsky, N. (1981). *Lectures on government and binding.* Dordrecht: Foris.

Chomsky, N. (1986). *Knowledge of language: Its nature, origin and use.* New York: Praeger.

Crain, S. (1986). *On the developmental autonomy of syntax.* Paper presented at the 11th Annual Boston University Conference on Language Development, Boston, MA.

Crain, S., & McKee, C. (1985). Acquisition of structural restrictions on anaphora. *Proceedings of the North Eastern Linguistics Society, 16,* 94–110.

Crain, S., & McKee, C. (1987). *Cross-linguistic analysis of the acquisition of coreference relations.* Paper presented at the 12th Annual Boston University Conference on Language Development, Boston, MA.

Deutsch, W., Koster, C., & Koster, J. (1986). What can we learn from children's errors of understanding anaphora? *Linguistics, 24,* 203–225.

Eisele, J. (1988). *Meaning and form in children's judgments about language.* Unpublished master's thesis, Cornell University, Ithaca, NY.

Eisele, J., & Lust, B. (1990). *Knowledge about pronouns: A developmental study using the 'truth value judgment task.'* Unpublished manuscript.

Finer, D. (1984). *The formal grammar of switch reference.* Unpublished doctoral dissertation, University of Massachusetts, Amherst.

Grimshaw, J., & Rosen, S. T. (1990). Knowledge and obedience: The developmental status of the binding theory. *Linguistic Inquiry, 21,* 187–222.

Grodzinsky, Y., & Reinhart, T. (in press). The innateness of binding and coreference: A reply to Grimshaw and Rosen. *Linguistic Inquiry.*

Hamburger, H., & Crain, S. (1984). Acquisition of cognitive compiling. *Cognition, 17,* 85–136.

Higginbotham, J. (1983). Logical form, binding, and nominals. *Linguistic Inquiry, 14,* 395–420.

Higginbotham, J. (1985). On semantics. *Linguistic Inquiry, 16,* 547–593.

Hyams, N., & Sigurjónsdóttir, S. (1988). *A cross-linguistic comparison of the development of referentially dependent elements.* Paper presented at the 13th Annual Boston University Conference on Language Development, Boston, MA.

Hyams, N., & Sigurjónsdóttir, S. (1990). The development of "long-distance anaphora": A cross-linguistic comparison with special reference to Icelandic. *Language Acquisition, 1,* 57–93.

Jakubowicz, C. (1984). On markedness and binding principles. *Proceedings of the North Eastern Linguistic Society, 14,* 154–182.

Jakubowicz, C. (1989). *Maturation or invariance of universal grammar principles in language acquisition.* Paper presented at the 14th Annual Boston University Conference on Language Development, Boston, MA.

Jakubowicz, C. (in press). Binding principles and acquisition facts revisited. *Proceedings of the North Eastern Linguistic Society, 21.*

Jakubowicz, C., & Olsen, L. (1988). *The acquisition of reflexive anaphors and pronominals in Danish.* Paper presented at the 13th Annual Boston University Conference on Language Development, Boston, MA.

Kaufman, D. K. (1987). *"Who's him?": Evidence for Principle B in children's grammar.* Paper presented at the 12th Annual Boston University Conference on Language Development, Boston, MA.

Kaufman, D. K. (1988). *Grammatical and cognitive interactions in the study of children's knowledge of binding theory and reference relations.* Unpublished doctoral dissertation, Temple University, Philadelphia, PA.

Kaufman, D. K. (1989). *Reference Aside: Children's judgments of I like me.* Unpublished manuscript, Temple University, Philadelphia, PA.

Lasnik, H. (1976). Remarks on coreference. *Linguistic Analysis, 2,* 1–22.

Lasnik, H. (1986). *On the necessity of binding conditions.* Paper presented at the Princeton Workshop on Comparative Grammar, Princeton, NJ.

Lasnik, H. (1989). *Essays on Anaphora.* Dordrecht: Kluwer.

Lee, H., & Wexler, K. (1987). *The acquisition of reflexive and pronoun in Korean: From the cross-linguistic perspective.* Paper presented at the 12th Annual Boston University Conference on Language Development, Boston, MA.

Limber, J. (1976). Unravelling competence, performance and pragmatics in the speech of young children. *Journal of Child Language, 3,* 309–318.

Lust, B., Eisele, J., & Mazuka, R. (1992). The Binding Theory module: Evidence from first language acquisition for Principle C. *Language, 68,* 333–358.

Lust, B., Loveland, K., & Kornet, R. (1980). The development of anaphora in first language: Syntactic and pragmatic constraints. *Linguistic Analysis, 6,* 217–249.

Lust, B., Mazuka, R., Martohardjono, G., & Yoon, J. (1989). *On parameter-setting in first language acquisition: The case of the Binding Theory.* Paper presented at GLOW, Utrecht.

Lust, B., Mazuka, R., Wakayama, T., & Oshima, S. (1986). *When is an anaphor not an anaphor?* Paper presented at the annual meeting of the Linguistic Society of America, New York, NY.

Maxfield, T., & McDaniel, D. (1991). *Principle B and contrastive stress.* Paper presented at the 16th Annual Boston University Conference on Language Development, Boston, MA.

McDaniel, D., Cairns, H. S., & Hsu, H. R. (1990). Binding principles in the grammars of young children. *Language Acquisition, 1,* 121–138.

McKee, C. (1992). A comparison of pronouns and anaphors in Italian and English acquisition. *Language Acquisition, 2,* 21–54.

Montalbetti, M. (1984). *After binding.* Unpublished doctoral dissertation, MIT, Cambridge, MA.

Montalbetti, M., & Wexler, K. (1985). Binding is linking. *Proceedings of West Coast Conference on Formal Linguistics, 4,* 228–245.

Otsu, Y. (1981). *Universal grammar and syntactic development in children: Toward a theory of syntactic development.* Unpublished doctoral dissertation, MIT, Cambridge, MA.

Padilla Rivera, J. A. (1985). *On the definition of Binding Domains in Spanish: The roles of the binding module and the lexicon.* Unpublished doctoral dissertation, Cornell University, Ithaca, NY.

Reinhart, T. (1976). *The syntactic domain of anaphora.* Unpublished doctoral dissertation, MIT, Cambridge, MA.

Reinhart, T. (1983). *Anaphora and semantic interpretation.* Chicago: University of Chicago Press.

Reinhart, T. (1986). Center and periphery in the grammar of anaphora. In B. Lust (Ed.), *Studies in the acquisition of anaphora: Vol. 1. Defining the constraints* (pp. 123–150). Dordrecht: Reidel.

Sigurjónsdóttir, S., & Hyams, N. (1991). *The acquisition of binding in Icelandic.* Paper presented at the 16th Annual Boston University Conference on Language Development, Boston, MA.

Solan, L. (1983). *Pronominal reference: Child language and the theory of grammar.* Dordrecht: Reidel.

Solan, L. (1987). Parameter setting and the development of pronouns and reflexives. In T. Roeper & E. Williams (Eds.), *Parameter setting* (pp. 189–210). Dordrecht: Reidel.

Solan, L., & Ortiz, R. (1982). *The development of pronouns and reflexives: Evidence from Spanish.* Paper presented at the Seventh Annual Boston University Conference on Language Development, Boston, MA.

Thornton, R., & Wexler, K. (1991). *VP ellipsis and the binding principles in young children's grammars.* Paper presented at the 16th Annual Boston University Conference on Language Development, Boston, MA.

Wexler, K., & Chien, Y.-C. (1985). The development of lexical anaphors and pronouns. In *Papers and Reports on Child Language Development, 24,* 183–149.

CHAPTER EIGHT

Problems With Pronoun Acquisition

Charlotte Koster
University of Groningen

THE TRADITIONAL BINDING THEORY

Knowledge of anaphora in relation to reflexives and pronominals is traditionally summed up in two of the principles of the Binding Theory (Chomsky, 1981). Principle A states that a bound anaphor, like the reflexive *himself*, must be bound in its governing category, and Principle B states that a free anaphor, like the pronominal *him*, must not be bound in its governing category.

Based on the Principles and Parameters view of language acquisition, it has been proposed that the principles of the Binding Theory should have an innate basis as part of what is often called Universal Grammar. Children's knowledge of the Binding Theory principles has been quite extensively investigated during the last decade, but the empirical evidence does not give as straightforward a picture as was originally expected.

Children's performance on anaphora tasks is more of a mixed success than had been predicted. Correct understanding of anaphoric reference with pronominals and reflexives is not instantaneously visible in very young children; but it does improve over time. Developmental patterns for sentences with reflexives and pronominals also do not necessarily run parallel. One of the more consistent results is that children relatively quickly and easily come to understand bound anaphors, such as reflexives. In the case of pronominals, development is usually (but not always) slow, often stagnating and problematic for many years, even up into middle childhood. In some experimental studies, children seem to be interpreting pronouns as

201

if they were reflexives, and this is the one error that they should not be making. To make the picture even more confusing, there are also situations in which children perform equally well on sentences with pronominals and sentences with reflexives, or even better on sentences with pronominals (Kaufman, 1992).

If both Binding Theory principles are presumed to be part of innate linguistic knowledge, how is it possible that children often, but not always, seem to apply one principle earlier and better than the other? Several proposals have been made as to what the problem is with the Binding Theory and the acquisition of anaphoric elements in general, or with Principle B and the acquisition of pronouns in particular (Grimshaw & Rosen, 1990; C. Koster, 1988).

The main focus of this chapter is the proposal that the traditional Binding Theory may be incorrectly stated and, specifically, that Principle B is in need of a reformulation that separates grammatical binding from intended coreference interpretations. This separation would entail a strict distinction between knowledge of a grammatical sort and knowledge of a pragmatic sort, the former presumed to be part of Universal Grammar and available from an early age, the latter presumed to be based on knowledge of the world that may be acquired only gradually, via experience.

In the traditional version of the Binding Theory, reflexives are always given a bound variable interpretation, whereas pronominals are open to either a bound variable interpretation that is grammatically determined or to an intended coreference interpretation that is in part pragmatically determined. The fact that pragmatic rules are brought into play for pronominals and not for reflexives could result in an imbalance between children's success with reflexives and pronouns.

THE REFORMULATED BINDING THEORY

A recent attempt to reformulate the Binding Theory centers specifically on problems with pronouns: What must be explained grammatically and what can be explained pragmatically (Montalbetti & Wexler, 1985; Reinhart, 1983, 1986). The suggestion is that the core issue of a syntactic Binding Theory should be bound variable interpretation, and not intended coreference, of pronominals as well as reflexives. The reformulated Principle B, therefore, would also be limited to grammatical binding. Constraints on intended coreference of pronouns, in this view, should not be considered part of a theory of grammar; they are, instead, limited to the domain of pragmatics.

In Reinhart's version of the reformulated Binding Theory, the anaphoric element must be syntactically bound, c-commanded by its antecedent, either within its governing category (for reflexives) or outside its governing category (for pronominals), in order to receive an interpretation. Reinhart's (1983) reformulated Binding Theory is as follows:

(1) *Binding Theory:*
Coindex a pronoun P with a c-commanding NP *alpha* (*alpha* not immediately dominated by COMP or S').

Conditions:
A: If P is an R-pronoun, *alpha* must be in its minimal governing category.
B: If P is a non-R-pronoun, *alpha* must be outside its minimal governing category.

For coreference, Reinhart (1983) described a Speaker's Strategy and a Hearer's Strategy, formulated as Rule I (Grodzinsky & Reinhart, 1993):

(2) *Rule I (inference):*
A free NP, *A*, can be intended as coreferential with NP *B*, in the same sentence, iff either
a. it is impossible to replace *A* with a (distinct) anaphoric expression that can be bound by *B*, or
b. the coreference interpretation needs to be distinguished from the bound interpretation.

Recently, Chien and Wexler (1990) stated the reformulation of Principle B in terms of only the local domain: Pronouns cannot have a bound variable reading with a c-commanding antecedent in the local domain. The key to reformulating the Binding Theory, according to them, lies in the role of indices: Anaphors must have the same index as the local c-commanding antecedent, whereas pronouns may not have the same index as the local c-commanding antecedent. The semantics and pragmatics must deal with the interpretation of these indices. In the case of Principle A, anaphors and their antecedents have the same index and are intended to refer to the same entity; coindexation implies intended coreference here. Principle B rules out the possibility of a pronoun and a local c-commanding NP having the same index. The pronominal cannot be locally bound.

The critical question for pronouns now is: When a pronoun has a different index from the local c-commanding NP, what does this noncoindexing imply? It can be demonstrated that it does not necessarily imply disjoint reference. Chien and Wexler gave the following example to demonstrate that disjoint reference is not always entailed:

(3) That$_i$ must be John$_j$.
(4) a. *At least he$_i$ looks like him$_i$.

b. At least he$_i$ looks like him$_j$.

Coindexing in (4a) is ruled out because *him* is bound in its governing category. In (4b), where the pronoun is not bound and no binding principle is violated, noncoindexing does not necessarily demand disjointness: *He* and *him* can both refer to the same entity, the NP *John*. Although two coindexed NPs must corefer, as in (4a), two noncoindexed NPs are simply free in reference, as in (4b). Chien and Wexler proposed a Principle P (P = pragmatics), like Reinhart's Rule I, to handle the pragmatic coreference cases like (4b), where *he* and *him* are not coindexed but nevertheless can be coreferentially interpreted.

The reformulated Principle B applies only to bound variable readings of pronouns and not to (4), which allowed a pragmatic, intended coreference interpretation of two noncoindexed NPs. In order for a pronoun to be interpreted as a bound variable, it must be coindexed with its antecedent and, as Principle B states, this must not occur in the local domain. Compare Reinhart's example (5) with (4).

(5) Each of the boys$_i$ brought his$_i$ bear.
    For all x (x is a boy), x brought x's bear.

The pronoun *his* is coindexed with the quantified phrase *each of the boys* and is interpreted as a variable bound by this antecedent. It does not have a fixed value here, because this value depends upon the choice of quantified antecedent. Quantified NPs have no reference.

Now, look at an example of a quantified NP and an object pronoun c-commanded by that NP. Compare Chien and Wexler's example (6) with (4) and (5):

(6) Every woman$_i$ looks like her·$_{i/j}$.

For the pronoun *her* to be interpreted as a variable bound by the quantified expression *every woman*, the two must be coindexed. Coindexing here is ruled out by Principle B. What is left is the noncoindexed reading: With a quantified antecedent, this must be interpreted as a non–bound variable reading, and the two cannot refer to one and the same entity. In such sentences with quantified antecedents only one principle applies, the reformulated Principle B. This grammatical principle is not confounded with pragmatic principles, as in (4).

The reformulated Principle B is meant to be a syntactic principle governing relationships between pronominals and their antecedents when both have identical syntactic indices. The interpretation of the relationships between NPs with different indices will be governed by pragmatic principles. It is then not

Principle B but the pragmatic principles that are not fully understood by children. If such rules are not available to a child, he or she will not know whether a noncoindexed pronominal and NP should have a coreference or a disjoint reference interpretation.

EXPERIMENTAL EVIDENCE

If a reformulation of the Binding Theory were the correct route to take, the problematic experimental acquisition results with pronouns could become more understandable. Many previous experiments have focused on intended coreference readings of antecedent-pronoun relations. If the Binding Theory and the rules for determining coreference are to be seen as stemming from separate knowledge sources, then it is possible that children can be expected to know the (reformulated) grammatical Principles A and B, but not necessarily the pragmatic rules of coreference. The fact that many errors are made with the coreference relations involving pronominals is then a problem for pragmatics and not for linguistic theory.

Quantified and Definite NP Antecedents in Simple Sentences

In experimental work, Chien and Wexler (1990) attempted to investigate the knowledge of children (2;6 to 7;0 years old) of the reformulated Binding Theory and the acquisition of bound variable versus coreferential interpretations. The sentences in (7)–(10) were designed specifically to test the child's knowledge of bound variable interpretations. They include either definite NPs or quantified NPs in the local c-commanding position.

(7) This is Goldilocks; this is Mama Bear.
Is Mama Bear touching herself?

(8) This is Mama Bear; this is Goldilocks.
Is Mama Bear touching her?

(9) This is Goldilocks; these are the bears.
Is every bear touching herself?

(10) These are the bears; this is Goldilocks.
Is every bear touching her?

Sentences (7) and (9) always give a bound variable reading. The antecedent and the reflexive have the same index and refer to the same entity. Recall that the claim of the proponents of reformulation was that interpretation of sentence type (8) confounds grammatical and pragmatic knowledge. So, even if a child understands that NPs are noncoindexed, the child can still allow a coreference interpretation if knowledge of pragmatic principles is lacking. Sentence (10), in contrast, is a clear test of syntactic knowledge only. In this case, noncoindexation cannot be confounded with coreference: In order for a pronoun to have a bound variable reading—which it must have if the antecedent is a quantifier—it must be coindexed with its antecedent. Because this is not the case in (10), there can be no coreference between the two NPs.

Using these sentences, the difference between children's understanding of intended coreference and that of bound variable interpretations can be compared. Sentences (7) and (9) showed the usual quick mastery of reflexives. Sentence (8) gave poor results with little or no improvement over age. Sentence (10), however, did not show the same results pattern as sentence (8); with this sentence type, children performed much better. The pattern for (10) closely resembled the response patterns obtained with the reflexive sentences (7) and (9); that is, a more consistent and rapid improvement over age, with only a slight acquisitional lag behind the reflexive sentences.

The children's success with (10) is attributed to the fact that in this sentence, the c-commanding NP in the local domain is a quantified NP. According to the reformulated Principle B based on the bound variable interpretation of pronouns, children know that grammatical binding of a pronominal and a quantified antecedent cannot occur in the local domain. The presence of the quantified NP in the local domain thus blocks the child's choice of an (incorrect) intended coreference interpretation: A reading of the quantified NP *every bear* as the antecedent of the pronoun *her* is claimed to be effectively prohibited by the reformulated Principle B.

These results on sentences with quantified NPs seem to support the claim that the core issue of Binding Principles A and B should be bound variable anaphora. More investigation into acquisition is called for, however, before such a distinction between bound variable interpretations and intended coreference can be assessed.

Quantified and Definite NP Antecedents in VP-Deletion Sentences

Reinhart (1986) pointed out that bound variable interpretation of pronominals is not limited to quantified NP antecedents. Pronominals can also have bound variable interpretations with definite NP antecedents, like names. The difference is that sentences with quantified antecedents allow only a bound variable interpretation, whereas sentences with definite antecedents allow both a bound variable interpretation and a pragmatic coreference interpretation.

The VP-deletion sentence, a coordinate construction where the verb phrase has been deleted in the second conjunct, reveals this ambiguity. If the first conjunct of a VP-deletion sentence contains a definite NP subject and a pronoun in the verb phrase, then the pronoun in the second conjunct can have both bound variable and intended coreference interpretations. This VP-deletion sentence type is also used in a test for true anaphoricity, the sloppy identity test. Reinhart (1986) gave the following examples:

(11) Charlie$_i$ talks to his$_i$ dog and Max$_j$ does too.
    a. Max$_j$ talks to his$_i$ dog too.
    b. Max$_j$ talks to his$_j$ dog.

One interpretation of the deleted conjunct in this example is that of (11a), the intended coreference *Max talks to Charlie's dog*: Reference has been fixed in the first conjunct and copied into the second conjunct. This is known as the *strict identity* reading. In the other interpretation, (11b) *Max talks to Max's dog*, the first conjunct contains an open formula, *x talks to x's dog*, which is satisfied by *Charlie* in the first conjunct and by *Max* in the second conjunct. This is the bound variable *sloppy identity* reading, and only this reading is considered to be provided by the reformulated Binding Theory.

The sloppy identity reading in (11b) shows that the application of the reformulated Principle B is not limited to sentences with quantified NPs as possible antecedents. This is the desired situation, because children's acquisition of pronominal use should not have to stand or fall on the presence or absence of a quantifier in a sentence. It would be a very narrow basis for Universal Grammar knowledge of the binding if success in understanding the use of pronominals was dependent upon such complex expressions as quantified NPs.

The following prediction can now be tested: If the reformulated Principle B is correct, then when dealing with a VP-deletion sentence without quantifiers, like (11), children should have no difficulties acquiring (11b), the bound variable interpretation. As for (11a), the intended coreference interpretation, children may or may not have the pragmatic strategies that are needed to understand this reading correctly.

VP-Deletion Experiments in Dutch

Recall that the classic error in previous experiments that is relevant for the reformulated Binding Theory is the incorrect interpretation of a pronominal as if it were reflexive. Both Wexler and Reinhart claimed that this classic error should not be a grammatical error (incorrectly coindexing the pronominal with a c-commanding antecedent from the same domain), but that it should be possible to expose this error as a pragmatic, intended coreference error (incorrectly allowing a noncoindexed pronominal and local c-commanding

NP to corefer). The VP-deletion sentences can critically test these questions about the source of pronoun errors in previous experiments.

The Dutch studies to be presented were designed to focus on how children resolve the reference problem in VP-deletion sentences containing the object pronoun *him*. A simplified form of a pronominal test sentence is given in (12):

(12) Bert wijst naar hem en Ernie ook.
'Bert points at him and Ernie (does) too.'

If the pronoun in the first conjunct of (12) is incorrectly interpreted as reflexive (*Bert points to Bert*), is this an intended coreference, pragmatic error or is it a grammatical error? The second, VP-deletion part of the sentence will give the answer. If a child does indeed interpret the nonreflexive *him* in the first conjunct as if it were reflexive, then the second conjunct can be given either an intended coreference or a bound variable reading. For example, when *Bert* incorrectly points to *Bert* in the first conjunct, then will *Ernie* also point to *Bert* (13b), or will *Ernie* point to *Ernie* (13c)? The former interpretation implies that the child has fixed the referent in the first conjunct and has copied it into the second conjunct; (13b) would be an incorrect strict identity, intended coreference response. The latter interpretation would imply that the child is using an open formula and is giving an incorrect sloppy identity, bound variable interpretation, as in (13c).

(13) a. *Correct indexing and coreference:*
Bert$_i$ points to him$_j$ (Pipo) and Ernie$_k$ points to him$_j$ (Pipo).
b. *Incorrect coreference/pragmatic error:*
Bert$_i$ points at him$_j$ (Bert) and Ernie$_k$ points at him$_j$ (Bert)
c. *Incorrect indexing/grammatical error:*
Bert$_i$ points at him$_i$ (Bert) and Ernie$_k$ points at him$_k$ (Ernie)

The incorrect intended coreference interpretation in the VP-deletion conjunct would indicate that the pronoun is being interpreted pragmatically in both parts of the sentence. The cause of this error should be sought outside the domain of grammar, according to the reformulated Binding Theory. An incorrect bound variable interpretation of the VP-deletion part would indicate that children are giving the sentence an incorrect reflexive, anaphoric interpretation, which should be impossible if the reformulated Binding Theory were correct.

Subjects and Experimental Task. The Dutch work presented here was carried out at the University of Utrecht in the spring of 1989 (Experiment 1) and in the spring of 1991 at the Netherlands Institute for Advanced Study

(NIAS) in Wassenaar (Experiment 2). Experiment 1 included 4- and 6-year-olds, 6 in each age group. Experiment 2 included 4-, 6-, and 8-year-olds, 10, 11, and 10 children in the respective age groups.

The experimental task was the same across experiments. The child listened to a sentence, repeated it, and then acted it out. This acting out task might have the disadvantage of only discovering a child's first preference, not absolute acceptance or rejection of a sentence's various grammatical and ungrammatical interpretations. But it has several advantages, too. The experimenter does not restrict the child's options of interpretation by offering only certain choices that are limited and possibly, from the child's perspective, all incorrect. Because no specific answers are offered, children know that they can give whatever interpretation they see fit to give. When children do not understand a sentence in an adult way, they may show a consistent deviant interpretation or they may randomly act out different scenes. Such answers are informative in pinpointing what the children's problems of interpretation may be.

Test Sentences. Experiment 1 included 6 sentences each of the types (14a), (14b), and (14c), and 15 filler sentences. In total, each child heard 33 sentences. Experiment 2 included 3 each of (15a) and (15b), 4 each of (16a) and (16b), and 3 each of (17a) and (17b), together with 22 filler sentences, 42 sentences in total.

Sentence (17) had a quantified NP, *iemand* 'someone', as a local c-commanding NP in the first conjunct. The other test sentences contained definite NPs, proper names, in this same position. The test sentences also varied as to how the possible recipient of the action was introduced, either in a lead-in sentence (*Here's Bert, Ernie, and Pipo*) or sentence-internally in several different positions. Basic examples are given here:

(14) a. Hier heb je Ernie, Pipo en Bert . . .
          Bert wijst naar zichzelf en Ernie ook.
          'Here's Ernie, Pipo, and Bert . . .
          Bert points at himself and Ernie (does) too.'
      b. Hier heb je Ernie, Pipo, en Bert . . .
          Bert wijst naar hem en Ernie ook.
          'Here's Ernie, Pipo, and Bert . . .
          Bert points at him and Ernie (does) too.'
      c. Hier heb je Ernie, Pipo en Bert . . .
          Bert wijst naar zijn auto en Ernie ook.
          'Here's Ernie, Pipo, and Bert . . .
          Bert points at his car and Ernie (does) too.'

(15) a. Bert wijst met Pipo's stokje naar zichzelf en Ernie ook.
          'Bert points with Pipo's stick at himself and Ernie (does) too.'
      b. Bert wijst met Pipo's stokje naar hem en Ernie ook.
          'Bert points with Pipo's stick at him and Ernie (does) too.'

(16) a. Pipo zegt dat Bert naar zichzelf moet wijzen en Ernie ook.
'Pipo says that Bert should point at himself and Ernie (should)
too.'

   b. Pipo zegt dat Bert naar hem moet wijzen en Ernie ook.
'Pipo says that Bert should point at him and Ernie (should) too.'

(17) a. Pipo zegt dat iemand naar zichzelf moet wijzen en Ernie ook.
'Pipo says that someone should point at himself and Ernie
(should) too.'

   b. Pipo zegt dat iemand naar hem moet wijzen en Ernie ook.
'Pipo says that someone should point at him and Ernie (should)
too.'

Sentence (17), with the quantified NP *iemand* '*someone*', had some special problems and is discussed in a later section dealing with quantified NP problems in general.

The sentence type (14c), with the possessive pronoun phrase *his car*, was included for a baseline investigation of Dutch children's understanding of VP-deletion constructions. Do the children have knowledge of the constituent structure of such VP-deletion sentences? Are they able to reconstruct the deleted VP in the second conjunct? It was indeed the case that the Dutch children were able to understand the underlying representations of these VP-deletion constructions. The children realized that these structures with possessive pronouns are ambiguous; they were able to fill in both the strict and the sloppy identity readings in the second conjunct, with a preference for the sloppy identity. At the same time, the children did not allow these sentences to have completely free readings—they obeyed constraints against impossible interpretations.

More support for children's knowledge of the constituent structure of VP-deletion sentences has recently come from Foley and others, who tested young English-speaking children between 2;10 and 5;8 years of age (Foley, Nuñez del Prado, Barbier, & Lust, 1992). They tested these children using sentences that involved either inalienable or alienable possession, like (18) and (19):

(18) Big Bird scratches his arm and Ernie does too.

(19) Scooter moves his penny and Bert does too.

These children also showed that they understood the underlying representations of these structures, with results similar to those of the Dutch study.

All in all, it can be concluded that children do have the grammatical competence necessary for understanding VP-deletion sentences. These findings point to the suitability of such VP-deletion sentences for the study of children's understanding of object position reflexives and pronominals.

Experimental Results and Discussion. The main contrast in the Dutch studies is between sentences containing reflexives and those containing pronominals. According to any interpretation of the Binding Theory, the deleted VP in (14a), (15a), and (16a) with the reflexive *himself* (*zichzelf* in Dutch), is open only to a bound variable interpretation: coindexing of the reflexive and the local c-commanding antecedent (*Bert points at Bert*, and *Ernie points at Ernie*). As long as the children understand the VP constructions, they should have no problems with these sentences.

The only acceptable interpretation of the sentences with the pronominal *him* (*hem*), (14b), (15b), and (16b), involves *Bert* and *Ernie* pointing to some person other than themselves. What is of interest in these sentences is: (a) does the child incorrectly interpret the pronoun in the first conjunct as if it were reflexive; and (b) if this actually does happen, then is it a case of incorrect coindexing or of letting noncoindexed entities incorrectly corefer? The standard Binding Theory already falls short in explaining (a). The reformulated Binding Theory is tested in (a) and (b) together.

The pronominal sentences with definite NPs, (14b), (15b), and (16b), give the children the critical option of making either of two error types. If the first conjunct gets a reflexive interpretation (*Bert* points at himself) and the second conjunct gets a nonreflexive interpretation (*Ernie* points at *Bert*) then this would be an incorrect pragmatic interpretation and outside the domain of grammar. The reason for this error response must be sought not in incorrect coindexing but in incorrect coreference and the child's lack of pragmatic knowledge. The other possible error response is associated with a critical test for the reformulated Binding Theory: It should be impossible for a child to give the pronominal a reflexive interpretation in both the first and second conjunct. This response would be evidence that a pronoun is coindexed with the local c-commanding NP and is interpreted as a bound variable, reflexive anaphor. Because the grammatical knowledge that a child is expected to have via the reformulated Binding Theory should forbid this response, its occurrence would be evidence against such a reformulation.

Some of the results of these studies are given in Table 8.1. The expected response for reflexive sentences is the *reflexive/reflexive* response and for pronominal sentences it is the *nonreflexive/nonreflexive* response.

Percentages in Table 8.1 do not always total at 100% per sentence type. This is due to rounded off subtotals and the exclusion of some responses that did not fit into the four response groups.

As is often the case, the children had no problems giving a grammatically correct interpretation to reflexive test sentences with definite NPs. The children were all relatively successful with these VP-deletion sentences including reflexives. The few errors that occurred were spread out over various response types, almost never exceeding 10% per error type.

TABLE 8.1
Percentages of Responses in First and Second Conjuncts of the Sentence,
per Age Group and per Sentence Type

First Conjunct Second Conjunct	Reflexive Reflexive			Nonreflexive Nonreflexive			Reflexive Nonreflexive			Nonreflexive Reflexive		
Age Group	4	6	8	4	6	8	4	6	8	4	6	8
Sentence												
(14a)-himself	100	100	—	0	0	—	0	0	—	0	0	—
(15a)-himself	83	85	93	7	3	7	3	12	0	0	0	0
(16a)-himself	88	84	90	10	4	7	0	8	4	0	4	0
(14b)-him	50	63	—	38	36	—	0	0	—	0	0	—
(15b)-him	53	18	40	47	64	57	0	6	3	0	3	0
(16b)-him	33	14	5	58	75	90	3	5	0	5	5	5

The only correct response to the sentences with the pronominal *him* was nonreflexive/nonreflexive. The pronominal–quantified NP results are discussed later. For the pronominal sentences with definite NPs, Table 8.1 shows that, for the youngest group, correct response rates are roughly equal to the incorrect response rates: around 50%. In general, correct pronoun performance on these sentences lags behind that of reflexives, with either no change or a slow improvement over age. These results for the VP-deletion sentences resemble the pattern often found in studies using other sentence constructions. This is, by now, the classic problem in anaphora acquisition research: How is the pronominal lag explained?

How does the proposed reformulation of Principle B fare as an explanation of the pronominal errors? Recall that a reformulated Binding Theory would apply only to bound variable interpretations. Because this knowledge would be considered to have an innate basis, all errors with pronominals should, ideally, be exposed as cases of incorrect pragmatic coreference and not as cases of incorrect coindexing. In VP-deletion sentences there should be no errors with pronominal sentences that resemble a double-reflexive, sloppy identity reading—the reflexive/reflexive pattern, because this error would show the child to be misinterpreting the pronominal as reflexive and giving it an incorrect bound variable interpretation in the second conjunct, too. For a reformulated Binding Theory, the only acceptable errors with pronominals would be the reflexive/nonreflexive combination, demonstrating that the error was to some degree unimportant grammatically, according to the reformulated Binding Theory, because it is beyond the domain of the grammar and must be explained via pragmatics.

Now let's look at the percentages of error responses in Table 8.1. The table shows that the error responses for pronominal VP-deletion sentences with definite NPs are exactly the kind of response that should not be possible, based on the reformulated Binding Theory. There are many reflexive/reflexive errors and basically no reflexive/nonreflexive errors. That is to say, the children regularly give pronominals a bound variable, reflexive interpretation over both parts of these VP-deletion sentences: The coindexed sloppy identity reading. The 4-year-olds actually score equally on incorrect and correct responses, roughly 50%. Rarely do the children first misinterpret the pronominal as a reflexive and then let the object of the second half of the sentence corefer with that in the first half, the pragmatic coreference solution. This is strong evidence against the reformulated Binding Theory.

In conclusion, these experiments do not motivate a reformulation of the Binding Theory as an improvement over the traditional Binding Theory in predicting or explaining children's acquisition of anaphoric relations. Children do make errors with pronominals, and this is problematic for the traditional theory. But when children make errors with pronominals in VP-deletion sentences they incorrectly interpret them as bound variable reflexives. This error is the one error that is not predicted by a Principle B based on bound variable pronominals. The reformulated version of Principle B was suggested as a better description of children's knowledge of pronominal-antecedent relations and seemed to be successful in studies with pronominals and quantified antecedents. But the results of these Dutch studies including VP-deletion sentences do not justify replacing the traditional version of Principle B with this reformulated version.

VP-Deletion Experiments in English

With respect to Dutch and English, the possible correct interpretations of VP-deletion sentences do not seem to be open to cross-linguistic variation. There are also no obvious reasons to presume any language-specific differences in children's understanding of this construction type. It is, therefore, surprising to ascertain that a recent English study does find different experimental results from the Dutch studies presented here.

Thornton and Wexler (1991) reported a study testing 19 4-year-olds on VP-deletion sentences with pronominals and reflexives in object position. The pronominal sentences had a possible antecedent at discourse level, whereas the antecedent for the reflexive was available sentence-internally. This difference could have affected this experiment but is not discussed here. A Yes/No judgment task was used: The children were first told a story and then asked to accept or reject a sentence as a description of that story. Sentences (20)–(23) are examples of their sentences:

(20) Batman cleaned himself and every turtle did too.

(21) Batman cleaned him and every turtle did too.

(22) Gonzo washed himself and Snuffy did too.

(23) Gonzo washed him and Snuffy did too.

As usual, the children did quite well with the reflexive sentences. The nonreflexive sentences gave the critical results in regard to the proposed reformulated Principle B.

Sentence (21) is a VP-deletion sentence with a quantified NP as local c-commanding NP in the second conjunct. If Principle B applies only to bound variable interpretations of pronouns, then it should be grammatically impossible for the quantified NP in the second conjunct to be coindexed with the pronominal from the first conjunct and pragmatically impossible for this quantified NP and pronominal to corefer.

Sentence (21) was tested in the following way: After hearing a story about *Batman* and *every turtle* washing themselves, the children were asked if (21) was an acceptable description of that story. The children incorrectly accepted sentence (21), a nonreflexive/nonreflexive sentence, as a description of this reflexive/reflexive story, only 10% of the time. These results with VP-deletion sentences involving quantified antecedents and pronominals were quite similar to the good results obtained with reflexives and were taken as support for reformulation of Principle B of the Binding Theory.

Sentence (23) does not involve quantified NPs. Thornton and Wexler did not report testing of a correct story-sentence match for sentence (23). As in the Dutch experiments, the critical cases involved children's reactions to this sentence type when they incorrectly accepted the first conjunct as reflexive. Will the second conjunct be accepted as reflexive (incorrect bound variable interpretation) or as nonreflexive (incorrect intended coreference)? Reformulated Principle B has no problems with nonreflexive responses in the second conjunct, because these would be considered proof that the whole sentence is being pragmatically (and incorrectly) interpreted. But a serious problem arises if there are many reflexive/reflexive responses, as were found in the Dutch studies.

Sentence (23) was therefore tested with two different stories. After one story in which *Gonzo* and *Snuffy* were washing themselves (reflexive/reflexive story), the 4-year-olds accepted sentence (23) (a nonreflexive/nonreflexive sentence) 22% of the time. This represents the rate at which the children allowed a sloppy identity, bound variable reading of the second conjunct after incorrectly interpreting the pronominal reflexively in the first conjunct. In contrast with the Dutch studies, the error rate here was still relatively low, but it was twice as high as for sentence (21), with a quantified NP.

The other testing of sentence (23) involved the acceptance of incorrect pragmatic coreferencing. After a different story, *Gonzo* washing himself and *Snuffy* washing *Gonzo* (a reflexive/nonreflexive story), the children accepted sentence (23) 43% of the time. This acceptance rate shows how often the children allowed a pragmatic coreference reading of VP-deletion sentences after incorrectly interpreting the pronominal as reflexive in the first conjunct. The error rate is seriously high (again, twice as high as the previous 22%). This error did not occur in the Dutch studies.

In summary, Thornton and Wexler concluded from their results that children do adhere to a reformulated Binding Theory: They make the most errors in pragmatic coreference interpretations of definite NP–pronominal sentences. According to Thornton and Wexler, the explanation for this error falls outside the domain of the reformulated Binding Theory.

EXPERIMENTAL DISCREPANCIES

Problems with VP-Deletion Experiments

Direct comparisons between Dutch and English children can be made only for the 4-year-olds, because this was the only age group tested by Thornton and Wexler. Developmental change cannot be compared. Direct comparisons of sentence types can be made only between the definite NP sentences, because the quantified NPs appeared in different conjuncts. If these studies were taxing the 4-year-olds in the same way, then the children's performance should be similar. But a comparison of results shows that they are in opposition: The Dutch results do not support a reformulated Binding Theory and the English results do. Such results call for a closer look at these experiments.

The Thornton and Wexler 4-year-olds gave only a 10% incorrect sloppy identity error rate for quantified NP sentences with pronominals, whereas definite NP sentences had either 22% (incorrect sloppy reading) or 43% (incorrect strict reading) error rates. Indeed, 10% is low and 43% is high, but what must be concluded about 22%? How important are the pronominal sentence error differences? Other studies have also shown more success with quantified NP–reflexive sentences than with quantified NP–pronominal sentences. Why are differences found between quantified NP–reflexive and quantified NP–pronominal sentences? What actually is the role of the quantified NP as a key to the "right answer"?

The difference in tasks may also have affected the children's performance. In the acting out task, the child heard the sentence, repeated it, and then acted out its meaning. When the Dutch children acted the sentences out, they had the option of showing that they did know the correct interpretation. They were also never forced to consider options that obviously were not topmost in their thoughts; for sentences with pronominals, they almost never spontaneously acted out the so-called pragmatic coreference combination (nonreflexive VP-deletion sentence and reflexive/nonreflexive action). The predominant acting out error for pronominal sentences was the reflexive/re-flexive interpretation.

The Yes/No judgment task for the English children involved hearing a story and then listening to and judging a sentence that did or did not match. For sentences with pronominals, the English children were forced to focus on two mismatch options. They accepted both incorrect pragmatic corefer-ence and the incorrect grammatical bound variable interpretations, but the pragmatic coreference error occurred more often.

It is possible to continue speculation on where the differences in these two studies lie, but a quick and easy answer is not at hand. Based on the information available, it is not fair to conclude that either the English study or the Dutch study is giving the true picture—support or rejection of a reformulation of Principle B. Before taking this point any further, it might prove useful to take a better look at these and other investigations of the viability of a reformulated Binding Theory and the effects of different test sentences and experimental tasks. Of interest is the robustness of this theory. Is there a strong tendency for experiments to support the reformulated Binding Theory? Or is the general pattern across experiments one of confused results, without obvious, theoretically interesting explanations? If this is the case, then there is something more—or something else—going on.

Problems with Quantified NPs

The Dutch study included sentences with a quantified NP as the local c-commanding NP in the first conjunct, and the English study had sentences with a quantified NP in the second conjunct. Whether or not this difference allows comparison of results can be debated. A comparison was not attempted, however, for quite different reasons. Although the English children could only say yes or no to their sentences, the Dutch children were free to act out their versions, repeated here. This acting out of sentences with quantified NPs turned out to be much more difficult to score than the acting out of sentences with definite NPs.

(17) Pipo zegt dat iemand moet naar zichzelf/hem wijzen en Ernie ook.
'Pipo says that someone should point at himself/him and Ernie (should) too.'

Both the reflexive and the pronominal versions of (17) should have been easy for children to understand properly, according to the reformulated Binding Theory. In the first conjunct, the antecedent-reflexive/pronominal relation is grammatically determined by the presence of the quantified NP, with no room for pragmatic coreference. But the results are a bit contradic-tory.

A surprise was that the reflexive version of (17) did not fare so well. It made an unexpectedly poor showing in comparison to the definite NP–reflexive sentences (15a) and (16a). Instead of the usual quite high percentages of reflexive/reflexive acting out responses, 4-, 6-, and 8-year-olds scored only 67%, 76%, and 83% on reflexive versions of (17). Nonreflexive/nonreflexive interpretations of this reflexive sentence were relatively high, 20%, 9%, and 13%. At the same time, the quantified NP–pronominal version of (17) showed 4-, 6-, and 8-year-olds giving 53%, 73%, and 90% nonreflexive/nonreflexive responses, with relatively low 26%, 6%, and 3% reflexive/reflexive responses. It should be cautioned that these scores cannot be directly compared with those in Table 8.1, as becomes clear in the next paragraphs.

A clue as to what may be going on with the quantified NP sentences can be found in the repetition task. Recall that after the experimenter said a sentence, the child was asked to repeat the sentence correctly before acting it out. In case of persistent errors, a maximum of three repetition trials were attempted, when necessary and if possible. In general, children were surprisingly successful in repeating the definite NP test sentences, but repetition errors occurred more often with the quantified NP sentences. For example, sentence (17) was repeated as (24):

(24) Pipo zegt dat hij naar iemand moet wijzen en Ernie ook.
'Pipo says that he should point at someone and Ernie (should) too.'

The child reconstructed sentence (17) as (24) by putting the quantified expression in the object position and eliminating the object reflexive/pronominal. With sentence (24) in mind, a child will act out a nonreflexive/nonreflexive scene, regardless of whether the original sentence was reflexive or pronominal.

This strategy could explain why reflexive/reflexive responses to the reflexive–quantified NP sentences are not as frequent as could have been expected, and the sizable rate of nonreflexive/nonreflexive responses to these reflexive sentences is also in line with the reconstructed version of the original reflexive test sentence. If the same reconstruction strategy is applied to the pronominal–quantified NP sentences, then there should be no or very few reflexive/reflexive responses to these pronominal sentences. The data show that, indeed, there still are reflexive/reflexive responses, but less than for the pronominal–definite NP sentences. It seems that the reconstruction strategy artificially reduces the error chances for the pronominal–quantified NP sentences and reduces the success chances for reflexive–quantified NP sentences.

Another clue that children were experiencing these quantified NP sentences differently appeared in their acting out. Children sometimes interpreted the second conjunct as meaning *and Ernie says . . . too* instead of *and Ernie points . . . too*, acting the sentence out as *someone* pointing to *himself/him* two times. During the practice session the children had been steered away from this interpretation, and the intonation of the test sentences was also against this interpretation. Children did not give the definite NP test sentences this interpretation.

These two ways of manipulating the quantified NP sentences suggest that children prefer a parallelism of the NP subject constructions in the two conjuncts. When these two are not identical, as in (17), the children will restructure the test sentence and act out a scene that matches their restructured version of the original test sentence. What the exact difficulty is here and why the children have the tendency to reconstruct these quantified NP sentences is beyond the scope of this chapter, but these observations do undermine the validity of the results on the quantified NP sentences, at least in the Dutch study. They also raise questions about the effects of quantified NPs in the English study.

Several studies have compared children's understanding of pronominals in other sentences, contrasting quantified NP constructions that call for bound variable interpretations and definite NP constructions with coreferential interpretations. In the case of pronominals, these studies show that the bound quantified NP sentences involving bound variable interpretation do not always have the predicted advantage over definite NP sentences involving pragmatic coreference. A sentence type that has often been investigated is one that includes an embedded locally c-commanding NP and a matrix nonlocally c-commanding NP. Several simplified variations of this sentence are given here. All these sentence variations have been tested in one study or another (Chien & Wexler, 1991; Jakubowicz, 1989, 1991; Kaufman, 1988; Leegstra & Melissen, 1992; McDaniel, Cairns, & Hsu, 1990; Wexler & Chien, 1985; and others).

(25) a. Bert wants Ernie to wash himself.
     b. Bert wants Ernie to wash him.

(26) a. Every bear wants Ernie to wash himself.
     b. Every bear wants Ernie to wash him.

(27) a. Bert wants every bear to wash himself.
     b. Bert wants every bear to wash him.

The traditional Binding Theory could predict no differences between reflexive (a) and pronominal (b) versions of these sentences. If they occur, such differences would have to be explained outside the grammar of the Binding Theory. It could also be possible that there are differences between the sentences with quantified NPs, (26a–b) and (27a–b), and sentences with definite NPs, (25a–b), but this would also have to be independently motivated outside the traditional Binding Theory.

A reformulated Binding Theory would predict that reflexive sentences should be understood by children. For pronominal sentences, it would predict that at least sentence (27b), with a local quantified NP, should be correctly understood. Sentence (26b), with the quantified NP in the nonlocal position, could probably also be correctly understood. But sentence (25b), with definite NPs, could show children making many errors.

The results of the studies including these sentence types are almost impossible to summarize succinctly. They are too varied to give a quick and simple picture, and therein lies the problem for the reformulated version of Principle B. A general impression of the problems confronting the interpretation of these studies can be given by making a limited comparison between the work of Jakubowicz and that of Chien and Wexler.

Jakubowicz (1989, 1991) tested French children between 3 and 7 years old with an act-out task on French versions of all of the sentence types in (25)–(27). In contrast with the predictions made by the reformulated Principle B, she found that the sentences with reflexives were significantly more often correctly acted out than any of the pronominal sentences. For the sentences with pronominals, the presence or absence of a quantified NP made no significant difference to the children, and it follows that the position of the quantified NP in these sentences also had no effect. For French children, the acquisition lag of pronominals in relation to reflexives persisted. In fact, the results showed a trend of more correct definite NP–pronominal sentences than quantified NP–pronominal sentences. These results certainly do not support the reformulated Binding Theory.

Wexler and Chien also investigated these sentence types and arrived at different conclusions. The children were of a comparable age range: between 3 and 8 years of age. The task was quite different: a Yes/No judgment task. A child was first shown a cartoon picture and then asked a test question (one of the sentences in (25)–(27), but in question form). The earlier study (Wexler & Chien, 1985) concentrated on the definite NP sentences (25) and (27) and showed the well-known difference that Jakubowicz also found— reflexive sentences were more successful than pronominal sentences. The later study (Chien & Wexler, 1991) investigated (25b), (26b), and (27b). On these pronominal sentences, Chien and Wexler found that (27b), with a quantified NP in the embedded position, provided a clear advantage compared to both the definite NP (25b) and the matrix quantified NP (26b) versions. This sentence (27b) was often correctly rejected as a match for a picture showing *every bear* washing himself. The children's relative success with sentence (27b) in comparison to the other pronominal sentences was taken as support for the reformulated Binding Theory. It would have been interesting to directly compare the quantified NP–pronoun sentence (27b) with a quantified NP–reflexive sentence (27a), but no reflexive sentences were included in this second study.

How is it possible that different experiments with quantified NPs lead to contradictory interpretations? Is it possible that quantifiers do somehow affect pronoun binding but in a way that is not central to Binding Theory issues? In review, compare the four sentences repeated here. Sentence (11) is from Chien and Wexler (1990), (21) is from Thornton and Wexler (1991), a version of (26b) can be found in Jakubowicz (1989) and Chien and Wexler (1991), and a version of (27b) can be found in Jakubowicz (1991) and Chien and Wexler (1991):

> (11) Is every bear washing her?
> (21) Batman helps him and every turtle (does) too.
> (26) b. Every bear wants Ernie to wash him.
> (27) b. Bert wants every bear to wash him.

A surprising result is that in almost all of these sentences, the children resisted binding the pronoun to a quantified antecedent, whether this binding was the correct solution or not.

With Chien and Wexler's sentence (11), children gave the correct rejection response in a sentence-picture mismatch task. The local quantified NP *every bear* was correctly rejected as the antecedent of the pronoun *her*; that is, a reflexive picture was not considered a match for a nonreflexive sentence.

With Thornton and Wexler's sentence (21), the children were asked to accept this nonreflexive sentence as if it corresponded to a story with the meaning *Batman helps himself and every turtle helps himself.* The children gave the correct rejection response. The story and sentence do not match, and the local quantified NP *every turtle* was correctly rejected as the antecedent of the pronoun *him.*

In contrast, sentence (26b) showed Jakubowicz's French children giving an incorrect response in an acting out test. But again it was the nonlocal quantified NP *every bear* that (incorrectly) was not chosen as the antecedent of the pronoun *him.* Chien and Wexler's children were asked whether this same sentence (26b) was a proper description of a picture showing *every bear* thinking that *Ernie* is washing himself. They often incorrectly accepted the mismatch, which entails that they did not choose *every bear* as the antecedent for *him.*

Sentence (27b) is the only case where children did not unanimously reject the quantified NP as the antecedent for the pronoun. Chien and Wexler's children followed the usual pattern of rejection. They were asked to reject a picture showing *every bear* as the antecedent of *him*, and they were often successful in doing so. In Jakubowicz's study, however, the French children incorrectly acted out the sentence. This is the only case where a quantified NP *every bear* was chosen as the antecedent for a pronominal *him*.

Taken together, responses to these sentences show an interesting overall pattern of rejecting quantified NPs as antecedents for pronominals. In the case of (11) and (21) and the correct rejection of a local c-commanding quantified NP as antecedent for the pronominal, these results support both Wexler's and Reinhart's reformulated Principle B. For (26b), with an incorrect rejection of the nonlocal c-commanding quantified NP as antecedent for the pronominal, Chien and Wexler (1991) suggested that this sentence is beyond the bounds of their reformulated Principle B, because the *every NP* phrase is outside the local domain and they stated only that a bound variable pronominal must not be bound within its local domain. Reinhart stated that a pronominal must be bound outside its local domain, so she must explain why the children do not accept a c-commanding, nonlocal, quantified NP as the antecedent to the pronoun here.

In summary, these sentences show that children generally do not accept a quantified NP as the antecedent of a pronominal, regardless of whether this is the correct or incorrect grammatical response. Such an across-the-board rejection does not match the predictions made by the reformulated version of Principle B.

There are other disturbing observations about quantifiers and their role in a reformulated Binding Theory. For example, it has been observed that it takes a relatively long time for children to succeed with quantified NP sentences, regardless of whether the sentence includes a reflexive or a pronoun. Chien and Wexler (1991) observed that children must be around 6 years old before they can competently handle test sentences with quantificational concepts like *every bear*. Also, the Dutch study presented earlier showed that children were having difficulties repeating and acting out VP-deletion sentences containing the quantified NP *iemand* (*someone*).

The fact that children show a late understanding of quantified NP sentences led Grimshaw and Rosen (1990) to suggest that Chien and Wexler's good results with children resisting binding between pronominals and quantified NPs in sentences like (27b) may have a quite different explanation. It is possible that these good results are not proof of knowledge of a reformulated Principle B but are, rather, a consequence of the fact that the bound variable interpretation of pronominals is actually not available to the child.

Recall that the measure of importance in Chien and Wexler's Yes/No judgment task was the percentage of correct rejections for a pronoun sentence and a reflexive picture/story combination. A correct rejection, however, might indicate something other than knowledge of the issue at hand. Grimshaw and Rosen claimed that children reject pronominal sentence–reflexive picture combinations for the wrong reasons. Children reject this combination because they fail to construct a bound variable reading of the quantified NP sentence, not because they know to reject the combination, based on the reformulated Principle B and knowledge of bound variables. It is thus the failure to understand the bound variable reading of this sentence that causes the child to reject it, not the knowledge of its bound variable reading and its mismatch with the picture. Recall that Jakubowicz's French children also showed, via the acting out task, that they did not correctly understand sentence (27b).

An experimental artifact explanation of the Yes/No judgment task results may also apply to the Thornton and Wexler study on VP-deletion sentences. Recall that in this study, the correct rejection rate for an incorrect bound variable interpretation was highest for sentences with quantified NPs and pronominals—90%. For referential NPs and pronominals, the incorrect bound variable interpretation had a correct rejection rate of 78%, and the incorrect coreference interpretation had a correct rejection rate of 57%. In all cases, the correct response was rejection, and this was most successful for quantified NP sentences. Grimshaw and Rosen would attribute this result to the nonavailability of a bound variable interpretation with quantified antecedents.

CONCLUSIONS

In the past, many empirical findings about the differences in the acquisition patterns of reflexives and pronominals have been difficult to understand in the light of the traditional Binding Theory. The reformulated Binding Theory was proposed to explain these differences by limiting the theory's domain of application to grammatical, bound variable interpretations of reflexives and pronouns. The child's grammatical knowledge of binding with pronominals would be part of his Universal Grammar knowledge. The reformulated Principle B would not be expected to cover the pragmatic, intended coreference interpretations of pronominals. This pragmatic knowledge of coreference would have to come from a different source, whether it be innate or learned.

The reformulation of the Binding Theory exclusively in terms of bound variable interpretations does not appear to solve the problems that it was intended to solve. The evidence is threefold. First, empirical justification for a reformulation of the Binding Theory should lie in the robustness of such a theory as a better explanation of acquisitional findings across many studies. But as demonstrated here, such consistent justification does not seem to be forthcoming. Results from the Dutch experiments using VP-deletion constructions do not support the reformulated theory and are in direct contrast with results from the English VP-deletion experiment. Results from other studies, using other types of sentences, also do not show the reformulated Binding Theory as a more explanatory theory than the traditional theory.

Limiting Principle B to bound variable interpretations of pronouns has not resolved the past experimental confusion surrounding the often problematic acquisition of pronominals.

A second problem for the reformulated theory is that children also demonstrate difficulties with a keystone element of bound variable interpretations, the quantified NP. The role that quantified NPs play in the acquisition of bound variable interpretations of pronominals is not very straightforward. The investigation of the reformulated Binding Theory has, to date, depended heavily upon the use of sentences with quantified NPs. Before attributing some of the more supportive results to a reformulated Principle B, it does seem appropriate to investigate children's general understanding of quantified expressions and the role this plays in children's understanding of pronominal-antecedent relations. Any further investigation of the reformulated Binding Theory should look into bound variable constructions that do not include quantified NPs in order to find out exactly where the child's problem lies. The influence of different tasks and the validity of interpreting their results as supportive of children's knowledge of bound variable interpretations has also been debated.

The third problem involves the linguistic evidence that calls into question the role of another central element of the theory, the c-command condition. It is not always necessary to have a c-command relation for bound variable interpretations of pronouns to succeed. Reinhart (1983) herself cited this as a problem for her bound anaphora analysis. As she pointed out, the c-command condition on bound variable interpretations of pronominals is systematically violated in three types of constructions: possessive NPs, psych-verbs, and certain PP types.

One of her examples is repeated here:

(28) Jokes about his wife upset Max, but not Felix.

The fact that a sloppy identity test can succeed with this sentence shows that it can have a bound variable interpretation without the pronoun having a c-commanding antecedent. Reinhart admitted that she had at best only ad hoc solutions for these c-command problems. If c-command is not crucial to bound variable interpretations of pronouns, then it is not clear what the reformulated Binding Theory can be based on.

A positive consequence of work on the reformulated Binding Theory is the focus on what aspects of pronominal-antecedent relations should be included in grammatical theory and what should be outside its scope. There seems to be a consensus that children do indeed know (something like) the syntactic Principles A and B, which govern relationships between syntactic indices. It does not seem possible that such principles mature over time or that children can learn them from primary linguistic data.

It is also the case that, with this knowledge, a child can come closer to correct usage of reflexives than to correct usage of pronominals. Syntactic knowledge about reflexive-antecedent relations is deterministic and focuses on the local domain and what the antecedent of the reflexive must be; in other words, what the coindexed elements are. Syntactic knowledge about possible pronominal-antecedent relations is usually focused on what elements must be noncoindexed in the local domain. In comparison to reflexives, what a child knows about pronominals is nondeterministic. Binding Theory tells the child that a pronominal cannot be coindexed with a c-commanding NP in the local domain, but it does not give him or her knowledge about what elements can be coindexed with the pronominal, and it does not give the child knowledge about how to interpret noncoindexed elements. As the proponents of the reformulated Binding Theory have once again shown, it is not clear what noncoindexing implies. They claim that it does not imply disjoint reference and that pragmatic principles are necessary to deal with noncoindexing.

The issues and problems surrounding a best possible Binding Theory are not at all resolved. There is as yet no general consensus about what the exact structure of the Binding Theory should be. The reformulated Binding Theory was an attempt to define both Principles A and B exclusively in terms of bound variables. This attempt does not receive support from language acquisition studies, and it also suffers from theoretical difficulties.

A child must not only know binding principles, whatever their correct formulation may be, but must also learn the properties of the lexical items to which these principles pertain. A Binding Theory must work in conjunction with an NP classification system of anaphoric elements (Chomsky, 1982). The child's problems with pronoun acquisition could involve some version of the Binding Theory, some version of the classification system, or both.

As far as classification goes, many languages have a more extensive set of anaphoric elements than does English. Dutch, for example, has at least two reflexives, *zich* and *zichzelf,* which cannot always be used interchangeably. Also, there are difficulties in classifying pronominals like *him* that sometimes appear to be used as reflexives, as in the well-known snake sentences and picture-NP sentences. Part of the problem in explaining children's difficulties may lie at this level of the lexicon. Just as in the investigation of a best possible Binding Theory, the best possible classification system can also be debated (cf. J. Koster, 1992).

In general, all the veils covering the real face of the knowledge involved in the acquisition of pronouns have, by far, not yet been lifted. In order to achieve this, it will be necessary to continue to identify and separate confounding factors, such as pragmatics and experimental design, from linguistically relevant factors, such as grammatical knowledge of anaphora. At the same time, continuous scrutiny of linguistic theory in relation to acquisition must continue at the level of binding and classification. There are theoretical linguistic and acquisitional problems with the traditional Binding Theory, but what is known as the reformulated version of the Binding Theory does not seem to solve these problems.

REFERENCES

Chien, Y.-C., & Wexler, K. (1990). Children's knowledge of locality conditions in binding as evidence for the modularity of syntax and pragmatics. *Language Acquisition, 1*, 225–295.

Chien, Y.-C., & Wexler, K. (1991). Children's knowledge of pronouns as bound variables in a long distance context. *Papers and Reports on Child Language Development, 30*, 25–38.

Chomsky, N. (1981). *Lectures on government and binding*. Dordrecht: Foris.

Chomsky, N. (1982). *Some concepts and consequences of the theory of government and binding*. Cambridge, MA: MIT Press.

Foley, C., Nuñez del Prado, Z., Barbier, I., & Lust, B. (1992). *On the strong continuity hypothesis: A study of pronoun coindexing in sloppy identity*. Paper presented at the annual meeting of The Linguistic Society of America,

Grimshaw, J., & Rosen, S. T. (1990). Knowledge and obedience: The developmental status of the binding theory. *Linguistic Inquiry, 21*, 187–222.

Grodzinsky, Y., & Reinhart, T. (1993). The innateness of binding and the development of coreference. *Linguistic Inquiry, 24*, 69–101.

Jakubowicz, C. (1989). *Maturation or invariance of universal grammar principles in language acquisition*. Paper presented at the 14th Annual Boston University Conference on Language Development, Boston, MA.

Jakubowicz, C. (1991). *Binding principles and acquisition facts revisited*. Paper presented at the Meeting of the North Eastern Linguistics Society, *21*.

Kaufman, D. K. (1988). *Grammatical and cognitive interactions in the study of children's knowledge of binding and reference relations*. Unpublished doctoral dissertation, Temple University, Philadelphia, PA.

Kaufman, D. K. (1992). *Grammatical or pragmatic: Will the real condition B please stand up?* Paper presented at the Symposium on Syntactic Theory and First Language Acquisition, Cornell University, Ithaca, NY.

Koster, Ch. (1988). An across-experiments analysis of children's anaphor errors. In G. De Haan & W. Zonneveld (Eds.), *Formal parameters of generative grammar, IV* (pp. 53–74). Dordrecht: ICG Printing.

Koster, J. (1992). *Strong and weak anaphors*. Paper presented at the Symposium on Syntactic Theory and First Language Acquisition, Cornell University, Ithaca, NY.

Leegstra, T. S., & Melissen, M. (1992). *Patronen in de verwerving van anaforen by nederlandstalige kinderen* [Patterns in the acquisition of anaphors in Dutch children]. Unpublished manuscript, University of Groningen.

McDaniel, D., Cairns, H. S., & Hsu, J. R. (1990). Binding principles in the grammars of young children. *Language Acquisition, 1*, 121–139.

Montalbetti, M., & Wexler, K. (1985). Binding is linking. *Proceedings of the West Coast Conference on Formal Linguistics, IV*, 228–245.

Reinhart, T. (1983). *Anaphora and semantic interpretation*. London: Croom Helm.

Reinhart, T. (1986). Center and periphery in the grammar of anaphora. In B. Lust (Ed.), *Studies in the acquisition of anaphora: Vol. I. Defining the constraints* (pp. 123–150). Dordrecht: Reidel.

Thornton, R., & Wexler, K. (1991). *VP ellipsis and the binding principles in children's grammars.* Paper presented at the 16th Annual Boston University Conference on Language Development, Boston, MA.

Wexler, K., & Chien, Y.-C. (1985). The development of lexical anaphors and pronouns. *Papers and Reports on Child Language Development, 24,* 138–149.

CHAPTER NINE

Commentary:
The Nonhomogeneity of
Condition B and Related Issues

Eric Reuland
University of Utrecht

Since its inception, the Binding Theory outlined in Chomsky (1981) has been confronted with an ever increasing range of data. Languages providing the foundation for its original formulation came to be known in greater depth and detail; the number of languages studied from a theoretical perspective increased dramatically; and, finally, research on language acquisition opened up vast areas of novel facts.

In its original formulation the theory is precise and simple: Apart from NPs with lexical content, it distinguishes between two types of argument expressions that are characterized by grammatical features only, namely, anaphors and pronominals. Anaphors are referentially defective and depend for their interpretation on a linguistic antecedent, which, furthermore, should not be 'too far away'; pronominals are not defective and can be interpreted independently. When they have a linguistic antecedent, it should not be 'too nearby'. The measure of distance is provided by the notion of governing category:

(1) β is the governing category of α iff β is the minimal category containing α, a governor of α and an (accessible) subject.

The (near) complementarity in distribution of pronominals and anaphors can then be captured in the following Binding Conditions:

(2) A. An anaphor is bound in its governing category.
B. A pronominal is free in its governing category.

From an acquisitional perspective, this theory is equally attractive. If the properties of anaphors and pronominals are uniform across languages, there is no need to assume that they have been learned; they may well reflect properties of the language faculty per se.

Since then, various facts have been discovered that necessitate revisions of this simple theory. Particularly important for the subsequent discussion are two facts. One is that in some languages anaphors may take their antecedents far beyond the domain defined in (1), with the actual binding domains also varying cross-linguistically. The other is that children do not seem to acquire Condition A and Condition B at the same time.

Illustrative of the first observation is the contrast between Icelandic, Norwegian, and Dutch in the binding possibilities of the cognate anaphors *sig*, *seg*, and *zich* (see also Giorgi, 1984, for a discussion of Italian).

In Dutch, the binding domain is almost strictly local (see Everaert, 1986; J. Koster, 1985, for discussion); only bare infinitives allow the anaphor *zich* to be bound from outside its clause. Thus, (3) is well formed under the indexing given.

(3) Jan$_i$ hoorde [Marie$_j$ een lied voor zich$_i$ fluiten].
Jan heard Marie a song for himself whistle
'Jan heard Mary whistle a song for him.'

The control infinitive in (4) is not well formed, nor is the finite clause in (5).

(4) *Jan$_i$ heeft Piet$_j$ gevraagd [PRO$_j$ een lied voor zich$_i$ te zingen].
Jan has Piet asked a song for himself to sing
'Jan$_i$ has asked Piet to sing a song for him.'

(5) *Jan$_i$ heeft gevraagd [of Piet$_j$ een lied voor zich$_i$ zingt].
Jan has asked if Piet a song for himself sings
'Jan$_i$ asked if Piet sings a song for him.'

Norwegian is like Dutch in not allowing binding into finite complements, but, unlike Dutch, it does allow binding into control complements. Such binding can cover a fair distance, as (6) shows (from Hellan, 1991).

(6) Jon$_i$ bad oss forsøke å få deg til å snakke pent om seg$_i$.
Jon$_i$ asked us to try to get you to talk nicely about seg$_i$

In Icelandic it seems that only indicative clauses are opaque for anaphor binding. Subjunctive clauses and both types of infinitival clauses are all transparent. The indicative-subjunctive contrast is illustrated in (7) (for discussion, see Anderson, 1986; Hellan, 1988; Maling, 1982; Pica, 1987; Thráinsson, 1991, to mention a few). (Note again that the long-distance reading may cross several clause boundaries with their intervening subjects.)

(7) a. *Jón$_i$ veit að María elskar sig$_i$.
    John knows that Mary loves INDIC him
 b. Jón$_i$ segir [að María telji [að Haraldur vilji [að Billi
    John says that Mary believes that Harald wants that Bill
    heimsaeki sig$_i$]]].
    visits him

Patterns such as these raise the question of what type of parameter is involved. Manzini and Wexler (1987) and Wexler and Manzini (1987) proposed that the differences are captured by parametrizing the opacity factor defining the governing category, as in (8).

(8) *b* is a *governing category for a* if and only if *b* is the minimal category containing *a*, a governor of *a*, and *F* (*F* an opacity factor).

F may assume values such as *(accessible) SUBJECT, Tense, AGR,* or *COMP.* These opacity factors are taken from a universal set, with particular anaphors differing in the value selected. This choice is represented in the lexical entry. (Anaphors with an opacity factor beyond the SUBJECT are then classified as long-distance anaphors.) Similarly, languages may differ in the opacity factors they make available.

An even more fundamental question is how a specific parameter setting can be acquired in the absence of negative evidence. Manzini and Wexler proposed that language acquisition is guided by the Subset Principle (see also Berwick, 1985). According to this principle, the child applies the following strategy. In case of a choice between two options for a specific setting of a parameter, if every structure that is grammatical under option A (the restricted option) is also grammatical under option B (the broader option), option A is chosen if it is compatible with the input. Wexler (1992) gave the following formulation:

(9) *Subset Principle:*
    Suppose parameter *P* has two values, *i* and *j*, such that for all derivations *D*, if *D* is grammatical under setting *i*, then *D* is grammatical under setting *j*. Then value *i* is unmarked with respect to value *j*.

If the value of a parameter is unmarked with respect to another value, the learner selects the unmarked value if the data do not contradict that choice. This is formulated in (10).

(10) *Markedness:*
    If (i) value *i* of parameter *P* is unmarked with respect to value *j*,

and (ii) the primary data (input) is consistent with value i, then the learner selects value i of parameter P.

Whereas the Subset Principle provides a solution to the problems posed by the variety in binding domains, the questions raised by the disparity between Binding Conditions A and B require a different type of answer. This issue can be summarized as follows.

If Conditions A and B together form one binding module, one would expect them to become available to the child together, at the same time. This, however, has turned out not to be the case. Children between 3 and 5 years of age show rapid improvement in their performance with respect to Condition A, but their command of Condition B develops much more slowly. Children violate Condition B frequently until they are well beyond the age of 6; in fact, their problems may well persist until they are 10 years old (see C. Koster, 1993, for extensive discussion and an overview of the literature). At this point there are two possibilities: Either Conditions A and B are far more different than the standard theory assumes, or they do indeed constitute one module, and there is a factor that may mask the effect of Condition B until a certain age, without masking Condition A. Much of the discussion in the contributions that were brought together in the present section focused on the latter possibility.

As background, note that for independent reasons it is necessary to distinguish between binding relations and coreference relations (see Reinhart, 1983). That is, the standard Binding Theory is concerned with the principles ruling out structures such as (11), with indexing as given.

(11) *Ernie$_i$ washes him$_i$.

However, that cannot be all there is to say, given the acceptability of sentences such as (12a), with *him* referring to Oscar.

(12) a. Everyone hates Oscar. Even Oscar hates him.
   b. Everyone hates Oscar. Even Oscar$_i$ hates him$_j$.

Such sentences have been taken to show that it must be possible for two NPs to corefer without being in a binding relation. A way to express this is by assuming that in the linguistic structure, *Oscar* and *him* bear different indices, say i and j, as in (12b), whereas in the semantics, *Oscar* and *him* are interpreted as the same individual. Clearly, under this indexing, (12b) does not violate Condition B, unlike (11). However, again, this cannot be all, because otherwise Condition B would be voided, contra the standard observation that (11) is ill formed. So, why cannot (11) be represented with different indices for *Ernie* and *him*? Then conditions have to be given restricting the coreference option. Grodzinsky and Reinhart (1993), modifying an earlier proposal by Reinhart (1983), formulated the following principle.

(13) *Rule I: Intrasentential Coreference*
      NP *A* cannot corefer with NP *B* if replacing *A* with *C*, *C* a variable A-bound by *B*, yields an indistinguishable interpretation.

Only under specific, presumably pragmatic, conditions, where coreference gives an interpretation that is distinguishable from the bound variable interpretation, can the coreference option bypass a Condition B violation. The question is then whether the assumption that (13) must be learned is necessary to explain the facts that have been observed. At this point it should be noted that all discussion so far involves the assumption that Condition B reflects a unitary and homogeneous phenomenon. However, as we see later, there is reason to assume that this is not so. As shown in Reinhart and Reuland (1993), facts standardly assumed to belong to the province of Condition B in fact result from the interaction of two different conditions, a condition on reflexive predicates, and a condition on coindexing chains.

The status of the Subset Principle as an explanatory principle and the question of what the real factor is behind the delay in the emergence of Condition B effects played a major role in the presentations in the section I am commenting on. Reading the chapters as they appear in this volume, I found these issues to play a less prominent role than I had expected on the basis of the oral presentations. Nevertheless, I take the liberty to revive some of the spirit of the discussion, if only by necessity, because the content of the contributions in this section is so rich, and their analyses so challenging, that it would lead me far beyond the allotted space if I were to try to do them all justice. So I take this as my lead and see if indeed it brings me, at least briefly, to each of the contributions in this section.

THE ISSUES

The Subset Principle

Three of the contributions address the status of the Subset Principle as an explanatory principle in language acquisition.

In her contribution, Hermon provides an extensive discussion of two types of approaches to domain differences between anaphors, what she calls parametric versus nonparametric approaches. Here I limit myself to one aspect of her chapter, namely, the nature of nonparametric approaches. I am not sure whether the choice of term is a lucky one. In her original presentation, more than in the written version, Hermon focused on the implications of newly acquired insights for the Subset Principle as a principle in language acquisition. It is clear that the nature of the observed variation puts parameters in a different light. Specifically, it is unlikely that variation in binding domains should directly refer to domain-related properties of lexical items. Consider, for instance, one of her examples, illustrating the blocking effects in long-distance binding that obtain in Chinese but not in Italian. The issue is illustrated in (14).

(14) [$_{CP}$ NP<+3rd>...[$_{CP}$ NP<+1st> I...[$_{CP}$...[<+Anaph,+3rd>]...]]]

As Hermon points out (following Batistella, 1987; Huang & Tang, 1991), in Chinese, an anaphor can be long-distance bound, but only if on the path between the anaphor and its antecedent all subjects are of the same person class. That is, in (14), the first person subject on the path between the anaphor and the highest subject prevents the latter from being a possible antecedent. If the intermediate subject had been third person as well, the higher subject would have been a possible antecedent (as would have been the intermediate subject itself). In languages like Italian or Icelandic, which allow long-distance anaphora as well, no such blocking effects have been observed. Hermon demonstrates, also on the basis of further cross-linguistic facts, that this can be related to another difference between Chinese and Italian, namely, that the latter has ϕ-features on Inflection, whereas in the former, Inflection by itself has no ϕ-features at all. If anaphor-antecedent links of this type are established by head movement, the crucial step is that in which the anaphor adjoins to the INFL node with the nonmatching subject. In a language where INFL has no ϕ-features, the features of the adjoined anaphor will count as the features of the newly created INFL node. Specifier-head agreement will now cause a clash between the features of the subject and those of the INFL node. Hence the structure is ruled out. If INFL has ϕ-features, the feature composition of the INFL node formed by adjunction will be the same as that of the original INFL node (by percolation). Hence, no clash obtains. Hermon's analysis raises interesting technical questions. In order to work properly, this analysis requires that checking of Specifier-head agreement follows the adjunction of the anaphor to INFL; that is, it requires a strictly derivational view, in accordance with the spirit of Chomsky's (1992) minimalist approach. It also raises a broader question. It implies a relation between parameters and binding domains that is far more indirect than under the standard view, in which parameters are associated with lexical properties of the elements in question. Whether or not an anaphor will be able to reach an antecedent in a certain position is at least as dependent on properties of the path, which can only be assessed in a more finely grained analysis, as on the lexical make-up of the anaphor itself.

Binding-theoretic differences may relate to all kinds of other differences between grammars. Consider, for instance, the nature of the differences between the binding domains of simplex anaphors (such as Dutch *zich*, Norwegian *seg*, or Icelandic *sig*) discussed earlier.

In Reinhart and Reuland (1991) it was shown that the contrast between Dutch, on the one hand, and Norwegian and Icelandic, on the other, with respect to binding into control infinitives, has nothing to do with lexical differences between these anaphors but can be explained as an effect of sentence extraposition. In an SOVI language like Dutch, but not in the Scandinavian SIVO languages, extraposition will destroy the configuration in which the anaphor can be linked to its antecedent. I later show in detail that Case, too, may affect binding possibilities. The upshot is that there are still parameters involved in establishing binding domains, only they are much more finely grained than is expressed in the parametrized Binding Theory stated in (8).

Thus, by themselves, these and similar results say nothing against parameters, nor against the Subset Principle, as reflecting a property of successive stages of a developing language. If the Binding Theory itself is not parametrized, but parameterlike effects are found that arise by interaction with components of the grammar that are parametrized, it is still logically possible that domain statements about anaphors can be derived as theorems. In turn, this leaves open the possibility that the Subset Principle holds as a theorem of a more finely grained theory stated in more primitive terms. Whether this is true in the end has yet to be determined.

In a very interesting contribution, which again raises far more issues than I could attempt to do justice to, Jakubowicz discusses the relation between morphosyntactic properties of an element (feature composition and X' status) and its functioning as an anaphor or a pronominal. The acquisition of the core properties of an element as either anaphoric or pronominal is instantaneous, given the fixation of its morphological properties. It is impossible to view long-distance binding as purely the consequence of an inherent property of an anaphor. Jakubowicz shows that in Danish, one and the same anaphor has a long-distance reading in one type of context, and an obligatorily local reading in another. The distinction is determined by the properties of the governing verb. It is assumed that the anaphor requires Case for its interpretation but cannot acquire it under government. The remaining option is to acquire Case by movement. If the verb is [+affective] it allows the anaphor to incorporate at Logical Form; with accusative Case thus acquired, the anaphor is licit. If the governing verb is [−affective] such incorporation is not allowed, and the anaphor has to move up to a higher position in order to become licensed. The long-distance reading is therefore the result of a last-resort process. Jakubowicz argues that French and Danish are minimally different with respect to the movement of *se* and *sig*. In French, movement applies in the overt syntax, due to the affixlike properties of *se*, whereas in Danish, movement applies covertly, at LF.

The analysis raises many interesting questions. One question is precisely why [+affected] verbs allow the anaphor to incorporate. Ideally, this should follow from an independent property of the verb. Given such an answer, one might find an explanation for how the distinction [+/−affected] relates to the [+/−intrinsic reflexive] contrast (Reinhart & Reuland, 1991, 1993). In discussing the interaction between logophoric interpretation and structural binding, Jakubowicz observes that in Danish, *sig selv* can never have a logophoric reading. This is the case in other languages as well. For instance, in Dutch, logophoric readings of *zichzelf* are hard to find; in Icelandic, logophoric readings of *sjalfan sig* have, to my knowledge, not been reported either. If one takes the view that in anaphors of the structure <*simplex anaphor*>-*SELF* both the simplex anaphor and the SELF-element are dependent elements, the generalization emerges that elements with two dependencies cannot be interpreted logophorically. (Note that this is consistent with the claim in Reinhart & Reuland, 1991, 1993, that the logophoric use of SELF-anaphors falls outside the scope of the grammar; the grammar defines the structural conditions under which logophoric use is possible but does not provide the interpretation mechanism itself.) Jakubowicz suggests that the impossibility of logophoric readings for <*simplex anaphor*>-*SELF*-type anaphors is due to their having to adjoin to IP at LF in order to receive ϕ-features (grammatical features such as number, person, and gender). From this position they could not move further without violating the ECP. This, however, presupposes that logophors get their interpretation by movement. This is unlikely, given that Icelandic 'sig' can receive a logophoric interpretation without any linguistic antecedent whatsoever. Further research will be necessary to clarify to what extent structural factors enter into a determination of logophoric interpretation.

I conclude my discussion of this chapter with a comment on Jakubowicz's suggestion that long-distance binding is a last resort operation. Conceptually, this would certainly be attractive. To my mind, this would predict that in all cases where long-distance binding is observed, any intervening subject should be in some sense unsuitable as a more local antecedent. However, empirical support for that consequence appears to be lacking. The blocking effects in long-distance anaphora in Chinese discussed by Hermon go against it (the presence of an unsuitable antecedent blocks, rather than facilitates, the possibility of reaching a higher suitable one), and also the long-distance binding facts in Germanic are incompatible, as is illustrated by the option of skipping the local PRO-subject, although it is a possible antecedent, in sentences like the following Icelandic example:

(15) Jón$_j$ skipadi Pétri$_i$ [ad PRO$_i$ raka$_{infinitive}$ sig$_{i,j}$ á hverjum degi]
     John ordered Peter to   shave   SIG every   day

It seems, therefore, questionable that a last resort analysis of long-distance anaphora can be maintained.

Mazuko and Lust discuss the problems that the existence of Japanese *zibun* poses for the standard classification of NPs into [+/−anaphor] and [+/−pronominal]. On the basis of the properties of this element, these authors argue against the commonly held assumption that in each language, lexical items must be defined as anaphors or pronouns or R-expressions independently and contrastively. Instead, they argue, a definitional approach should be adopted, where the properties of an element follow from the positions in which it occurs. The Binding Theory does not presuppose the lexicon but provides the linguistic foundations by which the child acquires the lexicon. This entails the possibility that some languages may not lexicalize the Binding Theory at all. The case of *zibun* is illustrative of a larger class of problems for the standard version of the Binding Theory (see, for instance, Sportiche, 1986; Wali, 1990). Mazuko and Lust argue that, on the one hand, *zibun* cannot freely occur in the core anaphoric domain (e.g., as an object bound by a subject); therefore, it cannot be [+anaphoric]. On the other hand, it does occur as a (subject-bound) object with some verbs, so that it does not obey Principle B either and hence cannot be [+pronominal]. It appears to be best in adjunct PPs. In addition, it can occur without a linguistic antecedent. Hence, it must have intrinsic reference. The authors clearly show that the classification of NPs as [+/−anaphoric, +/−pronominal] runs into serious problems. However, instead of concluding that the Binding Theory induces a classification of NPs by some kind of functional determination, it seems to me that an alternative is worth pursuing. Note, first, that *zibun* is not unique in not always requiring a linguistic antecedent. Many languages have anaphoric elements that under certain conditions may be used logophorically.

For instance, the understanding of binding relations in Icelandic has turned out to depend crucially on the ability to distinguish between anaphoric elements occurring as logophors (which depend for their interpretation on factors such as perspective and point of view), and anaphoric elements occurring as bound variables (whose interpretation is governed by purely structural factors, such as c-command and governing category). (See, among others, Anderson, 1986; Hellan, 1991; Sigurðsson, 1986; Thráinsson, 1991; and, for acquisition data, Sigurjónsdóttir & Hyams, in press, for discussion.) Taking the lexical element *sig* by itself and trying to classify it as an anaphor or a pronominal in terms of the canonical Binding Theory would be futile.

In some contexts *sig* can be locally bound, and in others it cannot, depending on lexical properties of the verb. In some contexts it must have at least a syntactic antecedent; in others it may depend for its interpretation on an element by which it is not c-commanded, or even on an element that is not linguistically expressed in the sentence. In illustration, I give two well-known examples of *sig* used logophorically.

(16) Skoðun Jonsᵢ er [að pu hafir svikið sigᵢ] . . .
     opinion John's is that you have betrayed self
                                             (Thráinsson, 1991)
(17) María var alltaf svo andstyggileg. Pegar Olafurᵢ kaemi segði hún sérᵢ/·ⱼ
     áreiðanlega að fara . . .
     'Mary was always so nasty. When Olaf would come, she would cer-
     tainly tell himself [the person whose thoughts are being presented—
     not Olaf] to leave.' (Note that (17) could not begin a story.)
                                             (Thráinsson, 1991)

But, of course, something similar could be said about English. If we did
not know English yet, and we were asked to classify *himself* either as an
anaphor obeying Condition A or as a pronominal obeying Condition B, the
data in (18) would simply make no sense.

(18) a. It angered him that she . . . tried to attract a man like himself.
     b. *It angered him that she tried to attract himself.
     c. Max boasted that the queen invited Lucie and himself for a drink.
     d. *Max boasted that the queen invited himself for a drink.

It is only when we notice that in the ungrammatical cases of (18), *himself*
is, by itself, a syntactic argument of the verb, and in the grammatical cases it
is not, that we can begin to make sense of these data (see Zribi-Hertz, 1989,
for an extensive overview of such data; and Reinhart & Reuland, 1991, 1993,
for discussion). Because certain anaphors can be used logophorically, one
should be very careful about using functional considerations as criteria. Also,
sensitivity to verbal class is not unique to *zibun*. The same holds true of
elements like Icelandic *sig* and Dutch *zich*. (See also Jakubowicz's chapter 5
in this volume.) In fact, it appears that the distribution of locally bound *zibun*
versus locally bound *zibun-zisin* is highly reminiscent of the distribution of
zich versus *zichzelf* in Dutch or *sig* versus *sjalfan sig* in Icelandic. For certain
verb classes there is even a direct match, although some verb classes behave
differently for some reason still to be investigated. (I am grateful to Takako
Aikawa for discussing with me her work in progress on this issue.) The pattern
found with *zibun* is not unexpected, from the perspective of the approach
developed in Reinhart and Reuland (1991, 1993). In this approach, the core
cases of binding are analyzed as involving a property of predicates: If a
predicate is reflexive (i.e., two of its arguments are coindexed), it must be
reflexive-marked. Reflexive-marking can be either intrinsic, as with a predicate
such as *behave* (one person cannot behave someone else), or extrinsic, such
that one of the arguments reflexive-marks the predicate. Referential defectiveness (a property related to an incomplete specification for ϕ-features) is hereby
distinguished from the property of being able to mark a predicate reflexive.

In languages like Dutch and Icelandic, only the complex anaphors *zichzelf* or *sjalfan sig* are able to reflexive-mark a predicate, not the simplex anaphors *zich* and *sig*. Thus, although in a sentence such as *Jan haat zich* 'John hates himself' the anaphor *zich* is correctly bound, the sentence is nevertheless ungrammatical, because *zich* cannot reflexive-mark the predicate formed by the verb *haten*. Thus, in this framework, the property [+anaphoric] by itself says nothing about occurrence in the core anaphoric domain. Nor does being able to overcome referential defectiveness, under specific discourse conditions, imply that an element is not [+anaphoric].

To my mind, it would be interesting to investigate further the various occurrences of *zibun*, with an eye to the precise discourse and environment factors governing its distribution and interpretation.

Coreference Versus Binding

Both C. Koster and Kaufman discuss the role of Reinhart's pragmatic principle in explaining the time lag in the Manifestation of Condition B effects. Kaufman presents an overview based on a variety of experiments involving different languages. She focuses on the general variability in the findings. Some investigators, including herself, report that children do well on Condition B, regardless of the nature of the antecedent. Others do find differences, but the overall results are too mixed, according to Kaufman, to warrant the conclusion that the pragmatic principle is supported. C. Koster presents a quite detailed argument, based on a comparison between an experiment by Thornton and Wexler (1991) on English children, and an experiment involving Dutch children carried out by herself.

Let us recapitulate the issue. Given some NP and a pronoun, which bear different indices and hence could not be in a binder-bindee relation, it is always possible that, on interpretation, they happen to pick out the same object in the domain of discourse and thus, accidentally, corefer. Thus, what may happen in the interpretation of the sentence (19a), is that the indexing assigned is not (19b), which violates Condition B, but rather (19c), with *him* accidentally interpreted as Bert rather than Ernie.

(19) a. {Bert, Ernie, . . .} Bert washes him.
   b. {Bert, Ernie, . . .} $Bert_i$ washes him_i.
   c. {Bert, Ernie, . . .} $Bert_i$ washes him_j & him_j=Bert.

To the observer, but not with respect to the internal grammar of the child, (19c) would be virtually indistinguishable from (19b). This strategy must be unavailable in the adult language, because otherwise, Condition B effects would generally be obscured. As I discussed earlier, Reinhart proposed that in the adult language, principle (13) is operative, restricting the use of pragmatic coreference to situations where it serves a specific function. If this principle must be learned and is not available to the child in the early stages, Condition B effects will be masked. But as soon as it has been acquired, these effects, which in fact were always there, will surface.

If it is the interference of coreference with binding facts that obscures what is actually happening in sentences such as (19a), one would expect that children make fewer, or no, mistakes if for some reason coreference as a factor is excluded. Chien and Wexler (1990) investigated this by using quantified antecedents; that is, they used sentences such as (20a). Because quantified NPs are not referring expressions, a representation such as (20b) makes no sense, and coreference can be dismissed as a possible interfering factor.

(20) a. Everyone$_i$ washes him$_i$.
b. *{everyone, . . .} Everyone$_i$ washes him$_j$ & him=everyone.

Hence, if children accepted (20a) in a situation with, let us say, three or four figures, where each figure washed himself, this would be a real Condition B violation. However, Chien and Wexler reported that children in fact do much better on sentences with quantified antecedents than on sentences with definite antecedents. This is in line with what one would expect if indeed a principle such as Rule I (given in (13)) interferes.

Subsequent discussion of these findings focuses on two aspects. First, do children of the relevant age group in fact understand quantificational expressions such as *everyone* well enough? Second, is the interpretation of these findings consistent with the existence of cross-linguistic variation? C. Koster discusses some experiments in Dutch where bound readings are guaranteed to arise due to the use of VP-deletion contexts, as in (21), comparing her results to those of Thornton and Wexler (1991), where the same strategy was used.

(21) a. Hier heb je Ernie, Pipo, and Bert. . . .
Bert wijst naar zichzelf en Ernie ook
'Here's Ernie, Pipo, and Bert. . . .
Bert points at himself, and Ernie (does) too.'
b. Hier heb je Ernie, Pipo, and Bert. . . .
Bert wijst naar hem en Ernie ook
'Here's Ernie, Pipo, and Bert. . . .
Bert points at him, and Ernie (does) too.'

She finds that children allow bound readings for (21b) rather regularly; that is, the sentence may be interpreted as (22).

(22) a. Hier heb je Ernie, Pipo, and Bert. . . .
Bert wijst naar hem [=Bert] en Ernie [wijst] ook [naar hem=Ernie]

'Here's Ernie, Pipo, and Bert. . . .
Bert points at him [=Bert], and Ernie [points to him=Ernie] too.'

As she notes, this is in contrast with the findings of Thornton and Wexler. Whereas Kaufman suggests that morphological and syntactic factors may be responsible for the variation she observes, C. Koster's position is that her results and Thornton and Wexler's results are incompatible; that is, UG should not allow results to diverge in this manner, which could imply that one of the experiments contains an artifact.

In the last section of this commentary I show that, in fact, languages can vary in this respect. That is, some languages demonstrably allow bound pronominals in positions where this is least expected from the perspective of the current Binding Theory. One such language is Frisian. Similar facts can be observed in various dialects of Dutch. Here, I limit myself to Frisian.

BOUND PRONOMINALS AND CASE

In this section I briefly review the discussion in Reuland and Reinhart (in preparation) of the anaphoric system of Frisian, a language spoken by about 150,000 inhabitants of the province of Friesland in the northern part of the Netherlands.

Like English, Frisian has a two-member system; there is an anaphor *himsels*, and a pronominal *him*. However, unlike Dutch and English, Frisian has locally bound pronominals. The generalization is that wherever Dutch allows *zich*, Frisian allows a bound pronominal. The paradigm is illustrated in (23)–(25).

(23) a. Willem$_i$ skammet him$_i$.
William shames him
b. Willem$_i$ wasket him$_i$.
William washes him

These are intrinsic reflexive verbs. Verbs that are not intrinsic reflexives must be SELF-marked, in accordance with the conditions on reflexive-marking discussed in Reinhart and Reuland (1993):

(24) Willem$_i$ bewûnderet himsels$_i$/*him$_i$.
William admires himself/him

Locative PPs allow locally bound pronominals, just as in Dutch and English.

(25) Klaas₁ treau de karre foar 'm₁ út.

'Klaas pushed the cart out before him.'

Frisian has bound pronominals as well as SELF-anaphors as subjects of ECM constructions as illustrated in (26).

(26) Jan₁ seach [ₛ him₁/himsels₁ yn 'e film de partij winnen].

Jan saw [him/himself in the film the match win]

These facts immediately fall out from the Binding Conditions as stated in Reinhart and Reuland (1993).[1] These conditions do not regulate the choice of anaphors versus pronominals per se but only govern the use of reflexive markings (either the presence of SELF or intrinsic reflexivization). With respect to these conditions, Frisian behaves just like Dutch.

In Dutch, however, an independently motivated condition on A-chains (a generalization of Chomsky's, 1986a, chain condition rules out the equivalents of (23) and (26), given as (23') and (26')).

---

[1]For ease of reference I give the relevant definitions here, but without discussion.

(i) *Definitions* (Reinhart & Reuland, 1993):

    a. The *syntactic predicate* formed of (a head) P is P, all its syntactic arguments, and an external argument of *P* (subject).

    The *syntactic arguments* of *P* are the projections assigned Θ-role or Case by *P*.

    b. The *semantic predicate* formed of *P* is *P* and all its arguments at the relevant semantic level.

    c. A predicate is reflexive iff two of its arguments are coindexed.

    d. A predicate (of *P*) is *reflexive-marked iff* either *P* is lexically reflexive or one of *P*'s arguments is a SELF-anaphor.

(ii) *Conditions:*

    A: A reflexive-marked syntactic predicate is reflexive.

    B: A reflexive semantic predicate is reflexive-marked.

In order to see how these work, consider (iii) and (iv).

(iii) a. *Max₁ criticized him₁.

    b. Max₁ criticized himself₁.

    c. *Max₁/he₁ criticized Max₁.

(iv) a. *Max₁ speaks with him₁.

    b. Max (\x (speaks with (x,x)))

In the cases of (iii), the revised Condition B is equivalent to the standard Condition B: In both (iiia) and (iiib) binding yields a reflexive predicate, so Condition B requires reflexive-marking. Although (iiib) is appropriately marked, the unmarked (iiia) is filtered out. In (iv), the PP is a grid argument of the verb. Binding yields, again, a reflexive predicate (represented, for convenience, with reanalysis in (ivb)). Because this predicate is not reflexive-marked, it is ruled out.

In locative PPs the NP in the PP is not an argument of the main verb:

(v) Max₁ saw a gun near him₁.

Therefore the predicate obtained by binding is not reflexive, so Condition B is met.

(23') a. Willem₁ schaamt *hem₁/zich₁.
     William shames him
  b. Willem₁ wast *hem₁/zich₁.
     William washes him

(26') Jan₁ zag [s *hem₁/zich₁ in de film de partij winnen].
    Jan saw [him in the film the match win]

A chain is now viewed as any appropriate sequence of coindexation (satisfying c-command and with no barrier between any of the links; see Everaert, 1990). Its links and its foot may be lexical or empty (trace); the stipulation that at most the head of an A-chain is nonempty has been dropped. So an A-chain is defined as in (27):

(27) *Generalized Chain:*
    $C = (\alpha_1 \ldots, \alpha_n)$ is a chain iff C is the maximal sequence such that
    (i) there is an index i such that for all j, $1 \le j \le n$, α_j carries that index, and
    (ii) for all j, $1 \le j \le n$, α_j governs α_{j+1}.

What grammatical A-chains, illustrated in (28)–(29), have in common is that the tail (all links and the foot) consists of referentially defective (−R) NPs, that is, NPs with an incomplete specification for grammatical features/φ-features.

(28) a. Felix was fired *t.*
  b. Felix fired himself.

(29) a. He is believed [*t* to be smart].
  b. He believes [himself to be smart].

(30) a. Felix was expected [*t* to be considered [*t* smart]].
  b. Felix expects [himself to consider [himself smart]].

The chain's head, in contrast, must be an NP that is not referentially defective (+R) (pronouns, including PRO and *pro*; and R-expressions, including WH-traces). Although an anaphor and an NP-trace can serve as an intermediate link in a chain, as in (30), they cannot head a chain, as in (31), where the chains are broken between *John* and *t*, and *Mary* and *herself.*

(31) a. *John seems that it appears [*t* to be smart].
  b. *Mary expected that [herself would be considered smart].

The chain condition is not definitional, as in Chomsky (1986a, 1986b); it is, instead, a condition on well-formedness. A-chains are subject to the well-

formedness condition (32). ((32) entails that a chain can contain only one [+R]
NP, and, because this is its head, the tail must consist of [−R] NPs.)

(32) *Condition on A-Chains:*
A maximal A-chain $(\alpha_l, \ldots, \alpha_n)$ contains exactly one link, α_l, that
is completely specified for ϕ-features.

Why, then, doesn't the chain condition rule out (23) and (26)? There is
good reason to assume that in the sentences displayed in (23) and (26), the
bound pronominal is not fully specified for ϕ-features. When a pronominal
is fully specified, the chain condition applies in Frisian just as in the other
languages discussed.

Consider the pronominal system of Frisian in more detail. Two pronominals, the third person singular feminine and the third person plural (common
gender), have two object forms: Both have *har* as well as *se* (the plural
pronoun has the form *harren* as well, but it behaves just like *har*). Often,
they are used interchangeably. This is illustrated in (33).

(33) a. Jan hat har juster sjoen.
        John has her/them yesterday seen
     b. Jan hat se juster sjoen.
        John has her/them yesterday seen

But unlike *har*, *se* is ungrammatical when locally bound.

(34) a. Marie₁ wasket harsels₁/har₁/*se₁.
        Mary washes herself/her
     b. De bern₁ waskje harsels₁/har₁/*se₁.
        the children wash themselves/them
     c. Marie₁ skammet har₁/*se₁.
        Mary shames her
     d. De bern₁ skamje har₁/*se₁.
        the children shame them

The ungrammaticality of the sentences with bound *se* shows that, for *se*, the
chain condition works in Frisian as it does in Dutch. As a consequence, it
remains to be explained in what respects *har* is different (assuming that this
explanation carries over to the cases of the pronominal paradigm where the
two object forms are not distinguished).

Hoekstra (1991) showed that *har* and *se* differ in Case. This point is
established on the basis of a variety of contexts, but I summarize his considerations. One significant context is the so-called free dative construction.

Frisian allows a free dative construction, that is, an (indirect) object NP that occurs independently of any specific lexical property of the predicate of the clause, as in (35).

(35) a. De blommen wiene harren ferwile.
　　 the flowers were them wilted
　 b. De kjitten steane har yn'e tún.
　　 the weeds stand her in the garden

In this context *har* may not be replaced by *se*, as is shown in (36).

(36) a. *De blommen wiene se ferwile.
　　 the flowers were them wilted
　 b. *De kjitten steane se yn'e tún.
　　 the weeds stand her in the garden

Se is also barred from adjunct PPs. As the argument of an adjective, moreover, *har* is preferred over *se*. Hoekstra concluded that the difference between *se* and *har* is that *se* requires structural Case, whereas *har* does not. That is, *har* is licensed with inherent Case. Suppose that structural Case is a truly grammatical Case (due to its being assigned by the functional system). Inherent Case, then, is Case that is licensed under government by a lexical projection.

Let us assume now that only structural Case, being related to the functional system, represents a ϕ-feature. That is, only a pronominal with structural Case is fully specified for ϕ-features and is hence [+R]. Pronominals with inherent Case are then ϕ-feature deficient and hence [−R]. Now, in order to account for the facts in (23) and (26), we only have to assume that in Frisian, but not in Dutch, the verb may assign inherent, rather than structural Case to its pronominal object.

But if this is possible in Frisian, any child learning a language will have to determine whether pronominals in that language may bear inherent Case. An incorrect hypothesis at this point will have the effect that locally bound pronominals are no longer (or, rather, not yet) ruled out with inherently reflexive predicates.

What about noninherently reflexive predicates? Note that in the adult language, too, the contrast between (37a) and (37b) is weaker than that between (37a) and (37c).

(37) a. Jan_i haat zichzelf_i.
　　 Jan hates himself
　 b. *Jan_i haat zich_i.
　　 Jan hates <simplex anaphor>
　 c. **Jan_i haat hem_i.
　　 Jan hates him

Even apart from other conceivable misanalyses (such as misanalyzing defective pronouns as instantiations of SELF, i.e., as reflexive markers), the weaker character of the violation in (37b) and the correspondingly weak character of the violation in (38), with *hem* incorrectly analyzed as Case-defective, may already be sufficient to account for children's mistakes.

(38) *Jan₁ haat hem₁.
      [inherent Case]

These facts indicate that the original Condition B is, in fact, not a homogeneous phenomenon but reflects, rather, the interaction of two different subsystems, one involving properties of predicates, the other grammatical features such as Case. But if this is so, the speed and ease with which the children master the exact properties of the Case system of their language may directly relate to their performance on Condition B. Therefore, precise conclusions with regard to the mastery of Condition B-type principles are dependent on a thorough investigation of the development of the Case system.

CONCLUSION

As should be clear from these comments, the chapters in this section all make challenging contributions to acquisition theory. I have tried here to sharpen the issues and identify possible confounding factors in the various arguments. Specifically, I pointed out that, as has been previously demonstrated for anaphor binding, pronominal binding is not a unitary phenomenon but, rather, reflects the workings of at least two different modules of the grammar. I hope that by isolating such factors further progress will become possible.

ACKNOWLEDGMENTS

I am very grateful to Peter Coopmans for his comments. I would also like to express my gratitude to the organizers of the Cornell workshop on language acquisition for giving me the opportunity to participate. Furthermore, I would like to thank them for their patience.

REFERENCES

Anderson, S. R. (1986). The typology of anaphoric dependencies: Icelandic (and other) reflexives. In L. Hellan & K. Koch Christensen (Eds.), *Topics in Scandinavian syntax* (pp. 65–89). Dordrecht: Reidel.

Batistella, E. (1987). *Chinese reflexivization.* Unpublished manuscript, University of Alabama, Birmingham.

Berwick, R. (1985). *The acquisition of syntactic knowledge.* Cambridge, MA: MIT Press.

Chien, Y.-C., & Wexler, K. (1990). Children's knowledge of locality conditions in binding as evidence for the modularity of syntax and pragmatics. *Language Acquisition, 1,* 225–295.

Chomsky, N. (1981). *Lectures on government and binding.* Dordrecht: Foris.

Chomsky, N. (1986a). *Barriers.* Cambridge, MA: MIT Press.

Chomsky, N. (1986b). *Knowledge of language: Its nature, origin, and use.* New York: Praeger.

Chomsky, N. (1992). A minimalist program for linguistic theory. *MIT Occasional Papers in Linguistics, 1.* Cambridge, MA: MIT, Department of Linguistics and Philosophy.

Everaert, M. (1986). *The syntax of reflexivization.* Dordrecht: Foris.

Everaert, M. (1990). Nominative anaphors in Icelandic: Morphology or syntax? In W. Abraham, W. Kosmeijer, & E. J. Reuland (Eds.), *Issues in Germanic syntax* (pp. 277–307). Berlin: Mouton de Gruyter.

Giorgi, A. (1984). Towards a theory of long distance anaphors. A GB approach. *The Linguistic Review, 3,* 307–359.

Grodzinsky, Y., & Reinhart, T. (1993). The innateness of binding and coreference. *Linguistic Inquiry, 24,* 69–101.

Hellan, L. (1988). *Anaphora in Norwegian and the theory of grammar.* Dordrecht: Foris.

Hellan, L. (1991). Containment and connectedness anaphors. In J. Koster & E. Reuland (Eds.), *Long-distance anaphora* (pp. 27–49). Cambridge: Cambridge University Press.

Hoekstra, J. (1991). *Pronouns and Case: On the distribution of* har(ren) *and se in Frisian.* Unpublished manuscript, Fryske Akademy, Ljouwert.

Huang, C.-T. J., & Tang, J. (1991). The local nature of the long-distance reflexive in Chinese. In J. Koster & E. J. Reuland (Eds.), *Long-distance anaphora* (pp. 263–282). Cambridge: Cambridge University Press.

Koster, C. (1993). *Errors in anaphora acquisition.* OTS dissertation series, Research Institute for Language and Speech, Utrecht University, The Netherlands.

Koster, J. (1985). Reflexives in Dutch. In J. Guéron, H.-G. Obenauer, & J.-Y. Pollock (Eds.), *Grammatical representation* (pp. 141–168). Dordrecht: Foris.

Koster, J., & Reuland, E. J. (Eds.). (1991). *Long-distance anaphora.* Cambridge: Cambridge University Press.

Maling, J. (1982). Non-clause-bounded reflexives in Icelandic. In T. Fretheim & L. Hellan (Eds.), *Papers from the Sixth Scandinavian Conference of Linguistics* (pp. 90–106). Trondheim: Tapir.

Manzini, R., & Wexler, K. (1987). Parameters, Binding Theory and learnability. *Linguistic Inquiry, 18,* 413–444.

Pica, P. (1987). On the nature of the reflexivization cycle. *Proceedings of the North Eastern Linguistics Society, 17,* 483–499.

Reinhart, T. (1983). *Anaphora and semantic interpretation.* London: Croom Helm.

Reinhart, T., & Reuland, E. J. (1991). Anaphors and logophors: An argument structure perspective. In J. Koster & E. J. Reuland, (Eds.) *Long-distance anaphora* (pp. 283–321). Cambridge: Cambridge University Press.

Reinhart, T., & Reuland, E. J. (1993). Reflexivity. *Linguistic Inquiry, 24,* 657–720.

Reuland, E. J., & Reinhart, T. (in preparation). *Pronouns, anaphors and Case.* Manuscript, Utrecht University and Tel Aviv University.

Sigurðsson, M. (1986). Moods and (Long Distance) reflexives in Icelandic. *Working Papers in Scandinavian Syntax, 25,* University of Trondheim.

Sigurjónsdóttir, S., & Hyams, N. (in press). Reflexivization and logophoricity: Evidence from the acquisition of Icelandic. *Language Acquisition.*

Sportiche, D. (1986). Zibun. *Linguistic Inquiry, 17,* 369–374.

Thornton, R., & Wexler, K. (1991). *VP ellipsis and the binding principles in children's grammars.* Paper presented at the 16th Annual Boston University Conference on Language Development, Boston, MA.

Thráinsson, H. (1991). Long-distance reflexives and the typology of NPs. In J. Koster & E. J. Reuland (Eds.), *Long-distance anaphora* (pp. 49–76). Cambridge: Cambridge University Press.

Wali, K. (1990). *On pronominal classification: Evidence from Marathi and Telugu.* Unpublished manuscript, Syracuse University and Cornell University.

Wexler, K. (1992). The subset principle is an intensional principle. In E. J. Reuland & W. O. G. Abraham (Eds.), *Knowledge and language, Vol. I, from Orwell's problem to Plato's problem* (pp. 217–239). Dordrecht: Kluwer.

Wexler, K., & Manzini, R. (1987). Parameters and learnability in Binding Theory. In T. Roeper & E. Willams (Eds.), *Parameter setting* (pp. 41–76). Dordrecht: Reidel.

Zribi-Hertz, A. (1989). A-type binding and narrative point of view. *Language, 65,* 695–727.

PART THREE

'PRO-DROP'

CHAPTER TEN

Early Null Subjects and Root Null Subjects*

Luigi Rizzi
Université de Genève

Around the age of 2, children freely drop subjects, irrespective of whether or not the target language is a null subject language. For instance, the phenomenon is typically found in the acquisition of English and French:

(1) ____ want more
____ find Giorgie
____ is broken

(Hyams, 1986)

(2) ____ boit café
____ fait un autre
____ est tombé

(Pierce, 1989)

Much recent work on the acquisition of English provides robust evidence for a selective drop of subjects: By and large, learners freely drop subjects but not obligatory objects (Hyams & Wexler, 1991; Valian, 1991; Wang, Lillo-Martin, Best, & Levitt, 1991). So the early null subject is not trivially amenable to an account in terms of some global strategy of structural reduction.

Hyams (1986) interpreted this state of affairs in terms of the Null Subject Parameter (Jaeggli & Safir, 1989; Rizzi, 1982, 1986): The initial setting is the

---

*This paper originally appeared in Hoeksta, T., and Schwartz, B. (Eds.), *Language Acquisition in Generative Grammar* (1994). John Benjamins Publishing Co.: Amsterdam/Philadelphia. Reprinted by permission.

null subject value. Learners of languages like English and French have to reset the parameter on the basis of experience, and this is normally done a few months after the second birthday. I would like to retain from Hyams' seminal approach the idea that the early null subject stage manifests a genuine grammatical option and cannot be reduced to an effect of extragrammatical factors (see Hyams & Wexler, 1991, for a detailed discussion of this issue). On the other hand, a number of structural properties of the early null subjects are emerging that suggest that this phenomenon is quite different from the drop of subjects in an adult grammatical system like Italian.

In the first part of this chapter I discuss some such properties and identify the major configurational constraint: By and large, the early null subject is possible in the first position of the structure, that is, in the specifier of the root. I then claim that such a configurational constraint is not specific to transitional systems in acquisition: Instances of root null subjects can be found in adult grammatical systems; hence they represent a genuine option of Universal Grammar.

Various questions are raised by the existence of root null subjects in acquisition, in special registers, and in normal adult languages: What is the status of the null element involved? How is it licensed and identified? How does it differ from a discourse-bound null operator (Huang, 1984)? Why is this option lost in the course of the acquisition of English and many other languages? I try to provide a partial answer to these questions by developing an analysis of root null subjects based on the typology of null elements proposed in Lasnik and Stowell (1991).

SOME STRUCTURAL PROPERTIES
OF EARLY NULL SUBJECTS

Valian (1991) pointed out that null subjects occur very rarely after a preposed WH-element in her corpus (natural production from 21 learners of English ranging from 1;10 to 2;8). There were only 9 null subjects in 552 WH-questions in which the WH-element was not a subject; that is, (3b) did not occur as a regular variant of (3a):

(3) a. Where daddy go?
     b. Where go?

This is a significant and surprising finding, especially in view of the fact that a null subject in this environment is perfectly acceptable in a null subject language (e.g., in Italian: *Dove va?* 'Where (he) goes?', *Cosa fai?* 'What (you) do?').

As Valian's observation is quite isolated in the acquisition literature, I tried to find confirmation elsewhere. A preliminary check of the standard

Brown (1973) corpora confirms the observed tendency (thanks to Rick Kazman for technical help). In the whole of Eve's corpus (20 recordings from 1;6 to 2;4) I counted 12 null subjects in 191 WH-questions with a nonsubject WH-element. Roeper (1991), addressing the issue, listed a number of examples with null subjects following a WH-element from the Adam corpus. Such cases indeed exist, but they are quite limited. If we look at the first 10 files of the Adam corpus, in which the proportion of null subjects in declaratives is well over 50% (57% according to Bloom, 1990; see also Hyams & Wexler, 1991), we find 21 cases of null subjects in 158 questions with nonsubject WH-elements. The proportion of null subjects in this environment thus drops to a percentage (13%) close to that of null objects in the same corpus (8%, according to Bloom, 1990).[1]

Also relevant is the apparent existence of WH-questions without movement in early English. The Adam corpus presents quite a few cases of WH in situ:

(4) They are for who? (Adam 25)
    It's a what? (Adam 26)
    He may do what to me? (Adam 33)

The majority of these cases (22 out of 34) involve a null subject; here is a sample:

(5) see what bear? (Adam 03)
    and do what? (Adam 25)
    use dat for what? (Adam 25)
    have what? (Adam 31)
    doing what? (Adam 35)
    cutting what? (Adam 35)
    close what? (Adam 36)
    fighting what? (Adam 36)
    sing what song? (Adam 38)

The existence of a consistent in-situ strategy in early English is, of course, far from being established by this small sample of examples (but see Radford, 1990; Whitman, Lee, & Lust, 1991, for supporting evidence and discussion). If confirmed, it would raise various interesting questions, as WH in situ is not a

---

[1]I leave open the question of the nature of the latter kind of omission. See also Hamann (1992), who found cases of nonroot (middle-field) null subjects in special contexts at a later stage of the acquisition of German. Nevertheless, the general trend in the acquisition of V-2 languages seems to involve null subjects located in the SPEC of the root. (See, in particular, De Haan & Truijhman, 1988, on Dutch; on early null subjects in German see Clahsen, 1991; Meisel, 1990; Weissenborn, 1992, and references cited there.) It remains to be determined whether French Early Null Subjects manifest similar occurrence restrictions. (See Pierce, 1989; Friedemann, 1992, for relevant discussion; preliminary results from Crisma, 1992, seem to strongly support an extension of our analysis to early French.)

property of the target language (apart from echo-questions): Why does it arise? How and when is it delearned? Let me put these questions aside for the moment.[2]

Note simply the high proportion of null subjects in in-situ questions, which suggests that early null subjects are affected not by the status of the sentence as a question, but by the preposing of the WH-element.

Another crucial property of the early null subject is that it is limited to main clauses. Roeper and Weissenborn (1990) pointed out that no cases of null subjects are produced by the learner of English in the first finite subordinate clauses. This observation was confirmed by Valian (1991), who found no cases of null subjects in the 123 examples of tensed subordinate clauses in her corpus. One could observe that this state of affairs may not be very significant for the analysis of the structural properties of early null subjects: After all, it could be that the child starts producing finite subordinate clauses after the end of the null subject stage. But this interpretation is strongly disfavored by the fact that we also find occasional cases in which a pronominal subject is dropped in the main clause and not in the embedded clause in the same utterance, or in two clauses in immediate succession, as in (6):

(6) a. ____ went in the basement # that what we do # after supper (Eve 19)
    b. ____ know what I maked (Adam 31)

Again, this observation invites a systematic verification; if confirmed on a larger scale, it strongly supports the hypothesis of a structural incompatibility between early null subjects and embedding, rather than that of a simple succession of acquisition stages.[3]

As in the previous case, this is quite different from what we find in a null subject language of the Italian type, in which a zero subject pronoun is equally possible in main and embedded subject position:[4]

---

[2] The delearning problem arises because the child apparently shifts from a system allowing both syntactic movement and in situ (like, say, French in main clauses) to a system requiring syntactic movement, apparently a move from a superset system to a subset system. Of course, the problem arises only if a substantial number of the in-situ examples are genuine questions. If they turned out to be analyzable as echo questions in the general case, there would be no delearning problem (even though a different question would presumably arise: Why so many echo questions in early English?). I return to this issue in the concluding remarks.

[3] It also rules out for this case the possibility that the child may be using two grammars interchangeably for some time (one with null subjects and no subordination and the other with subordination and no null subjects), a possibility suggested in a somewhat different context by A. Kroch, personal communication, 1992.

[4] If anything, a zero pronominal subject is even favored in embedded environments under coreference with the main subject, and compulsory when the embedded clause is adverbial:

(i) Gianni canta quando (lui) è contento.
    Gianni sings when (he) is happy

In (i), the zero pronoun must be selected to express coreference with the main subject.

(7) ____ so che cosa ____ hai detto.
    (I) know what (you) said

In conclusion, the early null subjects produced by learners of English appear to obey a strong distributional constraint: They occur in the first position of the structure. They tend not to appear after a preposed element and they do not appear in embedded clauses, two properties that are quite different from what we find in adult null subject languages.

What happens in the acquisition of Italian? Does the Italian learner around the age of 2 produce null subjects with the structural properties of early English? Or has the grammar already acquired the properties of adult Italian?

Even small production samples strongly suggest an early convergence with the properties of adult Italian. We typically find examples like the following, with a null subject following a preposed WH-element. (These examples were taken from the Martina corpus; see Cipriani, Chilosi, Bottari, & Pfanner, 1992, available on CHILDES, MacWhinney & Snow, 1985.)

(8) a. Ov'è? (1;8)
       'Where is?'
    b. Cos'è? (1;10)
       'What is?'
    c. Che voi? (2;3)
       'What (you) want?'
    d. Pecché piangi? (2;3)
       'Why (you) cry?'
    e. Quetto cosa fa? (2;5)
       'This what does?'

In the Martina corpus (13 recordings, roughly each month from 1;7 to 2;7) we find that, out of 35 questions with a nonsubject WH-element, 20 have a null pronominal subject.

Even though the data base is limited, the indication is quite clear: Early null subjects in the acquisition of Italian are not restricted to the first position. In this respect, the early system is just like adult Italian. The emerging picture thus seems to support the hypothesis of an early fixation of the Null Subject Parameter: Around the age of two, learners of English and Italian have already converged on the values of the parameter expressed by the adult languages. The early null subject manifested in the acquisition of English is a different phenomenon, structurally characterized by the fact that it is limited to the initial position, the specifier of the root.[5]

---

[5]Another observation of Valian's (1991) is potentially relevant in this context. She noted that early null subjects in Italian are about twice as frequent as early null subjects in English, given comparable age groups. Even if relative frequencies, as such, do not immediately bear on the

The next question we want to ask is whether such a root null subject is a special property of transitional systems in acquisition, or whether it is actually found in some adult grammatical systems, so that it corresponds to a genuine option of Universal Grammar.

SUBJECT DROP IN DIARIES

The closest analogue to the observed properties of the Early Null Subject is found in certain abbreviated varieties of English and other languages. Haegeman (1990) noticed the following cluster of properties in the register of diaries:

1. Subjects can be freely dropped even if the standard register of the language does not allow this. In English and French, for instance, dropped subjects are not necessarily first person, as the French example shows:

(9) A very sensible day yesterday. ____ saw noone. ____ took the bus to Southwark Bridge. ____ walked along Thames Street. . . .

(10) ____ m'accompagne au Mercure, puis à la gare . . .
'(he) takes me to Mercure, then to the station . . .'
____ s'est donné souvent l'illusion de l'amour . . .
'(he) often gave himself the illusion of love . . .'
____ me demande si . . . je lui eus montré les notes . . .
'(I) ask myself if . . . I would have shown him the notes'

Notice that the second and third line of the French example also show that a structurally represented null subject must be postulated; otherwise the anaphoric clitic would not be bound.

2. The subject cannot be dropped after a preposed element:

(11) a. ____ was so stupid!
b. * How stupid ____ was!

---

hypothesis of a structural difference (no frequency predictions are made directly by a structural hypothesis), the observed difference goes in the direction expected under a structural analysis of the sort advocated in the text. The null subject of Italian is possible in a larger set of structural environments; hence, all other things being equal, we would expect it to be more frequent than the Early Null Subject in English.

Do Italian learners possess the root null subject option, in addition to the early positive setting of the null subject parameter? I know of no empirical reason to exclude or confirm this possibility. On the other hand, if the suggestion of footnote 15 is correct, the availability of a *pro* subject may block the root null subject option in early Italian. I leave this question open.

3. Main subjects can be dropped; embedded subjects cannot:

(12) a. _____ can't find the letter that I need.
      b. * I can't find the letter that _____ need.
(See also the third line of (10).)

4. Subjects can be dropped; objects cannot:

(13) a. _____ saw her at the party.
      b. * She saw _____ at the party.

On the basis of Haegeman's (1990) description, subject drop in diaries appears to be ruled by the same structural constraints that characterize Early Null Subjects. Haegeman noticed that the root character of subject drop suggests a topic-drop-type analysis, involving a discourse-bound null operator in the matrix SPEC of C binding a variable in subject position. Under such an analysis, the null operator would be in competition with an overt preposed operator, whence the ungrammaticality of (11b). But she also noticed that under a topic-drop analysis, the subject-object asymmetry (13) is unexpected: Why couldn't the null operator bind a variable in object position? Of course, the same difficulty arises for an unqualified topic-drop analysis of the Early Null Subject. On the other hand, the structural conditions on root null subjects and topic-drop seem close enough to invite a detailed comparison.

TOPIC-DROP

In colloquial German (as well as in most V-2 Germanic varieties), it is possible to drop a main clause subject in the SPEC of C in a V-2 configuration like (14a). The option disappears in clause-internal position, that is, when the SPEC of C is filled by a preposed element, as in (14b), and in embedded clauses, no matter whether V-2 ((14c)) or not ((14d)):

(14) a. (Ich) habe es gestern gekauft.
         '(I)   have it yesterday bought.'
      b. Wann hat *(er) angerufen?
         'When has   he telephoned?'
      c. Hans glaubt *(ich) habe es gestern gekauft.
         'Hans believes I   have it yesterday bought.'
      d. Hans glaubt dass *(ich) es gestern gekauft habe.
         'Hans believes that I   it yesterday bought have.'

We thus seem to find the same structural restrictions operative on the Early Null Subject. Still, the dropping of arguments extends to preposed objects in colloquial German:

(15) (Das) habe ich gestern gekauft.
'This have I yesterday bought.'

This apparent subject–object symmetry led researchers to analyze the construction as involving topic-drop (Ross, 1982), or, in current terms, movement of a discourse-bound null operator to the SPEC of the root CP (Huang, 1984), from where it could bind a variable in subject or object position. Under this analysis, (14a) and (15) would have the following parallel representations:

(16) a. [OP habe [*t* es gestern gekauft]].
     b. [OP habe [ich *t* gestern gekauft]].

If this analysis was correct, the analogy with our Early Null Subjects would be partial at best. But Cardinaletti (1990) pointed out that there remains an important asymmetry between subject and object drop: Subject drop can involve pronouns with any person specification, provided that the dropped element is sufficiently salient in the context, whereas object drop is restricted to third person. For instance, a second person object pronoun cannot be dropped even in the most favorable case of contextual saliency, question-answer pairs:

(17) a. Hast du mich gesehen?
        'Have you me seen?'
     b. Dich habe ich nicht gesehen.
        'You have I not seen.'
     c. *____ habe ich nicht gesehen.
        '(you) have I not seen.'

If, in general, operators are intrinsically marked for third person (as is the case for interrogative operators, as we see later) the limitations on the object case follow from the structural analysis (16b). But then, Cardinaletti concluded, subject drop should not involve a null operator, and representation (16a) should be revised. If (14a) and (15) are to be dissociated as in Cardinaletti's proposal, then it becomes more plausible to partially assimilate the former case to the early English system.[6]

---

[6]Another reason for dissociating the dropping of local subjects in the specifier of the root from cases of topic-drop comes from Swedish. In this language, the dropping of the local subject can involve an expletive, as in (i), an element that cannot be topicalized, for instance, from the subject position of an embedded clause in (ii), whether or not it is dropped. Genuine cases of topic-drop are restricted to referential elements, which can be topicalized, as in (iii):

If the root null subject does not involve a discourse-bound null operator, we are then left with the questions: What is its status with respect to the typology of null elements? how can we express its minimal differences with respect to the null operator constructions? None of the currently assumed ECs seems to have the right intersection of formal and interpretative properties.

NULL CONSTANTS

A recent proposal by Lasnik and Stowell (1991), henceforth L&S, offers a new option that is worth exploring. In the context of a general discussion of the scope of Weak Crossover (WCO) effects, they observed that certain null operator constructions (and also some A'-dependencies involving overt operators, such as appositive relatives) differ significantly at the interpretative level from ordinary operator variable constructions, such as questions:

(18) a. John wonders who to please t.
  b. John is easy OP to please t.

The former involves quantification ranging over a possibly nonsingleton set. In the latter, the null element never ranges over a nonsingleton set; rather, it has its reference fixed to that of the antecedent. This interpretative difference correlates with a sensitivity to the WCO effect. Both kinds of A'-binding manifest sensitivity to Strong Crossover (SCO):

(19) a. * Who$_i$ did you get him$_i$ to talk to t_i?
  b. * John$_i$ is easy for us OP$_i$ to get him$_i$ to talk to t_i.

Only the former, however, manifests WCO effects:

(20) a. * Who$_i$ did you get his$_i$ mother to talk to t_i?
  b. John$_i$ is easy for us OP$_i$ to get his$_i$ mother to talk to t_i.

  (i) a. (Det) verkar som om . . .
      (it) seems as if . . .
    b. (Det) telefonerades mycket igaar.
      (it) was telephoned a lot yesterday
  (ii) a. * (Det) vet jag [t verkar som om . . .]
      it know I seems as if
    b. * (Det) visste jag [t telefonerades . . .]
      it knew I was telephoned
  (iii) (Det) visste jag [t skulle haenda].
      it knew I should happen

Cases of root null subjects in adult languages are occasionally reported in the literature (see Kenstowicz, 1989, on Levantine Arabic and Somali; Solà, 1992, on Corsican). The question whether such cases are amenable to an analysis along the lines proposed in the text is left open here.

L&S introduced a split between the two types of A′-bound traces in accordance with the semantic intuition. Only the trace bound by a genuine quantifier is a variable; the trace bound by the nonquantificational empty operator is not. It is a nonvariable R-expression to be assimilated to a null epithet or, more generally, to a null definite description. In order to distinguish it from the variable, I call this new type of null element the *null constant* (*nc*, terminological suggestion due to C. Hamann, personal communication, 1991). L&S then claimed that WCO is a property of variables; hence null operator constructions, not involving variables, are exempted from it. On the other hand, both kinds of A′-bound traces are R-expressions. As Principle C is a property of all R-expressions, the homogeneous behavior with respect to SCO is accounted for.

How is the new type of EC to be characterized? As a straightforward alternative to L&S's functional definition, let me simply propose that the feature [+/−v](ariable) combines with the familiar features [+/−a] and [+/−p], giving rise to eight cases:

(21)

$$
1. \begin{bmatrix} +a \\ +p \\ +v \end{bmatrix} = * \qquad
2. \begin{bmatrix} +a \\ +p \\ -v \end{bmatrix} = \text{PRO} \qquad
3. \begin{bmatrix} +a \\ -p \\ +v \end{bmatrix} = * \qquad
4. \begin{bmatrix} +a \\ -p \\ -v \end{bmatrix} = NP-t
$$

$$
5. \begin{bmatrix} -a \\ +p \\ +v \end{bmatrix} = pro(\text{res}) \qquad
6. \begin{bmatrix} -a \\ +p \\ -v \end{bmatrix} = pro \qquad
7. \begin{bmatrix} -a \\ -p \\ +v \end{bmatrix} = \text{variable} \qquad
8. \begin{bmatrix} -a \\ -p \\ -v \end{bmatrix} = nc
$$

Of these, 1 and 3 are presumably excluded by the inherent incompatibility of [+a] (requiring A-binding) and [+v] (requiring A′-binding): A single element cannot simultaneously belong to the A and the A′ systems.[7]

The remaining six combinations are all attested. 2, 4, 6, and 7 are the familiar types; 5 is *pro* used as a resumptive pronoun (as in Georgopoulos, 1991; Rizzi, 1982); and 8 is the null constant, a nonvariable R-expression.

---

[7]This conclusion is also supported by the fact that languages using resumptive elements (overt variables) always use pronouns, never anaphors: The feature [+v] can co-occur with [+p] but not with [+a]. G. Cinque and R. Clark (personal communication, 1991) have pointed out that PROs giving rise to so-called PRO gate effects (i.e., alleviating Weak Crossover violations in examples like *Who did PRO visiting his relatives annoy t?*, Higginbotham, 1980) may be analyzable as cases of [+v] PRO. If this is correct, then the incompatibility of [+v] with [+a] should be restricted to the pure anaphor, that is, the case of [+a] that is assigned a governing category.

We are now left with the question: What forces A'-binding of the null constant by a null operator? That is, as overt epithets and other definite descriptions can freely occur and directly pick up their referent in discourse, why can't the null variant do the same?

(22) I tried to visit John last week, but I was unable to persuade the guy / *EC to see me.

L&S's answer was: The null definite description, like all null elements, must satisfy an identification requirement that is fulfilled by the null operator. We can make this suggestion precise by assuming that the specific identification requirement on null constants is the same one that holds for variables and other types of traces, that is, the identification component of the ECP (in the sense of Rizzi, 1990), which holds for all nonpronominal empty categories:

(23) *ECP (Identification):*
EC [−p] must be chain-connected to an antecedent.

The antecedent can be an A or A' (or, irrelevantly here, X°) position, depending on the kind of chain.[8]

In sum, an EC [−a, −p] can be [+/−v]. If it is [+v] it is a variable and must satisfy (23) by being chain-connected to a genuine quantifier (e.g., a question operator), assigning it a range; if it is [−v] it is a null constant. It must still be chain-connected to an A' element to satisfy (23) (it could not be A-bound, as it is an R-expression), but a nonquantificational A' element, typically a null operator. The other combinations (a variable bound by a nonquantificational operator, a null constant bound by a quantificational operator) are excluded by the appropriate version of the Bijection Principle, the principle barring vacuous quantification, or whatever principle requires quantifiers to bind variables and variables to be bound by quantifiers (Chomsky, 1986; Koopman & Sportiche, 1982). Moreover, as the null constant is an R-expression, chain-connection to an element in A-position is barred by Principle C. A

---

[8] See Rizzi (1990); in the terms of that system, the chain-connection can be established via antecedent government or via binding, depending on the availability of referential indices. G. Cinque has suggested (personal communication, 1992) that our null constant may be assimilated to a variable bearing a referential index in the sense of Rizzi (1990), as sharpened by Cinque (1990), rather than to a variable unable to bear such an index, hence available for antecedent government connections only. If this reduction is correct, the [+/−v] feature is simply a descriptive label for an independently needed distinction (at least as far as [−a, −p] null elements are concerned).

nonquantificational operator thus remains as the only possible identifier of the null constant.[9]

DISCOURSE-IDENTIFIED NULL ELEMENTS REVISITED

L&S's proposal directly refers to cases of sentence-bound null operator constructions (*easy to please*, parasitic gaps, etc.) but can be immediately extended to the empty elements bound by discourse-identified null operators. In fact, if we apply L&S's diagnostic criterion for null constants, the EC bound by a discourse-identified null operator in German falls into this class: It is sensitive to SCO, but not to WCO:

(24) a. * Den Hans$_i$ hat er$_i$ t_i gesehen.
     'Hans has he seen.'
  b. * OP$_i$ hat er$_i$ t_i gesehen.

(25) a. Den Hans$_i$ hat [sein$_i$ Vater] t_i gesehen.
     'Hans has his father seen.'
  b. OP$_i$ hat [sein$_i$ Vater] t_i gesehen.

We can now go back to Cardinaletti's (1990) asymmetry between the local subject case and all the other cases. In all the other cases (e.g., the object case), the null constant (*nc*) is bound by a null OP, which as such has the intrinsic features of third person singular.

---

[9]A consequence of this system is worth noticing. It has been occasionally observed that, although the other three canonical types of ECs can (must) be the heads of A-chains, the purely anaphoric EC [+a, –p] cannot; it can only be an A-trace, a nonhead of a chain. In other words, natural languages do not seem to allow null variants of overt anaphors, which typically head their own chains:

(i) John saw himself / *EC.

Typically, however, they allow null R-expressions and null pronominals that head their A-chains, on a par with their overt counterparts. See, for instance, Brody (1985) for discussion. This gap follows from the proposed system, in fact from the interplay of the identification part of the ECP and the feature specification of the null elements. A [+a, –p] EC, qua [–p], is in the scope of (23), hence it must be chain-connected to an antecedent; qua [+a], it must be locally bound by an A-antecedent. Because the A and A' systems do not mix (see previous discussion), it follows that the EC must be chain-connected to an A-antecedent; hence it never is the head of an A-chain, Q.E.D. This conclusion does not hold for other types of ECs. [+a, +p], [–a, +p] are not in the scope of (23); hence chain formation with a higher element is not enforced. [–a, –p] is in the scope of (23) and must be chain-connected to an antecedent, but this antecedent can be in an A'-position, as the EC is [–a]. (In fact, the antecedent that the EC is chain-connected to must be an A'-position, because of Principle C.)

(26) [OP hat [er shon *nc* gesehen]].
has he already seen
(ihn, es, *mich, *dich . . .)
(him, it, *me, *you)

What about the local subject case? If the representation of (27) was (28), it would be hard to distinguish the two cases:

(27) ____ habe es shon gesehen.
(I) have it already seen

(28) [OP habe [*nc* es shon gesehen]].

One could not, for instance, simply claim that (27) can have a first person interpretation because the inflection endows OP with such features: If I had this capacity, what could exclude the possibility of non-third-person question operators in the appropriate contexts?[10]

(29) * Chi (di voi) sapete la risposta?
'Who (among you) know [+2d.pl.] the answer?'

But there is a possible alternative representation for (27). It has been repeatedly noticed that the SPEC of C position in V-2 languages can behave as an A position when the local subject is moved to it (with the trace in [SPEC, IP] behaving like an NP-*t*: Holmberg, 1986; Rizzi, 1991a; Taraldsen, 1986). Suppose then that (27) allows a representation with the null constant in the SPEC of C, binding an NP-*t* in [SPEC IP], and involving no null OP at all:

(30) [*nc* habe [*t* es shon gesehen]].

As the intrinsic limitation to third person is specific to operators, there is no reason to expect it in (30).

Still, (30) should violate the identification requirement of the ECP, as the null constant lacks a clause-internal identifier. Can (30) be made consistent with the ECP? A natural possibility is offered by an extension of an idea proposed by Chomsky (1986) in the context of the theory of binding. According to Chomsky's proposal, the governing category of an element is the

---

[10]Overt and null operators can inherit features other than third person, but only from a binding antecedent, not from AGR:

(i) Voi, OP che t sapete la risposta . . .
'You, who know [+2d.pl.] the answer . . .'

(ii) You are easy OP to please.

minimal domain with certain characteristics in which the binding requirements of the element are satisfiable in principle. Suppose that we extend and adapt this idea to the ECP by adding the following specification to (23):

(31) . . . if it can.

So an empty element must be identified in the way indicated by (23) if it can be, that is, if there is a potential identifier, a c-commanding maximal projection (possibly, a c-commanding $X°$ for an empty head). This has the effect of exempting from the identification requirement the specifier of the root, the highest position of the structure, the position that c-commands everything and is not c-commanded by anything. The specifier of the root then is the only position in which an empty element can fail to have a clause-internal identification and is available for discourse identification. Under this interpretation of (23), an unbound null constant can survive in the SPEC of the root in structures like (30) and receive its referential value in discourse.[11]

CROSS-LINGUISTIC VARIATION
AND DEVELOPMENTAL SEQUENCE

It is now natural to extend the proposed null constant analysis to all the observed cases of root null subjects, including the Early Null Subject. But why is the option lost in adult standard English and French, for instance? To deal with both the cross-linguistic variation and the observed develop-

---

[11](30) also violates the formal licensing part of the ECP, proper head government (Rizzi, 1990). If, following Moro (in press), we restrict the proper head government requirement to the case in which a head intervenes between a null element and its identifier, the requirement will not apply to (30).

Note that our interpretation of (23) also provides an explanation for the fact that embedded $C°$s generally are overt, whereas matrix $C°$s can (must) be null (assuming roots to be CPs in the general case; see later discussion). The head of the root lacks a potential identifier (a c-commanding head); hence it can be left empty. Consider also the possibility of dropping semantically empty fillers of I (*do, have, be*) in questions, but not in declaratives (Akmajian, Demers, & Harnish, 1984; Schmerling, 1973):

    (i) (Are) you going to lunch?
    (ii) (Have) you ever been to Chicago?
    (iii) (Does) she like her new house?

I-to-C movement raises the aux to the root head, where it can be null under our interpretation of (23). (The possibility of dropping a second person pronoun in this environment may involve incorporation of the pronoun into the null auxiliary and/or be related to the phenomenon of the null subject of imperatives.)

mental sequence, I propose that the possibility of a root null subject can arise when the SPEC of the root is an A-position and is lost in the varieties in which the SPEC of the root is an A'-position, not a suitable host for the null constant. Underlying this approach is the idea that the feature system [+/−a], [+/−p], (and [+/−v]) defines empty elements in A-position: Null elements belonging to the A'-system are not classified by this feature system, so the null constant (on a par with the variable, PRO, the NP-*t*, etc.) simply cannot be defined in an A'-position.

Let us start from a natural assumption about the nature of the root category. Following Stowell (1981), Radford (1988), and many others, I assume the following principle:

(32) Root = CP

This principle amounts to a claim that we normally speak through propositions, not fragments of propositions: In the unmarked case, the root category is the canonical structural realization of the proposition, the CP.

Let us first consider the case of the SPEC of C in a V-2 language such as German. I adopt the following definition of A-positions:

(33) *A-positions:*
      Theta positions and specifiers construed with AGR.
      (See Rizzi, 1991a, for discussion of the different cases.)

Under this definition, the SPEC of C in a V-2 language is an A-position when the local subject is moved into it, as in (34):

(34) [Ich habe [*t* es shon gesehen INFL]].

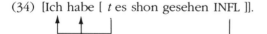

The subject is construed with the AGR specification of the highest inflectional head; if the latter is moved to C and the local subject is moved to the SPEC of C in V-2, the SPEC-AGR configuration is reconstituted at the CP level; hence the SPEC of C is an A-position under (33). The SPEC of C can therefore host our null constant, and structure (30) is well formed. If the language also possesses the discourse-linked null operator, as is the case in colloquial German, the null constant will also be possible in other structural positions (e.g., the object position, as in (26)), provided that it is bound by the discourse-identified null operator in the main SPEC of C, with the interpretative properties that we discussed earlier.

On the other hand, in English, French, and other non-V-2 languages, the structure of the root is as shown in (35):

(35)

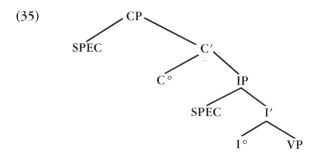

If the language possesses the discourse-identified null operator, a null constant in [SPEC, IP] (or in any other position) will be possible, being bound by the null operator in the SPEC of C (this may be the case of European Portuguese, according to Raposo, 1986). If the language does not have the discourse-identified null operator (as is the case in English or French) the null constant is not permissible in this configuration. The SPEC of C is not a possible host because it is an A′ position; the SPEC of I is not a possible host because it is not the SPEC of the root (but see the final section). There is a higher position that can be a potential antecedent, the SPEC of C; hence an unbound null constant in [SPEC, IP] is ruled out under (23).

Why is the root null subject option available in early English? Given the picture I have proposed, the most natural element to hold responsible for the developmental sequence is principle (32). Suppose that this principle is not operative initially; that is, the encircled part can be omitted in (35) (but does not have to be omitted; in fact, much recent work on the early manifestation of V-2, e.g., Boser, Lust, Santelmann, Whitman, 1991; Poeppel & Wexler, 1991, strongly suggests that the possibility of starting from CP is available from very early on). If the CP layer is omitted, then [SPEC, IP], an A-specifier of the root, becomes a suitable host for the null constant, and the root null subject is allowed. No other position is available for the null constant: If the CP layer is present in (35), for instance in a question with WH-movement, [SPEC, IP] ceases to be the SPEC of the root and an unbound null constant in this position is excluded by (23). Similarly, an unbound null constant in object position (or any other position) is excluded, as in (36):

(36) * I met *nc*.

This is because there are higher positions acting as potential identifiers (the subject position in (36)); hence (23) is enforced. As early English (like adult English) does not possess the discourse-identified null operator, the null constant is not permissible in any position other than the main subject position (when the CP layer is omitted); thus the observed subject-object asymmetry. As soon as principle (32) becomes operative (perhaps an event triggered by an inner maturational schedule, in the sense of Borer & Wexler, 1987), the conditions for the root null constant cease to be met, and the Early Null Subject disappears. (32) may remain a weak principle that can be "turned off" on abbreviated registers and, perhaps, under special contextual conditions (as in question-answer pairs).

SPECULATIONS ON DEVELOPMENTAL CORRELATIONS

If principle (32) is not operative initially, then root categories other than CPs are adequate starting points for early linguistic expressions. I have shown how the possibility of root null subjects follows from this property: If the CP layer can be omitted, then the structural conditions for the null constant in subject position are met. Do we expect other properties to correlate with root null subjects under this analysis? An immediate consequence of our proposal is that, if CP is not the compulsory starting point in early grammars, we would expect children to use a much wider variety of root categories, that is, simple NPs, PPs, APs, (nonfinite) VPs, different kinds of uninflected small clauses. Arguing for such a scenario goes beyond the limits of the present chapter; I simply note that the very high proportion of nominal or otherwise nonverbal utterances in children's production around the second birthday, as well as a sharp decline a few months later, is what the proposed approach leads us to expect. For instance, the proportion of utterances containing verbs in the production corpus of Valian's (1991) first group of English learners (age range 1;10–2;2) is only .27, a proportion that raises dramatically by over .70 in her third and fourth group (age ranges 2;3–2;6 and 2;6–2;8, respectively; the author has excluded imperative sentences from this calculation). In our terms, as soon as (32) becomes operative, the option of using (nonverbal) fragments of CPs as complete utterances ceases to be generally available and is confined to whatever special discourse contexts allow it in the adult grammar. See also Radford's (1990) comprehensive discussion of the early stages, particularly in connection with the early use of root small clauses.[12]

A less obvious property that may be related to early null subjects involves the apparent in-situ stage that was hinted at in the first section. Remember what the problem is: If learners of English go through a stage in which both

---

[12]Diary registers and other special abbreviated registers allowing root null subjects could now be characterized as retaining the nonoperativity of (32). We would then expect, among other things, that in these registers, discourse or textual units do not have to be full propositions and can be fragments of propositions. A quick perusal of Haegeman's (1990) corpus supports this hypothesis. We typically find in diaries chunks of propositions corresponding to maximal projections different from CP, as in (i):

(i) Après-midi à discuter, puis agréable.
    afternoon to discuss, then pleasant
                        (Léautaud, 1917–1930, quoted in Haegeman, 1990)

syntactic WH-movement and WH in situ are possible, how do they "delearn" the in-situ option, thus moving from a superset system to a subset system? Following a suggestion from M. Starke (personal communication, 1991), the real choice that the child has may not be between syntactic or LF WH-movement, but rather between CP or a different category as the root. If CP is chosen, then syntactic movement is obligatory, as in the adult English grammar; if a different category is selected, then WH-movement cannot take place, there being no appropriate host, so WH in situ is the only option (presumably with QR applying at LF to the WH element as a salvaging strategy to create the necessary operator-variable structure). Under this interpretation, when principle (32) becomes operative in English, then the (parametrized) principle requiring obligatory movement in this language applies in full force, and WH in situ is ruled out.[13]

Should one expect other co-occurrence relations between the root null subject and other properties of the early grammar? One could speculate that the delay in the operativity of (32) is related to the general parsimony of functional elements that the child's initial production manifests. Much recent work has shown that it is too radical to assume that the child's linguistic representations are purely lexical around the age of 2. Functional heads must be postulated in the child's grammar to account both for morphological analysis, the very presence of functional elements, and various word order phenomena (for instance, see Deprez & Pierce, 1990, on French; Poeppel & Wexler, 1991, and much other work on the acquisition of V-2 in German; Guasti, 1992, on Italian). Still, a residue of the idea that initial syntactic representations are purely lexical (Guilfoyle & Noonan, 1989; Lebeaux, 1988; Platzack, 1990; Radford, 1990) seems to remain valid: The child's production around the age of 2 manifests a liberty of omission of functional heads that is not found in the target languages (see also Kazman, 1990). Thus:

1. Determinerless NPs appear to alternate freely with full DPs in the early stages of languages in which the determiner is obligatory, such as French. (Examples are from Pierce, 1989; see Friedemann, 1992; Radford, 1990, who related this property to the freer distribution of nominals in the early stages.)

(37) a. Pas pousser chaise papa.
     'Not push the chair papa.'
   b. Fini café Madeleine.
     'Finished coffee Madeleine.'

---

[13]Notice that this approach requires that the principle in question, the WH Criterion of Rizzi (1991b), should also be interpreted as obligatory if satisfiable in principle. For the sake of argument, I have assumed that (4)–(5) are genuine questions. If a generalized echo question analysis is tenable, then the delearning problem does not arise.

2. The use of main clause participial sentences involves (at least) the omission of the functional head auxiliary (Bottari, Cipriani, & Chilosi, 1991):

(38) a. Fatto Diana. (Diana, 1;11)
done Diana
'Diana has done it.'
b. Che fatto la bimba? (Diana, 2;0)
what done the little girl
'What has the little girl done?'

3. The use of main clause infinitives found in many languages may involve the omission of tense (and/or of AGR). See Friedemann (1992), Guasti (1992), Wexler (1991), and references cited there for recent discussion (examples from Pierce, 1989).

(39) a. Monsieur conduire.
'Man (to) drive.'
b. Tracteur casser maison.
'Tractor break house.'

Some fundamental questions remain open in these cases, in particular the question whether the (partial) lack of phonetically realized functional elements in production reflects a blocking of spell-out for otherwise present categories, or the radical absence of the category. It is conceivable that different answers will be appropriate for different kinds of missing functional elements. If at least some cases of missing phonetic realization are to be analyzed as involving radical absence of the category, then the nonoperativity of (32) could be viewed as a special case of the overall parsimony of functional elements in the early grammar.[14]

ROOT EXPLETIVE SUBJECTS

As is well known, learners of English drop nonreferential subjects as well as referential subjects:

(40) Yes, _____ is toys in there.

(from Hyams, 1986)

---

[14]All other things being equal, we could then expect root null subjects to disappear concomitantly with the loss of main clause infinitives, for instance, even though one cannot a priori exclude the possibility that different principles enforcing the presence of different types of functional elements do not emerge simultaneously but, rather, follow a maturational schedule.

Can the null constant analysis be extended to cover this case? Notice first of all that some adult languages clearly extend the root null subject option to nonreferential elements, as in Swedish (examples due to C. Platzack):

(41) a. (Det) verkar som om . . .
    it   seems as if . . .
   b. (Det) telefonerades   mycket igaar.
    it   was telephoned a lot   yesterday

These appear to be genuine cases of root null subjects in that the zero variant of the expletive is possible only in initial position. When the SPEC of C is filled by a different element in a V-2 construction, the expletive cannot be dropped:

(42) Igaar   telefonerades *(det) mycket.
   yesterday was telephoned it   a lot

UG apparently allows the null constant to be an expletive. If the unmarked case for an expletive is to be null, then it is natural that the child will take the null constant option for the expletive.[15]

Some natural languages allow root null subjects only under the nonreferential interpretation. This is the case in colloquial French and may be true of some colloquial registers of English, even though the latter are less easy to tease apart from other registers in which referential subjects can also be dropped:

(43) a. ____ semble/paraît/s'avère que Marie est malade.
   b. ____ seems/appears/turns out that Mary is sick.

(44) a. * ____ dit/sait/pense que Marie est malade.
   b. * ____ says/knows/thinks that Mary is sick.

---

[15]Some languages allowing null constants (and null OPs) do not seem to like nonreferential null constants. Standard Dutch is an example:

(i) a. (Hij) praatte erover.
    'He talked there-about.'
   b. *? (Het) regent.
    'It is raining.'
   c. *(Er) werd lang gedanst.
    'It was long danced.'

This may be an irreducible property of the language, to be learned through indirect negative evidence, or it may be related to the fact that Dutch, unlike Swedish, allows some cases of expletive *pro*. It could be that natural languages do not like to have two different types of null elements functioning as expletives (Icelandic may be problematic for this conjecture; see Sigurðsson, 1989).

We find the root null subject properties again: If a WH-element is preposed, or if the structure is embedded, the expletive cannot be dropped.

(45) a. Pourquoi semble *(t-il) que . . .
     b. Why does *(it) seem that . . .
(46) a. Jean dit que *(il) semble que . . .
     b. John says that *(it) seems that . . .

Why is it that colloquial French and English retain the option of root null subjects but restrict this to certain types of expletives (here we gloss over the fact that not all types of expletives can be naturally dropped in the relevant context)? The hypothesis that these systems also possess a structural device to suspend the application of (32) (say, on a par with the abbreviated registers) would require an independent parametrization of the referential interpretation. (Diary French would take the option of discourse-identified referential interpretation; colloquial French would not.) This is not a very appealing possibility, for many reasons.

A somewhat more interesting possibility is the following. Suppose that specifiers are optional, in general, unless required by some special principle such as the Extended Projection Principle (EPP). Suppose then that the SPEC of the root C can be missing. Thus (35) can have the following shape:

(47)

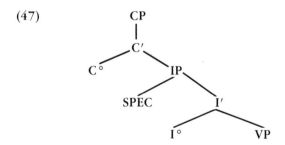

If this is correct, then an unbound null constant in [SPEC, IP] becomes possible again under (23), as there is no c-commanding maximal projection that may act as its antecedent. So the nonreferential *nc* is possible here, whereas it remains excluded from embedded contexts such as (46), or main contexts in which the SPEC of C is present, such as (45). But this now leaves us without our structural explanation for the impossibility of the referential *nc*.

We can observe that, over and above the constraints discussed so far, there are strong restrictions on discourse identification, illustrated by the fact that a discourse-linked null operator in German must be in the root SPEC of C. If it sits in an embedded SPEC of C (even in a V-2 structure), the sentence is excluded:

(48) OP habe ich *t* shon gesehen.
'(This) have I already seen.'
(49) *Hans glaubt OP habe ich *t* shon gesehen.
'Hans believes that (this) have I already seen.'

It appears that discourse identification of an empty category is restricted to the root and cannot look more deeply inside the structure apart from the immediate domain of the root.

An intuitively plausible way to express this constraint is to generalize the idea borrowed from Chomsky's Binding Theory and state it also as a constraint on discourse identification (while keeping it as a relaxing condition on principles of sentence grammar such as the ECP):

(50) A null element can be discourse-identified only if it is not c-commanded sentence-internally by a potential identifier.

So the null constant in [SPEC, IP] in (47) is formally licit (if no SPEC of C is selected, (23) is vacuous). But it cannot be discourse-identified because it is c-commanded by C, a potential identifier (typically, heads function as identifiers at least for one type of null element, *pro*). As is always the case for formally licit but unidentified null elements (cf. much current literature on *pro*), the null constant in this instance can function only as a nonargumental expletive.

ACKNOWLEDGMENTS

Versions of this chapter at different stages of elaboration were presented at the GLOW Workshop in the Development of Government and Inflection (Leiden, March 28, 1991), at the Symposium on Syntactic Theory and First Language Acquisition: Cross-Linguistic Perspectives (Cornell University, April 25, 1992), at the Certificat de Spécialisation of the University of Geneva, and at the Language Acquisition Seminar of SISSA, Trieste. I am grateful to the audiences of these events and to Adriana Belletti, Guglielmo Cinque, Marc-Ariel Friedemann, Teresa Guasti, Liliane Haegeman, and an anonymous reviewer for helpful comments and suggestions.

REFERENCES

Akmajian, A., Demers, R., & Harnish, R. (1984). *Linguistics*. Cambridge, MA: MIT Press.
Bloom, P. (1990). Subjectless sentences in child language. *Linguistic Inquiry, 21*, 491–504.
Borer, H., & Wexler, K. (1987). The maturation of syntax. In T. Roeper & E. Williams (Eds.), *Parameter setting* (pp. 123–172). Dordrecht: Reidel.
Boser, K., Lust, B., Santelmann, L., & Whitman, J. (1991). The syntax of CP and V-2 in early German child grammar. *Proceedings of the North Eastern Linguistics Society, 22*.
Bottari, P., Cipriani, P., & Chilosi, A. M. (1991). *Pre-syntactic devices in the acquisition of Italian free morphology*. Unpublished manuscript, Istituto Stella Maris, Pisa.

Brody, M. (1985). On the complementary distribution of empty categories. *Linguistic Inquiry*, *16*, 505–564.

Brown, R. (1973). *A first language: The early stages*. Cambridge, MA: Harvard University Press.

Cardinaletti, A. (1990). *Pronomi nulli e pleonastici nelle lingue germaniche e romanze* [Null pronouns and pleonastics in Germanic and Romance languages]. Unpublished doctoral dissertation, Università di Venezia.

Chomsky, N. (1986). *Knowledge of language*, New York: Praeger.

Cinque, G. (1990). *Types of A'-dependencies*. Cambridge, MA: MIT Press.

Cipriani, P., Chilosi, A. M., Bottari, P., & Pfanner, L. (1992). *L'acquisizione della morfosintassi in italiano: Fasi e processi* [The acquisition of morphosyntax in Italian: Phases and processes]. Padova: UniPress.

Clahsen, H. (1991). Constraints on parameter setting: A grammatical analysis of some acquisition stages in German child language. *Language Acquisition*, *1*, 361–391.

Crisma, P. (1992). *On the acquisition of Wh-questions in French*. Unpublished manuscript, Université de Genève.

de Haan, G., & Truijhman, K. (1988). Missing subjects and objects in child grammar. In Jordens & Halleman (Eds.), *Language development* (pp. 101–121). Dordrecht: Foris.

Deprez, V., & Pierce, A. (1990). *A cross-linguistic study of negation in early syntactic development*. Unpublished manuscript, Rutgers University and MIT.

Friedemann, M.-A. (1992). *The underlying position of external arguments in French: A study in adult and child grammar*. Unpublished manuscript, Université de Genève.

Georgopoulos, C. (1991). *Syntactic variables*. Dordrecht: Kluwer.

Guasti, M. T. (1992). *Verb syntax in Italian child grammar*. Unpublished manuscript, Université de Genève.

Guilfoyle, E., & Noonan, M. (1989). *Functional categories and language acquisition*. Unpublished manuscript, MIT and McGill University.

Haegeman, L. (1990). Understood subjects in English diaries. *Multilingua*, *9*, 157–199.

Hamann, C. (1992). Late empty subjects in German child language. *Technical Reports in Formal and Computational Linguistics*, *4*. Geneva: Université de Genève.

Higginbotham, J. (1980). Pronouns and bound variables. *Linguistic Inquiry*, *11*, 679–708.

Holmberg, A. (1986). *Word order and syntactic features*. Unpublished doctoral dissertation, University of Stockholm.

Huang, C.-T. J. (1984). On the distribution and reference of empty pronouns. *Linguistic Inquiry*, *15*, 531–574.

Hyams, N. (1986). *Language acquisition and the theory of parameters*. Dordrecht: Reidel.

Hyams, N., & Wexler, K. (1991). *On the grammatical basis of null subjects in child language*. Unpublished manuscript, UCLA and MIT.

Jaeggli, O., & Safir, K. (Eds.). (1989). *The null subject parameter*. Dordrecht: Kluwer.

Kazman, R. (1990). *The acquisition of functional categories and the lexicon: A psychologically plausible model*. Unpublished manuscript, CMU, Pittsburgh, PA.

Kenstowicz, M. (1989). The Null Subject Parameter in modern Arabic dialects. In O. Jaeggli & K. Safir (Eds.), *The Null Subject Parameter* (pp. 263–275). Dordrecht: Kluwer.

Koopman, H., & Sportiche, D. (1982). Variables and the Bijection Principle. *The Linguistic Review*, *2*, 139–161.

Lasnik, H., & Stowell, T. (1991). Weakest Cross-over. *Linguistic Inquiry*, *22*, 687–720.

Lebeaux, D. (1988). *Language acquisition and the form of the grammar*. Unpublished doctoral dissertation, University of Massachusetts, Amherst.

MacWhinney, B., & Snow, C. (1985). The Child Language Data Exchange System. *Journal of Child Language*, *12*, 271–296.

Meisel, J. (1990). *Infl-ection: Subjects and subject-verb agreement in early child language. Evidence from simultaneous acquisition of two first languages: German and French*. Unpublished manuscript, University of Hamburg.

Moro, A. (in press). Heads as antecedents: A brief history of the ECP. *Lingua e stile.*

Pierce, A. (1989). *On the emergence of syntax: A cross-linguistic study.* Unpublished doctoral dissertation, MIT, Cambridge, MA.

Platzack, C. (1990). A grammar without functional categories: A syntactic study of early Swedish child language. *Working Papers in Scandinavian Syntax, 45,* 13–34.

Poeppel, D., & Wexler, K. (1991). *The status of functional categories in early German grammar.* Unpublished manuscript, MIT, Cambridge, MA.

Radford, A. (1988). *Transformational grammar.* Cambridge: Cambridge University Press.

Radford, A. (1990). *Syntactic theory and the acquisition of English syntax.* Oxford: Basil Blackwell.

Raposo, E. (1986). The null object in European Portuguese. In O. Jaeggli & C. Silva-Corvalan (Eds.), *Studies in Romance linguistics* (pp. 373–390). Dordrecht: Foris.

Rizzi, L. (1982). *Issues in Italian syntax.* Dordrecht: Foris.

Rizzi, L. (1986). Null subjects in Italian and the theory of *pro. Linguistic Inquiry, 17,* 501–557.

Rizzi, L. (1990). *Relativized minimality.* Cambridge, MA: MIT Press.

Rizzi, L. (1991a). Proper head government and the definition of A positions. *GLOW Newsletter, 26,* 46–47.

Rizzi, L. (1991b). *Residual Verb Second and the Wh Criterion* (Technical Report in Formal and Computational Linguistics No. 3). Geneva: Université de Genève.

Roeper, T. (1991). *Why a theory of triggers supports the pro-drop analysis.* Unpublished manuscript, University of Massachusetts, Amherst.

Roeper, T., & Weissenborn, J. (1990). How to make parameters work. In L. Frazier & J. de Villiers (Eds.), *Language processing and language acquisition* (pp. 147–162). Dordrecht: Kluwer.

Ross, J. R. (1982). *Pronoun deleting processes in German.* Paper presented at the annual meeting of the Linguistic Society of America, San Diego, CA.

Schmerling, S. (1973). Subjectless sentences and the notion of Surface Structure. *Proceedings of the Chicago Linguistic Society, 9,* 577–586.

Sigurðsson, H. A. (1989). *Verbal syntax and the case in Icelandic.* Unpublished doctoral dissertation, University of Lund, Sweden.

Solà, J. (1992). *Agreement and subjects.* Unpublished doctoral dissertation, Universitat autonoma de Barcelona.

Stowell, T. (1981). *Origins of phrase structure.* Unpublished doctoral dissertation, MIT, Cambridge, MA.

Taraldsen, T. (1986). *Som* and the Binding Theory. In L. Hellan & K. K. Christensen (Eds.), *Topics in Scandinavian syntax* (pp. 149–184). Dordrecht: Reidel.

Valian, V. (1991). Syntactic subjects in the early speech of American and Italian children. *Cognition, 40,* 21–81.

Wang, Q., Lillo-Martin, D., Best, C., & Levitt, A. (1991). *Null subjects vs. null objects: Some evidence from the acquisition of Chinese and English.* Unpublished manuscript, Haskins Laboratories, New Haven, CT.

Weissenborn, J. (1992). Null subjects in early grammars: Implications for parameter setting theory. In J. Weissenborn, H. Goodluck, & T. Roeper (Eds.), *Theoretical issues in language acquisition* (pp. 269–299). Hillsdale, NJ: Lawrence Erlbaum Associates.

Wexler, K. (1991). *Optional infinitives, head movement and the economy of derivations in child grammar.* Unpublished manuscript, MIT, Cambridge, MA.

Whitman, J., Lee, O., & Lust, B. (1991). Continuity of the principles of Universal Grammar in first language acquisition: The issue of functional categories. *Proceedings of the North Eastern Linguistics Society, 21,* 283–297.

CHAPTER ELEVEN

Children's Postulation of Null Subjects: Parameter Setting and Language Acquisition

Virginia Valian

Hunter College and CUNY Graduate Center

This chapter covers three main points. The first is that, with respect to null subjects in young children's speech, the data collected thus far indicate no point at which the grammar of U.S. children speaking Standard English (henceforth, American children) clearly licenses null subjects, and no point at which IP and CP are clearly absent. In contrast, the grammars of children acquiring null subject languages do show clear evidence for null subjects and, equally, show evidence at least for IP. This is not to say that no American child ever has an incorrect grammar, but simply that the data thus far give us no grounds for claiming an incorrect grammar for most children. The data are briefly reviewed here.

The second point is that, in order to account for the diversity as well as the commonalities in acquisition within and across languages, theories must specifically include both a competence component and a performance component, and a model of how the two interact. Each component by itself is too weak in predictive power to handle the facts. A corollary of this is that there is no metatheoretic reason to prefer competence-deficit explanations over performance-deficit explanations.

The third point is that children's initial state is, with respect to parameters, unset. As I have argued in previous work (Valian, 1990a, 1990b), the child does not begin acquisition with one or another value preset; there is no default setting. Rather, the child entertains both options on an equal footing until sufficient evidence accrues to favor one over the other, and he or she remains with that value unless and until sufficient evidence accrues to switch to another value.

273

THE DATA

I first outline some of the data from my laboratory (Valian, 1991), concentrating on American English and Italian. Only fully intelligible, nonimperative, nonimitative utterances with verbs were used to calculate subject usage. Approximately $1\frac{1}{2}$ hours of speech from each of twenty-one 2-year-olds were taped and transcribed. The American children ranged in age from 1;10 to 2;8, and in MLU from 1.53 to 4.38. Even the lowest-MLU subgroup—five children between MLU 1.5 and 2.0, averaging 2 years in age and producing verbs in 27% of their intelligible utterances—used subjects almost 70% of the time. Children above MLU 2 produced subjects from 84% to 96% of the time. Furthermore, the majority of children's subjects were pronouns, even in the lowest-MLU group.

The lowest-MLU group's percentages contrast sharply with the performance of the five Italian children whose longitudinal data were analyzed. At Time I (roughly ages 1;6–1;11), the Italian children's verb use was the same as that of the American children in Group I—27%; at Time II (roughly ages 2;0–2;5), verb use had increased to 39%, still lower than the American children's verb use in Group II, which was 52%. The Italian children at Times I and II used subjects only 30% of the time, less than half as often as the American children. They used pronouns for a minority of their subjects and used them less than half as often as the American children. The 30% figure for subjects includes both pre- and postverbal subjects. If only preverbal subjects are included, the Italian children produced subjects only 15% of the time. From these data, then, even the very young American children, who used verbs in only 27% of their utterances, looked very different from Italian children.

As important as the differences in frequency of subject use between American and Italian children are the corresponding features of American children's speech. In our data (Valian, 1991), for example, American children, even below MLU 2, showed the rudimentary presence of inflectional elements (modals, past tense, third person singular present *s*) and showed consistent use of nominative case for pronominal subjects. Their lack of subjects does not seem due to an incomplete grammar. Because the Italian sample was smaller, and because of syntactic differences between English and Italian, the Italian children were compared to Americans only on modals, where they used modals somewhat less than did American children.

To enlarge the basis of our cross-linguistic comparisons, our laboratory also analyzed observational speech from five Greek children, ranging in age from 2;0 to 2;5 (unpublished data in collaboration with H. Arsenidou). Greek is a null subject language. The children produced subjects in about 20% of their clauses with verbs, again in contrast to the American children. Recently, Z. Eisenberg and I analyzed speech from 15 children acquiring Brazilian Portuguese, another null subject language. The children ranged in age from

2;0 to 2;10, and in MLU (measured in words rather than morphemes) from 1.58 to 4.92. The children below MLU 2 produced subjects in 29% of their utterances with verbs, and the children above MLU 2 produced subjects in 51% of such utterances. Again, the Brazilian Portuguese children contrasted with the American children.

Thus, in our comparative studies, American children looked very different from children acquiring null subject languages. They used subjects much more, used pronominal subjects more, and were different on many other measures. Contrary to claims by Guilfoyle and Noonan (1992), the children as a group could not be described as having an incomplete grammar (i.e., with a partial tree consisting of a VP and elements that can be contained within it). Contrary to claims by Hyams (1986), the children could not be described as having a grammar that included *pro*.

At the same time, the five American children below MLU 2 in Valian (1991) were variable, and there are data from other investigators suggesting that at the onset of combinatorial speech, some English-speaking children produce subjects less than 50% of the time. It is hard to evaluate those data because of differences in data analytic procedures and reporting. Clearly, more studies are needed of children who are just beginning to use verbs, as well as more cross-linguistic and longitudinal studies.

Data from two elicited imitation tasks with American children support the conclusions from the spontaneous production data by showing similarly high subject use. Gerken (1991) presented data for 18 children ranging in MLU from 1.25 to 3.74, and in age from 1;11 to 2;6. Children included subjects in 81% of their imitations. Valian and Hoeffner (1992) recently completed a similar study. We found that 10 children with a mean age of 2;3 and a mean MLU of 2.34 imitated subjects 70% of the time, while 9 children with a mean age of 2;4 and a mean MLU of 3.71 imitated subjects 91% of the time. Núñez del Prado, Foley, and Lust (1993) gave English- and Spanish-speaking children a variety of two-clause sentences to imitate. When the second clause was a tensed embedded clause, the American child dropped the lexical subject of that clause about 2% of the time, while the Puerto Rican children dropped it about 15% of the time.

In summary, the observational data from Valian (1991), and the elicited imitation data from Gerken (1991), Valian and Hoeffner (1992), and Núñez del Prado et al (1993) converge. They show spontaneous subject production at a rate ranging between 50% and 80% in utterances with verbs, in American children ranging in age from 1;10 to 2;6, and in MLU from 1.5 to 3.0. They show marked contrasts in the behavior of children learning null and non-null subject languages.

There is no evidence to support the hypothesis (e.g., Hyams, 1986) that American children have an incorrect grammar with respect to null subjects. American children give no evidence of having *pro* in their grammars.

Whether children's very early grammars are structurally incomplete, as Guilfoyle and Noonan (1992) and Radford (1990) proposed, is less clear. On the whole, I think the data suggest that American children's early grammars are *structurally* complete, including the functional projections of IP and CP, even if they are *lexically* incomplete.

A more recent proposal to explain children's inconsistent use of subjects was Rizzi's suggestion (this volume, chapter 10) that children have CP available but do not always use it to head a sentence; the absence of CP then licenses a null constant, which is also present in the adult language (see also Lillo-Martin, this volume, chapter 13, who suggested that some absent subjects are null epithets). On this proposal, the child mistakenly treats an obligatory projection as optional. This explanation could be extended to account for the absence of subjects in adult casual speech, because both referential and nonreferential subjects are sometimes missing in spoken English. The child and adult would thus differ only in the frequency with which they treat an obligatory projection as optional, a difference best explained on performance grounds. (Rizzi himself did not draw this conclusion, but it is a natural extension of his proposal.)

Another suggestion (Rizzi, this volume, chapter 10) was that specifiers are optional in the adult grammar unless required by another principle (such as the Extended Projection Principle). In a structure without a CP specifier, a null constant in subject position will be licit. In the adult grammar, only empty categories that do not require identification (nonargumental expletives) can be used; that allows for the existence of strings with nonthematic verbs and no subjects. Rizzi assumed that in adult English empty referential subjects must be excluded. In fact, however, as mentioned earlier, casual speech contains examples of missing referential as well as missing nonreferential subjects, suggesting that adults relax the identification requirements in casual speech. That in turn suggests that the child differs from the adult only in degree, relaxing the identification requirement more often than the adult does. That difference, again, is best explained on performance grounds. A reinterpretation of Rizzi's suggestions (this volume) is that children's "stripped" structures are the result of performance pressures. If either of Rizzi's suggestions were correct, the child would be quantitatively, rather than qualitatively, different from the adult.

A performance-based alternative to competence-deficit accounts of inconsistent use of subjects is that the child's limited performance system is responsible for omissions of subjects and other elements (P. Bloom, 1990; Gerken, 1991; Mazuka, Lust, Wakayama, & Snyder, 1986; Valian, 1991). As a result of their performance limitations, children produce strings that are ungrammatical from the point of view of their own grammars, not just from the point of view of the adult grammar. Several investigators (L. Bloom, 1970; L. Bloom, Miller, & Hood, 1975; P. Bloom, 1990; Crain, 1991; Gerken, 1991;

Valian, 1991) have presented data supporting relevant performance limitations.

Notice that all children, regardless of language, should have performance deficits. Thus, all children, regardless of language, should produce subjects less often than adults do. That is an important prediction of performance accounts and it has been verified. Italian children produce subjects less often than their parents do (Valian, 1991); Chinese children produce subjects less often than adults do (Wang, Lillo-Martin, Best, & Levitt, 1992); Greek children produce subjects less often than their parents do (unpublished data in collaboration with H. Arsenidou); Brazilian children produce subjects less often than their parents do (unpublished data in collaboration with Z. Eisenberg).

Even children learning null subject languages produce subjects less often than adults do, indicating that part of their nonproduction is due to performance factors. If all children increase their use of subjects in the course of development, that suggests that something other than, or in addition to, their grammars is influencing their initial rate of subject use.

There are also data suggesting that pronominal subjects are difficult for children, regardless of language. An analysis of Valian's (1991) observational data shows an interesting pattern. If one adds together the subjects that are absent and the subjects that are pronouns and divides by total number of subjects (absent plus pronominal plus lexical), that percentage is roughly constant across the MLU range. For Group I children, MLU 1.5–2.0, it is 84%; for Group II, MLU 2.0–3.0, it is 88%; for Group III, MLU 3.0–4.0, it is 86%; for Group IV, MLU 4.0–4.5, it is 85%. However, the percentage of pronouns out of the whole total increases dramatically from Group I to Group II, from 53% to 77%, an increase of 45%. The difficulty of pronouns is also apparent in imitation tasks. Both Gerken (1991) and Valian and Hoeffner (1992) found that low-MLU children fail to imitate pronominal subjects much more than they fail to imitate lexical subjects.

The pattern found in both the observational and the imitation data could be interpreted as supporting the view that children's early grammars contain *pro*. For that reason the children initially have a small percentage of pronouns; when *pro* is expunged the children use a pronoun in cases where they formerly would have used *pro*. There is, however, an alternative interpretation, namely, that pronominal subjects create difficulties for all children, and that low-MLU children fail, for pragmatic, prosodic, and performance reasons, to use pronouns uniformly in contexts where they later will use them.

How could one test the two interpretations? If the second interpretation is correct, then increased pronoun use should be observed in children acquiring all languages, null subject languages as well as non-null subject. The data confirm that prediction. The Italian children's data (Valian, 1991) were analyzed in the same way as the American children's. At Time I the five children (roughly ages 1;6–1;11) had a combined percentage of absent and pronominal subjects of 77%. At Time II (roughly ages 2;0–2;5) it was 81%. The percentage of pronouns out of the whole total goes from 7% at Time I to 10% at Time II. The increase is very small in absolute percentage points, but the relative increase—43%—is large. The Italian children thus show a similar pattern to the American children.

The data from our fifteen Brazilian Portuguese children are even clearer. The seven children below MLU 2 used absent plus pronominal subjects 89% of the time, and the eight children above MLU 2 used absent plus pronominal subjects 87% of the time, totals very similar to the American children's. The percentage of pronouns of the whole total increased from 18% to 38%. Again, there was a marked increase in use of pronominal subjects at higher MLUs.

The similarity across the language groups is striking. As development proceeds, children appear to increase their use of pronominals, whether their language is a non-null subject language like English or a null subject language like Italian or Brazilian Portuguese. The cross-linguistic pattern argues against an explanation based on the presence of *pro* in children's early grammars. If children increase their use of pronouns even when *pro* is continuously present, as the Italian and Brazilian Portuguese children do, then the American children's increase cannot be taken as evidence for a shift from a grammar with *pro* to a grammar without *pro*. Instead, the data show that children experience a difficulty with pronominal subjects that is independent of the target language, and that difficulty results in a selective absence of pronominal subjects at early stages of acquisition.

Difficulty in processing subject pronouns continues for quite some time. Read and Schreiber (1982) found that 7-year-olds had much more difficulty identifying and repeating the subject of a sentence when it was a pronoun, than when it was a multiword lexical NP. Similarly, Ferreira and Morrison (in press) reported that 5- and 6-year-olds had more difficulty identifying and repeating a pronominal subject than a proper name or Det-N subject. American children at those ages certainly do not have *pro* in their grammar, or any other grammatical deficit involving INFL subjects. The results with older children, like the cross-linguistic results, show that pronominal subjects are special in some way and cause processing difficulties unrelated to the Null Subject Parameter.

The data illustrate the importance of cross-linguistic information about children's use of subjects. Comparative data disentangle the strands of a child's productions. With only the speech of American children in hand, their increased use of subjects and pronominal subjects could mistakenly be attributed to a shift from having a grammar that licensed null subjects to a grammar that did not license null subjects. When, however, the same phenomenon appears in Italian and Brazilian Portuguese children, that potential explanation is demonstrated to be incorrect. Instead, two other factors, working simultaneously, seem to be operating. Children's performance pressures target subjects, regardless of language; pronominal subjects are particularly difficult for children.

COMPETENCE AND PERFORMANCE

The context within which to understand the results reviewed here is a theory of acquisition that integrates competence and performance. Such a theory starts with the truism that even a child with a complete grammar of, for example, English could not produce or understand sentences without a performance system. A grammar alone does not buy speech. The performance system that accesses the child's knowledge and puts it to use buys speech. Conversely, a performance system cannot operate in a competence vacuum. There must be a grammar to access. It is because of the interdependence of competence and performance that it is impossible to make predictions about the child's productions by reference to either component alone. A complete theory of acquisition must specify both components, specify how each develops, and specify how the two interact.

Recent work in acquisition is moving in the direction of developing such a theory of acquisition. What would a theory that incorporated competence and performance look like? Work with adults provides us with two approaches. One approach involves linguistically informed computational models of parsing, where a given theory of competence is assumed, and parsers access competence in different ways (e.g., Berwick & Weinberg, 1984; Fodor, 1989; Pritchett, 1991).

Another approach involves linguistically informed models of production such as that of Garrett (1975). This model, which proposes different levels of productive representation, is already being adapted to language acquisition. Gerken (1991), for example, used it to argue that children's non-production of subjects is due to overuse of a trochaic template at the foot assignment level; Demuth (1992) has made a similar proposal. Overuse of such a template will result in the omission of unstressed initial syllables and thus in the loss both of pronominal subjects and of unstressed determiners. In a different vein, Mazuka and Lust (1988, 1990) have been developing production models that are intimately interconnected with competence models.

Drawing on previous approaches, I proposed (Valian, 1992) that the child has a preferred D-structure template, used to guide the syntacticization of whatever message he or she wishes to express. The D-structure template will be a tree provided by X' syntax (including CP, IP, VP, etc., assuming that all those projections are universal). Each projection will take the form of a head, single-bar, and double-bar level.

The use of a template is a way of achieving cognitive economy. The child fits the message to the preferred template, and the template incurs very little cost (Gerken, 1991). Lexicalization of the template costs, and deviation from the template costs. In other words, the child can deviate, but the deviation will typically require economies elsewhere. Elements that will not fit into the template, such as those that would require iteration of bar levels, will tend not to be syntacticized, because syntacticization would require construction of a tree *de novo* rather than use of a prebuilt template. That predicts, for example, that auxiliary *be* will not be used as much as copula *be*, on the assumption that aux *be* requires iteration of bar levels (because two VPs are needed) and the copula does not (because only one VP is needed). That prediction is confirmed by data from both American and Italian children (Valian, 1992).

A template is parasitic on the child's grammar. For a usable template to exist, the child's grammar cannot be completely undecided. For example, the child cannot have a usable template for D-structure unless the grammar has a value for the head-direction parameter and the SPEC-direction parameter. Before the direction parameters are established, the child's template is like a mobile, with specifier and complement positions rotating around heads. In that mobile form, the template does not allow the child either to parse input or to produce speech. It is thus crucial for the child to quickly establish the direction parameters of his or her language. The paucity of word order errors even in children's earliest speech (Valian, 1986) is evidence that the direction parameters are in fact determined at the onset of combinatorial speech.

One general implication of the dependency between the parser and the grammar is that some parameters will be established before others, because they are crucial in allowing the child to produce and comprehend utterances (Kapur, this volume; Roeper & de Villiers, 1992). The child's need to parse the input and produce speech, and the nature of the target language, set priorities for grammar development. The parameters that are most frequently used in production and comprehension will be set first. The SPEC-direction parameter, head-direction parameter, and null subject parameter are candidates for parameters that will be set very early. And, as we have seen, the evidence from children's speech confirms that those parameters are indeed set early.

COMBINATORIAL EXPLOSION AND EVIDENCE SETS

In earlier work I introduced the *parsing constraint* as one constraint on an acceptable model of grammar development (Valian, 1990a). The child cannot appreciate the significance of input that contradicts the current parametric setting unless he or she is able to interpret that input as contradictory. But in order to interpret the input as contradictory the child needs access to the other, inactive, value (Valian, 1990a, 1990b), access which the standard parameter-setting account denies the child.

The obvious dilemma created by the parsing constraint can be solved by allowing both values of a parameter to feed the child's parser simultaneously

(Valian, 1990a, 1990b). In that way the child computes two inconsistent parses for relevant strings. For example, with the Null Subject Parameter, the child exposed to the string "Can't talk now" will perform one analysis on which the string is not a full sentence, and another on which the string is a full sentence with *pro* as its subject.

The dual value solution, however, creates in its turn a different problem. If the child's need for two parses is achieved by having all values of all parameters actively and simultaneously feed the parser, the child will have to perform hundreds of thousands of parses for each input. Providing the child with both values of each parameter leads to a combinatorial explosion.

The solution is to limit the occasions on which both values are activated in parsing either input or output. For the child's *output*, it will not matter which value feeds the parser because the child is not using his or her own speech as evidence. The value that feeds the output parser will either be the one for which the child has the most evidence to date (see below), or, if the grammar is completely undecided for that parameter, the value will be randomly chosen. Thus, no explosion occurs in parsing the child's output.

For the child's *input*, an explosion can also be avoided. The child's parser does not need access to both values for all of the input, but only for a relevant subset of the input. For the rest of the input it does not matter which value feeds the parser; it will either be the value for which there is the most evidence to date, or a randomly chosen value. Irrelevant input has no informational value. To understand how relevant subset is defined, it is necessary to introduce the notion of an *evidence set* for a parameter.

Each parameter defines an evidence set. Each value is associated with the structures whose presence or absence is directly entailed by the parameter. For the + value of the null subject parameter, the entailments are the presence of *pro* subjects with tensed verbs in both matrix and embedded clauses, and the absence of subjects with non-thematic verbs. (It is possible that the latter entailment does not hold across all null subject languages, see, e.g., Raposo & Uriagereka, 1990, but I am treating it here as universal.)

For the – value, the entailments are the absence of *pro* subjects with tensed verbs in either matrix or embedded clauses, and the presence of subjects with non-thematic verbs. The evidence set comprises the distinctive entailments of each value of a parameter, specifying both what should occur and what should not. (Other entailments no doubt also exist, but I concentrate on the two presented here.)

The evidence set tells the parser what to look for: (1) strings with tensed verbs but no overt subjects in both matrix and embedded position; (2) strings with non-thematic verbs. If the parser cannot identify tense or non-thematic verbs, only a single parse will result.

If the parser can identify tense, and encounters an input without an overt surface subject, a low-level parse is sufficient to recognize the absence of an overt subject. That will key in both parametric values, which in turn will provide two possible interpretations of the input. On one interpretation there is an underlying *pro*; on the other interpretation the string is not grammatical.

If the parser can identify a non-thematic verb, a low-level parse is sufficient to recognize the presence or absence of a subject. Either case will key in both parameter values. If the subject is absent, one interpretation will be that *pro* is the subject; the other is that the string is not grammatical. If the subject is present, one interpretation is that the string is not grammatical and that the subject is some sort of intrusion; the other is that *pro* subjects are impossible.[1]

Evidence sets limit the number of occasions on which the parser computes more than one parse. Only those strings which bear on the parameter's entailments receive more than one parse. A computational explosion is thereby avoided.

THE UNSET INITIAL STATE

We now consider how parametric values are established, and their effect on the parser. The usual metaphor for setting parameters is the switch metaphor. Parameters are set one way or the other as switches are. If a parameter is set incorrectly, input triggers a change to the other value. On most parameter-setting accounts, the switch is innately set to a particular value. The switch metaphor is incompatible with the view I am proposing.

A compatible metaphor is that of a balance or scale. Each parameter is a two-pan balance, with the scales initially balanced perfectly. Each value has the same potential; neither is preweighted and neither is the default value. Language development consists of gathering evidence which will establish the correct value for each parameter. Some evidence may fall on one side of the balance, and some on the other. Once evidence begins to be tabulated, one side will weigh more than the other. Gradually, the evidence weighs one side down very far. At the earliest stages, however, initial evidence in favor of one side could be outweighed a little later by more evidence in favor of the other side. Thus, the earliest grammars could change frequently, as evidence is tabulated.

---

[1]In English, for weather verbs, the expletive "it" can appear, as in "it's raining." Whether weather verbs are genuinely non-thematic may be an issue. For "seem"-type verbs, the subjects are more variable: "it," as in "it seems that she enjoys good food," or a raised pronoun or lexical NP, as in "she seems to enjoy good food," "Jane seems to enjoy good food," or "I seem to enjoy good food." In the latter cases the subject is forced to raise from the lower clause to the upper clause. While previous discussions have focused on expletives, the correct focus is more likely to be non-thematic verbs.

With respect to whatever property of INFL licenses null subjects, for example, the scales are perfectly balanced initially. For a few children, some features of the input, such as the nonappearance of subjects about 5% to 10% of the time in adult speech (Valian, 1991, in press), could temporarily weight the balance in favor of INFL licensing null subjects. Later, the uniform presence of subjects in embedded tensed clauses, the morphology of English verbs, the presence of expletives (Hyams, 1986), and perhaps other properties, will weight the scale against an INFL licenser. For some children, the initial syntactic production structure (template) would have an incorrect property in INFL. For most children, however, the evidence appears to weight the correct alternative from the onset of combinatorial speech (giving rise to a correspondingly correct template).

Whichever parametric value is at the moment more strongly weighted will determine the template the child will use for all the output, and the template the child will use for parsing input outside the evidence set.

If the incorrect value is more strongly weighted the child will misparse almost all of the input. The English-speaking child, for example, will be misattributing whatever property of INFL licenses *pro* to all tensed verbs. That error will have no deleterious consequences, however, because the child is not using the form of the template to draw conclusions about the form of the grammar.[2]

Exactly how the child's learning mechanism deals with multiple parses, and exactly how the input is stored, are important topics for future research. After the parser delivers two parses the language acquisition device can either make an immediate choice between the two interpretations, effectively placing a weight on just one pan of the balance, or can delay a choice by placing equal weights on both pans.

The storage of weights can be accomplished purely passively. A two-pan balance does not compute which side weighs more; it simply registers weight on each side. That the human learner has means of tracking the frequency of input forms is clear; frequency effects are ubiquitous in language learning and language processing (Brown, Cazden, & Bellugi, 1973; Brown & Hanlon, 1970; Gathercole, 1986; Valian, in press; Valian & Coulson, 1988).

---

[2]The actual evidence set relevant to null subjects might be different from the one I sketched. Although one consequence of setting the parameter is the possibility of *pro* as subject, the cause is some property of INFL, yet to be fully specified. I have been proceeding here on the assumption that there is no simple property, like morphological uniformity, which can be read directly off the surface string and used to conclude that *pro* is or is not possible. The diversity of the world's languages appears to preclude such a simple licenser. If, however, there were such a simple licenser, the evidence set would be different and might require the child to use both values of the parameter to parse every incoming string containing INFL. Because so much of the child's input contains INFL, the child would have to establish the null subject parameter almost as soon as he or she established the head-direction parameter.

SUMMARY OF PROPOSAL

Under the proposal presented here, each parameter is initially unset, with both values available to the child as equally unweighted alternatives, as on a two-pan balance. The development of grammatical competence consists in weighting the pans differentially, via analysis of the input. Each parameter defines an evidence set, consisting of input that, when analyzed, will weight one pan or the other. The child looks for that evidence. Parameters are established in an order determined by how frequently they are needed to parse the input. Some parameters, such as the head-direction and SPEC-direction parameters, must be set in order for the child to produce any speech at all.

Comprehension and production of speech is directly handled not by the grammar, but by the child's performance system, as it is for the adult. Parsing of input and output is handled in two ways:

1. Whenever possible, the child (or adult) uses performance templates based on the current grammar, with the more strongly weighted value of each parameter feeding the parser. Templates are low-cost and allow the child to syntacticize the message or analyze the input easily.

2. When input that is part of an evidence set for a parameter enters and, via a low-level parse, is registered as belonging to an evidence set, the parser constructs a parse for each value of the parameter. The child's acquisition mechanism evaluates the consequences of each parse and weights one pan or the other more heavily. The mechanism is a hypothesis-testing device which is not itself part of the grammar.

The proposal addresses four problems in language acquisition. The first problem is the need for an account that integrates the child's developing competence and his or her developing performance, so that their complex interaction can be properly analyzed and understood, and so that predictions about production and comprehension can be firmly grounded. The proposal addresses that problem by separating the mechanism that acquires grammatical competence from the mechanism that understands and produces speech.

The second problem is that the child's parser needs multiple interpretations of relevant input. The proposal addresses that problem by defining an evidence set for each parameter; when an evidence set member is identified, all values of the parameter are accessed.

The third problem is the need to prevent a combinatorial explosion. The proposal addresses that problem by providing multiple parses only when a member of an evidence set is encountered. All output, and all evidence-irrelevant input, receives only a single parse.

The final problem is the need to account for the data. The data on acquisition of the null subject parameter(s), which have been summarized here, show very early competence but imperfect performance. The data suggest that the child determines the correct status of his or her language, with respect to null subjects, very early in acquisition.

ACKNOWLEDGMENTS

Preparation of this chapter was supported in part by a grant from the National Institute of Child Health and Human Development (HD-24369) and in part by a grant from the City University of New York PSC-CUNY Research Award Program. My thanks to J. J. Katz for helpful discussion and to an anonymous reader for helpful comments. Address correspondence to Virginia Valian, Department of Psychology, Hunter College, 695 Park Avenue, New York, NY 10021, USA.

REFERENCES

Berwick, R., & Weinberg, A. (1984). *The grammatical basis of linguistic performance*. Cambridge, MA: MIT Press.
Bloom, L. (1970). *Language development: Form and function in emerging grammars*. Cambridge, MA: MIT Press.
Bloom, L., Miller, P., & Hood, L. (1975). Variation and reduction as aspects of competence in language development. In A. Pick (Ed.), *Minnesota Symposia on Child Psychology* (Vol. 9, pp. 3–55). Minneapolis: University of Minnesota Press.
Bloom, P. (1990). Subjectless sentences in child language. *Linguistic Inquiry, 21*, 491–504.
Brown, R., Cazden, C., & Bellugi, U. (1973). The child's grammar from I to III. In C. A. Ferguson & D. I. Slobin (Eds.), *Studies of child language development* (pp. 295–333). New York: Holt, Rinehart and Winston.
Brown, R., & Hanlon, C. (1970). Derivational complexity and order of acquisition in child speech. In J. R. Hayes (Ed.), *Cognition and the development of language* (pp. 11–53). New York: Wiley.
Crain, S. (1991). Language acquisition in the absence of experience. *Behavioral and Brain Sciences, 14*, 597–650.
Demuth, K. (1992). Accessing functional categories in Sesotho: Interactions at the morpho-syntax interface. In J. M. Meisel (Ed.), *The acquisition of verb placement: Functional categories and V2 phenomena in language acquisition* (pp. 83–107). Dordrecht: Kluwer.
Ferreira, F., & Morrison, F. (in press). Children's metalinguistic knowledge of syntactic constituents: Effects of age and schooling. *Developmental Psychology*.
Fodor, J. D. (1989). Empty categories in sentence processing. *Language and Cognitive Processes, 4*, 155–209.
Garrett, M. (1975). The analysis of sentence production. In G. Bower (Ed.), *Psychology of learning and motivation* (Vol. 9, pp. 133–177). New York: Academic Press.
Gathercole, V. (1986). The acquisition of the present perfect: Explaining differences in the speech of Scottish and American children. *Journal of Child Language, 13*, 537–560.
Gerken, L. A. (1991). The metrical basis for children's subjectless sentences. *Journal of Memory and Language, 30*, 431–451.

Guilfoyle, E., & Noonan, M. (1992). Functional categories and language acquisition. *Canadian Journal of Linguistics, 37*, 241–272.

Hyams, N. M. (1986). *Language acquisition and the theory of parameters.* Dordrecht: Reidel.

Mazuka, R., & Lust, B. (1988). Why is Japanese not difficult to process? A proposal to integrate parameter setting in Universal Grammar and parsing. *Proceedings of the North Eastern Linguistics Society, 18*, 333–356.

Mazuka, R., & Lust, B. (1990). On parameter setting and parsing: Predictions for cross-linguistic differences in adult and child processing. In L. Frazier & J. de Villiers (Eds.), *Language processing and language acquisition* (pp. 153–205). Dordrecht: Kluwer.

Mazuka, R., Lust, B., Wakayama, T., & Snyder, W. (1986). Distinguishing effects of parameters in early syntax acquisition: A cross-linguistic study of Japanese and English. *Papers and Reports on Child Language Development, 25*, 73–82.

Núñez del Prado, Z., Foley, C., & Lust, B. (1993). The significance of CP to the pro-drop parameter: An experimental study comparing Spanish and English. In E. Clark (Ed.), *The proceedings of the 25th annual Child Language Research Forum* (pp. 146–157). Stanford, CA: Center for the Study of Language and Information.

Pritchett, B. L. (1991). Head position and parsing ambiguity. *Journal of Psycholinguistic Research, 20*, 251–270.

Radford, A. (1990). *Syntactic theory and the acquisition of English syntax: The nature of early child grammars of English.* Oxford: Basil Blackwell.

Raposo, E., & Uriagereka, J. (1990). Long-distance case assignment. *Linguistic Inquiry, 21*, 505–537.

Read, C., & Schreiber, P. (1982). Why short subjects are harder than long subjects. In E. Wanner & L. Gleitman (Eds.), *Language acquisition: The state of the art.* Cambridge: Cambridge University Press.

Roeper, T., & de Villiers, J. (1992). Ordered decisions in the acquisition of *wh*-questions. In J. Weissenborn, H. Goodluck, & T. Roeper (Eds.), *Theoretical issues in language acquisition: Continuity and change in development* (pp. 191–236). Hillsdale, NJ: Lawrence Erlbaum Associates.

Valian, V. (1986). Syntactic categories in the speech of young children. *Developmental Psychology, 22*, 562–579.

Valian, V. (1990a). Logical and psychological constraints on the acquisition of syntax. In L. Frazier & J. de Villiers (Eds.), *Language processing and language acquisiton* (pp. 119–145). Dordrecht: Kluwer.

Valian, V. (1990b). Null subjects: A problem for parameter setting models of language acquisition. *Cognition, 35*, 105–122.

Valian, V. (1991). Syntactic subjects in the early speech of American and Italian children. *Cognition, 40*, 21–81.

Valian, V. (1992). Categories of First Syntax: *be, be+ing*, and nothingness. In J. M. Meisel (Ed.), *The acquisition of verb placement: Functional categories and V2 phenomena in language development.* Dordrecht: Kluwer.

Valian, V. (in press). *Parental replies: Linguistic status and didactic role.* Cambridge, MA: Bradford Books/MIT Press.

Valian, V., & Coulson, S. (1988). Anchor points in language learning: The role of marker frequency. *Journal of Memory and Language, 27*, 71–86.

Valian, V., & Hoeffner, J. (1992). *Young children's imitation of subjects.* Unpublished manuscript, Hunter College, New York, NY.

Wang, Q., Lillo-Martin, D., Best, C. T., & Levitt, A. (1992). Null subject vs. null object: Some evidence from the acquisition of Chinese and English. *Language Acquisition, 2*, 221–254.

CHAPTER TWELVE

Commentary: Null Subjects in Child Language and the Implications of Cross-Linguistic Variation

Nina Hyams
University of California at Los Angeles

A central point that has emerged from the chapters on null subjects is that although children universally omit subjects, there is also an interesting range of cross-linguistic variation in the young child's knowledge and use of null and overt pronouns. Pierce (this volume, chapter 14) notes, for example, that subject pronouns in early French and early English differ in distribution and frequency. Valian (this volume, chapter 11) observes that although American and Italian children both use null subjects, Italian children have a much higher frequency of null subject use than English-speaking children at a comparable developmental stage. Lillo-Martin (this volume, chapter 13) points out that although ·both English- and Chinese-speaking children have null subjects, only Chinese-speaking children drop objects, as is permissible in the adult language (cf. Wang, Lillo-Martin, Best, & Levitt, 1992). Finally, Rizzi (this volume, chapter 10) claims, based on claims in Valian (1991) and Roeper and Weissenborn (1990), that null subjects in early English are restricted to root contexts, whereas in null subject languages such as Italian, they are not so restricted. What these examples show is that child languages, like adult languages, show a complex interaction of universal and language-specific, that is, input-determined, properties.

In general, there are two perspectives from which to approach this kind of cross-linguistic variation. On the one hand, we might try to explain the variation we observe in child language the way we explain variation across adult languages, namely, as a reflex of differences and similarities in the underlying grammars. For ease of exposition, I refer to this as the *grammatical approach*. Pierce's analysis of subject pronouns is an example of such an approach. Pierce argues that subject pronouns in early French are inflectional heads, whereas in early English they are NPs. In this respect the early grammars mirror the adult grammars of these two languages, and the distributional differences in the acquisition data follow as a consequence of the different grammatical representations.

As noted earlier, there are also cross-linguistic differences in the child's use of null subjects. Although null subjects appear to be a universal property of early language, the structural conditions under which null arguments are licensed varies across child languages (as they do for adult languages). Thus, de Haan and Tuijnman (1988) and Poeppel and Wexler (1993) showed that children acquiring V-2 languages such as German and Dutch have topic-drop grammars; that is, null subjects (and objects) are licensed in Topic (i.e., [SPEC, CP]) position. This is in contrast to *pro*-drop languages such as Italian in which null subjects are licensed in [SPEC, IP]. Rizzi analyzes null subjects in early English as a kind of "diary drop," a phenomenon that also exists in adult English (Haegeman, 1990) and is distinct from both the *pro*-drop we find in Italian and the topic-drop of German and Dutch. Rizzi's grammatical analysis explains why English-speaking children omit subjects but not objects (in contrast to German and Dutch children) and also why null subjects in early English are restricted to root contexts.

In a similar vein, Hyams (1994) proposed that early English is a residual topic-drop language; that is, null subjects are licensed in [SPEC, CP], as in German and Dutch. However, null objects, which require licensing by a fronted verb in C (the V-2 effect) are excluded because English is not a V-2 language. According to this analysis, then, the difference between early English, in which only null subjects are licensed, and early German and Dutch, in which both null subjects and null objects are possible, is related to an independent difference in the two grammar types, the V-2 phenomenon.[1] In short, a grammatical approach to early cross-linguistic variation assumes that the differences that exist between child grammars (like the differences that exist between adult grammars) fall within well-defined limits. Thus, the goal is to: (a) tease apart the universal aspects of early grammar from those properties of early grammar that are fixed by experience with a particular input language, and (b) determine the limits of the language-particular variation.

In contrast to the grammatical approach, there is the view that cross-linguistic differences such as those that we find with respect to null arguments reflect the operation of different underlying cognitive mechanisms. Such a

---

[1]See also Jaeggli and Hyams (1988) and Hyams and Wexler (1993) for earlier related proposals concerning the subject-object asymmetry in English. More recently, Sano and Hyams (1994) argued that the null subject stage in early English is directly tied to the "root infinitive" phenomenon (see Wexler, 1992) and is thus distinct from both Italian pro-drop and Germanic topic-drop.

position is illustrated in what I understand to be Valian's proposal: that Italian children omit subjects as a grammatical option (Italian is a null subject language), whereas English-speaking children omit subjects due to performance limitations (cf. also P. Bloom, 1990). Let me refer to this as the *performance approach.*

In this commentary I argue that the performance approach to the null subject phenomenon is empirically inadequate and theoretically unmotivated. It fails to account for many of the basic statistical properties associated with null subjects in early English and it does not explain the cross-linguistic differences that it sets out to explain. The grammatical model fares better in both these respects. My discussion of the performance account is based on work that I have done in collaboration with Wexler (Hyams & Wexler, 1993).

A second related question that I address is whether the Null Subject Parameter comes preset at an initial default setting, as proposed, for example, in Hyams (1983, 1986). Both Lillo-Martin and Valian find the assumption of an initial [+null subject] setting problematic.[2] Lillo-Martin suggests that the English-speaking child may have different settings for different domains (i.e., root vs. embedded clauses). Valian proposes that the child initially entertains both a [+null subject] and a [–null subject] grammar, "until sufficient evidence accrues to favor one over the other." I compare the standard parameter-setting model to the scale model proposed by Valian.

THE INADEQUACIES OF A PERFORMANCE ACCOUNT

Performance accounts of the null subject phenomenon in child language (P. Bloom, 1990; Valian, 1991, chapter 11 in this volume) make two important assumptions. The first is that null subjects are not a grammatical option for young English-speaking children and hence do not appear in the grammatical representation of the sentence. Rather, sentence subjects are grammatically represented as either full NPs such as *John* (henceforth I refer to these as lexical subjects) or pronouns. The subject, whether lexical or pronominal, is subsequently dropped during the production of the sentence because of a constraint on output. A second crucial assumption of this approach, made explicit by P. Bloom, is that lexical subjects such as *John* impose a greater

---

[2]Lillo-Martin objects to the initial [+null subject] setting on learnability grounds; the child should not make the assumption that null pronouns are allowed until he or she has positive evidence in the form of sentences with null subjects. However, the learnability problem arises only if the two values of the Null Subject Parameter generate languages that fall into a Subset relation. Hyams (1986) and others have shown that this is not necessarily the case. Depending on the formulation of the Null Subject Parameter, there is positive evidence available that would force the English-speaking child to abandon the initial null subject grammar. I return to this issue.

TABLE 12.1
Proportion of Missing Subjects and Objects

Missing Term	Adam (2;5–2;8)	Eve (1;6–1;9)
Subjects	55%	39%
Objects	7%	13%

processing load than pronouns, and that omitting the subject imposes the least load. Thus, the probability of omission is a function of the "heaviness" of the subject selected. So lexical subjects are more likely to be omitted than pronoun subjects.

Hyams and Wexler (1993) developed a formal processing model incorporating these two assumptions, and we tested the model against a number of statistical properties of the null subject stage in early English. The processing model suffers several conceptual and empirical problems. First, it is simply unclear how dropping the subject reduces computational load, because the grammatical representation of the sentence (which, recall, contains a subject) is computed prior to the dropping of the subject, which happens during production. But even allowing that omission does reduce computational load for children, the processing model does not tell us why it is the subject that is omitted as opposed to the object, for example. The subject-object asymmetry is the most salient fact about the phenomenon. Table 12.1 reports the relative frequency of subject and object omission for Adam and Eve (CHILDES, MacWhinney & Snow, 1985). Thus, Adam (age 2;5 to 2;8) omits subjects 55% of the time, whereas objects are omitted in obligatory contexts only 7% of the time; Eve drops subjects at a lower rate, but there is still significantly more omission of subjects than of objects.[3] (Similar figures are reported in P. Bloom, 1990; and L. Bloom, Miller, & Hood, 1975; see also Valian, 1991, for comparable data on 21 subjects.)

To explain the subject-object asymmetry within the processing framework, some additional assumptions have to be made. One idea, due to P. Bloom (1990), is that the beginning of the sentence is harder to process than the end of the sentence. This assumption, however, is neither theoretically nor empirically motivated. There is no theory of performance from which such a result follows, and the scant empirical data that exists relevant to children's productive abilities fails to support the claim (Curtiss & Tallal, 1991; Ferreira & Morrison, 1990).[4] On the grammatical account, in contrast, the subject-object asymmetry follows without additional stipulation, because the hypothesis is that the English-speaking child (and all children) start out with a grammar that licenses null subjects.

---

[3] The differences reported in Table 12.1 are significant at the .05 level.
[4] See Hyams and Wexler (1993) for further discussion of this issue.

Another important statistical fact concerns the proportion of lexical subjects relative to pronominal subjects during the null subject stage. The grammatical hypothesis makes a precise prediction in this respect. In a null subject language, null subjects are used where pronouns are used in a non–null subject language (i.e., to refer to contextually specified information). Thus, we would expect that as English-speaking children switch from a [+null subject] to a [–null subject] grammar, there would be a marked increase in the proportion of pronominal subjects. In other words, the grammatical hypothesis predicts a trade-off between null subjects and pronouns over time, with the proportion of lexical subjects remaining roughly constant. Table 12.2 (adapted from Hyams and Wexler, 1993) reports the proportion of lexical subjects and pronoun subjects for Adam and Eve during the relevant stage of development.

As we can see from the columns headed P_L and P_P, the prediction of the grammatical model is confirmed. There is a steady increase in the proportion of pronouns over time, whereas the proportion of lexical subjects remains roughly constant from Adam 6 to Adam 30, though there are fluctuations. Similar considerations hold for Eve.[5] Notice, however, that this result is directly at odds with the predictions of the processing model. Recall that according to the processing model, lexical subjects are heavier than pronoun subjects and hence more likely to be omitted. We would therefore expect that in the early periods missing subjects would be more likely to result from the dropping of a lexical subject than from the dropping of a pronoun and thus, that once children grow out of the performance limitation and stop dropping subjects, we would see an increase in the proportion of lexical subjects. This prediction is in no way confirmed.

Notice, moreover, that we cannot explain the trade-off between null and pronominal subjects by saying, as Valian does, that there is some independent factor having to do with the difficulty of pronouns (relative to NPs) that makes them less likely to be used at the earlier ages. If this were the case, we would expect to see the same trends in object position that we see in subject position, that is, we should see an increase in pronominal objects over time. Hyams and Wexler showed that this is not the case. The proportion of pronominal to lexical objects remains roughly constant over time. (See Hyams and Wexler for further discussion.) Thus, the performance account fails to capture the relevant proportions of pronominal, null, and lexical NPs in the early stages, whereas the grammatical account makes precisely the right predictions.

---

[5] Valian finds the same result in her English data. She notes that the percentage of (null + pronominal) subjects remains constant across her different age groups (roughly 85%). Thus, as children develop, they tend to replace null subjects with pronominal ones and the rate of lexical NPs remains roughly constant, as the grammatical hypothesis would predict. Valian attributes this result to the young child's difficulty with pronouns, but see the following discussion in the text concerning pronoun difficulty.

TABLE 12.2
Proportions of Lexical (P_L) and Pronominal (P_P) Subjects

Child	Sample	P_L	P_P
Adam	06	.33	.11
	08	.23	.20
	10	.35	.20
	12	.14	.20
	14	.15	.15
	16	.12	.52
	18	.16	.60
	20	.11	.77
	30	.30	.67
Eve	02	.11	.29
	04	.12	.37
	06	.57	.14
	08	.47	.26
	10	.31	.37
	12	.21	.68
	14	.13	.74
	16	.23	.70
	20	.11	.82

What about the empirical data that seem to support the processing approach? First, there is the finding that the length of the VP varies as a function of the heaviness of the subject. P. Bloom (1990) did an analysis of the spontaneous speech of Adam, Eve, and Sarah and found that their VPs tended to be shortest with lexical subjects, longer with pronouns, and longest when the subject was omitted. These results are given in Fig. 12.1 (from P. Bloom, 1990).

Hyams and Wexler ran the same analysis on the spontaneous speech of Italian adults, that is, adult speakers of a null subject language, and, strikingly, we found the same result. Our results are given in Fig. 12.2. The similarity between the Italian adults and the English-speaking children shows that the VP length result has nothing to do with production constraints but, rather, is associated with some property of null subject languages, perhaps a pragmatic property that I will not speculate on here.[6]

A second major statistical fact offered in support of the processing model is Valian's finding that Italian children omit subjects at a rate of 70%, whereas English-speaking children omit subjects at a rate of 20% to 50% (depending on the study). According to Valian, this result is explained under the hypothesis that English-speaking children are dropping subjects for perform-ance reasons, whereas Italian children are taking advantage of the null

---

[6]See Hyams and Wexler (1993) for some suggestion as to the pragmatic nature of the VP length effect.

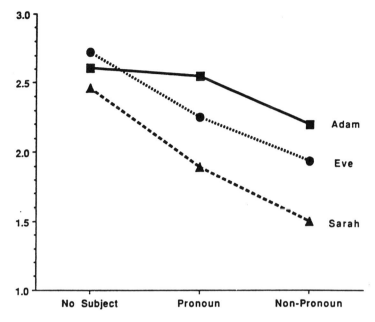

FIG. 12.1.   VP length as a function of subject size. Reprinted from *Linguistic Inquiry, 21*(4), 1990, by P. Bloom, "Subjective Sentences in Child Language," by permission of The MIT Press, Copyright © 1990.

subject option of their grammar. But Valian offers no theoretical reason why a performance constraint should yield fewer null subjects than a grammatical null subject option. In fact, the argument based on frequency differences is a spurious one, because neither the grammar nor the production model makes any prediction at all with respect to frequency. Thus, all Valian's analysis shows is that there is some difference between Italian- and English-speaking children with respect to the use of null subjects. It does not speak to the question of where the difference lies.[7]

To sum up, the processing model does not account for the major statistical properties observed during the null subject stage, whereas the grammatical model makes the right predictions with respect to these same properties.

---

[7]Although Valian reports that American children in her study drop subjects at a rate of 30% (averaging across studies), she asserts that "American children do not freely omit subjects." It is unclear what Valian's criteria are for "free subject omission." If frequency differences are criterial, why is the difference in the rate of subject omission between English- and Italian-speaking children (70% vs. 35%) more compelling for Valian than the difference in the rate of null subject use by English-speaking children versus English-speaking adults (30% vs. 0%). (The computation of the null subject rate for English-speaking children usually does not include those null subject sentences that would be grammatical in the adult language, e.g., *wanna leave?* Hence, for the purposes of this comparison, adult null subject use is 0%. [Valian, 1991, gives the figure, 0%–10%.])

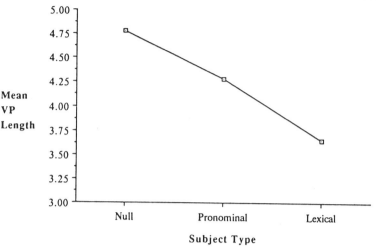

FIG. 12.2. VP length as a function of subject size for adult speakers of Italian.

Moreover, the processing model explains neither the VP length result (which exists for Italian adults as well as English-speaking children) nor the differences in frequency of null subject use, though these are the major empirical results offered in support of the model.

THE INITIAL STATE: TRIGGERS OR SCALES?

The grammatical approach to children's null subjects (e.g., Hyams, 1986, in press; Lillo-Martin, this volume, chapter 13; Pierce, 1989; Rizzi, this volume, chapter 10) holds that the initial grammar is a null subject grammar.[8] For children whose target language is not a null subject language, the switch to a [–null subject] grammar is triggered by input data that are not analyzable by the child's current null subject grammar. For example, in Hyams (1986) I proposed that lexical expletives such as *it* and existential *there*, or referential pronouns used in pragmatically neutral contexts, could trigger a parametric shift to a non–null subject grammar, because these elements would not be present in a null subject language.[9]

Valian argues against the idea of an initial setting and the trigger hypothesis, more generally. She proposes, instead, that the child "entertains

---

[8] The precise grammatical characterization of the null subject option—whether *pro*-drop (Hyams, 1986), topic-drop (Jaeggli & Hyams, 1988), diary drop (Hyams, 1994; Rizzi, this volume, chapter 10), or big PRO, as argued in Sano and Hyams (1994) and elsewhere—is irrelevant to the present discussion.

[9] What the particular triggers are depends on the precise grammatical characterization of the null subject phenomenon and is irrelevant to the present discussion, which is intended simply to illustrate the logic of the trigger hypothesis.

both options on an equal footing until sufficient evidence accrues to favor one over the other." I refer to this as the scale model, following Valian's metaphor.

The argument against an initial setting rests on what Valian calls the parsing constraint. That is, the child's parser (which is parasitic on his or her grammar) cannot analyze input not generated by the child's current grammar, and hence it cannot in principle analyze the triggers necessary to induce a parametric shift. Thus, in the case at hand, if the initial setting is [+null subject] the English-speaking child with a null subject grammar would not be able to analyze the lexical expletives or the infelicitous referential pronouns and hence would not be able to move to the correct [−null subject] grammar.

This particular criticism of the parameter model appears misguided, however. The parsing constraint that Valian describes does not block development. On the contrary, within parameter theory it is precisely the assumption of a failed parse under some parameter value that triggers the resetting to the other value. As typically conceived, the parameter-setting model views language development as a failure-driven process (Wexler & Culicover, 1980).[10] Thus, as noted earlier, the child progresses from one developmental stage (i.e., grammar) to the next when he or she encounters input data that are unanalyzable by the current grammar. We can also think of this as a parsing problem; that is, the child's parser (which incorporates a grammar) is unable to assign a well-formed representation to some input. A failed parse results and the relevant input is said to trigger a change from grammatical state A to grammatical state B. We can formally define *trigger* as follows (based on Clark & Roberts, 1991):

(1) A sentence *s* is a trigger for a parameter value *Px* just in case a grammar must have *P* set to *x* in order to assign a well-formed representation to *s*.

Although the parsing constraint poses no difficulty for the grammatical approach, it raises a vexing problem for the scale hypothesis. Valian argues that the child cannot use as triggering data any input that is not generated by his or her current grammar, that is, any input that results in a failed parse. Thus, the child is caught in an infinite loop, with a parser that is unable to analyze any input beyond the current grammatical stage and a grammar that depends on the analysis of new data in order to develop. The scale model "solves" this problem by providing the child with both grammars/parsers. Armed with both grammars/parsers, the child can parse all of the input

---

[10]Kim (1993), in his reply to Valian (1990), made a similar point concerning the parsing constraint. See his paper for a defense of parameter-setting models and arguments against Valian's hypothesis-testing model, which was very close to the current scale model.

necessary to determine whether the target is a null subject language or not (sentences with and without null subjects, lexical expletives, etc.). But the child at the initial state is faced with not one but many parametric options. Pursuing the logic of Valian's argument, it follows that in order for the child to parse all the triggering data for all parameters, he must start out with the entire set of possible adult grammars (null subject, non–null subject, head-first, head-last, verb raising, non–verb raising, etc.)—a rather implausible assumption, on the face of it.

Not only is the scale model conceptually flawed, but it also engenders serious learnability and computational problems. First, with respect to learnability, if the child starts out with both values of the Null Subject Parameter, he or she has a grammatical analysis for whatever input he or she receives. The child has, in effect, the union of two grammars. On what basis, then, would the child ever reject this "super grammar"? We are faced with a classic subset problem. The Italian child will hear sentences with and without null subjects, all of which, of course, are possible, given his [+null subject] grammar. The English-speaking child, in contrast, will never hear null subject sentences, but he or she could not exclude the null subject option on this basis unless we allow for direct or indirect negative evidence. Thus, adopting the scale model entails that we abandon either the Subset Principle or the assumption of no negative evidence, neither of which is desirable on a priori grounds.

The scale model is also implausible from a computational perspective. On this model, development consists of "gathering," "amassing," "tabulating" evidence in favor of one parameter value or the other until "gradually the evidence weighs down one side very heavily." Clearly, the psychological mechanisms necessary to tip the scales one way or the other require rather large computational resources. At the very least, the child must have an accurate memory for previous input data, past failed hypotheses, and parameter settings, as well as the ability to represent and compare the multiple representations of a sentence that are generated by the competing grammars. Thus, the scale model requires that we abandon yet another well-motivated assumption, namely, that the child is computationally bounded, to use a term of Clark and Robert's (1991). That is, he or she has a finite memory and a (small) finite amount of time in which to converge on the adult grammar. Moreover, the developmental picture that unfolds is one in which the younger you are, the more representations/grammars/parsers you must cope with. See Valian (this volume, chapter 11) for debate on this computational problem.

Quite apart from the plausibility of such a picture, Valian's assumptions concerning the child's computational abilities are clearly at odds with her proposal that the English-speaking child's use of null subjects is a performance effect, as discussed earlier. How is it possible that the child, who has such limited processing resources that he or she is unable to produce sentence subjects reliably, can at the same time compute multiple and in principle very large numbers of representations, for every (structurally ambiguous) sentence?[11]

In short, the parameter-setting model does not engender the kind of problem Valian discusses. It is a failure-driven model that assures rapid, deterministic learning. The scale model, in contrast, makes acquisition impossible under standard assumptions of a computationally bounded learner without access to negative evidence.

CONCLUSION

An ever-increasing body of cross-linguistic acquisition evidence (of which the papers in this section are a prime example), shows that environmental effects are felt quite early in language development. With respect to the null subject phenomenon, it now appears that Italian children *pro*-drop, Dutch, German and Chinese speaking children topic-drop (though Germanic topic-drop differs from Chinese topic-drop in certain respects), and English speaking children have yet a different analysis, one possibility being a kind of diary-drop, as Rizzi (this volume, chapter 10) proposes. The finding that children show an early sensitivity to language-specific properties of the input data is a welcome result in that it solves the rather thorny triggering problem of earlier accounts. One of the weaknesses of the parameter-setting analysis in Hyams (1983, 1986), which posited a universal early *pro*-drop stage, is that it did not explain why children acquiring non-*pro*-drop grammars fail to analyze the relevant input (triggering) data for as long as they do. Given the current picture, this problem no longer arises in the same way. On the other hand, the range of cross-linguistic variation that we observe very early in development raises the logical problem of language acquisition in a particularly perspicuous way; that is, how do children figure out the particular properties of their language, given such limited and fragmentary experience. Moreover, if we assume, as I think we must, that there is a uniform initial grammatical state (whatever it is) *prior to experience*, and if it is the case that linguistic input immediately (or almost immediately) alters that state, then the initial state becomes less amenable to direct empirical investigation. In this case, properties of the initial state will have to be determined logically

---

[11]According to the assumptions of the scale model, multiple representations would have to be computed only for sentences that are ambiguous (i.e., receive different analyses by the two grammars). However, this restriction does not actually reduce the computational load, because the set of sentences that is structurally ambiguous in this sense is still infinite. Moreover, it is unclear how the grammar/parser would know if a sentence is structurally ambiguous before assigning the structural descriptions.

rather than empirically, much in the way it is done in the study of adult grammars. We may ultimately find that the instantaneous model of development is closer to the truth than we have imagined.

ACKNOWLEDGMENTS

I would like to thank Robin Clark, Tom Cornell, Kyle Johnson, and Bonnie Schwartz for helpful discussion of a number of issues addressed in this chapter. Thanks also to Ken Wexler for a wonderful collaboration on Hyams and Wexler (1993), on which the first part of this commentary is based. Finally, my appreciation to Jeannette Schaeffer for editorial assistance.

REFERENCES

Bloom, L., Miller, P., & Hood, L. (1975). Variation and reduction as aspects of competence in language development. In A. Pick (Ed.), *Minnesota Symposia on Child Psychology* (Vol. 9, pp. 3–55). Minneapolis: University of Minnesota Press.

Bloom, P. (1990). Subjectless sentences in child language. *Linguistic Inquiry, 21*, 491–504.

Clark, R., & Roberts, I. (1991). *A computational model of language learnability and language change.* Unpublished manuscript, University of Geneva, Switzerland.

Curtiss, S., & Tallal, P. (1991). On the nature of the impairment in language impaired children. In J. Miller (Ed.), *New directions in research on child language disorders* (pp. 189–210). Boston: College Hill Press.

de Haan, G., & Tuijnman, K. (1988). Missing subjects and objects in child grammar. In P. Jordens & J. Lalleman (Eds.), *Language development.* Dordrecht: Foris.

Ferreira, F., & Morrison, F. (1990). *Children's knowledge of syntactic constituents.* Paper presented at the Annual Meeting of the Psychonomic Society, New Orleans.

Haegeman, L. (1990). Non-overt subjects in diary contexts. In J. Mascaro & M. Nespor (Eds.), *Grammar in progress* (pp. 167–179). Dordrecht: Foris.

Hyams, N. (1983). *Acquisition of parameterized grammars.* Unpublished doctoral dissertation, City University of New York.

Hyams, N. (1986). *Language acquisition and the theory of parameters.* Dordrecht: Reidel.

Hyams, N. (1994). V2, null arguments and C projections. In T. Hoekstra & B. Schwartz (Eds.), *Language acquisition studies in generative grammar.* Philadelphia: John Benjamins.

Hyams, N., & Wexler, K. (1993). On the grammatical basis of null subjects in child language. *Linguistic Inquiry.*

Jaeggli, O., & Hyams, N. (1988). Morphological uniformity and the setting of the Null Subject Parameter. *Proceedings of the North Eastern Linguistics Society, 18.*

Kim, J. J. (1993). Null subjects: Comments on Valian (1990). *Cognition, 46*, 183–193.

MacWhinney, B., & Snow, C. (1985). The child language data exchange system. *Journal of Child Language, 12.*

Pierce, A. (1989). *On the emergence of syntax: A crosslinguistic study.* Unpublished doctoral dissertation, MIT, Cambridge, MA.

Poeppel, D., & Wexler, K. (1993). The full competence hypothesis of clause structure. *Language, 69.*

Roeper, T., & Weissenbom, J. (1990). How to make parameters work. In L. Frazier & J. De Villiers (Eds.), *Language processing and acquisition* (pp. 147–162). Dordrecht: Kluwer.

Sano, T., & Hyams, N. (1994). Agreement, finiteness and the development of null arguments. *The Proceedings of North Eastern Linguistics Society, 24.*

Valian, V. (1990). Null subjects: A problem for parameter-setting models of language acquisition. *Cognition, 35,* 105–122.

Valian, V. (1991). Syntactic subjects in the early speech of American and Italian children. *Cognition, 40,* 21–81.

Wang, Q., Lillo-Martin, D., Best, C. T., & Levitt, A. (1992). Null subjects and objects in the acquisition of Chinese. *Language Acquisition, 2,* 221–254.

Wexler, K. (1992). *Optional infinitives, head movement, and the economy of derivation in child grammar* [Occasional paper #45]. MIT, Cambridge, MA.

Wexler, K., & Culicover, P. (1980). *Formal principles of language acquisition.* Cambridge, MA: MIT Press.

CHAPTER THIRTEEN

Setting the Null Argument Parameters: Evidence from American Sign Language and Other Languages

Diane Lillo-Martin
University of Connecticut and
Haskins Laboratories

Young children frequently omit the subject of their sentences. This general observation has been made for a number of languages, including English, Italian, and American Sign Language, among many others (e.g., Hyams, 1986; Lillo-Martin, 1991; Valian, 1991). Some examples from English are given in (1) (examples from Hyams, 1986, citing L. Bloom, 1970).

(1) Play it.
Eating cereal.
Shake hands.
See window.
Want more apple.
No go in.

This observation is by now widely known, although there have been a number of different proposals to account for it, and the accuracy of the generalizations has even been questioned. In this chapter, I contrast two types of accounts for this phenomenon, broadly known as grammatical versus performance accounts. Under grammatical accounts, it is hypothesized that the child's grammar, for various reasons, allows null subjects. Under some accounts children initially believe that their language is a null subject language, even if the target language does not display this characteristic (e.g., Hyams, 1986; Jaeggli & Hyams, 1988); under others, the child's grammar is incomplete in ways that will allow null subjects (e.g., Radford, 1990). Under performance accounts, children leave off subjects for nonlinguistic processing reasons (e.g., P. Bloom, 1990; Gerken, 1991; Valian, 1991). I evaluate these alternative proposals, bringing in data from the structure and acquisition of several languages, especially American Sign Language (ASL).

THE NULL ARGUMENT PARAMETERS

To evaluate the hypothesis that children's subjectless sentences are due to an incorrect setting on some null argument parameter(s), I have examined a range of null argument structures reported for adult languages (cf. Lillo-Martin, 1991). This study has led to the postulation of two separate parameters, one of which has two parts. I call the first parameter the Null Pronoun Parameter (NPP); it basically follows Rizzi's (1986) null pronoun parameter, with some modification. The Null Pronoun Parameter concerns null pronominal arguments (i.e., *pro*). As Rizzi (and others) observed, null arguments may require both licensing and identification. Often, the licenser of a null argument also provides its identification, as in rich verb agreement. There are also several cases in which rich agreement is not required to license null arguments, including *pro*. The Null Pronoun Licensing Parameter and the Null Pronoun Identification Parameter are given in (2) and (3).

(2) The Null Pronoun Licensing Parameter

    a. AGR when it Case-marks $\left\{\begin{array}{c}\text{is}\\\text{is not}\end{array}\right\}$ a licensing head for *pro*.

    b. V when it Case-marks $\left\{\begin{array}{c}\text{is}\\\text{is not}\end{array}\right\}$ a licensing head for *pro*.

    c. P when it Case-marks $\left\{\begin{array}{c}\text{is}\\\text{is not}\end{array}\right\}$ a licensing head for *pro*.

(3) The Null Pronoun Identification Parameter

    I. Let *X* be the licensing head of an occurrence of *pro*.
       Then *pro* has the grammatical specification of
       $\left\{\begin{array}{c}\text{no features}\\\text{the number features}\\\text{the person and number features}\end{array}\right\}$ on *X* coindexed with it.

    II. Null referential pronominal arguments require Identification by
       morphological marking of
       $\left\{\begin{array}{c}\text{no features}\\\text{the number features}\\\text{the person and number features}\end{array}\right\}$ on the licensing head.

As Rizzi observed, under standard assumptions of positive evidence only, for learnability reasons the initial settings on this parameter are expected to be those that do not allow null pronouns (i.e., AGR is not a licensing head for *pro*, etc.). Because languages do differ in which categories can be licensers, and how much identification is required, the child should not make any assumptions that null pronouns are allowed until he or she has positive evidence, in the form of sentences with null arguments.

The second parameter proposed is Huang's (1984) Discourse Oriented Parameter (DOP). The DOP captures a range of syntactic phenomena, including null arguments, discourse-bound anaphora, and topic-comment structures. No single statement of this parameter has been formulated to account for the full range of phenomena; likewise, I only discuss null arguments here. The discourse oriented languages, such as Chinese, allow null arguments without rich agreement; in these languages, the reference of the null argument is determined by a discourse topic. Formally, Huang proposes that a null sentential topic (binding an empty category in argument position) can be coindexed with a discourse topic in the discourse oriented languages. Thus, although this parameter depends on a discourse characteristic of languages, it has numerous syntactic consequences.

The nature of the null argument found in discourse oriented languages is still under considerable controversy. I assume that the empty category involved in null arguments in discourse oriented languages is not *pro*. I have argued previously for this distinction on the basis of evidence from American Sign Language (e.g., Lillo-Martin, 1986). I consider this null argument to be a variable rather than *pro*, or perhaps a null epithet (this category was introduced by Lasnik & Stowell, 1991; for discussion of its use as a null argument, see Lillo-Martin, 1991). Rizzi (this volume, chapter 10) also discussed the null epithet (which he called a null constant) as one type of null argument. (See later discussion.) The relevant part of the Discourse Oriented Parameter is given in (4).

(4) The Discourse Oriented Parameter (partial)

In the discourse grammar, an empty topic node $\begin{Bmatrix} \text{may} \\ \text{may not} \end{Bmatrix}$ be coindexed with an appropriate preceding topic.

Again considering learnability, the initial setting on this parameter is plausibly [−discourse oriented]. This is because positive evidence, in the form of sentences with null arguments, will be available to change the parameter setting to [+discourse oriented]. Because this parameter also controls several other constructions, not discussed here, there will also be other kinds of input to serve as triggering evidence for the parameter resetting. On the other hand, learning [− discourse oriented] would require consideration of the absence of expected constructions (i.e., indirect negative evidence; see Chomsky, 1981; Lasnik, 1989). Although indirect negative evidence may be available for children, I attempt here to account for the acquisition of the correct settings on the null argument parameters without it.

The two parts of the Null Pronoun Parameter and the Discourse Oriented Parameter allow for a variety of options with respect to the licensing and identification of null arguments. Most of these options are attested. The Appendix provides an explication of the options made available by these parameters, and examples of languages that display these options.

Earlier versions of the null argument parameters accounting for a narrower range of languages could be stated in such a way that positive evidence would be available to move from a [+null subjects] to a [−null subjects] setting (e.g., Hyams, 1986). However, given the cross-linguistic variation observed, new versions of the parameters seem to be needed, such as those given in (2)–(4), which require the initial settings not to allow null arguments (assuming positive evidence only).

EARLY NULL SUBJECTS AND CHILDREN'S GRAMMARS

The initial settings that are associated with these two parameters apparently do not account for the early null subject phenomenon. If, as the learnability arguments would suggest, the initial settings on the null argument parameters do not allow null arguments, then the grammatical explanation for the early null subject phenomenon would seem to be disconfirmed. Before completely ruling it out, however, let us consider the acquisition facts in more detail.

Valian (1991) questioned the accuracy of the generalization that early English shows frequent missing subjects like those found in null subject languages. She examined the utterances of 21 American (English-speaking) children, between the ages of 1;10 and 2;8. Their utterances were compared to those of 5 Italian children, who were observed longitudinally from the age of 1;6 to 2;5. Valian compared the American children to Italian children to test the hypothesis put forth by Hyams (1986), that early English is like Italian in grammatically allowing null subjects.

Valian tabulated the occurrence of subjects in sentences with and without verbs, and she calculated the proportion of overt pronominal subjects for these two groups. I have summarized these findings from her study in Table 13.1. The figures for the American children, although they do show inconsistent use of subjects, especially for Group 1, are nevertheless much different from the comparable figures Valian supplies for the acquisition of Italian. The Italian-speaking children use overt subjects much less frequently than the American children, at least in utterances with verbs. Their use of pronominal subjects is also much lower than that of the American children.

TABLE 13.1
Valian (1991): Null Subject Use in American and Italian Children

Group	All Utterances[a]	Sentences With Verbs	Overt Subjects With Verbs
American			
Group 1	23% overt	69% overt	73% pronouns
(MLU <2.0)	subjects	subjects	
Group 2	50% overt	89% overt	86% pronouns
(MLU 2.0–3.0)	subjects	subjects	
Italian			
Time 1	20% overt	30% overt	22% pronouns
(1;6–1;10)	subjects	subjects	
Time 2	23% overt	30% overt	35% pronouns
(2;0–2;5)	subjects	subjects	

[a]Excluding imitations and imperatives.

Valian's observations led her to believe that the youngest American children, despite their inconsistent use of subjects (in her terms), are not speaking a null subject language. If the American children were leaving off subjects because they considered it a grammatical option, they would be expected to leave off subjects at a higher rate than they do, and they would be expected to produce fewer pronominal subjects than they do.

Thus, there are reasons, in addition to the learnability considerations, to question whether young English-speaking children's frequent lack of subjects is due to a grammatical parameter missetting that makes early English Italian-like.

What if early English lacks subjects because children mistakenly believe that English is [+discourse oriented]? Jaeggli and Hyams (1988) made such a proposal, in part on the grounds that it allows children's early null subjects to be identified, via a discourse topic. Just as Hyams' earlier analysis predicted that early English would be like Italian in certain respects, the new analysis predicted that early English would be like Chinese in certain respects. This prediction was tested by Wang, Lillo-Martin, Best, and Levitt (1992).

Wang et al.'s main consideration in evaluating the predictions of Jaeggli and Hyams' proposal concerned the use of null objects. Chinese, as a discourse oriented language, allows null objects as well as null subjects. Thus, Wang et al. took one of the predictions of Jaeggli and Hyams' analysis to be that early English would allow null objects as well as null subjects. Because Hyams' previous work had showed that English-speaking children do not use null objects systematically, Jaeggli and Hyams proposed that null objects in children's grammars would require an empty category that children do not yet have (i.e., a variable). Thus, Jaeggli and Hyams tried to account for the fact that an adult discourse oriented language should allow null objects, but early English apparently does not. Wang et al. took this prediction a step further, coming to the conclusion that early Chinese ought to look like early English under this account. Thus, if the acquisition of English shows null subjects because the early grammar is discourse oriented, then the use of null subjects and objects should be similar for English- and Chinese-speaking children.

In the study by Wang et al., nine Chinese and nine American children between the ages of 2 and 4 were studied. The children were divided into groups on the basis of MLU, and the frequency of overt and null subjects and objects for each group was calculated. The results of this study did not confirm the predictions of the Jaeggli and Hyams analysis. Both the Chinese and the American children used null subjects at the youngest age, although even then there was a difference in frequency, showing an early effect of linguistic environment. Concerning objects, the youngest groups differed again: The youngest Chinese children dropped objects, but the youngest American children essentially did not. These results are summarized in Table 13.2.

A subject-object asymmetry was predicted by Jaeggli and Hyams, in part to support the argument that missing subjects in early grammars are a reflex of a grammatical parameter setting. Here, a subject-object asymmetry was found, but not with the details as predicted by Jaeggli and Hyams' proposal. As reported previously, English-speaking children were not found to use null objects systematically, although they did use null subjects. On the other hand, the Chinese-speaking children used both null subjects and null objects. They, too, displayed a subject-object asymmetry, however: Their use of null objects was much less frequent than their use of null subjects (similar results have been obtained for Japanese-speaking children; see Mazuka, Lust, Wakayama, & Snyder, 1986). This combination of results suggests that the use of null subjects by young English-speaking children is not due to an incorrect, [+discourse oriented] setting on the Discourse Oriented Parameter. Thus, the question why English-speaking children use null subjects (or what type of category the null subject represents) remains open.

The two studies overviewed here, in addition to reports from the acquisition of other languages (such as the study of the acquisition of French by Pierce, this volume, chapter 14), suggest that across a variety of language environments—perhaps universally—children use null subjects, including children whose linguistic environment does not allow any null arguments. However, children in linguistic environments that allow null subjects use them more frequently than children whose target language does not allow null arguments. Furthermore, only children who are exposed to languages that allow null objects use these empty categories systematically. Hence, there seems to be both an early effect of linguistic environment and a pervasive tendency for inconsistent subject use. This leads to the conclusion that the grammatical explanations for early subjectless sentences proposed so far do not seem to be sufficient.

TABLE 13.2
Wang et al. (1992):
Null Subjects and Null Objects in American and Chinese Children

Group	Null Subjects	Null Objects
American		
Group 1	26%	8%
Group 2	9%	1%
Chinese		
Group 1	56%	20%
Group 2	46%	21%
Group 3	38%	26%

Another type of grammatical explanation has been offered, which proposes that young English-speaking children's grammars are more strikingly different from the target grammar than under the accounts explored earlier. Although there have been several proposals made in this vein, I use Radford's (1990) for discussion. Radford argued that children in the early multiword stage of language acquisition have grammars with exclusively lexical, not functional, categories. Under one of his analyses, missing arguments in children's utterances are the reflex of a null NP, which he called *np* and which is not subject to constraints by functional categories. Alternatively, he proposed that children's null arguments are due to lexical saturation of the verb's theta-role, so that the syntactic position for the argument is not projected. I reject both of Radford's proposals. I do not find his arguments that children's early grammars do not contain functional categories convincing. There is now a growing body of evidence that young children in the early multiword stage do make use of (at least some) functional categories, even if their production of some of the elements contained in functional categories (e.g., agreement) is inconsistent (cf. Deprez & Pierce, 1989; Hyams, 1991; Whitman, Lee, & Lust, 1990; and several contributions to this volume; however, there is still some controversy regarding this). In addition, I reject his proposal that *np* is found in adult grammars, such as Japanese, given arguments that Japanese does have DP and other functional categories (e.g., Saito & Murasugi, 1990). Hence, *np* is not made available by Universal Grammar and, adopting the continuity hypothesis, it would not be available for children's grammars. Although I agree with Radford that children may occasionally have missing objects with verbs that are transitive in the adult grammar, I have just argued that English-speaking children do not systematically use null objects, and so I reject his lexical saturation analysis as well.

In sum, the grammatical explanations that have been proposed thus far encounter difficulties when a wider range of data are brought to bear on the question of the missing subjects in young children's utterances. I later discuss a newer grammatical proposal that fares much better. First, however, I would like to discuss an alternative type of explanation, under which children's early missing subjects are due not to nonadult grammars but, rather, to performance limitations.

EARLY NULL SUBJECTS AND PERFORMANCE LIMITATIONS

Several authors have proposed that young children's early subjectless sentences are due to some kind of performance limitation rather than a grammatical error. For example, P. Bloom (1990) suggested that children omit constituents at the beginning of a sentence, when under a heavy processing load. Gerken (1991) argued that children omit the unstressed syllable of an iambic foot in many constructions; subject pronouns will thus be omitted frequently because they often consist of unstressed syllables and are followed by a strong syllable. Valian (1991) also suggested that a performance limitation is the root of children's early subjectless sentences.

It is difficult to evaluate these processing limitation hypotheses directly, because they are somewhat vague as to the nature of the limitation involved, especially with regard to what constitutes a heavy processing load linguistically. (See Hyams & Wexler, 1993, for extensive discussion of processing limit accounts of the null subject phenomenon, especially that of P. Bloom.) However, they would seem to make an interesting cross-linguistic prediction for languages that are not subject-initial. Bloom and Valian both attempted to account for the observed subject-object asymmetry in missing arguments by arguing that sentence-initial position is especially heavy for processing load. This would predict that children acquiring a VOS language would not show missing subjects. (For Gerken, the pattern found in a VOS language would depend on further characteristics of stress patterns in the language.) However, Pye (1987) reported that children learning Quiche Mayan, a VOS language, do use null subjects productively from the earliest age tested. Unfortunately for this argument, however, Quiche Mayan is not the ideal test language, because the adult grammar does allow null arguments, and, as we have seen, there can be an effect of linguistic environment by the earliest ages. Therefore, it would be necessary to find evidence from the acquisition of a language that is not subject-initial and does not permit null arguments, in order to test this cross-linguistic prediction. If children learning such languages still go through a missing subject stage, like children learning English, then these processing limitation accounts will not be supported as they stand.

Further suggestive evidence against the current processing limitation accounts comes from my study of deaf children learning American Sign

Language (ASL) (Lillo-Martin, 1991). ASL does allow null arguments. In fact, I have argued that it allows null arguments licensed and identified by agreement or by discourse topic. (Because ASL allows null arguments, it, like Quiche Mayan, is not the perfect test case regarding early null argument use. However, the pattern of development found in ASL is suggestive, as discussed later.) A summary of the positions and status of null arguments found in ASL is given in Table 13.3.

Given the pattern of acquisition of null and overt arguments described here, it would be expected that deaf children learning ASL from deaf, signing parents would use null arguments from an early age. This is what I found, in a partially longitudinal study of 23 deaf children from the age of 1;7 to 8;11. However, the use of null arguments in children acquiring ASL is complicated by two factors. (a) the presence of discourse-identified null arguments in adult ASL; and (b) the acquisition of verb agreement morphology. I will discuss these in turn.

Deaf children learning ASL produce null subjects and objects which can be clearly related to an overt discourse topic from an early age. In this way, they are like the Chinese-speaking children studied by Wang et al. (1992). In addition, deaf children produce null arguments in other contexts. In the cases I studied, the identity of an unexpressed referent can usually be inferred from the situation, since the children were telling stories from a book. However, the children's use of null arguments without an overt discourse topic changed over time, in relation to their use of verb agreement. Thus, I examine these null arguments separately.

The 2-year-olds I studied do not systematically use the verb agreement system of ASL. Yet they use null arguments productively. The slightly older children are in the process of acquiring the verb agreement system. In contexts like telling stories from a book, they usually omit verb agreement markers altogether. At this time, they practically cease using null arguments, at least when verb agreement is not used. Yet older children use null arguments and verb agreement correctly. Under my analysis, many of the earliest null arguments used by 2-year-old deaf children are like the null

TABLE 13.3
Two Kinds of Null Arguments in ASL

Null Argument Type	Subject Position	Object Position	Identifier
pro	(a) when verb agreement is present; (b) embedded	when verb agreement is present	(a) verb agreement (b) matrix subject
variable (epithet)	bound by a null topic	bound by a null topic	null topic

subjects used by 2-year-old English-speaking children: They are not obviously identified by verb agreement or by an overt discourse topic. If young children under a processing limitation omit arguments for extra-grammatic reasons, then perhaps these null arguments are due to such performance limitations, whether or not the relevant parameters have been correctly set (since these null arguments are not apparently grammatically sanctioned). Some examples of sentences with null arguments produced by 2-year-old deaf children learning ASL are given in (5–6).

(5) (Steve, 2;3)
    a.[1] $_a$PRONOUN HAVE BALLOON.
       'He has balloons.'
    b. GIVE[uninflected] BALLOON.
       BOY GIVE[uninflected] BALLOON.
       '(He) gave (him) a balloon.'
       'The boy gave (him) a balloon.'
    c. HOLD, LET-GO
       '(He) held on (to it), then let go (of it).'

(6) (Brandi, 2;8)
    a. BOY GIVE, BOY GIVE(2h),[2] GIVE[on picture].
       'The boy gives, the boy gives, (he) gives (him) (one).'
    b. WALK OOPS CRY.
       '(He) walks, then oops!, and (he) cries.'
                              neg
    c. BALLOON, HOLD BALLOON.
       'The balloon, (he) didn't hold the balloon.'

In sum, deaf children display three relevant stages in their use of null arguments. The earliest stage shows null arguments without verb agreement. For children learning ASL, these may be topic-identified null arguments; or they may be nonidentified *pros*. Later, as children begin to learn the verb agreement system, the few null arguments that they use seem to be limited to the topic-identified variety, because *pro* would not be licensed in most of their utterances. Finally, both types are used appropriately.

With this background, I can bring up the evidence suggesting that the current processing limitation accounts are insufficient. According to Valian (1991), the performance limitation that leads to missing subjects is explicitly language-independent. Although other authors do not state this explicitly, I am led to believe that the performance limitation assumed by Bloom and

---

[1]Subscripts before or after signs indicate spatial locations, which are used to indicate reference or agreement.

[2]'2h' indicates that a normally one-handed sign was made with two hands.

Gerken would also be considered language-independent—that is, a general memory load or other cognitive limitation (although each author would also consider language-dependent factors in predicting exactly how the null arguments will pattern). Valian even stressed the relationship between age and subject use in arguing for this position. Given that older children are not under the same kind of processing limitations as younger children, then perhaps it would be expected that children learning language at an older age would also not be under the same kind of general processing limitations—hence, children learning language at an older age would not be expected to go through a missing subject stage.[3]

As it turns out, only 5%–10% of deaf children have deaf signing parents and go through the stages of the acquisition of ASL as just described. The remainder have hearing parents who do not know ASL when their deaf child is born. Many of these children do not receive any input in ASL until the age of 5 or later. Thus, for these children, first language acquisition is delayed. Unfortunately, much is not known about the course of language acquisition for these children. If it is correct to assume that the course of language acquisition in these children is comparable to the course of language acquisition in the normal situation in the relevant respects, we can use this group to test the hypotheses of the processing limitation account. These children will go through language acquisition at a later age than usual. Hence, their general, language-independent cognitive faculties will (presumably) be more developed when they are going through the early stages of language acquisition than are those of children acquiring their native language from birth. Hence, they might not be expected to go through the same missing subject stage as younger children do, under the processing limitation account.

At this time, I have data on the acquisition of ASL by 15 late-learning deaf children, ages 5;1–9;8, of nonsigning, hearing parents. These data are comparable to my data on deaf children learning ASL from deaf, signing parents. These children had a wide variety of experience in their exposure to ASL; yet the stages in their acquisition of ASL could be assimilated to the stages observed for the deaf children of deaf parents in my earlier study. In other words, each of these children responded to the study in a way comparable to the way the deaf children of deaf parents responded. In addition, each of the stages found in the earlier study was displayed by at least one child in this study. These findings support the comparison of these two groups.

---

[3]As noted by a reviewer, this prediction is based on a relatively simple view of the impact of processing limitations. It is quite possible that the relevant limitations apply at a certain stage of language development, rather than at a stage of cognitive development or a particular age. A greater degree of detail in such matters by the proponents of processing limitation accounts will make those accounts easier to evaluate.

Of interest here is the youngest child, age 5;1. This child's utterances were directly comparable to those of the 2-year-old native signers I tested earlier, and to those of one 2-year-old native signer tested in the same sessions as the late learners (Brandi, cited in example (6)). In particular, she exhibited the same null arguments without verb agreement that characterized the early group of native learners. Acknowledging that this is a single subject, from whom a limited quantity of data was collected, these results suggest that later learners of ASL go through a stage of null arguments without verb agreement. This is the pattern that might not be expected under some versions of the processing limitation account for the early null subject phenomenon. Examples of this child's productions are given in (7).

(7) (Lisa, 5;1)
   a. BOY PAINT-FACE.
      'The boy painted (her) face.'
   b. POUR-HEAD, GIRL POUR-HEAD
      '(She) poured on (his) head, the girl poured on (his) head.'
   c. MOTHER [index to picture] MAD.
      MOTHER SCOLD.
      'Mother, (she) is mad.
      'Mother scolds (them).'

In sum, the data presented here are only suggestive at best, as there are many caveats to consider. However, they do suggest that the use of null arguments that are not clearly identified is a property of a stage in language development, rather than a stage of cognitive development or a particular age. The results support a reconsideration of a grammatical account for early null arguments, rather than a performance account. I now return to this possibility.

DISCUSSION

I have shown that a consideration of the syntactic variation allowed cross-linguistically leads to formulation of null argument parameters whose initial settings are expected to be those that do not allow null arguments. Yet children seem to go through a stage of using null subjects, although even at the earliest ages there is an influence of linguistic environment. Because the form of the parameters and the differences between children learning different languages both argue against a grammatical account of early null subjects, the possibility that children's early subjectless sentences are due to processing limitations was explored. However, problems were found with this hypothesis, too. Hence, we remain in a paradox.

There are several possible routes out of this paradox. One is to reconsider the grammatical analyses of null arguments found in adult languages. Perhaps in another adult grammar a pattern of null arguments is found that more closely resembles that of the children's grammars. This possibility will be discussed later in this section.

An alternative approach reconsiders the notion of parameters and how they apply in language acquisition. Of the various grammatical phenomena that are subject to parametric variation cross-linguistically, it is the null argument parameters that have received the most attention in studies of language acquisition. Many other sources of cross-linguistic variation that have been analyzed as parametric do not seem to give rise to extended periods demonstrating an incorrect parameter setting in grammar acquisition (e.g., underlying word order, WH-movement). However, there may be evidence that children assume more than one parameter setting during some periods of development (e.g., Deprez, this work, volume 1, chapter 12; Valian, 1990). Perhaps children assume both null argument and non–null argument settings during the period in question, unless they have already analyzed their input as unambiguously leading to a positive setting on one of the null argument parameters. This could result in English-speaking children using null subjects, but at a rate lower than that of Italian- or Chinese-speaking children, who have already progressed to the adult parameter settings. Why would it take longer for the English-speaking children to move to the adult setting, and on what basis would they make such a move?

First, note that as Valian (1990) has pointed out, subjects are sometimes missing from sentences of adult English. Although subjectless sentences are not grammatical in adult English, part of the beginning of the sentence can be acceptably omitted, as in (8). Hence, the simple input that an English-speaking child receives is ambiguous with respect to the setting of the null argument parameters.

(8) a. She's there day and night.
   b. Runs the place with an iron hand.

However, an embedded tensed clause cannot have a missing subject, as illustrated in (9) (examples from Valian, 1990).

(9) * I think runs the place with an iron hand.

Furthermore, Roeper and Weissenborn (1990) provided evidence from the acquisition of French that although French-speaking children, like English-speaking children, do leave off subjects in matrix clauses at around 2 years of age, these children never leave off subjects in embedded clauses. This evidence indicates that children who appear to use an incorrect parameter setting in matrix clauses actually respect the correct parameter setting in embedded clauses. It is difficult to test this empirically, because children generally cease using null subjects by the time they use embedded clauses. However, if this observation is correct, it leads to the following possibility.

Following the syntactic analysis given earlier, suppose that the initial settings on the null argument parameters are those that do not allow null arguments. Children's utterances show that they respect these settings in embedded clauses. However, following Deprez (Vol. 1, chapter 12) somewhat, suppose in addition that outside of the embedded clause, additional parameter settings are available. Hence, null subjects would be available in matrix clauses only, until the proper parameter setting is achieved. In matrix clauses, we see that an initial parameter setting is not preset; rather, various parameter settings are manifested until the child determines the correct setting for his or her language. Thus, although children may hear conflicting evidence with regard to the presence of overt subjects in matrix clauses in English, they will not hear conflicting evidence from embedded clauses. For this reason, looking at the embedded clause as a triggering domain might be safer for the child's language acquisition process.

Although this is similar to the proposal made by Valian (1990), it is different in that under the present proposal, language acquisition is still a process of determining the correct settings on a range of parameters by using triggering data from the environment, rather than by hypothesis testing. However, it shares with Valian the notion that more than one parameter setting is available during a single stage of language development.

This proposal would require several new notions regarding parameter setting. First, it requires the notion that parameters have associated triggering domains. (Roeper & Weissenborn suggested that embedded clauses might be the triggering domain for all parameters, because embedded clauses are structure-preserving [cf. Emonds, 1976]. However, I am not making any proposals for parameters other than the null argument parameters at this point.) Second, it requires a view of initial parameter settings as tentative hypotheses, which need to be confirmed or disconfirmed. Third, it claims that although an initial setting is tentative, other settings may be available for the child outside of the triggering domain.

This proposal can be tested empirically by examining children's productions of embedded clauses in the acquisition of both null subject and non–null subject languages, to see whether there is any evidence that children learning a non–null subject language go through a null subject stage in embedded clauses. The proposal can also be tested by comparison to other potential instances of parameter setting in language acquisition. If the acquisition of other parameter settings also seems to require a particular triggering domain, and optionality of alternative parameter settings outside that domain, then the theory would be supported.

Is an alternative account available that does not require the postulation of these mechanisms? Perhaps yet another grammatical explanation will do. Rizzi (this volume, chapter 10) proposed that young English-speaking children's null subjects are a reflex of a grammatical parameter, but one that exists in addition to the parameters proposed earlier. This parameter is needed to account for null subjects in certain styles of English, French, and German: the so-called diary context. In certain contexts, adult English allows null subjects, which seem to have many of the same characteristics as the null subjects used by English-speaking children. In both cases, the identity of the null element seems to be different from *pro*. Rizzi argued that this null element is a null constant (*nc*), the [– anaphoric, – pronominal, – variable] null counterpart to the anaphoric epithet discussed by Lasnik and Stowell (1991).[1]

Rizzi's proposal is consistent with the data presented here. For children learning a language that allows null arguments, the evidence seems to indicate that this is acquired relatively early. Hence young Italian- and Chinese-speaking children use null arguments systematically; only the Chinese-speaking children use productive null objects. On the other hand, children learning a language like English or French might well use null subjects in root clauses, although still maintaining negative settings on the null argument parameters discussed earlier. The cause for their null subjects, under Rizzi's account, is not a performance limitation. Rather, these children use the *nc* even outside of the diary context in which it is allowed for adults. The reason, according to Rizzi, is that these children have not yet found that root clauses might be CP; *nc* will be licensed in SPEC of IP if IP is the root. Under Rizzi's proposal, the null constant will be licensed only for root subjects in English—its distribution corresponding to that of null subjects in the early grammar and in the diary context.

How well can Rizzi's proposal account for the ASL data? First, one must assume that the topic-identified null argument found in ASL, like that in Chinese, is distinct from the *nc* found in German and in English diary contexts and child grammars. (For one reason, ASL and Chinese, unlike German and English, allow null subjects in sentences with wh-movement.) Then, we find that children learning ASL, like children learning Chinese, set the discourse-oriented parameter relatively early. In addition, it seems that children learning ASL use the *nc* at an early age, before they have mastered the verb agreement system. Later, agreement-identified *pro* replaces *nc* as the null argument used without a discourse topic.

---

[1]This is the same null argument type that I independently proposed for different reasons as a possible alternative to the variable as the null argument found in discourse oriented languages (Lillo-Martin, 1991). Rizzi's analysis differs from mine in that he is not proposing the null constant as the null argument found in Chinese; rather, he assumes that Chinese retains a topic-drop analysis along the lines of Huang (1984).

CONCLUSION

I have argued that the grammatical and performance accounts presented previously for the early null argument phenomenon face empirical and/or conceptual difficulties. As an alternative, I discussed two possibilities. One is a reconsideration of the role of parameters and the means by which they are set. This possibility can be tested with further acquisition data, concerning both the null argument parameters and other proposed parameters. The second is a new grammatical account, proposed by Rizzi (this volume, chapter 10). This account can be tested with further exploration of the diary context null subjects found in adult English, and the distribution of early null arguments found in a variety of languages. Both possibilities expand the conception of language acquisition as parameter setting and call for further testing of this hypothesis.

ACKNOWLEDGMENTS

This work was supported in part by NIH Grant #DC-00183. I would like to thank the children and adults who participated in the studies on the acquisition of ASL, and I thank the personnel at the American School for the Deaf in West Hartford, CT, for allowing me to study children there. I have also benefited from the suggestions of several anonymous reviewers, although I have been unable to make use of all of their helpful suggestions.

APPENDIX

Cross-Linguistic Variation in Null Argument Constructions

LICENSING BY AGR
   Nonarguments only:
      German (also [+DO])
   Quasi-arguments and nonarguments:
      Insular Scandinavian
   All arguments; identification by no features:
      ?
   All arguments; identification by number features only:
      Chamorro
   All arguments; identification by person/number features:
      Italian, ASL (also [+DO])

LICENSING BY V
Referential arguments; identification by no features:
  Chamorro
Referential arguments; identification by arb person/number features:
  Italian
LICENSING BY P
Referential arguments; identification by no features:
  ?
Referential arguments; identification by arb person/number features:
  French

DISCOURSE ORIENTED
  Chinese, Portuguese

REFERENCES

Bloom, L. (1970). *Language development.* Cambridge, MA: MIT Press.
Bloom, P. (1990). Subjectless sentences in child language. *Linguistic Inquiry, 21,* 419–504.
Chomsky, N. (1981). *Lectures on government and binding.* Dordrecht: Foris.
Deprez, V., & Pierce, A. (1989). *Negation and functional projections in early grammar.* Unpublished manuscript.
Emonds, J. (1976). *A transformational approach to English syntax: Root, structure-preserving, and local transformations.* New York: Academic.
Gerken, L. (1991). The metrical basis for children's subjectless sentences. *Journal of Memory and Language, 30,* 431–451.
Huang, C.-T. J. (1984). On the distribution and reference of empty pronouns. *Linguistic Inquiry, 15,* 531–574.
Hyams, N. (1986). *Language acquisition and the theory of parameters.* Dordrecht: Reidel.
Hyams, N. (1991). The genesis of clausal structure. In J. Meisel (Ed.), *The acquisition of verb placement* (pp. 371–400). Dordrecht: Kluwer.
Hyams, N., & Wexler, K. (1993). On the grammatical basis of null subjects in child language. *Linguistic Inquiry, 24,* 421–459.
Jaeggli, O. and Hyams, N. (1988). Morphological uniformity and the setting of the Null Subject Parameter. *Proceedings of the North Eastern Linguistics Society, 18,* 238–253.
Lasnik, H. (1989). On certain substitutes for negative data. In R. Matthews & W. Demopoulos (Eds.), *Learnability and linguistic theory* (pp. 89–106). Dordrecht: Kluwer.
Lasnik, H., & Stowell, T. (1991). Weakest crossover. *Linguistic Inquiry, 22,* 687–720.
Lillo-Martin, D. (1986). Two kinds of null arguments in American Sign Language. *Natural Language and Linguistic Theory, 4,* 415–444.
Lillo-Martin, D. (1991). *Universal Grammar and American Sign Language: Setting the null argument parameters.* Dordrecht: Kluwer.
Mazuka, R., Lust, B., Wakayama, T., & Snyder, W. (1986). Distinguishing effects of parameters in early syntax acquisition: A cross-linguistic study of Japanese and English. *Papers and Reports on Child Language Development, 25,* 73–82.
Pye, C. (1987). *The acquisition of syntax in Quiche Mayan.* Paper presented at the Fourth International Congress for the Study of Child Language, Lund, Sweden.

Radford, A. (1990). *Syntactic theory and the acquisition of English syntax.* Oxford: Basil Blackwell.

Rizzi, L. (1986). Null objects in Italian and the theory of *pro. Linguistic Inquiry, 17,* 501–557.

Roeper, T., & Weissenborn, J. (1990). How to make parameters work: Comments on Valian. In L. Frazier & J. de Villiers (Eds.), *Language processing and language acquisition* (pp. 147–162). Dordrecht: Kluwer.

Saito, M., & Murasugi, K. (1990). N'-deletion in Japanese. *UConn Working Papers, 3.* Storrs, CT: University of Connecticut.

Valian, V. (1990). Logical and psychological constraints on the acquisition of syntax. In L. Frazier & J. de Villiers (Eds.), *Language processing and language acquisition* (pp. 119–146). Dordrecht: Kluwer.

Valian, V. (1991). Syntactic subjects in the early speech of American and Italian children. *Cognition, 40,* 21–81.

Wang, Q., Lillo-Martin, D., Best, C., & Levitt, A. (1992). Null subject vs. null object: Some evidence from the acquisition of Chinese and English. *Language Acquisition, 2,* 221–254.

Whitman, J., Lee, K., & Lust, B. (1990). Continuity of the principles of Universal Grammar in first language acquisition: The issues of functional categories. *Proceedings of the North Eastern Linguistics Society, 21,*

CHAPTER FOURTEEN

On the Differing Status of Subject Pronouns in French and English Child Language

Amy Pierce

This chapter compares the acquisition of subject pronouns in French and English. I claim that the comparative child language data support a syntactic distinction between subject pronouns in the two languages. While these pronominals behave as syntactic clitics in early French, they do not in early English. The acquisition data therefore serve as a surprising source of evidence for a particular analysis of these elements in the grammar of adult spoken French. Although this chapter does not address the null subject question directly, I suggest that French is a null subject language in both its child and, seemingly, its spoken adult forms. I also hope to show how a comparison between two child grammars leads to a clearer picture of individual child grammars.

BACKGROUND

The status of the class of subject pronouns in French known as weak forms (*je, tu, il, elle, nous, vous, ils, elles, on, ce*) is controversial. Kayne (1975) and Jaeggli (1982), for example, asserted that these elements are syntactic clitics, lacking the status of independent words in the syntax. Others have argued that although these elements may be clitics at the level of phonological form, they are in argument ([SPEC,IP]) position in the syntax (Brandi & Cordin, 1989; Burzio, 1986; Rizzi, 1986). I briefly review the arguments on both sides.

Jaeggli (1982), following Kayne (1975), pointed to five environments in French syntax in which subject clitics behave differently from strong form pronouns and lexical subjects. First, nothing except other clitics can intervene between the subject clitic and the verb:[1]

(1) a. *Il, souvent, va au cinéma.
'He/Jean, often, goes to the movies.'
b. Jean, souvent, va au cinéma.

Second, subject clitics cannot be conjoined, whereas lexical subjects can:

(2) a. *Jean et je voulons aller au cinéma.
'Jean and I want to go to the movies.'
b. *Ils et elles veulent partir en vacances.
'They (masc.) and they (fem.) want to take a vacation.'
c. Jean et Marie veulent partir en vacances.
'Jean and Marie want to take a vacation.'

Third, these clitics cannot be modified, whereas disjunctive (strong form) pronouns can:

(3) a. *Ils tous partiront bientôt.
'All of them will leave soon.'
b. Eux tous partiront bientôt.

Fourth, subject clitics cannot be contrastively stressed, whereas disjunctive pronouns can:

(4) a. *Il partira le premier.
'He will leave first.'
b. Lui partira le premier.

Fifth, subject clitics do not occur in other NP positions:

(5) a. *J'ai acheté ça pour tu.
'I bought this for you.'
b. J'ai acheté ça pour toi.

Based on these observations, Jaeggli contended that subject clitics are generated in INFL rather than in subject position, hence their obligatory closeness to the tensed verb.

---

[1] All examples in (1) through (5) are from Jaeggli (1982).

Arguments to the opposite effect focus on a set of facts that differentiate the behavior of subject clitics in French from that of subject clitics in certain Northern Italian dialects. It has been shown that subject clitics in these dialects represent a spelling-out of agreement (Brandi & Cordin, 1989; Burzio, 1986; Rizzi, 1986). Among the central points raised against viewing subject pronouns in French in the same light are the following. First, although subject clitics co-occur with lexical subjects in the Italian dialects, they do not in standard French:[2]

(6) a. Trentino: El Gianni el magna.
                   'John he eats.'
     b. French: *Jean il mange.

Note the sentence in (6b) is acceptable only as a left dislocation, when it is pragmatically or intonationally marked as such. Second, a conjunction of VPs can be predicated of a French but not an Italian subject clitic. The subject clitic in the Italian dialects must be repeated in the second conjunct:

(7) a. Trentino: La canta e la balla.
                   'She sings and she dances.'
     b. French: Elle chante et elle danse.
     c. Trentino: *La canta e la balla.
                   'She sings and dances.'
     d. French: Elle chante et danse.

Third, subject clitics in French precede the negative clitic *ne*, whereas other clitics follow it. In contrast, the subject clitic in Trentino occurs to the right of the equivalent negative, *no*:[3]

(8) a. Trentino: No la ghe l'ha dit.
                   'She has not said it to him.'
     b. French: Elle ne les aime pas/*Ne elle les aime pas.
                   'She doesn't like them.'

Fourth, the subject clitic is obligatory in the dialects, so that lexical subjects and clitics co-occur, whereas lexical and clitic subjects in standard French are in complementary distribution. Compare (6) with (9):

(9) a. Trentino:

---

[2]The Trentino examples in (6), (7), and (9) are from Rizzi (1986). That in (8) is from Brandi and Cordin (1989).

[3]Brandi and Cordin (1989) noted that subject clitics in Fiorentino can occur either to the left or to the right of the negative clitic.

                *El Gianni magna.
                'John eats.'
    b. French: Jean mange.

Many studying spoken French have argued that agreement and pronominalization should not be treated as distinct processes. Diachronic studies have indeed shown that pronominal elements undergo a process of phonological attrition due to their lack of stress. The cliticization of subject pronouns is thought to be a motivating factor in a syntactic reanalysis that took place between Old French and Middle French, when French lost the property of being verb-second (e.g., Adams, 1987; Kroch, 1989). Others have taken this view one step further, maintaining that cliticized subject pronouns in spoken Modern French are becoming obligatory subject agreement markers over the course of language change (Bailard, 1982; Barnes, 1985; Givon, 1976; Harris, 1978; Lambrecht, 1981; Larsson, 1979). Although I do not pursue this line of thought here (see Pierce, 1992), the study of child grammar can arguably shed light on language change, in the following way: Inconsistencies in the input (or adult) language are sometimes regularized in early child language, and this tendency to regularize, or fill out syntactic paradigms, may provide part of the answer to why dual-system grammars are found to be unstable in the study of language change.

    The so-called demotion of subject pronouns in French to inflectional prefixes has the effect that these clitics behave in certain respects like subject clitics in the Northern Italian dialects. For example, clausal conjunction in spoken French generally involves the repetition of the subject pronoun. According to Lambrecht (1981), the (a) examples in (10) and (11) are acceptable in written French, but the (b) examples are much more likely to be generated in speech:[4]

(10) a. Il mange et boit comme un cochon.
        'He eats and drinks like a pig.'
    b. I-mange et i-boit comme un cochon.
        'He eats and he drinks like a pig.'

(11) a. ?Je lis et puis écris.
        'I read and then write.'
    b. J-lis et puis j-écris.
        'I read and then I write.'

As understood from the English glosses in each case, (a) and (b) are equally acceptable in English; repetition of the pronouns, as in the (b) examples, simply adds emphasis. Note that the contrast between standard and nonstand-

---

[4]The examples in (10) and (11) are from Lambrecht (1981).

ard French does not maintain in cases of nonclausal conjunction, such as conjoined participial and infinitival phrases. In these structures, the locus of conjunction is below Inflection. If whole clauses of these types are conjoined, either both the auxiliary and the pronoun are repeated or neither are:

(12) a. Elle a mangé et dansé.
     'She ate and danced.'
   b. Elle a mangé et elle a dansé.
   c. *Elle a mangé et a dansé.

In examining the child language data presented later, we encounter evidence that Lambrecht's (1981) characterization of spoken French accounts for the French child's clausal conjunction, and that this contrasts with the English child's usage.

Another consequence of the analysis of subject pronouns as agreement prefixes is that they co-occur with other subject NPs. Sentences containing both a subject clitic and a coreferring NP or emphatic pronoun to its left or right occur quite frequently in spoken French. Left dislocations of the subject, as in (13a), were found by Ashby (1988) in a broad study of spoken French to be somewhat more common than right dislocations, such as (13b):

(13) a. Toi tu bois enormément.
     'You you drink enormous quantities.'
   b. Elle arrive rose ta soupe.
     'It (fem.) arrives pink your soup.'

In addition to the conjunction and dislocation facts, and those showing the weakness of subject pronouns in French, another parallel between spoken French and Northern Italian dialects with subject clitics is the near absence of simple NP subject–VP constructions like *Jean mange* 'John eats.' Linguists who have studied the colloquial language concur that this basic form is becoming strikingly rare (François, 1974; Lambrecht, 1981). This finding is echoed in the child language data, where I observed only a very small number of utterances containing preverbal lexical subjects. .

Transparently, it is the spoken language that the child receives as input during the first few years of life. Therefore, these observations about spoken French cannot be ignored in the study of French acquisition. In particular, what is the French child to make of right dislocations in the input if they lack pragmatic and prosodic marking, as many have argued? Without such marking, there is in effect no indication to the child to treat these structures as peripheral exceptions to core conditions on word order. If this is true, it would not be surprising to find that the developing grammar accommodates these structures. On the basis of natural production data from French child language, I argue that this is indeed the case. There is strong evidence, discussed later, both that subject clitics are in nonargument position in French child language and that postverbal subjects are generated by the French child's grammar (Pierce, 1992). The fact that the child's grammar accommodates these structures may itself be a force in the direction of change in French grammar that many linguists have remarked upon.

In sum, the distribution of subject clitics in spoken (or nonstandard) French, as discussed in the typological and functional literature, shows them to be closely aligned with subject clitics in the Italian dialects. But my concern here is with the acquisition facts, and specifically with the question of how subject pronouns in early French child speech line up with the analyses of subject pronouns I have just described. To the extent that it is still a controversial issue whether or not unstressed subject pronouns in French are syntactic inflectional clitics, I suggest that they are, based on the acquisition data.

SUBJECT PRONOUN USE AS A FUNCTION OF TENSE, POSITION, AND CASE

Subject pronouns are by far the most frequently used type of subject in English and French. In this respect the input to French and English children is similar. Also similar in the two languages is the fact that subject pronouns are unstressed elements. This may well have something to do with subject omission in child language. In both cases, full NP subjects and proper names are used relatively infrequently, as indicated in (14), based on data from four mothers in each language:[5]

(14) Overall percentage of maternal utterances containing full NPs in canonical subject position
English: 3–13%   French: 1–8%

Despite this apparent similarity, by about 2 years of age, French- and English-speaking children have acquired very different patterns of subject pronoun usage, that is, a different syntax of pronominal subjects. This is illustrated with some simple observations, outlined here.

French

As I have shown in previous work (Pierce, 1989, 1992), early child French is characterized by an optionality of finiteness. In (15) are some examples of finite and nonfinite sentences containing lexical subjects.[6]

---

[5]See Pierce (1992) for fuller accounts of the data and analyses discussed in this chapter.

[6]In the child language examples, the capital letter stands for the child's name, and age is given in years;months;weeks.

(15) Lexical subjects in preverbal position; [+/− finite]:
   a. encore dame tomber (D1;9;3), [−finite]
     'again lady fall'
   b. maman lit (D1;10;2), [+finite]
     'mother reads'
   c. papa réparer le tracteur (P2;1;3), [−finite]
     'father fix the tractor'
   d. papa travaille (P2;2;0), [+finite]
     'father works'

Unlike lexical subjects, pronominal subjects distribute exclusively with finite verbs. Some examples are given in (16), whereas (17) displays some nonoccurring nonfinite forms with a subject pronoun.

(16) Pronominal subjects in preverbal position; [+finite]:
   a. il est pas là (N2;2;2)
     'it is not there'
   b. et je veux (N2;2;2)
     'and I want'
   c. elle dort (D1;8;1)
     'she sleeps'
   d. il mange (G1;10;0)
     'he eats'

(17) Pronominal structures not observed; [−finite]:
   a. *il etre pas là
   b. *et je vouloir
   c. *elle dormir
   d. *il manger

Thus, for four French children roughly 20 to 27 months of age, subject pronouns were found to be dependent to a significant extent upon the co-occurrence of a finite verb. This is summarized in (18).

(18) Use of subject pronouns as a function of finiteness ($p < .025$)

	+ FINITE		− FINITE
Philippe	196	(99%)	3
Grégoire	143	(98%)	3
Nathalie	162	(96%)	7
Daniel	104	(88%)	14

From 88% to 99% of all subject clitics, depending on the child, occur in overtly tensed clauses. Not only does this indicate that very young children represent finiteness (or INFL), but it also shows that subject pronouns are not syntactically independent morphemes in early French grammar.

Another striking fact about subject pronouns in French child language is that they never appear in postverbal position. So, looking at (19), although French children are producing a majority of NP subjects in postverbal position (about 80% or 90%), regardless of whether or not the verb is finite, they never place a subject pronoun in postverbal position. That is, utterances like those in (20) are not observed.

(19) Lexical subjects in postverbal position; [+/− finite]:
    a. manger la poupée (N1;9;3), [−finite]
       'eat the doll'
    b. pleure bébé (N1;11;2), [+finite]
       'cries baby'
    c. manger salade Adrien (G1;9;2), [−finite]
       'eat salad Adrien'
    d. tombe Victor (G2;0;1), [+finite]
       'falls Victor'

(20) Pronominal structures not observed:
    a. *est pas là il
    b. *et veux je
    c. *dort elle
    d. *mange il

Just as they distinguish subject pronouns from lexical subjects in these ways, the children also use unstressed subject pronouns differently from accusative and disjunctive form pronouns, which occur in nonfinite clauses, as in (21).

(21) Disjunctive pronoun in nonfinite clauses:
    a. moi pousser (D1;9;3)
       'me push$_{-fin}$'
    b. moi dessiner la mer (D1;10;2)
       'me draw$_{-fin}$ the sea'
    c. vider la terre moi (P2;2;0)
       'empty$_{-fin}$ the ground me'
    d. aller dedans moi (G2;3;0)
       'go$_{-fin}$ inside me'
    e. toi venir (G2;3;0)
       'you go$_{-fin}$'

Tests of the relationship between subject type (weak or strong) and finite status produced highly significant results for each of the four children, showing that, although weak subject pronouns distribute almost always with finite verbs, strong form pronouns distribute in a significantly different manner in that they occur with both finite and nonfinite verbs.

Disjunctive pronouns also occur preferentially in postverbal position, as in (22), once again like lexical subjects and unlike pronominal subjects.

(22) Disjunctive pronoun in postverbal position:
    a. bois peu moi (D1;8;1)
        'drink little me'
    b. veux crayon moi (D1;10;2)
        'want pencil me'
    c. est tombé moi (P2;1;3)
        'is fallen me'
    d. va voir papa moi (P2;2;0)
        'goes to see papa me'
    e. moi fais tout seul moi (G2;1;3)
        'me do all by myself me'
    f. a peur moi (G2;3;0)
        'is scared me'

Finally, disjunctive pronouns can be dislocated and separated from the verb, as in (23), whereas unstressed pronouns cannot.

(23) Dislocated disjunctive pronoun:
    a. moi je vais faire café moi (D1;11;1)
        'me I go to make coffee me'
    b. moi je tousse encore (P2;2;2)
        'me I cough again'
    c. moi je veux regarder (G2;3;0)
        'me I want to watch'

In short, we observe the young French child making principled distinctions between unstressed pronominal subjects and other subject forms, by excluding the weak forms from nonfinite and postverbal positions, and by keeping them adjacent to the tensed verb. This contrasts with what is observed in English child language, to which I now turn, starting from the onset of pronoun use.

English

The child acquiring English often generates a subject pronoun next to a nonfinite verb, as the examples in (24) and (25) show. Subject pronouns are no less likely to occur in these environments than are lexical subjects. That is, there is no distinction, as there is in French child language, between the syntactic environments of pronominal and lexical subjects. If subject pronouns required finite INFL, as they appear to in early French, we would expect these constructions to be ruled out by the child's grammar.

(24) Subject pronouns with uninflected verbs:
   a. he sell ice cream (E1;8;0)
   b. it break (E1;6;2)
   c. she drink out a cup (E1;9;2)
   d. it hurt (Na1;10;3)
   e. she like it (Na2;0;3)
   f. he fall down (Ni1;11;2)
   g. he bite my fingers (Ni2;0;0)
   h. she have jamas on (Ni2;2;6)
   i. there it go (P2;2;1)
   j. she come back (P2;5;3)

(25) Subject pronouns with present participles:
   a. I banging (E1;7;2)
   b. he giving hay giraffe (E1;9;0)
   c. I washing (Na1;10;2)
   d. they all sleeping (Na2;1;2)
   e. I popping balloons (Ni2;0;2)
   f. it hard (Ni1;11;2)
   g. he walking (P2;1;0)
   h. it dirty (P2;1;3)

Unlike what is observed in French, the child acquiring English appears to be able to use nominative and accusative Case pronouns interchangeably for a time, although reports on the frequency of accusative pronouns in subject position vary (Radford, this work, volume 1, chapter 7; Valian, 1991). In (26) we see accusative pronouns occurring in the same environments in which we observe nominative Case subject pronouns in English child language, in both inflected and uninflected clauses.

(26) Accusative pronoun in subject position:
   a. him writing (E1;8;2)
   b. me come back (E1;10;0)
   c. me lay down (Na2;0;0)
   d. does him fish? (Na2;2;0)
   e. her holding a balloon (Ni2;0;0)
   f. him can't see (Ni2;2;0)
   g. her too cold (P2;1;0)
   h. no me take it off (P2;1;3)

I also found one instance in the English corpora, *I Adam don't sit* (2;4;3), in which the nominative pronoun is dislocated and separated from the verb. Recall that in French only disjunctive pronouns dislocate in this way.

SUBJECT PRONOUNS UNDER CLAUSAL CONJUNCTION

French

Another revealing distinction between French and English subject pronouns in child language concerns their behavior under coordination. In the case of French, the conjunction of tensed clauses with a pronominal subject invariably involves repetition of the subject pronoun. Although most of the examples, given in (27), come from one child, there were no exceptions to this generalization.

(27) Repetition of the subject pronoun:
    a. Moi je sautes et je descends. (P2;2;1)
       'Me I jump and I go down.'
    b. Il se ouvre et il se ferme. (P2;3;0)
       'It opens and it closes.'
    c. Je vais ouvrir le couvercule et je vais faire. . . (P2;9;0)
       'I'm going to open the cover and I'm going to. . .'
    d. Ben on ouvre et puis on, on prend le gateau. (P2;11;3)
       'One opens (it) and then one, one takes the cake.'
    e. Je le met dedans et puis je le tiens. (P3;0;1)
       'I put it inside and then I hold it.'
    f. Elle descend et elle remonte sur la main de maman. (G2;3;0)
       'It goes down and it goes back up on mommy's hand.'

In these examples, all preverbal clitics recur along with inflection in the second conjunct. With conjunction of untensed clauses, as in the case of conjoined past participles, the pronoun does not repeat. An example is given in (28). Repetition of the subject pronoun would clearly be ungrammatical here.

(28) J'ai joué et travaillé. (P2;6;3)
    'I (have) played and worked.'

I also observed no ungrammatical instances of conjoined subject pronouns of the type in (29).

(29) a. *Jean et il partiront bientôt.

b. *Tu et je mangeons.

English

Interestingly enough, the facts of English acquisition once again pattern differently. Although as in French the subject pronoun can be either repeated or not in this construction, from the point of view of grammaticality, unlike in French, it never is repeated. Instead, we find clausal conjunctions like those in (30), in which the subject pronoun occurs only in the first conjunct:

(30) Nonrepetition of the subject pronoun:
  a. We goed to the beach and saw. . . (E2;2;0)
  b. We goes to bed and wake up in the morning. (E2;3;0)
  c. You cut it in little pieces and bite it this way. (E2;1;0)
  d. I roll it up and put the band. (P2;6;2)
  e. They wake up and sleep in that bed. (P2;8;2)
  f. You take this off and take that off. (P2;3;3)
  g. I up by taking a bath and tell the story about. . . (Na3;5;0)
  h. And you walk around the house and look outside. (Na3;5;0)
  i. Could I sit down in chair and read the catalogue? (Na2;3;0)
  j. I go and pick them up. (Ni2;3;0)
  k. I have my eye and hurt. (Ni2;1;2)
  l. Me and all going. (Ni2;1;2)
  m. He puts his instruments and listens to my ear. (A2;9;0)
  n. I was falling down the stairs and went boom and hit my. . (M2;5;0)

And, in contrast to (29) for French, we also observe that subject pronouns can be conjoined in English child language. This is exemplified in (31).

(31) Subject pronouns in conjoined subjects:
  a. You and I have some grape juice. (Eve 2;2;0)
  b. Peter and he see Roy. (April 2;1;0)

From the beginning, then, French and English children have very different syntactic representations for subject pronouns. (32) summarizes the main properties of subject pronouns in French acquisition.

(32) Properties of subject pronouns in French child language:
  a. Appear adjacent to finite verbs.
  b. Do not occur in other NP positions.
  c. Cannot be conjoined.
  d. Co-occur with other lexical subjects.
  e. Repeated under clausal conjunction.

In short, the French child's subject pronoun is an inflectional clitic. The properties given in (32) are some of the defining characteristics of subject clitics in languages like the Northern Italian dialects. I am proposing that the French child represents the unstressed subject pronoun as in (33).

(33) Proposed S-structure for *il mange*.

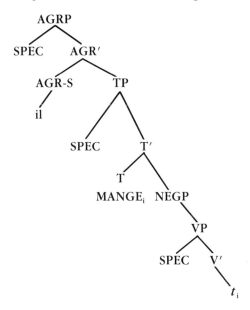

On this view, subject pronouns are syntactic affixes generated in AGR and requiring the presence of a tensed verb raised to INFL to avoid being filtered out. This contrasts with the analysis of subject pronouns in English, whose syntactic representation is presumably not distinguished from that of other subject forms. There is further suggestive evidence from one child for whom data at a later age is available. Philippe at 3 years includes subject pronouns in 95% of his utterances, largely by using left and right dislocation constructions to a greater extent than his parents (see also Clark, 1985). An interesting question for future research is whether this holds up for other older children, and whether in fact children first hypothesize obligatory subject clitics and then retreat from this hypothesis when they are exposed to more formal grammatical input during their school-age years.

One outcome of the analysis of subject pronouns as syntactic clitics in French is that French is then interpreted as a null subject language. This, in turn, leads us to expect that the proportion of subject omissions in French acquisition will not drop off at a young age, as it does in English. And, in fact, if sentences containing only a subject clitic are counted along with other null subject utterances, the rate of subject omission remains constant over the same developmental period in which it is found to drop off in English. This is illustrated in (34).

(34) Rate of full subject omission in French child language:
G1 (1;9;2) 57%/ G2 (1;10;0) 47%/ G3 (1;10;3) 56%/ G4 (1;11;3) 68%/ G5 (2;0;1) 69%/ G6 (2;1;3) 72%/ G7 (2;3;0) 62%
N1 (1;9;3) 47%/ N2 (1;10;1) 53%/ N4 (2;0;1) 65%/ N6 (2;2;2) 61%/ N7 (2;3;2) 88%
D1 (1;8;1) 87%/ D2 (1;8;3) 82%/ D3 (1;9;3) 90%/ D4 (1;10;2) 77%/ D5 (1;11;1) 79%
P1 (2;1;3) 70%/ P2 (2;2;0) 79%/ P3 (2;2;1) 63%/ P4 (2;2;2) 65%/ P7 (2;3;0) 79%

This result is akin to the consistency in subject drop that Valian (1991) observed in Italian children at a comparable age. In English acquisition, in contrast, the rate of subject omission drops off sharply during the period between 18 and 36 months (Pierce, 1992; Valian, 1991).

In sum, I have argued that French and English speakers have different syntactic representations for unstressed subject pronouns, starting from a very young age. Because it is the adult language as it is spoken or otherwise presented to children that shapes the early grammar, the findings presented here suggest that subject clitics in spoken French are analyzable as inflectional affixes, by children acquiring the language as well as by linguists studying these facts. Their syntactic clitic status in child French also serves as important evidence for the presence of INFL in early grammar.

REFERENCES

Adams, M. (1987). From Old French to the theory of pro-drop. *Natural Language and Linguistic Theory, 5,* 1–32.

Ashby, W. (1988). The syntax, pragmatics, and sociolinguistics of left- and right-dislocation in French. *Lingua, 75,* 203–229.

Bailard, J. (1982). Le francais de demain: VSO ou VOS? In A. Ahlqvist (Ed.), *Papers from the Fifth International Conference on Historical Linguistics* (pp. 20–28). Amsterdam: Benjamins.

Barnes, B. (1985). *The pragmatics of left detachment in spoken Standard French.* Amsterdam: Benjamins.

Brandi, L., & Cordin, P. (1989). Two Italian dialects and the null subject parameter. In O. Jaeggli & K. Safir (Eds.), *The null subject parameter* (pp. 111–142). Dordrecht: Kluwer.

Burzio, L. (1986). *Italian syntax.* Dordrecht: Reidel.

Clark, E. (1985). The acquisition of Romance with special reference to French. In D. Slobin (Ed.), *The crosslinguistic study of language acquisition* (Vol. 1). Hillsdale, NJ: Lawrence Erlbaum Associates.

François, D. (1974). *Francais parle: Analyse des unites phonetique et significatives d'un corpus recueilli dans la region parisienne* [An analysis of phonetic and signifying units from a corpus collected in the Paris region]. Paris: SELAF.

Givon, T. (1976). Topic, pronoun and grammatical agreement. In C. Li (Ed.), *Subject and topic.* New York: Academic Press.

Harris, M. (1978). *The evolution of French syntax.* London: Longman.

Jaeggli, O. (1982). *Topics in Romance syntax.* Dordrecht: Foris.

Kayne, R. (1975). *French syntax.* Cambridge, MA: MIT Press.

Kroch, A. (1989). Reflexes of grammar in patterns of language change. *Language Variation and Change, 1,* 199–244.

Lambrecht, K. (1981). *Topic, antitopic and verb agreement in non-standard French.* Amsterdam: Benjamins.

Larsson, E. (1979). La dislocation en francais: Etude de syntax generative [Dislocation in French: A study in generative syntax]. *Etudes Romanes de Lund, 28.* Lund: Gleerup.

Pierce, A. (1989). *On the emergence of syntax: A crosslinguistic study.* Unpublished doctoral dissertation, MIT, Cambridge, MA.

Pierce, A. (1992). *Language acquisition and syntactic theory: A comparative analysis of French and English child grammars.* Dordrecht: Kluwer.

Rizzi, L. (1986). On the status of subject clitics in Romance. In O. Jaeggli & C. Silva-Corvalan (Eds.), *Studies in Romance linguistics.* Dordrecht: Foris.

Valian, V. (1991). Syntactic subjects in the early speech of American and Italian children. *Cognition, 40,* 21–82.

CHAPTER FIFTEEN

Pragmatic Principles in Coreference

Carlota S. Smith
University of Texas

To understand the making of coreference, we must consider the principles that speakers follow in choosing among the relevant forms and interpretations of a language. The principles are complementary to those of the grammar. Principle B of the Binding Theory deals with the grammatical factors that block coreference (Chomsky, 1981), but not with coreference itself. I present some pragmatic principles of coreference and discuss their realization in Mandarin Chinese.

Children must acquire the pragmatic principles of coreference. We would like to know how and when the principles are acquired. The acquisition of these principles may not follow the same path as that of grammatical rules. Furthermore, understanding coreference from this viewpoint may be helpful in interpreting acquisition studies of Principle B.

Pronouns and other NPs used for coreference form a closed system, that is, they offer a limited set of contrasting possibilities. Closed systems were extensively studied by the linguists of the Prague School. Jakobson (1957/1971), for instance, was interested in the meanings associated with the members of such systems. He discussed them in terms of such notions as positive and negative values, symmetry, and contrastive information. In recent work I proposed an approach to closed systems that distinguishes between semantic and pragmatic information (Smith, 1991). Semantic information is associated with a linguistic form in the grammar of a language, whereas contrastive information about that form is part of the pragmatic knowledge of the speaker. A similar approach is appropriate for coreference.

Contrastive information must be relativized to a given language. Consider an example from the domain of aspect. Russian and English both have perfective and imperfective viewpoints in past tense sentences, but the full systems differ. In Russian the imperfective viewpoint is systematically dominant, whereas in English the perfective is dominant. There are conventions in the two languages that reflect this difference in aspectual structure. In Russian one frequently talks about a past, completed event with the imperfective viewpoint, though semantically the imperfective presents only part of the event. This convention is well known as the Statement of Fact convention. English does not have such a convention. Thus there is often a contrast in sentences presenting past, completed events in the two languages. The following examples illustrate this: Sentences like (1a) and (2a) are often translated into English as (1b) and (2b).

(1) a. Vojnu i mir pisal^{Impf} Lev Tolstoj.
   b. Lev Tolstoy wrote^{Perf} War & Peace.
(2) a. Ja govoril^{Impf} emu ob ètom.
   b. I told^{Perf} him about this.

Speakers of Russian know the pragmatic conventions underlying sentences such as (1a) and (2a), whereas English speakers know those associated with (1b) and (2b). This is only one Russian convention; there are others, of course.[1] Aspectual conventions were considered in Dahl (1985) and Smith (1991); general principles of inference were discussed in Grice (1975), and in neo-Gricean treatments such as Levinson (1991).

The forms indicating coreference in English are unstressed pronouns, stressed pronouns, full NPs, and anaphors. The conventions for using these forms are based partly on general principles and partly on the pattern of the language. In this chapter I consider some general conventions for using pronouns and their realization in English and in Chinese.

The work is directly relevant to the study of language acquisition. Recent experimental work on Mandarin Chinese by Wilcoxon showed an interesting discrepancy in children's knowledge of grammatical principles. The experiments focused on the Binding Theory in structures where pronouns precede NPs. The children knew Principle B, but they did not know an exceptional restriction on anaphora in Chinese. Moreover, their pattern of coreference choices suggested that they did not know the pragmatic principles that adult speakers follow for making coreference.

I first consider some pragmatic principles of coreference, sketching the relevant facts regarding Chinese. I then discuss Wilcoxon's acquisition experi-

---

[1]When the speaker wishes to emphasize that an event took place (rather than its completion), the Statement of Fact convention is used. The Russian aspectual system and conventions are discussed in chapter 10 of Smith (1991).

ments and interpret the results from a pragmatic point of view. I conclude with a general discussion of acquisition work pertaining directly and indirectly to coreference.

COREFERENCE WITH PRONOUNS

Pronouns are used to indicate coreference with a familiar entity, or for deixis; I am concerned here with coreference. It is common for languages to have pronouns that are syntactically in free variation. The variation is not really free, however, because the choice of a pronoun has semantic and pragmatic consequences. I discuss some of these choices. The most important factors are pronoun form, proximate or nonproximate referent, focal or neutral semantic structure, and discourse organization.

Pronoun forms are marked or unmarked, with contrasting interpretations. The unmarked forms are simpler morphologically than the marked and often have simpler or more general interpretations. The notion of markedness was introduced by linguists in the structural tradition; it is particularly useful for closed systems.[2] I discuss three patterns of contrasting form and interpretation in different languages and argue that they represent different versions of a general pragmatic principle. I also show that we need to recognize a discourse-based use of marked pronouns.

I begin by considering the information conveyed by marked and unmarked pronouns in English and some other languages, and I then discuss the contrasts conveyed in Chinese. Chinese is a language in which empty categories are salient. We find that the forms of Chinese make evident certain distinctions that are masked, or less obvious, in English. Chinese has a pronoun use that arises only in discourse, which I call *distinguishing* reference. It involves lexical pronouns, the marked form in Chinese. This use of coreference forms occurs in English, but it involves NPs rather than pronouns. Looking at languages with different forms illuminates the problem space, as has been shown recently with reflexives (cf. C. Koster, this volume, chapter 8; Reuland, this volume, chapter 9).

Marked and Unmarked Forms: The Principle of Obviation

In making coreference speakers must choose between marked and unmarked pronoun forms, a choice that has clear consequences. Pronouns allow or obviate coreference with an NP in a given linguistic context, depending on

---

[2] The logic of markedness extends beyond the closed systems studied by Jakobson and other Prague School theorists. The notion of neutral and nonneutral forms and interpretations is used extensively in modern linguistics.

their form. The unmarked pronoun refers neutrally (assuming grammatical and presuppositional constraints). The marked pronoun obviates neutral coreference. I pursue the hypothesis that there is a general principle of contrast between pronoun forms, which has somewhat different realizations in different languages. The discussion excludes coreference made with full NPs and with reflexives and other anaphors. I assume that the interpretation of pronouns in actual sentences involves several types of information, including verb semantics, contextual knowledge, and world knowledge. How this information is integrated is beyond the scope of this chapter.

The principle that marked forms block certain coreference interpretations was stated for Native American languages as the *principle of obviation* by Cuoq (1891).[3] Hopi, Algonquian languages, Hokan languages, Yup'ik Eskimo, and many others have contrasting forms that indicate reference and noncoreference between NPs in certain syntactic environments (Jacobsen, 1967; Voegelin & Voegelin, 1975). The unmarked pronoun form conveys coreference with a proximate NP, that is, an NP in the same multiclausal sentence. The marked form indicates coreference with an NP in another sentence. I call this type of system *positional obviation.*

Pragmatically, the choice of a proximate form indicates a familiar, expected referent that is the current center of attention (cf. Voegelin, 1946 on Delaware; Frantz, 1966 on Blackfoot; Wolfart, 1973 on Plains Cree, all Algonquian languages).[4] The marked pronoun form obviates proximate coreference, indicating a coreferent that is less prominent in the discourse. In both cases coreference is neutral: No particular semantic structure is associated with it. We can state these facts in terms of a pragmatic principle in which the unmarked pronoun form conveys proximate coreference and the marked form conveys obviative coreference. These brief remarks introduce one type of obviation; there are other systems that convey these notions, or related ones, in different ways.

In English the pronoun forms convey a somewhat different contrast. The unstressed pronoun indicates neutral coreference with another NP. The unmarked pronoun has a referent that is familiar, often predictable. This neutral coreference does not affect the scopal semantic structure of a sentence. It simply indicates a referent, and it maintains continuity with preceding

---

[3]The term *obviation* was proposed by Cuoq (1891). Obviation refers to a form indicating the less salient of two third person referents "to obviate confusion" (Voegelin & Voegelin, 1975, p. 385).

[4]Both Frantz and Wolfart noted that the proximate form has the pragmatic function of indicating a referent that is familiar, the current topic of the discourse: currently in focus, in the sense of discourse focus. Not all scholars agree that obviation is pragmatically significant. Hale (1978) suggested a grammatical account of obviation for relative clauses in Irish; Finer (1985) argued that switch reference, a closely related phenomenon, is grammatically rather than pragmatically based.

information and expectation. Extending the notion of obviation to English, we can say that this is a sense of proximate that does not necessarily involve a sentential domain; rather, it is a metaphorical notion in which the continuous and expected is metaphorically proximate.

In contrast, the marked, stressed pronoun obviates neutral coreference: It indicates focus, often with a nonproximate NP. Focused terms are put into opposition with other terms, usually by contrast or emphasis. Sentences with focused NPs have a distinctive semantic structure, which is organized into two parts. Semantically, focus "partitions (information) . . . into the part that is in focus and the complement part that is not in focus, commonly called the background" (Krifka, 1991, p. 1). The examples in (3) illustrate the English obviation contrast in two-clause sentences of English. In (3a) the pronoun is naturally taken to be coreferential with the NP in the main clause. The pronoun in (3b) cannot be so interpreted: it requires a different referent. Subscripts give the interpretations:

(3) a. When he_1 works, $John_1$ doesn't drink.
    b. When HE_2 works, $John_1$ doesn't drink.

As indicated, the referent of the stressed pronoun must be outside the sentence, in the linguistic or extralinguistic context. The unstressed pronoun neutrally indicates a proximate referent, in this case one that is internal to the sentence. The marked pronoun indicates focal coreference with an NP that is not proximate in the metaphorical sense. The referent may be literally proximate. For instance, it is not difficult to construct examples that have a sentence-internal referent for the stressed pronoun, as (4) illustrates:

(4) Although [his_1 colleagues]$_2$ think that they$_2$ understand John$_1$,
    HE$_1$ doesn't think that they$_2$ do.

The pronoun in the main clause must be stressed, because the NP *his colleagues* sets up a contrast set suggesting the focal interpretation of the pronoun.[5] Thus the marked and unmarked pronouns of English convey different semantic structures and in many cases different referents. The English system involves obviation, but with focus as the main factor; I call it focus obviation.

Context affects the interpretation of pronouns. In a context that gives appropriate information, for instance, the stressed pronoun in (3b) can be taken as coreferential with the following NP. In (5), (3b) is repeated as (5c).

---

[5]This sentence needs a context to make certain readings plausible. If a reading is indeed plausible in the appropriate context, it is semantically permitted by the sentence.

(5) a. John₁ insists that Tom₂ and Bill₃ abstain from drinking on the job.
   b. This isn't entirely unreasonable.
   c. After all, when HE₁ works, John₁ doesn't drink.

We can also construct examples in which information in the context changes the interpretation of an unstressed pronoun. In an appropriate context, an unstressed pronoun may be taken as coreferential with an NP in a different sentence. (5) illustrates; (6c) is similar to (3a). The subscripts indicate the external interpretation.

(6) a. My parents are coming to spend a week with us next month.
   b. Dad₁ is a strict teetotaler; he₁ doesn't even like to be around drinkers.
   c. When he₁ visits, John₂ doesn't drink.

The neutral referent for the pronoun in (6c) is *Dad*, in the context of (6a–b). There are also examples in which the referent of an unstressed pronoun is farther away, but they do not concern us here. Evidently, the position of referents is not limited: In these examples both focal and neutral referents may be either in the same sentence or in a different sentence, depending on information in a sentence or its context. The examples show that the distinction between proximate and obviative coreference is not formally marked in English. The basic generalization is that unstressed pronouns convey neutral coreference, whereas stressed pronouns convey focal coreference.

I suggest, then, that there is a significant difference in the information conveyed by the marked pronoun in different linguistic systems. In Native American languages it indicates positional obviation, whereas in English marked pronouns indicate focal obviation.

The focus type of obviation is also found in Spanish, a language with a different type of surface contrast between pronouns. In Spanish, null pronouns are unmarked, whereas lexical pronouns are marked. Focal coreference is associated with marked pronoun forms. (7) illustrates; it is the Spanish counterpart of (3) (from Lujan, 1985):[6]

(7) a. Cuando ø trabaja, Juan no bebe.
      'When he₁ works, Juan₁ doesn't drink.'

---

[6] Pronouns with heavy stress can be used to convey coreference in a way that overrides grammatical principles such as those of the Binding Theory. For instance, under certain circumstances a heavily stressed pronoun can corefer with an NP in a single clause, as in this well-known example from Evans (1980).

   (i) A: Nobody admires John.
      B: That's not true. (pointing to John) HE admires John.

In such cases the NP does not bind the pronoun. I do not consider them here.

    b. Cuando él trabaja, Juan no bebe.
      When HE$_2$ works, Juan$_1$ doesn't drink.'

Marked coreference is associated with a focal semantic structure similar to that proposed by Krifka (see Larson & Lujan, 1992, for a different treatment). Context affects the possibilities for referents similarly in Spanish and English. In (8b) the natural referent for the unmarked pronoun form is outside the sentence.

(8) a. Papa es muy estricto.
      'Papa$_1$ is very strict.'
   b. Cuando ø venga de visita, Juan no bebe.
      'When he$_1$ visits, John$_2$ doesn't drink.'

Stressed pronouns may also appear in Spanish; they are not discussed here.

    I assume that obviation contrasts are generally available in language, so that obviation is a general principle among other general principles of communication and linguistic form. Proximate or neutral coreference contrasts with positional or focal coreference, depending on the system. The domain in which focal obviation applies is not a syntactic one, although Principle B requires that at least two clauses be involved. The examples show that information that determines the referent for both neutral and focal coreference may appear in one multiclausal sentence, or in the context of a simple or multiclausal sentence. A sentence in isolation is simply one with certain pragmatic interpretations. The sentence may or may not have information that allows a sentence-internal interpretation of a pronoun. The null context is not neutral with respect to interpretation, but rather one in which referents are limited.

    Whether or not a pronoun naturally receives a sentence-internal interpretation depends on the type of pronoun and other information, including lexical and contextual information. However, people clearly prefer to give a sentence-internal interpretation of a pronoun if they can. This is partly due to a tendency, observed by Crain and Steedman (1985), for choice of referential interpretations that fulfill the presuppositional requirements of a sentence.[7]

Chinese

In Chinese the markedness contrast between pronouns is realized by lexical and null pronouns. Several characteristics of the language will be pertinent to this discussion. Empty categories are very common. There are null

---

[7]Speakers of certain dialects of Spanish may have interpretations other than the one given, as Paul Chapin pointed out (personal communication, 1992); dialects influenced by English are especially likely to allow such interpretations.

pronouns (*pro*) and null variables (as well as the empty category PRO, not relevant to this discussion). The language has structural topics, which are also commonly used.

Chinese has been called a discourse-oriented language (C.-T. J. Huang, 1984). The properties that lead to this characterization are null object constructions, topic chains (Tsao, 1977), topic prominence (Li & Thompson, 1976), and discourse anaphora (Yang, 1983). I discuss null object constructions briefly; a topic chain is a sequence of sentences that have the same topic. The topic is empty in all but the initial sentence. Topic-prominent languages have topic-comment sentences as basic forms (C.-T. J. Huang, 1984); discourse anaphora is the binding of an anaphor across discourse. Only the null object and topic chain properties are relevant to this discussion of coreference.

Pronominal Coreference. Pronouns must be free in their domain, according to Principle B of the Binding Theory. Generally, in Mandarin as in other languages, pronouns may not c-command their antecedents. Coreference is possible if this restriction is met (I follow the analysis of C.-T. J. Huang, 1984). Lexical and null pronouns contrast in many structures: They appear in the same environments and have the same grammatically based domains for coreference. (9)–(10) illustrate; the subscripts indicate possible coreference:

(9) a. Wang Xiansheng shuo ta youlan guo Changcheng.
    b. Wang Xiansheng shuo Ø youlan guo Changcheng.
       Wang Mr say he tour GUO Great Wall
       'Mr Wang$_1$ says that he$_{1,2}$ visited the Great Wall.'

(10) a. Xiaoming hai zai wu wai, ta jiu ba men guan shang le, zhen bu limao.
     b. Xiaoming hai zai wu wai, Ø jiu ba men guan shang le, zhen bu limao.
        X$_1$ still at house outside, he$_{1,2}$ then BA door close RVC le, really not polite
        'When Xiaoming is still outside, he closes the door; it's really impolite.'

For (9a–b), which appear without context, the natural reading is that the pronouns are coreferential with the main clause subject. For (10a–b), which have a short following context (*zhen bu limao*), the natural referent is outside the sentence. These sentences exemplify the dominant pattern of the language.

There is also a set of structures for which coreference is more restricted. These structures have lexical pronouns in the first clause and an NP in the following clause. Although the pronoun does not c-command the NP, it may not be coreferential with that NP. This restriction does not hold for null pronouns. The difference is shown in (11):

(11) a. [[ta deng-le sange zhongtou yihou], Zhangsan shuizhao-le]
3sg wait-LE 3CL hour after, Z. go-sleep LE
'After he$_1$ had waited 3 hours, Zhangsan$_2$ fell asleep.'
   b. [[ø deng-le sange zhongtou yihou], Zhangsan shuizhao-le]
3sg wait-LE 3CL hour after, Z. go-sleep LE
'After he$_{1,2}$ had waited 3 hours, Zhangsan$_2$ fell asleep.'

Coreference between the lexical pronoun and a following NP (*Zhangsan*) is blocked in (11a). But in (11b), which has a null pronoun, coreference is possible—though not, of course, required. For lexical pronouns to corefer with a following NP the pronoun must be relatively low in the syntactic structure of a sentence, as C.-T. J. Huang (1982) showed.[8]

The restriction on coreference with backwards anaphora holds only for lexical pronouns. Generally lexical pronouns and empty categories contrast in Chinese, so that the restriction constitutes an exception in the grammar. Chinese also allows stressed lexical pronouns, but this option is taken rarely.[9]

The Subject-Object Asymmetry. In Chinese empty categories may occur in all positions. But the distribution of null pronouns is constrained, due to the nature of topic structures. The constraint leads to a subject-object asymmetry (C.-T. J. Huang, 1982, 1984). The difference between subject and object affects the realization of the obviation principle, because the possibilities for the two syntactic positions are not the same.

There is a difference between the functions of an empty category (EC) in subject and object position in Chinese. In subject position an EC may be *pro* or a variable bound by the topic, or PRO; but ECs in object position are variables bound by a topic. Thus, although Chinese has ECs in both subject and object positions, they differ in noncoreference—and therefore in coreference—possibilities. The examples illustrate.

---

[8]C.-T. J. Huang (1984) defined a notion of cyclic c-command that accounts for cases when a pronoun may be coreferential with a following NP in the same multiclause sentence.

[9]There is a further option, taken relatively rarely in Chinese: Lexical pronouns may be stressed. Stressed pronouns are used in cases where pragmatic considerations override grammatical rules (cf. footnote 5). For instance:

(i) Dang ta zai jia de shihou, Lisi yige ren zongsh kizhe men shuijiao.
   when he at home DE time,   always open ZHE door sleep
   'When he$_1$ is at home, Lisi$_1$ alone always sleeps with the door open.'

In this sentence the phrase *yige ren* makes coreference pragmatically necessary.

(12) Embedded subject:
  a. Xiaoming shuo ta xiage yue jiehun.
     Xiaoming$_1$ say 3s$_{1,2}$ nextCL month marry
     'Xiaoming$_1$ says that he$_{1,2}$ will get married next month.'
  b. Xiaoming shuo ø xiage yue jiehun.
     Xiaoming$_1$ say EC$_{1,2}$ nextCL month marry
     'Xiaoming$_1$ says that he$_{1,2}$ will get married next month.'

(13) Embedded object:
  a. Xiaoming shuo Lisi bu renshi ta.
     Xiaoming$_1$ say Lisi$_2$ not know 3s$_{1,3}$
     'Xiaoming$_1$ says Lisi$_2$ doesn't know him$_{1,3}$.'
  b. Xiaoming shuo Lisi bu renshi ø.
     Xiaoming$_1$ say Lisi$_2$ not know EC$_3$
     'Xiaoming$_1$ says Lisi$_2$ doesn't know him$_3$.'

The subscripts show the different interpretations for subject and object ECs in these sentences. The variable ECs in object position are bound by empty topics. What is important for this discussion is that the object EC may not be coreferential with an NP in an A-position, that is, an NP in the matrix clause.[10]

Obviation in Chinese

I noted earlier that empty categories are very common in Chinese. In fact, ECs are so widespread they "must be regarded as normal, unmarked. . . . it is the *occurrence* of (lexical) pronouns in Chinese discourse that must be explained" (Li & Thompson, 1979, p. 322). It is generally agreed that ECs make neutral coreference; topic chains and other cases make it clear that the referent of an unmarked pronoun need not be literally proximate. The referent for a marked, lexical pronoun is unfamiliar, unexpected, highlighted in some way, or contrastive in some way. The category of marked coreference, then, is a complex one, which may include some types of focal coreference. Referents for both null and lexical pronouns may appear in the same sentence or in a different sentence (cf. Chen, 1983; Y. Huang, 1991; Li & Thompson, 1979, 1981; Pu, 1989; Tsao, 1977).

The Chinese version of obviation differs from both of the systems discussed earlier. It is unlike that in American Indian languages, because the system is not positional; it is unlike that in English, because focus is not necessarily associated with marked pronouns. Summarizing, in Chinese the null pronoun indicates neutral coreference and the lexical pronoun indicates marked

---

[10] There is some controversy in the literature about the analysis of object ECs in Chinese. It has been argued that some object ECs are pronouns (Zhang, 1988).

coreference, where marked coreference includes several different notions. I give in (14) a rough statement of obviation as a principle for pronoun use.

(14) *The obviation principle in Chinese:*
Use a null pronoun to convey neutral coreference;
use a lexical pronoun to convey marked coreference.

The principle is quite simple but its realization is rather complex, due to the pattern of the language. In this discussion I concentrate on the contrast between neutral and marked coreference, without distinguishing between types of marked coreference.

The subject-object asymmetry is significant for the coreference pattern of Chinese. If speakers want to make unmarked reference from object position to a topic, they use a variable EC. But for any kind of reference to an NP in the main clause of a complex sentence, they must use a lexical pronoun. Because there is no contrast in this position, the distinction between marked and unmarked pronouns is neutralized.

The possibility of topic chains is another factor that complicates obviation in Chinese. The sentences of a topic chain have anaphoric empty topics that bind one another in discourse. (15) illustrates; the first sentence introduces the topic and the subsequent sentences have an empty topic, which is identical with the subject.

(15) (1) Yang-Zhi qu-lu.
'Yang-Zhi$_1$ took to the road.
(2) Bu shu ri, ø lai-dao DongJing.
In a few days, he$_1$ arrived in DongJing.
(3) ø ru-de cheng-lai.
He$_1$ entered the city.
(4) ø xuan ge ke-dian.
He$_1$ found a hotel.
(5) ø an-xi xia.
He$_1$ settled down.'

This is a simple example. There are many other cases (cf. the discussions of Chen, 1983; Li & Thompson, 1979). According to these authors many different patterns of coreference occur, in conversation and in narrative.

The topic chain also affects the instantiation of the obviation principle in Chinese. It means that the lexical antecedent to a variable need not be literally proximate at all. In the preceding topic chains, for instance, the lexical referents are quite far away.

Realization of the obviation principle is somewhat complex in Chinese, then, for several reasons. The forms for neutral coreference vary. In subject position either marked or unmarked forms may appear. In object position a null variable must be used for a sentence-external referent, whereas if the referent is sentence-internal only a lexical pronoun may be used. Lexical pronouns may also be used for sentence-external referents.

The choice between null and lexical pronouns is also neutralized in single sentences of Chinese. There are both grammatical and pragmatic reasons for this. The grammatical point involves the subject-object asymmetry of Chinese. In object position only the lexical pronoun conveys coreference within a sentence. Therefore speakers cannot follow the simple principle of using an unmarked form to refer to an NP internal to a sentence. I have already noted that hearers generally seek to fulfill presuppositional requirements in understanding a sentence. For sentences in the null context, this has the effect of making people interpret reference as sentence-internal if they can do so. The tendency toward such interpretation is found in Chinese as well as English. For instance, consider (16), an example of Y. Huang (1991). According to Y. Huang, both pronouns have neutral referents internal to the sentence, as the subscripts indicate.

(16) a. Wang Xiaosheng shuo ta youlan guo Changcheng.
   Wang$_1$ Mr   say 3s$_{1,2}$ visit GUO Great Wall
   'Mr Wang$_i$ says that he$_i$ visited the Great Wall.'
   b. Wang Xiaosheng shuo ø youlan guo Changcheng.
   Wang$_1$ Mr   say 3s$_{1,2}$ visit GUO Great Wall
   'Mr Wang$_1$ says that he$_1$ visited the Great Wall.'

This reading is predictable according to the pragmatic principle that, in the absence of any other information, a sentence-internal reading is preferred. But in context, the pronoun in the complement clause may be taken to refer outside the sentence, as (17) shows; (17c) and (17c′) differ only the form of the pronoun and have the same interpretation.

(17) a. Fangjia de shihou, henduo ren dou chuqu wan le.
   'At vacation time, many people go away.'
   b. Xiaoming qu youlan-le naxie difang.
   'Where did Xiaoming$_1$ go?
   c. Wang Xiaosheng shuo ta youlan guo Changcheng.
   c′. Wang Xiaosheng shuo ø youlan guo Changcheng.
   'Mr Wang$_2$ says that he$_1$ visited the Great Wall.'

Both null and lexical pronouns are good in this context with the interpretation indicated, although the lexical pronoun is slightly preferred in this case by my informants. The examples show that when sentences are considered in and out of context they have different possibilities for coreference. Evidently, the null context is not neutral pragmatically: Rather, it is a context that maximizes internal coreference. The pressure for internal interpretation is indeed so strong that it overrides the principle of obviation. Given the artificiality of sentences in a null context and the fact that most pragmatic principles involve the use of language in context, this is not surprising.

Discourse Organization

I now point out a lexical pronoun use that is unlike those mentioned earlier. The case arises in discourse, where the organization of information is an important factor. Lexical pronouns are used in discourse to signal a new sub-unit or shift, essentially as discourse markers. This use brings the factor of discourse organization into the domain of pronoun choice. Lexical pronouns may be used for rather subtle shifts in point of view or subject, and to indicate a major discourse unit such as a paragraph.

Discourses of all kinds are organized hierarchically into units of different sizes. There are many devices that signal and accompany the beginning of a new discourse unit: particular words and phrases; changes of point of view, including place and time; temporal or typographical pauses. Li and Thompson (1979) argued convincingly that lexical pronouns also function as cues to discourse organization in Chinese. They gave a number of examples in which a lexical pronoun begins a new unit; (18) is one of their examples. (18) presents four sentences with the same topic, a young man named Wang-Mian. In the first three Wang-Mian is introduced and we are given some information about him; the fourth has an adverb and a pronoun that refers to Wang-Mian.

(18) (1) Zhe Wang-Mian tianxing congming.
'This Wang-Mian₁ was gifted.'
(2) ø nianji bu man ershi-sui.
(His₁) age didn't exceed 20 years.
(3) ø jiu ba na tianwen, dili, jingshi shang de da xuewen wu yi bu guantong.
(He₁) had already mastered astronomy, geography, and classics.
(4) Dan ta xingqing bu tong.
However he₁ had an unusual personality.'

At (4) a shift in point of view is signaled by the lexical pronoun. If this sentence simply continued the topic chain with a null pronoun, it would not be perceived as indicating a shift. The shift in this case is a small one, below the paragraph level. (19) exemplifies a different case (Li & Thompson, 1979).

(19) (1) Bai Xiansheng zai keting-li deng Lisi. (2) ø dai yanjing,
'Mr. Bai₁ waited for Lisi₂ in the livingroom. (He₁) was wearing glasses

zai nar kan baozhi. (3) ø haoxiang you dian bu naifan. (4) Ta shuo:
and reading a newspaper there. (He₁) seemed a little impatient. He₁
said:'

(4) shifts from background to foreground, again, with a lexical pronoun. It
might be indicated in a written text with a new paragraph. Similar discourse
uses of lexical pronouns in Polish are discussed in Flashner (1987).[11]

The same type of discourse shift appears in English. But we would expect
the marked forms to be full NPs, because lexical NPs are preempted for
neutral reference in the English system. In fact, examples of such cases are
given in a recent discussion of anaphora. Fox (1987) examined a number
of science fiction and mystery narratives and noted that "under certain
conditions full NPs are used where pronouns would have been possible.
. . . The key to this use of full NPs in the narrative texts lies in the structural
organization being displayed by the writer" (p. 67). Her account is very
close to the one sketched here. Fox proposed that "many full NPs in
narratives . . . function to signal the hierarchical structure of the text: in other
words . . . to demarcate new narrative units" (p. 168).

These examples show a use of coreference forms that is unlike those
discussed earlier. I call it the *distinguishing* use. The marked pronoun
complements the topic chain, in which the unmarked form signals continuity.
This use is closer to the obviative than the focal because it does not involve
a semantic scopal structure that partitions information. Distinguishing
pronouns may affect the way information is organized in representations of
discourse structure, a topic beyond the scope of this discussion.

In this exploratory discussion I have suggested that languages have a
pragmatic principle of obviation that contrasts the interpretation of marked
and unmarked pronoun forms. There are a number of different pronoun
interpretations. Unmarked coreference is neutral and may be literally as well
as metaphorically proximate; marked coreference may be obviative, marked,
or focal (*marked* is a complex category that includes several interpretations).
I have tentatively identified three patterns; there may be others. Languages
such as Algonquian and Eskimo have a contrast between proximate and
obviative; the English and Spanish systems contrast neutral and focal
obviation; the Chinese system contrasts neutral and marked obviation. The
fact that focus interacts with pronoun form in English and Spanish strongly
determines the possible interpretations. English does not distinguish between
the proximate and the nonproximate with unstressed and stressed pronoun
forms; it may do so in other ways. The relation between focus and obviation
remains to be sorted out. In some languages focus is marked with a distinct
morpheme rather than with stress. For them, the system of focus is orthogonal

---

[11]Flashner distinguished reference to *continuous themes*, marked by null pronouns, and
interrupted themes, which are more fully marked.

to that of obviation; the cases include languages with obviation morphemes (T. Woodbury, personal communication, 1992).

The distinguishing type of coreference does not necessarily involve contrasting pronoun forms, as we have seen. It is conveyed by full NPs in English, and marked pronouns in Chinese (full NPs may also be used for this purpose). There are other pronoun uses besides the ones discussed here. Pronouns may convey logophoric as well as coreference information (Sells, 1987). There is another pronoun use, the *distinctive*, which conveys weak emphasis that is neither contrastive nor focal (Rigau, 1986).[12]

At this point we do not know how many terms should be recognized in an idealized coreference space. The category of marked coreference in Chinese needs investigation. The notion of focus is complex; its components (e.g., contrast, strong emphasis, focus) should be differentiated in analysis, perhaps along the lines suggested in Krifka (1991).

The differences between systems discussed here suggest that the form of a marked pronoun may affect its possible interpretations. The marked pronoun in English is stressed and always conveys focal coreference. The marked pronoun in Chinese, which is lexical, may indicate several types of marked coreference. Extrapolating, the facts suggest that stressed pronouns are unlikely to have multiple functions. Perhaps the very salience of the strong stress on a pronoun limits its flexibility: As a strong cue, stress is unlikely to convey notions that differ greatly. We would then expect to find, across languages, that marked pronouns without strong stress may be available for several uses, whereas pronouns with strong stress are more limited.

ACQUISITION

Wilcoxon's Experimental Study

I now relate some of these ideas to a recent experimental study of the acquisition of syntax in Mandarin Chinese. The experiments were conceived and carried out by Wilcoxon. Wilcoxon was interested in whether young speakers of Chinese know the principles of backwards coreference; and, if they do, whether they know that lexical pronouns have an exceptional domain in backwards coreference (as discussed earlier). The results indicated relatively late learning of the exceptional restrictions, as predicted following C. Chomsky (1969). The study focused on syntax, not pragmatics, but some of the results are relevant to this discussion; I summarize them very briefly here. The experiments are reported in Wilcoxon (1991a, 1991b, in preparation).

---

[12]Distinctive pronouns involve the use of a contrast set, like focal pronouns. The notion of a distinctive pronoun is due to Ronat (1979).

Wilcoxon's study focused on sentences with temporal clauses in which lexical and null pronouns precede NPs. Temporal clauses precede the main clause in Chinese, so that the order of these sentences is basic rather than shifted. (20) illustrates:

(20) a. [[ta tiao guo zhu hou], niu da-le xiaoji]
          he jump GUO pig after, cow hit LE chicken
          'After he$_4$ jumps over the pig$_1$, the cow$_2$ hits the chicken$_3$.'
      b. [[ø tiao guo zhu hou], niu da-le xiaoji]
          ø jump GUO pig after, cow hit LE chicken
          'After he$_{2,3,4}$ jumps over the pig$_1$, the cow$_2$ hits the chicken$_3$.'

The subscripts indicate the coreference interpretations that are available in the adult grammar. In these structures the possibilities are different for lexical and null anaphora. A lexical pronoun can be coreferential only with an external NP, as in (20a), whereas a null pronoun may corefer with an NP in the main clause, as in (20b).

These and other stimuli were presented in a sequence of 10 sentences that formed a simple narrative. The same characters recurred, ensuring that presuppositions about existence were satisfied. The narrative had no internal structure: The particular actions and actors were not determined by story consideration at either the lexical or the global level. The subjects were children aged 3;6 to 7;2 years, and 24 adults. The stimuli were presented in an act-out task and a grammatical judgment task.

The results gave clear answers to the two experimental questions. The children were definitely aware that backwards coreference is possible in Mandarin Chinese: Even the youngest children tended to given an NP in the main clause as referent for a pronoun. However, many children allowed backwards coreference for both lexical and null pronouns. Their responses showed that they were unaware of the restriction on lexical pronouns in structures like (20a). Grammatical responses increased with age, but only the oldest children showed adult knowledge of the restrictions. From these results Wilcoxon was able to conclude that even the young children knew the basic Principle B of the Binding Theory, including the possibility for backwards coreference. This conclusion accords with that of other researchers (e.g., Chien, Lust, Chiang, & Eisele, 1991; Crain & McKee, 1985; Grimshaw & Rosen, 1990; Lust, Eisele, & Mazuka, 1992).[13] Wilcoxon also

---

[13]Chien et al. (1991) studied English and Chinese sentences with pronouns; their subjects included adults and children. Their work is relevant but not directly comparable to this. It is interesting, however, that the acquisition patterns they observed are consistent with the claims of this chapter. Pragmatic differentiation between null and lexical pronouns did not appear until the grammatical restriction was established on backwards coreference with lexical pronouns.

concluded that the younger children did not know the exceptional Chinese restrictions on lexical pronouns in backwards anaphora structures.

The adult responses consistently differentiated lexical and null pronouns. Adults always took lexical pronouns as coreferential with an NP in the preceding sentence, observing the restrictions noted earlier. They gave external interpretations of lexical pronouns in structures like (20a). These responses were grammatically based, because internal reference was blocked.

The adult responses to null pronouns were internal, in contrast to the other responses: The null pronouns were always interpreted as coreferential with an NP in the main clause. Now internal coreferents were not grammatically required for the null pronouns. Yet the adults chose them 100% of the time. Evidently, pragmatic as well as grammatical considerations were involved. The obviation principle straightforwardly explains the adult responses to sentences with null pronouns. Null pronouns are unmarked terms in the Chinese system. Adults gave the neutral interpretation of such pronouns, with internal referents that were proximate both literally and metaphorically. Internal referents were always appropriate in the context of the experiment.

Thus the adult responses to the two types of pronouns involved entirely different types of principles. Responses to lexical pronouns honored the restriction on backwards anaphora; responses to null pronouns were determined by the obviation principle.

The children, unlike the adults, chose internal and external referents for both pronouns. The responses of the children were understandable from the point of view of noncoreference—the children did not know the restriction on lexical pronouns in backwards anaphora. However, the responses are surprising from the point of view of coreference because they had no relation to the adult patterns. There are two possible explanations for the child patterns. One is simply that the children did not know the principle of obviation. If this is correct they would be expected to treat null and lexical pronouns in the same way. Another possibility is that, not knowing the relevant grammatical rules for noncoreference, the children were not in a position to use the principle of obviation. Knowledge of grammatical rules is a prerequisite to the realization of pragmatic principles. Grammatical rules are prior because they delimit the pragmatic choices that are available in a given structure. The Chinese speaker, therefore, needs to know the restrictions on coreference in the test structures in order to realize the principle of obviation. It seems likely that the children did not know the principle of obviation. If they had been trying to apply the principle we would expect to find distinct responses to the null and lexical pronouns.[14]

Children of this age are just learning how to deal with reference, especially in discourse. They may not have developed the concepts necessary for the

---

[14]As L. Baker pointed out (personal communication, 1992), the difficulties arise in learning that certain interpretations are impossible.

obviation principle. The Chinese version is relatively complex and subtle, which might contribute to relatively late learning.

COREFERENCE PRINCIPLES
AND LANGUAGE ACQUISITION

I now discuss briefly the acquisition of the pragmatic principles of coreference discussed in this chapter. There is a general question of learnability, and more specific questions about these particular principles. Children must learn the rules of Chinese grammar that pertain to noncoreference and to coreference. They must learn the general types of inference used in communication. They must also learn the concepts involved in obviation, focus obviation, and the other pronoun uses.

The logic of acquisition requires that rules and principles be learnable from positive evidence. The pragmatic principles discussed earlier are not problematic for learnability, because they associate particular forms with interpretations. The learner receives positive evidence as the principles are exemplified. The principle of obviation, for instance, associates linguistic forms with particular referents in a particular interpretation. When a given form is used, its interpretation is available in the extralinguistic context, often through overt activity; this is the logic of the toy-moving task. In fact, if children fail to follow established patterns for making coreference they are likely to receive direct evidence of error in the form of feedback (R. Meier, personal communication, 1992). Each form is paired with a different, nonoverlapping interpretation. As children learn how forms are paired with interpretations, they will discard the pairings that they do not encounter. As a result, they will learn that certain pairings of forms and interpretation cannot be made. Of course, to recognize the interpretation the learner must know the relevant concepts and inferences.

Conclusion

In this chapter I have discussed some questions concerning the pragmatic principles that underlie the use of pronouns. There is a good deal of work to be done before we understand these principles and their acquisition, as I have emphasized. Here as elsewhere it is clear that contextual factors must be included in both theoretical and empirical studies of language.

ACKNOWLEDGMENTS

I thank Hai Hua Pan and Meng Yeh for their judgments on Chinese, and Susan Wilcoxon for interesting discussions of her experiments. I would also like to thank Lee Baker and Richard Meier for very useful comments on substance and on the manuscript.

REFERENCES

Chen, P. (1983). *A discourse analysis of third person zero anaphora in Chinese*. Unpublished master's thesis, University of California at Los Angeles.

Chien, Y.-C., Lust, B., Chiang, C.-P., & Eisele, J. (1991). *Chinese and English children's interpretation of pronouns: A test of the linear procedence hypothesis*. Paper presented at the Third North American Conference on Chinese Linguistics, Columbus, Ohio.

Chomsky, C. (1969). *The acquisition of syntax in the child from 5 to 10*. Cambridge, MA: MIT Press.

Chomsky, N. (1981). *Lectures on government and binding*. Dordrecht: Foris.

Crain, S., & McKee, C. (1985). Acquisition of structural restrictions on anaphora. *Proceedings of the North American Linguistic Society, 16*, 94–110.

Crain, S., & Steedman, M. (1985). On not being led up the garden path. In D. Dowty, L. Karttunen, & A. Zwicky (Eds.), *Natural language parsing* (pp. 320–358). Cambridge: Cambridge University Press.

Cuoq, J. (1891). Grammaire de la langue Algonquine. *Proceedings and Transactions of the Royal Society of Canada, 1 Series*.

Dahl, O. (1985). *Tense and aspect systems*. Oxford: Basil Blackwell.

Evans, G. (1980). Pronouns. *Linguistic Inquiry, 11*, 327–362.

Finer, D. (1985). The syntax of switch reference. *Linguistic Inquiry, 16*, 35–56.

Flashner, V. (1987). The grammatical marking of theme in Polish narrative. In R. Tomlin (Ed.), *Coherence and grounding in discourse* (pp. 131–156). Amsterdam: Benjamins.

Fox, B. (1987). Anaphora in popular written English narratives. In R. Tomlin (Ed.), *Coherence and grounding in discourse* (pp. 156–174). Amsterdam: Benjamins.

Frantz, D. (1966). Person indexing in Blackfoot. *International Journal of American Linguistics, 32*, 50–58.

Grice, P. (1975). Logic and conversation. In P. Cole & J. Morgan (Eds.), *Syntax and semantics: Speech acts* (pp. 44–58). New York: Academic Press.

Grimshaw, J., & Rosen, S. (1990). Knowledge and obedience: The developmental status of the Binding Theory. *Linguistic Theory, 21*, 187–222.

Hale, K. (1978). *Obviation in modern Irish*. Unpublished manuscript.

Huang, C.-T. J. (1982). *Logical relations in Chinese and the theory of grammar*. Unpublished doctoral dissertation, MIT, Cambridge, MA.

Huang, C.-T. J. (1984). On the distribution and reference of empty pronouns. *Linguistic Inquiry, 15*, 531–574.

Huang, Y. (1991). A neo-Gricean pragmatic theory of anaphora. *Journal of Linguistics, 27*, 301–335.

Jacobsen, W. (1967). Switch-reference in Hokan-Coahuiltecan. In D. Hymes & W. Biddle (Eds.), *Studies in Southwestern ethnolinguistics* (pp. 238–263). The Hague: Mouton.

Jakobson, R. (1971). Shifters, verbal categories, and the Russian verb. *Selected Writings* (Vol. 2, pp. 130–147). The Hague: Mouton. (Original work published in 1957)

Krifka, M. (1991). A compositional semantics for multiple focus constructions. *Current issues in natural language processing*. Austin: University of Texas, Center for Cognitive Science.

Larson, R., & Lujan, M. (1992). *Focused pronouns*. Unpublished manuscript.

Levinson, S. (1991). Pragmatic reduction of the Binding Conditions revisited. *Journal of Linguistics, 27*, 107–161.

Li, C., & Thompson, S. (1976). Subject and topic: A new typology. In C. Li (Ed.), *Subject and topic* (pp. 457–490). New York: Academic Press.

Li, C., & Thompson, S. (1979). Third person pronouns and zero-anaphora in Chinese discourse. In T. Givon (Ed.), *Syntax & semantics: Vol. 12. Discourse and syntax* (pp. 311–334). New York: Academic Press.

Li, C., & Thompson, S. (1981). *Mandarin Chinese: A functional reference grammar.* Berkeley, CA: University of California Press.

Lujan, M. (1985). Binding properties of overt pronouns in null pronominal languages. In W. Eilford, P. Kroeber, & K. Peterson (Eds.), *Proceedings of the Chicago Linguistic Society, 21,* 424–438.

Lust, B., Eisele, J., & Mazuka, R. (1992). The Binding Theory module: Evidence from first language acquisition for Principle C. *Language, 68,* 333–358.

Pu, M. M. (1989). Topic continuity in written Mandarin discourse. In K. Hall, M. Meacham, & R. Shapiro (Eds.), *Proceedings of the Berkeley Linguistic Society, 15,* 256–267.

Rigau, G. (1986). Some remarks on the nature of strong pronouns in null-subject languages. In I. Bordelois, H. Contreras, & K. Zagona (Eds.), *Generative studies in Spanish syntax* (pp. 143–164). Dordrecht: Foris.

Ronat, M. (1979). Pronoms, topiques et distinctifs [Topical and distinctive pronouns]. *Langue Française, 44,* 106–128.

Sells, P. (1987). Aspects of logophoricity. *Linguistic Inquiry, 18,* 445–480.

Smith, C. (1991). *The parameter of aspect.* Dordrecht: Kluwer.

Tsao, F. (1977). *A functional study of topic in Chinese: The first step toward discourse analysis.* Unpublished doctoral dissertation, USC, Los Angeles, California.

Voegelin, C. F. (1946). Delaware: An Eastern Algonquian language. In C. Osgood (Ed.), *Linguistic structures of native America* (pp. 255–272). Viking Publications in Anthropology, No. 6, New York.

Voegelin, C. F., & Voegelin, F. M. (1975). Hopi (-qa). *International Journal of American Linguistics, 41,* 381–398.

Wilcoxon, S. (1991a). *The acquisition of interpretation patterns for subject pronouns in Mandarin.* Unpublished doctoral dissertation, University of Texas, Austin.

Wilcoxon, S. (1991b). *Development of discourse and syntactic constraints on anaphora in Mandarin.* Paper presented at the Conference on Language Development, Boston.

Wilcoxon, S. (in preparation). *The development of constraints on subject anaphora in Mandarin Chinese.*

Wolfart, H. C. (1973). *Plains Cree: A grammatical study.* Transactions of the American Philosophical Society, Philadelphia.

Yang, D. W. (1983). *The extended binding theory of anaphors.* Paper presented at GLOW, University of York.

Zhang, S. (1988). Argument drop and pro. *Proceedings of the West Coast Linguistic Society, 7,* 363–374.

PART FOUR

WH- AND QUANTIFIER SCOPE

CHAPTER SIXTEEN

Lexical Links in the WH-Chain

Thomas Roeper
University of Massachusetts at Amherst

Jill de Villiers
Smith College

A great deal of modern work in linguistic theory has been guided by the intuition that acquisition succeeds through an interaction of lexical knowledge and structural decisions.[1] Two pivotal elements exist in this process: (a) the direct application of principles of Universal Grammar to the input data that form the basis for a child's selection of a particular grammar, and (b) the determination of verb subcategorization from lexical knowledge. We refine these two uncontroversial observations in an exact way that allows us to account for the special stages in the acquisition of long-distance movement.

We argue that the child takes a circuitous path to long-distance movement in order to avoid potentially irreversible lexical decisions. If a set of decisions are irreversible, then we cannot guarantee that a child will fix the correct particular grammar unless he or she is in a position to make final lexical decisions with certainty. The application of UG takes two forms:

1. The definition of structures.
2. The setting of parameters.

It is sometimes assumed that children's grammars cannot exhibit structures not found in adult grammars (of course we have no guarantee that possible adult grammars happen to be represented on the planet or among the studied languages). Therefore the child can have no language-particular

---

[1]See Borer and Wexler (1987) and much subsequent work.

knowledge that does not represent a possible parametric choice. This perspective leaves no room for representations that are incomplete and that therefore must constitute grammars not found among adult languages, although they are defined by UG and in an important sense constitute subgrammars of the form discussed by Lebeaux (1988).

We argue that in order to structure the primary data that form the basis of parametric decisions, the child must apply structure-building principles of UG directly to the input. Our argument takes the following schematic form:

1. Input about subcategorization is ambiguous.
2. WH-movement requires proper government of intermediate traces via subcategorization.
3. German and English acquisition data reveal extraction from nonsubcategorized cases.
4. Our new proposal is that thematic government is sufficient to optionally allow a trace and therefore successive cyclicity.

The central claim addressed here is that subcategorization is likely to be difficult to acquire, given the myriad factors involved. We therefore propose a method by which the child might permit long-distance movement in questions before subcategorization gets fixed. We argue that the early grammar has a weaker form of government, *thematic government*, that is sufficient to license a trace but incapable of representing idiomatic information associated with subcategorization.

THE ACQUISITION OF LONG-DISTANCE MOVEMENT

Let us begin, then, by summarizing the results of our work on long-distance WH-movement. We began with a set of fundamental questions: At what stage do children allow long-distance extraction in questions? Do they distinguish between adjuncts and arguments? Do they respect conditions on extraction from WH-islands? In our first set of studies (de Villiers, Roeper, & Vainikka, 1990) we explored these questions with preschool children learning English; research has now been extended to French, German, Italian, Spanish, Greek, and Japanese.[2]

The heart of modern syntax has been the study of constraints on WH-extraction. Long-distance (LD) extraction requires the presence of a functional category, the Complementizer Phrase (CP), and the formation of chains of empty categories. An example is:

[2] This international research has received significant support from the Max Planck Gesellschaft, Netherlands ZWO, NIAS, NIH Training Grant to H. Seymour, and the Psycholinguistics Training grant (C. Clifton), and from individuals doing work in their native countries.

(1) Who did you say CP[*t* IP[you saw CP[*t* IP[Bill hit *t*]]]]?

Naturalistic data assembled by M. Takahashi showed that children as young as 3 exhibit LD rules, as in (2):

(2) Adam : What chu think.this gonna taste like?

But the naturalistic data do not allow us to ask a host of more refined questions about constraints and parameters. In particular, when do children know certain barriers to WH-movement (Chomsky, 1986)? Are they sensitive to the distinction between adjunct WH-questions (*why, how, when, where*) and argument WH-questions (*who, what*) so crucial to current theory concerning the Empty Category Principle (or ECP, Rizzi, 1990)? Therefore we developed a series of experiments to explore them. The technique involved presenting preschool children with a story that contained plausible answers for all potential interpretations (even disallowed ones) of a WH-question that followed the story, so the child could always find a grammatical interpretation for a question. For example, children freely give LD interpretations, as do adults, if no WH-word is in the lower clause CP:

(3) How$_i$ did she say [t_i to bake a cake t_i]? (=how-bake [with a spoon])

But they virtually never allow an adjunct to move over an argument WH-word:

(4) How did she say what to bake? (=how-say,*how-bake)
How$_i$ did she say t_i [what [to bake *t_i]]?

They will, however, freely allow an argument to move over an adjunct:

(5) What$_i$ did she know how to bake t_i?

The results for a group of 25 children aged 3;7 to 6;11 on all argument/adjunct[3] contrasts are summarized in Table 16.1, and an example of a story is

---

[3]One might ask why we find that arguments block arguments. In Rizzi's account, in fact, there should be no block because the pronominal binding relation of WH-arguments and their traces is independent of medial CPs. However, the intuitional data are not very clear. Adults also find argument-over-argument to be often of lower acceptability. The double object may add to this complexity. Consider this contrast:

(i) a. What did you wonder whether she bought?
   b. *What did you wonder who Bill gave?

We believe an extension of Rizzi's intuition, that an intervening category of the same type has a blocking effect, should be pursued here. This perspective, moreover, is compatible with Chomsky's minimalist proposals about local WH-movement.

TABLE 16.1
Preschool Children's Long Distance Interpretations of Questions

Percentages refer to answers interpreting the wh-question with that site.

Argument	0 medial
1. Who did the boy ask _____ to call _____ ?	
68%	32%
Adjunct	0 medial
2. When did the boy say _____ he hurt himself _____ ?	
50%	44%
Argument	Adjunct medial
3. Who did the boy ask _____ how to help _____ ?	
63%	30%
Adjunct	Argument medial
4. How did the girl ask _____ who to paint _____ ?	
23%	8%
Argument	Argument medial
5. Who did the girl ask _____ what to feed _____ ?	
70%	2%
Adjunct	Adjunct medial
6. When did the clown say _____ how he caught the ball _____ ?	
48%	6%

Note. From De Villiers, Roeper, and Vainikka (1990).

in Fig. 16.1.[4] To understand the nature of the constraint more precisely, we presented another group of children with questions in which the second question word was in final rather than in medial position:

(6) How did the girl decide [$_{CP}$to wear what]?

In this sentence the second WH-word is in situ and so does not occupy the medial SPEC of COMP, leaving the adjunct free to move long distance. Notice also that the question becomes one involving what we call a *bound variable reading*, in which the two question words are both answered: *She decided to wear this in this manner and that in that manner.* When the question word is in medial position, the bound variable reading is not usual for English speakers:

(7) How did she decide what to wear?

(7) can be answered, for instance, with *by looking in a magazine.* The children in the follow-up study were 21 children in the same age range,

---

[4]Extensive adult data on the same stories and questions is available in work by Li (1992) and confirms linguistic intuitions about English.

This boy loved to climb tree in the forest.

One day he slipped and fell to the ground. He picked himself up and went home.

That night when he had a bath he found a big bruise on his arm and he said to his Dad, "I must have hurt myself when I fell this afternoon". When did the boy say he hurt himself?

FIG. 16.1.

and they showed a clear distinction between their interpretations for the medial and final WH sentences. 36% of the time they answered as if the adjunct's trace were in the lower clause in (6), compared to only 5% for (7). Hence it is quite clear that it is the position of the WH-word in the lower SPEC of COMP that results in a barrier to movement.

Our central conclusions from this work are these:

1. By 4 years of age children make the distinction between adjuncts and arguments in movement, suggesting that they have some version of the ECP by this age.
2. Barriers to movement of the adjunct are introduced by the presence of a WH-complementizer in the SPEC of COMP.
3. The presence of a WH-word in situ in the lower clause does not create a barrier to movement from that clause.

We have shared our materials and methodology so that with the help of colleagues and students the basic results have been replicated in six different languages in experiments involving at least 150 children (see Table 16.2 for a summary of these results). In most of these cases, the children's behavior is in conformity with adult judgments of barriers in those languages, with a couple of exceptions. For instance, the adult grammar of German forbids extraction from a WH-island even for the case of the argument, unlike in English[5] (Bayer, 1992):

(8) *Wem hat er gefragt, wie er helfen soll?
     'Who$_i$ did he ask t$_i$ how to help t$_i$?'

Extraction in such a case entails a violation of Subjacency but not of the ECP (Rizzi, 1990). One explanation invoked for the contrast is that adult German has weaker lexical government than English, so that transitive verbs exercise less control in German over the argument trace. But German children find the extraction acceptable, as do English, French, Greek, and Spanish children of the same age. Children's grammars in all three languages permit extraction of an argument question over an adjunct medial (the numbers in the gaps refer to the percentages of children's choices of that reading):

---

[5]However, in English all extractions across adjuncts may not be equal. Compare the long distance interpretations of:

(i) a. Who did he ask how to help?
     b. Who did he ask when to help?

One indication that not all adjuncts are the same is the existence of nominalizations. We find the expression *know-how*, but no one says *know-when*. The existence of the first form suggests that *how* could be incorporated into the verb, making extraction easier.

TABLE 16.2
ECP Effects in Six Languages

	t_1	t_2
1. Arg-0 (untensed)		
Who did the boy ask t_1 to call t_2?		
English[1]	68	32
Black English[2]	46	46
French[3]	67	26
German[4]	49	48
Greek[5]	45	41
Spanish[6]	—	—
2. Adj-0 (untensed)		
How did the father say t_1 to cook t_2 the pie?		
English[7]	23	77
Black English	04	78
French	21	63
German	9	66
Greek	7	76
Spanish	23	77
3. Arg-comp (tensed)		
Who did the girl ask t_1 if she could call t_2?		
English[7]	52	48
Black English	—	—
French	53	33
German	75	16
Greek	—	—
Spanish	67	33
4. Arg-comp (tensed; subject extraction)		
Who t_1 said that t_2 must come?		
English	—	—
Black English	—	—
French	—	—
German		
Greek	10	69
Spanish	54	46
5. Adj-comp (tensed)		
How did the boy say t_1 that his balloon got popped t_2?		
English	15	85
Black English	—	—
French	27	36
German	28	40
Greek	17	83
Spanish	54	46

(Continued)

TABLE 16.2
(Continued)

6. Arg-adj (both tensed and untensed)
Who did the boy ask t_1 how to help t_2?

	t_1	med	t_2
English	63	04	32
Black English	58	01	30
French	56	17	21
German	44	26	30
Greek	44	27	20
Spanish	50	37	13

7. Adj-arg
How did the boy ask t_1 who to dress t_2?

		med	
English	23	68	08
Black English	40	41	09
French	11	55	02
German	06	92	02
Greek	07	59	19
Spanish	34	64	03

8. Adj-adj
When did the boy say t_1 how he fixed t_2 the bike?

		med	
English	48	40	06
Black English	30	50	08
French	21	26	09
German	07	60	13
Greek	19	43	18
Spanish	42	27	03

9. Arg-Arg
Who did the boy ask t_1 what to bring t_2?

		med	
English	70	28	02
Black English	61	36	00
French	—		—
German	54	46	00
Greek	26	49	14
Spanish	—		—

[1] de Villiers, Roeper, and Vainikka, 1990.
[2] Seymour, Bland, Champion, de Villiers, and Roeper, 1991.
[3] Weissenborn, Roeper, and de Villiers, 1991.
[4] Weissenborn, Roeper, and de Villiers, 1991.
[5] Leftheris, 1991. There is no infinitival in M.G.: These have the complementizer "na".
[6] Perez, 1991.
[7] de Villiers and Roeper, unpublished.

(9) *Argument—adjunct*
English: Who did the boy ask $(63)_{t_1}$ how to help $(30)_{t_2}$?
French: A qui le canard demande $(56)_{t_1}$ comment il peut donner un coup de main $(21)_{t_2}$?
'who does the duck ask how he can help?'
German: Wen fragt Bibo $(44)_{t_1}$, wie er malen soll $(30)_{t_2}$?
'who does Bibo ask how he should paint?'

The fact that they all block extraction of adjuncts is powerful evidence for the universality of the adjunct/argument distinction in early grammar. How German children eventually block argument extraction cries out for an explanation.

Does this evidence imply that the children's grammars contain appropriate clause attachment that permits LD movement? There are anomalies in English children's responses that suggest strongly that their grammars are not yet entirely like our own. The clearest evidence of a deviation comes from their responses to questions such as:

(10) How did Big Bird ask who to help?

A frequent answer is *Kermit*, that is, the answer to the medial question *who*. Children are particularly prone to answer medial arguments, but they also frequently answer medial adjuncts:

(11) When did Kermit say where he went?

(11), for instance, is answered with *to the store*. The incidence of these answers is shown in Table 16.3, and the result is replicated in all six languages to about the same degree (see Table 16.2). Once again, we seem to have evidence of a default option in children's grammars. But might this error in

TABLE 16.3
Incidence of Answering the Medial Question Word in COMP

Structures:	Arg-Arg	Arg-Adj	Adj-Arg	Adj-Adj
Subjects:				
Preschoolers	28%	4%	68%	40%
3rd grade	7.5%	0%	5%	5%
Adults	0%	0%	0%	0%

How did the boy say _____ he hurt himself _____ ?
33.3%   37.7%
How did the boy say _____ how he hurt himself _____ ?
34.1%   38.6%

fact be a performance difficulty, such as a parsing failure? It has been suggested several times to us that perhaps our questions are too complex, so that the children adopt some nongrammatical strategy such as answering the last question they hear, ignoring the matrix clause altogether. Several pieces of evidence convince us otherwise. First, the phenomenon was reported in production, using elicited production techniques (Thornton, 1991). There, children were observed to say such things as:

(12) What do you think what pigs say?

Less frequently, there were instances where the two WH-questions differed:

(13) What do you think which Smurf really has roller skates?
(14) Which animal do you think what really says, "Woof woof"?

Production evidence thus supports the idea that this is an option generated by the child's grammar at this stage, though later we discuss the differences between Thornton's account and our own.

Second, we have data from two different studies that tested the limits on the medial answer response. In the first, we asked whether children would ever answer the medial in *yes-no* questions with an embedded WH-question. So children were presented with short stories followed by a question such as:

(15) Did Mickey tell Minnie what he bought?

Only 1 child out of 20 answered a medial question under these conditions. Thus it seems clear that the medial question requires a WH-word at the front of the sentence, just as in the case of partial movement in German, detailed later. It is not the case that the child answers the last question word heard, and indeed, evidence from natural dialogues bears this out.

In the second study that bears on the issue, children received stories followed by questions containing relative clauses with the complementizer *who*, so that they superficially resembled the kinds of embedded questions used before. For instance, one such sentence was:

(16) How did the dog climb up who barked?

Notice that the extraposed relative with *who* occupies the same sentence position as the embedded question in:

(17) How did Kermit ask who barked?

TABLE 16.4
Adjunct Extraction from Relative Clauses

Subject relatives
13. How did the boy who sneezed _____ drink the milk _____ ?

4 yr olds	0%	0%	94%**
3 yr olds	0%	0%	58%

Subject relative extraposed
14. When did the woman sleep _____ who painted the picture _____?

4 yr olds	92%	0%	2%
3 yr olds	47%	0%	10.5%

Object relative
15. How did the woman help the man _____ who won the race _____ ?

4 yr olds	91.5%	0%	0%
3 yr olds	61%	0%	0%

*Percentages beneath the relative pronoun represent answers as if that were a question.
**The other reponses were answers to some other question, unrelated to the one asked (e.g., Where did they buy the milk?)

If children just answer the last question word they hear, they should answer the relative complementizer, but our evidence shows that they never do (see Table 16.4). In fact, they show a striking obedience to the barrierhood of relative clauses, virtually never allowing the adjunct question to connect inside the relative clause.

THE PROBLEM OF SUBCATEGORIZATION

We return now to the logical question of what children can decide in terms of what information they receive. The notion of subcategorization requires significant subdivisions, we argue, in order to be acquired and in order to fit the facts of acquisition that we and others have gathered.

Subcategorization has been regarded as a single phenomenon with four, in principle disparate, elements:

1. Thematic projection (e.g., theme).
2. Case projection (e.g., accusative).
3. Structural attachment site (e.g., sister NP or PP).
4. Idiosyncratic selectional character (e.g., +/− *that*).

It is instantly apparent that these features belong to different modules and bear different relations to input evidence. We believe that the acquisition of particular subcategorization frames is a very complex phenomenon that requires extensive exposure to language and has complex and sophisticated syntactic prerequisites. In this sense the debate over semantic and syntactic bootstrapping completely understates the problem.[6]

Pesetsky (1982), modifying Grimshaw (1979), argued that there is a link between constituent-selection (c-selection) and semantic-selection (s-selection).[7] These correlations no doubt facilitate acquisition: Minimally, there is an unmarked relation between c-selection and s-selection, what is called Canonical Structural Realization. For example, a verb that s-selects for a question usually takes an S' or an NP as its complement. Where the link is imperfect, Pesetsky argued, the theory of case assignment can account for special features. Pesetsky and Grimshaw made the important point that one can invest an NP with clausal content, as in *John asked the time* [=what time it is], or we might add *John tried the fish* [=tried to eat the fish]. However, certain verbs do not permit NP realizations of their s-selections, as in *He wondered the time*. Thus, there is not a perfect correlation between semantic content and syntactic complementation; for example, a proposition can be expressed as an NP or as a full clause. We take this as evidence that the projection of thematic information does not have an invariant stipulated link to a specific syntactic expression in UG.

We would argue, further, that these correlations exist at the VP level and do not capture the lexical idiosyncracies that are being projected at the V level. Hence the child could project the clausal content onto the typical form, called Canonical Structural Realization, without linking it to the specific verb in question, although the content is compatible with the verb's general meaning. Thus a child may say:

(18) I'm thinking why it is broken.

The notion of an indirect question is linked to a WH-tensed complement, which is compatible with a mental verb like *think* but not in fact projected by it in English. Such examples then demonstrate that the process of linking the verb and its subcategorization provides an intricate challenge on its own, which, not surprisingly, might not be executed in a single step.

It has long been known that children do not grasp subcategorization perfectly. Bowerman (1974, 1982) showed that there are overgeneralizations of the causative to a set of verbs that have a kind of causative potential but may fail to be subcategorized in that way.

Thus we find:

(19) a. Stay me here.
     b. That's what stays you up.

---

[6] The recent account in Chomsky and Lasnik (in press) redresses this simplicity somewhat but still understates the problem, in our estimation.

[7] See also Thornton (1991) for some discussion.

It is noteworthy that such overgeneralizations operate on plausible classes of verbs, but not on all verbs. There are no reported cases of causatives with verbs of being:

(20) a. *Seem me happy.
b. *Be me happy.
c. *Act me happy.

It is perfectly plausible, however, to imagine a causative with these verbs:

(21) d. Make me seem happy.
e. Make me be happy.
f. Make me act happy.

We conclude therefore that children have the ability to associate a thematic projection with a verb class. Although the topic is little discussed because it is clearest with older children, there are substantial mis-subcategorizations of complements at a syntactic level, though few radical mis-subcategorizations at the verb class level. There are languages in which *stay* is a causative, but, we suspect, few that allow *seem* or *be* to be causative.

Many other subcategorization overgeneralizations occur, precisely because there is idiosyncratic information associated with verbs. Consider these everyday statements in nursery school life:

(22) a. You are supposed to wear mittens.
b. Do you know how you are supposed to draw a picture?
c. We are supposed to all go out to play together.

However, the following version, though spoken by a 6-year-old, is ungrammatical:

(23) How do you suppose me to do that?

In other words, *suppose* takes an indirect object and an infinitive, but it can be used only in the passive for adults. The child who said (23) obviously acquired the set of possible thematic roles, but not the syntactic subcategorization restriction.

Consider these additional cases of incorrect subcategorization that we have collected:

(24) we were really high that it even had a telescope
I got a card how to get out of jail
did I seem that I was under the covers (2 times)

did you see this that I put it together
it's clear to hear (2 times)
listening what you think
listening what I whistled
I'm thinking why it's broken

Now the question that must be asked is how the thematic roles are linked to syntactic expressions. Recent work in the lexicon has led to a sharper dissociation than previously assumed. It has been extensively argued that implicit arguments are not associated with required projections (Roeper, 1987). In addition, Roeper (1993) argued that there is a class of implicit roles that prohibit syntactic expression but remain associated with a verb:

(25) a. *the push of John
     b. John needs a push (= push John/*John pushes)

Therefore it is natural to suppose that the child is capable of developing a representation within the thematic module that does not have a fixed association with phrase structure projections. In fact, Roeper (1992) argued that the last stage of acquisition occurs when a joint representation between the two modules is established. This has implications for the larger architecture of acquisition, but we extend it no further at the moment. One important consequence is that the Projection Principle, which requires uniform positions for thematic roles, is not observed under this formulation. As we show, this is particularly important for the analysis of German because it allows us to say that complements on either side of the verb can be thematically governed. In other words, in the extreme form, there may be no directionality of theta-assignment.

Attachment Ambiguity

To grasp the problem fully, let us consider some of the ambiguities that a child must resolve. Suppose a child hears, and must interpret, a sentence in which he or she can identify a verb and a complement; yet he cannot determine whether the complement is an adjunct or an argument. We argue that this is inevitable. The child must then project some representation. What would it be?

We argue that the default representation is a kind of adjunction.[8] An adjunct will be freely adjoinable without a lexically specific subcategorization. In a

---

[8] The theory of default projections has been argued for by Lebeaux (1988), Vainikka (1989), and Roeper and de Villiers (1992b). The essence of the idea is that UG provides a set of default analyses that a speaker has access to whenever parametric decisions are indeterminate or lexical decisions have not been made.

technical sense, however, this representation would violate UG because UG requires that a complement that bears a certain relation to a verb must be an argument and therefore must be adjoined directly under V':

(26) a. Adult representation:

John yelled [that Bill would be late]

b. Child's representation:

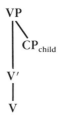

We propose specifically that it is at this VP level that verb-class characteristics are expressible but idiosyncratic features of verbs are inexpressible. Therefore it is natural for overgeneralizations to occur within a verb class. Lexical subcategorization occurs in a sister relation and reflects both arbitrary and systematic characteristics. The absence of subcategorization results in a failure of the proper government domain wherein lexical idiosyncracies can be expressed.

Systematic characteristics include:

(26) Mental verbs have propositional complements (*think, suppose, hope, intend*).

Idiosyncratic characteristics include:

(27) a. Some verbs allow *that*-deletion, others do not.
    1. a) John intended that we all should come.
       b) *John intended we all should come.
    2. a) John thought that we all should come.
       b) John thought we all should come.
  b. Some verbs undergo obligatory operations (e.g., passive):
    1. John was supposed to sing.
    2. *Someone supposed John to sing.

In other words, if the clause is attached at a higher level, then idiosyncracies cannot be expressed at that level. Each of the idiosyncratic features are, at times, not observed by children. They commonly delete obligatory *dass* in German or, in English, say such things as *How do you suppose me to do that?* We introduce this definition:

(28) *Thematic government:*
    a. There is thematic government by verb classes at the VP level.
    b. Thematic government is nondirectional.

We regard thematic government as a particular interpretation of Chomsky's (1992) and Webelhuth's (1989) suggestions that there is a notion of *broadly L-related* that applies at a higher V' level. It is present in all languages as a nondirectional form of government. In addition, some languages add directional subcategorization as a further requirement on complementation. This renders the nondirectional, higher percolation of thematic government invisible in those languages, although it is still present. The projection from individual verbs can be separated into two kinds: class information and idiosyncratic information. In a sense they are projected in different directions: The class information projects systematic complements and adjuncts upward to a higher V-node, whereas idiosyncratic information projects downward to subcategorized NPs and complements. The projection of adjuncts has always been positioned at a higher level than the projection of arguments. Therefore it is natural to propose that the verb-class information, which often includes adjuncts, percolates to a higher level. Thus we have the following alternatives:

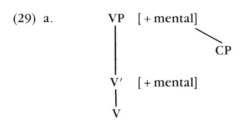

(29) a.
    VP [+ mental]
            CP
    V' [+ mental]
    V

b.
    VP [+ mental]
    V' [+ mental]
    V   CP
    [− WH] = > [− WH]

In (29a), the general verb-class feature [+mental] may percolate, whereas in (29b) the verb-specific feature [−WH] is projected onto a sister and therefore cannot percolate. This view is buttressed empirically by the fact that within verb classes there are overgeneralizations.

Now the child's provisional representation must undergo further modification in light of further information. It is often assumed that the adjunct/argument distinction is self-evident to the child. Chomsky and Lasnik (in press) pointed out that the child receives both lexical (contextual) information and syntactic complement information as a way to determine that a verb has both syntactic and semantic properties. However, this information does not settle the question: Is a complement an adjunct or an argument? This problem is very clear in the case of PPs:

(30) a. John put the plant [on the shelf]$_{argument}$.
  b. John found the plant [on the shelf]$_{adjunct}$.

In order to make the properties of *put* distinguishable from those of *find* one must develop a fairly complex learnability routine whereby one assumes first that all PPs are arguments and then reclassifies them as adjuncts if they are optional. The claim that such a process is obscure is bolstered by the fact that there is considerable debate over what is and what is not an argument for particular verbs (see Grimshaw, 1990).[9]

The same problem arises with sentential adjuncts, which, perhaps curiously, lack any distinguishing morphology or lexical clues. Infinitival sentences, for instance, are ambiguous:

(31) John helped Bill to be unselfish.
  (= Bill is unselfish)
  (= in order for John to be unselfish)

The same kind of ambiguity exists for tensed clauses in older forms of the language and, putatively, for child language:

(32) John yelled that Bill would be late.
  (= that he will be late [argument])
  (= so that he will be late [adjunct])

The child representation could fail to be an acceptable adult representation because it has the lexical content of a subcategorized clause (e.g., [that Bill would be late]), and the syntactic representation of an adjunct clause (e.g., [(so) that Bill would be late]). In general, the child may be able to impose

---

[9] See Randall (1992) for discussion.

an adjunctlike reading on an adult complement and arrive at an adequate interpretation of the sentence in context.

The syntactic representation of quotation is, likewise, not clearly determined by the fact that the proposition is introduced by a verb. The syntactic status of a quotation is still undecided in linguistic theory, but what is clear is that despite the connection of the proposition to the matrix verb, it is not a simple complement to the verb. It could be analyzed as involving an additional NP node, making it a barrier, or it could be analyzed as an adjunct, which would make it a barrier. There are significant syntactic differences between direct and indirect speech in the adult language. If quotation functions as an adjunct, then we have true complement semantics appearing in an adjunct position:

(33) John said, "Bill can do it."
John said that Bill can do it.

In fact we have evidence (to be presented) that children treat quotations as if they were complements with regard to pronoun subordination and extraction. This indicates that the child cannot instantly determine the syntax of quotation.

Prepositional phrases are also nonunique in their argument/adjunct status, as illustrated earlier. It is also evident that the meaning of these phrases can fail to be a clue. We find, for instance, that the following expressions have essentially the same meaning:

(34) a. observable by Bill
b. visible to Bill
c. *visible by Bill

Because -ible does not take argument structure, the agentlike role is picked up by the to-phrase, which is an adjunct. In essence, however, and certainly in the contexts available to the child, the meanings of to Bill and by Bill are not semantically distinguishable for the child. Moreover, the to-phrase is plausibly an argument in other cases like John spoke to me. Therefore the child cannot use other independent evidence that a to-phrase is always an adjunct.

In sum, the child cannot regard (a) syntactic position, (b) preposition choice, or (c) meaning as a perfect guide to adjunct or argument status. In fact, the decision requires several kinds of information (from several modules) and therefore fits our hypothesis that elements requiring joint representation will involve multiple acquisition steps.[10]

---

[10]Note, importantly, that we are referring to logical steps. This does not necessarily entail, though it may in some cases, the existence of temporal steps (i.e., separate discernible stages) in acquisition.

In order to make this discussion more precise, we need to differentiate two kinds of verbal selection and structural attachment. In effect there are three levels of attachment, each with a different relation to the verb. The precise points of attachment will be determined by the outcome of the current debate over whether all syntactic information should be in a binary format. But the primary distinctions are clear:

1. No relation to verb ⇒ S-level attachment.
2. Relation to verb class ⇒ VP-level attachment.
3. Relation to a particular verb ⇒ V'-level attachment.

This three-way distinction is meant to capture the fact that redundancy rules associate adjuncts with certain sets of verbs, but not with specific verbs.

Attachment and WH-Movement

What kinds of lexical decisions are at issue for LD movement? Lasnik and Saito (1992) pointed out that one can say (35a) but not (35b):

(35) a. Who thinks that John bought what?
     b. *Who thinks what John bought?

In order to prevent the appearance of (35b), which otherwise could have a meaning like (36), we must provide opposite specifications for the verbs *think* and *wonder*, and the child must realize them.

(36) Who wonders what John bought?

Moreover we must specify not only that *wonder* obligatorily selects a Q (WH-question)-morpheme, but also that *think* obligatorily selects a negative value, [–Q], for which the positive evidence is necessarily indirect.

We propose that lexical learning of this sort is irreversible and that because children must acquire negative information, they will project *a neutral default structure prior to the projection of a lexically specified structure*. The mistakes they make in subcategorization are seen as VP-level rather than V'-level attachments, that is, verb-class overgeneralizations.

Before the child decides on an irreversible lexical subcategorization, a number of points of language variation are involved and therefore must be subject to very specific kinds of acquisition. At least these kinds of selectional features are involved, some of them noted earlier: (a) + or – Q morpheme, (b) + or – tense dependency, (c) + or – pronoun dependency, (d) + or – scope equivalence (i.e., allowing NEG-hopping), (e) + or – factive.

Completely idiosyncratic features of complement subcategorization also exist: (a) choice of complementizer, (b) deletion of complementizer, and (c) choice of case assignment. For example:

(37) A. English and French allow tense subordination but German does not:
>
> English: Did you notice the coat that I *was* wearing?
> German: the coat that I *am* wearing

B. English, French, and German allow pronoun subordination but Navajo does not (M. Speas, personal communication, 1992).
>
> English: John said that he did it. (= John did it.)
> Navajo: John said that I did it. (= John did it.)

C. Spanish:
>
> a. Extraction is blocked if there is an *indicative* verb.
> b. Extraction is allowed if there is a *subjunctive* verb.

We demonstrate in the following that the available positive data are highly ambiguous with respect to many of these features. Therefore two consequences follow: (a) an unmarked form should exist, and (b) numerous steps may be involved in the acquisition of complete entries for lexical items.

Under the assumption of irreversibility, the child must await decisive contextual information before a decision is made about attachment. Consider the matter of tense dependency:

(38) Did you notice that my coat was brown?

By itself, the sentence is ambiguous: It could refer to a coat that was previously brown or is currently brown. But if this sentence is spoken in a context where one's coat is brown, then it could help the child realize that there exists tense dependency. Note that it is not easy to imagine an environment where neither tense dependency nor independence is true. The fact that my coat is now brown does not exclude the possibility that it was brown in the past as well. If the child must have a context where only the present is involved, but a past tense verb appears, in order to fix the tense dependency, and therefore the attachment site, then the right context may not be immediate.

Let us return to the central issue. Recall that in order for the child to correctly generate LD structures, the complement clauses must be subcategorized. Chomsky and Lasnik (in press) pointed out contrasts of the form in (39):

(39) a. Mary is too angry to hold a meeting. ⇒
>
> (ambiguous between: Mary holds meeting, we hold meeting)

b. What is Mary too angry to hold? ⇒
>
> (unambiguous: Mary holds meeting)

The disambiguation results from the fact that the PRO_{arb} ($\Rightarrow$ we) arises only in the adjunct context, whereas the controlled-PRO reading ($\Rightarrow$ *Mary*) arises under subcategorization, which in turn allows extraction. Therefore it would follow that a child should know automatically which verbs involve subcategorization when LD movement occurs, as it frequently does, in his or her environment.[11]

However, there is clear evidence from acquisition and from other languages that LD movement is more complex and may involve extraction from environments that are not clearly subcategorized. Therefore it no longer follows that traditional subcategorization is entailed by the presence of long-distance movement.

Long-Distance and Partial Movement

In German, Hungarian, and Romani there is a phenomenon (McDaniel, 1989; van Riemsdijk, 1983) involving LD movement from clauses that have been traditionally argued to be either extraposed or adjoined, but not subcategorized. We seek a more refined theory of subcategorization, forced upon us by the acquisition facts.

Here is the heart of the subcategorization problem. German governs to the left, being an SOV language, and therefore generates complements to the left at D-structure:

(40) a. Original position of complement:
         Er will Fussball zu spielen anfangen.
         he will football to play to start
     b. Extraposed complement:
         Er will Fussball anfangen, zu spielen.
         he will football to start to play
     c. Extraction from extraposed complement:
         Wie will er Fussball anfangen zu spielen *t*?
         how will he football start to play *t*
     d. Extraction without extraposition of complement:
         ?*Wie will er Fussball zu spielen anfangen?
         how will he football [to play *t*] start

Nevertheless extraction occurs after extraposition as in (40c) (and not before, or only marginally so, as in (40d)). Likewise, for tensed clauses, extraction occurs after extraposition:

---

[11]In fact, children have to acquire the control properties of particular constructions, and until they do, they extract freely from these environments (see de Villiers & Roeper, 1992).

(41) a. Wie hat er gesagt, dass er Fussball spielen will?
        'How did he say that he will play football?'

In fact, it is often argued that extraposition is obligatory for tensed clauses. How then do we account for the fact that extraction is excluded from the subcategorized position but allowed from an extraposed position? This has always been a prominent anomaly in the theory of movement.

Two facts correlate here[12] with the extraposition of the complement clause. *Dass*-deletion is prohibited:

(42) *Er glaubt er singen kann.
     *he believes he sing can
     Er glaubt dass er singen kann.

Partial movement occurs (McDaniel, 1989):

(43) Was$_i$ hat er gesagt wie$_i$ er Suppe isst?
     what did he say how he soup eats
     'How did he say he eats soup *t*?'

In (43), the question word *was* 'what' serves as a scope marker, and the real question word is the medial form *how*.[13] Alternatively, copying can occur, wherein the initial WH-word is repeated in the medial position:

(44) a. Wen hat er gesagt, wen er liebt?
        Was hat er gesagt, wen er liebt?
        who/what did he say who he loves
        'Who did he say he loves?'

How can we account for the fact that in German, both long-distance movement and partial movement are possible, whereas in English, only long-distance movement is possible? Suppose that under thematic government, either a trace or phonetic material is licensed, but under proper government, only a trace can appear. Our claim is that thematic government is distinct from full subcategorization (i.e., proper government). It is supported by a crucial fact: *Partial movement cannot occur where lexically specific syntactic subcategorization is present* (according to McDaniel, 1989). Where there is subcategori-

---

[12]An additional factor, which is difficult to incorporate in a precise way, is that LD extraction is slightly less acceptable for many speakers; it was specifically excluded in traditional grammars.

[13]W. Browne (personal communication, 1992) has provided us with evidence that *how* as well as *what* serves as a scope marker in several Slavic languages.

zation for a question (e.g., with the verb *fragen* 'wonder'), no partial movement can occur:

(45) *Wen hat er gefragt wen er einladen soll?
who did he wonder who he should invite

In English, partial movement is not allowed, just as it is disallowed for the subcategorized cases in German. We argue, in concert with Lasnik and Saito (1992), that English exhibits proper government of traces, but with a refinement. Proper government entails: (a) antecedent government, (b) thematic subcategorization, (c) syntactic subcategorization (word-specific). The indication of syntactic subcategorization in English is not inversion, but rather (a) the verb-specific deletability of *that*, and (b) the verb-specific presence of a [–Q] feature: the fact that we mark as ungrammatical a sentence like *who thinks what he bought.* We argue that the English children have not yet mastered the syntactic features of word-specific subcategorization. Therefore they have only thematic government, which means that partial movement is optionally available.

In other words, the environment where proper government occurs is precisely what is avoided when the complement is attached at a higher level. This attachment site, in turn, permits the generation of partial movement structures, precisely because the VP does not properly govern the CP, which allows a phonetic part of the chain to appear.

In sum, these facts show that the partial movement phenomenon occurs in a very precise domain: where thematic subcategorization is present but syntactic subcategorization is not. The approach in current literature on these questions in German is very close to the proposal made earlier: Koster (1987) and Bayer (1992) argued that government can be extended to extraposed clauses via a device called *domain extension.*

The domain extension approach does not, in any straightforward way, predict that partial movement should appear earlier in grammar or, if acquisition reflects core grammar, constitute a feature of core grammar. However, the claim that thematic subcategorization precedes syntactic subcategorization is intuitive and leads to this acquisition hypothesis very naturally.[14]

Our proposal to subdivide subcategorization is reminiscent of several treatments of thematic roles in morphology. In the lexicon, the thematic roles are assigned by the verb, but no directionality is entailed. We list here an example without a detailed discussion. In nominalizations the agent can appear as either a prenominal genitive or a postnominal PP:

---

[14]In Roeper and de Villiers (1992a) we provided more extensive discussion of the claim and extended it to predict a further change in the child's grammar with respect to the nature of traces at the point when proper government arises.

(46) a. the enemy's destruction of the city
b. the destruction of the city by the enemy

We argue here that if this approach to morphology and the projection of thematic arguments is correct, then it might logically extend to propositional thematic roles (i.e., complements). It is natural to assume that for children, complements are likewise subcategorized thematically, but without a necessary syntactic instantiation. Several syntactic factors are undetermined with purely thematic subcategorization:

1. Syntactic category of complements:
   feel it to me instead of *make me feel.*
2. Idiosyncratic complement type:
   suppose me to do that.
3. Idiosyncratic preposition type:
   watch out of it.
4. Idiosyncratic transformations; compare:
   (i) It was reasoned that Jane was late.
   *I reasoned it that Jane was late.
   (ii) It was believed that Jane was late.
   I believed it that Jane was late.
5. Idiosyncratic deletions:
   Know deletes *that, intend* does not.

In fact there is acquisition evidence that each kind of word-specific syntactic subcategorization may initially be absent, as discussed earlier.

In sum, we have made this argument for acquisition:

1. The acquisition device recognizes thematic government prior to the fixation of syntactic subcategorization frames.
2. The thematic government is nondirectional:
   [[that he is here] think [that he is here]]
   $CP \Leftarrow VP \Rightarrow CP$
3. Thematic government can license an empty category in an adjacent CP (Bayer, 1992).

SUPPORTING EVIDENCE FROM ACQUISITION

We are now in a position to connect the issue of partial movement in children's grammars to the problem of subcategorization and attachment just discussed. We have argued that the medial answers constitute a grammatical phenomenon for young children, and not a simple performance error. It obtains just where the option obtains in UG: where a scope marker appears at the front of the sentence. It is necessary to point out that the usual scope marker in German is *was* 'what', yet in the children's grammars any WH-word seems to be able to play that role (but see footnote 9 and Weissenborn, Roeper, & de Villiers, 1991, for further discussion).

We argue that children utilize a partial movement chain at the first stage. The status of such chains in linguistic theory is a topic of current interest, in part because of these data, and it raises several interesting questions. The first question is whether the partial movement chain belongs to a family of chains with the following property: They have intermediate phonetic material rather than a trace.

(47) WH . . . . WH . . . . *t*
     WH . . . . *t* . . . . *t*

Under this view, apparent copying phenomena at the same time involve the same kind of chain, although the WH-information is represented in both initial and medial positions. Thornton (1991) found examples of copying more frequently than examples of partial movement in children's production, and she interpreted those copies as a reflex of SPEC-head agreement. However, the fact that children answer the medial questions is not so clearly accommodated by such a view. In our view, the most important point is that at an abstract level the child does not project a properly governed trace in the medial position in both Thornton's data and our own.[15]

The nature of the scope marker introduces another question about the set of properties that a WH-word can have. In the case of partial movement, the content of the chain comes from the lower WH-word, not the upper

---

[15]One important feature of such chains is their capacity to allow another WH-word to function as an antecedent. In English, sequences of WH-words function as names and do not allow an antecedent connection:

(i) a. Who thinks who plays baseball?
    b. Who thinks he plays baseball?

The expression in (i) cannot mean (ia); it requires a set interpretation. However, in partial movement constructions, precisely this anaphoric property is allowed, as in this quotation from a child:

(ii) What do you think what she said?

Therefore, the WH-word has a property for children that makes it distinct from a pure name, and distinct from WH-words in some languages, like English. In Perez and Roeper (1992) it was argued that a WH-word can have the property of a WH-anaphor, as found in Chinese (Lin, 1994). They reported that children do in fact interpret sentences like (ia) as if they mean (ib).

one. Therefore the initial scope-marker WH-word, unlike any WH-word in adult English, inherits its content from the lower WH-word.

Now we see that the meaning of a chain can be derived from all of its positions:

(48) scope . . . . meaning . . . . origin (thematic role)

One can therefore argue that the chain is a theoretical entity whose parts must be composed in order to recover meaning. This division of content is particularly sharp in acquisition even though its initial default representation, partial movement, may not be found in some adult languages.

That option obtains in UG just where the verb does not subcategorize for an embedded question, so that the WH-chain is not of the usual form, but only short-distance movement occurs. That option coexists in German with long-distance movement, and it seems also to coexist in children's grammars with long-distance (successive cyclic) movement. Does it do so because the children are uncertain about the attachment of the clause to the verb? We have demonstrated that the subcategorization facts are subtle indeed, and that the child might wait to lexically subcategorize until he or she is certain of the appropriate properties of that verb. In the interim, the child may decide on a higher attachment, say to VP, and thus permit scope marking and medial copies.

As evidence that children block extraction from true adjuncts, witness the data in Goodluck, Sedivy, and Foley (1989) on extraction of WH-questions from temporal adjuncts, as in (49):

(49) *Who$_i$ did the elephant ask before helping t_i?

Their 3- to 5-year-old subjects showed striking obedience to the barrierhood of that adjunct, though the precise cue they were using must rest in the adverbial connective.

Quotation

The general theoretical claim is that thematic connection to the verb is sufficient for long-distance extraction, and that allows us to interpret otherwise puzzling evidence that we have collected on children's WH-extraction from quotation environments. In a series of studies we explored whether children extract questions from quotations, which are, in adult grammar, an absolute barrier to extraction, as in (50):

(50) How did he say, "Can I come"?

(50) cannot be answered with *by car*. In spoken form, the clue to quotation
can be provided by the inversion of the modal verb:

(51) a. How did the father say can Grandma ride a bike?
      b. How did father say Grandma can ride a bike?

It was this contrast we tested on 25 English speakers between the ages of
4 and 6. They once again allowed equal numbers of long-distance readings
for (55a) and (55b), ignoring the contrast carried by inversion of the modal.
In German a useful contrast is provided because there, the verb must be in
second position, and if it is displaced, then the result is a quotation: the
opposite of English. Weissenborn et al. (1991) detailed the facts: Discrimination was just as poor for German children, who also allowed extraction
from quotation environments:

(52) Wie sagt der Junge, "Das Mädchen kann trommeln"?
      'How did the boy say ___ "The girl can play the drums ___ "?'

53% of their interpretations were from the site inside the quotation. French
children did equally poorly, with the contrast carried by the absence of the
normally obligatory complementizer *que* signaling quotation:

(53) Comment est-ce que le garcon a dit, "La jeune fille va jouer du
      tambour"?
      'How did the boy say ___"The girl can play the drums ___"?'
(54) Quand est-ce que le garcon a dit qu'il s'est fait mal?
      'When did the boy say ___ that he hurt himself ___?'

36%–37% of the French children's answers violated the barrier of quotation.
Very clearly, children are not sensitive to the syntactic differences between
quotation and complementation, though the naturalistic data suggest early
command of the concept of quotation. Children hear and use inversion with
say, as demonstrated by several early examples in the CHILDES database
(*de little one said, "what cha doing?"* [Adam, sample 27]). Other naturalistic
examples (*I said, "Are you going to be my valentine?"* [Adam, sample 34])
indicate that quotation is understood and used early.
   In a further study, we showed that at least some children older than 4
years (5 out of 18 tested) have difficulty interpreting pronoun reference in
quotation and nonquotation environments, allowing coreference in both
(55) and (56) between Micky and *he*:

(55) Micky said he could sit there.

(56) He could sit there, said Micky.

In further work we plan to test whether giving multiple clues to the quotation status (say, verb inversion and pronoun switching) might increase children's obedience to extraction constraints, using sentences such as (57):

(58) How did Micky say, "Can I eat that"?

However, so far it seems that knowledge of the specific properties of complements and quotations are not mastered until quite late, as would be predicted from the earlier discussion about language variation.

Specific Complement Types

Knowledge of specific complements and where they can be used is the kind of subcategorization knowledge that reflects typical word-specific learning. There are two kinds of pertinent evidence that bolster the spontaneous speech evidence described earlier.

First, naturalistic data reveal that children fail to use the complementizer *that* even though they are exposed to it on a daily basis. In German, where *dass* is obligatory, it is not present in children's speech. Its absence therefore reflects lack of knowledge rather than deletion. Furthermore, there is the evidence cited earlier concerning the insensitivity to *que* in French to differentiate quotation from indirect speech.[16]

Second, in some very recent work, we have explored children's sensitivity to the different meanings carried by different complement types with the same verb. For example, we tell a story about Big Bird inviting people to a party and forgetting certain things. In the story, Big Bird is distracted and forgets to invite Bert, and then Big Bird goes to bed, forgetting that he invited Grover to a party. Then we follow the story with one of two questions:

(59) a. Who did Big Bird forget that he invited?
     b. Who did Big Bird forget to invite?

---

[16]A new experiment just completed demonstrates a possible insensitivity to the presence of the complementizer *that* for marking a clause boundary, though its full interpretation remains unclear. Children treated the following two sentences as equivalent:

(i) a. Sally said in the spring they would plant a pumpkin.
    b. Sally said that in the spring they would plant a pumpkin.

Eighteen children aged 4 and 5 years saw both sentences as ambiguous; that is, they allowed *in the spring* to modify the top verb *said* in both sentences as well as the lower verb *planted*. The conclusion that they are insensitive to the complementizer is not the only alternative, however. They could, equally, fail to respect barriers for the movement of prepositional phrases such as *in the spring*. We are exploring this further.

The answers to these questions are perfectly distinct for adults given the story, but children aged 4 and 5 years old confuse them. We have tested over 30 children with the verbs *forget, not remember, tell,* and *promise*; and with two adjectives, *is sorry* and *is happy,* as in (60):

(60) Who was Bert sorry to see?
Who was Bert sorry that he saw?

The story made the referents clear and distinct for the two questions. All of these forms have the two options for complementation, but children make many mistakes in answering the questions in which they must discriminate the complement forms; that is, they answer with the referent appropriate to the other complement. For instance, they are asked (59a):

(59) a. Who did Big Bird forget that he invited?

Children name *Bert,* who was the character Big Bird forgot to invite, not the character he did invite but then forgot about. The preliminary results suggest to us that children are still learning the complement properties of these common verbs at 5 years of age.

Relative Clauses as Adjuncts

Consider that the evidence from relative clauses discussed earlier is also consistent with this general formulation. Children did not extract from relative clauses, nor did they answer the relative pronoun *who.* What is the cue that allows them to differentiate the relative clause and WH-question constructions? Consider (16), repeated here:

(16) How did the dog climb up who barked?

In (16), the relative clause has to be an adjunct: It cannot be subcategorized by the verb *climb up.* Clearly the verb *climb up* has no thematic attachment to the relative clause, and it is this clue that allows the child to recognize that long-distance movement would be disallowed.

We have further evidence that children's discrimination of relative clauses and embedded clauses is not so good when the relative clause has a more plausible thematic relation to the verb: They do not seem able to use just the presence/absence of the complementizer as a sufficient clue. We tested 4- and 5-year-old children on the following contrast:

(61) a. Who did the dog know bought the cake?
b. Who did the dog know who bought the cake?

Their responses were entirely what would be expected by chance: no discrimination. (64a) was answered 30% of the time as if it were a relative clause with a missing complementizer (the subject complementizer is obligatory in relative clauses in English), and (64b) was answered 70% of the time as if it were an embedded clause with a redundant marker of the trace, as in German. Hence the discrimination between relative clauses and embedded clauses is vulnerable as the clues to the adjunct status of the relative clause are stripped away, in particular, as the thematic connection to the verb is made more plausible.

Learning Verb-Specific Properties

The foregoing evidence suggests that thematic licensing is sufficient for long-distance extraction for children. So how does the child take the further step to learn appropriate attachment and subcategorization? Take as a test case another example of mistaken overgeneralization: a failure to discriminate bridge from nonbridge verbs.

In this case (reported in Roeper & de Villiers, 1992a), we tested whether children would appropriately block long-distance extraction with nonbridge verbs such as *know*:

(62) When did the boy know he hurt himself?

In fact, (62) had exactly the same proportion of long-distance answers (about 65%) as did the bridge verb case (63):

(63) When did the boy say he hurt himself?

Hence children did not show any sensitivity to the difference in verb class. In recent work by Philip and de Villiers (1992) we have confirmation of this failure with more clearly factive verbs, such as *forget*. If the line of argument in that study is correct, the child will not learn the barrierhood of the factive verb until certain other logico-semantic properties of the verb are learned, in particular, its nonmonotonicity (Szabolsci & Zwarts, 1992).

In a second illustration of the prerequisite for certain lexical features, Roeper and de Villiers (1992b) asked whether children would allow extraction from small clauses, argued to have no CP node:

(64) How did the mother see him riding?

Adult subjects allow long-distance extraction freely, and it is argued to be different from successive cyclic movement because there is no CP. Instead, the exceptional case marking from the verb (that dictates the form *him* for the subject) opens up the clause for extraction. But superficially identical forms with other verbs do not permit LD extraction:

(65) How did the mother enjoy him running?

The distinction must therefore rest on knowing the exceptional case marking property of particular verbs. Children in fact block adjunct extraction from small clauses (see Table 16.5), and we argue it is because they have not yet acquired the exceptional case marking properties of the verbs in question. Until they do, they make the assumption that the small clause has a status akin to that of a temporal adjunct, attached high on the tree, as if the sentence were in fact (66):

(66) How did she see him, while he was riding?

They therefore forbid extraction. A crucial test of this idea (Radford, 1992) would be to use an unmarked verb instead of the gerund form:

(67) How did she see him ride?

This form would be unlikely to be construed as an adjunct. Then lower attachment might be forced and extraction might occur.

SUMMARY

In summary, the data on long-distance extraction suggest that children do not wait until attachment is resolved before allowing extraction from a complement, and the crucial feature for children seems to be whether the clause is thematically selected by the verb. This leads to a generally correct

TABLE 16.5
Long Distance Interpretations in Small Clauses and Nominalizations
(data from Roeper and de Villiers, 1991)

Argument	Small clause		
9. Who did the sister show _____	him copying	_____ ?	
Preschool (N = 16)	25%	62%	
Adult (N = 12)	12%	83%	
Adjunct	Small clause		
11. How did the mother see _____	him riding	_____ ?	
Preschool	81%	18%	
Adult	54%	45%	

constraint on LD movement out of extraposed relative clauses and temporal adjunct clauses (Goodluck, Sedivy, & Foley, 1989), but mistaken extraction from quotation environments and factive complements. The late fixing of the syntactic features of subcategorization also means that scope marking and partial movement continue to exist in the preschool years as grammatical options in English and other languages.

ACKNOWLEDGMENTS

We would like to thank the following people for their useful comments on this chapter or the work it contains: Josef Bayer, Noam Chomsky, Steve Crain, Jaklin Kornfilt, Jan and Charlotte Koster, Xiaoli Li, Dana McDaniel, Tom Maxfield, Bernadette Plunkett, Zvi Penner, Ana Perez-Leroux, William Philip, Luigi Rizzi, Peggy Speas, Ros Thornton, Anne Vainikka, Jurgen Weissenborn, and John Whitman. We are grateful to the audience at the Cornell conference and to two anonymous reviewers. The work was supported by a grant from NSF Linguistics #BNS 8820314 to Tom Roeper and Jill de Villiers.

REFERENCES

Bayer, J. (1992). *On the origin of sentential arguments in German and Bengali.* Unpublished manuscript, University of Dusseldorf.

Borer, H., & Wexler, K. (1987). The maturation of syntax. In T. Roeper & E. Williams (Eds.), *Parameter setting.* Dordrecht: Reidel.

Bowerman, M. (1974). Learning the structure of causative verbs: A study in the relationship of cognitive, semantic and syntactic development. *Papers and Reports on Child Language Development, 8,* 142–178.

Bowerman, M. (1982). Reorganizational processes in lexical and syntactic development. In E. Wanner & L. Gleitman (Eds.), *Language acquisition: The state of the art* (pp. 319–346). New York: Cambridge University Press.

Chomsky, N. (1986). *Barriers.* Cambridge, MA: MIT Press.

Chomsky, N. (1992). A minimalist program for linguistic theory. *MIT Occasional Papers in Linguistics, 1.* Cambridge, MA: MIT, Department of Linguistics and Philosophy.

Chomsky, N., & Lasnik, H. (in press). Principles and Parameters Theory. In J. Jacobs, A. von Stechow, W. Sternefeld, & T. Vennemann (Eds.), *Syntax: An international handbook of contemporary research.* Berlin: Walter de Gruyter.

de Villiers, J., & Roeper, T. (1992). *The acquisition of the CP.* Paper presented at the 17th Annual Boston University Conference on Language Development, Boston, MA.

de Villiers, J. G., Roeper, T., & Vainikka, A. (1990). The acquisition of long distance rules. In L. Frazier & J. de Villiers (Eds.), *Language processing and acquisition.* Dordrecht: Kluwer.

Goodluck, H., Sedivy, J., & Foley, M. (1989). Wh-questions and extraction from temporal adjuncts: A case for movement. *Papers and Reports on Child Language Development, 28,* 123–130.

Grimshaw, J. (1979). Complement selection and the lexicon. *Linguistic Inquiry, 10,* 279–326.

Grimshaw, J. (1990). *Argument structure.* Cambridge, MA: MIT Press.

Koster, J. (1987). *Domains and dynasties*. Dordrecht: Kluwer.

Lasnik, H., & Saito, M. (1992). *Move-alpha*. Cambridge, MA: MIT Press.

Lebeaux, D. (1988). *Language acquisition and the form of the grammar*. Unpublished doctoral dissertation, University of Massachusetts, Amherst.

Leftheri, K. (1991). *Learning to interpret wh-questions in Greek*. Honors thesis, Smith College, Northampton, MA.

Li, X. (1992). *Constraints on wh-long distance movement in adult Chinese for L2 acquisition and the implication for L2 teaching*. Unpublished doctoral dissertation, University of Massachusetts, Amherst.

Lin, J. (1994). *Chinese donkey anaphora*. Unpublished manuscript, University of Massachusetts, Amherst.

McDaniel, D. (1989). Partial and multiple wh-movement. *Natural Language & Linguistic Theory, 7*, 565–605.

Perez, A. (1991). The acquisition of long distance movement in Caribbean Spanish. In T. Maxfield & B. Plunkett (Eds.), *Papers in the acquisition of WH* (pp. 1–12). Amherst, MA. GLSA Publications.

Perez, A., & Roeper, T. (1992). *Copying wh-questions*. Paper presented at the 17th Annual Boston University Conference on Language Development, Boston, MA.

Pesetsky, D. (1982). *Paths and categories*. Unpublished doctoral dissertation, MIT, Cambridge, MA.

Philip, W., & de Villiers, J. (1992). *Monotonicity and the acquisition of weak wh-islands*. Paper presented at the 17th Annual Boston University Conference on Language Development, Boston, MA.

Radford, A. (1992). Comments on Roeper and de Villiers. In J. Weissenborn, H. Goodluck, & T. Roeper (Eds.), *Theoretical issues in language acquisition* (pp. 237–248). Hillsdale, NJ: Lawrence Erlbaum Associates.

Randall, J. (1992). The catapult hypothesis: An approach to unlearning. In J. Weissenborn, H. Goodluck, & T. Roeper (Eds.), *Theoretical issues in language acquisition* (pp. 93–138). Hillsdale, NJ: Lawrence Erlbaum Associates.

Rizzi, L. (1990). *Relativized minimality*. Cambridge, MA: MIT Press.

Roeper, T. (1987). Implicit arguments and the head-complement relation. *Linguistic Inquiry, 18*, 267–310.

Roeper, T. (1992). From the initial state to V2: Acquisition principles in action. In J. Meisel (Ed.), *The acquisition of verb placement* (pp. 333–370). Dordrecht: Kluwer.

Roeper, T. (1993). Explicit syntax and the lexicon. In J. Pustejovsky (Ed.), *Semantics and the lexicon* (pp. 185–220). Dordrecht: Kluwer.

Roeper, T., & de Villiers, J. (1992a). *The one feature hypothesis for acquisition*. Unpublished manuscript, University of Massachusetts, Amherst.

Roeper, T., & de Villiers, J. (1992b). Ordered decisions in the acquisition of wh-movement. In J. Weissenborn, H. Goodluck, & T. Roeper (Eds.), *Theoretical issues in language acquisition* (pp. 191–236). Hillsdale, NJ: Lawrence Erlbaum Associates.

Seymour, H., Bland, L., Champion, T., de Villiers, J., & Roeper, T. (1991). *The development of Wh-movement in Black English*. Paper presented at the Black Speech, Hearing and Language Association, Los Angeles.

Szabolsci, A., & Zwarts, F. (1992). *Unbounded dependencies and the algebraic semantics*. Lecture notes of the Third European Summer School in Logic, Language and Information, Saarbrucken, August 1991.

Thornton, R. (1991). *Adventures in long distance moving: The acquisition of complex wh-questions*. Unpublished doctoral dissertation, University of Connecticut, Storrs.

Vainikka, A. (1989). *Default case in acquisition*. Unpublished manuscript, University of Massachusetts, Amherst.

van Riemsdijk, H. (1983). Correspondence effects and the empty category principle. In Y. Otsu, H. van Riemsdijk, K. Inoue, & N. Kawasaki (Eds.), *Studies in generative grammar and language acquisition* (pp. 5–17). Tokyo: Monboshu Grant.

Webelhuth, G. (1989). *Syntactic saturation phenomena and the modern Germanic languages.* Unpublished doctoral dissertation, University of Massachusetts, Amherst.

Weissenborn, J., Roeper, T., & de Villiers, J. (1991). The acquisition of Wh-movement in German and French. In T. Maxfield & B. Plunkett (Eds.), *Papers in the acquisition of WH* (pp. 43–78). Amherst, MA: GLSA Publications.

CHAPTER SEVENTEEN

Structural Determinants of Quantifier Scope: An Experimental Study of Chinese First Language Acquisition

Yu-Chin Chien

In this chapter, we present the results of an experiment that was designed to examine Chinese-speaking children's interpretations of sentences containing the universal quantifier (*every*) and the existential quantifier (*one*). The data are used to evaluate some controversial predictions suggested by several recent theoretical analyses concerning Chinese scope relations. The test sentences are exemplified in (1) to (4). Sentences (1) and (2) are canonical constructions corresponding to the English constructions given in (5) and (6). These constructions preserve the canonical word order of Chinese; that is, the direct object is placed in a postverbal position. Sentences (3) and (4) are Chinese *ba*-constructions in which the direct object is placed in a preverbal position immediately following the preposition *ba* (cf. Huang, 1982; Li & Thompson, 1981).

(1) Xie $\begin{Bmatrix} \text{yige} \\ \text{meige} \end{Bmatrix}$ shuzi zai $\begin{Bmatrix} \text{meige} \\ \text{yige} \end{Bmatrix}$ gezi li.

    write $\begin{Bmatrix} \text{one-CL} \\ \text{every-CL} \end{Bmatrix}$ number at $\begin{Bmatrix} \text{every-CL} \\ \text{one-CL} \end{Bmatrix}$ box inside

(2) Zai $\begin{Bmatrix} \text{yige} \\ \text{meige} \end{Bmatrix}$ gezi li, (dou) xie $\begin{Bmatrix} \text{meige} \\ \text{yige} \end{Bmatrix}$ shuzi.

    at $\begin{Bmatrix} \text{one-CL} \\ \text{every-CL} \end{Bmatrix}$ box inside, (all) write $\begin{Bmatrix} \text{every-CL} \\ \text{one-CL} \end{Bmatrix}$ number

(3) Ba $\begin{Bmatrix} \text{yige} \\ \text{meige} \end{Bmatrix}$ shuzi (dou) xie zai $\begin{Bmatrix} \text{meige} \\ \text{yige} \end{Bmatrix}$ gezi li.

   ba $\begin{Bmatrix} \text{one-CL} \\ \text{every-CL} \end{Bmatrix}$ number (all) write at $\begin{Bmatrix} \text{every-CL} \\ \text{one-CL} \end{Bmatrix}$ box inside

(4) Ba $\begin{Bmatrix} \text{yige} \\ \text{meige} \end{Bmatrix}$ gezi, (dou) xie $\begin{Bmatrix} \text{meige} \\ \text{yige} \end{Bmatrix}$ shuzi.

   ba $\begin{Bmatrix} \text{one-CL} \\ \text{every-CL} \end{Bmatrix}$ box, (all) write $\begin{Bmatrix} \text{every-CL} \\ \text{one-CL} \end{Bmatrix}$ number

(5) Write $\begin{Bmatrix} \text{a} \\ \text{every} \end{Bmatrix}$ number in $\begin{Bmatrix} \text{every} \\ \text{a} \end{Bmatrix}$ box.

(6) In $\begin{Bmatrix} \text{a} \\ \text{every} \end{Bmatrix}$ box, write $\begin{Bmatrix} \text{every} \\ \text{a} \end{Bmatrix}$ number.

According to current literature (e.g., Aoun & Li, 1993; Huang, 1982; Lee, 1986), the scope facts concerning two quantifiers in a simple sentence do not hold across languages. In English, it is generally agreed that the scope relation of quantified noun phrases is free within the minimal sentence and thus allows various scope ambiguities. For example, when sentence (7) is interpreted as (7a), the universal quantified NP (Q-NP) *every child* takes scope over the existential Q-NP *a song*. When it is interpreted as (7b), the existential Q-NP *a song* is said to have scope over the universal Q-NP *every child*. In contrast to English, the corresponding Chinese sentences (e.g., (8)) are strictly unambiguous. Sentence (8) has only one meaning. It corresponds to the wide scope (WS) reading of the universal Q-NP *meige xiaohai*.

   (7) Every child sang a song.
       a. Different children sang different songs.
       b. The children all sang the same song.
   (8) Meige xiaohai dou chang le yishou ge.
       every-CL child all sing Asp. one-CL song
       'Different children sang different songs.'

EXPLANATIONS CONCERNING SOME SCOPE FACTS OF ENGLISH SENTENCES

May (1977, 1985) proposed the rule of Quantifier Raising (9) and the two conditions on it ((10) and (11)) to explain the scope ambiguity of sentence (7) and many other quantificational sentences. May argued that there is a level of Logical Form (LF) in syntax where generalizations concerning quantificational phenomena such as scope relations can be captured. In an

LF representation, if one quantified NP c-commands the other quantified NP, then the c-commanding one takes scope over the c-commanded one. The notion of *c-command* may be understood as it is stated in (12).

(9) Quantifier Raising Rule:
Chomsky-adjoin a quantificational NP to S.

(10) Condition on Proper Binding:
Every variable in an argument position of a predicate must be properly bound. (A is properly bound by B if A is coindexed and c-commanded by B.)

(11) Condition on Quantifier Binding:
Every quantified phrase must properly bind a variable.

(12) C-Command:
A c-commands B if and only if A does not dominate B, and every C that dominates A also dominates B, where C is taken to be
a. maximal projections (along the lines of Aoun & Sportiche, 1983; i.e., m-command, Chomsky, 1986), or
b. any branching category (c-command, along the lines of Reinhart, 1983).

By applying the rule of Quantifier Raising (QR) to the S-structure representation, the two quantified NPs in sentence (7) can be freely moved to adjoin successively to the S node. An S-structure like (7) can be transformed into the two well-formed LF representations given in (13) and (14).

(13) $[_S[\text{Every child}]_i \ [_S[\text{a song}]_j \ [_S x_i \text{ sang } x_j]]]$

(14) $[_S[\text{A song}]_j \ [_S[\text{every child}]_i \ [_S x_i \text{ sang } x_j]]]$

In the LF representation (13), the universal Q-NP *every child* c-commands the existential Q-NP *a song*. The universal Q-NP, therefore, takes scope over the existential Q-NP; (13) implies that different children might sing different songs. In (14), on the other hand, the existential Q-NP *a song* c-commands the universal Q-NP *every child*. In this situation, the existential Q-NP takes scope over the universal Q-NP; (14) implies that the children all sang the same song.

EXPLANATIONS CONCERNING SOME SCOPE FACTS OF CHINESE SENTENCES

There exist at least three proposals expressly designed to explain the scope facts of Chinese sentences. Considering a wide range of data, Huang (1982) examined quantifier scope in Chinese and claimed that although the QR rule and structural c-command are both relevant in the determination of scope relations in Chinese, the application of the QR rule in Chinese is not as free as in English. In order to interpret the scope phenomena of Chinese sentences and to account for the difference between Chinese and English shown in examples (7) and (8), Huang proposed a general condition on scope interpretation for Chinese. This general condition (also known as the Isomorphic Principle), given in (15), states that for Chinese quantificational sentences, the c-command relation between two quantified NPs at S-structure will stay the same at Logical Form.

(15) Huang's General Condition on Scope Interpretation in Chinese:
Suppose A and B are both QPs or both Q-NPs or Q-expressions, then if A c-commands B at S-structure, A also c-commands B at Logical Form.

According to Huang, sentence (8) is not ambiguous because at both S-structure and LF, the universal Q-NP *meige xiaohai* 'every child' c-commands the existential Q-NP *yishou ge* 'one song'.

A slightly different proposal was made by Lee (1986, 1991). Following Huang's proposal, Lee argued that the hierarchical relation between two quantified NPs in a sentence is relevant for the determination of scope relations in Chinese, but instead of c-command, the relevant hierarchical relation is that of *command*. In addition, Lee claimed that both the notion of linear precedence and that of hierarchical relation, namely command, are relevant to scope interpretation in Chinese. By incorporating these two notions, Lee revised Huang's general condition for scope interpretation as in (16):

(16) Lee's General Condition on Scope Interpretation in Chinese:
Given two quantified NPs A and B:
a. If A asymmetrically commands B at S-structure, A has scope over B at Logical Form.
b. If A and B command each other and A precedes B at S-structure, A has scope over B at LF.
(A commands B if neither dominates the other and the first S node dominating A also dominates B.)

In (8), *every child* and *a song* command each other. According to (16b) the preceding NP *every child* takes scope over the succeeding NP *a song*. Because, in Chinese sentences such as (8), the hierarchical relation of c-command is subsumed under that of *command and linear precedence*, additional data besides sentence (8) are required to evaluate these two analyses suggested by Huang and Lee. (We postpone the discussion of the related data until the experimental design and the outcomes are examined.)

Aoun and Li (1993) introduced another analysis in order to account for the scope phenomena of Chinese. They challenged Huang's and Lee's Isomorphic Principle by showing that there are instances in Chinese that do not exhibit this isomorphic effect. For example, Chinese passive sentences such as (17) are ambiguous. Yet, in the surface structure of (17), only the universal Q-NP *meige wanju* 'every toy' c-commands, or commands and precedes, the existential Q-NP *yige xiaohai* 'one child'. According to Huang and Lee, only the WS reading of *every toy* should be possible. However, this is inconsistent with the scope facts exhibited in (17).

(17) Meige wanju dou bei yige xiaohai nazou le.
every-CL toy all by one-CL child take-away Asp
'Every toy was taken by a child.'

To incorporate these scope facts, Aoun and Li advanced two requirements for scope interpretation, namely, the Minimal Binding Requirement and the Scope Principle given in (18) and (19), respectively. They argued that the NP-trace might play a significant role in determining quantifier scopes. As implied in (19), a quantifier A might have scope over a quantifier B if A c-commands B, or A c-commands a trace coindexed with B.

(18) The Minimal Binding Requirement:
Variables must be bound by the most local potential A'-binder. (An element is qualified as an A'-binder for a variable only if this element occupies an A'-position and c-commands the variable.)

(19) The Scope Principle:
A quantifier A has scope over a quantifier B in case A c-commands a member of the chain containing B.

Let us evaluate sentence (17) again. Its S-structure representation is illustrated in (20).

(20) [Meige wanju dou [bei yige xiaohai nazou le t]]. (*t*=trace)

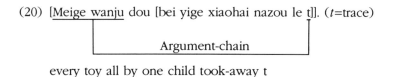

every toy all by one child took-away t

In (20), the surface structure subject *every toy* and the postverbal NP-trace form an argument-chain through an application of Move-α in mapping from

D-structure to S-structure. After QR, the universal Q-NP *every toy* takes scope over the existential Q-NP *one child* because the former c-commands the latter. The existential Q-NP may also have scope over the universal Q-NP because the former c-commands the trace of the latter. These two possibilities underlie the ambiguity of sentence (17). Notice that in both Huang's analysis and Aoun and Li's analysis, the relevant hierarchical relation is expressed in terms of c-command, rather than Lee's command. In order to differentiate Aoun and Li's analysis from Huang's analysis, one has to test Chinese passive sentences. In most active sentences, Aoun and Li's analysis and Huang's analysis yield the same prediction about scope relations. (Hereafter, Huang = H, Lee = L, and Aoun & Li = AL.)

THE EXPERIMENT

The purpose of the experiment was to acquire preliminary evidence about Chinese-speaking children's understanding of scope relations and to see whether they know which relations are possible for particular syntactic configurations. For the most part, linguists agree on the judgments of scope relations concerning most Chinese sentences. However, in some Chinese cases linguists seem to disagree on the adult judgments. Therefore, we also tested adults. Their judgments regarding the controversial cases were examined. Moreover, it was believed that some light might be shed on the validity of the experimental method through an examination of adult data.

Method

The Experimental Task. An act-out task was used to test Chinese-speaking subjects' interpretation of sentences involving two quantificational NPs. Each subject was first presented a sheet of paper with an array of three equally sized squares (1 in. × 1 in.) and a card (5 in. × 7 in.) with an array of three different numbers (or figures), or a set of three markers of different colors. The subject was then presented with a test sentence (e.g., *write one number in every box*) and asked to perform the action described in the presented sentence.[1] An example of the layout of the experimental materials is given in (21).

---

[1]The three numbers used in the Chinese study were 1, 2, and 3; the three figures were x, Δ, and o; the colors of the three markers were red, green, and blue. For those children who could not write or draw well, stamps with corresponding numbers or figures were used (one figure/number on one stamp). When stamps were adopted, the verb *stamp* replaced the verbs *write* and *draw*. For example, the sentence *Write every number in one box* became *Stamp every number in one box*.

(21)

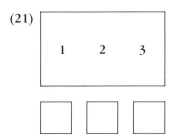

Note that the task adopted in the study allowed more than one token for each of the direct objects shown on the card. For example, when subjects were asked to write one number in every box, there was no restriction to how many numbers were to be used and how many times the same number (e.g., *1*) could be written.[2]

The Design and the Structural Analysis of the Test Constructions.
Sixteen different types of experimental sentences were tested, eight canonical constructions ((22)–(29)) and eight *ba*-constructions ((30)–(37)).

---

[2]The experimental setting of the current study is slightly different from the setting that has been considered when scope relationships are discussed. For example, the traditional setting might involve three Ninja Turtles (T, T, T) and three pizzas (P, P, P). Suppose somebody asked you to "give a pizza to every Ninja Turtle." A WS reading for *a pizza* implies that all three Ninja Turtles are sharing the same pizza, as illustrated in (ia); a WS reading for *every Ninja Turtle* implies that each Ninja Turtle has his own pizza, as illustrated in (ib), or it can accidentally imply the illustration given in (ia) (an accidental NS reading). In our task, when a subject was asked to "write one number in every box," the only way for him or her to represent the WS reading for *one number* was to write down the same number in each box, as in (ic). The representation given in (ic) resembles the one given in (ib) rather than the one given in (ia). The WS reading for *every box* obviously implies an interpretation illustrated in (id). However, because more than one token was available for each particular number, in contrast to the pizza case in which only one token was available for each particular pizza, one may say that the representation given in (ic) may also be viewed as a WS reading for *every box* rather than just an accidental NS reading. This possibility will be taken into account, when the data are discussed.

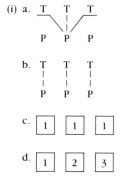

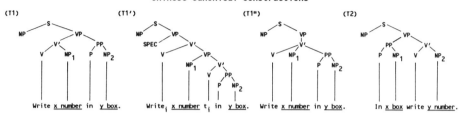

The Design
Chinese Canonical Constructions

(T1) (T1') (T1") (T2)

Write x number in y box.   Write$_i$ x number t$_i$ in y box.   Write x number in y box.   In x box write y number.

<u>PREDICTIONS</u>

Huang and Aoun & Li: <u>y box</u> has scope over <u>x number</u> (T1).   Huang and Aoun & Li: <u>x box</u> has scope over <u>y number</u> (T2).
Huang and Aoun & Li: <u>x number</u> has scope over <u>y box</u> (T1').
Huang and Aoun & Li: ambiguous (T1").
Lee: <u>x number</u> has scope over <u>y box</u> (T1, T1', & T1").   Lee: <u>x box</u> has scope over <u>y number</u> (T2).

(22) Xie yige shuzi zai meige gezi li.
Write one-CL number at every-CL box inside
'Write one number in every box.'

(23) Xie meige shuzi zai yige gezi li.
Write every-CL number at one-CL box inside
'Write every number in one box.'

(24) Xie meige shuzi zai meige gezi li.
Write every-CL number at every-CL box inside
'Write every number in every box.'

(25) Xie yige shuzi zai yige gezi li.
Write one-CL number at one-CL box inside
'Write one number in one box.'

(26) Zai yige gezi li xie meige shuzi.
At one-CL box inside write every-CL number
'In one box write every number.'

(27) Zai meige gezi li dou xie yige shuzi.
At every-CL box inside all write one-CL number
'In every box write one number.'

(28) Zai meige gezi li dou xie meige shuzi.
At every-CL box inside all write every-CL number
'In every box write every number.'

(29) Zai yige gezi li xie yige shuzi.
At one-CL box inside write one-CL number
'In one box write one number.'

The Design
Chinese Ba-Constructions

(T3)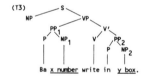

Ba x number write in y box.

(T4)

Ba x box write y number.

<u>PREDICTIONS</u>

Huang and Aoun & Li: <u>x number</u> has scope over <u>y box</u> (T3).   Huang and Aoun & Li: <u>x box</u> has scope over <u>y number</u> (T4).
Lee: <u>x number</u> has scope over <u>y box</u> (T3).   Lee: <u>x box</u> has scope over <u>y number</u> (T4).

(30) Ba yige shuzi xie zai meige gezi li.
Ba one-CL number write at every-CL box inside
'Write one number in every box.'

(31) Ba meige shuzi dou xie zai yige gezi li.
Ba every-CL number all write at one-CL box inside
'Write every number in one box.'

(32) Ba meige shuzi dou xie zai meige gezi li.
Ba every-CL number all write at every-CL box inside
'Write every number in every box.'

(33) Ba yige shuzi xie zai yige gezi li.
Ba one-CL number write at one-CL box inside
'Write one number in one box.'

(34) Ba yige gezi xie meige shuzi.
Ba one-CL box write every-CL number
'In one box write every number.'

(35) Ba meige gezi dou xie yige shuzi.
Ba every-CL box all write one-CL number
'In every box write one number.'

(36) Ba meige gezi dou xie meige shuzi.
Ba every-CL box all write every-CL number
'In every box write every number.'

(37) Ba yige gezi xie yige shuzi.
Ba one-CL box write one-CL number
'In one box write one number.'

398

According to their syntactic structures, we classified the eight canonical constructions into two major groups. Group 1 consisted of four constructions given in (22) to (25). Group 2 consisted of four constructions given in (26) to (29). The structural configuration representing the four constructions classified in Group 1 [(22)–(25)] is somewhat controversial and highly debated. These examples share the structural configuration illustrated in (T1) and at least two other alternative representations (T1′) and (T1″). The structural representation given in (T1′) is discussed in Huang (1988) and in Larson (1988). The structural representation given in (T1″) is discussed in Huang (1982). The four constructions classified in Group 2 [(26)–(29)] share the structural representation illustrated in (T2) (cf. Huang, 1982). Let us first examine the structural configuration given in (T1). Following Huang's (1982) proposal concerning the notion of c-command, if we assume that "c-command can be relaxed to allow for an NP object of a preposition to c-command across a dominating PP node" (Huang, 1982, p. 179), then, in (T1), NP_2 c-commands NP_1. According to H and AL, NP_2 (y *box*) takes scope over NP_1 (x *number*). However, if the structural representation for sentences (22) to (25) is that given in (T1′), then NP_1 c-commands NP_2. In this configuration, H and AL would predict that NP_1 (x *number*) has scope over NP_2 (y *box*). Finally, if the structure is analyzed as in (T1″), the two NPs c-command each other. Accordingly, H and AL would predict ambiguity for (22) to (25). In the configurations illustrated in (T1), (T1′), or (T1″), the first S node dominating NP_1 also dominates NP_2. Thus, according to L, these two NPs command each other and the preceding NP (x *number*) should have scope over the succeeding NP (y *box*), regardless of the structure chosen. The constructions in Group 1 make it difficult to evaluate H and AL. However, L may be evaluated by these constructions with no difficulty.

Consider the structural configuration given in (T2). In this structure, NP_1 c-commands NP_2. According to H and AL, NP_1 (x *box*) takes scope over NP_2 (y *number*). With regard to the notion of command, again, NP_1 and NP_2 command each other. In this case, L would predict that NP_1 has scope over NP_2. Considering (T2), a converging prediction for (26)–(29) is derived via all three analyses mentioned.

As can be seen from the examples given in (22) to (29), besides the configurational factor, we also varied the types of quantified NPs occupying the two object positions in each sentence. We included two types of quantified NPs in this study: the universal Q-NP such as *every box* or *every number* and the existential Q-NP such as *one box* or *one number*. In some sentences, the two quantified NPs were of the same type; in other sentences, the two NPs were not of the same type. Taking the order of the two quantified NPs into account, four possible combinations of these two types of quantified NPs were established for each group: the *one-every* construction, the *every-one* construction, the *every-every* construction, and the *one-one* construction. In order to facilitate comparisons among these conditions, we have included only one set of test sentences as examples. In the real test, three test items were included in each condition: one with the verb *hua* 'draw' and the direct object *tuxin* 'figure', one with the verb *xie* 'write' and the direct object *shuzi* 'number', and the final one with the verb *tu* 'mark/color' and the direct object *yanse* 'color'. There were 24 canonical sentences for each subject (3 items × 4 combinations of the two quantified NPs × 2 configurations = 24 items).

The design of the *ba*-constructions was parallel to the design of the canonical constructions. According to their syntactic structures, we classified the eight *ba*-constructions into two major groups. Group 1 consisted of four constructions, (30) to (33), which share the structural representation given in (T3). Group 2 consisted of four constructions, (34) to (37), which share the structural representation illustrated in (T4). Considering (T3) and (T4), NP_1 c-commands NP_2; NP_1 and NP_2 command each other. In these two configurations, H, AL, and L all predict that NP_1 (T3: *x number*, T4: *x box*) will take scope over NP_2 (T3: *y box*, T4: *y number*).

Within each group of the *ba*-constructions, we also included four different conditions, each containing one of the four possible combinations of the two quantified NPs (*every* and *one*). Again, for each condition three test items with different verbs and different direct objects were included, yielding a total of 24 *ba*-sentences for each subject. Together with the 24 canonical sentences, there was a total of 48 experimental items for each subject. The 48 items were organized into three test batteries (A, B, and C). Each consisted of 16 experimental items arranged in a random order. The three test batteries were given to each subject in a random order. At the end of each test battery, there were two control items (one with and one without the preposition *ba*). Altogether there were six control items. The control items were used to test the subjects' concept of *every*. For example, two of the control items simply asked the subject to "write every number on a blank sheet of paper" ("zai zhechang zhi shangmian, xie meige shuzi" or "ba meige shuzi dou xie zai zhechang zhi shangmian").

Several linguists have argued that quantification of postverbal theme/patient objects by *mei* 'every', as in *xie meige shuzi zai yige gezi li* 'write every number in one box', often results in unnatural sentences (e.g., Lee, 1991; Xu & Lee, 1989). The inclusion of some *ba*-constructions in which the theme/patient objects quantified by *mei* (e.g., (31)) were preverbal instead of postverbal permits us to evaluate the effect of the "unnaturalness" on the subjects' scope interpretations. Moreover, considering the structural representations given in (T1) (or (T1″), but not (T1′)) for the canonical constructions and the representation given in (T3) for the *ba*-constructions, we found that the hierarchical c-command relation between the two quantified NPs was not the same for these configurations ((T1) or (T1″) vs.

(T3)). However, the linear order of the corresponding two quantified NPs stayed the same. This allowed us to evaluate structural effect versus nonstructural effect on subjects' interpretations of scope relations.

Subjects. One hundred and eighty-six Chinese-speaking children between the ages of 3 and 10 and 42 adults were tested. Only those children who were acquiring Mandarin Chinese as their first language were included. The children were classified into seven developmental age groups of one-year periods. There were at least 24 children in each age group (except the first group, which had only 16 subjects). The children were sampled from preschools and elementary schools in Taipei, Taiwan. The 42 adults were undergraduate students attending National Chengchi University in Taipei, Taiwan.

Results and Discussions

The subjects' responses to the experimental constructions were classified into eight different types (A to H). An example of each of the eight response types is illustrated in (38).

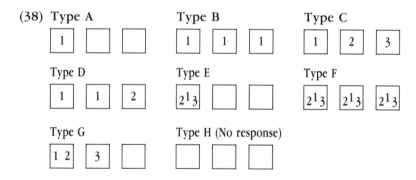

(38) Type A Type B Type C Type D Type E Type F Type G Type H (No response)

The subjects' responses to the control constructions were classified into three categories: correct, incorrect, and no response. In general, children 4 and older evidenced no difficulty in dealing with the concept of *every*. They gave correct answers to the control constructions more than 95% of the time. Some children between the ages of 3 and 4 had problems in dealing with the concept of *every*. About 18% of the 3-year-olds either gave incorrect responses or showed no responses to the control constructions.

Canonical Constructions. The results of the eight canonical constructions are illustrated in (39) to (42) and (43) to (46).

The Results
Chinese Canonical Constructions

(39) Xie yige shuzi zai meige gezi li.
      Write one-CL number at every-CL box inside
      'Write one number in every box.'

Type B	Type C
"one number"	"every box"
has wide scope	has wide scope

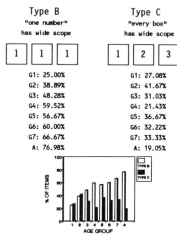

Type B	Type C
G1: 25.00%	G1: 27.08%
G2: 38.89%	G2: 41.67%
G3: 48.28%	G3: 31.03%
G4: 59.52%	G4: 21.43%
G5: 56.67%	G5: 36.67%
G6: 60.00%	G6: 32.22%
G7: 66.67%	G7: 33.33%
A: 76.98%	A: 19.05%

(41) Zai yige gezi li xie meige shuzi.
      At one-CL box inside write every-CL number
      'In one box write every number.'

Type E	Type C
"one box"	"every number"
has wide scope	has wide scope

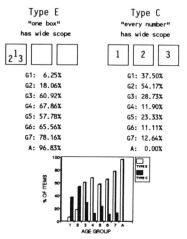

Type E	Type C
G1: 6.25%	G1: 37.50%
G2: 18.06%	G2: 54.17%
G3: 60.92%	G3: 28.73%
G4: 67.86%	G4: 11.90%
G5: 57.78%	G5: 23.33%
G6: 65.56%	G6: 11.11%
G7: 78.16%	G7: 12.64%
A: 96.83%	A: 0.00%

(40) Xie meige shuzi zai yige gezi li.
      Write every-CL number at one-CL box inside
      'Write every number in one box.'

Type C	Type E
"every number"	"one box"
has wide scope	has wide scope

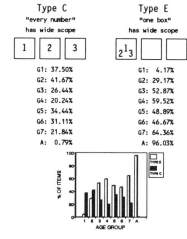

Type C	Type E
G1: 37.50%	G1: 4.17%
G2: 41.67%	G2: 29.17%
G3: 26.44%	G3: 52.87%
G4: 20.24%	G4: 59.52%
G5: 34.44%	G5: 48.89%
G6: 31.11%	G6: 46.67%
G7: 21.84%	G7: 64.36%
A: 0.79%	A: 96.03%

(42) Zai meige gezi li dou xie yige shuzi.
      At every-CL box inside all write one-CL number
      'In every box write one number.'

Type C	Type B
"every box"	"one number"
has wide scope	has wide scope

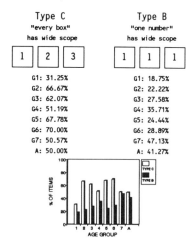

Type C	Type B
G1: 31.25%	G1: 18.75%
G2: 66.67%	G2: 22.22%
G3: 62.07%	G3: 27.58%
G4: 51.19%	G4: 35.71%
G5: 67.78%	G5: 24.44%
G6: 70.00%	G6: 28.89%
G7: 50.57%	G7: 47.13%
A: 50.00%	A: 41.27%

First, consider the subjects' responses to the four constructions with one universal Q-NP and one existential Q-NP. These results are summarized as follows:

1. Adults reacted to (39) *write one number in every box* with a Type B response 76.98% of the time and with a Type C response 19.05% of the time. Children allowed both Type B and Type C responses. However, as

illustrated in the figure given in (39), they assigned the WS reading more frequently to *one number* (Type B) than to *every box* (Type C), excepting Groups 1 and 2. The response pattern exhibited by children 5 and older followed the trend observed in adults; the response pattern exhibited by children younger than 5 did not.[3]

This set of results, at first glance, seemed to follow L's prediction but not the one provided by H or AL, if (39) had the structural configuration illustrated in (T1). However, it is important to note that a WS reading for *every* does allow a type B response, where the same number is written in each box (a kind of accidental narrow scope (NS) reading). Nothing about the syntax or the scope assignment makes it necessary to put a different number in each box. Moreover, as mentioned in the Method section, the task adopted in the current study allows more than one token for each of the direct objects shown on the card. When more than one token is available, a Type B response may be viewed as one of the several possible responses representing the WS reading for *every box*. (For more discussion, see footnote 2.) If this was indeed the case, that is, if the subjects gave Type B responses because they assigned the WS reading to *every box*, but not because they assigned the WS reading to *one number*, then we may argue that most subjects (both adults and children), when they were asked to determine scope relations, were not following L's scope principle given in (16b) (adults: WS *every box* = Type B + Type C = 96.03%; children: WS *every box* = Type B + Type C = 84.98%). In contrast, if the Type B response was actually treated by the subjects as a representation of the WS reading for *one number*, then it remains a problem for L's analysis that Type C responses were allowed by the adults about 19% of the time and by the children about 32% of the time. L predicted that no instances of Type C responses should be found. To summarize, if the structural representation for (39) is actually the one given in (T1), it seems that the results presented in (39) were more consistent with H or AL's analysis than with L's.

However, construction (39) may be analyzed as having the structural configuration given in (T1′), as discussed in Huang (1988) and Larson (1988). If (T1′) is indeed the correct analysis, a converging prediction is reached by the three different analyses; namely, subjects should allow only Type B responses. In this case, the problem for all three analyses is to explain why 19% of the adults and 32% of the children did accept Type C responses.

Still, there is another possibility. According to H's early analysis (1982), the structural representation for sentence (39) may be (T1″). In (T1″), the two Q-NPs c-command each other. As a result, according to both H and AL, (39) is predicted to be ambiguous. One reading corresponds to the Type B

---

[3] It should be pointed out that, in the present study, a high proportion of the young children tended to give only one particular response to all of the test questions they had received. The lack of differential responses to different sentence types has prevented us from drawing any clear-cut conclusions regarding these young subjects' scope knowledge.

response; one reading corresponds to the Type C response. One might say that the reading that implies the Type B response is the preferred reading for Chinese subjects. If the structural representation for (39) is truly (T1''), then the set of data confirms H and AL's analysis. According to L, the subjects should have allowed only Type B, but not Type C, responses. The problem again for L is to explain why 19% of the adults' responses and 32% of the children's responses were Type C. (See footnote 2 for discussion of the issue regarding multiple tokens.)

2. Adults consistently reacted to (40) *write every number in one box* with a Type E response (96.03%). Children 5 and older preferred Type E to Type C responses. Children younger than 5, on the other hand, preferred Type C to Type E responses.

If (40) has the structural configuration given in (T1), the results of our experiment followed from H and AL's analysis, but not from L's. However, if (T1') is the correct analysis, a converging prediction would be reached by all three analyses; namely, *every number* should have scope over *one box* (Type C). In this case, one might ask why the adults assigned the WS reading to *every number* less than 1% of the time and the children, less than 30% of the time. Finally, if (40) has the structural configuration given in (T1''), according to H and AL, sentence (40) is ambiguous. As a result, one might say that the preferred reading of sentence (40) for adult Chinese speakers and older children is that in which *one box* takes scope over *every number*. According to L, no matter what alternative configurations are assigned to sentence (40), the prediction is that *every number* takes scope over *one box*. Again, L has to explain why less than 1% of the adults and less than 30% of the children behaved as predicted.

3. Adults consistently gave Type E response (96.83%) to (41) *in one box, write every number*. Children 5 and older preferred Type E to Type C responses; they assigned the WS reading to *one box* more frequently than to *every number*. Children younger than 5 exhibited an opposite response pattern. The set of results from adults and older children was compatible with the predictions given by all three analyses.

4. Adults allowed both Type C (50%) and Type B (41.27%) responses to (42) *in every box, write one number*. (See footnote 2 for the alternative view concerning the Type B response.) The response pattern exhibited by children followed a similar trend observed in adults; they attributed the WS reading to *every box* more frequently than to *one number*. This set of results was compatible with all of the three scope analyses under discussion because the WS reading for the universal quantified NP *every box* does not imply that there must always be different numbers chosen.

To summarize, looking at the responses given by the adults and those given by children between the ages of 5 and 10 (i.e., G3–G7), a parallel between the children's and the adults' scope interpretations can be detected. The particular response distributions were somewhat different, yet the majority of the children's responses were consistent with the adults' responses. Assuming that constructions (39) and (40) have the structure given in (T1), the hypothesis that emphasizes the interaction between the notions of command and linear precedence (hereafter the *linearity hypothesis*) is not confirmed by the data. The two hypotheses that take into account the notion of c-command are confirmed by the data. On the other hand, assuming that constructions (39) and (40) have the structure given in (T1'), there exists a problem for all three scope analyses; that is, they all have to explain why, for construction (39), 19% of the adults and 32% of the children gave the unexpected Type C responses. Moreover, all three analyses have to explain why, for construction (40), less than 1% of the adults' responses and less than 30% of the children's responses were the expected Type C. Consider the third alternative. If constructions (39) and (40) have the structure given in (T1''), again the linearity hypothesis is not confirmed by the data, and the two hypotheses that take into account the notion of c-command are confirmed. As mentioned earlier, the structural configuration controversy has created some difficulties in evaluating H's and AL's scope principles by using constructions (39) and (40). However, no such difficulty was found when L's scope principle was evaluated. Based on the results presented so far, it seems clear that when more than one response was consistent with the syntactic analysis, the preferred response was not affected by L's linearity factor. Other nonsyntactic or performance factors should be considered. We will discuss this point in a more detailed manner when we examine the results of other constructions. The data listed in (41) and (42) confirmed all three analyses.

Let us examine the subjects' responses to the *every-every* constructions ((43) and (45)) and the *one-one* constructions ((44) and (46)). The results are summarized as follows:

The Results
Chinese Canonical Constructions (cont.)

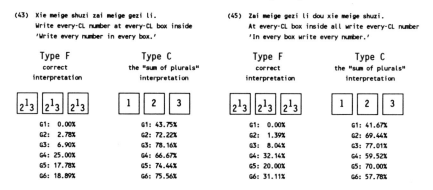

(43) Xie meige shuzi zai meige gezi li.
   Write every-CL number at every-CL box inside
   'Write every number in every box.'

Type F	Type C
correct interpretation	the "sum of plurals" interpretation
2^1_3 2^1_3 2^1_3	1 2 3
G1: 0.00%	G1: 43.75%
G2: 2.78%	G2: 72.22%
G3: 6.90%	G3: 78.16%
G4: 25.00%	G4: 66.67%
G5: 17.78%	G5: 74.44%
G6: 18.89%	G6: 75.56%

(45) Zai meige gezi li dou xie meige shuzi.
   At every-CL box inside all write every-CL number
   'In every box write every number.'

Type F	Type C
correct interpretation	the "sum of plurals" interpretation
2^1_3 2^1_3 2^1_3	1 2 3
G1: 0.00%	G1: 41.67%
G2: 1.39%	G2: 69.44%
G3: 8.04%	G3: 77.01%
G4: 32.14%	G4: 59.52%
G5: 20.00%	G5: 70.00%
G6: 31.11%	G6: 57.78%

G7: 22.99%   G7: 67.82%

A: 93.65%   A: 4.76%

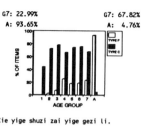

(44) Xie yige shuzi zai yige gezi li.
Write one-CL number at one-CL box inside
'Write one number in one box.'

Type A	Type C
correct	the "generic"
interpretation	reading

| 1 | | | | 1 | 2 | 3 |

G1: 37.50%   G1: 33.33%
G2: 62.50%   G2: 19.44%
G3: 79.31%   G3: 12.64%
G4: 82.14%   G4: 8.33%
G5: 76.67%   G5: 18.89%
G6: 61.11%   G6: 30.00%
G7: 85.06%   G7: 10.34%
A: 96.03%   A: 2.38%

G7: 21.84%   G7: 63.22%

A: 92.86%   A: 4.76%

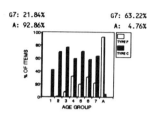

(46) Zai yige gezi li xie yige shuzi.
At one-CL box inside write one-CL number
'In one box write one number.'

Type A	Type C
correct	the "generic"
interpretation	reading

G1: 45.83%   G1: 33.33%
G2: 76.39%   G2: 12.50%
G3: 88.51%   G3: 9.19%
G4: 82.14%   G4: 14.29%
G5: 70.00%   G5: 27.78%
G6: 60.00%   G6: 33.33%
G7: 81.61%   G7: 16.09%
A: 76.19%   A: 18.25%

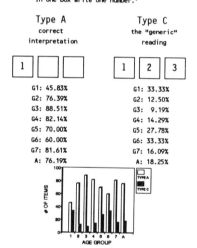

5. The only correct interpretation for the *every-every* sentences, (43) and (45), was to write all three numbers in each of the three boxes (Type F). As indicated, about 93% of the adults gave the correct interpretation to these two constructions. About 5% of the time, they mistakenly gave Type C responses by writing different numbers in different boxes. Children gave very few responses corresponding to the correct adult interpretation. In many cases, they wrote a number in a box and another number in another box until there were no numbers left and no boxes unused. Children seemed to know the concept of *every N* and tried to establish a relation between the members of the two sets of elements mentioned. However, instead of making one universal Q-NP enter the scope of another universal Q-NP, they assigned the *sum of plurals* reading to (43) and (45). For example, a sum of plurals reading for (43) corresponds to the following statement: *Write three numbers in three boxes such that each of the numbers is written and each of the boxes is written in* (Chien & Wexler, 1989). An alternative interpretation for this set of results is that children may produce this nonadultlike result because of some kind of mental set (or response set); for example, they might not want to use any number more than one time. Further research is necessary for validating this set of results and for

identifying the determining factors. If this response pattern is supported and can be viewed as a result of children's syntactic knowledge (rather than an artifact), then it might constitute an important empirical discovery that calls for theoretical explanations. (For some converging data in Japanese and English, see Chien, in preparation; Takahashi, 1990, 1991. Also see Philip, in press; Philip & Aurelio, 1991; Philip & Takahashi, 1991; Roeper & De Villiers, 1991; and Takahashi, 1991 for some syntactic analyses regarding children's responses to quantificational sentences involving *every*.)

6. Adults consistently gave Type A responses to (44) *write one number in one box* (96.03%). About 76% of the time, they reacted to (46) *in one box, write one number* with a Type A response. About 18% of the time, they assigned the generic reading to sentence (46) and interpreted the sentence as the following: *For every x, x=box, in x, write one y, y=number.* Like the adults, in most cases children reacted to the *one-one* sentences with a Type A response. In some cases the children assigned the generic reading to these sentences. However, they did so to both sentence (44) and sentence (46), whereas adults assigned the generic reading only to sentence (46). A more complete discussion and understanding of these and other results awaits further investigation.

Ba-constructions. The results of the four *ba*-constructions involving one universal Q-NP and one existential Q-NP are illustrated in (47) to (50). The major findings are summarized as follows.

The Results
Chinese Ba-Constructions

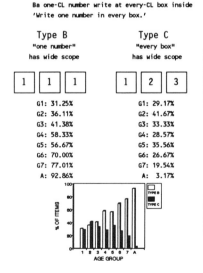

(47) Ba yige shuzi xie zai meige gezi li.
 Ba one-CL number write at every-CL box inside
 'Write one number in every box.'

Type B "one number" has wide scope	Type C "every box" has wide scope
`1 | 1 | 1`	`1 | 2 | 3`
G1: 31.25%	G1: 29.17%
G2: 36.11%	G2: 41.67%
G3: 41.38%	G3: 33.33%
G4: 58.33%	G4: 28.57%
G5: 56.67%	G5: 35.56%
G6: 70.00%	G6: 26.67%
G7: 77.01%	G7: 19.54%
A: 92.86%	A: 3.17%

(48) Ba meige shuzi dou xie zai yige gezi li.
 Ba every-CL number all write at one-CL box inside
 'Write every number in one box.'

Type C "every number" has wide scope	Type E "one box" has wide scope
`1 | 2 | 3`	`2¹3 |  | `
G1: 33.33%	G1: 10.42%
G2: 50.00%	G2: 25.00%
G3: 31.03%	G3: 54.02%
G4: 21.43%	G4: 60.71%
G5: 35.56%	G5: 50.00%
G6: 41.11%	G6: 43.33%
G7: 19.54%	G7: 71.26%
A: 0.79%	A: 92.86%

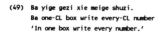

(49) Ba yige gezi xie meige shuzi.
Ba one-CL box write every-CL number
'In one box write every number.'

Type E	Type C
"one box"	"every number"
has wide scope	has wide scope

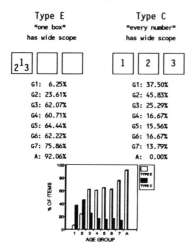

(50) Ba meige gezi dou xie yige shuzi.
Ba every-CL box all write one-CL number
'In every box write one number.'

Type C	Type B
"every box"	"one number"
has wide scope	has wide scope

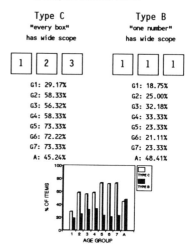

1. Adults reacted to (47) *ba one number write in every box* with a Type B response 92.86% of the time. To a large degree, the response pattern exhibited by children 5 and older followed the same trend observed in adults; they assigned the WS reading to *one number* (Type B) more frequently than to *every box* (Type C). The multiple-token issue concerning the Type B response, discussed in footnote 2, also applied in this case. If we put aside the possible alternative interpretation of the Type B response and assume that the Type B response was truly treated by the subjects as a representation of the WS reading of *one number*, then the set of results just presented is compatible with all three scope principles.

2. Adults reacted to (48) *ba every number all write in one box* with a Type E response 92.86% of the time. Children 5 or older preferred Type E responses to Type C responses but, apparently, permitted both types of responses. The structural configuration corresponding to (48) is illustrated in (T3). Given this configuration, all three proposals discussed predict that *every number* should have scope over *one box*. The data listed in (48) did not confirm this prediction. Of course, one might say that the WS reading for *every number* did not preclude the accidental NS reading corresponding to the Type E response. However, the question remains: why did the adult Chinese speakers assign a WS reading to the universal Q-NP in (48) less than 1% of the time?

3. Adults reacted to (49) *ba one box write every number* with a Type E response 92.06% of the time. Children 5 and older reacted to (49) by assigning the WS reading to *one box* (Type E) more frequently than to *every number*

(Type C). Children younger than 5 gave more Type C than Type E responses. The set of results (given by the adults and the children 5 and older) was compatible with all three analyses mentioned.

4. Adults allowed both Type C (45.24%) and Type B (48.41%) responses to (50) *ba every box all write one number.* Children reacted to (50) by assigning the WS reading to *every box* (Type C) more frequently than to *one number* (Type B). This set of results, to a certain degree, was compatible with all three scope analyses under discussion because the assignment of the WS reading to the universal quantifier does not imply that there must always be different numbers chosen. (Also, see footnote 2 for discussion of the multiple-token issue related to the Type B response.)

To summarize, considering the responses given by adults and those given by children 5 and older, a parallel between children's scope interpretation and adults' scope interpretation was found when *ba*-constructions (involving a universal Q-NP and an existential Q-NP) were examined. Again, the particular response distributions were somewhat different, and children seemed to be more flexible in terms of their scope interpretations than were adults (except in the case of (50)). However, the relative scope preferences exhibited by the children were consistent with those exhibited by the adults.

Let us consider the data of the *every-every* cases ((51) and (53)) and those of the *one-one* cases ((52) and (54)). The major findings concerning these *ba*-constructions are summarized as follows:

The Results
Chinese Ba-Constructions (cont.)

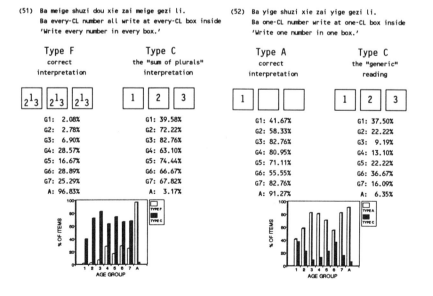

(51) Ba meige shuzi dou xie zai meige gezi li.
Ba every-CL number all write at every-CL box inside
'Write every number in every box.'

(52) Ba yige shuzi xie zai yige gezi li.
Ba one-CL number write at one-CL box inside
'Write one number in one box.'

Type F correct interpretation	Type C the "sum of plurals" interpretation	Type A correct interpretation	Type C the "generic" reading
$2^1 3$ $2^1 3$ $2^1 3$	1 2 3	1	1 2 3
G1: 2.08%	G1: 39.58%	G1: 41.67%	G1: 37.50%
G2: 2.78%	G2: 72.22%	G2: 58.33%	G2: 22.22%
G3: 6.90%	G3: 82.76%	G3: 82.76%	G3: 9.19%
G4: 28.57%	G4: 63.10%	G4: 80.95%	G4: 13.10%
G5: 16.67%	G5: 74.44%	G5: 71.11%	G5: 22.22%
G6: 28.89%	G6: 66.67%	G6: 55.55%	G6: 36.67%
G7: 25.29%	G7: 67.82%	G7: 82.76%	G7: 16.09%
A: 96.83%	A: 3.17%	A: 91.27%	A: 6.35%

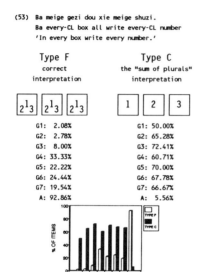

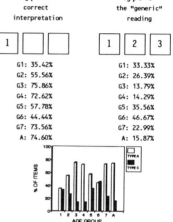

5. As with the canonical constructions, the only correct interpretation for the *ba*-constructions involving two universal Q-NPs is the Type F response. As can be seen from the data listed in (51) and (53), the majority of the adults gave the correct interpretation to these two constructions. When children were asked to interpret the two *every-every ba*-constructions, very few of them produced responses corresponding to the correct adult interpretation. In many cases, they gave Type C instead of Type F responses. Again, this set of results seemed to indicate that the children knew the concept of *every N* and tried to establish a relation between the members of the two sets of elements mentioned. However, instead of making one universal Q-NP enter the scope of another universal Q-NP, they assigned the sum of plurals reading to these *ba*-constructions.

6. Adults reacted to (52) *ba one number write in one box* with a Type A response 91.27% of the time. They reacted to (54) *ba one box write one number* with a Type A response 74.60% of the time and with a Type C response 15.87% of the time. Children (excepting G6) reacted to (52) and (54) by giving Type A responses more frequently than Type C responses. In some cases, they assigned the generic reading to these two sentence types.

SUMMARY AND CONCLUSION

The current study has provided a set of data regarding Chinese-speaking subjects' interpretations of quantificational constructions. It also provided some evaluation of the three scope principles that were proposed to account for the Chinese scope facts. A comparison between Chinese speakers' responses to the *ba*-constructions and their responses to the corresponding canonical constructions seems to indicate a high correspondence between these two sets of data. The arguments both for and against this high correspondence are summarized as follows:

1. As mentioned earlier in the design section, several Chinese linguists have argued that quantification of postverbal theme/patient objects by *mei* 'every'—as in (40) *xie meige shuzi zai yige gezi li* 'write every number in one box'—often resulted in unnatural sentences. The corresponding *ba*-construction with the preverbal theme/patient object quantified by *mei* (e.g., (48) *ba meige shuzi dou xie zai yige gezi li*, lit. 'ba every number all write in one box') is considered to be natural. The parallel between the results of these two constructions suggests that the potential effect of the unnaturalness on the subjects' scope interpretations should be regarded as minimal.

2. The high correspondence between the set of data from the canonical constructions and the set of data from the *ba*-constructions has strengthened the claim that linear precedence is not a stable determining factor for scope interpretations. According to the linearity hypothesis, the universal Q-NP should have scope over the existential Q-NP for both the canonical construction (40) *xie meige shuzi zai yige gezi li* 'write every number in one box' and the *ba*-construction (48) *ba meige shuzi dou xie zai yige gezi li* (lit. 'ba every number all write in one box'). However, as indicated, the data from the adults and the children (between the ages of 5 and 10) suggested the opposite. The linearity hypothesis also predicted that no Type C responses (with different numbers being written in different boxes) should have been observed for constructions (39) *xie yige shuzi zai meige gezi li* 'write one number in every box' and (47) *ba yige shuzi xie zai meige gezi li* (lit. 'ba one number write in every box'). However, the Type C responses did occur. The multiple-token issue with regard to the Type B response (i.e., putting a certain number in all three boxes) discussed in footnote 2 does not suggest a revision of this conclusion. Rather, it strengthens the argument that linearity cannot be a strong scope principle for Chinese.

3. The results of this study suggest that Chinese-speaking subjects, to a certain degree, are sensitive to the structure-dependent notion of c-command. They applied this concept when they were asked to provide scope interpretations. This claim is partially supported by the data given in (39) to (42). Although the structural configuration controversy (with regard to (39) and (40)) did create some problems in evaluating the importance of c-command in Chinese scope interpretation, these data (as discussed in the Results section), in general, are more consistent with the scope principles

that emphasize this structural notion of c-command than the one that emphasizes the interaction between the linearity factor and the notion of command. However, it should be pointed out that the high correspondence between the subjects' responses to the canonical and the *ba*-constructions has also raised some problems for the claim that c-command is a clear-cut determining factor for Chinese scope interpretations. The problem with regard to the structural configuration controversy observed in some of the canonical constructions did not occur in their corresponding *ba*-constructions. For example, *ba*-constructions (47) *ba yige shuzi xie zai meige gezi li* (lit. 'ba one number write in every box') and (48) *ba meige shuzi dou xie zai yige gezi li* (lit. 'ba every number all write in one box') have only one structural representation where the first Q-NP c-commands the second Q-NP. According to Huang's and Aoun and Li's analyses, the existential Q-NP should have scope over the universal Q-NP for (47), whereas the converse should be true for (48). However, only the data of (47) confirmed the prediction, whereas the adults and the children (between the ages of 5 and 10) appeared to violate the c-command constraint when they were asked to interpret (48).

Looking more closely at the response patterns, we found that the Chinese existential Q-NP (*one number* or *one box*) deserves additional discussion. According to Hornstein (1984), quantified NPs can be classified into two categories. One receives the [−operator] feature, with the associated sense of *a certain N*; the other receives the [+operator] feature and undergoes the quantifier raising process to form an operator-variable relation. It appears that the Chinese existential Q-NPs such as *one number* and *one box* can be classified in both categories. Moreover, it seems that the reading of *a certain N* is a strong reading in the Chinese existential Q-NPs. Thus, it is likely that the scope interpretation of sentences involving the existential Q-NPs are influenced by the application of this unique reading. It is still an open question to what extent and exactly how this unique property of the existential Q-NPs would interact with the structural factor of c-command (or other potential factors) to determine scope interpretations.

4. The results of the current study have also raised some problems for the Isomorphic Principle in general. Although the particular details of their scope analyses are different, Huang, Lee, and Aoun and Li (whose analysis may not obviously suggest this principle at first glance) all agree on some form of the Isomorphic Principle. As discussed earlier, the Isomorphic Principle states that the structural relation between two quantified NPs at S-structure will stay the same at Logical Form. This implies that, in Chinese, scope interpretations should reflect the surface syntactic relations of the two Q-NPs. Notice that the Isomorphic Principle is debatable if, according to a particular S-structure, only one scope interpretation was predicted, yet the subjects allowed various types of scope interpretations that imply different

syntactic relations between these two Q-NPs. As mentioned in the Results section, adults tended to give one particular interpretation to one particular construction. However, the lack of flexibility (or variability) in their responses did not necessarily suggest that they were applying the Isomorphic Principle when they were dealing with the quantificational constructions. This argumentation is partially based on the adults' data given in (47) and (48). As mentioned earlier, (47) and (48) share the same S-structure representation. However, only the results for (47) reflect the predicted surface syntactic relation between the two Q-NPs; the results for (48) do not. The data collected from the children also did not suggest a clear-cut isomorphic mapping between their scope interpretations and the surface syntactic relations. As discussed in the Results section, although, to a large degree, the responses given by the children resembled those given by the adults, the children seemed to be more flexible in terms of their scope interpretations than adults. They gave various scope interpretations to the same construction. In other words, they provided some scope interpretations that do not follow the predictions of the Isomorphic Principle.

5. Most children tested in this study indicated a high level of difficulty in dealing with the *every-every* sentences. They consistently gave non-adultlike responses to these constructions. Instead of making one universal Q-NP enter the scope of another universal Q-NP, they assigned the sum of plurals reading to these constructions.

To conclude, the major findings concerning Chinese-speaking subjects' scope interpretations are summarized as follows. First, surface linearity is not a determining factor for Chinese scope interpretation. Second, the structure-dependent notion of c-command, although not yet clear-cut in its role, is a potential determining factor for Chinese scope interpretation. The interaction between the structural concept of c-command and other nonstructural factors such as the unique meaning of the Chinese existential Q-NP should be considered. Third, the appropriateness of the Isomorphic Principle for Chinese scope interpretation is still debatable and requires further study.

Before one can make any clear-cut conclusions about the determining factors for Chinese scope interpretations, one would have to establish the definitive structural representation for the tested constructions. One may want to adopt a different approach; that is, assume that one of the scope principles such as Huang's principle or Aoun and Li's principle is correct and use the data presented in the current study and other studies to decide on the correct configuration for the as yet unresolved construction issue. The latter approach, however, has one prerequisite: More studies using different research methodologies and different linguistic materials should be designed in order to see whether convergent data can be obtained.

ACKNOWLEDGMENTS

This research was supported by NSF Grants BNS-8820439 and DBS-9120847. I would like to thank Dr. Barbara Lust for invaluable comments and constant support, Dr. John Whitman for useful commentaries, Dr. Ken Wexler for stimulating discussions, and three anonymous reviewers for valuable suggestions and detailed comments. I would also like to thank Dr. James Huang and Dr. Yen-Hui Audrey Li for thorough consultation on Chinese syntax and insightful remarks regarding the Chinese research. I am grateful to my research collaborators in Taiwan, Dr. Bonnie Chen and Dr. Chi-Pang Chiang, for coordinating the Chinese experiment, and to the research assistants at National Chengchi University for their assistance in data collection. Moreover, I would like to thank those children who took part in the experiments, and the school directors and principals for their cooperation in research. Finally, I would like to thank Richard J. Fogg for constructing tables and figures and for proofreading this chapter. A short version of this chapter, which included some results of the Chinese canonical constructions, was presented at the 20th Annual Child Language Research Forum at Stanford University in 1989.

REFERENCES

Aoun, J., & Li, A. (1993). *Syntax of scope*. Cambridge, MA: MIT Press.
Aoun, J., & Sportiche, D. (1983). On the formal theory of government. *The Linguistic Review, 2*, 211–235.
Chien, Y.-C. (in preparation). *English-speaking children's acquisition of quantificational concepts*.
Chien, Y.-C., & Wexler, K. (1989). Children's knowledge of relative scope in Chinese. *Papers and Reports on Child Language Development, 28*, 72–80.
Chomsky, N. (1986). *Barriers*. Cambridge, MA: MIT Press.
Hornstein, N. (1984). *Logic as grammar: An approach to meaning in natural language*. Cambridge, MA: MIT Press.
Huang, J. (1982). *Logical relations in Chinese and the theory of grammar*. Unpublished doctoral dissertation, MIT, Cambridge, MA.
Huang, J. (1988). Wo pao de kuai and Chinese phrase structure. *Language, 64*, 274–311.
Larson, R. (1988). On the double object construction. *Linguistic Inquiry, 19*, 335–392.
Lee, T. (1986). *Studies on quantification in Chinese*. Unpublished doctoral dissertation, University of California at Los Angeles.
Lee, T. (1991). Linearity as a scope principle for Chinese: The evidence from first language acquisition. In D. J. Napoli & J. A. Kegl (Eds.), *Bridges between psychology and linguistics* (pp. 183–206). Hillsdale, NJ: Lawrence Erlbaum Associates.
Li, C., & Thompson, S. (1981). *Mandarin Chinese: A functional reference grammar*. Berkeley: University of California Press.
May, R. (1977). *The grammar of quantification*. Unpublished doctoral dissertation, MIT, Cambridge, MA.
May, R. (1985). *Logical form: Its structure and derivation*. Cambridge, MA: MIT Press.

Philip, W. (in press). *Event quantification and the symmetrical interpretation of universal quantifiers in child language.* UMOP. Amherst, MA: GLSA Publications.

Philip, W., & Aurelio, S. (1991). Quantifier spreading: Pilot study of preschooler's "every." In T. L. Maxfield & B. Plunkett (Eds.), *Papers in the acquisition of WH* (pp. 267–282). Amherst, MA: GLSA Publications.

Philip, W., & Takahashi, M. (1991). Quantifier spreading in the acquisition of "every." In T. L. Maxfield & B. Plunkett (Eds.), *Papers in the acquisition of WH* (pp. 283–302). Amherst, MA: GLSA Publications.

Reinhart, T. (1983). *Anaphora and semantic interpretation.* London: Croom Helm.

Roeper, T., & de Villiers, J. (1991). The emergence of bound variable structures. In T. L. Maxfield & B. Plunkett (Eds.), *Papers in the acquisition of WH* (pp. 225–266). Amherst, MA: GLSA Publications.

Takahashi, M. (1990). *Children's interpretation of sentences containing "dono."* Unpublished manuscript. University of Massachusetts, Amherst.

Takahashi, M. (1991). Children's interpretation of sentences containing "every." In T. L. Maxfield & B. Plunkett (Eds.), *Papers in the acquisition of WH* (pp. 303–328). Amherst, MA: GLSA Publications.

Xu, L., & Lee, T. (1989). Scope ambiguity and disambiguity in Chinese. *Proceedings of the Chicago Linguistic Society, 25.*

CHAPTER EIGHTEEN

Scope and Optionality: Comments on the Chapters on WH-Movement and Quantification

John Whitman
Cornell University

Recent research has suggested that syntactic operations that are obligatory prior to the level of Phonetic Form are uniformly forced by morphological factors. Prime examples are operations such as verb raising to inflection in Romance and NP-movement. The former is forced by the need to support inflectional morphology, the latter by a need for Case in the surface syntax. Absent such essentially morphological requirements, the "procrastinate" principle (Chomsky, 1992) dictates that transformational operations are abstract, that is, delayed to the level of Logical Form (LF).

The hypothesis that directly observable movement occurs only to satisfy morphological requirements provides a clear characterization of many pervasive instances of cross-linguistic variation. Thus the variation between English and Romance with respect to surface verb placement results from a morphological difference: English verbs are base-generated together with verbal inflection, whereas tense and agreement morphology is generated separately in Romance, in the position of one or more inflectional heads above VP. The hypothesis also makes a prediction about how verb placement is acquired: The child must learn that English verbs are underlyingly generated with inflection. UG provides the remaining information necessary to acquire the two patterns of verb placement: the Stray Affix Filter (Baker, 1988; Lasnik, 1981) and the procrastinate principle. Failure to raise the verb in Romance would violate the former, a morphological requirement; illicit raising of the inflected verb prior to LF in English would violate the latter, a basic design feature of UG.

The chapters commented on here discuss two types of movement where cross-language variation has proven to be more difficult to correlate with morphological variation: WH-movement and Quantifier Raising (QR). Since Huang (1982), it has been held that languages may vary as to whether WH-movement occurs in the syntax or at LF. QR, as originally characterized by May (1977), is strictly an LF scope-fixing operation; but subsequent research on quantifier scope has proposed scope-fixing principles that reference surface position and introduce potential cross-linguistic variability. An example is Aoun and Li's (1989, 1993a) Scope Principle, discussed later.

In both of these cases it is not immediately clear how the morphologically motivated movement hypothesis could account for the observed variation. In the case of WH-movement, one might hypothesize that surface movement is forced by overt morphological marking of the question. But this hypothesis is immediately disconfirmed by the existence of WH-in-situ languages both with obligatory overt morphological marking (Japanese and Korean embedded clauses) and without such marking (Chinese). With QR, morphology plays no apparent role in forcing movement: QR is an adjunction operation and thus involves nothing like the specifier-head relationship evident in WH-movement, nor is QR accompanied by anything comparable to overt [+WH] marking of interrogative clauses.

This commentary focuses on WH-movement and QR in turn. Its general thrust is that Roeper and de Villiers (chapter 16) and Chien (chapter 17) support the view that these operations are subject to less variation than has been supposed, and they support rather than counterexemplify the morphologically motivated movement hypothesis.

WH-MOVEMENT

The preceding considerations have recently led to a serious re-examination of the alleged cross-linguistic variation regarding the level at which WH- movement takes place. Watanabe (1992), Chomsky (1992), and Aoun and Li (1993b) all proposed that WH-movement is syntactic, involving movement of an invisible WH-operator in contexts where the overt WH-phrase appears to be in situ. This approach solves the problem of cross-language variation, by declaring it spurious. However, it runs into a basic conceptual problem from the standpoint of the morphologically motivated movement hypothesis. Syntactic WH-movement may be characterized as forced by an agreement requirement, as originally proposed by Kuroda (1988). But agreement requirements do not force movement of all members of the relevant type (here, WH-phrases) in a particular domain. Instead, they are typically satisfied by movement of a single exemplar to a unique specifier position; and, under specific (if not completely understood) circumstances, they may be satisfied by insertion of an expletive, a nonmovement option in the syntax. The question that arises with respect to the universal syntactic movement account of WH-movement is: Why are these options not available here as well?

A potential answer to this question is provided the partial movement pattern in WH-questions studied by Roeper and de Villiers:

(1) Was$_i$ hat er gesagt wie$_i$ er Suppe $t_i$isst.
    what did he say   how he soup   eats
    'How did he say he eats soup?'

(2) a. What$_i$ do you think what$_i$ pigs say t_i?   (Cited from Thornton,1991)
    b. How$_i$ did Big Bird ask who$_i$ to help t_i?   (answer: *Kermit*)

The general characteristic of this pattern is that the scope of the interrogative operator is fixed by WH$_1$, whereas its content is determined by WH$_2$:

(3) [$_{CP}$ WH$_1$ . . . [$_{CP}$ WH$_2$ . . .]]

As (1) shows, partial movement is an option in adult German; (2a) shows that it occurs in child English production, whereas Roeper and de Villiers' (2b) shows that it occurs in comprehension of sentences designed to be WH-island violations. As Roeper and de Villiers argue, the tendency of children to answer the medial WH-word in questions like (2b) shows that they are employing a partial movement strategy parallel to that in the adult German (1), rather than simply copying the leftmost WH-word in the expected position of the medial trace in examples like (2a).

The partial movement pattern demonstrates the existence of an expletive WH strategy in UG, where semantically empty WH$_1$ stands in for WH$_2$. The pattern provides us with at least one clear instance where obligatory syntactic WH-movement, in the strict sense, does not occur. The rightmost WH-word in (1), for example, does move, but not to the position required by WH-movement, a [+WH] specifier position. Instead, the agreement requirements of the [+WH] matrix CP are satisfied by a base-generated dummy (i.e., expletive) WH-word. But this is a welcome result, because it shows that syntactic WH-movement indeed falls into the pattern of other types of morphologically induced movement. The morphological requirement (presence of a WH-phrase in the specifier of a [+WH] CP) can be satisfied by a base-generated expletive, and furthermore, it appears that only one WH-phrase is needed to satisfy the requirement.[1]

A second point about the partial movement strategy is more speculative, but equally important. Given the existence of this strategy, we might ask,

---

[1]This characterization of obligatory syntactic WH-movement is consistent with Watanabe's (1992) Two-Level Movement Hypothesis. Under this approach, one and only one WH-phrase per [+WH] Comp is affected at the first (syntactic) level of movement. The approach is inconsistent with Aoun and Li's (1993b) treatment, under which every WH-phrase is associated with an instance of syntactic movement. Here and throughout this discussion, *syntactic movement* refers to transformational operations that are subject to Subjacency and may be phonetically observable.

is something like a partial movement strategy operative in languages that have been analyzed as allowing all overt WH-phrases to remain in situ? Under this analysis the familiar Chinese and Japanese WH-in-situ contexts in (4)–(5) would be analyzed as having a null [+WH] operator—in effect, a null [+WH] expletive—in [SPEC, CP] in the syntax:[2]

(4) **Chinese**

[$_{CP}$OP$_{[+WH]}$ [Ni   mai-le   shenme]]?
             you buy-PERF what
'What did you buy?'

(5) **Japanese**

[$_{CP}$OP$_{[+WH]}$ [*pro* nani-o   kat-ta]   no]?
             you what-ACC buy-PERF Q
'What did you buy?'

This analysis extends the WH-expletive option by the partial movement pattern in (1)–(3) to the classical WH-in-situ pattern, under the general approach of morphologically motivated obligatory syntactic WH-movement. Following the assumption of this approach that a [+WH] specification requires the presence of a [+WH] operator in the CP specifier position in the syntax, this option permits that requirement to be satisfied by a null expletive WH-operator.

This analysis gives rise to a number of questions, not all of which can be answered here. One has to do with the licensing of the null expletive WH-operator in (4)–(5). In Chinese and Japanese, it seems plausible that the possibility of such an expletive operator is related to the general possibility of null expletives in these languages.[3] A second important question is whether the null expletive WH-operator pattern has an exact overt counterpart: one where the rightmost WH is actually in situ, rather than having been moved to an intermediate [SPEC, CP] as in the partial movement pattern of (1)–(2). An answer to this question is provided by Srivastav (1990), who described an overt expletive WH pattern in Hindi. In

---

[2]Aoun and Li (1993a) made essentially this proposal for WH in situ in Chinese.

[3]There is no question that Japanese, for example, has impersonal constructions that call for expletives if they are structural equivalents of their English counterparts:

(i) [pro kaer-ana-kereba] nar-ana-i
    go.home-NEG-if   become-NEG-IMP
    'It won't do if pro doesn't go home.'

Any type of overt (pronominal) expletive subject is disallowed in patterns like (i). This is consistent with the view that the expletive pronoun is obligatorily null. A radical alternative view holds that subject position in sentences like (i) is simply missing altogether; discussion of this alternative would take us beyond the realm of these comments.

the Hindi pattern, the contentful WH-phrase occurs in situ, but where it takes scope over a higher clause, this is marked by a pleonastic WH in that clause:

(6) [Tum kyaa$_{WH1}$ jaante ho [ki   usne kyaa$_{WH2}$ kiyaa]]
     you   what   know   that he   what   did
     'What do you know that he did?'

A final crucial question is how the null expletive WH analysis accounts for the locality effects evinced by the WH-in-situ pattern discussed by Watanabe and Aoun and Li (1993b), among others. Under the null expletive WH-operator analysis, these effects cannot result from syntactic movement of the operator. Whitman and Yanagida (1993) argued that locality effects with WH-in situ result not from movement of the WH- or associated operator phrase, but rather from head movement of the question marker (-*ka* or -*no* in Japanese) to COMP of the [+WH] CP. This approach explains, among other things, the apparent discrepancy between Japanese and Chinese with respect to WH-island effects. Although Watanabe (1992, and references cited there) assigned (7a) the status of a WH-island violation, Huang (1982) considered the corresponding sentence in Chinese, (7b), fully acceptable:

(7) a. Kimi-wa [dare-ga   nani-o   kat-ta ka]   siri-ta-i no?
        you-TOP who-NOM what-ACC buy-PERF Q know-want-IMP Q
        *'What do you want to know who bought?'
    b. Ni   xiang-zhidao [shei mai-le shenme]?
       you want-know   who buy-PERF what
       (?*)'What do you want to know who bought?'

Under Whitman and Yanagida's analysis, the matrix interrogative marker originates in a position adjacent to the WH-phrase *nani-o* 'what', a pattern actually realized in earlier forms of Japanese. Movement of the interrogative marker takes place in the syntax and violates Subjacency,[4] resulting in degraded acceptability. In Chinese, on the other hand, no interrogative marker need occur, so the corresponding violation does not result.

I have sketched an account of obligatory WH-movement in the syntax that ascribes to this operation the properties of morphologically motivated movement in general, in particular the possibility of an expletive strategy

---

[4] Movement of the interrogative marker also results in a violation of the Head Movement Constraint in the syntax; at this level of representation the interrogative marker is unable to antecedent-govern its trace. Whitman and Yanagida (1993) argued that subsequent LF movement of the WH-phrase containing the trace of the interrogative marker to [SPEC, CP] restores antecedent-government and rescues this violation.

as exemplified by partial WH-movement. The fact that early learners employ the partial movement strategy in English fits a central pattern of acquisition data recurring in these volumes, where the acquisition process attests a range of patterns permitted by UG but excluded in the adult language due to language-particular morphological properties. In the case of partial WH-movement, Roeper and de Villiers argue that the medial WH-phrase implicated in this pattern can occur only in CPs in a non–syntactically subcategorized position, such as extraposed complement CPs in German. The partial movement pattern in English occurs prior to acquisition of lexical (word-specific) subcategorization information. If the hypothesis associating the WH-in-situ pattern with a null WH-expletive is correct, we might predict that this pattern is available to early learners as long as their grammar permits null expletives.

QUANTIFIER RAISING

Aoun and Li (1989, 1993a) proposed a principle of UG to explain the apparent variation between Chinese and English with respect to quantifier scope. As outlined in Chien (this volume, chapter 17), the basic problem to be accounted for is that English sentences like (8) are ambiguous, whereas the corresponding (9) in Chinese is not:

(8) Every child sang a song
    a. Different children sang different songs.
    b. The children all sang the same song.

(9) Meige xiaohai dou chang le   yi-shou ge.
    each child   all   sing-PERF one-CL song
    Different children sang different songs.

Under Aoun and Li's Scope Principle, a quantifier may take scope over another quantifier if it c-commands the latter or its trace. Scope ambiguity in (8) is accounted for by exploiting the VP-internal subject hypothesis: Following LF adjunction of the object quantifier phrase to VP by QR, the object quantifier c-commands the VP-internal trace of the subject. The nonambiguity in (9) is explained by claiming that subjects in Chinese fail to undergo raising out of VP; in Aoun and Li's system, this makes it impossible for QR to derive a well-formed representation where the object quantifier has scope over the subject or its trace.

Aoun and Li's characterization of postverbal quantifier interaction in English is largely compatible with the Chinese data discussed by Chien. Their account predicts that the order Verb - Theme Argument - Nontheme is ambiguous, as in (10a), whereas the order Verb - Nontheme - Theme, as in (10b), is not:

(10) a. I assigned every problem to someone.   (ambiguous)
     b. I assigned someone every problem. (wide scope for *someone* only)

Aoun and Li assumed that the Verb - Theme - Nontheme order is derived by NP-movement of the theme argument from a lower position in the type of VP shell structure proposed by Larson (1988), leaving its trace c-commanded by the nontheme argument. This analysis can be extended to pairs of Chinese sentences like (11), discussed by Chien:

(11) a. Xie [$_{QP1}$ yi-ge   shuzi]   zai [$_{QP2}$ mei-ge gezi] li.
        write   one-CL number at   every-CL box inside
        'Write one number in every box.'
     b. Zai [$_{QP2}$ yi-ge   gezi] li   xie [$_{QP1}$ mei-ge   shuzi].
        at   one-CL box inside write   every-CL number
        'In one box write very number.'

Chien reports that 19.05% of adults[5] in her experiment assigned a wide scope interpretation to *every box* in (11a), whereas none assigned wide scope to this QP in (11b). If we apply Aoun and Li's analysis of English to (11a), the Verb - Theme - Nontheme order is derived by NP- (A-) movement of the Theme argument, predicting ambiguity under the Scope Principle. The order in (11b), on the other hand, is derived by A'-movement (fronting of the PP *in one box*); in this case no ambiguity is predicted.

Aoun and Li's approach thus appears to predict correctly, for this restricted set of data, that English and Chinese show the same scope facts with multiple postverbal quantifiers. Their theory also accounts for cross-linguistic variation in multiple quantifier interpretation by invoking a type of variation that is superficially compatible with the morphologically motivated movement hypothesis: whether or not surface NP movement of the subject out of VP is forced by a "strong agreement" requirement, in the terms of Chomsky (1992).

On closer consideration, however, this compatibility breaks down. Aoun and Li's theory assumes that subjects never raise out of VP in Chinese; if such raising occurred at LF, for example, the predicted result would be

---

[5]A slightly larger percentage of older children attested the wide scope interpretation for *every box*. In general, Chien's results for children show greater variability, with few or no unambiguous results, but with older children patterning like adults. As Chien discusses, this may be due to delay in learning the meanings of lexical quantifiers. I therefore focus on the adult results in this discussion.

ambiguity under the Scope Principle at LF, the level at which scope relations are computed. The core assumption of the morphologically motivated movement hypothesis, on the other hand, is that morphological requirements force surface syntactic movement: Morphological variation may result in the acceleration or delay of obligatory movement, but not its elimination. It should be further pointed out that the evidence for surface VP-internal position of subjects in Chinese is poor, and that this analysis is contraindicated by such basic facts as the relative order of subjects, negation, and adverbs, and the existence of VP fronting in Chinese (see Huang, 1993, for this and additional arguments against the surface VP-internal subject hypothesis for Chinese).

In fact Chinese and English exhibit another surface difference that may be correlated with the contrast in (8)–(9). Chinese marks the clausal scope of universally quantified phrases in preverbal position with the adverb *dou* 'all'. *Dou* may be analyzed as a pure adverb of quantification comparable to English quantificational adverbs such as *always, seldom* (Lewis, 1975), except that *dou* lacks the ability of the latter to bind a spatiotemporal context variable. *Dou* also has the interesting property that it cannot be associated with postverbal NPs.

A possible explanation for this property is that Chinese quantificational force is always provided by an adverb of quantification, overt (like *dou*) or covert. This would be a lexical property of Chinese, indicated to the language learner by the existence of overt adverbs like *dou* whose only function is to provide quantificational force for other sentence constitutents. Given this property, the quantificational force of postverbal indefinite NPs is provided by a covert existential operator, as in (12b), the LF representation of (12a) (=(9)):

(12) a. Meige xiaohai dou chang le [∃] yi-shou ge.
　　　each child all sing-PERF one-CL song
　　 b. dou$_x$ [child x] ∃$_y$ song y ∧ x sang y

A locality principle such as Aoun and Li's (1993a) Minimal Binding Requirement, which requires that variables be bound by the closest potential A'-binder, would then ensure that postverbal NPs are associated with the covert existential adverb of quantification.

Some support for this hypothesis is provided by Chien's data on NPs containing *meige* 'every' in postverbal position. As Chien observes, many previous researchers on Chinese have described such examples as ill formed. Chien, however, reports that speakers in her experiments were able to assign an interpretation to such sentences, as in (13):

(13) Xie mei-ge shuzi zai yi-ge gezi li.
　　 write every-CL number at one-CL box inside
　　 'Write every number in one box.'

What is remarkable about such examples is that the overwhelming majority of adult speakers assign wide scope to *one box* (96.03%) rather than *every number* (0.79%) in such examples. As Chien notes, this result is completely unpredicted by the Scope Principle; as we saw earlier, Aoun and Li's account predicts scopal ambiguity in a configuration like (13). Consider now the prediction made by the hypothesis that quantificational force in Chinese is always provided by adverbs of quantification. In the postverbal position of (13), only the covert existential adverb of quantification in (12) is available, but this is semantically incompatible with *meige* 'every'. For some speakers, the result may be ill formedness; for others, however, another possibility may be available: assigning *meige shuzi* 'every number' the interpretation of a nonquantificational plural or partitive NP, as in (14).

(14) Write the numbers   in one box.
          the group/set of numbers

This interpretation matches precisely the response provided by 96.03% of Chien's adult speakers, who wrote the complete set of available numbers in one and only one box.

The hypothesis that Chinese assigns quantificational force strictly through adverbs of quantification of course requires further exploration. Its most important feature is that this exemplifies the type of variation (variation in the distribution of a lexical class) that might be expected under an approach that restricts cross-language variation to morphological and lexical differences.

REFERENCES

Aoun, J., & Li, Y.-H. A. (1989). Constituency and scope. *Linguistic Inquiry, 20*, 141–172.

Aoun, J., & Li, Y.-H. A. (1993a). *Syntax of scope*. Cambridge, MA: MIT Press.

Aoun, J., & Li, Y.-H. A. (1993b). Wh-elements in situ: Syntax or LF? *Linguistic Inquiry, 24*, 199–238.

Baker, M. (1988). *Incorporation*. Chicago: Chicago University Press.

Chomsky, N. (1992). A minimalist program for linguistic theory. *MIT Occasional Papers in Linguistics, 1*. Cambridge, MA: MIT, Department of Linguistics and Philosophy.

Huang, C.-T. J. (1982). *Logical relations in Chinese and the theory of grammar*. Unpublished doctoral dissertation, MIT, Cambridge, MA.

Huang, C.-T. J. (1993). Reconstruction and the structure of VP: Some theoretical consequences. *Linguistic Inquiry, 24*, 103–138.

Kuroda, S.-Y. (1988). Whether we agree or not: A comparative syntax of English and Japanese. In W. Poser (Ed.), *Japanese syntax*. Stanford: CSLI.

Larson, R. (1988). On the double object construction. *Linguistic Inquiry, 19*, 335.

Lasnik, H. (1981). Restricting the theory of transformations: A case study. In N. Hornstein & D. Lightfoot (Eds.), *Explanation in linguistics*. London: Longman.

Lewis, D. (1975). Adverbs of quantification. In E. Keenan (Ed.), *Formal semantics of natural language* (pp. 3–15). Cambridge: Cambridge University Press.

May, R. (1977). *The grammar of quantification.* Unpublished doctoral dissertation, MIT, Cambridge, MA.

Srivastav, V. (1990). Hindi *wh* and pleonastic operators. *Proceedings of the North Eastern Linguistics Society, 20,* 443–457.

Thornton, R. (1991). *Adventures in long distance moving: The acquisition of complex wh-questions.* Unpublished doctoral dissertation, University of Connecticut, Storrs.

Watanabe, A. (1992). Subjacency and s-structure movement of wh-in-situ. *Journal of East Asian Linguistics, 1,* 255–291.

Whitman, J., & Yanagida, Y. (1993). *Wh-head movement.* Unpublished manuscript, Cornell University, Ithaca, NY.

PART FIVE

LEARNABILITY

CHAPTER NINETEEN

How to Obey the Subset Principle: Binding and Locality

Janet Dean Fodor
Graduate Center, City University of New York

LEARNING AMBIGUITIES

A language learner lacking systematic negative evidence could rely on the Subset Principle (SP) to avoid adopting an overgenerating grammar. But SP will be effective in fending off overgeneration only if learners are able to *determine*, reliably and across the board, whether two candidate grammars stand in a subset/superset relation, and if so, which of them gives the subset language. Whether this is easy or difficult depends in part on the assumptions we make about the form in which grammars are mentally represented. I take it as obvious that learners do not assess potential subset relations by generating languages and comparing them; rather, they must be able to settle the matter by comparing grammars.[1] So learning would be facilitated if subset relations between languages were reliably associated with some readily accessible relationship between grammars. On traditional hypothesis-testing models of learning, which assumed rich grammars needing to be constructed from scratch, no such transparent relationship could be identified; that is, the search for an evaluation metric was a failure. The parameter setting model offers a

---

[1]See Fodor (1989). Kapur, Lust, Harbert, and Martohardjono (1993) contrasted an extensional SP defined over languages, with an intensional choice principle defined over grammars that does *not* select the subset language. They did not note the possibility of an intensional principle that does reliably select the subset language, as I suggest here. (Incidentally, it is not clear that they have a true exception to SP in extension, for though they draw attention to a potential problem involving parametrization of Principle B, their own intensional solution to it presupposes that the selected grammar does not generate a superset language.)

welcome solution. Because parameters and their values are assumed all to be innately specified, it can be assumed also that whenever two values of a parameter stand in a subset/superset relation, they are innately ordered, with priority given to the subset value. Then a learner can satisfy SP very easily, just by obeying the injunction: Select the earliest (highest priority) value of a parameter that is consistent with the available evidence.

Innate ordering of parameter values thus resolves an ambiguity in the input-to-grammar mapping: ambiguity about which value of a parameter to adopt when more than one is compatible with the evidence. But there are other ambiguities that a learner is faced with besides this. In all of these cases, a learner could be utterly committed to obeying SP and yet not know how to do so. Clark (1988) observed that ordering parameter values is successful only if the learner already knows *which* parameter to reset at each step, but this may be underdetermined by the input. Also, a matter of obvious concern is that ungrammatical input (also, grammatical input mistakenly assigned an ungrammatical analysis by the child) might trigger the setting of a parameter to an incorrect value (see Grodzinsky, 1989; Valian, 1990). Here, there is uncertainty for the learner about which input is to be learned from, and which input should be discarded. Yet another kind of indeterminacy that may trouble learners concerns the distinction between input that should trigger parameter setting in the core grammar, and input that calls for elaboration of the peripheral grammar.

In what follows I briefly discuss parameter-parameter ambiguity (Clark's problem) as background for a more extensive discussion of core/periphery ambiguity, which I believe has not been addressed before.[2] I then set out the nature of the problem, illustrate it with binding theory examples, and examine some standard sorts of solutions to it, which I argue are not effective in this case. A wider range of possible solutions is discussed in Fodor (1992c), including the one that I believe to be correct. About the problem of sorting valid from invalid input I have nothing useful to say. Assuming that there are no interesting constraints on *which* ungrammatical sentences a child might hear (or think he has heard),[3] this problem seems completely insoluble as long as one-trial learning is assumed to occur. (See Kapur, this volume, chapter 22.) Of course there *must be* some mechanism for coping with this; and it is conceivable that, if we knew what it is, we would see that it also contributes to the differentiation of periphery from core (roughly: of exceptions from

---

[2]Roeper and Weissenborn (1990) dealt with a related problem in their search for an unambiguous trigger for the positive value of the null subject parameter. Though they did not discuss peripheral grammar, they had a similar concern about the danger of a nontrigger (in their case, subject omission in root clauses) being mistaken for a trigger.

[3]To refer to learners I use the pronouns, *he, his,* and *him* throughout, to avoid the clumsiness of disjunction, and also the common practice of reserving feminine pronouns for those who have not yet achieved full linguistic competence.

generalizations). In that case, the learning problems presented here may not be quite so bad as I have painted them.

PARAMETER/PARAMETER AMBIGUITIES

For safe learning, a parametric model in which the values of each parameter are innately specified has the following advantages:

A. Values of the same parameter are mutually exclusive; setting to one value automatically switches off other values. For values not in a subset relation (whose selection is therefore not governed by SP), this allows recovery from a misselection, because positive evidence for one value has the effect of negative evidence for the other(s).

B. Values of a parameter that do stand in a subset relation can be innately ordered; as noted earlier, SP can then be obeyed without need for extensional computation of subset relations. (Ordering of nonsubset values is also possible and might cut learning time.)

C. Input triggers can be innately specified in association with each value. The learning mechanism then does not need to compute on-line which input sentences require which parameter settings. Also (see later discussion) certain indeterminacies can be resolved.

What Clark observed is that the sorts of learning uncertainties that are resolved by properties (A–C) for values *within* a parameter can also arise where the competition is between values of two *different* parameters.

Clark's example of a cross-parameter indeterminacy involves an ambiguity between exceptional case marking (ECM) and structural case assignment (SCA) to the subject of a nonfinite complement clause. An input such as (1) is compatible with either.

(1) John believes Bill to have left.

In English, (1) exhibits ECM, not SCA; the NP *Bill* is assigned case by the matrix verb *believes*. A superficially similar sentence in Modern Irish is licensed by SCA, not ECM; the second NP is assigned accusative case from within the lower clause.[4] Clark assumed that ECM follows from a marked setting of a government parameter, and SCA follows from a marked setting of a distinct parameter in the case theory module; though there are other

---

[4]Clark was drawing on the work of Chung and McCloskey (1987), who maintained that Modern Irish has a productive rule of accusative case assignment that applies even to an ungoverned subject of a small clause that contains no Infl. The subject of a nonfinite full clause (as in the Irish counterpart of (1)) is governed by Infl. Whether its case is assigned by Infl or by the rule that covers small clauses does not matter for present purposes; what is important is only that there is no clause-external case assigner.

possibilities, let us accept this as correct. Then a learner who hears a sentence like (1) that is not yet licensed by his grammar must decide which of these two parameters to (re)set. Sentence (1) provides no basis for a decision. And SP does not determine the right choice since this is not a subset situation. The learner must apparently just guess, and he might guess wrong. It is essential, therefore, that his error will be revealed to him by subsequent input, as under Point A. The trouble is, as Clark observed, that once a wrong move has been made, the import of subsequent data may be distorted.

ECM and SCA predict different patterns of binding, as illustrated in (2) and (3).

(2) John$_i$ believes himself$_i$ to be clever.   ECM

(3) John$_i$ believes him$_i$ to be clever.   SCA

These look like just the right sorts of sentences to guide learners to the proper analysis of (1). But they do not reliably do so, because they too are learning-ambiguous. Imagine that the target language has ECM, not SCA. And imagine a learner who opts for SCA on encountering the ambiguous (1). Later he hears (2). He might take (2) as a cue to switch to ECM. But he might instead see it as an instance of long-distance anaphor binding (LDA) in an SCA construction. In that case the original error would remain uncorrected, and a new error would have been added to it (leading possibly to yet others as further inputs are misconstrued by the learner in light of his false assumptions). And, as Clark noted, *this* error constitutes a violation of SP. The ECM/SCA choice did not violate SP; nor does the assumption of LDA *given* the assumption of SCA. But the two steps together violate SP and result in overgeneration: SCA plus LDA gives (1), (2), and (3), whereas ECM gives only (1) and (2). The learner cannot apply SP to avoid this error, if we assume with Clark that SP governs only individual steps of acquisition (i.e., that children aren't required to consider subset languages that would have been achievable if different choices had been made previously).

This problem results from the learner's selecting the SCA analysis in the absence of evidence either way. Let us assume, then, that learners never do this, that is, that they have an innate predisposition to assume ECM for examples like (1), until (if ever) they encounter evidence of SCA, such as (3). Unfortunately this proposal won't do either. It offers an ordering solution (= Type B). And for competing values of *different* parameters, a Type B solution presupposes some sort of innate cross-wiring between parameters. This seems to be the only way that a value of one parameter could be priority-ordered relative to a value of another.[5] But it conflicts with the

---

[5]There is another way. Clark (1988) suggested innate input filters, which would disappear as the learner matures, and which would indirectly determine the order in which parameters could be set. But such filters can themselves create learning problems, as Clark noted, and I will not consider them further here. See Fodor (1992b) for discussion.

standard assumption that parameters are independent of each other.[6] The independence postulate could be given up in order to permit cross-parameter interactions, but that would be an unwelcome complication of the standard parameter model. (See Fodor & Crain, 1990; Travis, 1984.)

A second problem with the Type B solution for (1) is that it doesn't work. In fact, *neither* analysis can safely be given priority. We have seen that opting first for SCA is not safe, because the positive evidence for subsequent correction to ECM is ambiguous and could lead the learner further down the garden path. Now a similar point can be made about ECM. Suppose the target language has SCA. A learner who adopted ECM for (1) and then encountered (3) might recognize it as evidence against ECM. But he might instead treat it as evidence for SCA as *well* as ECM. Or he might hold onto ECM and conclude that his target language permits local binding of pronouns, as some languages do (see later discussion). In either case his grammar would overgenerate (2), irremediably in the absence of negative data.

Thus, neither giving priority to SCA nor giving priority to ECM would guarantee learnability for both English and Irish (assuming no global, extensional subset computations). At the very least, SCA and ECM need to be made mutually exclusive, at least as a default until or unless there is ample evidence for both phenomena. This would be a Type A solution. But once again, a solution that is acceptable for within-parameter competitions becomes uncomfortable when extended to between-parameter decisions, because it implies nonindependence of parameters. That would increase the expressive power of the model and undermine the central idea of parameters as encapsulated orthogonal dimensions of variation.

A variety of other potential solutions to Clark's problem are examined in Fodor (1992b). Special attention is given to Type C solutions, which exploit the mechanism of specific UG-designated triggers associated with parameter values,[7] because these, unlike solutions based on mutual exclusion or ordering, do *not* threaten the independence postulate. We could suppose that learners discard all parameter-ambiguous input: Nothing counts as a trigger unless it is uniquely assigned to just one value of one parameter.[8]

---

[6]This notion of independence is fairly standard but is not identical to that discussed by Manzini and Wexler (1987), which has to do with whether subset relations among the values of one parameter can differ depending on the setting of another parameter.

[7]The remedy for core/periphery indeterminacy proposed in Fodor (1992c) stresses the importance of innately *specifying* triggers, rather than adopting the general criterion that *any* member of a set of triggered sentences qualifies as a trigger for that set. This is also argued for by Roeper and Weissenborn (1990). See later discussion.

[8]How does a learner *know* that there is a parameter-parameter ambiguity? In unambiguous cases the learner somehow determines which parameter to reset. One possible mechanism is: If parsing with the current grammar fails, try to reparse the input with each parameter reset (serially, or in separate but parallel computations); if just one attempt is successful, retain the new setting. If more than one parse succeeds, a choice must be made, or (as suggested here)

Then (1) will have no effect on learning, and nor will (2) or (3). What is needed then is some unambiguous triggers for ECM and SCA. There are distributional differences between these constructions that can reveal what is governing the subject NP of the nonfinite clause and can thus select between the analyses. However, it becomes clear, as the details of this triggering approach are worked out, that it can succeed only if combined with mutual exclusion and priority ordering relationships across parameters. For instance, ordering is required because the distributional evidence provides a positive trigger only for SCA, not for ECM; therefore a learner encountering (1) must adopt ECM in preference to SCA until or unless the SCA triggers occurs. (See Fodor, 1992b, for details.) Some cross-parameter relations thus seem to be inescapable.

It appears, then, that the classic parameter-setting model could sustain some real damage from the kind of surface merger of distinct phenomena that Clark drew attention to. Clark's own response to this situation (see Clark, this volume, chapter 21) has been to give up the standard switch-setting conception of parameters and shift to a genetic model in which natural selection evaluates every possible combination of parameter values as a whole. This is a somewhat drastic, but effective, way of getting by without independence of parameters. One may wonder why UG does not make short work of the whole problem by stipulating it away, e.g., by simply forbidding neutralization of distinct triggers. But arguably it is powerless to enforce this. UG is concerned only with mechanisms (principles, etc.) and is blind to their surface consequences and interactions. Ambiguity (of word strings, of structure, of parametric responsibility) occurs when derivations happen to converge, but this is not under UG's control.[9] This defenselessness of UG against accidental neutralization of distinctions that are important to learners becomes even more apparent when we turn to the comparable learning problem for indeterminacies of descriptive responsibility between core grammar and peripheral grammar. Peripheral aspects of the grammar are assumed not to be innately prefigured, but to be constructed by the learner. So there appears to be no way in which peripheral constructions (idioms, etc.) could be prevented from resembling core triggers or could be innately interordered with core parameter settings. Thus core/periphery ambiguities constitute an escalation of Clark's problem: Information that learners need is obscured, as in the case of parameter/parameter ambiguities, but there are even fewer resources available for composing a solution.

---

neither (none) of the new settings is retained. Triggering offers a more automatic version of the same idea: Encounter with a trigger sentence immediately flips the parameter switch that it is wired up to, but if it is wired to more than one there is a deadlock that prevents either (any) of them from being affected.

[9]There do seem to be some no-ambiguity constraints, motivated by the practical problems of left-to-right parsing, but these are somewhat marginal; UG constraints are not characteristically ambiguity-sensitive.

CORE/PERIPHERY AMBIGUITIES

To make a *prima facie* case that core/periphery ambiguities do arise in natural language, I need to set up a working example comparable to Clark's example (1). What we need is a case where the trigger for a (nondefault) value of some parameter is identical to (or is not distinguishable by learners from) a possible peripheral construction. Then the learner will be faced with the decision: Reset the parameter or add descriptive devices (e.g., rules, lexical entries) to the peripheral grammar? I argue here that neither move is acceptable as a general strategy. If we try out the usual remedies A–C for parametric indeterminacies, we see that a learner in the clutch of a core/periphery ambiguity cannot be rescued by remedy A (mutual exclusion), or B (ordering), or C (deterministic triggers).

English contains constructions in which a pronoun appears though an anaphor would have been expected; (4)–(6) is a sample.

(4) I'm gonna make me a sandwich.

(5) Sit you down. (some dialects)

(6) Let's (let us) go to the zoo.

These are acceptable English sentences, yet they apparently violate Binding Principle B, which dictates disjoint reference between a pronoun and a c-commanding NP in its governing category (except in special discourse contexts). The governing category for an object NP (direct or indirect) in English is normally its clause; (4)–(6) contrast with the more typical (7)–(9), which are ungrammatical (though this would of course not be evident in the primary linguistic data available to learners).

(7) a. *I'm gonna improve me.
   b. *I sent me a copy of the memo.

(8) *Put you in my shoes.

(9) *We'll let us relax once the exam is over.

The oddity of (4)–(6) does not lie in the subject NP; even where it is phonologically null, there are various indicators of its identity, as in (10) and (11).[10]

---

[10]These tests do not exclude the possibility that the pronoun is the subject, not the object, of the preceding verb. In other idioms such as *Mind you* or *Mark you*, the *you* may be the subject. For instance, the British dialect of my childhood allowed also *Mark you my words* and *Mark you me* (also *Believe you me* though not *Mind you me*). The (marginal?) acceptability of indicative first and third person *I sat me down*, *He sat him down* suggests that the *you* of (5) is the direct object. Also note *Sit yourself down* but not *Sit you yourself down*. (In earlier forms of English the case marking of *thee* versus *thou* permitted a nice distinction between *Go thou to Cumberland* (subject) and *Get thee to Cumberland* (object).) The accusative case in (6) suggests that *us* is the object. It is also compatible with *us* being an ECM subject, but loose usages such as *Let's US go too* or *Let's you and I go early and Tom can catch up later* or even *Let's you two guys fight and I'll hold the coats* suggest that it is not.

(10) a. Sit you down, won't you?
     b. Sit you down, and make yourself at home.

(11) a. Let's go, shall we?   *Let's go, will/won't you?
     b. Let us go then, you and I. . . (T. S. Eliot)

At first sight, then, (4)–(6) are exceptions to the standard Binding Principles as parametrized for English. In Fodor (1992c), I consider the possibility that they can be incorporated into core grammar nevertheless. But for the sake of setting up the problem, let us take them here at face value as exemplifying a peripheral construction in English. (They might not all be the *same* peripheral construction, but for simplicity we can assume this also for now.) Then we can conclude that local binding of object pronouns is a possible peripheral phenomenon in natural language.

Now it needs to be established that local binding of pronouns (LBP) is also a possible core phenomenon. This was not acknowledged by Manzini and Wexler (1987) in their parametrization of the definition of governing category. They posited as the smallest of their five possible governing categories a constituent containing a subject; this entails that a pronominal must be free within its clause (or in a nominal with a subject NP as its specifier). The requirement that a governing category be a complete functional complex (CFC; Chomsky, 1986) also normally makes IP (or NP with subject) the binding domain for an object pronoun (though Hestvik, 1991, noted that for objects of prepositions the binding domain is PP if the PP is a CFC). But for examples like (4)–(6) to be well-formed, the binding domain for the pronoun would have to be not IP but VP. VP has been contemplated as a possible binding domain by Varela (1989, see also McKee, 1992), who proposed dropping the CFC requirement in favor of a maximal projection requirement. With VP as domain, an object pronoun need not be free of its subject but only of a fellow object. However, Varela proposed this as a hypothesis that might be adopted by learners; no adult language is cited as exhibiting this pattern of binding.[11]

Without tampering with the binding domain, examples like (4)–(6) could be generated if some pronouns were just immune to Principle B. One place

---

[11]This pattern of binding would include direct object anaphors bound by the subject for lack of a potential antecedent within VP, but an oblique object anaphor could be bound only by the direct object if one is present. Thus, as Varela (1989) noted, *Daddy told Mommy about himself* would be sufficient to trigger a shift to IP as binding domain for learners of English. An oblique object pronoun would have to be free of the direct object, though not of the subject. Such restrictions are not entirely without precedent; subject- and antisubject-orientation are attested for anaphors and pronouns (see Reuland & Koster, 1991, for a review). Hestvik (1991) also allowed VP as a binding domain but only when it is a CFC, as when it is a bare VP complement to a verb. Hestvik gave an example from Norwegian, but his footnote 9 showed some inclination to withdraw it on the grounds that the complement may not be bare VP, but IP with PRO subject. In any case, Hestvik's proposal is not relevant to examples like (4)–(6), for which the CFC is IP.

to find this is in languages that have no anaphors. Keenan (1975) cited Maori and Tahitian as examples. Maori, for instance, uses a single pro-form (*'ia* in third person singular) to cover the whole range of anaphor and pronoun use in languages that have both. The same was true of Middle English. (No doubt this is the source of examples like (4)–(6), which appear to be fairly isolated relics of older dialects. But of course, this does not change the status of these examples for learners unaware of their history.) In a language without anaphors there is obvious practical motivation for lifting the restriction on pronominals: If *'ia* were subject to either Principle A or Principle B, some propositions would become inexpressible in Maori. Of course there are other ways of looking at these data. Because the situation is symmetric, one might suppose that Maori has no pronoun but only a long-distance anaphor. However, the fact that *'ia* does not have to be bound tells against this. Another possibility is that in a language with only one pro-form, the distinctive features that invoke Principle A and Principle B are inactive, so that there is just one undifferentiated pro-form, neither pure pronoun nor pure anaphor, that can be bound locally, nonlocally, or not at all.[12,13] There are other languages, however, that exhibit what might be LBP even though they also have a distinct anaphor. Possible candidates for LBP are the *zich* of Dutch and the *seg* of Norwegian, which co-exist with the anaphors *zichzelf* and *segselv*, respectively, and the genitive *his* of modern English in contrast to *his own* (see Burzio, 1992). Each of these might be argued to be pronominal, and each can be locally bound in at least some contexts, though elsewhere it can be nonlocally bound. However, the relevant definitions of *local*, and the exact status of these forms (e.g., LBP or LDA, core or peripheral), are intricate topics that there is no space to discuss here. These constructions are examined in Fodor (1992c), where their relation to English LBP as in (4)–(6) is explored. For present purposes I

---

[12]Note that freedom from both Principles A and B does not result, as perhaps it should, from neutralization of a *single* featural distinction, as long as one feature ([+anaphoric]) is used to drive Principle A and a different feature ([+pronominal]) is used to drive Principle B; but other feature systems are imaginable (cf. Everaert, 1991; J. Koster, this volume, chapter 1). Lust, Mazuka, Martohardjono, and Yoon (1989) assumed that an undifferentiated pro-form subject to neither principle, hence bindable both locally and nonlocally, results from the positive feature specifications [+anaphoric] and/or [+pronominal]. They claimed that it is favored by learners until the negative values of these features have been acquired on the basis of indirect negative evidence. However, their argument rests on an unconventional interpretation of the binding principles as allowing, rather than requiring, anaphors to be bound and pronouns to be free, and it assumes that learners fail to exploit the inference that [+anaphor] entails [−pronominal], and [+pronominal] entails [−anaphor], when their respective governing categories clash (e.g., when they are the same).

[13]This is syntactic neutralization. A distinct but also plausible idea is phonological neutralization (that is, that Maori does have both an anaphor and a pronoun in the syntax but they are homophonous so the dividing line between them is indiscernible). I consider this idea further in Fodor (1992c). Everaert (1991) rejected it for the proform *him* of Frisian, which he noted behaves in some contexts like an anaphor and in other contexts like a pronominal, but his reasoning is elusive.

set them aside and use Maori as the working example of core LBP. Fortunately, the choice of descriptive terminology is not crucial to the general project; it can be shown that the fundamental learnability problem remains whether we take Maori *'ia* to be a pronoun that can be locally bound, or a syntactically undifferentiated proform, or syntactically distinct but homophonous pronoun and anaphor. For the sake of discussion I will continue to present it as an instance of LBP. Then Maori can serve as our existence proof for languages in which LBP occurs as a core construction, not just in lexical or constructional idioms. For concreteness I will also assume here (though all of these points deserve re-examining; see Fodor, 1992c) that to be locally bound is to be bound within a minimal CFC, that whether or not a pronoun can be locally bound is a parametric difference between languages, that the default setting of this parameter is the negative value, and that the trigger for the positive value is any LBP construction. I will also simplify by ignoring, throughout, the possibility that a language could have two pronominals that behave differently with respect to LBP.

The core/periphery indeterminacy problem has now been set up. Examples like (4)–(6) could be a sample drawn from English, or a sample from Maori. A learner has to decide which. Random guessing is no solution; learners need a systematic strategy for resolving such ambiguities. The logic of learnability applies as usual: If the alternatives are in a subset relation, learners should be able to make a decision based on SP; if the alternative languages are not in a subset relation, there should be positive data to decide the issue. However, Clark's problem teaches us to be wary of these in-principle solutions; we have seen that they do not always work in practice.[14]

Preemption by the Periphery: 1

With respect to LBP, English is a proper subset of Maori; hence SP should be applicable to the learner's choice between them. Peripheral LBP in English is limited to specific idioms like (5) and (6), and the "ethical dative" construction (4), which occurs with a range of verbs but not all.[15] Core LBP in Maori is widespread, occurring in all contexts. Clearly, then, SP entails

---

[14]Note that the problem posed by peripheral constructions is essentially the problem of positive exceptions, which is familiar from discussions of lexical learning (e.g., Bowerman, 1987; Fodor, 1985; Pinker, 1989). Positive exceptions have sometimes been taken to be benign (Mazurkewich & White, 1984) but in fact are deeply dangerous (even in very small numbers) because they could tempt learners to overgeneralize. Though I have not worked it through, I think that something like the solution for the periphery problem outlined here might be adapted to acquisition of lexical rules also.

[15]The term *ethical dative* seems to be common usage for a similar construction in other languages, but to avoid confusion I note that (4) corresponds to what Borer and Grodzinsky (1986) called the *reflexive dative* in Hebrew, and *not* to what they called the *ethical dative*. With *reflexive* ambiguous between form and function, I do not think it would be helpful to rebaptize the English construction to match the Hebrew. The details and status of this construction are discussed in Fodor (1992c).

that a learner encountering an LBP input should accommodate it by expanding his peripheral grammar, *not* by switching the relevant parameter to the Maori setting that inactivates Principle B across the board. In this respect, LBP seems to be quite typical; that is, it seems likely that a core analysis of *any* phenomenon would generalize it more broadly than a peripheral analysis would. By definition, the core is the locus of general principles, while the periphery houses idiosyncrasies that do not fall under the principles. The setting of a core parameter is supposed to have broad consequences. By contrast, learners are evidently extremely cautious about generalizing within the peripheral grammar, for otherwise they would never learn any idiomatic constructions at all.

The greater generalizing tendency of core over periphery, in conjunction with SP, clearly entails the learning principle: Where there is a choice, incorporate a novel input by modifying the peripheral grammar rather than by (re)setting core parameters. But this principle should give us pause, for it is not a principle conducive to the health of parameter theory. The periphery includes the most marked aspects of a language. It seems distinctly odd that learners should be innately advised to favor a marked over an unmarked description whenever possible, that is, to construe the language they are exposed to as a "worse" (less natural) language than their sample of it necessitates. This flies in the face of the idea that what makes a language a natural language is that it is favored by human learners.

Thus a favor-the-periphery learning strategy, required by SP, provokes some serious conceptual concerns about the theory of markedness as it relates to learning and linguistic description. Let us nevertheless play out the idea a little further, to see how it fares at a descriptive level. In fact it runs into immediate empirical trouble: Under reasonable assumptions, it renders Maori unlearnable. Though it has never been quite clear what descriptive devices are available in the periphery, the general picture is that these will differ from the principles and parameters of the core in being more open-ended though also more costly. In order to proceed we need to make some more specific working assumptions about what the descriptive power of the periphery is. Let us first consider the possibility that there is no limit to what phenomena could be characterized by a peripheral grammar.[16] Then a favor-the-periphery learner who abides by the learning principle would assign *every* new input to the periphery; no parameter would ever be set. Clearly this won't do. If all the work were done in the periphery, grammars would be huge, generalizations would be missed, and

---

[16]The periphery may not fall completely within the language module. To the extent that it does, its descriptive apparatus may be subject to certain limitations (e.g., on the metavocabulary available for naming syntactic categories, writing rules, etc.). But for present purposes that is not important; it is sufficient if the periphery can characterize (even if more effortfully) everything that the core can.

acquisition would not be effected by switch-setting. The whole mechanism of parameters would be lying idle. And Maori would be unlearnable. A language that sounds like Maori could be learned, but (with respect to pronouns) it would be just a mass of idioms—like (4)–(6) in English, but vastly more of them. This is sketched in Fig. 19.1. Language B is a "pure Principle B" language with no LBP. E(nglish) differs from it only in permitting some peripheral LBP. M(aori) is a superset of both B and E and permits LBP in all contexts. Unlike E, both M and B are core languages, whose peripheral grammars are null (with respect to pronoun binding). We can assume for convenience that a learner first encounters pronouns that respect Principle B, and will thus assume the target language is B. (Of course, exactly the same question arises concerning how B could have been acquired as core, rather than as a set of idioms, but we can ignore that for now.) By SP, any instances of LBP that are observed are then put into the periphery. If the target is E, just (4)–(6) will go into the periphery. If the target is M, all of the x's in Fig. 19.1 will be swallowed into the periphery one by one as they are encountered, and core M will never be attained. This model can surely be rejected. If it were true, parameter theory would be false of all known languages; it could be true only of humanly unattainable (un-learnable) languages.[17]

Preemption by the Periphery: 2

Having just observed the dire consequences of assuming that the descriptive power of the periphery includes that of the core, let us now suppose instead that some possible sentence structures lie beyond the descriptive power of the peripheral grammar. Then in a bias-toward-periphery system, SP would allow a core parameter to be set just in case its trigger were one of these inherently nonperipheral constructions. Other parameter values, those whose triggers were still ambiguous with possible peripheral constructions, would never be set. Thus, some parameter values in UG would be evident in the languages that people learn, while others would never be humanly realized. In particular: All parameter values that linguists actually wish to posit to account for observed language facts would have to be such that their triggers could not be accommodated by any peripheral mechanisms, or else they would never have resulted in parameter setting. So learning

---

[17]This conclusion is too severe if it could be the case that constructions are initially sent to the periphery, but after a temporary sojourn there they move into the core. Perhaps after the periphery silts up too heavily, the learning mechanism tries to restructure the grammar by shifting phenomena over to the core wherever it can find a collection of peripheral constructions that is coextensive with the effect of some core parameter setting. But that would be a reversion to something more like a traditional inductive learning model.

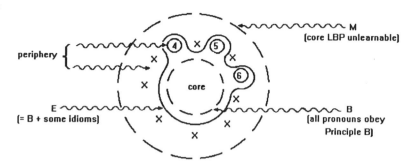

FIG. 19.1. Preemption by periphery.

theory now predicts a language universal: For any parameter value exemplified in any actual language, at least one of its triggers lies outside the set of all possible peripheral constructions. This disqualifies examples like (4)–(6), which occur peripherally in English, from being the triggers for core LBP as in Maori. Therefore there must be some *other* trigger for core LBP in Maori, a trigger that is not confusable with a possible peripheral construction. In general: Given that SP entails preemption by the periphery of all core/periphery ambiguous inputs, core and peripheral constructions may overlap in natural language if and only if every learnable language that has the core construction contains a learning-unambiguous, inherently nonperipheral, example of it that can serve as its trigger.

For LBP it is not clear what the unambiguous core trigger could be. The one thing we know is that it cannot resemble (4)–(6). Because of (4), the trigger cannot be an ethical dative, which seems reasonable enough. Presumably the most central instance of LBP would be a direct object bound by its local subject. However, this is also off limits as a core trigger because of (5) and (6). Pronominal objects of prepositions won't do, because they can be bound within a clause even in a non-core-LBP language such as English, as in (12).

(12) John$_i$ saw a snake near him$_i$.

But in a PP argument, rather then adjunct, a locally bound pronoun might perhaps be exclusive to a core LBP language. A possible trigger, then, would be some such construction as in (13).

(13) a. *John$_i$ talks to him$_i$.
  b. *John$_i$ introduced me to him$_i$.
  c. *I mentioned John$_i$ to him$_i$.

These are clearly core-ungrammatical in English,[18] though their counterparts are grammatical in Maori. I know of no idioms in English that have this form. So here is a small window within which current data may offer some hope of finding an unambiguous trigger for core LBP. But the hope is pretty thin, I think. It requires that there could *never* be a language in which an example like (13a–c) occurs as an idiom. And for a general solution, it would require likewise for *all* cases of core/periphery overlap.

We should not be surprised if it turns out to be difficult to find a trigger for a core parameter that is not ambiguous with the periphery. Consider what would have to be incapable of peripheral description: not constructions that are so wild that they do not qualify as human language even in an extended sense, but constructions that are so apparently normal that they look just like core constructions. So the restrictions that would have to be imposed on peripheral descriptive devices are highly suspicious. These restrictions, in UG, would have to tailor peripheral devices to be exactly complementary in their descriptive powers to the total set of core triggers. Explicit restrictions having this effect would undoubtedly be complex; more importantly, their existence would be unexplained.

There is only one account of core/periphery complementarity that is plausible, and this is that the descriptive load is carried by the parameters wherever possible; only what is left over after parameter setting would be submitted to peripheral analysis. But this is not a favor-the-periphery acquisition strategy. It is just the opposite—a strategy that gives priority to the core. Because this is in direct opposition to SP, we are entering here on dangerous ground. Either some very basic long-standing assumptions about learners and their data would have to be revised, or else we can anticipate serious empirical trouble: All the learning problems we thought had been solved by previous research might now turn out to be resolved in the wrong direction. In other respects, though, favor-the-core is a much more appealing strategy than favor-the-periphery, and so it is worth thinking through, even if only to reject it eventually.

Preemption by the Core

Suppose a learner's input is first submitted to the parameter-setting device. (Or suppose it is input to the parameters and the periphery acquisition

---

[18]Like other Principle B violations, the examples in (13) may be acceptable in special discourse contexts. It is important that learners should be able to factor out effects of contrast, parallel structure, and so forth, or else any contextually appropriate Principle B "violation" in English (e.g., *I consider ME the perfect choice for team captain*) would incorrectly trigger cancelation of Principle B. I will not address this context problem here though it is a close neighbor of the periphery problem for learnability. It is also related to the concerns of Roeper and Weissenborn (1990).

device in parallel, and whichever one provides the most economical analysis wins.) Then everything in a construction that could follow from core principles would be attributed to core principles. Possibly, nothing would remain unaccounted for. If something did, and if no resetting of a core parameter would allow it to be absorbed, then just that aspect of the construction would be recorded as an oddity in the peripheral grammar.[19] This picture is ideal from a linguistic point of view, because it allows the recognition of core properties even within sentences that are odd in some limited respect; a partly exceptional construction does not have to be put bodily into the periphery. It is also an improvement from the viewpoint of design of the learning mechanism, because it allows the peripheral devices to be left unconstrained, even while eliminating core/periphery overlap. There would be some broad natural class of peripheral mechanisms, which might be capable, in principle, of characterizing core phenomena. Indeed, core phenomena might even be *simpler* for the periphery to characterize than exclusively peripheral phenomena are. But no learner would ever draw on the resources of peripheral grammar unless a core description was unavailable. This seems most in keeping with the defining conception of the core as that which is unmarked and acquired by minimal exposure to the language, while the periphery is a collection of less orderly accretions, possibly not even purely linguistic. Thus, unlike preemption by the periphery, preemption by the core is an inherently plausible strategy. It would not make grammars more untidy than they are forced to be; on the contrary, it would smarten them up. A child exposed to a target language containing a construction with a costly peripheral description would regularize it into a "better" language in which that construction had been absorbed into the core and was described much more cheaply. Only where peripheral devices were unavoidable would they be called into play.

This is all as we would want it to be. Nonetheless, the favor-the-core strategy is untenable. It faces just the same empirical problem as we observed earlier, but seen now from the other side. It seems to be a fact that one and the same phenomenon (or two superficially indistinguishable phenomena)

---

[19]Fodor (1992a) worked out this idea in a Phrase Structure Grammar framework, using universal principles of feature distribution to factor apart predictable ("core") from idiosyncratic properties of an input construction. The work of distinguishing them is essentially done by the parser. Any feature value that the construction contains that the parser can account for as due to universal principles or defaults, or to the current grammar for the language, is checked off; anything that remains is a marked feature value and is recorded as such in the grammar. The construction automatically generalizes to just that set of sentences that are derivable by interaction of this cluster of marked feature values with universal feature instantiation principles. (Beyond that, the only other possible mechanism for generalization would be the collapsing of one marked feature specification with another, into a more schematic and comprehensive rule. To prevent overgeneralization in learning the periphery, a system of this sort would therefore need to constrain severely any such rule-collapsing process.)

can fall under core grammar in one language and under the peripheral grammar in another. The problem is to think of some kind of learning strategy that could allow acquisition of *both* kinds of language. Preemption by the periphery fails in one direction; preemption by the core, which we are considering now, fails in the other. It would fail for any target language which contains a genuinely peripheral construction that resembles a core construction. The peripheral input would be construed as core by the learner and would trigger resetting of the relevant parameter. (And if that parameter were a subset/superset parameter, no retreat from the reset value would be possible.) Hence the input in question would never be submitted to the peripheral learning mechanism. So it would never occur in the periphery of any actual (acquired) human language. Therefore no such target language as we have imagined would ever actually occur. Children would never be exposed to it, and if they were they would mislearn it.

Note that the flaw in this model stems entirely from the fact that the core analysis of a construction typically generalizes over it more broadly than a peripheral analysis does. We pictured the core as taking its bite of the phenomenon, and the periphery mopping up the leftovers. But this is not how things would work. Instead, in many cases the core grammar would swallow up a genuinely peripheral phenomenon from the target language and overgeneralize it; in the case of LBP, a favor-the-core learner exposed to English would acquire Maori instead. In Fig. 19.2, an encounter with (4)–(6) or any of the *x*'s would shift the learner's grammar directly from B to M, and E would not be attainable.

From this failure of the favor-the-core strategy on top of the failure of the favor-the-periphery strategy we can derive a reductio ad absurdum conclusion: No learner ever faces such a choice. If core and periphery are both to be learnable, there can never be (in actually occurring languages) any superficial overlap between peripheral constructions in one language and the trigger for a core construction in another. Thus, as before, the learnability problem leads to a linguistic prediction: There cannot be any

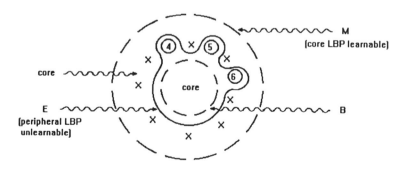

FIG. 19.2. Preemption by core.

overlap between English and Maori with respect to LBP. The problem is that the prediction is apparently false. All we have gained by shifting to favor-the-core is a more plausible mechanism for regulating the competition between core and peripheral devices.

Summary

Input that is ambiguous between core and periphery leaves learners susceptible to inadvertent SP violations, however well-motivated they are to learn conservatively. To give priority to the periphery would be to spurn the significant advantages of the core (speed of learning, simplicity of description, etc.); most or all of every language would be treated as peripheral, quite unnecessarily. The (true) grammar of Maori would be unlearnable. To give priority to the core is a much more sensible strategy but would in (most or) all cases result in overgeneralization. Idiosyncrasies of the target language would be misperceived as evidence for regularities. English LBP would be unlearnable. Putting the two halves of this argument together, we see that the core/periphery problem has no ordering solution (Type B solution). Innate ordering of the alternative choices is a standard solution to subset problems within the core (within one parameter, perhaps across different parameters), but we have discovered that it will not regulate a subset situation extending across core and periphery.

Why is the core/periphery situation different in this way from core/core indeterminacies? Obedience to SP requires learners always to start by assuming the narrowest possible language and to creep up on a richer language step by step by step, passing along the way through every intermediately rich language that UG allows (and that is compatible with the learner's data at that time). As long as this model is limited to the core, and as long as UG provides a limited set of core options, this stepwise progress does not strike us as too impracticable. Not only are the intermediate languages relatively few, but also it is not too implausible to suppose that the more steps it takes to arrive at a given target language, the more marked or unnatural that language is (see Berwick, 1985; Williams, 1981). But the logic of SP is not specific to the core; it must apply equally to the periphery. And adding the periphery into the model vastly increases the number of languages to be passed through in a typical case. Worse still, it is now impossible to claim that the more accessible ones are "better" languages than the ones that it is more arduous to attain: The former have a heavier reliance on the periphery, while the latter have broader, more principled generalizations.

This is what an ordering implementation of SP entails. If we do not find it tolerable, we must either give up SP or we must find some very different way of imposing it on learners. There is little comfort to be found in the other approaches sketched earlier: mutual exclusion and deterministic triggers. The only contribution of mutual exclusion would be to force learners to give up a peripheral analysis upon subsequently adopting a core analysis, but this is not a great help if we do not know how to persuade a conservative learner to adopt a core analysis in the first place.[20] Deterministic triggers cannot provide a general solution, as we have seen, unless there are never any core/periphery ambiguous examples at all, which gives every appearance of being false. Thus, the traditional remedies for subset problems seem to be ineffective here.

OTHER SOLUTIONS

The standard moves (A–C) for eliminating indeterminacies within the core do not transfer well to core/periphery choices, but perhaps it was a mistake to expect them to do so, since the architectual relations between core and periphery are so unlike those among components within the core. The bright side of this observation is that there might be a solution just for core/periphery problems, one that somehow manages to turn the peculiar status of the periphery to advantage. Fodor (1992c) examines seven possibilities:

1. Peripheral input is delayed until after core grammar is acquired.
2. Peripheral constructions are superficially recognizable as such.
3. Only one new fact can be acquired from each input sentence.
4. There are positive triggers for retreat from overgeneral parameter settings.
5. Nonoccurrence of predicted constructions serves as indirect negative evidence for retreat.
6. The Uniqueness Principle provides indirect negative evidence.
7. All positive exceptions to core syntactic patterns are lexical and are learned item by item.

Though I can do no more than list these suggestions here, I believe that none of them is completely satisfactory as a general solution, though each may have application to some particular instances of the problem.

---

[20]Even without built-in mutual exclusivity it is not difficult to account for a learner's giving up a peripheral analysis if a core analysis is available. There is considerable evidence that the parsing mechanism adopts the simplest available parse for any input. And there is reason to believe that rules, principles, and lexical entries become more accessible, the more frequently they are used. So in cases of competition between core and peripheral analyses, the core analysis would be increasingly favored, and the specially recorded peripheral analysis would eventually wither away from disuse.

For want of a convincing alternative, we may be tempted to reconsider the unpalatable linguistic universal that kept emerging earlier: that the set of (learnable) peripheral constructions must be disjoint from the set of all core triggers. Setting aside the fact that it seems to be false, this has much to commend it. First, it costs the model nothing; it would come about of its own accord as long as we assume that triggers cannot help triggering. Note that this is just a version of the assumption that priority is given to the core, which we have seen is independently the most desirable strategy. Second, given one additional assumption, this can provide the mechanism we have been looking for, which will permit a construction to occur as core in one language and peripheral in another. This would be so if the construction in question is not a trigger for the core generalization it falls under. If it were, it would trigger the generalization in every language in which it occurs, and could never be acquired as an idiom. But a construction *c* that is *not* a trigger for any parameter value can be acquired in two ways. If *c* is encountered by a learner, it will be recorded as an individual item in the periphery, since it triggers no generalization. Alternatively, *c* can become part of the core language if the learner encounters a *different* construction that *is* a trigger for a parameter value that licenses *c*.

Thus the trick is to distinguish between a trigger sentence and the (larger) set of sentences whose introduction into the language it triggers. Any or all of the sentences (more precisely, throughout: sentence *types*) in the domain of a core generalization induced by some parameter setting *might* serve as a trigger for it, but no one of them *must* be a trigger, and perhaps very few of them actually are. We may assume that UG associates with each (nondefault) parameter value a characterization of what sentence type(s) trigger it, and stipulates that nothing else is a trigger. Note that now the disjointness prediction becomes much less sweeping, and so might perhaps be true after all. Possible peripheral constructions only need to be distinct from core *triggers*, not from all possible core sentences. In fact the only empirical burden of this model is that for every learnable core generalization there must exist at least one trigger that differs in some specifiable way from any construction that can occur peripherally in any other natural language. For the case of LBP, this implies that there must be some example of LBP in languages like Maori, which can serve as the trigger for LBP, and which can be characterized in such a way as to differentiate it from the nontrigger instances of LBP that occur in languages like English. This is sketched in Fig. 19.3, where *m* is the trigger for core LBP as in Maori.

To complete the solution of the core/periphery indeterminacy problem, all we have to do is identify, for each core parameter value, the characteristic property that divides the sentences it licenses into triggers and nontriggers (where this distinction is coextensive with impossible versus possible peripheral constructions). In Fodor (1992c) I have proposed that for LBP,

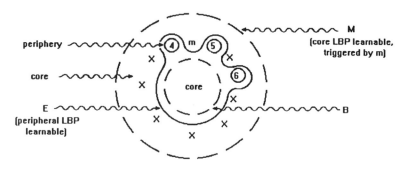

FIG. 19.3. Designated trigger.

the trigger is a sentence such as *John$_i$ kicked him$_i$,* differentiated from (4)–(6) by the fact that its pronoun object is fully thematic, whereas those in (4)–(6) have non-canonical thematic roles or none at all.[21]

The evidence for this, and its ramifications for other aspects of binding theory and theta theory, cannot be presented here. And it is of course an open-ended project to show that triggers can be distinguished from nontriggers for *all* linguistic phenomena that exhibit apparent overlap of core and periphery (e.g., word order, overt complementizers, etc.). On the other hand, the designated-trigger hypothesis, unlike the other seven proposals listed earlier, does cut to the heart of the problem of core/periphery indeterminacy and offers an in-principle solution to it. So the investment of effort in searching for narrow linguistic characterizations of triggers versus nontriggers may be worthwhile. As the search proceeds, we may begin to discern a generalization about which constructions UG tends to select as triggers. Roeper and Weissenborn (1990) proposed the generalization that triggers (for phenomena common to root and nonroot clauses) are nonroot constructions. In Fodor (1992c) I have suggested the generalization that the trigger for phenomenon *X* is unmarked with respect to everything other than *X*.

Finally, it should be noted that this in-principle solution to the core/periphery problem shows no respect for SP. Though the project began with a question about how to obey SP, it has ended with the conclusion that learners should not obey SP. The designated trigger model flouts SP by allowing trigger inputs to induce generalizations that are broader than is necessary (on the

---

[21]Note that the property that singles out the trigger from the nontriggers need not be the property that is projected by the parameter value that it triggers. In the case of LBP, the property that is projected is *locality* of pronoun binding, but the qualifying property of the trigger is *thematicity* of the pronoun. This is an important difference from the more traditional view of triggering according to which *all* constructions licensed by a parametric setting qualify as triggers for that setting. On that assumption, the trigger for more local binding would have to be an instance of more local binding. This was what made it difficult in the earlier discussion of preemption by the periphery to find a distinctive trigger for core LBP. Because nontrigger examples like (5) and (6) are maximally local, we could not find a *more* local case to serve as trigger.

reasonable assumption that the input could have been accommodated in the periphery, where it would have been generalized very narrowly or not at all). Violation of SP seems shocking. How could learners possibly get away with it, without recourse to negative data in one form or another that could motivate retreat from the resulting overgeneration? The answer is that there is no great harm in violating SP as long as everyone does it alike.

The penalty for an SP violation is that the grammars thereby passed over are unlearnable even though (by assumption) they are possible grammars in the sense of being compatible with UG principles. But that is perfectly acceptable, and is quite likely true of a great many UG-compatible grammars. Because linguists observe only the languages that someone has succeeded in learning, we have no way of knowing how many UG-permitted grammars are impossible to learn. What we have seen here is that, given that natural languages can contain idioms whose properties seem not to be limited by UG, every trigger for a core parameter is an exception to SP and results in the unlearnability of some UG-compatible grammar. In the case of LBP, what is unlearnable is a grammar such that *John_i kicked him_i* is licensed in the periphery but not in the core. But this seems a good empirical bet; at least none of the evidence considered here tells against it. SP would prevent this grammar from being unlearnable, but that merely suggests that the role of SP has been overestimated in previous research. SP embodies a logical truth about relationships among *learnable* grammars, but it need not be true of all UG-*possible* grammars, and it need not be *obeyed* by learners facing subset/superset choices; indeed, we have seen a case where obedience to SP would make it impossible to learn a learnable grammar (Maori). Violations of SP make UG-possible languages unlearnable, but they do no harm as long as those languages are not target languages for any learner. And this is guaranteed to be true as long as all learners violate SP for the same languages, for then those languages will have no speakers. Hence SP violations are perfectly tolerable as long as they do not occur at random but follow from some general principle that everyone abides by. The general principle I have proposed here is that all and only UG-designated triggers violate SP, by bypassing peripheral descriptive mechanisms and inducing broader generalizations in the core.

ACKNOWLEDGMENTS

This research was supported by a fellowship from the John Simon Guggenheim Memorial Foundation, and by the Center for the Study of Language and Information at Stanford University whose hospitality made it possible and pleasurable to prepare the final draft. I thank Richie Kayne who in the shortest time imaginable provided an extraordinary amount of help. Discussion with Stephen Crain, as always, helped to consolidate my thoughts. Gaby Hermon,

Cecile McKee, and an anonymous reviewer read and understood an early draft and made wise suggestions for improvements.

REFERENCES

Berwick, R. C. (1985). *The acquisition of syntactic knowledge.* Cambridge, MA: MIT Press.

Borer, H., & Grodzinsky, Y. (1986). Syntactic cliticization and lexical cliticization: The case of Hebrew dative clitics. In H. Borer (Ed.), *Syntax and Semantics: The syntax of pronominal clitics* (Vol. 19, pp. 175–217). New York: Academic Press.

Bowerman, M. (1987). The 'no negative evidence' problem: How do children avoid constructing an overly general grammar? In J. A. Hawkins (Ed.), *Explaining language universals* (pp. 73–101). Oxford: Oxford University Press.

Burzio, L. (1992). *Weak anaphora.* Paper presented at Graduate Center, City University of New York.

Chomsky, N. (1986). *Knowledge of language: Its nature, origin, and use.* New York: Praeger.

Chung, S., & McCloskey, J. (1987). Government, barriers, and small clauses in Modern Irish. *Linguistic Inquiry, 18,* 173–237.

Clark, R. (1988). On the relationship between the input data and parameter setting. *Proceedings of the North Eastern Linguistics Society, 19,* 48–82.

Everaert, M. (1991). Contextual determination of the anaphor/pronominal distinction. In J. Koster & E. J. Reuland (Eds.), *Long-distance anaphora* (pp. 77–118). Cambridge: Cambridge University Press.

Fodor, J. D. (1985). *Why learn lexical rules?* Paper presented at the 10th Annual Boston University Conference on Language Development, Boston, MA.

Fodor, J. D. (1989). Learning the periphery. In R. J. Matthews & W. Demopoulos (Eds.), *Learnability and linguistic theory* (pp. 129–154). Dordrecht: Kluwer.

Fodor, J. D. (1992a). Learnability of phrase structure grammars. In R. Levine (Ed.), *Formal grammar: Theory and implementation* (pp. 3–68). Oxford: Oxford University Press.

Fodor, J. D. (1992b). How to obey the subset principle: Case assignment. In D. Bhattarchargee, T. Hashimoto, & R. Hollander (Eds.), *CUNYForum, 17* (pp. 55–84). New York: City University of New York.

Fodor, J. D. (1992c). *Designated triggers versus the subset principle.* Unpublished manuscript, City University of New York.

Fodor, J. D., & Crain, S. (1990). Phrase structure parameters. *Linguistics and Philosophy, 13,* 591–633.

Grodzinsky, Y. (1989). The language learner: A trigger-happy kid? *Behavioral and Brain Sciences, 12,* 342–343.

Hestvik, A. (1991). Subjectless binding domains. *Natural Language & Linguistic Theory, 9,* 455–497.

Kapur, S., Lust, B., Harbert, W., & Martohardjono, G. (1993). Universal grammar and learnability theory: The case of binding domains and the 'subset principle.' In E. Reuland & W. Abraham (Eds.), *Knowledge and language: Issues in representation and acquisition* (pp. 185–216). Cambridge: Cambridge University Press.

Keenan, E. L. (1975). Logical expressive power and syntactic variation in natural language. In E. L. Keenan (Ed.), *Formal semantics and natural language* (pp. 406–421). Dordrecht: Kluwer Academic Press.

Lust, B., Mazuka, R., Martohardjono, G., & Yoon, J. M. (1989). *On parameter setting in first language acquisition: The case of the binding theory.* Paper presented at GLOW, Utrecht.

Manzini, R. M., & Wexler, K. (1987). Parameters, binding theory and learnability. *Linguistic Inquiry, 18*, 413–444.

Mazurkewich, I., & White, L. (1984). The acquisition of the dative alternation: Unlearning overgeneralizations. *Cognition, 16*, 261–283.

McKee, C. (1992). A comparison of pronouns and anaphors in Italian and English acquisition. *Language Acquisition, 1*, 21–55.

Pinker, S. (1989). *Learnability and cognition: The acquisition of argument structure*. Cambridge, MA: MIT Press.

Reuland, E., & Koster, J. (1991). Long-distance anaphora: An overview. In J. Koster & E. Reuland (Eds.), *Long-distance anaphora*. Cambridge: Cambridge University Press.

Roeper, T., & Weissenborn, J. (1990). How to make parameters work: Comments on Valian. In L. Frazier & J. de Villiers (Eds.), *Language processing and language acquisition* (pp. 147–162). Dordrecht: Kluwer.

Travis, L. (1984). *Parameters and effects of word order variation*. Unpublished doctoral dissertation, MIT, Cambridge, MA.

Valian, V. (1990). Logical and psychological constraints on the acquisition of syntax. In L. Frazier & J. de Villiers (Eds.), *Language processing and language acquisition* (pp. 119–145). Dordrecht: Kluwer.

Varela, A. (1989). A structural account of children's apparent failure to respect Condition B. Paper presented at the 14th Boston University Conference on Child Language Development, Boston, MA.

Williams, E. S. (1981). Language acquisition, markedness and phrase structure. In S. L. Tavakolian (Ed.) *Language acquisition and linguistic theory* (pp. 8–34). Cambridge, MA: MIT Press.

CHAPTER TWENTY

Degree-0 Learnability

David Lightfoot
University of Maryland

Universal Grammar, it is often said, consists of principles and a set of option-points or parameters. If this is so, then we need a separate theory that will complement UG in order to yield an account of language acquisition; specifically, something needs to be said about how parameters are set. I argue here for a principle of degree-0 learnability, which says something about how parameters are set and does not belong to Universal Grammar, if UG consists only of grammatical principles and parameters. The idea is that parameters are set only by structurally simple data. I contrast this idea with another proposal in the literature, which addresses some similar problems: the idea that children set their parameters primarily on the basis of data from embedded clauses (Roeper & Weissenborn, 1990).

Consider the following data, first pointed out by Clark (1989). Subjects of English infinitives sometimes appear in the accusative case (1a), and most linguists under the age of 40 say that there is some exceptional device that permits the matrix verb (here *expect*) to govern and assign case to the infinitival subject (perhaps a device that deletes the lower CP node). It is supposed that children learn the existence of this device or set the relevant parameter on the basis of hearing some simple expression like (1a). But it cannot be that simple. Latin had structures like (1b), with an infinitival subject in the accusative case, which seem to be essentially identical to English (1a). However, sentences corresponding to (1b) do not set the same parameter as in English, because we know that the accusative case on *eam* is unrelated to government by the higher verb *spero*. We know this because we also find accusative subjects where they are not governed by a higher verb, as in the sentential subject in (1c). This means that English-speaking children cannot set the parameter of exceptional case marking unless they know that structures corresponding to (1c) do not occur in their language. Similarly, (1b), although effectively a word-for-word translation of the English (1a), did not set a comparable exceptional case marking parameter for Latin speakers, presumably because of the presence of (1c).

(1) a. I expect [her to win].
    b. Spero [eam vincere].
       I-hope her to-win
       'I hope for her to win.'
    c. [Eam vincere] mihi semper libet.
       'For her to win always pleases me.'
    d. Is cuimhneach leo [iad a bheith ar seachran].
       [copula] mindful with-them [they to-be lost]
       'They remember being lost.'
    e. *Shil siad [a cheile a bheith breoite].
       'They thought each other to be ill.'

Irish shows that matters are still more complex. Irish also shows infinitives with lexical subjects, as in (1d); but, unlike in English and Latin, those subjects may not always be bound by an element in the higher clause, as in (1e).

This shows that the relationship between primary data and the parameters that they set may be complex. It is not enough to say merely that the English-speaking child sets the relevant parameter on the basis of hearing something like (1a). We need not only to identify the parameters but also to say how they are set, specifying why the English child does not adopt the Irish setting and vice versa.

One can illustrate the point also by considering the operations that associate inflectional features with the appropriate verb. Most grammars raise their verbs to the position containing the inflectional elements, as in (2c–d), but English grammars, unusually, have an operation that lowers I onto an adjacent verb, as in (2a). It seems reasonable to construe the English lowering operation as a morphological phenomenon: In general, lowering operations are unusual in the syntax, a lowering operation here would leave behind a trace that would not be bound or properly governed, and one would expect a morphological operation but not a syntactic operation to be subject to a condition of adjacency. Therefore the representation in (2a), reflecting a morphological operation, contains no trace of the lowered I. In any case, the English lowering needs to be taken as the default setting; there is, as far as I can see, no nonnegative evidence available to the child that would force him or her to select an I-lowering analysis over a V-raising analysis as in (2b) for English. In that case, let us take the morphological I-lowering analysis as the default setting, always available to children and requiring no particular triggering experience. Then one can ask what triggers a syntactic V-to-I raising operation in grammars where it applies.

(2) a. Jill [$_{VP}$ leave+past].
b. Jill [$_I$ leave$_I$+past] [$_{VP}$ e_i].
c. Jeanne [$_I$ lit$_i$] [$_{VP}$ toujours e_i les journaux].
d. Lit$_i$ [$_{IP}$ elle e_i [$_{VP}$ toujours e_i les journaux]].

Some generalizations have emerged over the last several years. One is that languages with rich inflection have V-to-I operations in their grammars, and rich inflection could be part of the trigger. So standard English has one verb that is richly inflected, the verb *be*, and this element raises to I (and may therefore move on to C, as in *is George president now?*, and may occur to the left of *not*). Some forms of the language show no inflection here and use *be* uniformly regardless of context, as in (3b). These forms of English (Black English Vernacular and some forms of children's speech) use negatives and interrogatives like (3c–d) and not (3e); (3e) is what would be expected if the uninflected *be* raised to I.

(3) a. George is president now.
b. George be president now.
c. George don't be president now.
Do George be president now?
What do George be?
d. Did it be funny?
Do clowns be boys or girls?
I don't be angry.
e. *George ben't president now.
*Be George president now?
*What be George?

The contrast between these forms of the language strongly suggests that the inflected *be* raises to I, whereas the uninflected form does not raise. So rich inflection and V-to-I raising are linked in some way.

However, we cannot simply link the presence of V-to-I raising with rich inflection in a one-to-one fashion. It may be the case that if a language (or, as we have just seen, part of a language) has rich inflection, it has V-to-I raising. If there is no rich inflection, a grammar may have the raising operation (Swedish) or may lack it (English). In that case, there will need to be a syntactic triggering experience. So, for example, a verb occurring in C, that is, to the left of the subject NP (as in a verb-second language or in interrogatives), could get there only by raising first to I, and therefore inversion forms like (2d) in French could be syntactic triggers for V-to-I.[1] This suggests to me that the V-to-I operation applies only where necessary; otherwise, the morphological operation may suffice to link inflectional elements with the appropriate verb (this is consistent with the way that Chomsky, 1992, implemented his economy idea in this domain). In that case, one can ask how robustly the parameter setting by which V raises to I is "expressed"; it is expressed robustly if there are many simple expressions that can be analyzed by the child only by applying the V-to-I operation. A particular parameter setting may be triggered if it is expressed appropriately in the primary linguistic data. So, for example, the sentences corresponding to (2c–d) can be analyzed by the French child only if the V *lit* raises to I. *Jeanne lit les journaux* 'Jeanne reads the newspapers,' on the other hand, could be analyzed with *lit* raised to I or with the I lowered down into the VP in the English fashion and therefore it does not express the V-to-I parameter setting. [By quantifying the *expression* of a parameter, we can understand why English grammars lost the V-to-I operation and why they lost it as the periphrastic *do* form became increasingly common; this is discussed at some length in Lightfoot (1993), where it is shown that, as the new *do* forms came into the language, they eliminated constructions which had expressed the V-to-I operation.] My general point here is that it is not enough to identify whether a grammar has or lacks the V-to-I operation; one must ask also how the analysis is triggered.

I have suggested that we ask which simple utterances express any given parameter setting, and that brings us to degree-0 learnability. I argued in Lightfoot (1991) that grammars are degree-0 learnable in the sense that parameters are set by simple data, specifically by data drawn from unembedded binding domains. The literature contains reasonably well-understood parameters that seem to require that children have access to very complex structures. For example, in the first discussion of grammatical parameters, Rizzi (1982) argued that the Subjacency Condition was parametrized such that the bounding nodes might be NP and IP in English and NP and CP in Italian. Such a parameter would account for the fact that *a cui* may move from its trace position in Italian (4a), whereas the comparable sentence is ill formed in English, where the *to whom* would need to move across two instances of IP, each a bounding node. Sportiche (1981) made a similar argument for French, that the bounding nodes are NP and CP, on the basis of structures like (4b).

---

[1]Swedish is sometimes analyzed as lacking the V-to-I operation. So Vikner (1990), for example, had verbs move directly to C, because negatives precede finite verbs in embedded clauses: . . . *om Jan inte köpte boken* 'if John didn't buy the book'. But this indicates that *inte* 'not' and other such adverbs occur to the left of I and does not provide evidence against the application of V-to-I. Occurrence of verbs in C is strong evidence of movement through I, given almost any version of the proper government condition on traces.

(4) a. Tuo fratello, [a cui$_i$ [$_{IP}$ mi domando [$_{CP}$ che storie$_j$ [$_{IP}$ abbiano raccontato e_j e_i]]]], era molto preoccupato.
'your brother, to whom I wonder which stories they told, was very troubled.'

b. C'est à mon cousin$_i$ [que je sais [lequel$_j$ offrir e_j e_i]].
'It's to my cousin that I know which one to offer.'

These analyses have parameters being set by data of degree-2 complexity (two levels of embedding), but I showed (Lightfoot, 1991) that the desired result can be obtained by invoking simple triggers. (5a), a monoclausal structure, shows a movement across NP and IP and thus demonstrates that IP can not be a bounding node. The biclausal (5b) has the same effect for Italian.

(5) a. Combien$_i$ as [$_{IP}$ tu vu [$_{NP}$ e_i [$_{N'}$ de personnes]]]?
How many have you seen people
'How many people have you seen?'

b. Ne$_i$ ho visti [$_{IP}$ [$_{NP}$ molti e_i] corregli incontro].
'Of them (I) saw many run toward him.'

Similarly, Koopman (1983) showed in effect that the operation of the Doubly Filled COMP Filter can be learned from maximally simple structures. (6a) is ungrammatical because the complementizer projection contains something (*that*) that is not the head of that projection. (I use the formulation of Aoun, Hornstein, Lightfoot, & Weinberg, 1987; if *that* were the head, i.e., if the indexing were [[e_i that$_j$]$_j$ e_i . . .], then the subject trace would fail to be properly governed and fail to be locally bound.) The Dutch child comes to know that the Doubly Filled COMP Filter, whatever its precise form, does not hold, as shown by (6b). Koopman showed that this can be learned from a very simple structure, namely (6c), which must be a legitimate structure (Dutch is underlyingly verb-final and finite verbs are fronted to a C position in matrix clauses.) English has nothing corresponding to (6c) and, therefore, English-speaking children have no simple basis for unlearning the Doubly Filled COMP Filter.

(6) a. *Who$_i$ did Jay say [[e_i that]$_i$ e_i saw Kay]?

b. Wie$_i$ denk je [[e_i dat]$_i$ e_i het boek gelezen had]?
Who think you that the book read had?
'Who do you think had read the book?'

c. [Wie$_i$ heeft$_j$]$_i$ [e_i het boek gelezen e_j]?
Who had the book read?
'Who had read the book?'

d. [Who]$_i$ [e_i has read the book]?

e. *[Who$_i$ did$_j$]$_i$ [e_i e_j read the book]?

English does have structures like (6d), but there is no reason to believe that *has* moves to the C projection; in fact, the ungrammaticality of (6e) shows that the I element does not move to C where the subject position is a trace. Again we see that a very simple structure can serve to set a parameter whose effects are seen in embedded domains.

The hypothesis of degree-0 learnability, as formulated in Lightfoot (1991), says that parameters are set on the basis of data from matrix clauses and from the positions in an embedded clause given in (7).

(7) Degree-0 learnability
  . . . [$_{CP}$SPEC C [(NP) I . . .]]

The exact form of the generalization may be a matter of debate. For example, the elements of (7) are precisely the elements for which the binding domain is not the clause that immediately contains them, but the next clause up. I assume, again with Aoun et al. (1987), that an element's binding domain is the first CP that contains an accessible SUBJECT. An accessible SUBJECT is the first c-commanding NP or AGR with which the item may be coindexed without violating Principle C of the Binding Theory. In the case of a SPEC of CP and a C, there can be no NP or AGR within its own clause that c-commands it. This is true as well for the subject of an infinitive (the parenthesized NP in (7)), because infinitival verbs in English occur only when there is no AGR in I. Furthermore, if one takes I to be the head of the whole clause, it is reasonable to suppose that the only element that may c-command it is something outside that clause. Consequently, Lightfoot (1991) argued that a degree-0 learner sets parameters on the basis of data not from unembedded clauses, which would obviously be too restrictive, but from unembedded binding domains.

An alternative way of construing things, not discussed in Lightfoot (1991), would be to say that degree-0 learners have access to data from unembedded clauses together with their *connection points* with embedded clauses. By connection points, I mean those elements that feature in subcategorization frames, in selectional restrictions, or in linking time reference. So verbs are subcategorized in terms of whether they may have complements introduced by a [+WH] element in SPEC of CP, a *that* complementizer, or a lexical subject of an infinitive. Likewise, the reference of an I may be determined in part by properties of the higher I; we traditionally refer to this as a sequence-of-tenses phenomenon (see Hornstein, 1990, for discussion). On the other hand, there are no such relations between the subject of a finite verb and an upstairs element, or the direct object of a transitive verb, and so such elements play no role in setting parameters when they occur in embedded clauses.

For most purposes these two ways of viewing (7) and the definition of degree-0 complexity are equivalent, but there are some empirical considerations that could require one formulation rather than the other. Here I will hold to the restriction given in (7), that parameter setting is sensitive only to the elements of an embedded clause specified there, leaving the interpretation open.

There are many phenomena in the literature that appear to be counter-examples to the hypothesis of degree-0 learnability. Some can be analyzed away straightforwardly and some are more genuinely problematic.

It was said for some time that the verb *serve* selected a complement containing a transitive verb, distinguishing (8a–b). That generalization would not be learnable by our degree-0 child because the direct object of an embedded clause is not one of the items in (7); it has an embedded binding domain and is not one of the connection points between clauses. It therefore cannot influence parameter setting. Higgins (1973), however, showed that this generalization is not the real one; rather, the subject of *serve* and the corresponding PRO subject of the embedded infinitive must be an instrument, as indicated by (8c). Furthermore, Higgins noted that in English all verbs with instrumental subjects are transitive. This generalization could hold universally for principled reasons; but, if it has to be learned, it can be learned from simple clauses with instrumental subjects. Therefore the apparent restriction on *serve* is an epiphenomenon of something that is straightforwardly learnable.

(8) a. *The ice served to melt.
     b. The ice served to chill the beer.
     c. *Edison served [PRO to invent the light bulb].

Other cases are more trivial. Wasow (1989) pointed to (9) as a problem for degree-0 learnability; an embedded conditional clause may contain a subjunctive verb, and he assumed that this is learned by children in the usual fashion. It is unclear whether these subjunctive forms are acquired in the usual fashion or whether they are archaisms that are perpetuated by educational systems. But if they are acquired normally, they can be acquired by degree-0 learners, who have access to the I of an embedded clause by (7). I discussed some other cases of this type in (Lightfoot, 1989) my "Author's response" in the *Behavioral and Brain Sciences* (12.2) debate on degree-0 learnability.

(9) If I were the boss, I would . . .

Andersson and Dahl (1974) offered the facts of (10a–c) as a counterexample to the Penthouse Principle of Ross (1973); and, prima facie, the facts would be problematic for degree-0 learnability. They pointed out that the Swedish auxiliary verb *ha* is deletable in embedded clauses, as in (10c), but not in main clauses, as in (10a–b). However, Platzack (1986) showed that the generalization is incorrect and that *ha* may be deleted in matrix clauses if the second position to which it would ordinarily move is already occupied by an adverb like *kanske* 'perhaps', as in (10d). This suggests that the correct generalization is that *ha* may be deleted quite generally, but in fact it fails to be deleted when moved to C (recall that Swedish is a V-2 language, in which finite verbs typically move to C in matrix clauses). The restriction that it may not be deleted in C can then be understood in terms of the ECP: If *ha* were deleted in that position, its trace would fail to be properly governed. This suggests, as N. Hornstein (personal communication, 1991) pointed out, that *ha* may be deleted only in its base-generated position, where it is not needed in order to properly govern a trace. Hornstein noted as well that this would also explain the nondeletability of a moved *do* or modal in English, as in (11a); compare the nonmoved *can* in (11b). Under this view the Swedish facts are not as peculiar as one might have thought, and there are certainly no special conditions that have to be learned.

(10) a. Han hade sett henne.
          'He had seen her.'
      b. *Han *e* sett henne.
      c. . . . att han (hade) sett henne.
          '. . . that he had seen her.'
      d. Allan kanske redan (har) skrivit sin bok?
          'Allan perhaps already has written his book?'

(11) a. *Who did Jay greet and who Ray treat?
          *Who can Jay visit and who Ray eat with?
      b. Jay can visit Fay and Ray eat with Kay.

Another potential problem concerns so-called long-distance anaphors, of the kind that occur in Chinese and other languages. So in (12) the anaphor *ziji* may be coindexed with any c-commanding subject NP, including the long-distance *John.*

(12) John$_i$ xiangxin [Bill$_j$ dui Sam$_k$ shuo [ziji$_{i/j/*k}$ taoyan Mary]].
      'John believes that Bill said to Sam that self hated Mary.'

Long-distance anaphors used to be viewed as reflecting a parametrization of binding domains: some grammars would require that anaphors be bound within binding domains that are larger than in other grammars (Manzini & Wexler, 1987). But this view has now been generally abandoned in favor of an analysis first put forward by Battistella (1989) and elaborated by Cole, Hermon, and Sung (1990) in a *Barriers* framework, whereby anaphors may move to I. The parametrization concerns not the size of the binding domain but the lexicality of I: In languages like Chinese, I is lexical and thus *ziji* may move to I. I lexically governs and thus licenses a trace that it locally c-commands and is coindexed with; in languages like English, I is not a lexical governor and therefore could not license the trace of an anaphor, explaining why English does not show comparable long-distance effects. Two central facts receive a natural explanation if *ziji* moves to I and remain mysterious if binding domains are parametrized. First, *ziji* is always subject-oriented and may not be coindexed with a nonsubject, as in (12). Second, its interpretation is subject to blocking effects, such that it may not corefer with a subject NP if another subject NP of a different person intervenes, as in (13).

(13) *John$_i$ xiangxin [wo shuo [ziji$_i$ taoyan Mary]].
     'John believes that I said that self hated Mary.'

In fact, there are reasons to suppose that *ziji* moves to I after S-structure on the PF side of the grammar. Under this view *ziji* is not interpreted via the Binding Theory, but it is interpreted on the PF side of the grammar as anaphoric to the subject NP to which it is adjacent after movement (perhaps through a predication operation; for the notion of interpretation at PF, see Hornstein, 1987, who also takes predication to be a PF operation). This would predict correctly that the interpretation of *ziji* is not subject to reconstruction, if, as is usually assumed, reconstruction is an LF property. So *ziji* must be interpreted in its surface position in (14a) and not in its D-structure position, unlike *taziji*, which is a conventional anaphor interpreted via the Binding Theory at LF and therefore subject to reconstruction, as in (14b).

(14) a. Zhangsan$_i$ shuo [ziji$_{i/*j}$ de shu [Lisi$_j$ zui xihuan]].
        'Zhangsan said that self's books, Lisi likes most.'
     b. Zhangsan$_i$ shuo [taziji$_{i/j}$ de shu [Lisi$_j$ zui xihuan]].

Furthermore, elements interpreted by the Binding Theory at LF are affected by the focus marker *shi*, which changes the domain in which binding properties must hold. So *qitaren* must be A-free within its binding domain, which accounts for the ungrammaticality of (15a) (Chuang, 1990). However, the presence of *shi* changes the coindexing possibilities, as in (15b).

(15) a. *Mali$_i$ zhidao [qitaren$_i$ zuo le Lisi de zuoyie].
        'Mali knew some others did Lisi's homework.'
     b. Mali$_i$ zhidao [shi [qitaren$_i$ zuo le Lisi de zuoyie]].

Similarly, the interpretation of *taziji* is affected by the focus marker, in (16), but *ziji* is not, in (17).

(16) a. Zhangsan jeude [Lisi$_j$ xihuan taziji$_j$].
        'Zhangsan feels that Lisi likes self.'
     b. Zhangsan$_i$ jeude [shi Lisi$_j$ xihuan taziji$_{i/j}$].

(17) Zhangsan$_i$ jeude [shi Lisi$_j$ xihuan ziji$_{i/j}$].
'Zhangsan feels that it is Lisi who likes self.'

In any case, the best analyses of long-distance anaphors suggest that the relevant parametrization has nothing to do with the size of binding domains but, rather, relates to properties of I, perhaps to the lexicality of I. Various matters need to be resolved, but the phenomenon does not yet raise any particular problems for the hypothesis of degree-0 learnability.

On the other hand, there are some more genuinely problematic cases. One was pointed out by Baker (1989). Some languages have resumptive pronouns in embedded object positions, where other languages allow empty elements, as in (18). As noted earlier, this position should not influence parameter setting by the hypothesis of (7).

(18) a. John is too tired to invite [him] for dinner.
b. The woman who we met [her] lives in DC.

Cinque (1990a) analyzed such alternations in Italian and argued that the real difference between expressions with overt resumptive pronouns and expressions with empty elements lies in how the clause is introduced. He argued that ordinary complements participate in a predication relation, which he outlined, and may have empty objects, as in (19a), but clauses introduced by a preposition may not participate in the relevant predication relation and therefore do not permit empty objects, as in (19b). Under this analysis, what has to be learned is the constituent membership of the infinitival clause, whether or not it is introduced by a preposition; and that is straightforward for our degree-0 learner.

(19) a. Il problema non è facile [$_{CP}$ da risolvere e subito].
b. Questo libro è troppo di parte [$_{PP}$ [$_{P'}$ per [$_{CP}$ C
[$_{IP}$ adottarlo]]]].

It is unclear whether this analysis will generalize appropriately. For example, some forms of Brazilian Portuguese show the comparable alternations in (20), as described by Tarallo (1985). Here we seem to have a case of a diachronic change that is currently in progress: Resumptive pronouns are increasingly common in contexts like (20a–b). Conversely, another change seems to be taking place more or less in parallel, whereby empty objects are increasingly common in simple clauses like (20c). It is unclear whether these phenomena actually represent a single change abstractly and what the implications are for empty/filled objects in embedded domains.

(20) a. Eu conheço um hotel$_i$ perto da rodoviária [que e$_i$ chama Pensão
Ita].

'I know a hotel near the bus station that is called Pensao Ita.'
b. Eu tenho uma comadre$_i$ minha [que ela$_i$ mora na esquina da minha casa].
'I have a friend of mine that she lives around the corner from my house.'
c. Eu vi *e* no Rio.
'I saw him/her in Rio.'

Whatever the correct analysis of the Brazilian facts, Cinque's treatment of Italian is an analysis of the right kind from the perspective of a degree-0 learner.

Consider now another problem for degree-0 learnability, which may raise more substantial issues. Many languages allow finite verbs to move to some second position, often analyzed as the head of CP. So (21a) is an analysis of such a sentence in Dutch; the verb moves first to I and then the I element moves to C, taking the verb along with it. This is a main clause phenomenon and verbs do not move to C in embedded clauses: One finds (21b–c), but not corresponding structures with the verb in the embedded C.

(21) a. [$_{CP}$ Den Haag$_i$ [bezoek$_j$+t]$_k$ [$_{IP}$ hij [$_{VP}$ *e*$_i$ *e*$_j$] *e*$_k$]].
The Hague visits he
b. Ik vraag me af [$_{CP}$ of [$_{IP}$ hij den Haag bezoekt]].
'I wonder whether he is visiting The Hague.'
c. Ik vraag me af [$_{CP}$ wie$_i$ [$_{IP}$ hij *e*$_i$ bezoekt]].

Modern Greek is an SVO language that also allows verbs to move to C optionally as in (22), as shown by Efthimiou and Hornstein (1992).

(22) a. Enas neos andras eklise tin porta.
a   young man closed the door
b. Eklise enas neos andras tin porta.

In Greek the verb must move to C if a WH-item occurs initially, as in (23) (there is some dialectal variation concerning which WH-items trigger movement; we can ignore this here). Furthermore, unlike in Dutch, this movement takes place in embedded clauses; (23b) has the structure of (23b').

(23) a. Pou pije o Yanis?
Where went John
b. Anarotjeme [$_{CP}$ pjon idhe i Maria].
'I wonder whom Maria saw.'
b'. Anarotjeme [$_{CP}$ pjon$_j$ idhe$_i$ [$_{IP}$ i Maria *e*$_i$ *e*$_j$]]

Efthimiou and Hornstein also showed that a WH-trace in SPEC of CP triggers verb movement to C, as in (24a) and movement takes place as well in a relative clause that is introduced by the invariant element *pou*, as in (24b).

(24) a. Pjon nomizi o Yanis [cp oti idhe i Maria]?
'Whom does John think that Maria saw?'
b. Vrika to vivlio [cp pou erapse o Yanis].
'I-found the book that John wrote.'

This is all straightforward; and the grammars of Dutch and Greek, as I have sketched them, can be attained by a learner who sets parameters having access to an embedded SPEC of CP and C in accordance with (7). Our degree-0 child analyzes (24a) with *idhe* in C, preceded by a WH-trace in SPEC of CP. In particular, relative clauses reflect complement structures like (24a) and nothing special has to be learned about them. The problem, however, comes with Spanish, as described by Torrego (1984). Torrego pointed out that a preposed WH-argument requires the finite verb to move, even in an embedded clause, as in (25).

(25) a. No sabía qué querian esos dos.
'I didn't know what those two wanted.'
b. Es impredecible con quién vendra Juan hoy.
'It is unpredictable who John will come with today.'

Furthermore, as in Greek, the trace of a WH-item in the SPEC of CP also entails movement of the verb, as in (26).

(26) Qué pensaba Juan [que le habia dicho Pedro
[qué habia publicado la revista]]?
'What did John think that Peter had told him that the journal had published?'

The problem is that Greek relative clauses parallel other embedded clauses in requiring verb movement if a WH-item has been preposed, but this is not so in Spanish. Torrego (1984) noted that verb movement is only optional in relative clauses. Consequently one finds sentences like (27), where the verb is not moved to the left of the subject NP.

(27) Encontre el libro que Juan le dio a Maria.
'I-found the book that Juan gave-it to Maria.'

This suggests that children need to have access to the C of a relative clause in order to learn the difference between Greek and Spanish; and this position is generally taken to have an embedded binding domain, namely, the complex NP that contains the relative clause and its head. This is an area that requires further analysis, and at this stage I have nothing concrete to suggest.[2]

So far I have been considering potential problems for the notion of degree-0 learnability and suggesting solutions or approaches to solutions consistent with that notion. There are independent reasons to believe not just that degree-0 learnability is possible but that something like this must hold. Before I give those reasons, let us step back a moment and consider the distinction that Emonds (1976) drew between root and structure-preserving transformations. He distinguished transformations that yielded constituent structures that could in principle have been derived directly by the phrase structure rules without the application of transformations; these were structure-preserving. In contrast, other transformations, such as subject-auxiliary inversion, yielded outputs that could not have been derived directly by phrase structure rules and therefore deformed structures in a way that structure-preserving transformations did not; these transformations applied only to root domains. A similar idea lay behind Ross' (1973) Penthouse Principle, which said that what goes on downstairs may also go on upstairs, but not vice versa. The insight that operations in embedded clauses constitute some subset of operations in matrix clauses is now well established. However, current theories that do not permit transformational operations like subject-auxiliary inversion and restrict us to Move-something or Affect-something cannot state the distinction of rule types drawn by Emonds. If the insight cannot be captured by grammatical theory, it must follow from something else that embedded clauses manifest only a subset of the operations seen in matrix clauses. A natural candidate would be the acquisition theory, which characterizes how parameters are set.

There are two approaches to this in the literature. One is degree-0 learnability. If parameters are set on the basis of data from unembedded binding domains, it follows that whatever affects embedded domains is a by-product of what is seen in matrix domains. So, for example, there is good reason to believe that Dutch and German children learn that their grammars have underlying object-verb order (which is manifested superficially in embedded clauses) from data from matrix domains (which typically show the verb in second position). Lightfoot (1991) showed how this happens, how Dutch children endowed with a version of X′ theory that requires verbs and their complements to be adjacent at D-structure must

---

[2]This case may entail that children have access to the C projection of a relative clause for the purposes of setting parameters, but there may also be alternative analyses. For example, it might be the case that Spanish has the option of a resumptive *pro* in a relative clause (and elsewhere), which would entail that there is no movement to SPEC of CP in (27) and therefore no V-movement; Cinque (1990b) provided such an analysis for some relative clauses in Italian.

conclude that verbs move in Dutch, how sentences like (28a–c) show the source of verb movement, as in (28b'). Furthermore, the examples in (28d) are instances of simple colloquial expressions manifesting the verb in its base-generated position.

(28) a. Jan belt de hoogleraar op.
     'John calls the professor up.'
   b. Jan moet de hoogleraar opbellen.
     John must the professor up-call.
     'John must call up the professor.'
   b'. $[_{CP}$Jan$_i$ moet$_i$ $[_{IP}$ e_i $[_{IP}$ PRO de hoogleraar $e_k]$ e_i opbellen$_k]]$.
   c. Jan bezoekt de hoogleraar niet/soms/morgen/vaak.
     John visits the professor not/sometimes/tomorrow/often.
   d. En ik maar fietsen repareren.
     'I ended up repairing bicycles.'
     hand uitsteken
     'hand outstretch' = signal
     Jantje koekje hebben?
     'Johnnie has a cookie?'
     Ik de vuilnisbak buiten zetten? Nooit.
     'Me put the garbage out? Never.'

There can be differences between matrix and embedded domains that affect only the elements listed in (7). So our degree-0 learner, having access to a lower SPEC of CP and C, can learn that verbs do not move to embedded Cs in Dutch but they do in Greek and Spanish.

The other existing approach to this problem is sketched by Roeper and Weissenborn (1990), who postulated that children follow a subordinate clause strategy and set their parameters on the basis of data from embedded clauses: "Parametric decisions have no local exceptions in subordinate clauses. Therefore subordinate clauses provide the locus for unique triggers which can set the primary parameter . . . children will not get conflicting input involving tensed embedded clauses." (Roeper & Weissenborn, 1990, p. 154). They pointed to discrepancies between matrix and embedded clauses and argued that in the case of such discrepancies it is the embedded clause that manifests the true generalization. For example, they pointed to (29) and claimed that the alternation in (29a) gives contradictory data with reference to the presence/absence of null subjects in English, whereas embedded clauses uniformly manifest the correct generalization that null subjects are not possible.

(29) a. (It is) raining out today.
   b. *I think that raining out today.

Similarly, it is, they argued, only embedded clauses that manifest the generalization that French has WH-movement constructions and that WH in situ does not manifest a full, exceptionless generalization.

(30) a. Il est où, papa?
b. Où il est, papa?
c. Il me demande où je vais.
d. *Il me demande je vais où.

The partial, exceptional generalizations that are manifested in main clauses are not, in their view, a function of parameter setting; instead they reflect "subparameters," a notion that they do not define.

Degree-0 learnability and the subordinate clause strategy of Roeper and Weissenborn represent starkly contrasting efforts to capture through acquisition theory what Emonds (1976) captured through grammatical theory. I point to some data from three quite different empirical domains, which militate in favor of degree-0 learnability and against Roeper and Weissenborn's subordinate clause strategy.

First, consider some data from language change. Historical linguists have long been aware that word order changes affect main clauses before embedded clauses, and they affect embedded clauses catastrophically. Lightfoot (1991) discussed in some detail the loss of object-verb order in English, showing that the relevant parameter was reset in the 13th century. At that time embedded clauses changed rather rapidly from object-verb order to verb-object. Prior to the 13th century, embedded clauses were uniformly OV, and they were uniformly VO after that time; there was nothing gradual about this change. If the parameter was reset in the 13th century, one can ask what changes took place before that time. One wants to find what might have changed in the triggering experience for the OV/VO parameter. I pointed to a number of gradual changes in simple structures affecting the distribution of separable particles and main clause instances of OV order and found, for example, a slow but significant decrease in the frequency of matrix clause OV order. If children are degree-0 learners, one would expect those changes in matrix domains to lead to a new parameter setting, which in turn would lead to new patterns in embedded clauses. And that is what one finds. On the other hand, if children set their parameters by following a subordinate clause strategy, one would again expect to find gradual small-scale changes in the triggering experience leading up to the new parameter setting, but Roeper and Weissenborn would expect to find these preliminary changes in embedded domains. That is not what one finds.

Second, Lightfoot (1991) discussed the Guyanese creole language Berbice Dutch, which has a subject-verb-object order, although it is based on two languages that are underlyingly subject-object-verb, Dutch and the Kwa language of Eastern Ijo. The two input languages are similar in that they are underlyingly SOV but have a verb-fronting operation in main clauses, so that the underlying SOV order is manifested at the surface, uniformly in embedded clauses but almost never in matrix clauses. If the Guyanese children are like other children, then Roeper and Weissenborn would expect them to set their parameters on the basis of embedded clause data. The embedded clauses that the first creole speakers heard, whether drawn from Dutch, Ijo, or some kind of pidgin, would have been uniformly object-verb. Therefore Roeper and Weissenborn would presumably expect the first creole speakers to generalize that pattern, certainly in embedded clauses. But this is not what happened. The relevant parameter was set to verb-object, and the verb-movement operation was lost. This is not surprising if parameters are set on the basis of data from unembedded domains, and particularly if the properties of verb syntax are acquired as I indicated earlier, namely, by attending to data from matrix domains and using indirect indicators like particles and negation markers to determine the underlying position of the verb. Under this view, the uniform object-verb order of embedded clauses in Dutch and Ijo could not influence parameter setting. If the first speakers of Berbice Dutch did not have robust evidence about the distribution of the separable particles, or if negative elements were not retained in their D-structure position (marking the D-structure position of the verb), then there would not be adequate data to trigger the object-verb setting. Negation, for example, works differently in Dutch and Ijo. In Dutch the negative element occurs to the right of an object NP, marking the position from which the verb moves, but in Ijo the negative particle "is adjoined directly to the verb in its proposition-negating role" (Smith, Robertson, & Williamson, 1987) and moves with it, as in (31); it therefore does not reveal the underlying position of the verb.

(31) Á nimi-γá.
  'I know not.'

Ijo provided the negative marker for the creole, *kane*, although it is a free-standing morpheme in Berbice Dutch and not a clitic. Because Ijo provided the basis for negation patterns, one of the Dutch indicators of underlying object-verb order was obscured. If children acquire the verb syntax of languages like Dutch and Ijo by relying on indirect evidence from unembedded domains, then minor shifts in those patterns could produce very different effects. What constitutes one piece of indirect evidence for one of the languages might be obscured if the other language is dominant with respect to that construction type, as we saw with negation. Consequently, one can understand how a creole language might emerge with quite different properties from the two input languages, if one assumes that the relevant data for language acquisition are structurally limited and that some of the simple data might be analyzed differently by children as a result of the contact situation. (See Lightfoot, 1991, for further discussion of this case.)

Third, there is good reason to believe that Dutch and German children actually determine the underlying verb-final nature of their grammars on the basis of simple structures. Clahsen and his collaborators (see, for example, Clahsen & Smolka, 1986) have identified four major stages in the acquisition of the syntax of the German verb, given in (32). Strikingly, from the earliest relevant stage children identify sentence-final position as one of the possible positions for verbs, including finite verbs, despite the fact that they are almost never heard in this position in main clauses. At Stage 3 there is a dramatic increase in the frequency of verb-second structures: In Stages 1 and 2 they are used in only 20%–40% of the utterances, but at Stage 3 they are used in 90%. Clahsen and Smolka reported that this increase takes place explosively, within a month for all the children studied. At this stage children seem to have the object-verb D-structure order and an operation moving a finite verb obligatorily to some fronted position. Most importantly for our present concerns, when they begin to use embedded structures (Stage 4), the finite verbs are invariably in final position and there seems to be no experimentation or learning based on embedded clause data, contrary to what Roeper and Weissenborn lead us to expect. The relevant learning seems to be complete before children begin using embedded structures.

(32) *Stage 1 (25–29 months):* All verbal elements (including verbal complexes) occur in first/second and final position, with a preference for final position.
Stage 2 (31–33 months): Verbal elements with particles occur regularly in final position; other finite verbs occur in both first/second and final position.
Stage 3 (36–39 months): All and only finite verbs occur in first/second position; verbal complexes with finite and nonfinite parts appear in discontinuous positions.
Stage 4 (41–42 months): As soon as embedded sentences are produced, their finite verbs are in final position.

I have just pointed to three arguments in favor of degree-0 learnability and against any form of subordinate clause strategy (the details of these arguments are elsewhere). These arguments seem to me to be persuasive, and they show that it is no accident that one can point to simple triggers for parameters that had seemed to require access to complex structures, as I showed earlier in the context of bounding nodes for Subjacency and deletability of *ha* in Swedish, and so forth. In that case, it is worthwhile to seek new analyses of phenomena that are prima facie counterexamples to degree-0 learnability, such as the distribution of resumptive/empty pronouns and the properties of verb movement in Spanish and Greek. In this way the hypothesis of degree-0 learnability not only makes a claim about the nature of language acquisition but, in suggesting the need for new analyses of certain phenomena and some properties that those analyses should have, also provides another diagnostic for linguists to use as they construct their grammatical hypotheses.

ACKNOWLEDGMENTS

Thanks to Norbert Hornstein for comments on a preliminary draft of this chapter.

REFERENCES

Andersson, A.-B., & Dahl, D. (1974). Against the penthouse principle. *Linguistic Inquiry, 5*, 451–454.

Aoun, J., Hornstein, N., Lightfoot, D., & Weinberg, A. (1987). Two types of locality. *Linguistic Inquiry, 18*, 537–577.

Baker, C. L. (1989). Some observations on degree of learnability. *Behavioral and Brain Sciences, 12*, 334–335.

Battistella, E. (1989). Chinese reflexivization: A movement to INFL approach. *Linguistics, 27*, 987–1012.

Chomsky, N. (1992). A minimalist program for linguistic theory. *MIT Occasional Papers in Linguistics, 1*. Cambridge, MA: MIT, Department of Linguistics and Philosophy.

Chuang, L. (1990). *Disjoint reference of qitaren*. Unpublished masters thesis, University of Maryland, College Park.

Cinque, G. (1990a). Complement object deletion. In J. Mascaro & M. Nespor (Eds.), *Grammar in progress*. Dordrecht: Foris.

Cinque, G. (1990b). *Types of A' dependencies*. Cambridge, MA: MIT Press.

Clahsen, H., & Smolka, K.-D. (1986). Psycholinguistic evidence and the description of V2 in German. In H. Haider & M. Prinzhorn, (Eds.), *Verb-second phenomena in Germanic languages* (pp. 137–167). Dordrecht: Foris.

Clark, R. (1989). Causality and parameter setting. *Behavioral and Brain Sciences, 12*, 337–338.

Clark, R. (1990). *Papers on learnability and natural selection*. (Technical Report in Formal and Computational Linguistics No. 1). Geneva: University of Geneva.

Cole, P., Hermon, G., & Sung, L.-M. (1990). Principles and parameters of long-distance reflexives. *Linguistic Inquiry, 21*, 1–22.

Efthimiou, H., & Hornstein, N. (1992). *Verb movement in Modern Greek*. Unpublished manuscript, University of Maryland, College Park.

Emonds, J. (1976). *A transformational approach to English syntax*. New York: Academic Press.

Higgins, R. (1973). *The pseudo-cleft construction in English*. Unpublished doctoral dissertation, MIT, Cambridge, MA.

Hornstein, N. (1987). Levels of meaning. In J. Garfield (Ed.), *Modularity in knowledge representation and natural language understanding* (pp. 133–150). Cambridge, MA: MIT Press.

Hornstein, N. (1990). *As time goes by.* Cambridge, MA: MIT Press.

Koopman, H. (1983). ECP effects in main clauses. *Linguistic Inquiry, 14,* 346–350.

Lightfoot, D. W. (1989). The child's trigger experience: Degree-0 learnability. *Behavioral & Brain Sciences, 12,* 321–334.

Lightfoot, D. (1991). *How to set parameters.* Cambridge, MA: MIT Press.

Lightfoot, D. (1993). Why UG needs a learning theory: Triggering verb movement. In C. Jones (Ed.), *Historical linguistics: Problems and perspectives* (pp. 190–214). New York: Longman.

Manzini, R., & Wexler, K. (1987). Parameters, binding theory and learnability. *Linguistic Inquiry, 18,* 413–444.

Platzack, C. (1986). Comp, Infl, and Germanic word order. In L. Hellan & K. Koch Christensen, (Eds.), *Topics in Scandinavian syntax* (pp. 185–234). Dordrecht: Reidel.

Rizzi, L. (1982). Violations of the wh island constraint and the Subjacency condition. In L. Rizzi, *Issues in Italian syntax* (pp. 49–76). Dordrecht: Foris.

Roeper, T., & Weissenborn, J. (1990). How to make parameters work. In L. Frazier & J. de Villiers (Eds.), *Language processing and language acquisition* (pp. 147–162). Dordrecht: Kluwer.

Ross, J. R. (1973). The penthouse principle and the order of constituents. In C. Corum, T. C. Smith-Stark, & A. Weiser (Eds.), *You take the high node and I'll take the low node.* Chicago: Chicago Linguistic Society.

Smith, N. S. H., Robertson, I., & Williamson, K. (1987). The Ijo element in Berbice Dutch. *Language in Society, 16,* 49–90.

Sportiche, D. (1981). On bounding nodes in French. *The Linguistic Review, 1,* 219–246.

Tarallo, F. (1985). The filling of the gap: Pro-drop rules in Brazilian Portuguese. In L. D. King & C. A. Maley (Eds.), *Selected papers from the 13th Linguistic Symposium on Romance Languages.* Amsterdam: John Benjamins.

Torrego, E. (1984). On inversion in Spanish and some of its effects. *Linguistic Inquiry, 15,* 103–129.

Vikner, S. (1990). *Verb movement and the licensing of NP-positions in the Germanic languages.* Unpublished doctoral dissertation, University of Geneva.

Wasow, T. (1989). Why degree-0? *Behavioral and Brain Sciences, 12,* 361–362.

CHAPTER TWENTY-ONE

Finitude, Boundedness, and Complexity: Learnability and the Study of First Language Acquisition

Robin Clark
University of Pennsylvania

AUTOMATION AND LANGUAGE ACQUISITION

The nature of the relationship between the formal theory of learnability (Gold, 1967; Osherson, Stob, & Weinstein, 1986), the theory of grammar, and the theory of acquisition poses a difficult conceptual problem. Ideally, the various studies should reinforce each other in such a way as to converge toward a complete theory of language acquisition. Thus, one would hope to find a great deal of collaboration between the three disciplines. In recent years, developmental psycholinguists have been able to draw on work in generative grammar to inform their research on child language acquisition. Relations have not been so close with formal learning theory, where the mathematical formalism seems to have acted as a hindrance to communication between the disciplines. I argue here, perhaps unoriginally, that the three disciplines cannot be easily separated and that each can draw on the others for insights about the language faculty.

Before turning to more specific questions, we should consider the general character of the problem of language learning. A fundamental question for cognitive science is whether or not certain mental faculties are amenable to algorithmic analysis.[1] That is, it could be that certain mental processes can

---

[1] An anonymous reviewer marveled that anyone would question the possibility that mind is algorithmic. In fact, the matter is very much under debate, as the growing literature on intentionality amply demonstrates. Witness, for example, the recent book by Penrose (1989), where it is argued that mental faculties lie outside the domain of the recursive functions. If this is correct, then mental faculties cannot be modeled with algorithms. This is also the point

be usefully modeled using algorithms, whereas others would inherently defy such an analysis. The vision faculty is arguably in the former class, whereas understanding the use of the objects in the visual field may lie in the latter class. Thus, it is important to ask whether language learning lies in the class of faculties that can be usefully modeled via an algorithm. Preliminary evidence suggests that language acquisition can, in fact, be usefully modeled algorithmically. In particular, the human capacity to acquire language seems to be largely automatic, outside the conscious control of the learner. In other words, children within a certain range of ages will automatically acquire a basic knowledge of a given language upon sufficient exposure to that language. This basic knowledge includes aspects of the syntax, morphology, phonology, and semantics of the target language. The child need not intend to acquire this knowledge and, furthermore, need not have any special intellectual gifts in order to succeed.

I assume, as seems reasonable, that such automatic processes can be modeled algorithmically. This entails that it should be possible to embody the learner as an explicit procedure; that is, the learner can be described as a sequence of instructions. Such an algorithm would specify how the learner, when exposed to data from the target language, moves from the initial state through a sequence of hypotheses to a final hypothesis that corresponds to the adult state of grammatical knowledge. Above all, this process must be nonvolitional; the learner should not be faced with a nonquantitative choice between competing analyses. For present purposes, the important point is that a theory of automatic processes should be explicitly mechanical and, above all, not make appeal to any sort of mental force analogous to the (now discredited) notion of life force in biology. An example of one such mental force would be in Searle's (1984) appeal to *intentionality*. In Searle's usage, intentionality is a property of brains that, by its very nature, cannot be modeled via an algorithm. Notice, however, that we need not reject Searle's arguments entirely. Automatic processes are inherently nonintentional because they make no appeal to qualitative choices or understanding. Thus, a good part of our mental life can still make appeal to intentionality; the intentional mind would, nevertheless, be supported by a nonintentional substratum of automatic processes.[2]

The claim that the learning mechanism is free from any notion of qualitative choice between hypotheses does not entail that the learner makes no choices. Choices could be based on quantitative aspects of hypotheses

---

behind Searle's Chinese Room Argument (Searle, 1984), if I understand him correctly. Searle argued that intentionality cannot be modeled with algorithms and thus places the mind outside of the recursive functions. See Dennett (1991) for one response. I take the issue to be largely mathematical. What mental faculties, if any, can be modeled with recursive functions (i.e., algorithms)? What properties would prevent a faculty from being so modeled?

[2] See, in particular, the entertaining discussion of this point in Poundstone (1988).

or on stochastic mechanisms. The claim is, rather, that there is nothing about the learner that is beyond the purview of mathematics and biology at least as far as the acquisition of the core components of grammar are concerned. Again, we must be careful to distinguish types of knowledge. There could be vast individual differences between speakers as to their knowledge of lexical items and rhyming pairs. If mutual communication is to be possible, however, they must share a central backbone of syntactic, semantic, morphological, and phonological structure. It is this structure that is the output of the automatic process of language acquisition.

With the foregoing in mind, let us turn to the fundamental observation that the acquisition of knowledge, grammatical or otherwise, is a process that is inherently bounded by the availability of computational resources. That is, the learner has at its disposal a finite amount of time, memory, or both. Anything that cannot be learned within the bounds set by the available computational resources cannot, for all practical purposes, be learned. Suppose, for example, that an individual who is a detective is given a set of 100 assertions (e.g., *John is tall, Mary is a counterfeiter, the atomic weight of plutonium is 6*) and a further proposition that is compatible with the set of 100 under some particular assignment of truth values (e.g., *John is tall = 1, Mary is a counterfeiter = 0, the atomic weight of plutonium is 6 = 0*). Our hypothetical detective is faced with an imposing task, because the number of possible truth-value assignments to the initial set is 2^{100} or 1,267,650,600,228,229,401,496,703,205,376 possibilities. A brute-force search through such an enormous number of possibilities is clearly impossible. Thus, unless there is some clever method of discovering the correct assignment of truth values to the initial set, the question of compatibility between the initial set of propositions and the new assertions is, for all practical purposes, unknowable. Note that a method exists that will find the truth eventually; but the method is so extravagant in terms of computational costs as to forbid its use. In order to find the truth of the matter, one must first find an economical method for discovering the truth.

One might wonder whether a special cost-efficient algorithm is needed for language acquisition. Instead of a list of 100 propositions, suppose that our hypothetical detective now has a list of 100 possible grammatical rules. We then give him an arbitrarily selected language that can be characterized by some subset of the set of rules. Notice that our poor detective is again confronted with a space of 2^{100} possibilities. If he has no other method at his disposal than a brute-force search through the enormous, albeit finite, hypothesis space, his search may well require unimaginably large computation before the appropriate set of rules is discovered. If this method were taken as a model of learning we would be legitimately disappointed by it as a theory of actual language acquisition, because only immortal babies would ever find the method useful.

Crucially, the foregoing problem did not require an infinite space of possible grammars; finite spaces can quickly become so large that sorting through them becomes a practical impossibility. The present considerations are ones of pure economic feasibility and not those of "in principle" learnability. We have added an additional, and very stringent, criterion to that of explanatory adequacy.[3] Our theory must provide an account of learning that explains how it is that children are capable of locking onto the correct grammar in a relatively short period of time. As I argue, the investigation of computational thrift, properly the domain of formal learning theory, will inform both linguistic theory and psycholinguistic theory, because constraining the learning algorithm will inevitably constrain the class of things that can be learned and the type of data needed to learn them. (Recall that we are making the hypothesis that language acquisition is a mental faculty that can be modeled algorithmically.) If we are unable to give a tractable algorithm for syntactic acquisition, then our hypothesis is in serious trouble. Furthermore, the general conjecture that automatic mental processes are algorithmic (within the domain of recursive function theory) begins to collapse, since no tractable algorithm could simulate a mind. When viewed in this light, questions of economic feasibility become central to the formal theory of mental processes.

MODELING PARAMETRIC SYSTEMS

In this chapter, I assume the Principles and Parameters (*P&P*) approach to Universal Grammar.[4] Here, a central core of principles is common to all languages; grammatical variation is treated as a function of a finite set of parameters. For example, all languages might share the property that certain lexical heads can assign case but they differ as to the grammatical category of the case assigners. The learner would fix the parameters by discovering the grammatical categories of the case-assigning heads. Thus, typological diversity is bounded; the learner is faced with a finite space of hypotheses.

The learner's hypotheses can be coded in binary form by (a) encoding parameters as descriptive statements about the grammar that may bear a truth value (for example, *Nominative Case is assigned under SPEC-Head agreement with Tense*), or (b) fixing an order of the parameters. Any given string of *0*'s and *1*'s may then be interpreted as a particular grammar and mapped onto a parsing device that accepts the language associated with

---

[3]The problem of feasibility or accessibility is discussed both in Chomsky (1965) and in Wexler and Culicover (1980).

[4]See Chomsky (1981) and Chomsky (1985) for some nontechnical discussion of *P&P* systems. See Clark (1992) and Clark and Roberts (1993) for more detailed expositions of the formal properties of such systems.

that grammar. A small parametric space is shown in (1), an example of a hypothesis string is shown in (2a), and its interpretation is given in (2b) (see Clark & Roberts, 1993, for discussion of some of the following parameters):

(1) a. Nominative Case is assigned under SPEC-Head agreement with Tense.
   b. Nominative Case is assigned under government with Tense.
   c. Exceptional Case Marking is possible.
   d. Structural Case Marking is possible.
   e. Verb-Second is obligatory in the root.

(2) a. 1 0 1 0 1
   b. Nominative Case is assigned under SPEC-Head agreement with Tense but not under government; the language allows ECM but not SCM; V-2 is obligatory in the root.

We can assume that the learner comes endowed with a general language processing device. The central core of the device could be treated as a program missing certain lines of code. The parameters specify these missing bits of the program. The bit string in (2a) would, then, tell the learner how to fill in the missing pieces of its parsing device and thus get a working processor. The main hypothesis of a *P&P* approach is that there is only a finite number of ways of filling in the missing pieces and, therefore, only a finite number of different grammars/processors.

As we saw earlier, however, a finite hypothesis space does not guarantee economical learnability. Instead, we must be able to provide an algorithm that will correctly set parameters within some bounded amount of time (for example, correctly setting 50 parameters in 3 years' time). Common sense seems to dictate that parameter setting must involve some form of natural deduction.[5] For example, the learner might attempt to deduce the well-formedness of an input example from a set of parameter settings. The reasoning would be along the lines of (3):

(3) If parameter p_n is set to value v_j, then the current input example, σ_k, receives a well-formed structural analysis.

---

[5]Although some form of logic provides an appealing model of the human capacity for learning, some caution is necessary here. There is an extensive literature in psychology on the mismatch between logic and human reasoning. Tversky and Kahneman (1983), for example, showed quite persuasively that even statistically sophisticated subjects will violate basic rules of inductive logic. I have argued elsewhere (Clark, 1990, 1992) for a learning system that dispenses with deduction altogether. One might speculate that the mismatch between logic and human reasoning arises from the fact that the mind simulates logical systems in a cost-effective way; that is, it dispenses with logic.

The approach in (3) is based on a derivational system. That is, it attempts to deduce a grammatical structure corresponding to a particular utterance from the core grammatical principles plus the set of properly instantiated parameters. Although this system provides a plausible basis for deriving grammaticality judgments, it seems exactly backwards for modeling the process of parameter setting. This is because it uses possible sequences of parameter settings to discover grammatical utterances rather than using the input data to discover the target sequence of parameter settings. One would expect that the learner would reason as follows:

(4) Given that the utterance s_k occurs in the input stream, then parameter p_n must be set to value v_j.

The utterance s_k is a *trigger* to set parameter p_n to value v_j. The reasoning in (4) seems to ground the learner's hypotheses in its linguistic environment; (4) is data driven in a way that (3) is not.

Our folk-theoretic intuition, then, is that each parameter is associated with a trigger that automatically causes the learner to set a parameter to some value immediately upon exposure to it. A trigger for a parameter, P_i, would be an element drawn from some class of structures; intuitively, these structures would be associated with sentences that could be represented only if P_i is set to some particular value, v_j.

Consider, for example, the parameters that govern word order. Let us suppose, for the sake of discussion, that the core word order parameters involve Case and θ-role assignment:

(5) a. Assign Case to the left.
    b. Assign θ-roles to the left.

Assigning the value *1* to both of the parameters in (5) would result in a head-final language. Assigning *0* to both would result in Case and θ-role assignment to the right and, hence, a head-initial language.[6] Intuitively, triggers for the parameters in (5) would include any structure from the following classes, where elements of the class described by (6a) trigger head-initial order and those from the class described by (6b) trigger head-final order:

(6) a. $[_{X'} X^0 \text{ Compl}]$
    b. $[_{X'} \text{ Compl } X^0]$

---

[6] Notice that the separation of Case assignment from θ-role assignment in (16) also allows for the generation of other types of word orders. See Travis (1984) and Koopman (1983) for discussion of the possible word orders, given the parametrization in (16).

Thus, the example in (7) is an element of the class described by (6a) and would be sufficient to trigger head-initial order, given that the learner has mastered the appropriate lexical items and their argument structure:

(7) a. Kiss Dolly.
b. $[_{V'} [_{V^0} \text{kiss}] [_{DP} \text{Dolly}]] = [_{X'} X^0 \text{ Compl}]$

Assuming that the learner is in a state where one or more of the word order parameters in (5) are incorrectly set, encountering an example like (7a) will constitute evidence for the correct settings.

The task faced by the learner, when considered in terms of this trivial model, seems simple enough. Suppose, however, that the learner must explore a more complex space of possible grammars. For example, suppose that the target system is head-final but has root verb-second (V-2) structures. In this case, the following example would not be a trigger for head-initial ordering:

(8) John kissed Dolly.

Instead, the head-final ordering has been obscured by another grammatical process. Thus, (8) would receive from the target grammar the following representation (abstracting away from the details of the representation):

(9) [John [kissed$_i$ [$_{VP}$ Dolly t_i]]]

If (8) were taken in isolation from other examples in the input stream, we might expect the learner to be temporarily misled by it; in fact, this does not seem true. Rather, evidence indicates that learners are sensitive to the context in which a datum occurs. Thus, examples with auxiliary and modal verbs would indicate to the learner that additional processes are at work.[7]

Similar examples are easy to create. Scrambling, for example, does not cause the learner to reset word order parameters with each new example from the input stream. Eventually, the learner must be able to record the presence of word order variation within the input text and interpret that variation with respect to those parameters that regulate scrambling. Equally, the learner must not be misled by the presence of topicalization or heavy NP shift into incorrect

---

[7]An anonymous reviewer observed that the learner would somehow have to keep track of the various alternative hypotheses. This complexity, however, is exactly what the theory of learnability must grapple with, as observed in the first section. For one proposal on how to deal with this type of complexity, see Clark (1992), where a parallel algorithm that locally evaluates the performance of hypotheses is discussed. For a very different approach, see Gibson and Wexler (1992).

settings for word order. The learner recognizes that other processes may obscure basic orders and analyzes the input stream accordingly.

If this analysis is on the right track, then individual examples are not taken in isolation but rather are interpreted relative to the stream of input data in which they occur. The idea that a datum is a trigger simply by being an element of the relevant class of structures is misleading; instead, we must complicate our notion of trigger so that the relevant class of structures is defined relative to a value v_j for parameter P_i and an input text σ_k. This, in turn, implies that the learning system is able to simulate memory for past examples.[8] Note, however, that the learner must be able to compute an interpretation for each potential trigger with respect to the input data. If he or she cannot do so, then the memory will be of little use.

The intuitive solution has been to assume that hypothesis formation involves deductive steps designed to find the best set of parameter settings relative to an input text. The best set of parameter settings would be the sequence of parameter settings that maximizes the learner's ability to represent the input text. Increased deductive capacities on the part of the learner entail increases in complexity because each deductive step will require either an additional unit of time or, if some parallel processing is admitted, an additional processor to search some part of the hypothesis space.

INTERACTIONS BETWEEN PARAMETER VALUES

The previous section considered the interpretation of a datum relative to an input text and showed that the learner could not consider each datum in absolute isolation. In this section, I consider the interpretation of data relative to sets of possible parameter settings. A fundamental property of parametric systems of grammar is that they have an extremely rich deductive structure; the grammar can be seen as a set of axioms, divided into a set of grammatical modules, which interact to prove grammatical structures as theorems. The problem of parameter setting can be seen as tuning the set of axioms (along lines prescribed by the parameters) so that the correct set of grammatical structures is derived.

It is tempting to allow the learning algorithm to exploit the deductive structure of the grammar by turning on its head the procedure for deriving sentences. That is, one would like to diagnose the error in the learner's current hypothesis by examining the proofs that the learner's grammar

---

[8] This can be done indirectly via a Bayesian model that gradually alters a weight associated with each hypothesis. This weight would correspond to the learner's confidence in the hypothesis. The model proposed in Clark (1990, 1992) and Clark and Roberts (1993) exhibits similar behavior by using a Genetic Algorithm (Goldberg, 1989; Holland, 1975) to search the space of available grammars.

produces. Although this idea, however vaguely formulated, holds a good deal of attraction, its computational costs will, upon further analysis, prove to be too great to be acceptable. The unacceptable cost of this procedure is largely due to the fact that parameters are not insulated from each other. The learner, in attempting to unravel a derivation, is faced with a complex problem of credit/blame assignment.

In general, any given grammatical construction in a language has its particular form as the result of the interaction between a number of different elements of grammar, including the values of various parameters. Furthermore, as shown in Clark (1990, 1992), a single string can support different structural analyses and thus, on occasion, different parameter settings. For example, as noted earlier, the order SVO may be base-generated and, thus, result from a particular set of values for θ-role assignment and Case assignment. On the other hand, the surface SVO order may be a result of V-2 applied to a completely different base structure and, thus, would originate from a completely different set of parameter values. More formally, there exist input examples, s, that receive well-formed, but distinct, structural representations from hypothesis h_1 and h_2, where h_1 is a sequence of parameter values $<p_1, \ldots, p_i, \ldots, p_j, \ldots, p_n>$ and h_2 is $<p_1, \ldots, \bar{p}_i, \ldots, \bar{p}_j, \ldots, p_n>$. Because h_1 and h_2 contain contradictory parameter settings (p_i and p_j as opposed to $\bar{p}_i$ and $\bar{p}_j$), there must be examples where h_1 and h_2 predict conflicting acceptability judgments; thus, the learner has some stake in selecting either hypothesis. In particular, there will be further possible input sentences s', s'', and so on, which will distinguish between h_1 and h_2; the learner must be sensitive to the presence of such examples in the input text.[9]

This situation seems amenable to a deductive treatment; the learner could apparently use the parameter settings in the current hypothesis to make predictions that could be confirmed or disconfirmed by the evidence. This position becomes less attractive when we consider that the conflicting parameter settings can interact in complex ways.[10] Thus, the learner will have to consider increasingly complex interactions between parameters when

---

[9]An anonymous reviewer pointed out that such examples seem difficult to construct. Although I agree with his or her assessment, it would seem that the difficulty arises from the fact that, to date, relatively few parameters have been formulated in the literature. Many of the cases that arise are easily resolved, as is the case with the V-2 example in the text. Others are more complex; see the example discussed in Clark (1992). Examples of the latter type will no doubt become easier to find as our knowledge of comparative grammar and the typology of the parameter space increases.

[10]This analysis is originally discussed in Clark (1992) who, nonetheless, failed to note the relationship with the Tower of Hanoi and Hamiltonian circuits. The classic work on complexity theory and NP-Completeness is Garey and Johnson (1979). Poundstone (1988) provided an amusing and accessible discussion of complexity and cognition. Rawlins (1992) is also to be recommended.

deducing predictions; where n is the number of parameters and k is the number of possible interactions, the learner will have to consider the following number of possibilities:

$$f(n) = \sum_{k=1}^{n} \binom{n}{k} \tag{1}$$

This number is equal to $2^n - 1$, roughly the size of the hypothesis space to begin with. Two observations are worth making. First, we concluded earlier that a brute-force search of n elements could not be the correct approach to the learning problem because, in the worst case, it required an impractical 2^n steps. Because $2^n - 1$ is only a very marginal improvement, the deductive theory is not doing much better than the brute-force search. This is sufficient to show that the mathematical theory of learning has an important place in the study of language acquisition. It will provide the boundaries of feasibility within which a plausible theory of first language acquisition must place itself.

The second observation is that the function $f(n) = 2^n - 1$ has an interesting history connected with it. It is worth lingering for a moment first to consider its properties and second to discover why the deductive method for parameter setting should be associated with it. A standard problem in the analysis of algorithms is the analysis of methods for solving the Tower of Hanoi game (see, for example, the lucid analysis in Graham, Knuth, & Patashnik, 1989). The game consists of three pegs and a number (usually eight) of disks, graduated in size. Legend (disseminated by the game's inventor, the French mathematician Edouard Lucas) has it that temple priests in the holy city of Benares are occupied in transferring a set of 64 golden disks from one peg to the next. Only one disk may be transferred at a time and a larger disk may never be placed upon a smaller disk. Still according to legend, when the 64 disks have been successfully displaced, the world will vanish. Because $2^{64} - 1 = 18,446,744,073,709,551,615$ is an awfully large number, the end of the world is not yet in sight. As Gardner (1959/1991) pointed out, the Tower of Hanoi has the same mathematical structure as a Hamiltonian circuit; given a graph, a Hamiltonian circuit is one that starts at an arbitrary vertex and, following only edges, visits each vertex once and only once (this is perhaps better known as the Traveling Salesman problem). As Garey and Johnson (1979) showed, this problem is itself NP-Complete.

The preceding discussion strongly suggests that the problem of parameter setting is itself NP-Complete. If this is correct, then we have raised a serious problem for the algorithmic approach to parameter setting and first language acquisition. How are children able to solve an intractable problem with such accuracy and uniformity? Having recognized where we stand mathematically, we can now ask what the source of complexity is. Why should it be that setting parameters is like playing the Tower of Hanoi? Obviously, they're not at all alike, so something in our notion of how parameters are being set must be wrong. The problem with the Tower of Hanoi is that, in order to move the nth disk on a peg, all the $n - 1$ disks above it on the peg must be moved. Notice that all combinations of the $n - 1$ disks will occur on the other pegs. The complexity of the game arises from the fact that one must systematically move through all of these combinations according to the foregoing rules.

COMPLEXITY AND LEARNABILITY

An analysis similar to that of the Tower of Hanoi can be applied to the problem of parameter setting. Intuitively, each parameter corresponds to a disk. Assuming, as before, that parameters are binary-valued, then the two pegs that are empty at the start state of the puzzle correspond to the values 0 and 1 for the parameters. Thus, we can convert the Tower of Hanoi game into a memory storage for a machine that sets parameters deductively. The disks on the 0 and 1 pegs will be mapped onto parameters set to 0 and 1. The interactions of these parameters will be checked by deriving a set of structures that must be tested against the input stream. The complexity problem arises because the learner must test all possible combinations of parameters and values, just as the temple priests must move all the golden disks through all possible combinations on the pegs before completing their task.

No input sentence ever exhibits the action of one and only one parameter. Even the simplest sentences involve combinations of parameter settings. A simple transitive sentence in English, for example, involves the action of parameters regulating the direction and form of Case assignment, the attachment of verbal morphology, agreement, and θ-role assignment. Thus, sentences look the way they do because principles and parameters form coalitions to derive the language. In order to represent the input stream and properly set parameters to their target values, the learner must untangle these coalitions of parameters. The learner is testing to find sentences that can be represented only if certain combinations of parameters are fixed at certain values. If these sentences appear in the input stream, then the learner has substantial evidence for particular parameter settings. In the simple deductive model, the learner is testing every possible combination of parameter values.

We can now move from an apparently whimsical analogy between the Tower of Hanoi and the logical problem of language acquisition to a serious constraint on parametrized grammatical systems. The complexity problem arises because all the possible coalitions of parameters apparently must be tested. Thus, if some principled upper bound can be placed on n, the number of possible interactions per derivation, the complexity of the problem will decrease. Notice that, if $n = 100$, then:

$$\sum_{k=1}^{100} \binom{100}{k} = 1,267,650,600,228,229,401,496,703,205,375 \qquad (2)$$

If, on the other hand, the size of coalitions between parameters is limited to 5 then:

$$\sum_{k=1}^{5} \binom{100}{k} = 79,375,495 \qquad (3)$$

The foregoing illustrates that the complexity of the learner's task can be reduced several orders of magnitude by limiting the size of the coalitions that may form between parameters. In other words, the learner has a much better chance of discovering the target within severely bounded time limits if it can assume that the interactions between parameters have an upper limit that is bounded by a constant.

THE SIMPLICITY OF THE TRIGGERING DATA

It is intuitively plausible to suppose that the learner has a chance of discovering the correct parameter settings for its target grammar just in case those parameter settings have some tangible effects on the form of sentences in the input stream. This suggests the following definition of parameter expression (see Clark, 1992):

(10) *Parameter Expression*
A sentence ρ expresses a parameter P_i just in case a grammar must have P_i set to some definite value in order to assign a well-formed representation to ρ.

A sentence, then, will be a trigger for some parameter just in case it expresses that parameter.

Clark (1992) argued that parameters must have an upper bound on the syntactic complexity of their triggers. Head-Complement order, as we saw above, can be encoded in trees of a very shallow depth, essentially just the $\overline{X}$ level. SPEC-Head relations (ordering and agreement, for example) are exemplified in trees of a slightly greater depth, the $\overline{\overline{X}}$ level. Still other parameters, for example those regulating complementizers or anaphora, would require trees of a slightly greater complexity in order to be expressed. In any event, because there are a finite number of parameters, there must be an upper limit on the structural complexity that can be encoded by a parameter and, thus, a limit on the size of the smallest structure needed to express that parameter:

(11) *Boundedness of Parameter Expression*
For all parameter values v_i in a parameterized system P, there exists a syntactic structure τ_j that expresses v_i where the complexity $C(\tau_j)$ is less than or equal to some constant, U.

This intuition is common to much recent work on learnability. Wexler and Culicover (1980) expressed the insight in terms of the boundedness of the syntactic complexity of structures upon which the learner will make a detectable error.[11] Lightfoot (1989, 1991) argued that triggering data must be of degree 0; parameters are expressed by sentences of minimal syntactic complexity.

We have already noted, however, that parameters always form coalitions; that is, any given input sentence shows the results of the interaction between several different parameters. Thus, the notion that parameters have an upper bound on their syntactic complexity is not yet sufficient to guarantee learnability within bounded time. It must also be the case that parameter coalitions are bounded; thus, parallel to (11) is (12):

(12) *Boundedness of Parameter Coalitions*
Let $\Re(\iota)$ be a measure of the number of parameters triggered by the syntactic structure ι. Then for all syntactic structures, τ_j, such that the complexity $C(\tau_j) \leq U$, there is an upper bound V such that $\Re(\tau_j) \leq V$.

Boundedness of Parameter Expression places an upper bound, U, on the syntactic complexity of the minimal structure required to express a parameter. Boundedness of Parameter Coalitions places an upper bound, V, on the number of parameters that may interact in the generation of a structure of complexity at most U.[12]

The two constraints make claims about the nature of the input evidence adequate for parameter setting and may seem quite parallel. Notice, however, that Boundedness of Parameter Expression places a constraint on the complexity of a representation, whereas Boundedness of Parameter Coalitions places a constraint on interactions in the derivation of a structure. Thus, the

---

[11]See the Boundedness of Minimal Degree of Error (BDE) in Wexler and Culicover (1980).

[12]In recent work, Gibson and Wexler (1992) assumed the maturation hypothesis such that parameters are extrinsically ordered with respect to the setting operation. The learner has only some parameters available for setting at any given time. Their hypothesis presupposes that interactions between parameters are limited in much the way that the Boundedness of Parameter Coalitions formalizes. Space limitations prevent a detailed discussion of their work.

latter condition implies that parameters can be set from sentences of simple derivational structure; although all sentences in the input stream show the effects of parameter coalitions, the coalitions must be small enough that the learner can untangle them quickly.

From the point of view of syntactic analysis, Boundedness of Parameter Expression and Boundedness of Parameter Coalitions place strong bounds on the minimal syntactic structures required to determine a grammar. Thus, it should be possible to enumerate a minimal set of syntactic trees the complexity of which is bounded by the constants U and V. Syntactic structures of greater complexity would, of course, exist, but they could be excluded from the learner's primary evidence without preventing convergence. Indeed, structures outside the bounds defined by U and V would be created by finite adjunctions of trees drawn from this minimal set.[13]

TOWARD AN ECOLOGY OF LANGUAGE

Because the set of all trees within the bounds set by the principles and parameters made available by Universal Grammar and the complexity constants U and V has finite cardinality, there will be some most complex structure in the minimal set. We can use this structure to define an upper bound on a description language for syntactic trees. The learner would be faced with the task of specifying the subset of this minimal set that corresponds to the basic structures of the target language. On an even more speculative level, we might take the specification for each basic tree as the phenotype for an automaton that builds syntactic trees (call it a "treebot").[14] For example, one could use a string of binary digits to describe the form of the subtree and various conditions on the nodes. The string could be broken into substrings that describe the grammatical category of the root node, the daughters of the node, linear ordering of the daughters, and so forth. The core language would consist of a "hive" of such automata. The members of the hive would cooperate to create syntactic representations for linguistic input. In general, the behavior of the hive would be constrained by economic considerations that would prefer compact, simple representations. The language, itself, would emerge from the interactions of automata; that is, it would result from the ways in which the basic trees would combine to form more complex structures.

---

[13] The idea here owes much to the work of Joshi and others on Tree Adjoining Grammar. See Joshi (1987) and the references cited there. Similar ideas can be found in Chomsky (1992).

[14] The idea here owes much to Holland's (1975) notion of a *broadcast language*. In general, the specification of the treebot would be much like a *classifier system* as described in Holland (1986) and Booker, Goldberg, and Holland (1990). Thus, each treebot would be equivalent to a production rule in a classifier system. See Booker, Goldberg, and Holland (1990) and the references cited there.

More specifically, we can imagine an environment of tree-building creatures, one type of which would be specialized for mapping lexical items onto predefined subtrees. Upon encountering a noun like *boy*, this type of treebot would map it to:

(13) $[_{NP} [_{\bar{N}} [_{N} boy]]]$

Other treebots might be specialized for combining available subtrees. Thus, one might take the tree fragment in (13) and combine it with the fragment in (14) to yield the fragment in (15):

(14) $[_{DP} [_{\bar{D}} [_{D} the]]]$
(15) $[_{DP} [_{\bar{D}} [_{D} the [_{NP} [_{\bar{N}} [_{N} boy]]]]]]$

Thus, all representations would be built by the combination of subtrees. Each subtree would be built by an agent, a treebot, whose behavior is determined by some phenotype. By phenotype I mean an encoded representation of the actions performed by the agent. In the preceding examples, these include:

(16) a. If the current lexical item is a determiner, project a *DP* in accordance with the $\bar{X}$ schema.
      b. If the current lexical item is a noun, project an *NP* in accordance with the $\bar{X}$ schema.
      c. If both a *DP* and an *NP* are available and if the *NP* satisfies the lexical requirements of the head *D* of the *DP*, then combine the two with the *NP* as a right-sister of the *D*.

Notice that the preceding production rules could be encoded, given a suitable set of conventions, in a binary form; that is, as a string of binary digits. This representation would be analogous to the representation developed in Clark (1992). The cooperation of these agents would determine the set of representations built by the community of treebots.

The result of the foregoing would be a community of beings whose behavior is genetically fixed. This community would form a genetically related population over which natural selection could apply. In other words, learning could be achieved via a Genetic Algorithm in much the same way as described in Clark (1992). An initial population of treebots would reproduce relative to their behavior on the input stream. Because the behavior of the automata is fundamentally cooperative—several treebots must cooperate to parse an input string—those automata that worked together to create the best representation for an input string would share an increase in fitness, perhaps via a "bucket-brigade" algorithm (Holland, 1986). The members of the hive would interbreed, the most fit combining together their phenotypic specification via the genetic operators (see Clark, 1992; Goldberg, 1989; Holland, 1975) with occasional innovations arising due to mutation. Because members of the hive would interbreed, we would expect a great deal of cross-categorial similarity, because the treebots would share genetic material. However, although such a system would prefer similarities across categories, cross-categorical variation would be tolerated. Thus, languages like German that have head-final order in *VP*, but prepositional (rather than postpositional) phrases would be easily derived.

CONCLUSION

I have argued here that the feasibility of parameter setting is ultimately a function of two factors: first, the complexity of the simplest tree required to express a parameter, and second, the types of coalitions that naturally occur when independent modules of grammar work together to derive linguistic structures. If the reasoning here is correct, then notions of feasibility and the study of behavior of complex, autonomous systems are fundamental to our understanding of the acquisition and implementation of linguistic knowledge. Although the account of learning discussed here remains programmatic, it does show that there is a rich connection between the formal learning theory, the theory of linguistic typology, and the study of acquisition.

ACKNOWLEDGMENTS

This chapter is a highly revised version of a paper delivered at the Cornell University Symposium on Syntactic Theory and First Language Acquisition in April 1992. I would like to acknowledge the helpful input I received from audiences at the Symposium and at a talk given at the University of Pennsylvania, and from the students in my seminar at the University of Geneva. I have greatly benefited from the comments made by two anonymous reviewers. The research was funded by Grant 11-25362.88 from the Fonds National Suisse pour la Recherche Scientifique and by a grant from the Fondation Ernst et Lucie Schmidheiny.

REFERENCES

Booker, L. B., Goldberg, D. E., & Holland, J. H. (1990). Classifier systems and genetic algorithms. In J. Carbonell (Ed.), *Machine learning: Paradigms and methods* (pp. 235–282). Cambridge, MA: MIT Press.

Chomsky, N. (1965). *Aspects of the theory of syntax.* Cambridge, MA: MIT Press.

Chomsky, N. (1981). Principles and parameters in syntactic theory. In N. Hornstein & D. Lightfoot (Eds.), *Explanation in linguistics: The logical problem of language acquisition* (pp. 123–146). London: Longman.

Chomsky, N. (1985). *Knowledge of language.* New York: Praeger.

Chomsky, N. (1992). A minimalist program for linguistic theory. *MIT Occasional Papers in Linguistics, 1.* Cambridge, MA: MIT, Department of Linguistics and Philosophy.

Clark, R. (1990). *Papers on learnability and natural selection* (Technical Report in Formal and Computational Linguistics No. 1). Geneva: University of Geneva.

Clark, R. (1992). The selection of syntactic knowledge. *Language Acquisition, 2,* 83–149.

Clark, R., & Roberts, I. (1993). A computational model of language learnability and language change. *Linguistic Inquiry, 24,* 299–345.

Dennett, D. (1991). *Consciousness explained.* Boston: Little, Brown.

Gardner, M. (1991). The Icosian Game and the Tower of Hanoi. In M. Gardner, *Mathematical puzzles and diversions* (pp. 56–61). London: Penguin Books. (Original work published 1959)

Garey, M., & Johnson, D. (1979). *Computers and intractability: A guide to the theory of NP-Completeness.* New York: W. H. Freeman.

Gibson, E., & Wexler, K. (1992). *Triggers.* Unpublished manuscript, MIT, Cambridge, MA.

Gold, E. M. (1967). Language identification in the limit. *Information and Control, 16,* 447–474.

Goldberg, D. (1989). *Genetic algorithms in search, optimization, and machine learning.* Reading, MA: Addison-Wesley.

Graham, R. L., Knuth, D. E., & Patashnik, O. (1989). *Concrete mathematics.* Reading, MA: Addison-Wesley.

Holland, J. (1975). *Adaptation in natural and artificial systems.* Ann Arbor, MI: University of Michigan Press.

Holland, J. (1986). Escaping brittleness: The possibilities of general-purpose learning algorithms applied to parallel rule-based systems. In R. Michalski, J. Carbonell, & T. Mitchell (Eds.), *Machine learning II* (pp. 593–623). Los Altos, CA: Morgan Kaufmann.

Joshi, A. (1987). An introduction to tree adjoining grammars. In A. Manaster-Ramer (Ed.), *Mathematics of language* (pp. 87–114). Amsterdam: John Benjamins.

Koopman, H. (1983). *The syntax of verbs.* Dordrecht: Foris.

Lightfoot, D. (1989). The child's trigger experience: Degree-0 learnability. *Behavioral and Brain Sciences, 12,* 321–334.

Lightfoot, D. (1991). *How to set parameters: Arguments from language change.* Cambridge, MA: MIT Press.

Osherson, D., Stob, M., & Weinstein, S. (1986). *Systems that learn: An introduction to learning theory for cognitive and computer scientists.* Cambridge, MA: MIT Press.

Penrose, R. (1989). *The emperor's new mind: Concerning computers, minds, and the laws of physics.* New York: Oxford University Press.

Poundstone, W. (1988). *Labyrinths of reason: Paradox, puzzles and the frailty of knowledge.* London: Penguin Books.

Rawlins, G. J. E. (1992). *Compared to what? An introduction to the analysis of algorithms.* New York: W. H. Freeman.

Searle, J. R. (1984). *Minds, brains and programs.* Cambridge, MA: Harvard University Press.

Travis, L. (1984). *Parameters and effects of word order change.* Unpublished doctoral dissertation, MIT, Cambridge, MA.

Tversky, A., & Kahneman, D. (1983). Extensional versus intuitive reasoning: The conjunction fallacy in probability judgements. *Psychological Review, 90,* 293–315.

Wexler, K., & Culicover, P. (1980). *Formal principles of language acquisition.* Cambridge, MA: MIT Press.

CHAPTER TWENTY-TWO

Some Applications of Formal Learning Theory Results to Natural Language Acquisition

Shyam Kapur
James Cook University, Queensland, Australia

In this section, I provide some background to my work. The primary goal of this research is to provide a mathematical foundation on which various ideas in the study of natural language acquisition can be assessed. I believe that such theoretical modeling moving side by side with empirical investigations would be ideal for solving the ultimate problem of linguistic theory, learnability (Chomsky, 1986). In this way, my research complements that in linguistics and psychology.

Progress has been made with regard to the development of ideas in learning theory with applications to natural language acquisition (Berwick, 1985; Gold, 1967; Osherson, Stob, & Weinstein, 1984, 1986; Wexler & Culicover, 1980). However, the theoretical results have often been applied without adequate justification.

Consider first the pioneering work of Gold (1967), who proposed a model of inductive inference termed *identification in the limit*. In this paradigm, as applied to language learning, the learner is presented with the *text* of a language (all grammatical sentences in any order with possible repetitions) that belongs to a specified family of languages. The learner is said to learn a language if, on all texts for it, the learner's guess *converges* to the target language, that is, from some point onwards, the guess coincides with the language being presented. The learner is said to learn the family if it learns each language in the family.

Gold showed that a family of languages that contains all finite languages and any infinite language is not learnable. There has been a significant (direct or indirect) impact of this nonlearnability result. Today, linguistic theory has been substantially altered so as to negate this learnability problem. For example, within the Principles and Parameters framework (Chomsky, 1981), the child does not learn rules as such but simply sets a finite number of parameters associated with innate principles. Further, it has been argued that parameters can take only a finite number of values, so that there are only a finite number of possible languages. Any family of a finite number of distinct languages is trivially learnable (Osherson et al., 1986). Of course, there were independent reasons for and other advantages to this shift. Ultimately, however, if learnability is the real problem of linguistic theory and learnability can be shown to be as easy for infinite families as for finite ones, some force to this shift will be diminished.

Along with showing nonlearnability given positive evidence, Gold also showed learnability given both positive and *negative evidence* (evidence about what is ungrammatical, maybe in the form of repetitions, corrections, etc.). Around the same time, some work concluded that the child acquires language from positive evidence alone (Braine, 1971; Brown & Hanlon, 1970). Consequently, the absence of negative evidence in the input became a central issue for research in natural language acquisition. (For example, see Marcus, 1993, and the references therein.) Consider the following:

> "In sum, the 'no negative evidence' problem is not a myth, but a very real and serious challenge for the construction of an adequate theory of language acquisition" (Bowerman, 1988, p. 96).

> "Much of the recent discussion of language learnability has centered around the absence for the learner of negative evidence and the implications of that absence" (Lasnik, 1990, p. 184).

Because, even in the absence of negative evidence, learning must take place, it has been argued that this must be reflected both in the form of the learning mechanism and in the parameter space structure. Consider the extensive discussion of the problem of *overgeneralization* (also called the *subset problem*), which arises only in those situations where negative evidence is absent. The problem of overgeneralization is simply stated as follows:

> If in the course of making guesses the inference process makes a guess that is overly general, i.e., specifies a language that is a proper superset of the true answer, then with positive and negative data there will eventually be a counterexample to the guess, i.e., a string that is contained in the guessed language but is not a member of the true language. No such conflict with examples will occur in the case of inference from positive data. (Angluin, 1980, p. 118)

To a certain degree, there has been an unnecessarily severe impact of this observation. It has been viewed as though overgeneralizations must be avoided completely to ensure successful learning. Ironically though, Angluin (1980) also showed that learning can take place with overgeneralizations; in fact, in some cases it must, because there are families of languages that can be learned only by learners that overgeneralize.

The Subset Principle (Berwick, 1985; Manzini & Wexler, 1987; Wexler & Manzini, 1987) (henceforth, the SP) was proposed as a solution to the problem of overgeneralization. The learner is stipulated to guess the least language (in terms of inclusion of strings/derivations). Because this learning strategy allows no overgeneralization, it is argued that learning must take place. There are some studies in psycholinguistics that argue in favor of the SP being operative in child language acquisition (for example, Chien & Wexler, 1989). There are other studies presenting a different picture (for example, Hermon, this volume, chapter 4; Jakubowicz, this volume, chapter 5; Jakubowicz & Olsen, 1988).

Parameters in contemporary linguistic theory are generally devised so that they can be learned from positive evidence alone. Invoking even a minimal amount of negative evidence in any acquisition proposal tends to draw scorn from a significant quarter of researchers. Likewise, there is an effort to explain away any overgeneralizations in child input (Baker, 1979; Pinker, 1989) and to show that the SP is (sometimes must be) operative (Fodor, this volume, chapter 19; Wexler, 1993).

I give the following summary of some objections to the formal aspect of the SP:[1]

1. It can be argued that the SP is no more than a description of a particular developmental sequence. Because, in general, the subset relation between languages cannot be computed, the subset relationships must be known beforehand. However, in that case, the observation that the child is learning without overgeneralization does not give the SP any causal/explanatory power. In other words, the SP cannot explain the constraints on the acquisition sequence nor those on the linguistic theory. On the contrary, it is at best a description of the empirical situation.

2. The SP is a unique solution to the problem of overgeneralization only if a subset-superset relationship holds between the languages generated by alternative parameter values and the *conservativeness* constraint holds, that is, the learner is not allowed to change its guess unless there is explicit contradiction in the input data.[2] The conservativeness constraint has never

---

[1]For detailed formal and empirical argumentation against the status of the SP, see Kapur, Lust, Harbert, and Martohardjono (1993, in preparation).

[2]Learning under the conservativeness constraint and error-driven learning are not necessarily identical because an error-driven learner need not be conservative.

been shown to have any independent basis. The SP can then be viewed as an obvious solution to a problem that is unjustifiably created in the first place (by imposing the conservativeness constraint), leaving it as the only solution.

3. Some proposals for an SP presuppose the finiteness of the language family (Wexler, 1993). (Even though there are infinite families that can be learned without overgeneralization, in general, learning algorithms more sophisticated than the SP are needed [Kapur, 1991; Kapur & Bilardi, 1992b].) In the finite parameter situation, it is significant only to show feasible learning, because learning from positive evidence alone is always possible. (See the next section.) Because the SP fails even to address that question, it is quite irrelevant.

4. The SP crucially works only when there are *subset* parameters, that is, the parameters that give rise to languages that are in a subset-superset relationship. Clearly, not all parameters in any natural language theory satisfy this extensional relationship (e.g., head direction). Thus, there will have to be separate learning mechanisms stipulated in case of the other parameters. Given that there are many other possible algorithms that can set parameters of either type in a uniform fashion, this calls into question the stipulation of the specialized SP.

5. There are other learning algorithms that are general, simple, and natural (like the SP, according to Wexler, 1993) and that work in case there are only a finite number of languages. Thus, the SP is not even necessary for learning. There are other algorithms that work equally well for the finite case, and although some of them extend to the infinite case, others do not. The SP is not even special in the sense that it crucially exploits the finite cardinality of the language family.

In summary, we have seen that learning theory has made an impact on research in language acquisition and linguistics, but at least some of the influence is of a controversial nature.

Some recent work has shown that there can be no computable translation from the description of a learnable class of languages to a learner for it (Kapur, 1991; Kapur & Bilardi, 1992c). However, if the notion of learning is weakened to include the possibility of failure with probability 0 (i.e., failure on presentations that are infinitely unlikely to appear), a learner can always be obtained (Kapur, 1991; Kapur & Bilardi, 1992a). In this setting, a stochastic assumption on the input is shown to compensate for the lack of direct negative evidence. In the next section, I discuss the requirements that a plausible language learning algorithm must meet. Then in another section, on the basis of these new developments in formal learning theory, I develop an alternative model of parameter setting.

FEASIBLE PARAMETER SETTING

Consider the following picture of the child's learning task: Universal Grammar consists of a certain finite set of principles, and there are a finite number of variations permitted in the form of parameters, each of which can take a finite number of values. The core of each possible natural language is uniquely determined by the values to which these parameters are set. All the principles are innate to the child, and learning consists in setting the parameter values appropriate for the language he or she is exposed to.

Because, in this way, the possible natural languages are heavily restricted, it appears plausible that there can be an easy explanation for learning. However, looking at the space of possible languages in the form of a parameter space by itself does not get you any advantage. For example, if there are 20 binary parameters, there are still more than a million possible parameter settings. In my view, for feasible learning, you need to have more specific information about the structure of this space.[3] (For relevant argumentation, see Frank & Kapur, 1992.) The additional structure on the space of parameters can be defined on the basis of both linguistic generalizations and learning principles. The SP as such places absolutely no constraint on this space. In contrast, a principle such as the *Independence Principle* (Manzini & Wexler, 1987; Wexler & Manzini, 1987), although of doubtful empirical validity, offers a clear description of the space that the parameters create and for that reason is more meaningful. Likewise, ideas based on economy of derivation (Chomsky, 1989, 1992) structure the parameter space. I next sketch a simple algorithm that achieves in principle, albeit infeasible, learning without making any use of the structure of the parameter space.

The following simple *enumeration-based* learning scheme can easily be shown to learn the parameter space. Imagine that all the possible parameter value tuples (over a million if there are 20 or more parameters) are laid out on a line with one node corresponding to each specific setting. Further, suppose the corresponding languages form a topological order with respect to the subset-superset inclusion relation ($\subseteq$). Imagine a learner that continues to maintain its guess unless it is inconsistent with the input evidence. Only in case of inconsistency does it proceed to guess the next language on that line.

Even given just positive evidence, this scheme would work. Because we can compute such a learning machine uniformly given a family of languages, learning is shown to take place without any additional (noncomputable) information. (In general, this is impossible; cf. Kapur, 1991; Kapur & Bilardi, 1992c.) Further, we do not need to store any input evidence at all (directly or

---

[3]We acknowledge that Clark (1990, 1992) took a different approach. However, that required him to forgo deductive, linguistically motivated learning.

indirectly) as long as it is guaranteed that every bit of evidence will be repeated arbitrarily often in the input. Such a guarantee is a direct consequence of the assumption that the input is generated from some unknown *stochastic source* (Angluin, 1988; Kapur, 1991; Kapur & Bilardi, 1992a; Osherson et al., 1986).

In spite of its obvious intuitive appeal, there are two crucial aspects in which such an algorithm appears implausible. For one, there is the issue of the time required to converge on the right guess. Because the target language could be the millionth element in the chain, it would take an unreasonable amount of time to get there. There is also the issue of noise in the input. Imagine that after the machine reached the right language, there appeared a single string in the input that could not be understood on the basis of the current guess. The machine would be forced to change the guess and this can lead to delayed convergence or even convergence to the wrong language.

Motivated by this simple example, I state what I regard as the basic properties any algorithm appropriate for the child must satisfy. (My formulation may be related to the proposal in Pinker, 1979.)

(1) **Definition** 1 A *feasible* learning algorithm must satisfy the following constraints:

   a. *Limited Space*—it should save at most a few items of input from one stage to the next.

   b. *Limited Time*—it should take a reasonably small amount of time, because the child acquires most of his or her syntax within the first 3 or 4 years of life.

   c. *Robustness*—it should behave uniformly in a wide variety of circumstances (including those with noisy, degenerate input) to which the child may be exposed.

   d. *Simplicity*—no complex functions/statistics should be computed on the basis of the input data.[4]

I denote an algorithm that meets all these constraints as belonging to the *type STRS*. In case an algorithm fails to meet one or more of these requirements, I substitute *X* in the corresponding position of its type.

A requirement that I have ignored is consistency with current psycholinguistic findings. Because, quite often, these findings are interpreted solely within the theoretical framework under which they are obtained, I do not make it a primary initial criterion. However, among algorithms of the same type, an algorithm consistent with robust psycholinguistic findings is to be preferred.

---

[4]Because simplicity is a relative notion, I propose this as a requirement of the same kind as Occam's Razor. In any case, the amount of computation that the child can perform on a single input must be bound by some reasonably tight space and time constraints.

It is clear that if we drop one or more of the preceding requirements, learning algorithms can easily be constructed. In my notation, the simple enumeration-based learning algorithm is of type *SXXS*. Clearly, as such, the SP-based algorithm meets neither the limited time nor the robustness requirement. In the worst scenario, it may even be viewed as an algorithm of type *XXXX*, because we may need to save all the evidence and make a complicated computation of the least language.

In the next section, I build up to a parameter setting algorithm of type *STRS*.

PARAMETER SETTING PROPOSAL

In this section, I sketch the new model for setting parameters. I first provide some motivation for it.

Motivation

Even if the child can be shown to get simple data to set parameters, he or she should not set them hastily for the following reasons:

1. If parameters can be reset, then the child's guess may never converge (at least within reasonable time).
2. In case of subset parameters (under the conservativeness assumption), the child may end up with wrong settings.

Therefore, the child must build up confidence with regard to a parameter value before making the choice. The only way the child can build confidence is by observing repeated occurrence of the same phenomena. Without loss of generality, one can view it as though the child entertains a set of hypotheses and maintains a record of the occurrence of certain sets of phenomena that confirm those hypotheses. This wait for corroboration of the hypotheses must be for some well-defined, reasonable duration. Surely, just as some hypotheses get confirmed, there must be others that get disconfirmed. These hypotheses fail precisely because indirect negative evidence (in its most general sense) has been used to invalidate them, which means that nonoccurrence can reveal as much as occurrence. Thus, we conclude that although there is positive evidence aplenty available in the world, the child must use it very carefully. Interestingly, the only way to use it judiciously is such that indirect negative evidence comes for free.

Even if there were negative evidence available in the world, it would suffer from the same drawbacks as positive evidence and hence would not be directly useful for learning. So my claim at this point is that there is neither decisive positive nor decisive negative evidence available in the child's environment. (With regard to setting the null subject parameter, Valian, 1990, reached a similar conclusion on different grounds.) Of course, this is a strong claim. I withdraw from this extreme position at a later stage, but the strength of my argument consists in showing that quite a lot is possible even if I maintain this radical assumption.

The Proposal

I next describe the core of my proposal, but I begin with a couple of caveats. First, the following description is only a subpart of the entire construction necessary to achieve learning of type *STRS*. Also, in spite of the use of expressions such as "the child looks at the next input" in my presentation, it must be recognized that I am describing a fully deterministic, automatic process and do not imply that any conscious effort on the part of the child is involved. Here is a skeleton of the proposal:

1. All parameters are unset initially (i.e., there are no preset values). The parser is organized to obey only the universal principles.

2. Both the values of each of the parameters are competing to make themselves established.[5]

3. Corresponding to a binary parameter (values + and −), the child generates a pair of hypotheses:[6]

    (a) Hypothesis H_+: Expect not to observe phenomena from a small, fixed set O_- of phenomena that support the parameter value −.

    (b) Hypothesis H_-: Expect not to observe phenomena from a small, fixed set O_+ of phenomena that support the parameter value +.

4. Next, these hypotheses are tested on the basis of input evidence. Let w and k be two small numbers (for concreteness, say 10 and 100, respectively). Testing the hypothesis H_+ involves the following procedure:

    (a) A window of size w sentences is constructed and the child records whether or not a phenomenon from within the set O_- occurred among those w sentences.

    (b) The child repeats this construction of the window k different times and a tally c is made of the fraction of times the phenomena occurred at least once in the duration of the window.

    (c) The hypothesis H_+ succeeds if and only if the ratio of c to k is less than .5.

---

[5] The view of parameter values in competition with each other is quite similar to that adopted by Clark (1990, 1992).

[6] In case the parameter values are in a subset-superset relationship, at most one of the two hypotheses may turn out to be spurious.

5. If H_- fails or H_+ succeeds, the child sets the parameter's value to +. Otherwise, he or she sets it to −.

The following comments help to explain the various steps of this learning procedure. It is assumed that in the initial state the child's parser accepts all sentences that are compatible with the universal principles. In other words, at least everything that is acceptable in any possible language is permissible. Testing the hypothesis H_- involves exactly a parallel procedure to that given for the hypothesis H_+. Although the requirement for setting the parameter value to + appears asymmetric, in fact it is not: It is guaranteed that, with high probability, H_+ and H_- cannot both succeed or both fail.

Within the parametrization of V-2 and word order given by Gibson and Wexler (1992) for the parameter that determines head-specifier order (+, specifier-first; −, specifier-final), the set O_+ could be the patterns Adv-Adjunct SOV, Adv-Adjunct SVO and Adv-Adjunct VSO, whereas the set O_- could be Adv-Adjunct VOS and Adv-Adjunct OVS. Of course, this is an idealization, but it gives an idea of the kind of phenomena the child is observing.

Using adequate window sizes and standard probabilistic techniques, the child can ensure that if the actual parameter value for the language is +, then the probability that H_- does not fail and H_+ does not succeed is very small (e.g., one in a billion). There are two key ideas that make this approach work. For one, there is the window size, w, which has to be set appropriately so that the probabilities for the alternative hypotheses fall on opposite sides of .5. Then, the number of repetitions of trials (i.e., the quantity k) needs to be chosen so as to push up the probability that is greater than .5 to an appropriately large value close to 1. (For an investigation of the formal aspects of this parameter setting algorithm, see Kapur, 1992.)

The idea of using windows to estimate the occurrence or nonoccurrence of phenomena is a simple but powerful technique by which we ensure that just the relevant bit of information is extracted and maintained.[7,8] Notice that the window size is large enough so that there is no need to take relative relevance of phenomena into account. Also, note that because the child does not need to store any evidence, only a small amount of storage is required. Further, the child can disregard any evidence that does not bear upon the hypotheses he or she is entertaining. In this way, raw input data are converted via sophisticated internal processing mechanisms into statistically salient data.

The procedure I have outlined so far can easily be argued to be of type *SXRS*. I later incorporate the fourth constraint—limited time—as well.

---

[7]Windows were originally used in Kapur (1991) and Kapur and Bilardi (1992a) in an algorithm that showed that any arbitrary family of languages could be learned with probability 1 from stochastic input.

[8]One could speculate that the window sizes may be related to some decay characteristics of the neurons.

Properties of This Proposal

Here are some features of the present construction that make it a candidate worthy of further investigation:

1. Parameter setting may not be instantaneous and few errors will be made.

2. The child is capable of handling a considerable amount of noise in the input. Because the child determines what to look for in the input, much of the evidence will pass by him or her without having any impact. Further, because only phenomena that repeat themselves with some regularity can influence the child, random noise will not.[9] Even the input that is actually used by the child is not constrained to be specific or *complete*. (Along with the absence of negative evidence, the fact that the positive evidence is incomplete is a part of the poverty of the stimulus.)

3. Because parser-failure/parser-success are not criteria used to change/ maintain a guess, interpretability of input evidence, as discussed by Valian (1990), is not an issue. The child focuses precisely on what he or she can analyze given the cognitive/linguistic constraints at that particular stage of development. In fact, at any stage, there is a strict correspondence between the possibilities that the child is still considering and the part of the input he or she selectively uses.

4. The language need not be *recursive* (Hopcroft & Ullman, 1979), that is, grammaticality of every sentence need not be decidable. Thus it can be the most general kind of grammar. This follows because it is not necessary for the child to analyze every bit of the input.

5. The learning algorithm is computationally trivial and psychologically plausible. There are no unnatural memory requirements and no unnatural tasks to be undertaken. For instance, sensitivity to nonoccurrence has been found in infant perception. Notice also that initially, everything is possible (provided it is permitted by the universal principles), but infrequently used options gradually disappear. This is analogous to aspects of acquisition of phonology, where some studies have shown that the absence of experience leads to loss of sensitivity.

6. The extensional relation among the strings (or derivations) in the languages is no longer important for learning. No markedness needs to be associated with parameter values on extensional (or any other) basis. Because indirect negative evidence is available and is used, overgeneralization and its solutions such as the SP are completely irrelevant. Subset and

---

[9] There must be a limit as to how frequent a phenomenon must be in order for it to make an impact on parameter settings. Clearly, the noise at the stage at which a phenomenon makes an impact must be an order of magnitude smaller.

nonsubset parameters are not distinguished; and, in this sense as well, learning is uniform.

7. It has been observed that repetitions/corrections, by and large, make no apparent impact on the child (Brown & Hanlon, 1970; Demetras, Nolan Post, & Snow, 1986). In our construction as well, direct negative evidence of this (or any) form will need to be systematic and very frequent to have any impact. (A similar general point is made by Marcus, 1993.)

8. It has been shown that there is insignificant correlation between caretaker's speech patterns and a child's language development. It may be that just as corrections (negative evidence) do not seem to have an impact, positive evidence also does not work directly. Because the progress of the child in our construction is strongly determined by his or her internal biases, this is not surprising.

Why Parameter Setting May Not Be Error Driven

Clearly, our learning algorithm is not of the error-driven variety. Although Wexler and Culicover (1980) and Gibson and Wexler (1992) maintained that it is standardly assumed that language learning is error driven, Clark (1990) recognized that it is not an absolute requirement.

I believe that there cannot be a learning algorithm of type *STRS* that is of the error-driven kind and that works in the situation in which the child is placed. For one, due to the great variability in input, there will always be sentences that will make the child unsure about his or her hypothesis. Thus, there will not be a convergence to the target grammar in the necessary sense. This point is brought out even more strongly in special circumstances such as the ones discussed in Bowerman (1988). It is also an illusion to believe that error-driven learning is maximally economical in any real sense. After all, when evidence points to a failure in the analysis (and it must frequently), it is not easy to determine what alternatives should be considered and in what order. In contrast, in our proposal there is less work, distributed evenly across the entire growth period.

For the following additional reasons, I believe, my proposal is more attractive than one based on error-driven learning:

1. There is no *credit-blame* problem (Clark, 1990, 1992), that is, given inconsistency, the problem of which parameter(s) ought to be reset. The credit-blame problem is also complicated by the fact the child needs to generate a number of parsers that reflect the change in one or the other parameter value. It is debatable whether a universal parser is feasible and can undertake such a mammoth task (Clark, 1992).

2. The child is especially sensitive to occurrence as well as nonoccurrence of expected events, not to occurrence of unexpected events.

3. The child is not expected to interpret every bit of input and can get away with sloppiness.

Finally, I note that any extension of error-driven learning to make it robust will need to incorporate a hypothesis-testing kind of mechanism for reasons suggested earlier.

The Limited Time Requirement

So far, I have shown that learning is possible under realistic assumptions on the input in a uniform, simple, robust fashion without storage of any evidence. We also observe that the learner need not create developmental sequences that are in accordance with the SP.

Let us suppose that there are 20 binary parameters in all that need to be set. If we use the algorithm outlined here, there is a good reason why it would not meet the time requirement. Because the search space consists of a million different languages and the input is noisy, there is bound to be substantial delay in setting all the parameters, especially because some of the parameters may apply only to sentences that are rather infrequent in the input. For setting the latter parameters with a high degree of confidence, we would need relatively large window sizes. We would not be able to achieve a setting for all the parameters in the available time. Consider the following crude analysis:

Let us say that the child is exposed to an order of a million sentences during the first 4 years. That much input needs to suffice for setting the parameters to their target value. Of course, as I have argued, we make only two (noncontroversial) assumptions about the nature of the input: that it is generated from a stochastic source and that it contains a certain level of random noise. Simply put, the assumptions amount to saying that the input is not maliciously constructed. Let us also say that a window of an order of 1,000 sentences is about the maximum window size that is reasonable. Suppose we list the principles and parameters of UG. Let us say there are 80 principles and 20 parameters. Suppose we assume that a particular principle is applicable to a sentence/derivation if negating the principle (or, in case of a parameter, flipping the value of the parameter) changes the grammaticality of that sentence. Clearly, different principles and parameters will be applicable to different subsets of sentences. Suppose we rank the principles and parameters in order of the expected sizes of these subsets. It is to be expected that there will be a substantial slope and that there may be parameters that apply to almost all the sentences, whereas others apply to as few as 1,000 sentences. We partition the parameter space into two main groups—those that apply to a substantial fraction of sentences and others. For illustration, let us assume that there are 10 parameters in the first group and about 10 in the second. It is quite clear that although our algorithm can succeed in setting the 10 frequent parameters within a reasonable time, it will fail to do so for the other parameters. In order to remedy this defect, that is, to overcome the sparse data problem for the less frequent parameters, I propose the following modification to our procedure:

As before, all parameters are initially unset. Now the parameters are divided into, for example, three groups of say five, seven, and eight parameters, according to decreasing levels of expression. Suppose the first task the child needs to accomplish is to set the first five frequent parameters. Initially, the child sets up windows of various sizes for these five parameters and waits for the various predictions to hold. These five parameters are set to their target value concurrently and a new grammar is compiled that incorporates the effect of this setting of the first five parameters. Now the child considers the next seven parameters. Considering parameters in groups of this form allows the impact of an individual parameter to be isolated. Primarily, the interaction with other parameters in the same group needs to be minimized in order to make unambiguous predictions. Because the new grammar will not allow any input that is inconsistent with the first five parameters, the predictions that the child must now try to verify must deal with forms that satisfy the settings of the first five parameters. Notice that this allows the possibility that if the first five parameters were set to other values, the predictions could be very different. As the data would tend to get sparser, the child would have to enhance his or her sensitivity to them.[10] The child might also be willing to diminish the level of confidence up to which he or she needs to establish the value of the less frequent parameters. In this way, the process proceeds right up to the end.

The division of parameters into groups based on their frequency of expression is not peculiar to the particular model I have proposed and may have independent merit. In our model, the parameters in the less frequent groups are set later for the following reasons:

1. These parameters can be expressed only in terms of structural notions that the original parser is incapable of analyzing. Only after the previous parameters have been set is the redefined parser able to carry out the necessary sophisticated analysis of its input.

2. Some hypotheses can be formed only as a function of the settings of the parameters in the earlier groups. Evidence can be decisive in different ways, depending on the previous settings.

3. Because the parameters in the less frequent groups make finer distinctions, any attempt to set them earlier will be thwarted by noise. However, once some of the random noise is filtered out by setting the

---

[10]Notice that due to growing cognitive skills, data that the child may use will not be getting sparse that quickly.

parameters in the previous groups, the parameters in these groups can be set efficiently.

4. Even though these parameters are expressed more sparsely, the degree of expression in the input may actually be nearly constant, because the input can be used in a more efficient and sophisticated way once the previous parameters are set (see footnote 10). The noise in the input may actually facilitate learning by ensuring that identical window sizes are applicable across the board.

Notice that in my proposal, the child is endowed with the ability to make linguistically motivated judgments as to what evidence to look for, what to keep track of and what to ignore completely. This determination is crucial for success within tight space and time bounds.

Connections and Implications

Even though my proposal appears to be radically different from any of the existing ones, there are points at which it makes links with some of them. For example, consider some recent work that argues that every parameter must have unambiguous evidence as a trigger (Roeper & Weissenborn, 1990; Weissenborn, 1992). My proposal is one response to the following conclusion in Weissenborn, Goodluck, and Roeper (1992): "To sum up, the ambiguity of the input suggests that the learner needs an efficient data-sorting device if he or she is to use either principles of Universal Grammar or learning principles effectively" (p. 12).

There have been other recent discussion of trigger-based learning where each value of each nonsubset parameter comes with a trigger. When the child sees this trigger, he or she can reliably set the corresponding parameter (Gibson & Wexler, 1992). However, even in the presence of triggers, showing feasible learnability is not trivial (Frank & Kapur, 1992). Although trigger-based strategies appear superficially similar to my proposal, the fact that the strategy proposed here is not error driven remains a crucial distinction.

This algorithm also provides justification for some of the constraints suggested recently. Consider the following constraint in Roeper and de Villiers (1992):

> We propose one constraint on an acquisition mechanism that guarantees this result: *ordered parameters.*
> (2) A decision in Parameter B is not executed until Parameter A is fixed. (pp. 192–193)

Our learning algorithm of the type *STRS* makes some predictions that must hold for any theory of language. For one, there must be a substantial difference in the frequency of a particular form in different languages that arises due to different settings of parameters. As a corollary, we also expect (somewhat in the sense of Chomsky, 1986) that different languages carve out the space so as to maintain distance from each other. Previously, this distance was assumed to be extensional (i.e., only in terms of sets of strings/derivations). I claim that this distance may also be in terms of frequencies (probabilistic distance) to which different phenomena are used. (For possible connections with language change, see Kroch, 1989.)

Further, because the order of acquisition of parameters is fixed (governed by the frequency of appearance as well as "granularity" of distance), in a strong form the following claim can be made: A linguistic phenomenon that appears in two different languages but is very frequent in one, and much less frequent in the other, must actually be different phenomena in the two languages, that is, the parameter value must be set differently. This is because if the algorithm chose to set the corresponding parameter by observing the frequency of this particular phenomenon, the parameter value is likely to be set differently. Of course, this claim can be relativized in the sense that two radically different languages may have phenomena that violate this hypothesis, but two languages that are close to each other (in many parameter settings) must not.

CONCLUSION

I have sketched a proposal for parameter setting motivated by formal learning theory and considerations of computational plausibility. I have also tried to maintain faithfulness to psycholinguistic aspects of the issue. At this point, this is an investigation into the nature of possibilities and it is hoped that future work will investigate further the value of this proposal. For some recent progress, see Brill and Kapur (1993), Kapur (in press), and Kapur and Clark (1994). Various components of the model—such as the technique to handle absence of negative evidence and to achieve robustness, or the idea of parameter groupings—may have independent merit, because the proposal is only one specific way (by no means the only reasonable one) of putting things together.

ACKNOWLEDGMENTS

I am indebted to Bob Frank, Lila Gleitman, Barbara Lust, Isabella Barbier, Eric Brill, Aravind Joshi, and Scott Weinstein along with the audience at the University of Pennsylvania and Cornell University for useful comments on parts of this work. I am especially indebted to an anonymous referee for various suggestions. This work was supported in part by ARO Grant DAAL

03-89-C-0031, DARPA Grant N00014-90-J-1863, NSF Grant IRI 90-16592, and Ben Franklin Grant 91S.3078C-1.

REFERENCES

Angluin, D. (1980). Inductive inference of formal languages from positive data. *Information and Control, 45,* 117–135.

Angluin, D. (1988). *Identifying languages from stochastic examples* (Tech. Rep. No. 614). New Haven: Yale University.

Baker, C. L. (1979). Syntactic theory and the projection problem. *Linguistic Inquiry, 10,* 533–581.

Berwick, R. (1985). *The acquisition of syntactic knowledge.* Cambridge, MA: MIT Press.

Bowerman, M. (1988). The 'no negative evidence' problem: How do children avoid constructing an overly general grammar. In J. Hawkins (Ed.), *Explaining linguistic universals* (pp. 73–101). Oxford: Basil Blackwell.

Braine, M. (1971). On two types of models of the internalization of grammars. In D. I. Slobin (Ed.), *The ontogenesis of grammar* (pp. 153–186). New York: Academic Press.

Brill, E., & Kapur, S. (1993). *An information-theoretic solution to parameter setting.* Paper presented at the Georgetown University Roundtable on Language and Linguistics: Pre-session on Corpus-based Linguistics, Washington, DC.

Brown, R., & Hanlon, C. (1970). Derivational complexity and order of acquisition in child speech. In J. R. Hayes (Ed.), *Cognition and the development of language* (pp. 11–53). New York: Wiley.

Chien, Y.-C., & Wexler, K. (1989). Children's knowledge of relative scope in Chinese. *Papers and Reports on Child Language Development, 28,* 72–80.

Chomsky, N. (1981). *Lectures on government and binding.* Dordrecht: Foris.

Chomsky, N. (1986). *Knowledge of language.* New York: Praeger.

Chomsky, N. (1989). Some notes on economy of derivation and representation. *MIT Working Papers in Linguistics, 10,* 43–74.

Chomsky, N. (1992). A minimalist program for linguistic theory. *MIT Occasional Papers in Linguistics, 1.* Cambridge, MA: MIT, Department of Linguistics and Philosophy.

Clark, R. (1990). *Papers on learnability and natural selection* (Technical Report in Formal and Computational Linguistics No. 1). Geneva: University of Geneva.

Clark, R. (1992). The selection of syntactic knowledge. *Language Acquisition, 2*(2), 83–149.

Demetras, M., Nolan Post, K., & Snow, C. (1986). Feedback to first language learners: The role of repetitions and clarification questions. *Journal of Child Language, 13,* 275–292.

Frank, R., & Kapur, S. (1992). *On the use of triggers in parameter setting.* Paper presented at the 17th Annual Boston University Conference on Language Development, Boston, MA.

Gibson, E., & Wexler, K. (1992). *Triggers.* Paper presented at GLOW, Lisbon, Portugal.

Gold, E. M. (1967). Language identification in the limit. *Information and Control, 10,* 447–474.

Hopcroft, J., & Ullman, J. (1979). *Introduction to automata theory, languages, and computation.* Reading, MA: Addison-Wesley.

Jakubowicz, C., & Olsen, L. (1988). *Reflexive anaphors and pronouns in Danish.* Paper presented at the 13th Annual Boston University Conference on Language Development, Boston, MA.

Kapur, S. (1991). *Computational learning of languages.* Unpublished doctoral thesis, Cornell University, Ithaca, NY. (Computer Science Department Technical Report 91-1234)

Kapur, S. (1992). *Parameter setting from stochastic input.* Unpublished manuscript.

Kapur, S. (in press). How much of what? Is this what underlies parameter setting? *Cognition.*

Kapur, S., & Bilardi, G. (1992a). Language learning from stochastic input. In *Proceedings of the Fifth Conference on Computational Learning Theory* (pp. 303–310). San Mateo, CA: Morgan-Kaufman.

Kapur, S., & Bilardi, G. (1992b). Language learning without overgeneralization. In *Proceedings of the Ninth Symposium on Theoretical Aspects of Computer Science* (pp. 245–256). New York: Springer-Verlag.

Kapur, S., & Bilardi, G. (1992c). On uniform learnability of language families. *Information Processing Letters, 44*, 35–38.

Kapur, S., & Clark, R. (1994). *The automatic identification and classification of clitic pronouns.* Paper presented at the Berne workshop on the L1 and L2-acquisition of clause-internal rules: Scrambling and cliticization, Berne, Switzerland.

Kapur, S., Lust, B., Harbert, W., & Martohardjono, G. (1993). Universal Grammar and learnability theory: The case of binding domains and the Subset Principle. In E. Reuland & W. Abraham (Eds.), *Knowledge and language: Issues in representation and acquisition* (pp. 185–216). Boston: Kluwer Academic.

Kapur, S., Lust, B., Harbert, W., & Martohardjono, G. (in preparation). *On relating Universal Grammar and learnability theory: Intensional and extensional principles in the representation and acquisition of binding domains.*

Kroch, A. S. (1989). Reflexes of grammar in patterns of language change. *Language Variation and Change, 1*, 199–244.

Lasnik, H. (1990). On certain substitutes for negative data. In *Essays on restrictiveness and learnability* (pp. 184–197). Boston: Kluwer Academic.

Manzini, M. R., & Wexler, K. (1987). Parameters, binding theory and learnability. *Linguistic Inquiry, 18*, 413–444.

Marcus, G. (1993). Negative evidence in language acquisition. *Cognition, 46*, 53–85.

Osherson, D. N., Stob, M., & Weinstein, S. (1984). Learning theory and natural language. *Cognition, 17*, 1–28.

Osherson, D. N., Stob, M., & Weinstein, S. (1986). *Systems that learn: An introduction to learning for cognitive and computer scientists.* Cambridge, MA: MIT Press.

Pinker, S. (1979). Formal models of language learning. *Cognition, 7*, 217–283.

Pinker, S. (1989). *Learnability and cognition.* Cambridge, MA: MIT Press.

Roeper, T., & de Villiers, J. (1992). Ordered decisions in the acquisition of wh-questions. In J. Weissenborn, H. Goodluck, & T. Roeper (Eds.), *Theoretical issues in language acquisition: Continuity and change in development.* Hillsdale, NJ: Lawrence Erlbaum Associates.

Roeper, T., & Weissenborn, J. (1990). How to make parameters work. In L. Frazier & J. de Villiers (Eds.), *Language processing and language acquisition* (pp. 147–162). Boston: Kluwer Academic.

Valian, V. (1990). Logical and psychological constraints on the acquisition of syntax. In L. Frazier & J. de Villiers (Eds.), *Language processing and language acquisition* (pp. 119–145). Boston: Kluwer Academic.

Weissenborn, J. (1992). Null subjects in early grammars: Implications for parameter-setting theories. In J. Weissenborn, H. Goodluck, & T. Roeper (Eds.), *Theoretical issues in language acquisition: Continuity and change in development* (pp. 269–299). Hillsdale, NJ: Lawrence Erlbaum Associates.

Weissenborn, J., Goodluck, H., & Roeper, T. (1992). Introduction: Old and new problems in the study of language acquisition. In J. Weissenborn, H. Goodluck, & T. Roeper (Eds.), *Theoretical issues in language acquisition: Continuity and change in development* (pp. 1–23). Hillsdale, NJ: Lawrence Erlbaum Associates.

Wexler, K. (1993). The subset principle is an intensional principle. In E. Reuland & W. Abraham (Eds.), *Knowledge and language: Issues in representation and acquisition* (pp. 217–239). Boston: Kluwer Academic.

Wexler, K., & Culicover, P. (1980). *Formal principles of language acquisition.* Cambridge, MA: MIT Press.

Wexler, K., & Manzini, M. R. (1987). Parameters and learnability in Binding Theory. In T. Roeper & E. Williams (Eds.), *Parameter setting.* Dordrecht: Reidel.

CHAPTER TWENTY-THREE

Commentary: Some Remarks on the Subset Principle

Aravind K. Joshi
University of Pennsylvania

These remarks are based on my comments after the presentations of earlier versions of the chapters by Fodor, Clark, and Kapur. These chapters address various issues in the learnability theory and, in one way or another, deal with the so-called Subset Principle (SP). My remarks here deal with only certain aspects of the SP.

The SP is invoked to prevent overgeneralization. Overgeneralization is avoided by the use of SP if we assume that only positive evidence is available to the learner, an assumption that is standardly made in learnability theory (Kapur excluded, in the sense that he allows indirect negative evidence in his model). Given two grammars G_1 and G_2, if every sentence (structured sentence) w that is grammatical with respect to G_1 is also grammatical with respect to G_2, then the learner chooses G_1 instead of G_2 because the language of G_1, $L(G_1)$ is contained in the language of G_2, $L(G_2)$. If the learner had chosen G_2 and if G_2 is the incorrect choice, then no further positive evidence will enable the learner to return to G_1. If the SP is obeyed then this situation can be avoided. By a language of a grammar G, $L(G)$ we mean the string language of G. We could, of course, consider $T(G)$, the tree language of G, that is, the set of structured sentences (derivation trees, for example). In either case, the statement of the Subset Principle will be the same. Later we return to the question whether we should consider the string language or the tree language when we discuss how the SP is to be instantiated.

The SP clearly has an intuitive appeal, especially when only positive input is available to the learner. Many questions arise, however, when we consider in detail how the SP can be instantiated.

COMPUTING THE STRING LANGUAGE

An obvious way to check the subset relationship is to check directly whether, with respect to the string languages, $L(G_1) \subseteq L(G_2)$. Of course, as far as I know, no one in the learnability theory has proposed that the string language extensions of the grammars are computed for checking the subset relationship, which, in general, is undecidable. It is decidable if one assumes that the grammars are finite state grammars. However, if the grammars are context-free or more powerful than context-free then the problem of checking subset relationship is, in general, undecidable. Even if for particular grammars the question is decidable, no one is seriously suggesting that the string language extensions are being computed by the learner in order to instantiate the SP. So, somehow, the SP has to be checked by appealing to some other criterion.

COMPUTING THE TREE LANGUAGE OR THE DERIVATIONS

Instead of considering the string languages we could consider the tree languages or the derivations. It is in this sense that Wexler (1991) considered the SP as an intensional principle. I do not comment directly on that paper here. I briefly pursue the case when the SP is defined in terms of derivations. In this case the SP can be instantiated by checking that the set of derivations under G_1 are contained in the set of derivations under G_2. The grammars may be parametrized, say with a parameter P that takes one of two possible values, say g_1 and g_2, corresponding to the two grammars, G_1 and G_2. An intensional definition can then be formulated as follows. If any derivation under g_1 that has a property Q also has the same property under g_2, then by the SP the learner chooses G_1. Of course, the learner needs to check this for "all" derivations. Unless the learner can check this containment indirectly, we have once again the problem of checking subset relationships, this time the sets being derivations (trees) and not strings. Again, as far as I can tell, no one is really saying that the learner is computing the tree sets of the grammars. One is hoping for some indirect way of checking this subset relationship. There are some suggestions along these lines in Wexler (1991).

In the case of string language extensions, I have pointed out that if we are dealing with finite state grammars then indeed, in principle, the learner can compute the subset relationship. Of course, no one is assuming that the grammars are only finite state. If the grammars are context-free (or more powerful than context-free) then the question whether the subset relationship holds is undecidable, as has been already stated. There is one interesting fact, however, that is not very well known among linguists and perhaps not among researchers in learnability. I describe it for whatever it is worth. If we assume that the grammars are context-free then the question whether the subset relationship holds for the tree sets (derivations) is indeed decidable. This result follows from the fact that finite state tree automata can be defined analogous to the finite state string automata (Thatcher, 1971). These tree automata take labeled trees as their inputs. All terminal symbols of a tree are assigned some initial states. The transitions of the automata are defined in terms of the states of the daughters of nodes in the tree, the label of the mother node, and the state assigned to the mother node as a result of the transition. This automaton walks over the tree bottom-up and finally ends at the root node of the tree. If the state assigned to the root node by the transition function, as the automaton reaches the root node, is one of the final states of the automaton, then the tree is accepted; otherwise it is rejected. Finite state string automata correspond to finite state string languages (regular sets). Similarly, finite state tree automata correspond to finite state tree languages, but these are exactly the tree languages (derivation trees) of context-free grammars (Thatcher, 1971).[1] As a consequence of this equivalence, it can be shown that the problem of checking subset relationship for the tree sets of context-free grammars is decidable. Therefore, if we assume that the learner is dealing with context-free grammars, then the SP can be instantiated, in principle. Of course, I am not suggesting this is what the learner is actually doing. All I want to point out is that if the grammars are context-free (an assumption that is much more respectable than the assumption that the grammars are finite state grammars) then instantiation of the SP is possible with respect to the tree sets (derivations).

ORDERING OF THE PARAMETER VALUES

If the parameter values are already innately ordered for the learner in some way, then, of course, the SP can be instantiated very easily. In this case, the learner need not compute the subset relationship (with respect to the string sets or the tree sets). The subset relationship is implicitly encoded in the ordering of the parameter values. Thus, in our earlier example, g_1 will be ordered before g_2. If the given data licenses both the values, the learner will choose the value g_1, that is, the grammar G_1. In this case, however, the SP is not a strategy the learner uses but rather a description of a particular developmental sequence that is guided by the innate knowledge of the ordering of the values of a parameter.

---

[1]Strictly speaking, the equality between the trees sets accepted by the bottom-up finite state tree automata and the derivation trees of context-free grammars holds up to relabeling of the nodes. This detail is not relevant to our present discussion.

There appears to be some confusion about whether the SP covers only the case when a parameter has two values and the SP tells us how to choose one of these values, or whether it also covers the case when we have two parameters and the SP tells us how these parameters are ordered. Our discussion of the SP so far is concerned with only the first case. If we consider the second case, there are problems with parameter ordering that arise with input that is ambiguous with respect to the so-called core grammar and periphery grammar. This problem and its implications for the very distinction between core and periphery have been discussed by Fodor in her chapter.

NEGATIVE EVIDENCE

The use of the SP to prevent overgeneralization works if we assume that only positive evidence is available to the learner. If negative evidence is available directly or indirectly then, of course, the SP is not relevant. This is the position Kapur takes in presenting a general purpose learning model that is also stochastic. In his model, roughly speaking, if a piece of evidence is not seen over a window of certain size then it is highly unlikely that the evidence will appear later, and therefore, this lack of positive evidence is taken as negative evidence, indirect evidence to be sure. In this model, the parameter values can flip back and forth (at least for those parameters whose values are determined at a later stage); however, learning is achieved if convergence to the right value can be shown. This approach is more in the spirit of a general hypothesis-testing paradigm. The success of this approach depends on whether convergence to the right values can be shown and whether the time course of acquisition can emerge as a corollary. The approach is more general and in some sense independent of a specific linguistic theory, therefore difficult to falsify, in contrast to an approach based on specific learning strategies tied to specific linguistic theories and therefore easily falsifiable if they are ultimately wrong.

COMPLEXITY OF COMPUTATION

Complexity of computation is obviously crucial in determining the appropriateness of learning strategies. As far as I can tell, at this stage of the development of learnability we do not have very sharp results about complexity, whether or not one adheres to the SP.

CONCLUSION

I have commented briefly on the SP. The SP has an intuitive appeal, but there are problems in instantiating it. These considerations have led to two research strategies—one trying to adjust the definitions and strategies of instantiation of SP, a conservative strategy, and the other a more general and radical one that just ignores the SP. The conservative strategy is easily falsifiable if wrong. However, it can often suggest some new interesting questions as the strategy is modified. The general strategy is not easily falsifiable. The success depends on showing the convergence and the emergence of the observed time course of development, something that is not firmly established yet. So the jury is out and it may be out for a long time!

REFERENCES

Thatcher, J. W. (1971). Characterizing derivation trees of context-free grammars through a generalization of finite automata theory. *Journal of Computer System Science, 5,* 365–396.

Wexler, K. (1991). The Subset Principle is an intensional principle. In E. Reuland & W. Abraham (Eds.), *Knowledge and language: Issues in representation and acquisition* (pp. 217–239). Dordrecht: Kluwer Academic.

Author Index

Subject Index

Language Index